ACCOUNTING THEORY

Third Edition

AHMED RIAHI BELKAOUI

University of Illinois at Chicago,
Illinois, USA

ACADEMIC PRESS

Harcourt Brace Jovanovich, Publishers
London   San Diego   New York
Boston   Sydney   Tokyo   Toronto

This book is printed on acid-free paper.

ACADEMIC PRESS LIMITED
24–28 Oval Road
London NW1 7DX

Copyright © 1992 by
ACADEMIC PRESS LIMITED

This edition is not for sale in the United States of America or Canada.
A separate North American edition (ISBN 003 096 5659) is available from
The Dryden Press, Harcourt Brace Jovanovich College Publishers,
Suite 3700, 301 Commerce Street, Fort Worth, Texas, 76102, USA.

A catalogue record for this book is available from the British Library.

ISBN 0-12-084785-X

Filmset by Bath Typesetting Ltd., Bath, Avon
Printed in Great Britain by The University Press, Cambridge.

Contents

Preface

A single generally accepted accounting theory does not exist at this time. Several attempts have been made to formulate such a theory. Starting with different assumptions and using different methodologies, the various attempts have resulted in different frameworks for financial reporting standards.

The construction of an accounting theory requires the justification or refutation of existing accounting practices. Under the traditional approach, construction and verification of a theory were considered virtually synonymous. In the past ten years, however, a new approach that employs a distinct verification process has emerged. The underlying objective of both approaches is the same: to develop a conceptual framework for what accountants do or are expected to be doing. A coherent system of objectives and assumptions is necessary for the promulgation of consistent standards that define the nature, function, and scope of financial statements and the techniques for producing them. In other words, the standard-setting process, or generally accepted accounting principles, must be guided by a generally accepted accounting theory.

Constructing and verifying an accounting theory consists of defining and selecting the objectives of accounting and financial statements and delineating the elements of financial statements, the attributes of these elements, and the appropriate unit of measure to be used.

Given the diversity of assumptions within the accounting environment, writers, researchers, and practitioners have tackled the task of theory construction in various ways. The result has been a state of continual crisis or revolution within accounting, in which (1) various accounting paradigms, or models, have competed for primacy, (2) vested interest groups have argued for the domination of their particular paradigms and resultant theories, and (3) a gradual politicization of the standard-setting process has taken place.

Accounting Theory, Third Edition, is intended for junior, senior, and graduate courses in financial accounting, financial accounting theory, seminars in asset valuation and income determination, and contemporary issues in accounting. The textbook should be helpful to those who wish to study for professional accounting examinations and to those who wish to keep up to date with current accounting research and education.

Accounting Theory,, Third Edition, consists of seventeen chapters. Chapter 1 describes the history and development of accounting. Chapter 2 covers the nature and uses of accounting. Chapter 3 describes the traditional approaches to the formulation of an accounting theory. Chapter 4 elaborates on the regulatory approaches to an accounting theory. Chapter 5 presents the events, behavioral, and human information processing approaches to the formulation of an accounting theory. Chapter 6 examines the predictive and positive approaches to the formulation of accounting theory. Chapter 7 discusses the development of a conceptual framework for financial accounting and reporting. Chapter 8 identifies and explains the theoretical structure of accounting.

Chapter 9 commences the examination of the asset valuation/income determination issue by focusing on current value accounting. Chapter 10 presents general price-level accounting as an alternative accounting approach. Chapter 11 offers a synthesis of the asset-valuation and income-determination models; a clear differentiation is made between the attributes to be measured and the unit of measurement to be used. Chapters 12, 13 and 14 discuss the issues surrounding the main financial statements: the income statement, the balance sheet and the statement of cash flows. A glimpse into the future of accounting is provided in Chapter 15. Chapter 16 looks at international accounting. Finally, Chapter 17 concludes with a philosophical and scientific view of accounting as a multiple paradigm science.

I wish to express appreciation to the officers of the American Institute of Certified Public Accountants (AICPA), the Financial Accounting Standards Board (FASB), and the American Accounting Association for their kind permission to reprint some of their material.

I am indebted to numerous people for their help in reviewing the manuscript for the third edition. Literally scores of changes have been made in the third edition as a result of comments and suggestions received from anonymous reviewers and others who provided insightful reviews of the manuscript at various stages.

I wish to thank Kalliopi Karabatsos, Veena Rao, Shiela Decena and Pei-to of the University of Illinois at Chicago for their cheerful and intelligent assistance. Finally, Jennifer Pegg and Fiona Murphy of Academic Press and Jain Simmons of Harcourt Brace Jovanovich are to be congratulated for a professional job.

Ahmed Riahi Belkaoui

CHAPTER 1

THE HISTORY AND DEVELOPMENT OF ACCOUNTING

1.1 INTRODUCTION

The study of the history and development of accounting is very important to an understanding and appreciation of present and future practices, as well as of the institutional structure of the discipline. This chapter presents the important facets of the history and development of accounting that should be known by every serious student of the accounting discipline.

1.2 EVOLUTION OF DOUBLE-ENTRY BOOKKEEPING

1.2.1 Early History of Accounting

Various attempts have been made to locate the place and time of the birth of the double-entry system, resulting in various scenarios.[1] Most of these scenarios recognize the presence of some form of record-keeping in most civilizations dating back to about 3000 BC. Included are the Chaldean-Babylonian, Assyrian and Sumerian civilizations, the producers of the first organized government in the world, some of the oldest written languages, and the oldest surviving business records;[2] the Egyptian civilization, where scribes formed the "pivots on which the whole machinery of the treasury and other departments turned",[3] the Chinese civilization, with government accounting playing a key and sophisticated role during the Chao Dynasty (1122–256 BC); the Greek civilization, where Zenon, a manager of the great estate of Appolonius, introduced in 256 BC an elaborate system of responsibility accounting;[4] and the Roman civilization, with laws requiring taxpayers to prepare statements of their financial positions, and with

1

civil rights depending on the level of property declared by the citizens.[5] The presence of these forms of bookkeeping in the ancient world has been attributed to various factors, including the invention of writing, the introduction of Arabic numerals and of the decimal system, the diffusion of knowledge of algebra, the presence of inexpensive writing material, the rise of literacy, and the existence of a standard medium of exchange. In fact, A. C. Littleton lists seven preconditions for the emergence of systematic bookkeeping:

> The Art of Writing, since bookkeeping is first of all a record; Arithmetic, since the mechanical aspect of bookkeeping consists of a sequence of simple computations; Private Property, since bookkeeping is concerned only with recording the facts about property and property rights; Money (i.e., among economy), since bookkeeping is unnecessary except as it reduces all transactions in properties or property rights to this common denominator; Credit (i.e., incompleted transactions), since there would be little impulse to make any record whatever if all exchanges were completed on spot; Commerce, since a merely local trade would never have created enough pressure (volume of business) to stimulate men to coordinate diverse ideas into a system; Capital, since without capital commerce would be trivial and credit would be inconceivable.[6]

Each of the ancient civilizations mentioned earlier included these prerequisites, explaining the presence of some form of bookkeeping.

What is still missing is a scenario of the history of accounting, from the isolated pieces of information in early bookkeeping treatises. One plausible scenario, attributed to Gordon, goes as follows:

> Were we to trace this important science [accounting] back to its original, we would be naturally led to ascribe the first invention to the first considerable merchants; and there are none who have a fairer claim to precedency in point in time than those of Arabia. The Egyptians, who for many ages made a glorious appearance in the commercial world, derived their first notions of trade from their intercourse with these ingenious people; and, of consequence, from them likewise they must have received their first form of accountantship, which in the natural way of trade, was communicated to all the cities on the Mediterranean. When the western empire had been over-run by the Barbarians, and all the countries of which it had been composed, took that opportunity of asserting their own independency, commerce fled quickly after liberty; and immediately Italy, which had formerly been the court of the Universe, became the seat of trade, to which the ruin of the eastern empire by the Turks, into whose genius or constitution the arts of commerce never entered, did not a little contribute. The business of exchange, by which the Lombards connected all the trading cities of Europe, likewise introduced their method of keeping accounts, by double entry; whence, at this day, it gets the name of Italian book-keeping.[7]

This Italian bookkeeping prospered with the development of the commercial republics of Italy and the use of the double-entry method in the fourteenth century. The first double-entry books known to exist are those of Massari of Genoa, dating back from the year 1340.[8] This double-entry bookkeeping preceded Paciolo by some two hundred years. Raymond de Rover describes as follows the early development of accounting in Italy:

> The great achievement of the Italian merchants, roughly between 1250 and 1400, was to fuse all these heterogeneous elements into an integrated system of classification in which the pigeon holes were called accounts and which rested on the principle of dual entries for all transactions. One should not, however, assume that balancing the books was a primary objective of medieval accounting. On the contrary, in Italy at least, the

merchants had begun by 1400 to use accounting as a tool of management control. To be sure, they were not so far advanced as we are today and they were even far from realizing all the potentialities of double-entry bookkeeping. Nevertheless, they had made a start by developing the rudiments of cost accounting, by introducing reserves and other modes of adjustments, such as accruals and deferred items, and by giving attention to the audit of balance sheets. Only in the analysis of financial statements did the merchants of that time make little progress.[9]

It is also fair to mention that a rudimentary form of double-entry accounting existed among the ancient Incas in 1577.

1.2.2   Luca Pacioli's Contribution

Luca Pacioli, a Franciscan friar, is generally associated with the introduction of double-entry bookkeeping. In 1494 he published his book, *Summa de Arithmetica, Geometria, Proportioni et Proportionalita* which include two chapters—*de Computis et Scripturis*—describing double-entry bookkeeping. His treatise reflected the practices of Venice at the time, which became known as "the Method of Venice" or "the Italian method." Therefore, he did not invent double-entry bookkeping, but described what was being practiced at the time. He stated that the purpose of bookkeeping was "to give the trader without delay information as to his assets and liabilities."[10] Debit (adebeo) and credit (credito) were used for the entries to secure a double-entry. He said, "All entries . . . have to be double entries, that is, if you make one creditor, you must make someone debtor."[11] Three books are used: a memorandum, a journal and a ledger. The entries are quite descriptive. Pacioli suggested that "not only was the name of the buyer or seller recorded, as well as the description of the goods with its weight, size or measurement, and price, but the terms of payment were also shown," and "wherever cash was received or disbursed, the record was shown of the kind of currency and its converted value . . .".[12] At the same time, given the short duration of business ventures, Pacioli advised the computation of a periodic profit and the closing of the books. The following advice is given:

> It is always good to close the books each year, especially if you are in a partnership with others. Frequent accounting makes for long friendship.[13]

Pacioli's book was translated in several languages, contributing to the spread and popularity of the Italian method.

1.2.3   Development of Double-Entry Bookkeeping

The "Italian method" spread throughout Europe in the sixteenth and seventeenth centuries, later acquiring new characteristics and developments, to become what we know as the double-entry model. In an effort to show that the double-entry model has evolved in ways that closely resemble the descriptions of normal science, Cushing outlines a series of developments.[14] They include the following:

1 Around the sixteenth century a few changes were made in bookkeeping techniques.

Noticeable changes were the introduction of specific journals for the recording of different types of transactions. According to Yamey:

> This involved the use of specialized subsidiary books, for example, for recording cash transactions, bills transactions or particular types of expenditures. The purpose was to keep detail out of the journal and also the ledger, so as to avoid filling them up too quickly . . . . It seems to have been fairly common practice to have had at least a separate cash book, with periodic postings of totals to the cash account in the ledger, with or without a summarized entry in the journal.[15]

2 The sixteenth and seventeenth centuries saw the evolution of the practice of periodic financial statements.[16] In addition, the seventeenth and eighteenth centuries saw the evolution of the personification of all accounts and transactions, in an effort to rationalize debit and credit rules that are applied to impersonal and abstract accounts.[17]

3 The application of the double-entry system was extended to other types of organizations. According to Peragallo:

> In the second cycle, extending from 1559 to 1795, a new element appeared—the critique of bookkeeping. This is also the period when double-entry extended its field of application to other types of organizations, such as monasteries and the state. With the critique and the widening sphere of bookkeeping, began theoretical research into the subject.[18]

4 The seventeenth century saw the use of separate inventory accounts for different types of goods. According to Yamey:

> . . .various goods accounts together with other goods on consignment accounts, goods in partnership ("company") accounts, and voyage accounts may make up a large part of a ledger. And one would look in vain for a single collective trading account, in which the results of all buying-and-selling activity are brought together for a period, preparatory to transfer to the general profit-and-loss account. One must conclude that many merchants found it useful to have many separate goods accounts, even where there was no question of accounting to partners or principals for the disposal of their goods.[19]

5 Beginning with the East India Company in the seventeenth century and continuing with the growth of the corporation following the industrial revolution, accounting acquires a better status, characterized by the need to inform absentee investors, the need for auditing, the need for cost accounting, and a reliance on concepts of continuity, periodicity and accrual.[20]

6 Three methods of treating fixed assets evolved by the eighteenth century. According to Yamey:

> First, the asset is carried forward at original cost, the difference between "revenue" payments and receipts (e.g., house repairs and rents received), which generally were entered in the asset account, being transferred to the profit-and-loss account at balancing date. Second, the asset account, containing entries for original outlay and other expenditures and receipts (including receipts from the sales of part of the asset), is closed at balancing date and the difference between total debits and total credits is carried forward as the account balance. There is no debit or credit to the profit-and-loss account. Third, the asset is revalued, upwards or downwards, at balancing date; the revised value is carried forward in the account, and the balancing difference (including the gain or loss on revaluation) is carried to profit-and-loss account.[21]

7 Up to the early nineteenth century, depreciating property was accounted for as unsold merchandise. In the last half of the nineteenth century, depreciation in the railroad industry was considered unnecessary unless the property was deemed to be in improper working condition. While still not heavily used, there is evidence, provided by Saliero in 1915, of the existence of the following depreciation methods: straight-line, reducing balance method, sinking fund and annuity methods, and unit cost method.[22] It is only following the 1930s that depreciation charges became more common.[23]

8 Cost accounting emerged in the nineteenth century as a product of the industrial revolution. It originated in fifteenth-century textile factories. D. R. Scott noted the consequences of factory developments in *The Cultural Significance of Accounts:*

> Before the industrial revolution, accounting was mainly a record of the external relations of one business unit with other business units, a record of relations determined in the market. But with the advent of large-scale productive operations ... necessity arose for more emphasis upon the accounting for interests within the competitive unit and upon the use of accounting records as a means of administrative control over the enterprise .... The appearance of cost accounting in manufacturing ... is [an] example.[24]

The records of early fifteenth century textile mills and of giant manufacturing firms are used to support two hypotheses:
  a. The first hypothesis is that the increased use of fixed assets prompted the development of industrial cost accounting.[25,26]
  b. The second hypothesis is that changes in the way economic activity was organized, not just changes in the temporal structure of their costs, prompted the development of internal cost accounting procedures in the fifteenth century.[27]

9 The latter half of the nineteenth century saw the development of techniques of accounting for prepayments and accruals, to allow the computation of periodic profit.[28]

10 The latter nineteenth and twentieth centuries saw the development of funds statements.[29]

11 The twentieth century saw the development of accounting methods for complex issues, ranging from the computation of earnings per share, accounting for business computations, accounting for inflation, long-term leases, and pensions, to the crucial problem of accounting for the new products of financial engineering.

1.3 THE DEVELOPMENT OF ACCOUNTING PRINCIPLES IN THE USA

Various groups in the USA, implementing a mix of approaches, have subjected accounting theory and principles to a constant reexamination and critical analysis. Four phases of this process may be identified. In the first phase (1900–33), management had complete control over the selection of financial information disclosed in annual reports; in the second phase (1933–59) and third phase (1959–73), the professional bodies played a significant role in developing principles; and in the fourth phase, which continues to the present, the Financial Accounting Standards Board (FASB) and various pressure groups are moving toward a politicization of accounting.

1.3.1 Management Contribution Phase (1900–33)

The influence of management in the formulation of accounting principles arose from the increasing number of shareholders and the dominant economic role played by industrial corporations after 1900. The diffusion of stock ownership gave management complete control over the format and content of accounting disclosures. The intervention of management may be characterized best by the adoption of ad hoc solutions to urgent problems and controversies. The consequences of the dependence on management initiative include:

1 Given the pragmatic character of the solutions adopted, most accounting techniques lacked theoretical support.
2 The focus was on the determination of taxable income and the minimization of income taxes.
3 The techniques adopted were motivated by the desire to smooth earnings.
4 Complex problems were avoided and expedient solutions were adopted.
5 Different firms adopted different accounting techniques for the same problem.[30]

This situation generated dissatisfaction during the 1920s. Two men, William Z. Ripley and J. M. B. Hoxley, were particularly outspoken in arguing for an improvement in standards of financial reporting.[31] Similarly, Adolph A. Berle and Gardiner C. Means pointed to corporate wealth and the power of industrial corporations, and called for the protection of investors.[32]

The main players of the time were a professional association of accountants, The American Institute of Accountants (AIA), which in 1917 established a Board of Examiners to create a uniform CPA examination, and The New York Stock Exchange, which from 1900 required all corporations applying for listing to agree to publish annual financial statements. A theoretical and controversial debate of the period was the question of accounting for interest costs. The FASB's Discussion Memorandum on "Accounting for Interest Costs" traces the background of the "interest as a cost" controversy:

> Towards the end of the nineteenth century, the issue of accounting for interest arose as part of a larger concern with developing realistic product costs to serve as a basis for establishing selling prices and measuring manufacturing efficiency. The increasing complexity of business, the increasing reliance on machinery and the consequent need to invest large amounts of capital for long periods of time greatly increased the amount of overhead. The inclusion of overhead in product cost therefore became a major accounting issue.[33]

The position of the AIA at the request of the Federal Trade Commission was that "no selling costs, interest charges, or administrative expenses are included in the factory overhead costs."[34] Opposition to the Institute's position was met by the statement in a report that "the inclusion in production cost of interest is unsound in theory and wrong, not to say absurd, in practice."[35] The opposition lost, as the Institute yielded to the call for uniform accounting practices by the FTC and a "horrifying" call by its chairman, Edward N. Hurley, that "consideration might be given to the possibility of developing a register of public accountants whose audit certificates would be acceptable to the Commission and the [Federal Reserve] Board."[36] It is interesting to note, however, that the dispute on accounting for interest costs was viewed later by Previts and Merino as a conflict between the entity and proprietary theories.[37]

Another important event of the era was the growing effect on accounting theory of taxation of business income. While the Revenue Act of 1913 provided for the calculation of taxable income on the basis of cash receipts and disbursements, the 1918 Act was the first to recognize the role of accounting procedures in the determination of taxable income. As stated in Section 212(b) of this act:

> The net income shall be computed upon the basis of the taxpayer's annual accounting period (fiscal year or calendar year, as the case may be) in accordance with the method of accounting regularly employed in keeping the books of such taxpayer; but if no such method of accounting has been so employed, or if the method employed does not reflect the income, the computation shall be made upon such basis and in such manner as in the Opinion of the Commissioner does clearly reflect the income.

It set the stage for the beginning of a harmonization between tax accounting and financial accounting.

1.3.2 Institution Contribution Phase (1933–46)

This phase was marked by the creation and the increasing role of institutions on the development of accounting principles. It includes the creation of the Securities and Exchange Commission (SEC); the approval by the AIA of "six rules or principles;" and the new role of the Committee on Accounting Procedures. Each is reviewed below.

1 In 1934 Congress created the SEC to administer various federal investment laws including the Securities Act of 1933 that regulates the issuance of securities in the interstate markets, and the Securities Act of 1934 that regulates the trading of securities. With regard to its role in the development of accounting principles, Section 13(b) of the 1934 Securities Exchange Act provides that:

> The Commission may prescribe, in regards to reports pursuant (sic) to this title, the form or forms in which the required information shall be set forth, the items or details to be shown in the balance sheet and the earnings statement, and the methods to be followed in the preparation of reports, in the appraisal or valuation of assets and liabilities, in the determination of depreciation and depletion, in the differentiation of reoccurring and nonreoccurring income . . . .

And to make things pretty clear on April 25, 1938, the SEC sent a definitive message that unless the profession established a standard-setting body, the SEC would use its mandate and develop accounting principles. Witness the following statement from Accounting Series Release (ASR) no. 4:

> In cases where financial statements filed with the Commission . . . are prepared in accordance with accounting principles for which there is no substantial authoritative support, such financial statements will be presumed to be misleading or inaccurate despite disclosures contained in the certificate of the accountant or in footnotes to the statements provided the matters are material. In cases where there is a difference of opinion between the Commission and the registrant as to the proper principles of accounting to be followed, disclosure will be accepted in lieu of correction of the financial statements themselves only if the points involved are such that there is substantial authoritative support for the practices followed by the registrant and the position of the Commission has not previously been expressed in rules, regulations, or other official releases of the Commission, including the published opinions of its chief accountant.[38]

It set the stage for the role of the SEC as a creative irritant in the development of accounting principles in the USA.

2 Following the publication by Zipley of an article criticizing reporting techniques as deceptive, George O. May, an Englishman, proposed that the AICPA begin a cooperative effort with the stock exchange so that:

> ... standards might be established for balance-sheets and income accounts which would be welcomed by many corporation executives and accountants who desire to be guided by the best practice, if they can be assured what that practice is.[39]

As a result, the AICPA's Special Committee in cooperation with the Stock Exchange suggested the following general solution to the NYSE Committee:

> The more practical alternative would be to leave every corporation free to choose its own methods of accounting within ... very broad limits ... but require disclosure of the methods employed and consistency in their application from year to year ... .
> Within quite wide limits, it is relatively unimportant to the investor which precise rules or conventions are adopted by a corporation in reporting its earnings if he knows what method is being followed and is assured that it is followed consistently from year to year ... .[40]

In addition, the Committee proposed the first formal attempt to develop generally accepted accounting techniques. Known as May's "broad principles," they include the following:

a. That income accounts should not include unrealized profit, and expenses ordinarily chargeable against income should not be charged instead against unrealized profit.

b. That capital surplus (additional paid-in capital) should not be charged with amounts chargeable ordinarily to income.

c. That earned surplus (or retained earnings) of a subsidiary company created prior to acquisition was not part of the consolidated earned surplus of the parent.

d. That dividends on treasury stock may not be credited to the company's income.

e. That amounts receivable from officers, employees, and affiliated companies should be shown separately.

A good evaluation of this joint effort goes as follows:

> The recommendations [all aspects of the original NYSE/AICPA document] were not fully implemented, but the basic concept which permitted each corporation to choose those methods and procedures which were most appropriate for its own financial statements within the basic framework of "accepted accounting principles" became the focal point of the development of principles in the United States.[41]

3 Following the SEC's issuance of ASR no. 4, which challenged the profession to provide "substantial authoritative support" for accepted accounting principles, and the increasing criticism from the newly created American Accounting Association and its members, the Institute decided in 1938 to empower the Committee on Accounting Procedure (CAP) to issue pronouncements. CAP issued twelve Accounting Research Bulletins (ARBs) during the 1938–9 period alone, and continued doing so during the war years. The post-war period was one of intense activity for the CPA, with the issuance of eighteen ARBs from 1946 to 1953, with a strategy of eliminating questionable and suspect accounting practices, and focusing

on particular reporting problems, including accounting for the effects of price-level changes, and recommending the current operating performance concept in ARB 32. In spite of these efforts, the period 1957 to 1959 was marked with an intensive criticism of the CAP for various reasons including failure to give adequate hearings to financial executives and accounting practitioners; failure to work on unpopular issues; failure to develop a comprehensive statement of basic accounting principles;[42] and crossing swords several times with the SEC, which was displeased by the CAP's preference for the "current-operating performance" conception of income statement and by the failure of the CAP to limit the alternatives available to management.[43]

1.3.3 Professional Contribution Phase (1959–73)

The discontent with the CAP was best expressed by the then president of the AICPA, Alvin R. Jennings, with the question "how successful we have been in narrowing areas of difference and inconsistency in the preparation and presentation of financial information."[44] A Special Committee on Research Program set up in 1957 and 1958 proposed the dissolution of the CAP and its research department.[45] The AICPA accepted the recommendations of the committee and established in 1959 the Accounting Principles Board and the Accounting Research Division with the mission to advance the written expression of what constitutes generally accepted accounting principles. The Accounting Research Division proceeded with the publication of rigorously argued positions that depend on deductive reasoning.

The APB issued also various Opinions dealing with controversial issues, amounting to 31 Opinions between 1959 and 1973. The American Accounting Association also participated in the process through several research studies and attempts to develop an integrated statement of basic accounting theory. The efforts were not always successful. The APB found itself embattled and criticized for a) limited controversial or ad hoc Opinions, including APB 8 on pension accounting, APB 11 on income tax allocation, and APBs 2 and 4 on investment tax credit; and b) failing to solve problems of accounting for business combinations and goodwill. The suspected link of the profession to the APB did not help. The intervention of professional associations and agencies in the formulation of an accounting theory was spurred on by efforts to eliminate undesirable techniques and to codify acceptable techniques. Again, dependence on such associations and agencies has not been without consequences, which include the following:

1 The associations and agencies did not rely on any established theoretical framework.
2 The authority of the statements was not clear-cut.
3 The existence of alternative treatments allowed flexibility in the choice of accounting techniques.

The dissatisfactions with the results of professional intervention, as expressed in the writings of Briloff, were quite effective in bringing to the attention of the general public the accounting abuses that dominated certain annual reports.[46]

1.3.4   Politicization Phase (1973–present)

The limitations of both professional associations and management in formulating an accounting theory led to the adoption of a more deductive approach as well as to the politicization of the standard-setting process—a situation created by the generally accepted view that accounting numbers affect economic behaviour and, consequently, that accounting rules should be established in the political arena. In the same view, Horngren states:

> The setting of accounting standards is as much a product of political action as flawless logic or empirical findings. Why? Because the setting of standards is a social decision. Standards place restrictions on behaviour; therefore, they must be accepted by the affected parties. Acceptance may be forced or voluntary, or some of both. In a democratic society, getting acceptance is an exceedingly complicated process that requires skillful marketing in a political arena.[47]

Since its inception, the FASB has adopted a deductive and a quasi-political approach to the formulation of accounting principles. The FASB's conduct is better marked, first, by an effort to develop a theoretical framework or accounting constitution and, second, by the emergence of various interest groups, the contribution of which is required for the "general" acceptance of new standards. The standard-setting process, therefore, has a political aspect. The following statement by the FASB indicates its awareness of this new situation:

> The process of setting accounting standards can be described as democratic because, like all rule-making bodies, the Board's right to make rules depends ultimately on the consent of the ruled. But because standard setting required some perspective, it would not be appropriate to establish a standard based solely on a canvass of the constituents. Similarly, the process can be described as legislative because it must be deliberative and because all views must be heard. But the standard setters are expected to represent the entire constituency as a whole and not be representatives of a specific constituent group. The process can be described as political because there is an educational effort involved in getting a new standard accepted. But it is not political in the sense that an accommodation is required to get a statement issued.[48]

That the process of formulating accounting standards is becoming political is better expressed by a report released by the Senate Subcommittee on Reports, Accounting, and Management, entitled *The Accounting Establishment*. Known as the "Metcalf Report," it charged that the "big eight" accounting firms monopolize the auditing of large corporations and control the standard-setting process. The relationship of the major organizations suggests the "big eight" and the AICPA have control over accounting standards approved by the SEC. After emphasizing the need for the federal government to ensure that publicly-owned corporations are properly accountable to the public, the report made the following recommendations aimed at enhancing corporate accountability:

1 Congress should exercise stronger oversight of accounting practices promulgated or approved by the federal government, and more leadership in establishing proper goals and policies . . . .
2 Congress should establish comprehensive accounting objectives for the federal government to guide agencies and departments in performing their responsibilities . . . . A comprehensive set of federal accounting objectives should encompass

such goals as uniformity, consistency, clarity, accuracy, simplicity, meaningful presentation, and fairness in application. In addition, Congress should establish specific policies abolishing such "creative accounting" techniques as percentage of completion income recognition, inflation accounting, "normalized" accounting, and other potentially misleading accounting methods . . . .

3 Congress should amend the federal securities laws to restore the right of damaged individuals to sue independent auditors for negligence under the fraud provisions of the securities laws . . . .

4 Congress should consider methods of increasing competition among accounting firms for selection as independent auditors for major corporations . . . .

5 The federal government should establish financial accounting standards for publicly-owned corporations . . . .

6 The federal government should establish auditing standards used by independent auditors to certify the accuracy of corporate financial statements and supporting records . . . .

7 The federal government should itself periodically inspect the works of independent auditors for publicly-owned corporations . . . .

8 The federal government should restore public confidence in the actual independence of auditors who certify the accuracy of corporate financial statements under the federal securities laws by promulgating and enforcing strict standards of conduct for such auditors . . . .

9 The federal government should require the nation's fifteen largest accounting firms to report basic operational and financial reports annually . . . .

10 The federal government should define the responsibilities of the independent auditors so that they clearly meet the expectations of the Congress, the public, and courts of law . . . .

11 The federal government should establish financial accounting standards, cost accounting standards, auditing standards, and other accounting practices in meetings open to the public. . . .

12 The federal government should act to relieve excessive concentration in the supply of auditing and accounting services to major publicly-owned corporations . . . .

13 The federal government should retain accounting firms which act as independent auditors only to perform auditing and accounting services . . . .

14 The Securities and Exchange Commission should treat all independent auditors equally in disciplinary and enforcement proceedings under the federal securities laws . . . .

15 The Membership of the Cost Accounting Standards Board should not be dominated by representatives of the industry and accounting firms which may have vested interests in the standards established by the Board . . . .

16 Federal employees should not serve on committees of the American Institute of Certified Public Accountants or similar organizations that are assigned directly or indirectly to influence accounting policies and procedures of the federal government . . . .[49]

1.4 ACCOUNTING AND CAPITALISM

Accounting and capitalism have been linked by some economic historians with the general claim that double-entry bookkeeping has been vital to the development and evolution of capitalism. Max Weber emphasizes the argument as follows:

> The modern rational organization of capitalistic enterprise would not have been possible without two other important factors in its development: the separation of business from the household . . . and, closely connected with it, rational bookkeeping.[50]

This thesis was best expanded by Sombart as follows:

> One cannot imagine what capitalism would be without double-entry bookkeeping: the two phenomena are connected as intimately as form and content. One cannot say whether capitalism created double-entry bookkeeping as a tool in its expansion; or perhaps, conversely, double-entry bookkeeping created capitalism.[51]

This link between accounting and capitalism became known as the Sombart thesis or argument. It argues that the transformation of assets into abstract values and the quantitative expression of the results of business activities, systematic accounting in the form of double-entry bookkeeping, made it possible a) for the capitalistic entrepreneur to plan, conduct and measure the impact of his/her activities, and b) for a separation of owners and the business itself, thus allowing the growth of the corporation. The following four reasons are generally advanced to explain the role of double-entry in the economic expansion following the close of the Middle Ages:

1 *Double entry contributed to a new attitude toward economic life.* The old medieval goal of substance was replaced by the capitalistic goal of profits. The spirit of acquisition was promoted and encouraged. Double-entry bookkeeping was imbued with the search for profits. The goals of the enterprise could be placed in a specific form and the concept of capital was made possible.

2 *This new spirit of acquisition was aided and propelled by the refinement of economic calculations.* The use of an integrated system of interrelated accounts made it possible for the entrepreneur to pursue profits rationally. Rationalization could now be based on a rigorous calculation. Present economic status could be readily determined and rational plans for future operations could be developed.

3 *This new rationalism was further enhanced by systematic organization.* Systematic bookkeeping promotes order in the accounts and organization in the firm. Its very duality provides for a check on accuracy, and its mechanization and objectivity contribute to an orderly and continued recording of business affairs. It is a unique system of classification.

4 *Double-entry bookkeeping permits a separation of ownership and management and thereby promotes the growth of the large joint stock company.* By permitting a distinction between business and personal assets it makes possible the autonomous existence of the enterprise. Its standardized techniques make it a means of communication readily understood by many rather than by just the owner-manager and his bookkeeper.[52]

The thesis is not surprising. It is derived from a general conclusion at that time that trade was the natural consequence of the adoption of double-entry bookkeeping. Whether or not double-entry in systematic accounting was indispensable for the success of commercial enterprises is not easy to determine.[53] While it is possible to find general statements made about the urgency of keeping books, historical evidence provided by Yamey indicates that businessmen in the sixteenth through eighteenth centuries did not use double-entry bookkeeping to keep track of profits and capital, but simply as a record of transactions.[54] He states:

... double-entry system does little more than provide a framework into which accounting data can be fitted and within which the data can be arranged, grouped and regrouped. The system does not itself determine the range of data to be included in a particular setting, nor impose a particular pattern of internal ordering and re-ordering of data.[55]

He also makes the points that a) double-entry bookkeeping is not necessary for determining profits and capital, b) double-entry bookkeeping is only useful for routine problems, and c) it is not necessarily useful for the selection from the opportunities available to the businessmen.

The differences of views between Sombart and Yamey lie basically "on the interpretation of the significance of early double-entry techniques and the use to which early double-entry records were put."[56] Accordingly, Winjum tried to give an interpretation that contradicts Yamey's, by providing evidence as early as the sixteenth century where profit and loss determination was an important facet of double-entry bookkeeping. He concludes as follows:

Sombart was correct in directing attention to the relationship between accounting and the use of capitalism. The system of double-entry bookkeeping does have the capability of making a positive contribution towards economic growth. Although the ability of double entry to reveal the success or failure of a business enterprise for a specific period of time was not valued by the early English merchants, double entry's capacity to accumulate data on individual operating activities, combined with its ability to bring order to the affairs and accounts of these merchants, stimulated and rationalized the economic activities of the early English merchant.[57]

1.5   RELEVANCE OF ACCOUNTING HISTORY

Accounting history is important to accounting pedagogy, policy and practice. It makes it possible to "better ... understand our present and to forecast or control our future."[58] Accounting history may be narrative by relating episodes of accounting history in a particular, specific, non-analytic manner, "with descriptions of theories of knowledge, the unique work of individuals, their systems of values and the criticisms of their related works,"[59] or interpretational by providing explanations of these episodes.[60] A good definition of accounting history follows:

Accounting history is the study of the evolution in accounting thought, practices and institutions in response to changes in the environment and societal needs. It also considers the effect that this evolution has worked on the environment.[61]

It is a study of the heritage of accounting and its contribution to accounting pedagogy, policy and perspective.

With regards to pedagogy, accounting history can be very helpful to a better understanding and appreciation of the field of accounting and its evolution as a social science. A good rationale for the relevance of history in pedagogy goes as follows:

First, a profession based on traditions built over many centuries should educate its members to appreciate their intellectual heritage. Second, the import of advances in thought, of major contributors to the literature, and of crucial positive studies may be lost, fragmented, or inadequately recognized in the longer term unless they are documented and incorporated by scholars who have historical skills. Third, without access to analyses and interpretations of historical developments in accounting thought and practice, today's empiricists risk basing their investigations upon incomplete or unjustified claims about the past.[62]

With regards to policy perspective, accounting history is instrumental to a better understanding of the accounting problems and their institutional contexts as well as the formulation of public policy.

With regards to accounting practice, accounting history could provide a better assessment of the existing practices by a comparison with the methods used in the past.

The relevance of accounting history to accounting practice, policy and pedagogy call for more accounting history inquiry. The subject matter of this historical research will include such areas as biography, institutional history, development of thought, general history, critical history, taxonomic and bibliographic databases, and historiography.[63] These are defined in Exhibit 1.1. They constitute an ideal tool for a historiography of accounting and promise to provide important knowledge to a better conduct of accounting research, practice and policy.

EXHIBIT 1.1
Historical Research Subject Matter

Area	Principal aspects
Biography	Influence of key individuals on accounting concepts, practice, and institutions
Institutional history	Traditions of the accounting profession and organizations. Considers influence on the social, economic, and political environments; source of data for explanatory research in other accounting history subjects
Development of thought	Identifies and explicates conceptual foundations and individuals and institutions related thereto. Traces and models conceptual development; impact of schools of thought on practice and other disciplines and institutions
General history	Macroperspective of accounting development; traditional and/or national emphasis; develops specific areas (e.g. cost accounting)
Critical history	Adopts a perspective inclined toward criticism in examining the role of an historical factor in the context of conflicting social, political, economic and institutional interaction
Databases – taxonomies and bibliographies	Source of primary information; support for contemporary and historical research
Historiography	The structure of historical research; evaluates accounting history research; perspective on methods for conducting and interpreting accounting history research

Source: Previts, Gary John, Parker, Lee D. and Edward N. Coffman, "An Accounting Historiography: Subject Matter and Methodology," *Abacus* (September, 1990), p. 142.

1.6   CONCLUSIONS

This chapter has presented the important facets of the history and development of accounting. The historical evolution of accounting provides clues and explanations for most of the important events that shaped the rise of double-entry bookkeeping and the development of modern accounting. It increases the ability of people interested in the accounting discipline to make judgements on a broader and more informed basis. It allows us to relate the past to what is practised and to what ought to be practised, in other words a link between the historical state and both the positive and normative state,[63] a link that supports the view of history as a cultural product acquired within the full context of social, political, economic and temporal environments.[64,65]

NOTES

[1] Yamey, B.S., "Early Views on the Origins and Development of Book-keeping and Accounting," *Accounting and Business Research* (Special Accounting History Issue, 1980), pp. 81–92.

[2] Brown, R. (ed.), *A History of Accountants and Accountancy* (Edinburgh: Jack, 1905; reprinted by B. Franklin, NY, 1966), p. 16.

[3] Woolf, A.H., *A Short History of Accounting and Accountants* (London: Gee and Coy, 1912), p. 6.

[4] Hain, H.P., "Accounting Control in the Zenon Papyri," *The Accounting Review* (October, 1966), pp. 700–2.

[5] Penndorf, B., "The Relation of Taxation to the History of the Balance Sheet," *The Accounting Review* (December 1930), p. 244.

[6] Littleton, A.C., *Accounting Evolution to 1990* (New York: American Institute Publishing Company, 1933; reprinted by Russell and Russell, NY, 1966), p. 12.

[7] Yamey, B.S., "Early Views on the Origins and Development of Book-keeping and Accounting," Op. cit., p. 84.

[8] Peragallo, Edward, *Origin and Evolution of Double Entry Bookkeeping* (New York: American Institute Publishing Co., 1938).

[9] De Rover, Raymond, "The Development of Accounting Prior to Luca Pacioli According to the Account Books of Medieval Merchants," in *Studies in the History of Accounting*, A.C. Littleton and B.S. Yamey (eds), (Homewood, Ill.: Richard D. Irwin, Inc., 1956).

[10] Green, Wilmer L., *History and Survey of Accountancy* (New York: Standard Text Press, 1930), p. 91.

[11] Geijsbeek, J., *Ancient Double-Entry Bookkeeping* (Scholars Book Co., 1976). p. 25.

[12] Green, Wilmer L., *History and Survey of Accounting*, p. 8.

[13] Geijsbeek, J., *Ancient Double-Entry Bookkeeping*, Op. cit., p. 67.

[14] Cushing, Barry E., "A Kuhnian Interpretation of the Historical Evolution of Accounting," *The Accounting Historians Journal* (December 1985), p. 17.

[15] Yamey, B.S., "Some Topics in the History of Financial Accounting in England, 1500–1900," in *Studies in Accounting*, Edited by W.T. Baxter and S. Davidson (London: The Institute of Chartered Accountants in England and Wales, 1977), p. 18.

[16] Littleton, A.C., *Accounting Evolution to 1900* (New York: American Institute Publishing Co., Inc., 1933), pp. 123–40.

[17] Ibid., p. 49.

[18] Peragallo, Edward, *Origin and Evolution of Double-Entry Bookkeeping* (New York: American Institute Publishing Co., Inc., 1938), p. 54.

[19] Yamey, B.S., "Some Topics in the History of Financial Accounting in England, 1500–1900," Op. cit., p. 19.

[20] Chatfield, Michael, *A History of Accounting Thought* (Hinsdale, The Dryden Press, 1974), Chapters 7–8.

[21] Yamey, B.S., "Some Topics in the History of Financial Accounting in England, 1500–1900," Op. cit., p. 23.

[22] Saliero, Earl A., *Principles of Depreciation* (New York: The Ronald Press, 1915), pp. 134–74.

[23] Hatfield, Henry Rand, *Accounting, its Principles and Problems* (New York: D. Appleton & Co., 1927), p. 140.

[24] Scott, D.R., *The Cultural Significance of Accounts* (Henry Holt and Company, 1931), p. 143.

[25] Garner, S.P., *Evolution of Cost Accounting to 1925* (University of Alabama Press, 1954), p. 28.

[26] Chatfield, M., *A History of Accounting Thought* (Hinsdale: The Dryden Press, 1974).

[27] Johnson, H. Thomas, "Toward a New Understanding of Nineteenth-Century Cost Accounting," *The Accounting Review* (July 1981), pp. 510–18.

[28] Yamey, B.S., "Some Topics in the History of Financial Accounting in England," Op. cit., pp. 24–5.

[29] Rosen, L.S., and DeCoster, Don T., " 'Funds' Statements: A Historical Perspective," *The Accounting Review* (January 1969), pp. 124–36.

[30] Skinner, R.M., *Accounting Principles: A Canadian Study* (Toronto: Canadian Institute of Chartered Accountants, 1973), p. 314.

[31] Ripley, W.Z., *Main Street and Wall Street* (Boston: Little and Brown, 1927) and *Railroads, Finance and Organization* (New York: Longmans, Green and Co., 1915); Hoxley, J.M.B., "Accounting for Investors," *Journal of Accountancy* (October 1930), pp. 251–81.

[32] Berle, Adolph A., and Means, Gardiner C., *The Modern Corporation and Private Property* (New York: Macmillan, 1933).

[33] Financial Accounting Standards Board, "Accounting for Interest Costs," *Discussion Memorandum* (FASB, 1977), para. 174.

[34] "Uniform Accounts," *Federal Reserve Bulletin* (April 1, 1917), p. 267.

[35] "Report of the Special Committee on Interest in Relation to Cost," *1918 Yearbook of the American Institute of Accountants* (AIA, 1918), p. 112.

[36] Carey, John L., *The Rise of the Accounting Profession: From Technician to Professional: 1896–1936* (New York: American Institute of Certified Public Accountants, 1969).

[37] Previts, Gary John, and Merino, Barbara D., *A History of Accounting in America* (New York: The Ronald Press, 1979).

[38] Securities Exchange Commission, "Administrative Policy on Financial Statements," *Accounting Series Release No. 4* (Securities and Exchange Commission, 1938), p. 5.

[39] May, George O., "Corporate Publicity and the Auditor," *The Journal of Accountancy* (November 1926), p. 324.

[40] American Institute of Accountants, *Audits of Corporate Accounts* (American Institute of Certified Public Accountants, 1934), p. 9.

[41] Storey, Reed K., *The Search for Accounting Principles—Today's Problems in Perspective* (New York: AICPA, 1964), p. 12.

[42] Spacek, Leonard, *Business Success Requires an Understanding of Unsolved Problems of Accounting and Financial Reporting* (Arthur Andersen & Co., 1959).

[43] Storey, Reed K., *The Search for Accounting Principles—Today's Problems in Perspective* (American Institute of Certified Public Accountants, 1964), pp. 48–51.

[44] Jennings, Alvin R., "Present-Day Challenges in Financial Reporting," *Journal of Accountancy* (January 1958), pp. 25–34.

[45] "Report to Council of the Special Committee on Research Program," *Journal of Accountancy* (January 1958), pp. 62–8.

[46] Briloff, Abraham J., *Unaccountable Accounting* (New York: Harper and Row, 1972).

[47] Horngren, Charles T., "The Marketing of Accounting Standards," *Journal of Accountancy* (October 1973), p. 61.

[48] Structure Committee, *The Structure of Establishing Financial Accounting Standards* (Stamford, CT: Financial Accounting Foundation, April 1977), p. 15.

[49] US Senate Committee on Government Operations, Subcommittee on Reports, Accounting, and Management, summary of *The Accounting Establishment, A Staff Study* (New York: National Association of Accountants, December 1976), pp. 20–4.

[50] Andreski, S. (ed.), *Max Weber on Capitalism, Bureaucracy and Religion* (London: George Allen, 1983), p. 26.

[51] Sombart, Werner, *Der Moderne Kapitalismus* (Munich: Dunker and Hurnblot, 1919), Vol. II, p. 118.

[52] Winjum, James O., "Accounting and The Rise of Capitalism: An Accountant's View," *Journal of Accounting Research* (Autumn, 1971), pp. 336–7.

[53] Yamey, B.S., "Scientific Bookkeeping and the Rise of Capitalism," *The Economic History Review* (1, 1949), pp. 99–113.

[54] Yamey, B.S., "Accounting and the Rise of Capitalism: Further Notes on a Theme by Sombart," *Journal of Accounting Research* (Autumn, 1964), pp. 47–136.

[55] Ibid., p. 177.

[56] Yamey, B.S., "Introduction," *Studies in the History of Accounting*, (eds) A.C. Littleton and B.S. Yamey (Homewood, Ill.: Richard D. Irwin, Inc., 1956), p. 9.

[57] Winjum, J.O., "Accounting and the Rise of Capitalism: An Accountant's View," Op. cit., p. 350.

[58] Haskins, C.W., *Business Education and Accountancy*, F.A. Cleveland (ed.) (Harper and Brothers, 1904, reprinted by Arno Press, 1978), p. 141.

[59] Previts, G.J., Parker, L.D., and Coffman, E.N., "An Accounting Historiography: Subject Matter and Methodology," *Abacus* (September, 1990).

[60] Degler, L.N., "Should Historians Be Skeptical about Using Psychological Methods?," *The Chronicle of Higher Education* (27, May 1987).

[61] Committee on Accounting History, *Report of the Committee*, *The Accounting Review* (Supplement to Vol. XLV, 1920), p. 53.

[62] Previts, G.J., Parker, L.D., and Coffman, E.N., "Accounting History: Definition and Relevance," *Abacus* (26, 1, 1990), pp. 3–4.

[63] Previts, G.J., "Methods and Meanings of Historical Interpretation for Accounting," *The Accounting Historians' Notebook* (Fall, 1984).

[64] Lister, R.J., "Accounting as History," *The International Journal of Accounting Education and Research* (Spring, 1983).

[65] Hopwood, A., and Johnson, H.T., "Accounting History's Claim to Legitimacy," *The International Journal of Accounting Education and Research* (Spring, 1986).

REFERENCES

The Development of Accounting Principles in the USA

Blough, Carmen, "Development of Accounting Principles in the United States," *Berkeley Symposium on the Foundations of Financial Accounting* (Los Angeles: University of California, 1967), pp. 1–14.

Chatfield, Michael, *A History of Accounting Thought* (Hinsdale, Ill.: Dryden Press, 1974).

Moonitz, Maurice, "Three Contributions to the Development of Accounting Principles Prior to 1930," *Journal of Accounting Research* (Spring, 1970), pp. 145–55.

Previts, Gary John, and Merino, Barbara D., *A History of Accounting in America* (New York: The Ronald Press, 1979).

Storey, Reed K., *The Search for Accounting Principles—Today's Problems in Perspective* (American Institute of Certified Public Accountants, 1964).

Accounting and Capitalism

Sombart, Werner, *The Quintessence of Capitalism* (Dutton & Co., 1915).

Winjum, James O., "Accounting and the Rise of Capitalism: An Accountants's View," *Journal of Accounting Research* (Autumn, 1971), pp. 333–50.

Yamey, B.S., "Scientific Bookkeeping and the Rise of Capitalism," *The Economic History Review* (1, 1949), pp. 99–113.

Yamey, B.S., "Accounting and the Rise of Capitalism: Further Notes on a Theme of Sombart," *Journal of Accounting Research* (Autumn, 1964), pp. 117–35.

Relevance of Accounting History

American Accounting Association, "Committee on Accounting History," *The Accounting Review* (Supplement, Vol. XLV, 1970).

Cushing, B.E., "A Kuhnian Interpretation of the Historical Evolution of Accounting," *The Accounting Historians' Journal* (December, 1989), pp. 1–41.

Merino, B., and Neimark, M.D., "Disclosure Regulation and Public Policy: A Sociohistorical Reappraisal," *Journal of Accounting and Public Policy* (Fall, 1982).

Merino, B., Kock, B.S., and MacRitchie, K.R., "Historical Analysis—A Diagnostic Tool for Archival Research: The Impact of the 1933 Securities Act," *The Accounting Review* (Fall, 1987).

Parker, L.D., "The Classical Model of Control in the Accounting Literature," *The Accounting Historians' Journal*, Spring 1986a.

Parker, L.D., "Henry Fayol, Accounting and Control: An Environmental Reflection," *The Accounting Historians' Notebook*, Spring 1986b.

Parker, L.D., *Developing Control Concepts in the Twentieth Century* (Garland Press, 1986c).

Parker, L.D., "An Historical Analysis of Ethical Pronouncements and Debate in the Australian Accounting Profession," *Abacus*, September, 1987.

Parker, R.H. (ed.), *Bibliographies for Accounting Historians* (Arno Press, 1980).

Parker, R. H., "The Study of Accounting History," in A. Hopwood and M. Bromwich (eds), *Essays in British Accounting Research* (London: Pitman, 1981).

Parker, R.H. *The Developments of the Accountancy Profession in Britain to the Early Twentieth Century*, Monograph No. 5, The Academy of Accounting Historians, 1986.

Peloubet, M.E., "The Imprint of Personalities on the Accounting Profession," *Fifty Years of Service, 1898–1948*, New Jersey Society of Certified Public Accountants, 1948.

Peragallo, E., *Origin and Evolution of Double Entry Bookkeeping*, American Institute Publishing Company, 1938.

Peragallo, E., "Development of the Compound Entry in the Fifteenth Century Ledger of Jachomo Badoer, A Venetian Merchant," *The Accounting Review*, January 1983.

Previts, Gary John, Parker, Lee D., and Coffman, Edward N., "An Accounting Historiography: Subject Matter and Methodology," *Abacus* (September 1990), pp. 136–58.

Previts, Gary John, Parker, Lee D., and Coffman, Edward N., "Accounting History: Definition and Relevance," *Abacus* (26, 1, 1990), pp. 1–13.

Previts, G.J., "The SEC and Its Chief Accountants: Historical Impressions," *Journal of Accountancy*, August 1978.

Previts, G.J., *A Critical Evaluation of Comparative Financial Accounting Thought in America, 1900 to 1920* (Arno Press, 1980).

Previts, G.J., "Methods and Meanings of Historical Interpretations for Accountancy," *The Accounting Historians' Notebook*, (Fall, 1984).

Previts, G.J., *The Scope of CPA Services: A Study of the Development of the Concept of Independence and the Profession's Role in Society* (John Wiley, 1985).

Previts, G.J., and Merino, B.D., *A History of Accounting in America: An Historical Interpretation of the Cultural Significance of Accounting* (New York: The Ronald Press, 1979).

Weilenmann, P., "The Evolution of Accounting Theory in Europe From 1900 to the Present Day and Its Implications on Industrial Management of Tomorrow," in E.N. Coffman (ed.), *The Academy of Accounting Historians Working Paper Series*, Vol. 2, The Academy of Accounting Historians, 1979.

Zimmerman, V.K. (ed.), *Written Contributions of Selected Accounting Practitioners, Volume 1: Ralph S. Johns* (Center for International Education and Research in Accounting, University of Illinois, 1976).

Zimmerman, V.K. (ed.), *Written Contributions of Selected Accounting Practitioners, Volume 2: Paul Grady* (Center for International Education and Research in Accounting, University of Illinois, 1978).

Zimmerman, V.K. (ed.), *Written Contributions of Selected Accounting Practitioners, Volume 3: Andrew Barr* (Center for International Education and Research in Accounting, University of Illinois, 1980).

Evolution of Double-Entry Bookkeeping

Baxter, W.T., and Davidson, S., *Studies in Accounting* (London: The Institute of Chartered Accountants in England and Wales, 1977).

Cushing, B.E., "A Kuhnian Interpretation of the Historical Evolution of Accounting," *The Accounting Historians' Journal* (December, 1985), pp. 1–41.

Garner, S.P., *Evolution of Cost Accounting to 1925* (University of Alabama Press, 1954).

Geijsbeek, J., *Ancient Double-Entry Bookkeeping* (Scholars Book Co., 1974).

Green, Wilmer L., *History and Survey of Accountancy* (New York: Standard Text Press, 1930).

Johnson, H.T., "Towards a New Understanding of Nineteenth Century Cost Accounting," *The Accounting Review* (July, 1981), pp. 510–18.

Littleton, A.C., *Accounting Evolution to 1900* (New York: America Institute Publishing Co. Inc., 1933).

Peragallo, E., *Origin and Evolution of Double Entry Bookkeeping* (New York, AICPA, 1938).

Rosen, L.S., and DeCoster, Don T., " 'Funds' Statement: A Historical Perspective," *The Accounting Review* (January, 1969), pp. 124–36.

QUESTIONS

1.1 Describe the evolution of double entry bookkeeping.

1.2 Discuss the development of accounting in the USA.

1.3 What is the link between capitalism and accounting?

1.4 What is the relevance of accounting history?

1.5 Standard Setting

When the Accounting Principles Board was founded in 1959, it planned to establish financial accounting standards using empirical research and logical reasoning only; the role of political action was little recognized at this time. Today, there is wide acceptance of the view that political action is as much an ingredient of the standard-setting process as is research evidence. Considerable political and social influence is wielded by user groups, those parties who are most interested in or affected by accounting standards.

Two basic premises of the Financial Accounting Standards Board (FASB) are that (1) it should be responsive to the needs and viewpoints of the entire economic community and (2) it should operate in full view of the public, affording interested parties ample opportunity to make their views known. The extensive procedural steps employed by the FASB in the standard-setting process support these premises.

Required

Describe why financial accounting standards inspire or encourage political action and social involvement during the standard-setting process (*CMA adapted*).

1.6 Securities and Exchange Commission

The US Securities and Exchange Commission (SEC) was created in 1934 and consists of five commissioners and a staff of approximately 1,900. The SEC professional staff is organized into four divisions and several principal offices. The primary objectives of the SEC are to support fair securities makets and to foster enlightened shareholder participation in major corporate decisions. The SEC has a significant presence in financial markets and corporation-shareholder relations and has the authority to exert significant influence on entities whose actions lie within the scope of its authority. The SEC chairman has identified enforcement cases and full disclosure filings as major activities of the SEC.

Required

1 The SEC must have some "license" to exercise power. Explain where the SEC receives its authority.
2 Discuss in general terms the major ways in which the SEC:
   a. supports fair securities markets.
   b. fosters enlightened shareholder participation in major corporate decisions.
3 The major responsibilities of the SEC's Division of Corporation Finance include full disclosure filings. Describe the means by which the SEC attempts to assure the material accuracy and completeness of registrants' financial disclosure filings (*CMA adapted*).

CHAPTER 2

THE NATURE AND USES OF ACCOUNTING

One hears different definitions of accounting, encounters different debates about whether it is an art or a science, and so many who are puzzled or confused about its role. This chapter intends to bring some answers and restore some order to these issues concerning the nature of accounting, its links to management, its reliance on double-entry accounting and generally accepted accounting principles. This order, however, brings more questions about its uses, as evidenced by the frequency of accounting changes and the evidence of earnings management: such is the relative complexity of the nature and uses of accounting that this chapter introduces.

2.1 DEFINITIONS AND ROLE OF ACCOUNTING

2.1.1 Definitions of Accounting

The Committe on Terminology of the American Institute of Certified Public Accountants defined accounting as follows:

> Accounting is the art of recording, classifying, and summarizing in a significant manner and in terms of money, transactions and events which are, in part at least, of a financial character, and interpreting the results thereof.[1]

The scope of accounting from the above definition appears limited. A broader perspective was offered, by the following definition of accounting as:

> The process of identifying, measuring, and communicating economic information to permit informed judgments and decisions by users of the information.[2]

More recently, accounting has been defined with reference to the concept of quantitative information:

Accounting is a service activity. Its function is to provide quantitative information, primarily financial in nature about economic entities that is intended to be useful in making economic decisions, in making resolved choices among alternative courses of action.[3]

These definitions refer to accounting as either an "art" or a "service activity" and imply that accounting encompasses a body of techniques that is deemed useful for certain fields. *The Handbook of Accounting* identifies the following fields in which accounting is useful: financial reporting; tax determination and planning; independent audits; data processing and information systems; cost and management accounting; national income accounting; and management consulting.[4] Since then the list has expanded to include interesting new developments such as international accounting, behavioral accounting, socio-economic accounting, governmental accounting, not-for-profit accounting, and third world accounting, to name only a few. In fact, research as well as practice have taken accounting to new frontiers, making accounting a full pledged social service.

2.1.2   Accounting: An Art or a Science?

The accounting literature developed at one point in time a long drawn out debate of whether accounting is a service.[5,6,7] Those who argue that accounting is an art or a trade suggest that the accounting skills necessary to be a good tradesman should be taught, and that a "legalistic" approach to accounting is warranted. The advocates of accounting as a science suggest instead the teaching of the accounting model of measurements to give the accounting students more conceptual insight in what conventional accrual accounting is attempting to do to meet the general objectives of serving users' needs; and to provoke critical thought about the field and the dynamics of change in accounting.[8] How accounting is taught, as a trade or as a science, will affect the views of the field and the preparedness of those students electing to major in accounting and to join ultimately the ranks of the accounting profession. Theory, in both the normative and positive sense, and the science of accounting, placed at the front and not only at the back of the curriculum may prepare the students to understand better the accounting practices, to be prepared for changes in these practices, and ultimately to make better policy decisions. This last argument fits perfectly to the now widely-held view that accounting is a full-pledged social science. This argument was eloquently made by Mautz as follows:

Accounting deals with enterprises, which are certainly social groups; it is concerned with transactions and other economic events which have social consequences and influence social relationships; it produces knowledge that is useful and meaningful to human beings engaged in activities having social implications; it is primarily mental in nature. On the basis of the guidelines available, accounting is a social science.[9]

2.1.3   The Role of Accounting

The role of accounting is to produce information about the economic behavior resulting from a firm's activities within its environment. The result of accounting is best

EXHIBIT 2.1
Information Spectrum

All Information Useful for Investment, Credit and Similar Decisions
(Concepts Statement 1, paragraph 22; partly quoted in footnote 6)

Financial Reporting
(Concepts Statement 1, paragraphs 5–8)

Area Directly Affected by Existing FASB Standards

Basic Financial Statements
(In AICPA Auditing Standards Literature)

Scope of Recognition and Measurement Concepts Statement

Financial Statements	Notes to Financial Statements (& parenthetical disclosures)	Supplementary Information	Other Means of Financial Reporting	Other Information
Statement of Financial Position	Examples:	Examples:	Examples:	Examples:
Statements of Earnings and Comprehensive Income	■ Accounting Policies	■ Changing Prices Disclosures (FASB Statement 33 as amended)	■ Management Discussion and Analysis	■ Discussion of Competition and Order Backlog in SEC Form 10-K (under SEC Reg. S-K)
Statement of Cash Flows	■ Contingencies	■ Oil and Gas Reserves Information (FASB Statement 69)	■ Letters to Stockholders	■ Analysts' Reports
Statement of Investments by and Distributions to Owners	■ Inventory Methods			■ Economic Statistics
	■ Number of Shares of Stock Outstanding			■ News Articles About Company
	■ Alternative Measures (market values of items carried at historical cost)			

Source: FASB Statement of Financial Accounting Concepts No. 5, *Recognition and Measurement in Financial Statements of Business Enterprises* (December 1984), p. 5. Reprinted with permission.

represented by what the FASB calls "the information spectrum." It is shown in Exhibit 2.1, and is composed of the financial statements, the notes to the financial statements, other means of financial reporting and other information. Only the financial statements, including the notes thereto, of a firm are audited, in the sense that an auditor has exercised independent judgment to attest to the fact that these statements fairly represent the firm's position and performance in accordance with generally accepted accounting principles.

Prakash and Rappaport provide an interesting frame of reference, based on information flows, that shows the role of accounting in providing the kind of information that ties together the managerial processes and links the firm to its environment.[10] This frame of reference is shown in Exhibit 2.2. It shows the internal structure of the firm as composed of five informational processes — planning, decision making, implementation-cum-observation, data structuring, and performance evaluation. They all interlink in such a way as to provide the necessary information to management. It also shows the various informational links of the firm to its environment, allowing a) factor and product markets coupling, b) external evaluation complying, and c) economic feedback and regulatory complying. The soudness of this frame of reference is its ability to show:

> ...that the firm, in functioning as a system within the parameters determined by its environment, itself functions as an element in a higher level system, namely the economy, wherein it interacts and interrelates with other elements and so takes part in the process of determining the very parameters within which it must function internally.[11]

2.2 MEASUREMENT IN ACCOUNTING

2.2.1 Nature of Measurement in Accounting

It is generally considered that accounting is a measurement as well as a communication discipline. By measurement is meant "the assignment of numerals to objects or events according to rules."[12] The first step in accounting is to identify and select these objects, activities or events and their attributes that are deemed relevant to users before actual measurement takes place. Naturally, limitations of availability of data as well as specific characteristics of the environment, like uncertainty, lack of objectivity and verifiability, may create constraints to measurement. Notwithstanding these constraints, measurement in accounting traditionally involves the assignment of numerical values to objects, events or their attributes in such a way as to insure easy aggregation or disaggregation of the data. Where measurement is inadequate or infeasible, nonquantifiable or nonmonetary information may be provided in the footnotes.

2.2.2 Types of Measures

Various types of measures are possible in accounting:

1 Accounting measures can be either direct or indirect. Direct or primary measures are actual measures of an object or its attributes. Indirect or secondary measures are

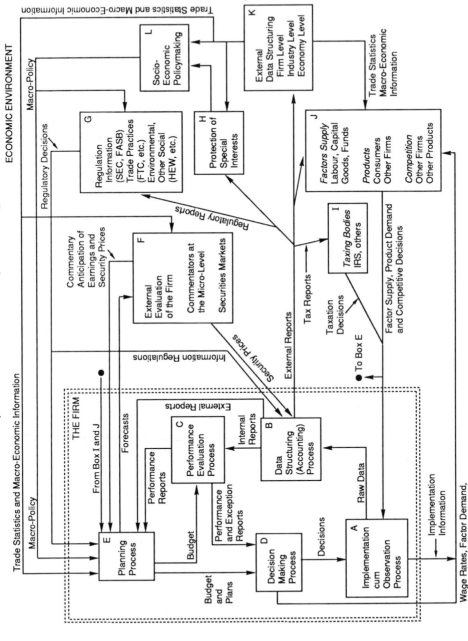

EXHIBIT 2.2
System Structure Induced by Accounting Information

Source: Prakash, Prem, and Alfred Rappaport, "Informational Interdependencies: System Structure Induced by Accounting Information," *The Accounting Review* (October 1975), p. 727. Reprinted with permission.

derived indirectly by an algebraic transformation of a set of numbers that themselves represent direct measure of some objects or attributes. These objects or attributes are the *intrinsic objects* of an indirect or secondary measure. Their primary measures are transformed into the indirect measure. The unit cost of production that is derived by dividing the total production by the volume of production is an indirect or secondary measure. Most measures used in accounting are indirect measures resulting from some transformation. It is the degree of transformation that provides the distinction between what is perceived as a direct or an indirect measure, and defines the source of the measurement error. Thus, a measurement error would occur either in a) the original primary quantification or b) the transformation process.[11]

2 With respect to decision time dimension, accounting measures can be classified as a past measure, a present measure, or a future measure to refer respectively to a measure of a future event.

3 To refer to whether the accounting object or its attribute measures belong to a past, present or future event relative to the time at which measurement is made, the accounting measures can be classified as a retrospective measure, a contemporary measure, or a prospective measure. This makes it possible to have:

   a. Three kinds of past measures: retrospective past measures, contemporary past measures and prospective past measures.

   b. Two kinds of present measures: contemporary present measures and prospective present measures.

   c. All future measures to be prospective.[14]

4 Measurements can be either:

   a. Fundamental measurements where the numbers can be assigned to the property by reference to natural laws, and do not rely on the measurement of any other variables.

   b. Derived measurements which rely on the measurement of two or more quantities and depend on the existence of a verified empirical theory linking the given property to other properties.[15]

5 Measurements can be either a) made when confirmed empirical theories may be used to support their existence, or b) made by fiat, based on arbitrary definitions.[16] Most accounting measurements are measurements by fiat, although a scientific approach to accounting theory construction and verification attempts to provide the necessary empirical testing, and thereby reduce and even eliminate some of the arbitrariness in definition and measurement of accounting concepts. Mattessich states:

> [measurement by fiat] is the least desirable since it depends greatly in the intuition of the experimenter and offers frequently too large a number of definitional possibilities or alternatives. We might measure the value of an asset by its purchase price (historic cost basis), by its discounted expected net revenues, by the potential of its liquidation yield, or many other variations and confirmations. There neither exists at present the possibilities to infer accounting values through "natural laws" (i.e., by fundamental measurement) nor through a combination of two or more fundamental measures that result in derived measurement. Most of the economic and accounting measures belong in the category of measurement by fiat, which is reflected in a certain definitional arbitrariness of our discipline.[17]

2.2.3   Types of Scales

Every measurement is made on a scale. Scales can be described in general terms as nominal, ordinal, interval or ratio.

A nominal scale assists in the determination of equality, like the numbering of footballers. It is a simple classification or labeling system like the case of a chart of accounts. The numbers reflect the objects themselves, rather than their properties.

An ordinal scale assists in the determination of greater or lesser, like grades of wool or street numbers. It is an order of preference system. One problem with the ordinal scale is that the differences or intervals between the numbers are not necessarily equal.

An interval scale assists in the determination of the equality of intervals or differences, like temperature and time. It assigns equal values to intervals between assigned numbers.

A ratio scale assists in the determination of the equality of ratios, with the additional feature of the existence of a unique origin, a natural zero point, where the distance from it for at least one object is known.

Accounting relies on each of the scales of measurements:

> The nominal scale although basic to the accounting process is neither the only nor the most important scale pertaining to our discipline. The evaluation process — the core of theoretical accountancy — utilizes the ratio scale; statement analysts primarily work with ordinal scales; and certain aspects of cost accounting can be considered as applying the *interval scale*.[18]

2.3   RATIONALE BEHIND DOUBLE-ENTRY ACCOUNTING

Double-entry accounting achieved its most serious notoriety with Friar Luca Pacioli's treatise on bookkeeping. In one of the five sections of his book *Summa de Arithmetica, Geometria, Proportioni et Proportionalita*, published in 1494, he provided a description of double-entry bookkeeping, known then as "the method of Venice". In its most simple formulation, double entry is a formulation of "where-got, where-gone," a two-dimensional system that permits classification within one set of classes. It calls for a dual classification along a duality principle. This is best defined by Mattessich as:

> the assertion that a transaction or flow has basically two dimensions: an aspect and a counter-aspect (to avoid the terms *input* and *output* which have too concrete a flavor, or the terms *debit* and *credit* which have too strong a flavor of the technical recording process). More precisely, the principle asserts that *there exists economic events which are isomorphic to a two-dimensional classification of a value within a set of classes* [Author's italics].[19]

Double-entry accounting consists of two kinds: a classificational double-entry accounting and a causal double-entry accounting. Both kinds rely on the equality of debits and credits.

A classificational double-entry accounting is aimed at maintaining the fundamental accounting equation that summarizes the classificational position:

$$Assets = Liabilities + Owners' \ Equity$$

In this classificational double-entry accounting a debit portrays a classification, while a credit portrays another classification. Two different classifications are made. For example, the purchase of inventory on credit for $20,000 is recorded as

	Dr	Cr
Inventory	$20,000	
Accounts Payable		$20,000

Two classifications were made by this entry, one based on the new asset acquired and the other based on the new liability incurred; both belong to different sides of the accounting equation.

A causal double-entry accounting describes the cause–effect relationship between an increment and a decrement. The value of an increment (debit) is offset by an equal value of a decrement (credit). For example the purchase of the same inventory for cash is recorded as

	Dr	Cr
Inventory	$20,000	
Cash		$20,000

In assessing both kinds of double-entry bookkeeping, we cannot avoid regarding the classificational double entry as merely a special case of multiple-entry bookkeeping, and unlike what Arthur Cayley thought, it is not absolutely perfect. How about the causal double-entry bookkeeping? Ijiri makes the most eloquent case as follows:

> Contrary to classificational double entry, the duality in causal double entry has a much deeper root. In causal double entry, an increment (debit) is matched with a decrement (credit). If we were to add a third element to make it a triple entry, what would this element be? It is hard to conceive of such an element because the duality stems not from a selection of two classifications out of many, as in classificational double-entry, but from our perception of change in the resource set as being an addition and a subtraction. If the positive is matched with the negative, nothing else is left to be matched unless we introduce additional dimensions to the change.[20]

2.4   GENERALLY ACCEPTED ACCOUNTING PRINCIPLES (GAAP)

2.4.1   The Meaning of GAAP

Accounting is practiced within an implicit framework. This framework is known as generally accepted accounting principles. Statement No. 4 of the Accounting Principles Board of the American Institute of Certified Public Accountants (hereafter AICPA Accounting Principles Board) stated that GAAP are noted in "experience, reason, custom, usage, and...practical necessity"[21] and they "... encompass the conventions, rules, and procedures necessary to define accepted accounting practice at a particular time."[22] They are a guide to the accounting profession in the choice of accounting techniques and the preparation of financial statements in a way considered to be good accounting practice.

The conventions, rules, and procedures have acquired the special status of being included in GAAP, because they have *substantial authoritative support*. The APB referred to this term in Chapter 6 of the APB Statement No. 4:

> In as much as generally accepted accounting principles embody a consensus they depend on notions such as general *acceptance* and *substantial authoritative support* which are not precisely defined.[23]

One way to give a recognizable meaning to the term "generally accepted" is to describe the conditions under which an accounting method will be deemed as generally accepted. For example, Skinner argues that the accounting method must meet at least one, and usually some of the following conditions, to qualify as generally accepted:

> — The method will be in actual use in a significant number of cases where the circumstances are suitable.
> — The method would have support in the pronouncements of the professional accounting societies, or other authoritative bodies such as the Securities and Exchange Commission in the United States.
> — The method would have support in the writing of a number of respected accounting teachers and thinkers.[24]

The literature pertaining to GAAP has expanded in time to include volumes of statements, opinions, and other pronouncements from a variety of authoritative sources. It includes the pronouncements currently in force of the various standard-setting bodies, namely the Financial Accounting Standards Board (FASB) statements of financial accounting standards (SFAS) and the interpretations, along with the Accounting Principles Board (APB) opinions and the American Institute of Certified Public Accountants (AICPA) accounting research bulletins.

Other common sources of the GAAP are:

1 AICPA industry audit and accounting guides and statements of positions and AICPA accounting interpretations.
2 Other identified publications of the FASB, such as its technical bulletins, and those of its predecessors, such as APB statements.
3 Publications of the Securities and Exchange Commission (SEC), such as accounting series releases.
4 Recognized and prevalent practices as reflected in the annual AICPA publication *Accounting Trends and Techniques*.
5 AICPA issues papers, FASB concepts statements, textbooks, and articles.

This profusion of sources may be viewed as a hierarchy. Exhibit 2.3 looks at the hierarchy as a four-storey-house — the house of GAAP. The authoritativeness of accounting guidance rests on the various official positions of the profession and the SEC.

Use of the term "general acceptance" remains a source of confusion, especially in a new situation or when a standard is mandated. As stated by Skinner:

> In a new situation, obviously there is not generally accepted principle. If different entities adopt different policies, there is no mechanism for judging which is generally accepted. (In practice, it is not impossible that all will be considered generally accepted.) On the other hand, a recommendation of a standard-setting body is automatically deemed generally accepted to the exclusion of other practices, no matter how unpopular the recommendation is.[25]

EXHIBIT 2.3
The House of GAAP

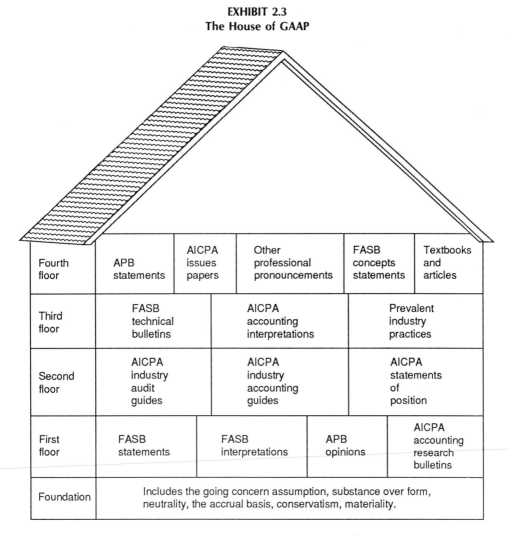

Fourth floor	APB statements	AICPA issues papers	Other professional pronouncements	FASB concepts statements	Textbooks and articles
Third floor	FASB technical bulletins		AICPA accounting interpretations		Prevalent industry practices
Second floor	AICPA industry audit guides		AICPA industry accounting guides		AICPA statements of position
First floor	FASB statements		FASB interpretations	APB opinions	AICPA accounting research bulletins
Foundation	Includes the going concern assumption, substance over form, neutrality, the accrual basis, conservatism, materiality.				

Source: Stevin, Rubin, "The House of GAAP," *Journal of Accountancy* (June 1984), p. 123. Reprinted with permission.

2.4.2 What should it be? GAAP, Special GAAP, or OCBOA?

There is a change of perception of the GAAPs. They are not seen as being a rigid set of measurement rules. Their numerous applications differ, in fact, depending on the circumstances. On the one hand, we have the widely-known GAAP for business enterprises; on the other hand, we have various and different special GAAPs, such as the GAAPs for governmental organizations, the GAAPs for regulated business enterprises, the GAAPs for non-profit organizations, the GAAPs for investment companies, and the GAAPs for banks. There is even serious debate in favor or a special set of GAAPs for small enterprises. This has been officially adopted by the FASB, which has either given small and closely-held business some relief from certain financial-statement disclosure requirements — like the suspension in 1978 of the requirements to disclose earnings per share and segment information for companies whose securities are not publicly traded — or has distinguished between disclosure that should be required for all enterprises, and that which should be required for only certain designated types of enterprise.

There is also more interest in alternatives to the GAAP, basically in financial statements prepared in accordance with other comprehensive bases of accounting (OCBOA). The impulse to switch to the OCBOA came from changes in the tax laws made by the Economic Recovery Act of 1981 and the increasing separation of tax accounting from the GAAP accounting, the increase in the number of partnerships, the subchapter S corporations and other entities that prefer to present tax or cash-basis financial statements, and the tentative conclusions of the AICPA accounting standards overload-study special committee in favor of the increased tax basis of accounting. Guidance to practitioners faced with the OCBOA statements is provided in the 1976 AICPA Statement on Auditing Standards No. 14 *Special Reports*. Of the four types of report identified, one is based on the OCBOA. To be classified as OCBOA, one of the following four criteria must be met:

1 A basis of accounting necessary to meet regulatory requirements. It is basically GAAP for regulated companies.
2 A basis of accounting that may be used for income tax returns. It is basically the tax basis of accounting.
3 A basis of accounting based on cash receipts and disbursements with or without some accrual support. It is basically the cash basis or the modified cash basis of accounting.
4 A basis of accounting resulting from the application of a definite set of criteria. Current-value financial statements or price-level adjusted financial statements are good examples.

The use of the OCBOA statements presents more problems to both users and CPAs:

1 To the users, they may not appear as an acceptable or known alternative to the GAAP. This may be aggravated by the requirement that the auditor's report includes a middle paragraph that:
   a. States, or preferably refers to the note to the financial statements which states, the basis of presentation of the financial statements on which the auditor is reporting.
   b. Refers to the note to the financial statements that describes how the basis of presentation differs from the GAAP and that may state the monetary effect of such differences.
   c. States that the financial statements are not intended to be presented in conformity with the GAAP.
   This middle paragraph may be perceived by the less-than-sophisticated user as a qualification by the auditor, rather than an informational statement.
2 To the practitioner, the OCBOA statements may present problems due to the lack of comprehensive guidance similar to the one available for the GAAP statements. To alleviate the situation the AICPA Technical Information Service (TIS), a consultation services department, may be used by an AICPA member to obtain assistance on any accounting or auditing problem by letter or toll-free telephone call.

But what should it be: GAAP, special GAAP, or OCBOA? Those in favor of more uniformity and comparability would argue for the GAAP; those in favor of more flexibility and better avenues to deal with varying circumstances would argue for the special GAAP. Those arguing for unique circumstances or against standards overload would argue for the OCBOA.

2.4.3   Little GAAP vs. Big GAAP

Accounting is facing the problem of small business being overburdened by administrative and accounting costs in order to comply with irrelevant rules, and the need for relief in the form of exemptions. When one considers that more than one-half of the USA's manufacturing, trade, and retail sales are produced by medium-sized and small businesses that are not listed on the New York or American stock exchanges, the gravity of the problem is further magnified. The question is whether any real difference exists between large and small businesses and among the needs of their respective information users to justify differences in the accounting rules in the form of two GAAPs: a little GAAP for smaller and/or closely held businesses, and a big GAAP for large companies.

Differences Between Large and Small Businesses

With respect to the differences between large and small businesses, the question is to identify those companies for which more relief from existing financial-reporting require-ments should be made. A definition is needed to distinguish between small and large companies on the basis of the real differences between them. The FASB tentatively defined a small company as follows:

> A company whose operations are relatively small, usually with total revenues of less $5 million. It typically (a) is owner-managed, (b) has few other owners, if any, (c) has all owners actively involved in the conduct of enterprise affairs except possibly for certain family members, (d) has infrequent transfer of ownership interest, and (e) has a simple capital structure.[26]

It also defined a public company as follows:

> A company (a) whose securities trade in a public market on a stock exchange or in the over-the-counter market or (b) that is required to file financial statements with the Securities and Exchange Commission. A company is also considered a public company if its financial statements are issued in preparation for the sale of any class of securities in a public market.[27]

It follows that a large company is any company that is other than the above-defined small company, and a private company is any company that is other than the above-defined public company. Although these definitions show the real differences between small and large companies and public and private companies, they do not indicate whether the disclosure and reporting relief should be provided to private companies, to small companies, or to private and small public companies.

Differences among Users of Financial Statements

With respect to the differences among users, the issues are to identify (a) whether there are real differences between the needs of users of financial statements of public companies and users of financial statements of private companies, and (b) whether there are real differences among users regarding the degree of their reliance on financial statements of private companies as sources of information. Empirical research on both questions presents conflicting evidence. Evidence asserts that financial analysts and public stock-holders are the primary users of the financial statements of public companies, whereas owner-managers and creditors are the primary users of financial statements of private companies. It follows that different groups may be perceived to have different information needs. Another evidence, however, asserts that bank loan officers and security analysts have a high degree of similarity of preferences for various types of information that are typically included in the financial statements. It attributed the few instances in which those two groups might have a difference in preference for information to a difference in focus (for example, cash-flow analysis for bankers versus earnings per share for security analysts). This last finding has been the prevalent position of standard-steerers when it comes to defining the needs of users. Statement No. 4 of the Accounting Principles Board identified the following different user groups: owners, creditors and suppliers (both present and potential), management, taxing authorities, employees, customers, financial analysts and advisors, stock exchanges, lawyers, regulatory or registration authorities, financial press and reporting agencies, trade associations, and labor unions. Although it acknowledged that these groups have different needs, the statement observed that:

> . . . the problem of ascertaining specialized needs of a large number of users, the cost of attempting to serve those needs on an individual basis, and the confusion that might result from disseminating more than one set of information about the financial results of an enterprise's operation militate against attempting to serve all needs of users with special-purpose reports.

It also identified one of the basic features of financial accounting as the presentation of "general-purpose financial information that is designed to serve the common needs of present and potential owners and creditors." This basic feature of financial accounting is based on the presumption that "a significant number of users need similar information." As we might expect, the FASB adopted similar positions. Its stated objective for financial reporting is to serve the needs of users of financial statements in general and not the particular needs of specific users.

Another indication of the FASB's view was expressed in an FASB exposure draft issued before the issuance of FASB Statement No. 14, *Financial Reporting for Segments of a Business Enterprise*:

> The Board believes, however, that there is no fundamental difference in the types of decisions and the decision-making process of those who use the financial statements of smaller or privately held enterprises . . . . Information of the type required to be disclosed by this statement is as important to users of the financial statements of those enterprises as it is to users of the financial statements of a large or publicly held enterprise. Accordingly, this statement applies to all financial statements that present financial position or results of operations in conformity with generally accepted accounting principles.

There seems to be no awareness by the standard setters that small and closely held companies are in an economic environment completely different from that of large and publicly held companies.

Many, however, will disagree with the APB Statement No. 4 and the FASB positions on the nature of the user and his or her further needs and with most of the empirical findings that there may be no basic differences in the needs of users of financial statements. The intuitive and at the same time accurate view is that principal users of public company financial statements are financial analysts and public stockholders, and financial statements of smaller and/or closely held businesses are usually directed toward owner-managers and bankers and other credit grantors.

Official Positions on "Little GAAP"

The need for differential measurement, reporting, and disclosure on the basis of either size (small versus large) or ownership (public versus private) has been a concern of the profession since 1952. More recently, the AIPCA's accounting standards division began a study of the application of the GAAP to smaller and/or closely held businesses by forming in 1974 the Committee on Generally Accepted Accounting Principles for Smaller and/or Closely Held Businesses (the "little GAAP" Committee). Four basic questions were asked in a discussion paper distributed to more than 20,000 members:

1 Are any differences in the application of the generally accepted accounting principles appropriate?
2 If there were differences in the application of the generally accepted accounting principles, on what basis should the different applications be determined?
3 If there were differences in the application of the generally accepted accounting principles, what differences would be appropriate?
4 If there were differences in the application of the generally accepted accounting principles, what impact would this have on the independent CPA?

The "little GAAP" Committee studied the response and concluded generally in its 1976 report that there was strong support within the profession as a whole for reconsideration of existing practices with respect to the application of the generally accepted accounting principles to the financial statements of smaller and/or closely held businesses, and with respect to standards for reports of CPAs on such statements. More specifically, the report (pages 8 and 9) contained the following conclusions and recommendations directly related to the issues being considered:

[Conclusions]

■ ...The same measurement principles should be applied in the general-purpose financial statements of all entities, because the measurement process should be independent of the nature of users and their interest in the resulting measurements.
■ ... The nature of the information disclosed and the extent of detail necessary for any particular disclosure may well vary depending on the needs of users.
■ ... [There should be a distinction between] disclosures ... required by GAAP [and] additional or analytical [disclosures] in the financial statements of all entities.

[Recommendations]

■ ...The Financial Accounting Standards Board should develop criteria to distinguish disclosures that should be required by GAAP ... from disclosures that merely provide additional or analytical data .... The criteria should then be used in a formal review of disclosures presently considered to be required by GAAP and should also be considered by the Board in any new pronouncements.

■ ...The AICPA auditing standards division should reconsider pronouncements concerning a CPAs report on (a) unaudited financial statements, including those accompanied by an "internal use only" disclaimer, (b) financial information presented on prescribed forms, and (c) interim financial statements of smaller and/or closely held businesses.

■ ...The Financial Accounting Standards Board should amend APB Opinion No. 15 [Earnings Per Share], to require only publicly traded companies ... to disclose earnings-per-share data.

The official reactions to these recommendations were positive. The AICPA created the Accounting and Review Services Committee (ARSC) and gave it the status of a senior committee. Its objective was to reconsider all aspects of AICPA pronouncements applicable to the association of CPAs with unaudited financial statements, a project that is basically small-business oriented. Since then the ARSC has issued statements on standards for accounting and review services (SSARs), which establish and delineate the CPA's involvement with unaudited financial statements of companies. The ultimate result is to give to small businesses the possibility of appearing "unaudited but OK."

The FASB reacted favorably to the report. In 1978 it issued Statement No. 21 *Suspension of the Reporting of Earnings per Share and Segment Information by Nonpublic Enterprises*, which suspends the earnings-per-share and segment disclosures as requirements for reporting by private companies. It also started including in its pronouncements size tests that exempt small and private companies from certain requirements.

The AICPA, however, was not impressed with the FASB efforts. Thus in 1980 the Technical Issues Committee of the AICPA Private Companies Practice Section began a project to identify significant measurement and disclosure requirements of the generally accepted accounting principles that either (a) were not relevant to the financial statements of most small and medium-sized privately owned businesses (private companies) or (b) did not provide benefits to the users of those statements sufficient to justify the costs of applying the principles.

In 1982 the committee issued its report, *Sunset Review of Accounting Principles*. It recommended changing or eliminating eleven accounting and disclosure requirements that the committee believed either should not apply to private companies or do not sufficiently benefit the users of private companies' financial statements to justify their costs. The eleven issues examined were:

1 deferred income taxes;
2 leases;
3 capitalization of interests;
4 imputed interests;
5 compensated balances;
6 business combinations;
7 troubled debt restructuring;
8 research and development costs;
9 discounted operations;
10 tax benefit of operating loss carryforward;
11 investment tax credits.

The ball was once more in the FASB's court. Would it go toward the creation of a "little GAAP", or would it treat the problems faced by small business within the standards-overload problem? The more logical approach for the FASB would be to treat the standards-overload problem first, which would alleviate the problems faced by small business. Creating a "little GAAP" would be practically and logically unsound. Most of the objections to having two sets of GAAPs are convincing.

Examples of objections are as follows:

1 Improvements in reporting to one group of users should also result in improving the reporting to other groups.
2 All companies operate in the same environment, face similar economic conditions, and could have the same types of transactions.
3 Most companies belong to either trade associations or industry groups that typically summarize financial statements of companies in the association or the group, and different accounting requirements for different companies within the same group could distort financial comparisons.
4 Most private companies would eventually become public.

2.5   ACCOUNTING POLICY AND CHANGES

Firms need to make choices among the different accounting methods in recording transactions and preparing their financial statements. These choices as dictated by generally accepted accounting principles represent the accounting policies of the firm. They are best defined by the Accounting Principles Board in its Opinion 22, *Disclosure of Accounting Policies* (April 1972), paragraph 6:

> The *accounting policies* of a reporting entity are the specific accounting principles and the methods of applying those principles that are judged by the management of the entity to be the most appropriate in the circumstances to present fairly financial position, changes in financial position, and results of operations in accordance with generally accepted accounting principles and that accordingly have been adopted for preparing the financial statements.

Firms also make accounting changes as part of their accounting policies. The general belief is that firms make accounting changes to mask performance problems. The accounting literature explains the changes in accounting principles and estimates in terms of management's desire to reach definite objectives such as income smoothing,[28] or the reduction of agency costs associated with a violation of debt covenants. A summary of existing research results suggests that as the tightness of debt covenant increases, firms are more likely to loosen the tightness of covenant restrictions through appropriate accounting changes.[29] In fact two studies that examined the accounting changes of a) successful and unsuccessful firms[30] and b) firms facing or experiencing bond rating changes,[31] provide some evidence consistent with the assertion that managers can modify income through judicious accounting changes.

Accounting regulators have tried to limit management's ability to use accounting changes to increase or decrease net income. Since 1970, APB No. 20 has stipulated that accounting changes should be accounted for as a cumulative effect change, requiring the reporting in the comparative income statements of the cumulative effect of change in the net income of the period of the change as well as the disclosure in the notes of the effect of adopting the new accounting principle on income before extraordinary income and net income (and on related per share amounts) of the period of change. Similarly, the SEC's accounting Release No. 177 required that accounting changes be made to more preferable accounting methods, using reasonable business judgement in the choice. While both pronouncements act as a control mechanism, they do not eliminate management's ability to increase and/or decrease income through accounting changes.

2.6   INCOME SMOOTHING HYPOTHESIS

2.6.1   Nature of Income Smoothing

Income smoothing may be viewed as the deliberate normalization of income in order to reach a desired trend or level. As far back as 1953, Heyworth observed "... more of the accounting techniques which may be applied to affect the assignment of net income to successive accounting periods ... for smoothing or leveling the amplitude of periodic net income fluctuations."[32] What followed were arguments made by Mousen and Downs[33] and Gordon[34] that corporate managers may be motivated to smooth their own income (or security), with the assumption that stability in income and rate of growth will be preferred over higher average income streams with greater variability. More specifically, Gordon theorized on income smoothing as follows:

Proposition 1: The criterion a corporate management uses in selecting among accounting principles is the maximization of its utility or welfare.

Proposition 2: The utility of a management increases with (1) its job security, (2) the level and rate of growth in the management's income, and (3) the level and rate of growth in the corporation's size.

Proposition 3: The achievement of the management goals stated in Proposition 2 is dependent in part on the satisfaction of stockholders with the corporation's performance; that is, other things being equal, the happier the stockholders, the greater the job security, income, etc., of the management.

Proposition 4: Stockholders' satisfaction with a corporation increases with the average rate of growth in the corporation's income (or the average rate of return on its capital) and the stability of its income. This proposition is as readily verified as Proposition 2.

Theorem: Given that the above four propositions are accepted or found to be true, it follows that a management would within the limits of its power, that is, the latitude allowed by accounting rules, (1) smooth reported income, and (2) smooth the rate of growth in income. By "smooth the rate of growth in income," we mean the following: if the rate of growth is high, accounting practices that reduce it should be adopted, and vice versa.[35]

The best definition of income smoothing was provided by Beidelman as follows:

Smoothing of reported earnings may be defined as the intentional dampening of fluctuations about some level of earnings that is currently considered to be normal for a firm. In this sense smoothing represents an attempt on the part of the firm's management to reduce abnormal variations in earnings to the extent allowed under sound accounting and management principles.[36]

Given the above definition, what needs to be explicated are the motivation of smoothing, the dimensions of smoothing and the instruments of smoothing.

2.6.2 Motivations of Smoothing

As early as 1953 Heyworth claimed that motivations behind smoothing include the improvements of relations with creditors, investors and workers, as well as dampening of business cycles through psychological processes.[37] Gordon proposed that:

1 The criterion a corporate management uses in selecting among accounting principles is to maximize its utility or welfare.
2 The same utility is a function of job security, the level and rate of growth of salary and the level and growth rate in the firm's size.
3 Satisfaction of shareholders with the corporation's performance enhances the status and rewards of managers.
4 The same satisfaction depends on the rate of growth and stability of the firm's income.[38]

These propositions culminate the need to smooth as explained in the following theorem:

> Given that the above four propositions are accepted or found to be true, it follows that a management should within the limits of its power, i.e., the latitude allowed by accounting rules, (1) smooth reported income and (2) smooth the rate of growth in income. By smooth the rate of growth in income we mean the following: If the rate of growth is high, accounting practices which reduce it should be adopted and vice versa.[39]

Beidelman considers two reasons for management to smooth reported earnings.[40] The first argument rests on the assumption that a stable earnings stream is capable of supporting a higher level of dividends than a more variable earnings stream, having a favorable effect in the value of the firm's shares as overall riskiness of the firm is reduced. He states:

> To the extent that the observed variability about a trend of reported earnings influences investors' subjective expectations for possible outcomes of future earnings and dividends, management might be able favorably to influence the value of the firm's shares by smoothing earnings.[41]

The second argument attributes to smoothing the ability to counter the cyclical nature of reported earnings and likely reduce the correlation of a firm's expected returns with returns on the market portfolio. He states:

> To the degree that auto-normalization of earnings is successful, and that the reduced covariance of returns with the market is recognized by investors and incorporated into their evaluation process, smoothing will have added beneficial effects in share values.[42]

It results from the need felt by management to neutralize environmental uncertainty and dampen the wide fluctuations in the operating performance of the firm subject to an intermittent cycle of good and bad times. To do so, management may resort to organizational slack behavior,[43] budgetary slack behavior,[44] or risk-avoiding behavior.[45] Each of these behaviors necessitates decisions affecting the incurrence and/or allocation of discretionary expenses (costs) which result in income smoothing.

In addition to these behaviors intended to neutralize environmental uncertainty, it is also possible to identify organizational characterizations that differentiate among different firms in their extent of smoothing. For exaple, Kamin and Ronen[46] examined the effects of the separation of ownership and control on income smoothing, under the hypothesis that management-controlled firms are more likely to be engaged in smoothing as a manifestation of managerial discretion and budgetary slack. Their results confirmed that income smoothing is higher among management-controlled firms with high barriers to entry.

Management was also assigned to circumvent news of the constraints of generally accepted accounting principles by attempting to smooth income numbers so as to convey their expectations of future cash flows, enhancing in the process the apparent reliability of prediction based on the observed smoothed series of numbers.[47] Three constraints are presumed to lead managers to smooth:

1 the competitive market mechanisms, which reduces the options available to management;
2 the management compensation scheme, which is linked directly to the firm's performance; and
3 the threat of management displacement.

This smoothing is not limited to high management and external accounting, it is also presumed to be used by lower-level management and internal accounting in the form of organizational slack and slack budgeting.[48]

More recently the terminology changed from "income smoothing" to "earnings management." Earnings management is shown to be motivated by management's desire to increase annual corporate income,[49,50] to influence proxy contests[51] and the likelihood of foreign trade regulation.[52]

2.6.3   The Dimensions of Smoothing

The dimensions of smoothing are basically the means used to accomplish the smoothing of income numbers. Dascher and Malcolm distinguished between real smoothing and artificial smoothing as follows:

> Real smoothing refers to the actual transaction that is undertaken or not undertaken on the basis of its smoothing effect on income, whereas artificial smoothing refers to accounting procedures which are implemented to shift costs and/or revenues from one period to another.[53]

Both types of smoothing may be indistinguishable. For example, the amount of reported expenses may be lower or higher than previous periods because of either deliberate actions on the level of the expenses (real smoothing) or the reporting methods (artificial smoothing). For both types, an operational test proposed is to fit a:

> ... curve to a stream of income calculated two ways,
> a) excluding a possible manipulative variable and
> b) including it
>   If the variations of the observations around the curve are smaller in the latter case, income smoothing has been the consequence of transaction in the account.[54]

Artificial smoothing was also considered by Copeland and defined as follows: "Income smoothing involves the repetitive selection of accounting measurement or reporting rules in a particular pattern, the effect of which is to report the stream of income with a smaller variation from trend than would otherwise have appeared."[55]

Besides real and artificial smoothing, other dimensions of smoothing were considered in the literature. A popular classification adds a third smoothing dimension, namely classificatory smoothing. Barnea *et al.* distinguished between three smoothing dimensions, as follows:

> 1. *Smoothing through events' occurrence and/or recognition:* Management can time actual transactions so that their effects on reported income would tend to dampen its variations over time. Mostly, the planned timing of events' occurrences (e.g., research and development) would be a function of the accounting rules governing the accounting recognition of the events.
>
> 2. *Smoothing through allocation over time*: Given the occurrence and the recognition of an event, management has more discretionary control over the determination over the periods to be affected by the events' quantification.
>
> 3. *Smoothing through classification (hence classificatory smoothing)*: When income statement statistics other than net income (net of all revenues and expenses) are the object of smoothing, management can classify intra-income statement items to reduce variations over time in that statistic.[56]

Basically real smoothing corresponded to the smoothing through events' occurrence and/ or recognition, while artificial smoothing corresponded to the smoothing through the allocation over time.

2.7   CONCLUSIONS

One is left after reading this chapter with a sense of bewilderment that a discipline that appears so mundane and practical to some can be so complex, so ridden with issues and meanings. The definition and uses of accounting leaves us with the certain fact that indeed accounting is a social science, a science with practical rules and supporting theories. The reader is assumed to have mastered the practical rules elsewhere. He/she is introduced to the theories of accounting and to the realms of a full-pledged social science that aspires to be at the core of the working of society and the economy.

NOTES

[1] "Review and Resume," *Accounting Terminology Bulletin No. 1* (New York: American Institute of Certified Public Accountants, 1953), paragraph 5.

[2] American Accounting Association, *A Statement of Basic Accounting Theory* (Evanston, Ill.: American Accounting Association, 1966), p. 1.

[3] Accounting Principles Board, *Statement No. 4*, "Basic Concepts and Accounting Principles Underlying Financial Statements of Business Enterprises" (New York: American Institute of Certified Public Accountants, 1970), paragraph 40.

[4] *The Handbook of Accounting*, (Fifth Edition) (New York: The Ronald Press, 1970).

[5] Beams, Floyd A., "Implications of Pragmatism and Empiricism in Accounting Thought," *The Accounting Review* (April 1965), pp. 382–8.

[6] Sterling, R.R., "Toward a Science of Accounting," *Financial Analysts Journal* (September–October, 1975), pp. 28–36.

[7] Sterling, R.R., *Toward a Science of Accounting* (Scholars Book Co, 1979).

[8] Burton, John C., "Intermediate Accounting from a User Perspective," in Jensen, D.L. (ed.), *The Impact of Rule-Making on Intermediate Financial Accounting Textbooks* (Columbus, Ohio: College of Administrative Sciences, 1982).

[9] Mautz, R.K., "Accounting as a Social Science," *The Accounting Review* (April, 1963), p. 319.

[10] Prakash, Prem, and Rappaport, Alfred, "Informational Interdependencies: System Structure Induced by Accounting Information," *The Accounting Review* (October, 1975), pp. 723–34.

[11] Ibid., p. 723.

[12] Stevens, S.S., "On the Theory of Scales of Measurement," *Science* (June 7, 1946), p. 677.

[13] Committee on Foundations of Accounting Measurement, *Report of the Committee on Foundations of Accounting Measurement*, *The Accounting Review*, Supplement to Vol. XLVI, 1971, pp. 20–1.

[14] Ibid., pp. 27–8.

[15] Campbell, Norman, *Physics, the Elements* (Cambridge University Press, 1920); Campbell, N., *An Account of the Principles of Measurement and Calculations* (London: Longman, Green, 1928).

[16] Torgeson, Warren, *Theory and Methods of Scaling* (John Wiley, 1958), pp. 22–4.

[17] Mattessich, Richard, *Accounting and Analytical Methods* (Homewood, Ill.: Irwin, 1964), p. 79.

[18] Ibid., p. 68.

[19] Ibid., p. 26.

[20] Ijiri, Yuji, *Theory of Accounting Measurement*, Studies in Accounting Research No 10 (Sarasota, Florida: American Accounting Association, 1975), p. 83.

[21] Accounting Principles Board, Statement No 4, *Basic Concepts and Accounting Principles Underlying Financial Statements of Business Enterprises* (New York: American Institute of Certified Public Accountants, 1970), p. 9084.

[22] Ibid., p. 9084.

[23] Ibid., footnote to paragraph 137.

[24] Skinner, Ross, *Accounting Principles: A Canadian Viewpoint* (Toronto: The Canadian Institute of Chartered Accountants, 1972), p. 26.

[25] Skinner, Ross M., *Accounting Standards in Evolution* (New York: Holt, Rinehart and Winston of Canada, Ltd., 1987), p. 52.

[26] Financial Accounting Standards Board, *Financial Reporting by Private and Small Companies* (Stanford, CT, 1981), pp. 3–4.

[27] Ibid.

[28] Belkaoui, Ahmed, *Accounting and Public Policy* (Westport, CT: Quorum Books, 1985).

[29] Christie, A., "Aggregation of Test Statistics: On Evaluation of the Evidence as Contracting and Size Hypotheses," *Journal of Accounting and Economics* (12, 1990).

[30] Lilien, S., Mellman, M., and Pastena, V., "Accounting Changes: Successful or Unsuccessful Firms," *The Accounting Review* (October, 1988), pp. 642–51.

[31] Belkaoui, A., "The Effect of Bond Ratings on Accounting Changes," Unpublished pages, University of Illinois at Chicago, 1990.

[32] Heyworth, S.R., "Smoothing Periodic Income," *The Accounting Review* (January, 1953), p. 32.

[33] Mousen, R.J., and Downs, A., "A Theory of Large Managerial Firms," *The Journal of Political Economy* (June, 1965), pp. 221–36.

[34] Gordon, M.J., "Postulates, Principles, and Research in Accounting," *The Accounting Review* (April, 1965), pp. 251–63.

[35] Gordon, M.J., "Postulates, Principles, and Research in Accounting," *The Accounting Review* (April, 1964), pp. 261–2.

[36] Beidelman, Carl R., "Income Smoothing: The Role of Management," *The Accounting Review* (October, 1973), p. 653.

[37] Heyworth, S.R., "Periodic Income Smoothing," *The Accounting Review* (January, 1953), p. 34.

[38] Gordon, Myron, J., "Postulates, Principles, and Research in Accounting," *The Accounting Review* (April, 1964), pp. 251–63.

[39] Ibid.

[40] Beidelman, C.R., "Income Smoothing: The Role of Management," *The Accounting Review* (October, 1973), pp. 658–67.

[41] Ibid., p. 654.

[42] Ibid., p. 654.

[43] Ceyert, R.N., and March, J.G., *A Behavioral Theory of the Firm* (Prentice-Hall, 1967).

[44] Schiff, M., and Levin, A.Y., "Where Traditional Budgeting Fails," *Financial Executive* (May, 1968), pp. 57–62.

[45] Thompson, J.D., *Organizational in Action* (New York: McGraw-Hill, 1967).

[46] Kamin, J.Y., and Ronen, J., "The Smoothing of Income Numbers: Some Empirical Evidence in Systematic Differences Among Management-Controlled and Owner-Controlled Firms," *Accounting, Organizations and Society* (3,2,1978), pp. 141–53.

[47] Barnea, A., Ronen, J., and Sadan, S., "Classificatory Smoothing of Income with Extraordinary Items," *The Accounting Review* (January, 1976), pp. 110–22.

[48] Belkaoui, Ahmed, *Behavioral Accounting* (Westport, CT: Greenwood Press, 1989).

[49] Healy, P., "The Effects of Bonus Schemes on Accounting Decisions," *Journal of Accounting and Economics* (April, 1985), pp. 85–107.

[50] McNichols, M., and Wilson, G., "Evidence of Earnings Management from the Provision for Bad Debts," *Journal of Accounting Research* (Supplement, 1988), pp. 1–31.

[51] DeAngelo, L., "Managerial Competition, Information Costs, and Corporate Governance. The Use of Accounting Performance Measures in Proxy Contests," *Journal of Accounting and Economics* (January, 1988), pp. 3–36.

[52] Jones, J., "The Effect of Foreign Trade Regulation on Accounting Choices and Production and Investment Decisions," Working Paper, the University of Michigan (1988).

[53] Dascher, Paul E., and Malcolm, Robert E., "A Note on Income Smoothing in the Chemical Industry," *Journal of Accounting Research* (Autumn, 1970), pp. 253–4.

[54] Gordon, M.J., "Discussions of the Effects of Alternative Accounting Rules for Nonsubsidiary Investments," *Empirical Research in Accounting: Selected Studies, 1966*, Supplement to Vol. 4, *Journal of Accounting Research* (1966), p. 223.

[55] Copeland, R.M., "Income Smoothing, Empirical Research in Accounting: Selected

Studies," Supplement to Vol. VI, *Journal of Accounting Research* (1968), p. 101.

[56] Barnea, A., Ronen, Joshua, and Sincha Sadan, "Classificatory Smoothing of Income with Extraordinary Item," *The Accounting Review* (January, 1976), p. 111.

REFERENCES

Double-Entry Bookkeeping

Cayley, Arthur, *The Principles of Book-Keeping by Double-Entry* (Cambridge: Cambridge University Press, 1984).

Hatfield, Henry Rand, "A Historical Defense of Bookkeeping," *Journal of Accountancy* (April, 1938), pp. 293–302.

Ijiri, Yuji, *Theory of Accounting Measurement*, Studies in Accounting Research No. 10 (Sarasota, Florida: American Accounting Association, 1975).

Kafer, Karl, *Theory of Accounts in Double-Entry Bookkeeping* (Illinois: Centre for International Education and Research in Accounting, 1966).

Mattessich, Richard, *Accounting and Analytical Methods* (Homewood, Ill., 1964).

William, John J., "A New Perspective on the Evolution of Double-Entry Bookkeeping," *The Accounting Historians' Journal* (Vol. 5, No. 1), pp. 29–39.

Measurement in Accounting

American Accounting Association, "Report of the Committee on Foundations of Accounting Measurements," *Accounting Review Supplement* (1971), pp. 1–48.

American Accounting Association, "Report of the Committee on Foundations of Accounting Measurements," *Accounting Review Supplement* (1975), pp. 535–73.

Bierman, Harold, "Measurement and Accounting," *The Accounting Review* (July, 1963), pp. 501–7.

Chambers, Raymond, J. "Measurement and Misrepresentation," *Management Science* (January, 1960), pp. 141–8.

Chambers, Raymond J., "Measurement in Accounting," *Journal of Accounting Research* (Spring, 1965), pp. 32–62.

Chambers, Raymond J., "Asset Measurement and Valuation," *Cost and Management* (March–April, 1971), pp. 30–35.

Chambers, Raymond J., "Measurement and Valuation, Again," *Cost and Management* (July–August, 1971), pp. 12–17.

Chambers, Raymond J., "Measurement in Current Accounting Practices: A Critique," *The Accounting Review* (July, 1972), pp. 488–509.

Devine, Carl, T. "Accounting — A System of Measurement Rules," *Essays in Accounting Theory*, Vol. 1, *Studies in Accounting Research* No. 22 (American Accounting Association) (1985), pp. 115–26.

Ijiri, Yuji, *The Foundations of Accounting Measurement: A Mathematical, Economic, and Behavioral Inquiry* (Prentice-Hall, 1967).

Ijiri, Yuji, "Measurement in Current Accounting Practices: A Reply," *The Accounting Review* (July, 1972), pp. 510–26.

Ijiri, Yuji, "Theory of Accounting Measurement," *Studies in Accounting Research* No. 10 (American Accounting Association).

Jaedicke, Robert, Yuji Ijiri, and Oswald Nielsen (eds), *Research in Accounting Measurement* (American Accounting Association, 1966).

Mattesich, R., "On the Perennial Misunderstanding of Asset Measurement by Means of 'Present Values'," *Cost and Management* (March–April, 1970), pp. 29–31.

Mattesich, R., "On Further Misunderstandings About Asset 'Measurement' and Valuation," *Cost and Management* (March–April, 1971), pp. 36–42.

Mattesich, R., "Asset Measurement and Valuation — A Final Reply to Chambers," *Cost and Management* (July–August, 1971), pp. 18–23.

Mock, Theodore, "Measurement and Accounting Information Criteria," *Studies in Accounting Research* No. 13 (American Accounting Association, 1976).

Moonitz, Maurice, "Price-Level Accounting and Scales of Measurement," *The Accounting Review* (July, 1970), pp. 465–75.

Vickrey, Don, "Is Accounting a Measurement Discipline?" *The Accounting Review* (October, 1970), pp. 731–42.

Generally Accepted Accounting Principles

Accounting Principles Board, Statement No. 4. *Basic Concepts and Accounting Principles Underlying Financing Statements of Business Enterprises* (New York: American Institute of Certified Public Accountants, 1970).

Alderman, C.W., Guy, D.M. and Meals, D.R., "Other Comprehensive Bases of Accounting: Alternate GAAP?, *The Journal of Accountancy* (August, 1982), pp. 52–62.

Benson, B., "Fitting GAAP to Smaller Businesses," *The Journal of Accountancy* (February, 1978), pp. 45–51.

Chazen, Charles and Benson, Benjamin, "Fitting GAAP to Smaller Businesses," *Journal of Accountancy* (February, 1978), pp. 46–7.

Larson, R.E. and Kelly, T.P., "Differential Measurement in Accounting Standards: The Concept Makes Sense," *The Journal of Accountancy* (November, 1984), pp. 78–86.

Robbins, Barry P., "Perspectives on Tax Basis Financial Statements", *Journal of Accountancy* (August, 1985), pp. 89–100.

Rubin, Steven, "The House of GAAP," *Journal of Accountancy* (June, 1984).

Skinner, Ross, *Accounting Principles: A Canadian Viewpoint* (Toronto: The Canadian Institute of Chartered Accountants, 1972).

Income Smoothing and Earnings Management

Beidelman, Carl R., "Income Smoothing: The Role of Management," *The Accounting Review* (October, 1973).

DeAngelo, L. "Managerial Competition, Information Costs, and Corporate Covenance: The Use of Accounting Performance Measures in Proxy Contest," *Journal of Accounting and Economics* (January, 1988), pp. 3–36.

Gordon, M.J., "Postulate, Principles, and Research in Accounting," *The Accounting Review* (April, 1965), pp. 251–63.

Healy, P., "The Effects of Bonus Schemes on Accounting Decisions," *Journal of Accounting and Economics* (April, 1985), pp. 85–107.

Heyworth, S.R., "Smoothing Periodic Income," *The Accounting Review* (January, 1953), pp. 32–9.

Koch, Bruce C., "Income Smoothing: An Experiment," *The Accounting Review* (July, 1981), pp. 574–86.

McNichols, M. and Wilson, G., "Evidence of Earnings Management from the Provision for Bad Debts," *Journal of Accounting* (Supplement, 1988), pp. 1–31.

Accounting: An Art or a Science?

Beams, Floyd A., "Implications of Pragmatism and Empiricism in Accounting Thought," *The Accounting Review* (April, 1965). pp. 382–8.

Jensen, D.L., *The Impact of Rule-Making on Intermediate Financial Accounting Textbooks* (Columbus, Ohio: College of Administrative Science, 1982).

Kelly, Arthur C., "Can Corporate Incomes Be Scientifically Ascertained?" *The Accounting Review* (July, 1951), pp. 289–98.

McCowen, George B., "The Accountant as Artist," *The Accounting Review* (April, 1946), pp. 204–11.

Mautz, R.K., "Accounting as a Social Science," *The Accounting Review* (April, 1963), pp. 317–25.

Sterling, R.R., "Toward a Science of Accounting," *Financial Analysts Journal* (September–October, 1975), pp. 28–36.

Sterling, R.R., *Toward a Science of Accounting* (Scholars Book Co., 1979).

Wilson, D.A., "On the Pedagogy of Financial Accounting," *The Accounting Review* (April, 1979), pp. 396–401.

QUESTIONS

2.1 Discuss some of the issues surrounding the definition, nature and role of accounting.

2.2 Discuss the measurement issue in accounting.

2.3 What is the rationale behind double-entry bookkeeping?

2.4 Discuss the major issues surrounding the GAAP concept.

2.5 Discuss the phenomena of income smoothing.

2.6 Financial Statement Violations of GAAP. The following are the financial statements issued by Allen Corporation for its fiscal year ended October 31, 1992:

ALLEN CORPORATION
Statement of Financial Position
October 31, 1992

Assets	
Cash	$ 15,000
Accounts receivable, net	150,000
Inventory	120,000
Total current assets	$285,000
Trademark (Note 3)	250,000
Land	125,000
Total assets	$660,000
Liabilities	
Accounts payable	$ 80,000
Accrued expenses	20,000
Total current liabilities	$100,000
Deferred income tax payable (Note 4)	80,000
Total liabilities	$180,000

Stockholders' Equity

Common stock, par $1 (Note 5)	$100,000	
Additional paid-in capital	180,000	
Retained earnings	200,000	480,000
Total liabilities and stockholders' equity		$660,000

ALLEN CORPORATION
Earnings Statement
For the Fiscal Year Ended October 31, 1992

Sales		$1,000,000
Cost of goods sold		(750,000)
Gross margin		$ 250,000
Expenses:		
Bad debt expense	$ 7,000	
Insurance	13,000	
Lease expenses (Note 1)	40,000	
Repairs and maintenance	30,000	
Pensions (Note 2)	12,000	
Salaries	60,000	(162,000)
Earnings before provision for income tax		$ 88,000
Provision for income tax		(28,740)
Net earnings		$ 59,260
Earnings per common share outstanding		$ 0,5926

ALLEN CORPORATION
Statement of Retained Earnings
For the Fiscal Year Ended October 31, 1992

Retained earnings, November 1, 1991	$150,000
Extraordinary gain, net of income tax	25,000
Net earnings for the fiscal year ended October 31, 1992	59,260
	$234,260
Dividends ($0.3426 per share)	(34,260)
Retained earnings, October 31, 1992	$200,000

Notes to Financial Statements:

1. *Long-Term Lease.* Under the terms of a 5-year noncancelable lease for buildings and equipment, the Company is obligated to make annual rental payments of

$40,000 in each of the next four fiscal years. At the conclusion of the lease period, the Company has the option of purchasing the leased assets for $20,000 (a bargain purchase option) or entering into another 5-year lease of the same property at an annual rental of $5000.

2. *Pension Plan.* Substantially all employees are covered by the Company's pension plan. Pension expense is equal to the total of pension benefits paid to retired employees during the year.

3. *Trademark.* The Company's trademark was purchased from Apex Corporation on January 1, 1990, for $250,000.

4. *Deferred Income Tax Payable.* The entire balance in the deferred income tax payable account arose from tax-exempt municipal bonds that were held during the previous fiscal year, giving rise to a difference between taxable income and reported net earnings for the fiscal year ended October 31, 1992. The deferred liability amount was calculated on the basis of past tax rates.

5. *Warrants.* On January 1, 1991, one common stock warrant was issued to stockholders of record for each common share owned. An additional share of common stock is to be issued upon exercise of ten stock warrants and receipt of an amount equal to par value. For the six months ended October 31, 1992, the average market value for the Company's common stock was $5 per share and no warrants had yet been exercised.

6. *Contingent Liability.* On October 31, 1992, the Company was contingently liable for product warranties in an amount estimated to aggregate $75,000.

Required

Review the preceding financial statements and related notes. Identify any inclusions or exclusions from them that would be in violation of generally accepted accounting principles, and indicate corrective action to be taken. Do *not* comment as to format or style. Respond in the following order:

1 Statement of Financial Position
2 Notes
3 Earnings Statement
4 Statement of Retained Earnings
5 General (*AICPA adapted*)

2.7 Accounting Changes
It is important in accounting theory to be able to distinguish the types of accounting changes.

Required

1 If a public company desires to change from the sum-of-the-years'-digits depreciation method to the straight-line method for its fixed assets, what type of accounting change would this be? Discuss the permissibility of this change.
2 When pro forma disclosure is required for an accounting change, how are these pro forma amounts determined?
3 If a public company obtained additional information about the service lives of

some of its fixed assets that showed that the service lives previously used should be shortened, what type of accounting change would this be? Include in your discussion how the change should be reported in the income statement of the year of the change, and what disclosures should be made in the financial statements or notes.

4 Changing specific subsidiaries comprising the group of companies for which consolidated financial statements are presented is an example of what type of accounting change, and what effect does it have on the consolidated income statements? (*AICPA adapted*).

2.8 Accounting Changes

The various types of accounting changes may significantly affect the presentation of both financial position and results of operations for an accounting period and the trends shown in comparative financial statements and historical summaries.

Required

1 Describe a change in accounting principle and how it should be reported in the income statement of the period of the change.

2 Describe a change in accounting estimate and how it should be reported in the income satement of the period of the change.

3 Describe a change in reporting entity and how it should be reported. Give an appropriate example of a change in reporting entity. (*AICPA adapted*).

2.9 Accounting Changes

Berkeley Company, a manufacturer of many different products, changed its depreciation method for its production machinery from the double-declining balance method to the straight-line method effective January 1, 1992. The straight-line method was determined to be preferable.

In addition, Berkeley changed the salvage values used in computing depreciation for its office equipment. This change was made on January 1, 1992 because additional information was obtained.

On December 31, 1992 Berkeley changed the specific subsidiaries comprising the group of companies for which consolidated financial statements are presented.

Required

1 What kind of accounting change is each of the preceding three situations? For each situation indicate whether or not each should show:

a. The cumulative effect of a change in accounting principle in net income of the period of change.

b. Pro forma effects of retroactive application.

c. Restatement of the financial statements of all prior periods.

2 Why does a change in accounting principle have to be disclosed by the company? (*AICPA adapted*).

CHAPTER 3

THE TRADITIONAL APPROACHES TO THE FORMULATION
OF AN ACCOUNTING THEORY

Various approaches have applied over time to the formulation of an accounting theory. Some of these approaches are known as "traditional" approaches, because they are characterized by the absence of a vigorous process of verification in the attempt to develop an accounting theory. Traditional approaches constitute conventional research rather than new streams of research that rely on traditional reasoning to formulate a conceptual accounting framework. Among these approaches we may distinguish (1) the nontheoretical approaches, (2) the deductive approach, (3) the inductive approach, (4) the ethical approach, (5) the sociological approach, and (6) the economic approach. In this chapter, each of these approaches is examined in terms of its contribution to the formulation of an accounting theory and in terms of its relative advantages of accounting, the differences between theory construction and verification, the nature of an accounting theory, and the methodologies for the formulation of an accounting theory.

3.1 THE NATURE OF ACCOUNTING: VARIOUS IMAGES

The Committee on Terminology of the American Institute of Certified Public Accountants originally defined accounting as follows:

> Accounting is the act of recording, classifying, and summarizing, in a significant manner and in terms of money, transactions and events which are, in part at least, of a financial character, and interpreting the results thereof.[1]

More recently, accounting has been defined with reference to the concept of information:

> Accounting is a service activity. Its function is to provide quantitative information, primarily financial in nature, about economic entities that is intended to be useful in making economic decisions, in making reasoned choices among courses of action.[2]

These definitions refer to accounting as either an "art" or a "service activity" and imply that accounting encompasses a body of techniques that is deemed useful for certain fields. *The Handbook of Accounting* identifies the following fields in which accounting is useful: financial reporting; tax determination and planning; independent audits; data processing and information systems; cost and management accounting; national income accounting; and management consulting.[3]

Accountants draw on different images of the accounting process to elaborate different theories of accounting.[4] Before examining the traditional approaches to the formulation of accounting theory, it would be useful to examine some of the images that have shaped developments in financial accounting. These images are accounting as a *language*, accounting as a *historical record*, accounting as a *current economic reality*, accounting as an *information system*, accounting as a *commodity*, and, finally, accounting as an *ideology*.

3.1.1 Accounting as an Ideology

> Ideologies are world views which, despite their partial and possible crucial insights, prevent us from understanding the society in which we live and the possibility of changing it. They are world views which correspond to the standpoint of classes.... [5]

Accounting has been perceived as an ideological phenomenon — as a means of sustaining and legitimizing the current social, economic, and political arrangements. Karl Marx maintained that accounting perpetrates a form of false consciousness and provides a means for mystifying rather than revealing the true nature of the social relationships that form productive endeavor.[6] Accounting has also been perceived as a myth, symbol, and ritual that permits the creation of a symbolic order within which social agents can interact. Both perceptions are also embodied in the prevalent view of accounting as an instrument of economic rationality and as a tool of a capitalistic system.

The perception of accounting as an instrument of economic rationality is best exemplified by Weber, who defines the formal rationality of economic action as "the extent of quantitative calculation or accounting which is technically possible and which is actually applied."[7] The same point is well emphasized by Heilbroner when he states that

> Capitalist practice turns the unit of money in a tool of rational cost–profit calculations, of which the towering monument is double-entry bookkeeping ... primarily the product of the evolution of economic rationality, the cost–profit calculus, in turn reacts on that rationality; by crystallizing and defining numerically, it powerfully propels the logic of enterprise.[8]

3.1.2 Accounting as a Language

Accounting has been perceived as the language of business. It is one means of communicating information about a business.

ion of accounting as a language is emphasized in most popular accounting
example, Ijiri contends that

> guage of business, accounting has many things in common with other
> The various business activities of a firm are reported in accounting
> state... s using accounting language, just as news events are reported in newspapers
> in the English language. To express an event in accounting not only does one run the
> risk of being misunderstood but also risks a penalty for misrepresentation, lying or
> perjury. Comparability of statements is essential to the effective functioning of a
> language whether it is in English or in Accounting. At the same time, language has to
> be flexible to adapt to a changing environment.[9]

This perception of accounting as a language is also recognized by the accounting
profession, which publishes accounting terminology bulletins. It is acknowledged in the
empirical literature, which attempts to measure the communication of accounting
concepts.

What makes accounting a language? To answer this question, let us look at the
potential parallels between accounting and language. Hawes defines a language as
follows:

> Man's symbols are not randomly arranged signs which lead to the conceptualization of
> isolated and discrete referents. Rather, man's symbols are arranged in a systematic or
> patterned fashion with certain rules governing their usage. This arrangement of symbols
> is called a language, and the rules which influence the patterning and usage of the
> symbols constitute the grammar of the language.[10]

This definition and others indicate that there are two components of a language, namely
symbols and *grammatical rules*. Thus, the recognition of accounting as a language rests on
the identification of these two components as the two levels of accounting. It may be
argued as follows:

1 The *symbols* or *lexical characteristics* of a language are the "meaningful" units or
 words identifiable in any language. These symbols are linguistic objects used to
 identify particular concepts. Symbolic representations do exist in accounting. For
 example, McDonald identifies numerals and words and debits and credits as the
 only symbols accepted and unique to the accounting discipline.[11]
2 The *grammatical rules* of a language refer to the syntactic arrangements in any given
 language. In accounting, grammatical rules refer to the general set of procedures
 used that are followed to create all financial data for the business. Jain establishes the
 following parallel between grammatical rules and accounting rules:

> The CPA (the expert in accounting) certifies the correctness of the application
> rules as does an accomplished speaker of a language for the grammatical
> correctness of the sentence. Accounting rules formalize the inherent structure of a
> natural language.[12]

Given the existence of these identified components, symbols and grammatical rules,
accounting may be defined a priori as a language.

3.1.3 Accounting as a Historical Record

Generally, accounting has been viewed as a means of providing the history of an organization and its transactions with its environment. For either the owner or the shareholders of a company, accounting records provide a history of the manager's *stewardship* of the owner's resources. The stewardship concept is basically a feature of the principal–agent relationship, whereby the agent is assumed to safeguard the resources of the principal. The measuring of the stewardship concept has evolved over time. Birnberg distinguishes between four periods:

1 The pure custodial period.
2 The traditional custodial period.
3 The asset-utilization period.
4 The open-ended period.[13]

The first two periods refer to the need for the agent to return the resources intact to the principal by performing minimal tasks to fulfill the custodial function. In these two periods, the disclosure of balance sheet data is considered to be adequate. The third period refers to the need for the agent to provide initiative and insight in using the assets to conform to agreed plans. In addition to the balance sheet, this period requires the acquisition of performance-evaluation data on the effectiveness of the use of the assets. Finally, the open-ended period differs from the asset-utilization period by providing more flexibility in the use of the assets and allowing the agent to chart the course of asset utilization. Birnberg elaborates on this last concept as follows:

> This involves not only the initial direction, but also ascertaining the critical point in time when such directions must be changed. Like strategic control, the stewardship function requires that a significant degree of responsibility be assumed by the servant. The task force is probably characterized by a lack of structure and a significant amount of uncertainty. This suggests that we may find our reporting system to the master caught between the rock and hard place of communication. The need for the detail on one hand and the risk or overload and excessive complexity on the other.[14]

3.1.4 Accounting as Current Economic Reality

Accounting has also been viewed as a means of reflecting current economic reality. The central thesis of advocates of this view is that both balance sheets and income statements should be based on a valuation basis that is more reflective of economic reality than historical costs. The method considered to be most reflective of economic reality focuses on current and future prices rather than on historical prices. The main objective of this image of accounting is the determination of *true income*, a concept that reflects the change in the wealth of the firm over a period of time. Which methods best measure the economic values of assets and liabilities and the related measurement of income is a theoretical and empirical question that has generated the most prolific debate in the accounting literature. In Chapters 7–9 we will elaborate on the relative advantages and limitations of some of the asset-valuation methods proposed.

3.1.5 Accounting as an Information System

Accounting has always been viewed as an information system. It is assumed to be a process that links an information source or transmitter (usually the accountant), a channel of communication, and a set of receivers (external users). Basically, when considered as a process of communication, accounting can best be defined as "the process of encoding observations in the language of the accounting system, of manipulating the signs and the statements of the system and decoding and transmitting the reuslt."[15] This view of accounting has important conceptual and empirical overtones. First, it assumes that the accounting system is the only formal measurement system in the organization. Second, it raises the possibility of designing an optional accounting system capable of providing *useful* information (to the user). The behavior of the sender is important in terms of both the reaction to the information and the use made of the information. Both behaviors are the subject of conceptual and empirical research in the field of behavioral accounting (see Chapter 3). The superiority of the image of accounting as an information system is stated as follows:

> Alternative accounting systems need no longer be justified in terms of their ability to generate "true income" or on the faithfulness with which they represent history. As long as the different users find the information useful, the utility of the system can be established.[16]

3.1.6   Accounting as a Commodity

Accounting is also viewed as a commodity that results from an economic activity. It exists because specialized information is in demand and accountants are willing and capable of producing it. As a public commodity, accounting provides ideal ground for regulation, making an impact on public policy and monitoring of all types of contracts between the organization and its environment. The choice of accounting information and/or accounting technique then may have an impact on the welfare of various groups in society. As a result, there is a market for accounting information with its derived demand and supply. This image of accounting as a commodity is having and will continue to have a profound impact on accounting thought and research. For example:

> The emergence of the image of accounting as a commodity again provides a striking example of the manner in which accounting thought reflects its social content. It has arisen in an era of mushrooming regulation and increasing concern with the public interest in a situation of scarce resources and many competing demands. It has provided the rationale for accounting policies which seek to aid the allocation of resources in the service of the public interest.[17]

3.2   THEORY CONSTRUCTION AND VERIFICATION

Although accounting is a set of techniques that can be used in specified fields, it is practiced within an implicit *theoretical* framework composed of principles and practices that have been accepted by the profession because of their alleged usefulness and their logic. These "generally accepted accounting principles" guide the accounting profession in the choice of accounting techniques and in the preparation of financial statements in a way considered to be good accounting practice. In response to changing environments, values, and information needs, generally accepted accounting principles are subject to constant reexamination and critical analysis. This is reflected in APB Statement No. 4, which describes the principles as follows:

> Present generally accepted accounting principles are the result of an evolutionary process that can be expected to continue in the future. Changes may occur at any level of generally accepted accounting principles... . Generally accepted accounting principles change in response to changes in the economic and social conditions, to new knowledge and technology, and to demands of users for more serviceable financial information. The dynamic nature of financial accounting — its ability to change in response to changed conditions — enables it to maintain and increase the usefulness of the information it provides.[18]

Changes in the principles occur mainly as a result of the various attempts to provide solutions to emerging accounting problems and to formulate a theoretical framework for the discipline. Thus, a definite link exists between accounting theory construction attempts either to justify or to refute existing practice. Accounting theory construction stems from the need to provide a rationale for what accountants do or expect to be doing.

The process of accounting theory construction should be completed by theory verification or theory validation. Machlup defines this process as follows:

> Verification in research and analysis may refer to many things, including the correctness of mathematical and logical arguments, the applicability of formulas and equations, the trustworthiness of reports, the authenticity of documents, the genuineness of artifacts or relics, the adequacy of reproductions, translations, and paraphrases, the accuracy of historical and statistical accounts, the corroboration of reported events, the completeness in the enumeration of circumstances in a concrete situation, the reproducibility of experiments, the explanatory or predictive value of generalizations.[19]

This statement implies that theory should be subject to a logical or empirical testing to verify its accuracy. If the theory is mathematically based, the verification should be predicted based on logical consistency. If the theory is based on physical or social phenomena, the verification should be predicted based on logical consistency. If the theory is based on physical or social phenomena, the verification should be predicted based on the relationship between the deduced events and observations in the real world.[20]

Accounting theory, therefore, should be the result of both a process of theory construction and a process of theory verification. A given accounting theory should explain and predict accounting phenomena: when such phenomena occur, they should be regarded as verification of the theory. If a given theory is unable to produce the expected results, it is replaced by a "better" theory.[21] This well-accepted idea in the philosophy of science also applies to and is accepted in accounting, as shown by the following statement from the Committee on Accounting Theory and Verification:

> Scientific theories provide certain "expectations" or "predictions" about phenomena and, when these expectations occur, they are said to "confirm" the theory. When unexpected results occur, they are considered to be anomalies which eventually require a modification of the theory or the construction of a new theory. The purpose of the new theory or the modified theory is to make the unexpected expected, to convert the anomalous occurrence into an expected and explained occurrence.[22]

To date, this line of thinking has not been strictly followed in accounting. Instead, two approaches have been used. In the traditional approach to accounting theory construction, accounting practice and verification are considered synonymous; in the new approaches to accounting theory construction, attempts are made to logically or empirically verify the theory. In this chapter, we will elaborate on the nature and contribution of the traditional approaches to accounting theory construction. Chapters 2–4 cover the same issues for the new approaches to accounting theory construction. Before we are introduced to the traditional approaches, however, we will examine the nature of an accounting theory and the methodologies adopted for the formulation of an accounting theory. The traditional approaches we will examine are the nontheoretical, pragmatic, and authoritarian approach; the deductive approach; the inductive approach; the ethical approach; the sociological approach; the economic approach; and the eclectic approach.

3.3   THE NATURE OF AN ACCOUNTING THEORY

The primary objective of accounting theory is to provide a basis for the prediction and explanation of accounting behavior and events. We assume, as an article of faith, that an accounting theory is possible. A *theory* is defined as "a set of interrelated constructs (concepts), definitions, and propositions that present a systematic view of phenomena by specifying relations among variables with the purpose of explaining and predicting the phenomena."[23]

It must be recognized at the outset that no comprehensive theory of accounting exists at the present time. Instead, different theories have been and continue to be proposed in the literature. Many of these theories arise from the use of different approaches to the construction of an accounting theory or from the attempt to develop theories of a *middle ranger*, rather than one single comprehensive theory. Accounting theories of a middle range result from differences in the way researchers perceive both the "users" of accounting data and the "environments" in which the users and preparers of accounting data are supposed to behave. These divergences led the American Accounting Association's Committee on Concepts and Standards for External Financial Reports to conclude that:

1 No single governing theory of financial accounting is rich enough to encompass the full range of user-environment specifications effectively; hence,
2 there exists in the financial accounting literature not a theory of financial accounting, but a *collection of theories* which can be arrayed over the differences in user-environment specifications.[24]

Despite the presence of accounting theories of a middle range, few authors of these theories have attempted to prove that an accounting theory is possible. Two exceptions deserve our attention.

E.S. Hendriksen used a definition of "theory" that may be applied to accounting. According to *Webster's Third New International Dictionary*, "theory" represents "the coherent set of hypothetical, conceptual, and pragmatic principles forming the general frame of reference for a field of inquiry." Hendriksen therefore defines *accounting theory* as "a set of broad principles that (1) provides a general frame of reference by which accounting practice can be evaluated and (2) guides the development of new practices and procedures."[25] This definition allows us to perceive accounting theory as providing a coherent set of logically-derived principles that serve as a frame of reference for evaluating and developing accounting practices.

McDonald argues that a theory must have three elements: (1) encoding of phenomena to symbolic representation, (2) manipulation or combination according to rules, and (3) translation back to real-world phenomena.[26] Each of these theory components is found in accounting. First, accounting employs symbolic representations or symbols; "debit," "credit," and a whole terminology are proper and unique to accounting. Second, accounting employs translation rules; encoding (symbolic represenations of economic events and transactions) is a process of translation into and out of symbols. Third, accounting employs rules of manipulation; techniques for the determination of profit may be considered as rules for the manipulation of accounting symbols.

3.4 METHODOLOGIES FOR THE FORMULATION OF AN ACCOUNTING THEORY

We have now established that an accounting theory is possible if (1) it constitutes a frame of reference, as suggested by Hendriksen, and (2) it includes three elements: encoding of phenomena to symbolic representation, manipulation or combination according to rules, and translation back to real-world phenomena, as suggested by McDonald.

As in any other discipline, a methodology is required for the formulation of an accounting theory. The divergence of opinions, approaches, and values between accounting practice and accounting research has led to the use of two methodologies. One is descriptive; the other, normative.

In the professional world of accounting, the belief is widely held that accounting is an art that cannot be formalized and that the methodology traditionally used in the formulation of an accounting theory is an attempt to justify *what is* by codifying accounting practices. Such a theory is labeled *descriptive accounting* or a *descriptive theory of accounting*.[27]

The descriptive accounting approach has been criticized by proponents of a normative methodology. Normative accounting theory attempts to justify what ought to be, rather that what is. Such a theory is labeled *normative accounting* or a *normative theory of accounting*.[28]

At the risk of oversimplifying, we may assume that, given the complex nature of accounting phenomena and issues, both methodologies may be needed to formulate an accounting theory. The descriptive methodology will attempt to justify some of the accounting practices that are deemed useful, and the normative methodology will attempt to justify some of the accounting practices that ought to be adopted. Among the descriptive theories of accounting are Grady's "Inventory of Generally Accepted Accounting Principles for Business Enterprises," Accounting Principles Board Statement No. 4, and the works of Skinner and Ijiri.[29] Ijiri's book differs from the other attempts to formulate a theory, in that it is not only a descriptive but also an analytic examination of accounting through (1) a mathematical inquiry to examine the logical structure, (2) an economic inquiry to examine what is measured, and (3) a behavioral inquiry to examine how accounting is practiced and used. A distinction is made between two different orientations. One, called *operational accounting* is aimed at providing useful information for management and investor decisions, especially decisions concerning resource allocation; the other, called *equity accounting*, is aimed at reconciling the equities of shareholders and other interested parties inside or outside an organization to achieve an equitable distribution of the proceeds or benefits from operations.

Among the normative theories of accounting are the studies by Noonitz, Sprouse and Moonitz, the American Accounting Association's *A Statement of Basic Accounting Theory*, the theory of Edwards and Bell, and the Chambers study.[30] A good review of the descriptive and normative methodologies and of the resulting theories is provided by McDonald and the American Accounting Association's *Statement on Accounting Theory and Theory Acceptance.*[31]

3.5 APPROACHES TO THE FORMULATION OF AN ACCOUNTING THEORY

Although there is no single comprehensive theory of accounting, various accounting theories of a middle range have resulted from the use of different approaches. For the sake of clarity, we will limit our discussion in this chapter to the traditional approaches to the formulation of an accounting theory. These traditional approaches have reached a higher level of acceptance and exposure than the new approaches, which will be presented in Chapters 2–4. The traditional approaches are:

1 Nontheoretical, practical, or pragmatic (informal).
2 Theoretical:
   a. deductive;
   b. inductive;
   c. ethical;
   d. sociological;
   e. economic;
   f. eclectic.

We will examine each of these approaches in the following sections.

3.5.1 Nontheoretical Approaches

The nontheoretical approaches are a *pragmatic* (or practical) approach and an *authoritarian* approach.

The *pragmatic approach* consists of the construction of a theory characterized by its conformity to real-world practices that is useful in terms of suggesting practical solutions. According to this approach, accounting techniques and principles should be chosen on the basis of their usefulness to users of accounting information and their relevance to decision-making process. *Usefulness*, or *utility*, means "that property which fits something to serve or to facilitate its intended purposes."[32]

The *authoritarian approach* to the formulation of an accounting theory, which is employed primarily by professional organizations, consists of issuing pronouncements for the regulation of accounting practices.

Because the authoritarian approach also attempts to provide practical solutions, it is easily identified with the pragmatic approach. Both approaches assume that accounting theory and the resulting accounting techniques must be predicted on the basis of the ultimate uses of financial reports, if accounting is to have a useful function. *In other words, a theory without practical consequences is a bad theory.*[33]

The use of utility as a criterion for the choice of accounting principles links accounting theory construction to accounting practices, which may explain the lack of enthusiasm generated by the pragmatic approach. In fact, the pragmatic and authoritarian approaches have been largely unsuccessful in reaching satisfactory conclusions in their attempts to construct an accounting theory. For instance, Skinner claims that:

> In essence, the pragmatic approach to the development of accounting principles has been followed by accounting authority in the past, and attempts to reduce conflicting practices have until recently been extremely cautious and tentative. It is apparent on the basis of experience that this approach will never, by itself, come close to solving the problem of conflicts in accepted accounting principles.[34]

Utility is cited as a main objective of accounting by various writers in the literature, including Fremgen and Prince.[35] Mueller also argues that accounting principles should be developed through a pragmatic approach.[36] The practical attempts should not be discarded simply because they are basically nontheoretical. Practical approaches are necessary to any theory with an operational utility. In fact, pragmatic considerations permeate the field of accounting through the generally accepted standard of relevance.[37]

We may also think of the pragmatic approach as including a *theory of accounts*. The approach, which rests on a rationalization of double-entry bookkeeping, was contained in Luca Pacioli's *Summa De Arithmetica, Geometria, Proportioni et Proportionalita*, published in Venice in 1494. Although the *Summa* was a review of the literature of the then-current mathematical technology, it included thirty-six short chapters on bookkeeping, called *De Computis et Scripturis* (Of Reckonings and Writings).[38]

The theory of accounts approach rationalizes the choice of accounting techniques on the basis of the maintenance of the accounting equations, namely the balance sheet equation and the accounting profit equation.

> The balance sheet equation is usually stated as:
> Assets = Liabilities + Owner's Equity
> The accounting profit equation is usually stated as:
> Accounting Profit = Revenues − Costs

These two equations in the theory of accounts approach led to the development of two positions within the standards-setting bodies, namely, a balance-sheet-oriented position and a profit-oriented position. In any case, the theory of accounts approach, like the pragmatic and authoritarian approaches, suffers from the absence of theoretical foundations.

3.5.2   Deductive Approach

The deductive approach to the construction of any theory begins with basic propositions and proceeds to derive logical conclusions about the subject under consideration. Applied to accounting, the deductive approach begins with basic accounting propositions or premises and proceeds to derive by logical means accounting principles that serve as guides and bases for the development of accounting techniques. This approach moves from the general (basic propositions about the accounting environment) to the particular (accounting principles first and accounting techniques second). If we assume at this point that the basic propositions about the accounting environment consist of both objectives and postulates, the steps used to derive the deductive approach will include:

1 Specifying the objectives of financial statements.
2 Selecting the "postulates" of accounting.
3 Deriving the "principles" of accounting.
4 Developing the "techniques" of accounting.

In a deductively derived accounting theory, therefore, the techniques are related to the principles, postulates, and objectives *in such a way that if they are true, the techniques must also be true*. The theoretical structure of accounting defined by the sequence of objectives, postulates, principles, and techniques rest on a proper formulation of the objectives of accounting. A proper testing of the resulting theory is also necesary. According to Popper, the testing of deductive theories could be carried out along four lines:

> First, there is the logical comparison of the conclusions among themselves, by which the internal consistency of the system is tested. Secondly, there is the investigation of the logical form of the theory with the object of determining whether it has the character of an empirical or scientific theory, or whether it is, for example, tautological. Thirdly, there is the comparison with other theories, chiefly with the aim of determining whether the theory would constitute a scientific advance should it survive our various tests, and finally, there is the testing of the theory by way of empirical applications of the conclusions which can be derived from it.[39]

The last step is necessary to determine how the theory stands up to the demand of practice. If its predictions are acceptable, then the theory is said to be *verified* or *corroborated* for the time being. If the predictions are not acceptable, then the theory is said to be *falsified*.

Although they do not necessarily adopt the same steps that we have defined for the deductive process, some accounting writers who have dealt primarily with the conceptual underpinnings of accounting may be categorized as "deductive theorists." Such writers as Paton, Canning, Sweeney, MacNeal, Alexander, Edwards and Bell, Moonitz, and Sprouse and Moonitz[40] are deductive theorists. In addition to them, research writers unanimously agree that users should use current price information in their resource-allocation decisions. In fact, the search for rigor in the formalization of the structure of accounting theory has led some deductive theorists to resort to the *axiomatic method* found in the writings of Mattessich and Chambers, which involves mathematical, analytic representations and testing.[41]

3.5.3 Inductive Approach

The inductive approach to the construction of a theory begins with observations and measurements and moves toward generalized conclusions. Applied to accounting, the inductive approach begins with obervations about the financial information of business enterprises and proceeds to construct generalizations and principles of accounting from these observations on the basis of recurring relationships. Inductive arguments are said to lead from the *particular* (accounting information depicting recurring relationships) to the *general* (postulates and principles of accounting). The inductive approach to a theory involves four stages:

1 Recording all observations.
2 Analysis and classification of these observations to detect recurring relationships ("likes" and "similarities").
3 Inductive derivation of generalizations and principles of accounting from observations that depict recurring relationships.
4 Testing the generalizations.

Unlike the deductive approach, the truth or falsity of the propositions does not depend on other propositions, but must be empirically verified. In induction, the truth of the propositions depends on the observation of sufficient instances of recurring relationships.

Similarly, we may state that accounting propositions that result from inductive inference imply special accounting techniques only with more or less high probability, whereas the accounting propositions that result from deductive inference lead to specific accounting techniques with certainty.

Some accounting theorists rely on observations of accounting practice to suggest a theoretical framework for accounting. Inductive theorists include Hatfield, Gilman, Littleton, Paton and Littleton, and Ijiri.[42] The underlying objective of most of these authors is to draw theoretical and abstract conclusions from rationalizations of accounting practice. The best defense of the inductive approach is provided by Ijiri in his attempts to generalize the goals implicit in current accounting practice, and to defend the use of historical cost:

> This type of inductive reasoning to derive goals implicit in the behavior of an existing system is not intended to be proestablishment to promote the maintenance of the status quo. The purpose of such exercise is to highlight where changes are most needed and where they are feasible. Changes suggested as a result of such a study have a much better chance of being actually implemented. Goal assumptions in normative models or goals advocated in policy discussions are often stated purely on the basis of one's conviction and preference, rather than on the basis of inductive study of the existing system. This may perhaps be the most crucial reason why so many normative models or policy proposals are not implemented in the real world.[43]

It is interesting to note that although the deductive approach starts with general propositions, the formulation of the propositions is often accomplished by inductive reasoning, conditioned by the author's knowledge of and experience with accounting practice. In other words, the general propositions are formulated through an inductive process, but the principles and techniques are derived by a deductive process. Yu suggests that inductive logic may presuppose deductive logic.[44] It is not surprising, therefore, that inductive theorists sometimes interpose deductive reasoning and that deductive theorists sometimes interpose inductive reasoning. It is also interesting to note that when Littleton, an inductive theorist, and Paton, a deductive theorist, collaborate, the results are of a hybrid nature, indicating a compromise between the two approaches.

3.5.4   Ethical Approach

The basic core of the ethical approach consists of the concepts of fairness, justice, equity, and truth. Such concepts are D.R. Scott's main criteria for the formulation of an accounting theory.[45] Scott equates "justice" with equitable treatment of all interested parties, "truth" with true and accurate accounting statements without misrepresentation, and "fairness" with fair, unbiased, and impartial presentation. Accountants since Scott have considered these three concepts to be equivalent. Yu, in contrast, perceives only justice and fairness as ethical norms, and views truth as a value statement.[46] The "fairness" concept has become implicitly ethical; in general, the "fairness" concept implies that accounting statements have not been subject to undue influence or bias. "Fairness" generally implies that the preparers of accounting information have acted in good faith and employed ethical business practices and sound accounting judgement. "Fairness" is a value statement that is variously applied in accounting. Patillo ranks "fairness" as a basic standard to be used in the evaluation of other standards, because it is the only standard that implies "ethical considerations."[47] Spacek goes one step further in asserting the primacy of the "fairness" concept:

> A discussion of assets, liabilities, revenue, and costs is premature and meaningless until the basic principles that will result in a fair presentation of the facts in the form of financial accounting and financial reporting are determined. This fairness of accounting and reporting must be for and to people, and these people represent the various segments of our society.[48]

Whatever it may connote, fairness has become one of the basic objectives of accounting. The Committee on Auditing Procedures refers to the criteria of "fairness of presentation" as (1) conformity with generally accepted accounting principles, (2) disclosure, (3) consistency, and (4) comparability.[49] In an unqualified report, the auditor not only states compliance with generally accepted accounting principles and generally accepted auditing standards but also expresses an opinion with the words "present fairly." Thus, the conventional auditor's report reads as follows:

> We have examined the consolidated balance sheet of XYZ, as of June 30, 1978, and consolidated statements of income, retained earnings, and changes in financial position for the year then ended. Our examination was made in accordance with generally accepted auditing standards, and accordingly, included such tests and other procedures as we consider necessary in the circumstances.
>
> In our opinion, these consolidated financial statements present fairly the financial position of the company as of June 30, 1978, and the results of its operations and the changes in financial position for the year then ended in accordance with generally accepted accounting principles applied on a basis consistent with that of the preceding year.

On close examination of this standard auditor's report, we see that the statement "present fairly" is included in addition to the auditor's expressed compliance with generally accepted accounting principles and generally accepted auditing standards. This may be seen as psychologically desirable, because it may increase the user's confidence. On the other hand, it may imply a double standard, because the concept of "fairness" is substituted for the tests of generally accepted accounting principles and generally accepted auditing standards.

"Fairness" is a desirable objective in the construction of an accounting theory if whatever is asserted on its basis is logically or empirically verified and if it is made operational by an adequate definition and identification of its properties.

3.5.5 Sociological Approach

The sociological approach to the formulation of an accounting theory emphasizes the social effects of accounting techniques. It is an ethical approach that centers on a broader concept of fairness — *social welfare*. According to the sociological approach, a given accounting principle or technique is evaluated for acceptance on the basis of its reporting effects on all groups in society. Also implicit in this approach is the expectation that accounting data will be useful in making social-welfare judgments. To accomplish its objectives, the sociological approach assumes the existence of "established social values" that may be used as criteria for the determination of accounting theory.[50] It may be difficult to identify a strict application of the sociological approach to accounting-theory construction, due to the problems associated with determining acceptable "social values" for all people and with identifying the information needs of those who make welfare judgments. We may, however, identify cases in which accounting is expected to serve a useful social role. Belkaoui and Beams and Fertig,[51] among others refer to the necessity of "internalizing" the social costs and social benefits of the private activities of the business firm. Ladd, and Littleton and Zimmerman[52] make several assertions that accounting should serve the public interest and evolve in anticipation of public inputs, minority viewpoints, and even disagreements among groups. Bedford goes one step further by arguing that the maximization of social well-being is related to a measure of income determination that is best for society. Bedford says the measurement of operational income

> . . . plays the role of a lubricant, facilitating the functioning of society in an operational sense. Specifically, measured income is used as a computed amount to accomplish objectives necessary for the operation of society.[53]

The sociological approach to the formulation of an accounting theory has contributed to the evolution of a new accounting subdiscipline, known as *socioeconomic accounting*. The main objective of socioeconomic accounting is to encourage the business entities that function in a free-market system to account for the impact of their private production activities on the social environment through measurement, internalization, and disclosure in their financial statements. Over the years, interest in this subdiscipline has increased as a result of the social responsibility trend espoused by organizations, the government, and the public. Social-value-oriented accounting — with its emphasis on "social measurement," its dependence on "social values," and its compliance to a "social-welfare criterion" — will probably play a major role in the future formulation of accounting theory.

3.5.6   Economic Approach

The economic approach to the formulation of an accounting theory emphasizes controlling the behavior of macroeconomic indicators that result from the adoption of various accounting techniques. While the ethical approach focuses on a concept of "fairness" and the sociological approach on a concept of "social welfare," the economic approach focuses on a concept of "general economic welfare." According to this approach, the choice of different accounting techniques depends on their impact on the national economic good. Sweden is the usual example of a country that aligns its accounting policies with other macroeconomic policies.[54] More explicitly, the choice of accounting techniques will depend on the particular economic situation. For example, the last in, first out (LIFO) method will be a more attractive accounting technique during periods of continuing inflation than the first in, first out (FIFO) or average cost methods, because LIFO is assumed to produce a lower annual net income by assuming higher, more inflated costs for the goods sold.

The general criteria employed in the macroeconomic approach are, firstly, that accounting policies and techniques should reflect "economic reality,"[55] and secondly, that the choice of accounting techniques should depend on "economic consequences."[56] "Economic reality" and "economic consequences" are the precise terms being used to argue in favor of the macroeconomic approach.

Until the advent of the Financial Accounting Standards Board, the economic approach and the concept of "economic consequences" were not much used in accounting. The professional bodies were encouraged to resolve any standard-setting controversies within the context of traditional accounting. Few people were concerned with the economic consequences of accounting policies. In one case, the accounting treatment of the investment tax credit generated a debate among the Accounting Principles Board, the industry respresentative, and the administrations of Presidents Kennedy, Johnson, and Nixon. The government contested the use of the deferral method on the basis that it diluted the incentive effect of an instrument of fiscal policy.[57] The economic approach and the concepts of "economic consequences" and "economic reality" have been revived since the creation of the Financial Accounting Standards Board.[58] Most of the questions examined during the short life of the Board have been the subject of a critical examination in terms of the economic consequences of possible recommendations. Some examples are accounting for research and development, self-insurance and catastrophe reserves, development-stage companies, foreign currency fluctuations, leases, the restructuring of troubled debt, inflation accounting, and accounting in the petroleum industry.

In setting accounting standards, therefore, the considerations implied by the economic approach are more economic than operational. Although reliance has been on technical accounting considerations in the past, the tenor of the times suggests that standard setting encompasses social and economic concerns as well.

3.6   THE ECLECTIC APPROACH TO THE FORMULATION OF AN ACCOUNTING THEORY

In general, the formulation of an accounting theory and the development of accounting principles have followed an eclectic approach, or a combination of approaches, rather than only one of the approaches presented here. The eclectic approach is mainly the result of numerous attempts by individuals and professional and governmental organizations to participate in the establishment of concepts and principles in accounting. This eclectic approach has given rise to the new approaches being debated in the literature — the regulatory approaches (covered in Chapter 4), the behavioral approaches (covered in Chapter 5), and the event, predictive, and positive approaches (covered in Chapter 6).

3.7 CONCLUSIONS

The traditional approach to the formulation of an accounting theory has employed either a normative or a descriptive methodology, a theoretical or a nontheoretical approach, a deductive or an inductive line of reasoning, and has focused on a concept of "fairness," "social welfare," or "economic welfare." The traditional approach has evolved into an eclectic approach and is beginning to be replaced by newer approaches, to be examined in Chapters 4–6 (namely, the regulatory, behavioral, event, predictive, and positive approaches). Whatever approach is chosen, it is important to remember that an accounting theory must be confirmed to be accepted.

NOTES

[1] Accounting Terminology Bulletin No. 1, *Review and Résumé* (New York: American Institute of Certified Public Accountants, 1953), paragraph 9.

[2] APB Statement No. 4, *Basic Concepts and Accounting Principles Underlying Financial Statements of Business Enterprises* (New York: American Institute of Certified Public Accountants, 1970), paragraph 40.

[3] *The Handbook of Accounting* (Fifth Edition) (New York: American Institute of Certified Public Accountants, 1970), paragraph 9.

[4] Davis, S.W., Menon, K., and Morgan, G., "The Images That Have Shaped Accounting Theory," *Accounting, Organizations, and Society* (December, 1982) pp. 307–18.

[5] Shaw, M., "The Coming Crisis of Radical Sociology," in *Ideology in Social Science*, R. Blackburn (ed.) (New York: Fontana, 1972), p. 33.

[6] Burchell, S., Clubb, C., Hopwood, A., Hughes, J., and Nahapier, J., "The Roles of Accounting in Organizations and Society," *Accounting, Organizations, and Society* (June, 1980), p. 19.

[7] Weber, M., *Economy and Society*, Vol. 1 (New York: Bedminster Press, 1969), p. 85.

[8] Heilbroner, R.L., *Business Civilization in Decline* (New York: Penguin Books, 1977), pp. 123–4.

[9] Ijiri, Yuji, Accounting Research Study No. 10, "Theory of Accounting Measurement" (Sarasota, Fl.: American Accounting Association, 1975), p. 14.

[10] Hawes, L.C., *Pragmatics of Analoging* (Reading, Ma.: Addison-Wesley, 1972).

[11] McDonald, Daniel, L., *Comparative Accounting Theory* (Reading: Ma.: Addison-Wesley, 1972).

[12] Jain, Tribhowan, N., "Alternative Methods of Accounting and Decision Making: A Psycholinguistic Analysis," *The Accounting Review* (January, 1973), p. 101.

[13] Birnberg, J.G., "The Role of Accounting in Financial Disclosure," *Accounting, Organizations, and Society* (June, 1980), p. 73.

[14] Ibid., p. 74.

[15] Chambers, R.J., *Accounting, Evaluation, and Economic Behavior* (Houston: Scholars Book Company, 1974), p. 184.

[16] Davis, S.W., Menon, K., and Morgan, G., The Images That Have Shaped Accounting Theory, op. cit., p. 312.

[17] Ibid., p. 313.

[18] APB Statement No. 4, paragraphs 208 and 209.

[19] Machlup, Fritz, "The Problem of Verification in Economics," *The Southern Economic Journal* (July, 1955), p. 1.

[20] "Report of the Committee on Accounting Theory Construction and Verification," *The Accounting Review*, supplement to Vol. 46 (1971), p. 54.

[21] Kuhn, Thomas S., "Anomaly and the Emergence of Scientific Discoveries," *The Structure of Scientific Revolution* (Chicago: University of Chicago Press, 1962), pp. 52–65.

[22] "Report of the Committee on Accounting Theory Construction and Verification," p. 53.

[23] Kerlinger, F.N. *Foundations of Behavioral Research* (New York: Holt, Rinehart & Winston, 1964), p. 11.

[24] *Statement of Accounting Theory and Theory Acceptance* (Sarasota, Fl.: American Accounting Association, 1977), pp. 1–2.

[25] Hendriksen, E.S., *Accounting Theory* (Third Edition) (Homewood, Ill.: Richard D. Irwin, 1977), p. 1.

[26] McDonald, Daniel L., *Comparative Accounting Theory*, op. cit., pp. 5–8.

[27] Ibid., p. 8.

[28] Ibid., p. 8.

[29] Grady, Paul, Accounting Research Study No. 7, *Inventory of Generally Accepted Accounting Principles for Business Enterprises* (New York: American Institute of Certified Public Accountants, 1965); Skinner, R.M., *Accounting Principles: A Canadian Study* (Toronto: Canadian Institute of Chartered Accountants, 1973); Ijiri, Yuji, *The Foundations of Accounting Measurement: A Mathematical, Economic, and Behavioral Inquiry* (Englewood Cliffs, N.J.: Prentice-Hall, 1967).

[30] Moonitz, Maurice, *The Basic Postulates of Accounting* (New York: American Institute of Certified Public Accountants, 1961); Sprouse, R.T., and Moonitz, Maurice, Accounting Research Study No. 3, *A Tentative Set of Broad Basic Accounting Principles for Business Enterprises* (New York: American Institute of Certified Public Accountants, 1962); *A Statement of Basic Accounting Theory* (Evanston, Ill.: American Accounting Association, 1966); Edwards, E.O., and Bell, P.W., *The Theory and Measurement of Business Income* (Berkeley: University of California Press, 1961); Chambers, R.J., *Accounting, Evaluation, and Economic Behavior*.

[31] McDonald, Daniel L., *Comparative Accounting Theory; Statement of Accounting Theory and Theory Acceptance*.

[32] Fremgen, James M., "Utility and Accounting Principles," *The Accounting Review* (July, 1967), p. 457–67.

[33] Hendriksen E.S., *Accounting Theory* op. cit., p. 23.

[34] Skinner, R.M., *Accounting Principles* op. cit., p. 302.

[35] Fremgen, James, M., "Utility and Accounting Principles," op cit.; Prince, T.R., *Extension of the Boundaries of Accounting Theory* (Cincinnati: South-Western, 1973).

[36] Mueller, Gerhard G., *International Accounting* (New York: Macmillan, 1967) pp. 27–30.

[37] *A Statement of Basic Accounting Theory*, p. 9.

[38] Geijsbeek, J.B., *Ancient Double-Entry Bookkeeping: Luca Pacioli's Treatise* (Denver: University of Colorado, 1914).

[39] Popper, I., *The Logic of Scientific Discovery* (London: Hutchinson, 1959), p. 33.

[40] Paton, W.A., *Accounting Theory* (New York: The Ronald Press, 1922); Canning, J.B., *Tax Economics of Accountancy* (New York: The Ronald Press, 1923); Sweeny, Henry W., *Stabilized Accounting* (New York: Hayer & Brothers, 1936); MacNeal, Kenneth, *Truth in Accounting* (Philadelphia: University of Pennsylvania Press, 1939); Alexander, Sidney S., "Income Measurement in a Dynamic Economy," *Five Monographs of Business Income* (New York: American Institute of Certified Public Accountants, 1950); Edwards, E.O., and Bell, P.W., *The Theory and Measurement of Business Income*; Moonitz, Maurice, *The Basic Postulates of Accounting*; Sprouse, R.T., and Moonitz, Maurice, "A Tentative Set of Broad Basic Accounting Principles for Business Enterprises," op. cit.

[41] Mattessich, R., *Accounting and Analytical Methods* (Homewood, Ill.: Richard D. Irwin, 1964); Chambers, R.J., *Accounting, Evaluation, and Economic Behavior*, op. cit.

[42] Hatfield, H.R., *Accounting* (New York: D. Appleton & Company, 1927); Gilman, S., *Accounting Concepts of Profit* (New York: The Ronald Press, 1939); Littleton, A.C., "Structure of Accounting Theory," *Monograph No. 5* (Evanston, Ill.: American Accounting Association, 1953); Paton, W.A., and Littleton, A.C., "An Introduction to Corporate Accounting Standards," *Monograph No. 3* (Evanston Ill.: American Accounting Association, 1940); Ijiri, Yuji, "Theory of Accounting Measurement," *Studies in Accounting Research No. 10* (Evanston, Ill.: American Accounting Association, 1975).

[43] Ijiri, Yuji, "Theory of Accounting Measurement," op. cit., p. 28.

[44] Yu, S.C., *The Structure of Accounting Theory* (Gainesville: The University Presses of Florida, 1976), p. 20.

[45] Scott, D.R., "The Basis for Accounting Principles," *The Accounting Review* (December, 1941), pp. 341–9.

[46] Yu, S.C., *The Structure of Accounting Theory*, op. cit.

[47] Patillo, James, W., *The Foundations of Financial Accounting* (Baton Rouge: Louisiana State University Press, 1965), p. 11.

[48] "Comments of Leonard Spacek," in R.T. Sprouse and Maurice Moonitz, *Accounting Research Study No. 3*, "A Tentative Set of Broad Basic Accounting Principles for Business Enterprises" (New York: American Institute of Certified Public Accountants, 1962), p. 78.

[49] Statement on Auditing Procedure No. 33, *Auditing Standards and Procedures* (New York: American Institute of Certified Public Accountants, 1963), pp. 69–74.

[50] Rappaport, A., "Establishing Objectives for Published Corporate Accounting Reports," *The Accounting Review* (October 1964), pp. 954–61.

[51] Belkaoui, A., "The Whys and Wherefores of Measuring Externalities," *The Certified General Accountant* (January–February 1975), pp. 29–32; Beams, Floyd A., and Fertig, Paul E., "Pollution Control Through Social Cost Conversion," *Journal of Accountancy* (November 1971), pp. 37–42.

[52] Ladd, D.R., *Contemporary Corporate Accounting and the Public* (Homewood, Ill. Richard

D. Irwin, 1963), p. ix; Littleton, A.C., and Zimmerman, V.K., *Accounting Theory: Continuity and Change* (New York: Prentice-Hall, 1962), pp. 261–2.

[53] Brooks, L.L., Jr. "Accounting Policies Should Reflect Economic Reality," *The Canadian Chartered Accountant Magazine* (November, 1976), pp. 39–43.

[54] Mueller, Gerhard, G., *International Accounting*, op. cit., pp. 27–30.

[55] Brooks, L.L., Jr. "Accounting Policies Should Reflect Economic Reality," *The Canadian Chartered Accountant Magazine* (November, 1976), pp. 39–43.

[56] Zeff, A.S., "The Rise of 'Economic Consequences'," *Journal of Accountancy* (December, 1978), pp. 56–63.

[57] Moonitz, Maurice, "Some Reflections on the Investment Credit Experience," *Journal of Accounting Research* (Spring, 1966), pp. 47–61.

[58] Conference on the Economic Consequences of Financial Accounting Standards (Stamford, Ct.: Financial Accounting Standards Board, 1978).

REFERENCES

Images of Accounting

Belkaoui, A., "Linguistic Relativity in Accounting," *Accounting, Organizations, and Society* (October, 1978), pp. 97–104.

Birnberg, J.G., "The Role of Accounting in Financial Disclosure," *Accounting, Organizations, and Society* (June, 1980), pp. 71–80.

Buckley, J.W., "Policy Models in Accounting: A Critical Commentary," *Accounting, Organizations, and Society* (June 1980), pp. 49–64.

Burchell, S., Clubb, C., Hopwood, A., Hughes, J., and Nahapier, J., "The Roles of Accounting in Organizations and Society," *Accounting, Organizations, and Society* (June, 1980), pp. 5–28.

Chambers, R.J., "The Myths and the Science of Accounting," *Accounting, Organizations, and Society* (June, 1980) pp. 167–80.

Davis, S.W., Menon, K., and Morgan, G., "The Images That Have Shaped Accounting Theory," *Accounting, Organizations, and Society* (December, 1982), pp. 307–18.

Jain, Tribhowan N., "Alternative Methods of Accounting and Decision Making: A Psycholinguistic Analysis," *The Accounting Review* (January, 1973), pp. 95–104.

Morgan, G., "Paradigms, Metaphors and Puzzle Solving in Organization Theory," *Administrative Science Quarterly* (1980), pp. 605–22.

Theory Construction and Verification

American Accounting Association, "Report of the Committee on Foundations of Accounting Measurement," *The Accounting Review*, supplement to Vol. 46 (1971), pp. 37–45.

American Accounting Association, "Report of the Committee on Accounting Theory Construction and Verification," *The Accounting Review*, supplement to Vol. 46 (1971), pp. 53–79.

Buckley, J.W., Kircher, Paul, and Mathews, Russell L., "Methodology in Accounting Theory," *The Accounting Review* (April, 1968), pp. 274–83.

Gonedes, N.J., "Perception, Estimation, and Verifiability," *International Journal of Accounting Education and Research* (Spring, 1969), pp. 63–73.

McDonald, Daniel L., *Comparative Accounting Theory* (Reading, Ma.: Addison-Wesley, 1972).

Schrader, William J., and Malcolm, Robert E., "Note on Accounting Theory Construction and Verification," *Abacus* (June, 1973), pp. 93–8.

Sterling, Robert R., "An Explication and Analysis of the Structure of Accounting," Part 1, *Abacus* (December, 1971), pp. 137–52; Part 2, *Abacus* (December, 1972), pp. 145–62.

Sterling, Robert R., "On Theory Construction and Verification," *The Accounting Review* (July 1970), pp. 444–57.

Nontheoretical Approach

Beams, Floyd, A., "Indications of Pragmation and Empiricism in Accounting Thought," *The Accounting Review* (April, 1968), pp. 382–97.

Cowan, T.K., "A Pragmatic Approach to Accounting Theory," *The Accounting Review* (January, 1968), pp. 94–100.

Fremgen, James, M., "Utility and Accounting Principles," *The Accounting Review* (July, 1967), pp. 457–67.

Geijsbeek, J.B., *Ancient Double-Entry Bookkeeping: Luca Pacioli's Treatise* (Denver: University of Colorado, 1914).

Mueller, Gerhard G., "Accounting and Conventional Business Practices," *International Accounting* (New York: Macmillan, 1967), pp. 718–23.

Prince, R.T., *Extensions of the Boundaries of Accounting Theory* (Cincinnati: South-Western, 1963).

Deductive, Inductive, and Axiomatic Approaches

Bedford, N.M., and Dopuch, N., "Research Methodology and Accounting Theory: Another Perspective," *The Accounting Review* (July 1972), pp. 351–61.

Demski, Joel, S. "The General Impossibility of Normative Accounting Standards," *The Accounting Review* (October, 1973), pp. 718–23.

Devine, C.T., "Research Methodology and Accounting Theory Formation," *The Accounting Review* (July, 1960), pp. 387–99.

Hakansson, Nils H., "Normative Accounting Theory and the Theory of Decision," *International Journal of Accounting Education and Research* (Spring, 1969), pp. 33–47.

Langenderfer, H.Q., "A Conceptual Framework for Financial Reporting," *Journal of Accountancy* (July, 1973), pp. 45–55.

Mattessich, R., *Accounting and Analytical Methods* (Homewood, Ill.: Richard D. Irwin, 1964).

Mattessich, R., "Methodological Preconditions and Problems of a General Theory of Accounting," *The Accounting Review* (July, 1972), pp. 469–87.

Moonitz, Maurice, "Why Do we Need 'Postulates' and 'Principles'?" *Journal of Accountancy* (December, 1963), pp. 42–6.

Pellicelli, Georgio. "The Axiomatic Method in Business Economics: A First Approach," *Abacus* (December, 1969), pp. 119–31.

Vernon, Kam, "Judgment and Scientific Trend in Accounting," *Journal of Accountancy* (February, 1973), pp. 57–67.

Ethical Approach

Arnett, Harold E. "The Concept of Fairness," *The Accounting Review* (April, 1967), pp. 291–7.

Burton, John C. (ed.), *Corporate Financial Reporting: Ethical and Other Problems* (New York: American Institute of Certified Public Accountants, 1972), pp. 17–27 ff.

Patillo, James W., *The Foundation of Financial Accounting* (Baton Rouge: Louisiana State University Press, 1965).

Scott, D.R., "The Basis for Accounting Principles," *The Accounting Review* (December, 1941), pp. 341–9.

Spacek, Leonard, *A Search for Fairness in Financial Reporting to the Public* (Chicago: Arthur Andersen & Co., 1965), pp. 38–77 and 349–56.

Sociological Approach

Alexander, Michael O., "Social Accounting, If You Please!" *The Canadian Chartered Accountant Magazine* (January, 1973), pp. 23–7.

American Accounting Association, "Report of the Committee on Measures of Effectiveness for Social Programs," *The Accounting Review*, supplement to Vol. 47 (1972), pp. 337–98.

American Institute of Certified Public Accountants, *Social Measurement* (New York: American Institute of Certified Public Accountants, 1972).

Andrews, Frederick, "Puzzled Businessmen Ponder New Methods of Measuring Success," *The Canadian Chartered Accountant* (March, 1972), pp. 58–61.

Beams, Floyd, A., and Fertig, Paul E. "Pollution Control Through Social Cost Conversion," *Journal of Accountancy* (November, 1971), pp. 37–42.

Belkaoui, A., "The Whys and Wherefores of Measuring Externalities," *The Certified General Accountant* (January–February 1975), pp. 29–32.

Estes, Ralph, W., "Socioeconomic Accounting and External Diseconomies," *The Accounting Review* (April, 1972), pp. 284–90.

Gambling, Trevor, *Societal Accounting* (London: George Allen & Unwin, 1974).

Ladd, D.R., *Contemporary Corporate Accounting and the Public* (Homewood, Ill.: Richard D. Irwin, 1963).

Mobley, Sybil C., "The Challenges of Socioeconomic Accounting," *The Accounting Review* (October, 1970), pp. 762–8.

Economic Approach

Brooks, L.L., Jr., "Accounting Policies Should Reflect Economic Reality," *The Canadian Chartered Accountant Magazine* (November, 1976), pp. 39–43.

Enthoven, Adolf, J.H. *Accountancy and Economic Development Policy* (New York: American Elsevier, 1973).

FASB Conference on the Economic Consequences of Financial Accounting Standards (Stamford, Ct.: Financial Accounting Standards Board, 1978).

Moonitz, Maurice, "Some Reflections on the Investment Credit Experience," *Journal of Accounting Research* (Spring, 1966), pp. 47–61.

Meuller, Gerhard G. "Accounting Within a Macroeconomic Framework," *International Accounting* (New York: Macmillan, 1967), pp. 27–30.

Zeff, A.S. "The Rise of 'Economic Consequences'," *Journal of Accountancy* (December, 1978), pp. 56–63.

QUESTIONS

3.1 Define *accounting* and identify its fields of applications.

3.2 What is mean by *generally accepted accounting principles*?

3.3 What is the difference between *accounting theory construction* and *verification*?

3.4 What is the main difference between the traditional and new approaches to accounting theory construction and verification?

3.5 What is an *accounting theory*?

3.6 Define a *middle-range accounting theory*?

3.7 Elaborate on the differences between a *descriptive* and a *normative* methodology for the fomulation of an accounting theory.

3.8 What is the main difference between a theory *of* accounting and a theory *for* accounting?

3.9 Define and evaluate the following approaches to the fomulation of an accounting theory:
   a. Deductive approach
   b. Inductive approach
   c. Nontheoretical approach
   d. Theory of accounts approach
   e. Axiomatic approach
   f. Sociological approach
   g. Ethical approach
   h. Economic approach
   i. Eclectic approach

3.10 Contrast general-purpose financial statements, specific-purpose financial statements, and differential disclosure.

3.11 The following statements are made by S.C. Yu in *The Structure of Accounting Theory* (Gainesville: The University Presses of Florida, 1976), p. 45:

In one sense, a discipline may mean a body of specific instructions and exercises designed to train to proper conduct, behavior, or action; or it may mean a set of established rules and regulations and guiding or controlling action or performance. Alternatively, a discipline may be viewed as a branch of learning requiring the use of proper methodology.

Which of the above definitions applies to accounting?

3.12 The following statements were made by Arthur H. Woolf in *A Short History of Accountants and Accountancy* (London: Gee & Co., 1912), pp. xxix–xxx:

In one important respect, bookkeeping differs from other sciences, in that it is not in the least theoretical, but essentially and fundamentally practical. It is based on expediency, and upon the actual needs and requirements of everyday life. It was invented because man wanted it, because he found that he could not get on without it. It is essentially utilitarian. It is not the result of the work of *dilletanti*, of men who conceived some theory and labored to prove the truth of it.

Do you agree with the above statements? Why or why not?

3.13 The following statements were made by David Solomons in "The Politicization of Accounting," *Journal of Accountancy* (November 1978), p. 70:

Information cannot be neutral — it cannot therefore be reliable — if it is selected or presented for the purpose of producing some chosen effect on human behavior. It is this quality of neutrality which makes a map reliable: and the essential nature of accounting, I believe, is cartographic. Accounting is financial mapmaking. The better the map, the more completely it represents the complex phenomena that are being mapped.

What are the strengths and limitations of the analogy between accounting and cartography?

3.14 The following four statements have been taken directly or with some modification from the accounting literature. All of these statements are quoted out of context, involve circular reasoning, or contain one or more fallacies, half-truths, erroneous comments or conclusions, or inconsistencies (internally or with generally accepted principles or practices).

Statement 1: Accounting is a service activity. Its function is to provide quantitative financial information that is intended to be useful in making economic decisions about and for economic entities. Thus, the accounting function might be viewed primarily as a tool or device for providing quantitative financial information to management to facilitate decision making.

Statement 2: Financial statements that were developed in accordance with generally accepted accounting principles, which apply the conservatism convention, can be free from bias (or can give a presentation that is fair with respect to continuing and prospective stockholders as well as to retiring stockholders).

Statement 3: When a company changes from the LIFO to the FIFO method of valuing ending inventories, and this change results in a $1 million increase both in income after taxes and in income taxes for the year of change, the increase would stem from the elimination of LIFO reserves established in prior years.

Statement 4: If the value of an enterprise were to be determined by the method that computes the sum of the present values of the marginal (or incremental) expected net receipts of individual tangible and intangible assets, the resulting valuation would tend to be less than if the value of the entire enterprise had been determined in another way, such as by computing the present value of total expected net receipts for the entire enterprise (that is, the resulting valuation of parts would sum to an amount that was less than that for the whole). This would be true even if the same pattern of interest or discount rates were used for both valuations.

Required

Evaluate each of these statements as follows:

a. List the fallacies, half-truths, circular reasoning, erroneous comments or conclusions, and inconsistencies.
b. Explain by what authority or on what basis each item listed in (a) may be considered fallacious, a half-truth, circular, an erroneous comment or conclusion, or inconsistent. If the statement or a portion of the statement is merely out of context, indicate the context(s) in which the statement would be correct.

(AICPA adapted)

3.15 At the completion of the Darby Department Store audit, the president asks about the meaning of the phrase "in conformity with generally accepted accounting principles" that appears in your audit report on the management's financial statements. The president observes that the meaning of the phrase must include more than what he considers to be "principles."

Required

a. Explain the meaning of the term "accounting principles" as it is used in the audit report. (Do not discuss the significance of "generally accepted" in this part.)

b. The president wants to know how you determine whether or not an accounting principle is generally accepted. Discuss the sources of evidence for determining whether an accounting principle has substantial authoritative support. (Do not merely list the titles of publications.)

(AICPA adapted)

THE REGULATORY APPROACH TO THE FORMULATION OF AN ACCOUNTING THEORY

The establishment and enforcement of standards is an important problem to the accounting profession and to interested users. Determining the best mechanism to employ in establishing uniform accounting standards may be essential to the acceptability and usefulness of accounting standards. Should the free-market approach, the private-sector approach, or the public-sector approach be employed? Chapter 4 is intended to provide a discussion of the merits and utility of each of these approaches. First, however, it explicates the nature of accounting standards, determines the entities concerned with accounting standards, and traces the development of accounting principles. In conclusion, the chapter elaborates on the legitimacy of the standard-setting process as well as the standards overload problem.

4.1 THE NATURE OF ACCOUNTING STANDARDS

Accounting standards dominate the accountant's work. These standards are being constantly changed, deleted, and/or added to, both in the United States and abroad. They provide practical and handy rules for the conduct of the accountant's work. They are generally accepted as firm rules, backed by sanctions for nonconformity.

Accounting standards usually consist of three parts:

1. A description of the problem to be tackled.
2. A reasoned discussion (possibly exploring fundamental theory) or ways of solving the problem.
3. Then, in line of decision or theory, the prescribed solution.[1]

In general, standards — especially auditing standards — have been restricted to point 3, which has generated a lot of controversy about the absence of supporting theories and the use of an ad hoc formulating approach. The general trend, however, is to include points 1 and 2, thereby providing a concise, theoretically-supported rule of action.

In considering the subject matter of standards, Edey divides requirements under standards into four main types:[2]

1. *Type 1* states that accountants must tell people what they are doing by disclosing the methods and assumptions (accounting policies) they have adopted.
2. *Type 2* aims at achieving some uniformity of presentation of accounting statements.
3. *Type 3* calls for the disclosure of specific matters in which the user may be called to exercise his or her own judgment.
4. *Type 4* requires implicit or explicit decisions to be made about approved asset valuation and income determination.[3]

Are standards of Type 4 — first, based on broad, debated principles and on a comparison of the pros and cons of rival theories and, second, selected on that basis by an authority (a standard-setting body) — possible? A lot of people will express serious doubt. In any case, all these types of standards continue to be promulgated. Some good reasons to establish standards are that they:

1. Provide users of accounting information with information about the financial position, performance, and conduct of a firm. This information is assumed to be clear, consistent, reliable, and comparable.
2. Provide public accountants with guidelines and rules of action to enable them to exercise due care and independence in selling their expertise and integrity in auditing firms' reports and in attesting the validity of these reports.
3. Provide the government with data bases on various variables that are deemed essential to the conduct of taxation, regulation of enterprises, planning and regulation of the economy, and enhancement of economic efficiency and other social goals.[4]
4. Generate interest in principles and theories among all those interested in the accounting disciplines. The mere promulgation of a standard generates a lot of controversy and debate both in practice and in academic circles, which is better than apathy.

4.2 GOALS OF STANDARD SETTING

The enactment of a standard may benefit some and hurt others. It is a social choice. It forces the standard setters to adopt a political process in order to find some accommodations. If any social welfare criteria is used to justify the enactment of a standard, then a serious question is raised about the legitimacy of any non-elected standard-setting body.[5] The question then becomes to determine the right approach to accounting policy questions. Two approaches exist:

1 a representational faithfulness approach;
2 an economic consequences approach.

The first approach favors neutral reporting and the pursuit of faithful representations through the standard-setting process. Under such an approach, accounting is compared to financial map-making, where maps have to be accurate and faithful. The second approach favors the adoption of standards with good rather than bad economic consequences. Under such an approach, standards are enacted that have a positive, or at least nonnegative, impact on social welfare. The differences between the two approaches are best expressed as follows:

> If economic consequences are to be pursued, then accounting policy makers must provide information signals that will direct the decisions of information users. Pragmatically, this results in the policy makers acting as decision makers. If a use-oriented measurement objective is to be pursued, then accounting policy makers must provide information to facilitate users' decision making. Pragmatically, if the information provided is faithful and chosen based on user needs, it is the user that is acting as the decision maker.[6]

A new approach has emerged recently to argue for the recognition of an explicit political economy of accounting.[7,8] As stated by Cooper and Sherer:

> Our position, that the objectives of and for accounting are fundamentally contested, arises out of the recognition that any accounting contains a representation of a specific social and political context. Not only is accounting policy essentially political in that it derives from the political struggle in society as a whole, but also the outcomes of accounting policy are essentially political in that they operate for the benefit of some groups in society and to the detriment of others . . . . Social welfare is likely to be improved if accounting practices are recognized as being consistently neutral; that the strategic outcomes of accounting practices consistently (if not invariably) favor specific interests in society and disadvantage others.[9]

4.3 ENTITIES CONCERNED WITH ACCOUNTING STANDARDS

4.3.1. Individual and Public Accounting Firms

Individual and public accounting firms are responsible through their auditors for independently certifying that corporate financial statements present fairly and accurately the results of business activities. The most influential of these firms, which make up most of the accounting establishment, are the following:

1 Ernst & Young
2 Arthur Andersen
3 Coopers and Lybrand

4 KPMG Peat Marwick
5 Price Waterhouse
6 Deloitte Haskins & Sells
7 Touche Ross
8 Laventhol & Horwath

Independent auditors are expected to be truly independent of the interests of their corporate clients. The work of public accounting firms consists principally of the performance of auditing, accounting, tax, and management advisory services. The accounting and auditing services assist in the design of reliable record-keeping systems, check the systems periodically to ensure their effectiveness, prepare financial statements that convey accurate information, and certify financial statements for accuracy.

4.3.2   The American Institute of Certified Public Accountants (AICPA)

The American Institute of Certified Public Accountants (AICPA) is the professional coordinating organization of practicing Certified Public Accountants in the United States. Its two important senior technical committees — the Accounting Standards Executive Committee (AcSec) and the Auditing Standards Committee (AuSec) — are empowered to speak for the AICPA in the areas of financial and cost accounting, and auditing, respectively. These committees issue Statements of Positions (SOPs) on accounting issues. These SOPs clarify and elaborate on controversial accounting issues and should be followed as guidelines if they do not contradict existing FASB pronouncements. Through its monthly publication, the *Journal of Accountancy*, the AICPA communicates with its members on controversial accounting problems and solutions. In fact, since its inception in 1887, its Committee on Accounting Procedures (CAP) has striven to "narrow the areas of difference in corporate reporting" by eliminating undesirable practices. Rather than developing a set of generally accepted accounting principles, the CAP adopted an ad hoc and pragmatic approach to controversial problems. Over a period of twenty years, through 1958, the CAP issued fifty-one Accounting Research Bulletins (ARBs) suggesting accounting treatments for various items and transactions. At the time, these Accounting Research Bulletins were supported by the Securities and Exchange Commission (SEC) and the stock exchanges, and consequently represented the only source of generally accepted accounting principles in the United States.

After the Second World War, the coexistence of many alternative accounting treatments, the new tax laws, and financing techniques and complex capital structures, such as business combinations, leasing, convertible debts, and investment tax credit, created the need for a new approach to the development of accounting principles. In 1959, the AICPA created a new body, the Accounting Principles Board (APB), "to advance the written expression of what constitutes generally accepted accounting principles." In addition, the AICPA appointed a director of accounting research and a permanent staff. Between 1959 and 1973, the APB issued opinions, intended to be used as guidelines for accounting practices unless superseded by FASB Statements. In addition to the opinions, the APB published four statements and a series of Accounting Interpretations intended to expand on the opinions or to communicate recommendations related to accounting problems. The statements are:

1 APB Statement No. 1, a report on the receipt of Accounting Research Studies No. 1 and No. 3.
2 APB Statement No. 2, *Disclosure of Supplementary Financial Information by Diversified Companies*, issued in September 1967.
3 APB Statement No. 3, *Financial Statements Restated for General Price-Level Changes*, issued in June 1969.
4 APB Statement No. 4, *Basic Concepts and Accounting Principles Underlying Financial Statements of Business Enterprises*, issued in October 1970.

To stimulate discussion of controversial topics before the APB acts on them, the Research Division of the AICPA commissions research studies by independent investigators or by members of the research staff under the guidance of the director of research and an advisory committee. Accounting Research Study No. 1, entitled *The Basic Postulates of Accounting*, and Accounting Research Study No. 3, entitled *A Tentative Set of Broad Accounting Principles for Business Enterprises*, were published in 1961 and 1962, respectively. Maurice Moonitz and R. T. Sprouse[10] used a deductive approach in both studies. In the first study, the authors supported exit-value accounting; in the second study, they suggested that it might be necessary to account for both general and specific price-level changes. As might have been expected at the time, the AICPA rejected both studies, claiming that they were radically different from generally accepted accounting practices and therefore unacceptable. A new study was commissioned to review existing accounting principles. Thus, Accounting Research Study No. 7 by Paul Grady, entitled *Inventory of Generally Accepted Accounting Principles for Business Enterprises* was nothing more than an inventory of existing accounting principles, practices and methods of the APB and the CAP (that is, APB and ARB's opinions). After the AICPA's rejection of Accounting Research Studies No. 1 and No. 3, the remaining studies reflected the assumptions and findings of the particular researcher who conducted the study. The APB opinions did not, in general, follow the recommendations of Accounting Research Studies No. 1 and No. 3. The other twelve Accounting Research Studies (ARS) are:

1 ARS No. 2, *Cash Flow Analysis and the Funds Statement*, by Perry Mason (1961).
2 ARS No. 4, *Reporting of Leases in Financial Statements*, by John H. Myers (1962).
3 ARS No. 5, *A Critical Study of Accounting for Business Combinations*, by Arthur B. Watt (1963).
4 ARS No. 6, *Reporting the Financial Effects of Price-Level Changes*, by the staff of the Research Division (1963).
5 ARS No. 8, *Accounting for the Cost of Pension Plans*, by Ernest L. Hicks (1966).
6 ARS No. 9, *Interperiod Allocation of Corporate Income Taxes*, by Howard A. Black (1966).
7 ARS No. 10, *Accounting for Goodwill*, by George R. Catlett and Norman O. Olson (1968).
8 ARS No. 11, *Financial Reporting in the Extractive Industries*, by Robert R. Field (1968).
9 ARS No. 12, *Reporting Foreign Operations of US Companies in US Dollars*, by Leonard Lorenson (1972).
10 ARS No. 13, *The Accounting Basis of Inventories*, by Horace G. Barden (1973).
11 ARS No. 14, *Accounting for R & D Expenditures*, by Oscar S. Gellein and Maurice S. Newman (1973).
12 ARS No. 15, *Stockholders' Equity*, by Beatrice Melcher (1973).

4.3.3 The American Accounting Association (AAA)

The American Accounting Association (AAA) is an organization of accounting academics and any individuals interested in the betterment of accounting practice and theory. Its quarterly journal, the *Accounting Review*, is devoted to the exchange of ideas and results among accounting researchers. The AAA serves as a forum within which academics express their views on various accounting topics and issues, either individually or through the organization's special appointed committees. In fact, the AAA has attempted through such special committees to provide a framework for corporate financial statements. These efforts, which have met with varying degrees of success, comprise the following studies:

1 *A Tentative Statement of Accounting Principles Underlying Corporate Financial State-ments*, published in 1936 and revised successively in 1941 and 1948, with eight supplementary statements prepared between 1950 and 1954 that clarify or expand on the 1948 statement: revised again in 1957, with five supplementary statements appearing between 1957 and 1964.
2 *An Introduction to Corporate Accounting Standards*, by W. A. Paton and A. C. Littleton, published in 1940.
3 *An Inquiry into the Nature of Accounting*, by Louis Golberg, published in 1964.
4 *A Statement of Basic Accounting Theory*, published in 1966.
5 *A Statement on Accounting Theory and Theory Acceptance*, published in 1977.

Initially based on an inductive approach, these attempts by the AAA to develop an accounting framework gradually shifted to a deductive approach with the 1957 revision, entitled *Accounting and Reporting Standards for Corporate Financial Statements — 1957 Revision*. The members of the AAA, primarily college and university professors, play one of the greatest roles in the formulation of accounting theory, through continuous innovative research and active participation in the principal standard-setting bodies. The enthusiasm of AAA members is indicated by their research output in the various accounting journals.

4.3.4 The Financial Accounting Standards Board (FASB)

The Financial Accounting Standards Board (FASB) replaced the APP in 1973 as the body responsible for establishing accounting standards. The demise of the APB was due mainly to the following factors:

1 The continuing existence of alternative, accounting treatments that allowed companies to show higher earnings per share, specially as a result of corporate mergers and acquisitions.
2 The lack of adequate accounting treatments for such new accounting problems as the investment-tax credit, accounting for the franchising industries, the land-development business, and long-term leases.
3 A number of cases of fraud and lawsuits implicating the accounting methods, which failed to disclose relevant information in many cases.
4 The failure of the APB to develop a conceptual accounting framework.

After investigating the situation, a committee appointed by the AICPA, known as the Wheat Committee, proposed a new structure for establishing accounting standards. The proposed new structure consisted of a nonprofit organization, the Financial Accounting Foundation (FAF), that would operate the FASB and would be cosponsored by five interests groups:

1 The Financial Executive Institute;
2 The National Association of Accountants;
3 The American Accounting Association;
4 The Financial Analysts Federation;
5 The Security Industry Association.

Exhibit 4.1 illustrates the FASB structure adopted in 1973.

EXHIBIT 4.1
Structure of the Financial Accounting Standards Board (FASB)

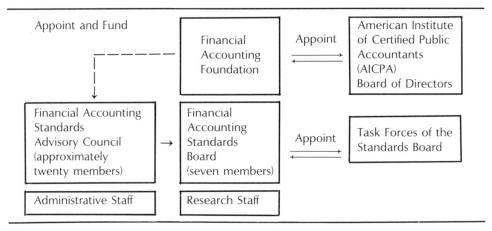

Source: American Institute of Certified Public Accountants, *Report of the Study on Establishment of Accounting Principles* (New York: AICPA, 1972).

The FASB is the authoritative, independent body charged with establishing and improving financial accounting and reporting standards — that is, those standards concerned with recording meaningful information about economic events and trans-actions in a useful manner in financial statements. The members of the FASB are assumed to represent most parties interested in financial accounting. More specifically, four members are CPAs in public practice, and three members are from areas related to accounting (government, industry, and education). Although APB members had been permitted to retain their positions with firms, companies, and institutions, FASB members must sever all such ties. Finally, FASB members are well-paid, full-time members, appointed for renewable five-year terms. This broader representation, increased indepen-dence, and smaller full-time remunerated membership should make the FASB more successful than the APB.

The relationship of the accounting profession to the FASB was clarified by Rule 203 of the AICPA's Code of Professional Ethics which holds that a member of the AICPA may not express an opinion that financial statements are presented fairly in conformity with generally accepted accounting principles if these statements depart from an FASB Statement or Interpretation or an APB Opinion or Accounting Research Bulletin, unless the member can demonstrate that, due to unusual circumstances, the financial statements would otherwise be misleading. Rule 203 constitutes an endorsement of the FASB, with the reservation that recognizes that, in unusual circumstances, literal compliance with presumptively-binding, generally accepted accounting principles issued by a recognized standard-setting body may not invariably ensure that financial statements are presented fairly.

Since its inception, the FASB has adopted the following due-process procedure:

1 A reporting problem is identified and placed on the Board's agenda.
2 A task force composed of a group of knowledgeable individuals in the accounting and business community is appointed. The technical staff of the FASB, in consultation with the task force, prepares a Discussion Memorandum (DM) on the reporting problem. The DM exposes the principal questions and alternatives to be considered by the Board.
3 The DM is made available to the public for examination for a period of at least 60 days.
4 A public hearing is staged, during which viewpoints regarding the merits and limitations of various possible positions are presented to the Board.
5 Based on the oral and written comments received, the Board issues an Exposure Draft (ED) of a Proposed Statement of Financial Accounting Standards. Unlike the DM, the ED sets forth the definite position of the Board on the reporting problem.
6 The ED is made available to the public for examination for a period of at least thirty days.
7 Another public hearing is staged, during which viewpoints regarding the merits and limitations of the positions set forth in the ED are presented to the Board.
8 Based again on the oral and written comments received following the issuance of the ED, the Board may take any of the following actions:
   a. Adopt the Proposed Standard as an Official Statement of Financial Accounting Standards (SFAS)
   b. Propose a revision of the proposed standard, again following the due-process procedure.
   c. Postpone the issuance of a standard and keep the problem on the agenda.
   d. Not issue a standard, and eliminate the issue from the agenda.

Public participation does not alter the fact that the actual decisions regarding accounting standards are made by the members of the FASB.

4.3.5   The Securities and Exchange Commission (SEC)

Created by an Act of Congress in 1934, the Securities and Exchange Commission (SEC) is primarily responsible for the administration of various laws intended to regulate securities and to ensure proper financial reporting and disclosure by American firms. Briefly, the various acts and their respective general registration requirements are:

1 *Securities Act of 1933:* Requires registration of new securities offered for public sale.

2 *Securities Exchange Act of 1934:* Requires continuous reporting of publicly-owned companies, and registration of securities, security exchanges, and certain brokers and dealers.
3 *Public Unity Holding Act of 1935:* Requires registration of trust indenture documents and supporting data.
4 *Trust Indenture Act of 1939:* Requires registration of trust indenture documents and supporting data.
5 *Investment Company Act of 1940:* Requires registration of investment companies.
6 *Investment Advisers Act of 1940:* Requires registration of investment advisers.[11]

The Securities Acts of 1933 and 1934 gave the SEC the power to determine accounting standards. As Horngren explains, the SEC was the top management and the APB was the lower management.[12] Although the SEC has the power to regulate accounting practices and disclosure, in general the SEC has relied on the accounting profession and used its power to set constraints and exert veto power. John C. Burton better expressed this position while he was chief accountant of the SEC:

> We are in partnership and our best interests are served in an atmosphere of mutual nonsurprise. The SEC does not view itself as being in a position of absolute authority and the FASB working for it.[13]

Thus, the SEC has generally concurred with the profession's pronouncements, APB opinions, and FASB statements. Nevertheless, the SEC has retained its rights to express its views in the following five ways:

1 Regulation S-X, which prescribes the form and content of the reports filed with the SEC. (The most important of these SEC corporate reports are the 10-K annual report, the 10-Q quarterly report, and the 8-K report of unscheduled material events or corporate exchanges of interest to shareholders or the SEC.)
2 Accounting Series Releases, which are pronouncements on accounting matters.
3 SEC Decisions and Reports.
4 The SEC Annual Report.
5 Speeches and articles by members of the Committee and its staff.

The SEC has not always concurred with the accounting profession's pronouncements. Some of its Accounting Series Releases (ASRs) on accounting, auditing, and financial matters have been in conflict with, or have in fact amended or superseded, standards set by the standard-setting bodies. Three notorious examples are:

1 ASR No. 96, in which the SEC rejected APB Opinion No. 2 and granted acceptance to several methods of handling the investment credit.
2 ASR No. 147, in which the SEC characterized lessee disclosures required by APB No. 31 as inadequate and imposed additional disclosure requirements of its own.
3 ASR No. 146, in which the SEC provided an interpretation of APB Opinion No. 16 which prompted a CPA firm to sue the SEC.

After the failure of the APB and the creation of the FASB, the SEC issued a policy statement, Accounting Series Release No. 150, which specifically endorsed the FASB as the only standard-setting body whose standards would be accepted by the SEC as satisfying the requirements of the federal securities laws. The release states that "principles, standards, and practices promulgated by the FASB will be considered to have no such support." It also states, however, that "the Commission will continue to identify areas where investor information needs exist and will determine the appropriate methods of disclosure to meet these needs." The SEC continues to permit the establishment of accounting standards by the private sector, and the Commission's intervention as the federal government's major participant in the accounting standard-setting process is in the form of cooperation, advice, and occasional pressure, rather than in the form of rigid controls. In other words, the SEC endorses the FASB with some reservations, in that it has not delegated any of its authority or given up any right to reject, modify, or supersede FASB pronouncements through its own rule-making procedures.

4.3.6 Other Professional Organizations

Although the previously-cited organizations traditionally have been involved with the development of accounting theory, other organizations in the United States and abroad have recently become active participants. A list of some of these organizations is shown in the Appendix to this chapter.

Each of these organizations is actively involved in setting accounting standards in its respective country and in furthering the basic foundations of accounting.

4.3.7 Users of Financial Statements

The different groups interested in the results of the activities of a profit-oriented organization have been classified as direct users and indirect users.

Direct users include:

1 the owners of a corporation and its shareholders;
2 the creditors and suppliers;
3 the management of a firm;
4 the taxing authorities;
5 the laborers in an organization;
6 the customers.

Indirect users include:

1 the financial analysts and advisers;
2 the stock exchanges;
3 lawyers;
4 regulatory or registration authorities;
5 the financial press and reporting agencies;
6 trade associations;
7 labor unions;
8 competitors;
9 the general public;
10 other governmental departments.

Direct and indirect users have diverse and conflicting sets of objectives. Basically, these two types of users have different information needs. Three kinds of financial statements may be prepared:

1 General-purpose financial statements meet the common needs of the users. In designing the financial statements presented in most annual reports, accountants assume that the reports will meet the common needs of users.
2 Specific-purpose financial statements meet the needs of specific user groups.
3 Differential disclosures present different figures for the user to select.

Whatever kind of financial statement is used, most users act as pressure groups to influence the development of accounting principles in such a way that their objectives are met.

4.4   WHO SHOULD SET ACCOUNTING STANDARDS?

4.4.1   Theories of Regulation

Regulation is generally assumed to be acquired by a given industry and is designed and operated primarily for its benefit. There are two major categories of theories of regulation of a given industry:

1 public-interest theories;
2 interest-group or capture theories.[14,15]

The *public-interest* theories of regulation maintain that regulation is supplied in response to the demand of the public for the correction of inefficient or inequitable market prices. They are instituted primarily for the protection and benefit of the general public.

The *interest-group* or *capture* theories of regulation maintain that regulation is supplied in response to the demands of special-interest groups, in order to maximize the income of their members. The main versions of this theory are:

1 the political ruling-elite theory of regulation;[16]
2 the economic theory of regulation.[17]

The political ruling-elite theory concerns the use of political power to gain regulatory control; the economic theory concerns economic power.

Which of these theories better describes accounting standard setting? Unfortunately, the theory of what constitutes maximizing behavior in an accounting regulatory agency is in its infancy. Benston attempted to explain the behavior of the SEC according to the economic theory's predictions of agency conservatism:

> An active regulatory agency has an incentive for insisting on conservative, explicit, even rigid accounting standards. Such standards reduce the risk to the agency that it will be criticized for "accepting" statements that, when viewed with the benefit of hindsight, appear misleading or fraudulent.
>
> It is not surprising that the SEC tends to want uniform, conservative reporting by corporations.[18]

Needless to say, this statement by Benston is inconsistent with the behavior of the SEC since the early 1970s.

Similarly, Hussein and Ketz examined and rejected the plausibility of the political ruling-elite version of the theory of regulation.[19] More empirical evidence is needed to develop a theory of regulation of accounting standards.

4.4.2   Should We Regulate Accounting?

A debate exists as to whether accounting should or should not be regulated.

Those arguing for an unregulated market use agency thereby to question why incentives should exist for reliable and voluntary reporting to owners. To solve the conflict between owners and managers financial reporting is used to monitor employment contracts, to judge and reward managers. In addition, firms have an incentive to report voluntarily to the capital market, because they compete for resources with other firms in a competitive capital market, and failure to report might be interpreted as bad news. Even if firms do not report voluntarily, those seeking the information may resort to private contractors for the information.

Those arguing for a regulated market use a public interest argument. Basically, either market failures or the need to achieve social goals dictate a regulation of accounting. Market failures, as suboptimal allocation of issuances, may be the result of:

1 A firm's reluctance to disclose information about itself, as it is a monopoly supplier of information about itself;
2 the occurrence of fraud;
3 the underproduction of accounting information as a public good.

The need to achieve desired social goals also argues for a regulation of accounting. These goals include fairness of reporting, information symmetry, and the protection of investors, to name only a few.

While the debate on the benefits and limitations of regulation continue, standard-setting is a reality of the accounting environment. The advantages and limitations of various forms of standard-setting — regulatory or nonregulatory — may be assessed as a way of improving the process. In the following section, each of the approaches to standard-setting will be examined.

4.4.3   The Free-Market Approach

The free-market approach to the production of accounting standards starts from the basic assumption that accounting information is an economic good, much the same as other goods or services. As such it is subject to the forces of demand by interested users, and supply by interested preparers. What results is an optimal amount of information disclosed at an optimal price. Whenever a given piece of information is needed and the right price is offered for it, the market will generate the information if the price exceeds the cost of the information. The market is thus presented as the ideal mechanism for determining the types of information to be disclosed, the recipients of the information, and the accounting standards to govern the production of such information.

Advocates of a regulatory approach (whether private or public) maintain that there are both *explicit* and *implicit* market failures in the private market for the information:

1 In general, explicit market failure is assumed to happen when either the quantity or the quality of a good produced in an unregulated market differs from the private costs of and benefits derived from that good, and the market solution results in a non-Pareto resource allocation. The same explicit market failure is also applied to the private market for the accounting information, with the assumption that the quantity and the quality of the accounting information differ from the social optimum. More explicitly, accounting information is viewed as a public good, and due to the inability to exclude nonpurchasers (free riders), there is a non-Pareto optimal production of the information of firms.[20]

2 Implicit market failure theories focus on one or more of the following claimed defects of the private markets for accounting information:

a. monopoly control over information by management:
b. naive investors:
c. functional fixation:
d. misleading numbers:
e. diversity of procedures:
f. lack of objectivity.[21]

Each of these alleged defects is briefly examined next.

a. Monopoly control over information by management: the hypothesis claims that accountants possess a monopolistic influence over the data provided and used by the market. As a result, the market cannot really distinguish between real and accounting effects, and may be misled by the accounting changes.[22]

b. Naive investor hypothesis: the hypothesis claims that those investors who are not well versed in some of the complex accounting techniques and transformations may be "fooled" by the use of different techniques by comparable firms and may not be able to adjust their decision-making process to take the diversity of accounting procedures into account.

c. Functional fixation: it is argued that under certain conditions investors may be unable to change their decision-making processes in response to a change in the underlying accounting process that provided them with the data. The failure of these investors to change their decision-making processes to conform to a change in accounting methods is attributed to the phenomenon of functional fixation.

d. Misleading numbers: because accounting relies heavily on various asset-valuation bases and various allocation procedures deemed arbitrary and incorrigible, the accounting output is at best meaningless or misleading for the purpose of decision-making.

e. Diversity of procedures: given the flexibility in the choice of accounting techniques used to report particular events and the inclination of management to present a "desired" picture, the accounting output from one firm to another firm is less than comparable and useful.

f. Lack of objectivity: no objectivity criteria are available on which management can base its choice of accounting techniques: incomparable output is the obvious result.

Based on these alleged defects, those who favor some form of regulation of accounting criticize the market approach as ineffective and claim that regulation is superior in improving accounting output. These allegations have not gone uncontested. The best challenge to the market failure theories as they affect accounting information is summarized by Leftwich:

> Market failure theories contain a fundamental flaw. The output identified by those theories as optimal is optimal in name only — it is defined independently of any institutional arrangements that can produce the output. None of these theories identifies a level of output which is optimal, given the existing technology of markets, regulations or any other regimes. Thus, unless market failure theories incorporate attainable institutional arrangements, they can yield no policy implications. It is illogical to condemn the actual output of an existing market (or government agency) merely because the quantity or quality of that output differs from an unattainable norm that is falsely described as optimal.[23]

The question of what would happen to financial accounting in the absence of regulation remains. Kripke proposes the following two possible consequences:

> First, there would continue to be adequate accounting disclosure, as issuers negotiated with lenders, investors, and underwriters in the new issue market and felt the pressure of analysts in the trading market. Second, the accounting would be less uniform than it is now, because vast differences in views as to the appropriate interpretation and abstraction of events are concealed by the mandated system. But the pressures would be such that the disclosure would be adequate to enable the reader to make his own judgment.[24]

4.4.4   Private-Sector Regulation of Accounting Standards

The private-sector approach to the regulation of accounting standards rests on the fundamental assumption that the public interest in accounting is best served if standard-setting is left to the private sector. Private standard-setting in the United States has included the Committee on Accounting Procedures (1939–59), and the Financial Accounting Standards Board (1973–present). Given the FASB is the ongoing, standard-setting body in the private sector, it will be used to illustrate the advantages and the limitations of private-sector regulation of accounting standards.

Advocates of the private-sector approach cite the following arguments in support of their position:

1 The FASB seems to be responsive to various constituents. First, it is composed of members of various interested groups in addition to the public accounting profession. Second, its financial support is derived from the contributions of a diverse group of individuals, companies, and associations. Third, it has adopted a complex due-process procedure that relies heavily on the responses of all interested constituents. Fourth, the due-process procedure generates an active concern about the consequences of its actions on the constituents.

2 The FASB seems to be able to attract, as members or as staff, people who possess the necessary technical knowledge to develop and implement alternative measurement and disclosure systems. As a unit, the standards are more likely to be acceptable to CPA firms, business firms, and external users.

3 The FASB seems to be successful in generating responses from its constituency base and in responding to such input. The volume of responses to controversial topics shows that the constituents have been expressing interest by participating and voicing their concern through at least three different mediums:

(1) written responses to a discussion memorandum

(2) oral responses to an exposure draft, and

(3) written responses to an exposure draft.

Such participation is deemed essential to the accounting standard-setting process. A former staff member of the FASB describes the importance of the constituent's input:

> The FASB represents a legislative body in the private sector that must pay careful attention to the views of all the elements of its constituency. Each constituent potentially affects formulation of the FASB decisions by providing thoughtful and theoretically sound input for the Board members to comprehend and evaluate, weigh against other constituent input, and synthesize with their own educated views on the particular issue of concern. The decision-making process, however, does not merely involve tallying these constituent preferences and resolving the issue by majority consensus. The FASB's responsibility in reaching its decision entails careful consideration of all constituent interests; it does not entail numerical-count comparisons or attempts to serve specific constituents over others.[25]

Opponents of the private-sector approach cite the following arguments in support of their position:

1 The FASB lacks statutory authority and enforcement power and faces the challenge of an override by either Congress or a governmental agency. Kaplan states the case as follows:

> Acceptance of FASB standards requires voluntary agreement from the AICPA and the benevolent delegation of authority from the SEC. Lacking true statutory authority, the private standard-setting agency is always susceptible to end runs by aggrieved constituents when they feel their particular ox is about to be gored.[26]

This situation is a result of the positions taken by Congress and the SEC on accounting standard-setting. Following the Securities Act of 1933 and the Securities Act of 1934, Congress became the legal authority for standard-setting. It then delegated its authority to the accounting profession. Finally, in Accounting Series Release No. 150, the SEC recognized the authoritative nature of the pronouncements of the FASB and at the same time retained its role as adviser and supervisor as a constant threat of override.

2 The FASB is often accused of lacking independence from its large constituents — public accounting firms and corporations. This lack of independence translates into a lack of responsiveness to the public interest. This theme gained popularity as a result of assertions made in the Metcalf Report that the accounting and financial reporting standard-setting process is dominated by the "big eight" accounting firms.[27] One way in which this domination may manifest itself is through pressure in the FASB to avoid standards that would involve subjective estimates, especially standards that would require the use of current-market prices. Kaplan states the case as follows:

> Because practitioners from CPA firms are primarily auditors, the auditing implications of any standard will receive a great deal of attention from a private standard-setting agency. There will be strong pressure for rules that can be

implemented without requiring subjective estimates that are difficult to audit and even more difficult to defend should the financial statements be subject to question in a judicial proceeding. Given the present litigious climate, auditors wish to avoid having to certify figures for which objective verifiable evidence is unavailable. These feelings are reinforced by corporate executives, another principal constituency of the private standard-setting agency, who may also fear the repercussions from issuing "soft" data. In addition, the production of subjective data is expensive and introduces a degree of uncontrolled volatility to a company's financial statements.[28]

3 The FASB is often accused of responding slowly to major issues that are of crucial importance to some of its constituents. This situation is generally attributed to the length of time required for due process and extensive deliberations of the Board. The defenders of the Board maintain, however, that these extensive deliberations may allow the Board to correct the unintended side-effects of some of its pronouncements. This brings to mind the additional problem that the proposed standards have a slim chance of being implemented without general support. Horngren provides the following details on problems associated with the Accounting Principles Board's issuance in October 1971 of an exposure draft supporting the deferral method:

Without public support, which usually means without the widespread support of industry, significant changes are seldom possible. Perhaps the situations would be better expressed negatively. If there is widespread hostility to a suggested accounting principle, there is a small chance of implementing it — regardless of how impeccable or how heavy the support within the Board.

The investment tax credit is a clear example of the impotency of both the SEC and the APB when hostility is rampant. Let me describe the events without getting tangled in the pros and cons of the conceptual issues:

The APB did not use its exposure draft of October 22, 1971, until receiving two written commitments. The SEC said it would support the APB position, and the Department of the Treasury indicated that it "will remain neutral in the matter." The Senate Finance Committee issued its version of the 1971 Revenue Act of November 9. In response to lobbying, the Committee clearly indicated that companies should have a free choice in selecting the accounting treatment of the new credit.

On November 12, the Treasury sent a letter to the chairman of the Senate Finance Committee that stated:

"Since any change in the preexisting, well-established financial accounting practice might operate to diminish the job-creating effect of the credit, the Treasury Department strongly supports a continuation of the optimal treatment." Congress then cut the ground out from under the APB and the SEC by passing legislation that stated:

"No taxpayer shall be required, without his consent, to use . . . any particular method of accounting for the credit."

The APB's unanimous denunciation of congressional involvement was issued on December, 9, 1971.[29]

4.4.5 Public-Sector Regulation of Accounting Standards

Public-sector regulation of any activity is always the subject of heated debate between advocates and opponents. Without a doubt, public-sector regulation has gained a high degree of legitimacy and become part of American and international traditions and legal frameworks. To be effective, however, regulation must ascribe to certain general principles. Elliot and Schuetze present the following:

> First, regulation must not violate constitutional rights or statutes. Second, it should be designed to prevent real or probable social change. Third, regulation must be in the public interest. A corollary to this principle is that costs must not exceed benefits and the regulation itself ought not to be superfluous. If the forces of the marketplace can resolve a question adequately, regulation is superfluous. Fourth, regulation should not be adopted by the public sector if its purpose can be achieved by private-sector institutions. Fifth, the potential regulatee should not bear the burden of proving regulation is warranted; rather, advocates of regulation must demonstrate that regulation is warranted. Sixth, regulatory action should not be used to correct occasional lawbreaking, which is the task of law enforcement; nor should regulatory responsibilities be established to combat occasional antisocial behavior that can be proscribed by statute.[30]

Even if all of these principles were met, regulation is still perceived to be suffering from various failures. Buckley and O'Sullivan identify the *zero-cost phenomenon*, the *regulatory lag* or *nonfeasance*, the *regulatory trap*, and the *tar-baby effect* as some of the observed regulatory failures.[31] The zero-cost phenomenon results from the fact that regulators do not bear the costs of their failures. The regulatory lag or nonfeasance results from delays in regulation. The regulatory trap refers to the difficulties of reserving a given regulation. Finally, the tar-baby effect results from the tendency of regulation to expand continually.

Given these strong arguments about regulation in general, what about public-sector regulation of accounting specifically? As we might expect, arguments for and against public-sector regulation of accounting standards abound in the literature. These arguments center generally around the role of the SEC.

Advocates of public-sector regulation of accounting standards cite the following arguments in favor of their position:

1 It is generally maintained that the process of innovation in accounting rests on the role of a governmental agency such as the SEC as a "creative irritant." Burton, a former chief accountant of the SEC, makes this point:

    > Since its inception in 1943, the Securities and Exchange Commission has been a principal source of creative irritation in accounting, and the practicing public accounting profession has generally served as the host that builds upon it. It is the hypothesis of this paper that this combination of SEC stimulation and professional reaction is one which emerges logically from the historical and economic forces at work that is likely to continue, and that the result is likely to be a satisfactory balancing of diverse interests and objectives. In the financial reporting environment as it exists today, substantial change will not occur in the absence of SEC stimulation.[32]

    The implication here is that the SEC is the most important catalyst for change, and that the private sector and market forces do not provide the leadership necessary to effect such change. The SEC has been instrumental in guiding the field from "safe" or "conservative" methods of accounting toward more innovative and realistic methods of accounting.

2 It is argued that the structure of securities regulation established by the Securities Acts of 1933 and 1934 serves to protect investors against perceived abuses. Thus public-sector regulation of accounting standards is motivated by the need to protect

the public interest. It provides mechanisms to offset the preparer bias that institutionally exists in the standard-setting process, as well as to offset the economic limitations of investors seeking adequate information.[33] The mechanisms include suggestions through speeches, the exercise of rule-making powers granted by Congress under the Securities Act of 1933 and 1936, the use of a review and comment process, and the power not to accelerate the effectiveness of a registration statement and to discourage accounting applications in cases judged to be inappropriate, given the circumstances.[34]

3 The SEC is motivated by the desire to create a level of public disclosure deemed necessary and adequate for decision making. Burton suggests:

> The SEC has as its objective achieving a level of public disclosure at least equivalent to the disclosure that would likely be sought by a provider or capital user. If it errs in this objective, it seeks to do so on the side of providing more information rather than less, since an underlying premise of its regulatory purpose is to assure the existence of adequate information so that the capital-allocating mechanism of the marketplace will work effectively.[35]

To do so the SEC assumes the role of advocate for investors and attempts to determine their needs by continuously surveying analysts and other interested users.

4 Unlike the FASB, the SEC is secured greater legitimacy through its explicit statutory authority. Added to that is a greater enforcement power than a private agency and the absence of an explicit constituency that may "feel their particular ox is about to be gored." Kaplan provides the following illustration:

> For example, the replacement cost disclosure of Accounting Series Release No. 190 and the recently announced Reserve Recognition Accounting for oil and gas companies were accomplished by the SEC with little prior discussion and with considerable speed. Neither of these initiatives, which represented major departures from the conventional, historical, cost-based system, could have been accomplished by the FASB nearly so quickly or with so little public debate.[36]

In short, the SEC is better able to conduct experiments in disclosure policy when they are enforceable and can go uncontested by all participants in the standard-setting process.

5 Some claim that the private sector has to be watched and controlled, given that its objectives may sometimes contradict the public interest. A minimum of governmental intervention is deemed necessary to avoid the extreme and negative behaviors. Chetkovich emphasizes the same point:

> The private sector does not have all the answers; it is not immune to excesses, to shortsightedness, to deficiencies, and to failures. We need surveillance and prodding and, at times, intervention by government. Left totally to our own devices, I am afraid we might destroy ourselves. On the other hand, government must exercise great restraint and not just because increasing governmental involvement is inconsistent with the concept of a free society, although that should be reason enough.[37]

There are, however, strong arguments against public-sector regulation of accounting standards:

1 It is generally maintained that there is a high corporate cost for compliance with government regulation of information. The problem is a matter of concern to

opponents of public-sector regulation of accounting standards. The financial reports required by the federal government keep increasing to comply with such legislation as the Sherman Act, the Robinson-Patman Act, DOE pricing rules, OSHA, EPA, EEOC, NHTSA, NRC, NLRB, FDA, FTC, ICC, CPSC, FHLBB, MSHA, and NTSB. All of these reports have an impact on business organization in terms of paper costs and in terms of constant changes in organizational structure that cause the formation of new positions or departments. Added to these complaints are the following as yet unanswered questions:

a. What happens to the reports once they are sent to the federal government?
b. Do they end up in some agency's files never to be looked at again?
c. Or is the information from this one company's reports actually used, along with that from thousands of other corporations, to make important policy decisions?

A study of attempting to follow up on some of this information and see what happens to it would be interesting. Perhaps such a study would also give some indication of the possible benefits to society from such information-gathering.[38]

2 Some have argued that bureaucrats have a tendency to maximize the total budget of their bureau.[39] Applied to the SEC, this argument assumes that the SEC is staffed with people who tend to maximize their own welfare with no consideration for the costs and benefits of additional disclosures. Watt makes the same point:

> If the SEC's budget is determined by politicians more concerned with appearance than substance, I would expect the SEC's actions to be more concerned with appearance rather than fact. The SEC's function is to issue regulations and to prosecute — to appear to be acting to remedy "perceived" abuses. Allowing serious calculations of costs to affect those regulations would be dysfunctional. That is why the SEC spends a small fraction of its budget on estimating costs and benefits and a large fraction on the lawyers who produce and enforce regulation.[40]

3 There is the danger that standard-setting may become increasingly politicized. Special-interests groups may possess the added initiative to lobby the governmental agency for special treatment. Moreover, political appointees may feel that "witch hunts" are necessary to protect the public interest. Another fear is that "uninformed populists" may want some of the action at the expense of accounting standards and the accounting profession.[41]

4 Some have questioned the need for a governance system backed by a police power. It is claimed that such a situation may hinder the conduct of research and experimentation of accounting policy and is not essential to achieve standardization of measurement. For example, David Mosso, then a member of the FASB, claimed that

> ...the police power is not necessarily required for balancing the conflicting interests of the various parties in the capital-allocation process, including the interests of the state itself. The vast majority of interest conflicts in our society are resolved through systems of self-restraint.[42]

4.5 LEGITIMACY OF THE STANDARD-SETTING PROCESS

4.5.1 The Pessimistic Prognosis

The legitimacy of the standard-setting process was sometimes linked to its ability to produce an optimal accounting system, that is "one for which the expected payoff to a user employing an optimal decision strategy is greater than or equal to the corresponding payoff for any other alternative system.[43] The implication is that no alternative financial statement presentations based on any other set of accounting rules can lead to a better user-utility. Improved debate in the accounting literature concerns the attainability of such an optimal accounting system. The debate was sparked by Demski's use of the impossibility theorem to argue that:

1 an accounting standard-setting process must satisfy Arrow's condition[44] to be legitimate; and
2 no set of standards exists that will always seek alternatives in accordance with preferences and beliefs.[45]

He concludes as follows:

> We have interpreted accounting theory as providing a complete and transitive ranking of accounting alternatives at the individual level. It was then proven that no set of standards (applied to the accounting alternative *per se*) exist that will rank accounting alternatives in relation to consistent individual preferences and beliefs."[46]

This pessimistic prognosis was expanded to show:

1 that the selection of financial reporting alternatives 'ultimately must entail trading off one person's gain for another,'[47] and
2 that the resolution of financial reporting alternatives will require 'value or ethical judgments as to whose well-being will be traded off — and in what dimensions for whose.'[48] What appears from these efforts is that rational choice theory offers no hope for solutions to the issues of choice among financial reporting alternatives. As stated by Cushing:

> Consider now an accounting policy-maker who implores this literature in searching for help in the discovery of optimal accounting principles. Under certain assumptions and conditions which seem logical and desirable, the policy maker finds that attempts to use standards apparently will be fruitless, that optimal accountng principles apparently do not exist and that she/he must reconcile herself or himself to a political role of trading off conflicting objectives of financial statement user groups.[49]

4.5.2   The Optimistic Prognosis

In fact, Cushing gave an optimistic prognosis about the sheer responsibility of optimal accounting principle, provided that the assumption of heterogeneous users is dropped, and that the assumptions underlying the Arrow Paradox are challenged, namely the assumptions:

(1) that Arrow's definition of a social welfare function requires that social choices be transitive, and
(2) that Arrow's condition of "independence or irrelevant alternatives" is of questionable merit.[50]

Another optimistic prognosis is offered by Bromwich on the possibility of partial accounting standards; standards for one or more accounting problems, enacted in isolation from standards or other accounting problems.[51]

Chambers chose to counteract Demski's economic school and impossibility thesis by proposing a necessity school that assumes the existence of an ideal norm or standard that cuts across specific situations.[52] The norm is the information that represents the current money and money's worth of assets and the amount currently owing to others at any time.[53] Even if that norm is not available, Chambers suggests that the feasible alternative that most closely produces the necessary measure is the preferred alternative.

Cushing, Chambers and Bromwich, in demonstrating that under certain restrictive conditions it was possible to select accounting standards without isolating Arrow's conditions (or by violating only some minor aspects of one or more conditions), could have argued the legitimacy of the FASB by focusing on its feasibility and the irrelevancy of Arrow's Impossibility Theorem to the assessment of the legitimacy of the FASB standard-setting process. They would have used Tullock's argument when he examined the relevance of Arrow's Impossibility Theorem for purposes of assessing the legitimacy of certain voting processes, and concluded in these terms:

> One of the real problems raised by Arrow's look was why the real world democracies seemed to function fairly well in spite of the logical impossibility of rationally aggregating preferences. [Although] no decision process will meet Arrow's criteria perfectly, many [processes] meet them to a very high degree of approximation [and, therefore, the ability of a process to meet the strictly mathematical requirements imposed by Arrow is largely irrelevant in the real world].[54]

The problem remaining, however, is to assert the legitimacy of the FASB. To achieve that task, Johnson and Solomons relied on the "individualistic constitutional calculus."[55] This process involved mainly the economics/political science literature.[56]

It is defined as follows:

> Individualistic constitutional calculus is based on the premise that a process or institution is legitimate if it continues to be acceptable to its constituency in spite of the challenges posed to its credibility by the inevitable crisis that surrounds the exercise of such authority. In short, legitimacy implies acceptability in the face of uncertainty, and that, in turn, implies institutional durability.[57]

Basically institutional constitutional calculus established the legitimacy of the FASB based on:

1 its ability to provide adequate procedural safeguard;
2 its ability to impose constraints on the choice set that are adequate to ensure an acceptable outcome;
3 the balance of procedural and outcome controls possessed by the standard setting process of the FASB. The ability of the FASB to meet these conditions was assessed by showing that the FASB possess sufficient authority, ensure substantive due process and ensure procedural due process.[58]

4.6 ACCOUNTING STANDARDS OVERLOAD

David Moss describes best the gravity of the standards overload issue by the following statement:

> When I first encountered the subject, "standards overload" looked like the legendary

Gordian knot, so intricate it couldn't be untied by any ordinary mortal. After five years of wrestling with the problem, however, I think maybe it isn't a Gordian knot after all — it looks like a hangman's noose.[59]

The accounting standards overload is generally associated with the proliferation of accounting standards. The following situations have also been identified with accounting standards overload:

1 Too many standards.
2 Too detailed standards.
3 No rigid standards, making selectivity of application difficult.
4 General-purpose standards failing to provide for differences in the needs of preparers, users, and CPAs.
5 General-purpose standards failing to provide for differences between:
   a. public and nonpublic entities;
   b. annual and interim financial statements;
   c. large and small enterprises; and
   d. credited and nonaudited financial statements.
6 Excessive disclosures, complex measurements, or both.

The situation took years to develop to the stage of becoming a serious problem. Various factors contributed to the standards-overload problem. First, with the numerous questions raised about what to disclose and what not to disclose, accountants began to issue a greater number of standards, which tended to leave less to judgment and to reduce the amount of litigation involving accounting principles. Second, the need to protect the public interest and to assist the individual investor generated various and numerous governmental and professional regulations and disclosures. Finally, the desire to satisfy the needs of many users required more detailed standards and disclosures.

What resulted is a complex and cumbersome situation. Mandated GAAP increased in number, complexity, and specificity, affecting the costs of preparing financial statements for both small and large firms. Some believe the GAAP are becoming intolerable to some firms, their auditors, and the users of information. Others think that the new and detailed GAAP requirements are more designed to serve the informational needs of investors and creditors at the expense of the particular users of financial statements of small or closely held business. This is in direct conflict with the accepted argument that serving the needs of users of financial statements is, or should be, the primary objective of financial reporting. In effect, that is exactly the main emphasis of FASB's Statement of Financial Accounting Concepts No. 1, *Objectives of Financial Reporting by Business Enterprises*:

> Financial reporting should provide information that is useful to present and potential investors and creditors and other users in making rational investment, credit, and similar decisions. The information should be comprehensible to those who have a reasonable understanding of business and economic activities and are willing to study the information with reasonable diligence.

The problem of overload is aggravated by the proliferation of standard-setting bodies. In addition to the FASB, the development of the GAAP and related disclosures are influenced by other bodies such as the SEC; the AICPA, including the Accounting Standards Executive Committee (AcSEC) and the Auditing Standards Board (ASB); and to some extent Congress. Examples of congressional actions having accounting consequences are the investment tax credit and the enactment of the Foreign Corrupt Practices Act. In addition, the standards themselves are not only excessive in number, but too narrow in their application to cover all possible situations, and requiring too much detailed guidance.

4.6.1 Effects of Accounting Standards Overload

The large number, narrowness, and rigidity of accounting standards can have serious effects on the work performed by accountants, the value of financial information to users, and business decisions made by management. The accountants may lose sight of their real jobs because of the excessive data required when complying with existing standards. Audit failures may result, because the accountant may lose the focus of the audit and may forget to perform basic audit procedures. The proliferation of complex accounting regulations may lead to noncompliance with those regulations by business, with the tacit agreement of CPAs. The embattled practitioner is in fact caught in the middle between the demands of professional standards and the discontent of small business clients with the burden these standards impose on them. This situation will undoubtedly have serious implications for legal liability, erosion of professional ethics, loss of public support, and dissonance within the accounting profession.

One way out for practitioners faced with the GAAP departures is to give a modified opinion. Most CPAs, however, resist a modified opinion for the GAAP omissions in audited financial statements, because they think the negative connotation is not acceptable. What may be needed is an education of the public to greater acceptance of CPA reports that take note of omitted GAAP requirements.

The users may also be confused by the number and complexity of the notes used to explain the requirements under the existing standards. Users of financial reports of small businesses generally are concerned with the complexity introduced by the Financial Accounting Standards Board pronouncements. The jargon used in the notes can be understood only by accountants and other financial persons. Consider, for example, the following note from the 1981 United Leasing Corporation's Form 10-K, describing the company's method of recognizing revenue from a lease used to finance an asset:

> *Direct financial leases* — At the time of closing a direct financing lease, the company records on its balance sheet the gross sale receivable, estimated residual valuation of the leased equipment, and unearned lease income. The unearned lease income represents the excess of the gross lease receivable plus the estimated residual valuation over the cost of the equipment leased. A portion of the unearned income equal to the initial direct costs incurred in consummating the lease plus an amount equal to the provision for losses is recognized as revenue at the time the lease is closed. Commencing with the second month of the lease, the remainder of the unearned lease income is recorded as revenue over the lease term so as to approximate a constant rate of return on the net investment in the lease.

The note can be understood only by a seasoned veteran familiar with the accounting jargon and body of knowledge.

The managers may also be overwhelmed by the number and complexity of the standards. In fact, they may be tempted to rewrite contracts and change business practices so as not to have to comply with some of the accounting standards. It is possible to restructure the terms of leases to avoid capitalization and the intricate requirements of Statement of Financial Accounting Standards No. 13 on lease. The major motivation for the restructuring of transactions by managers of small businesses is to avoid not only the detailed requirements of some accounting standards, but the excessive costs of preparing and verifying the information. Besides, the costs of complying with the standards may outweigh the benefits, given that users of financial reports of small businesses may be more interested in cash-flow projections than in the other financial-statement information. In fact, because users of financial reports of small businesses have more immediate contact with management, they do not need to rely on financial reports as much as users of reports or large businesses.

4.6.2   Solutions to the Standards-Overload Problem

The gravity of the standards-overload problem led various interest groups to address the problem and suggest solutions. The AICPA Special Committee on Accounting Standards evaluated the following possible approaches to dealing with accounting standards overload:

1 No change; retain status quo.
2 A change from the present concept of a set of unitary GAAP for all business enterprises to two sets of GAAP, thus creating a separate set of GAAP for certain entities, such as small nonpublic businesses.
3 Changes in GAAP to simplify application to all business enterprise.
4 Establishing differential disclosure and measurement alternatives.
5 A change in CPA's standards for reporting on financial statements.
6 An alternative to the GAAP as an optional basis for presenting financial statements.

Of all of these approaches, the committee recommended either establishing disclosure and measurement alternatives or adopting an alternative to the GAAP.

The approach based on differential disclosure and measurement alternatives for small nonpublic enterprises is a good solution to the standards-overload problem, in that it considers relevance to users and cost-benefit considerations with respect to small nonpublic entities. This is in line with the FASB's Statement of Financial Accounting Concepts No. 2, which states:

> The optimal information for one user will not be optimal for another. Consequently, the Board which must try to cater to many different users while considering the burdens placed on those who have to provide information, constantly treads a fine line between requiring disclosure of too much information and requiring too little.

The approach calls for a flexible concept of the GAAP with differential measurement alternatives to serve the specialized needs of small nonpublic companies. One way of implementing this approach would be for the standard-setting body to adopt a basis for exemption from the detailed requirements of each standard. The basis might be public versus private, or a size test based on asset values.

The approach that relies on an alternative to the GAAP rests on three possibilities:

1 a new basis accounting method (BAM);
2 the cash or modified cash basis;

3 the income tax basis.

A BAM is out of the question, because it would create more costs than benefits. Some of the conclusions of the committee include the following:

1 BAM will contain the essentials of the GAAP and allow significant departures from the measurement principles of the GAAP. As such, it would confuse everybody and undermine the GAAP in the process.
2 BAM will add rather than reduce the overload problem, given that it will create new requirements in addition to the GAAP.
3 BAM will require a position on each of the GAAP issues, which will be costly and time consuming.
4 BAM will need to be prepared by a new standard-setting body.
5 BAM will be perceived not as a subset of the GAAP but as a search set of the GAAP for special entities.

Given these constraints, the committee suggested that the issuance, in accordance with existing reporting standards, of compiled, reviewed, or audited other comprehensive-bases-of-accounting (OCBOA) financial statements, including income tax-basis financial statements, can help alleviate the burden of accounting standards overload for small nonpublc entities.

4.7   CONCLUSIONS

The establishment and enforcement of accounting standards are emerging as complex problems. First, it does not appear that standards are based on broad, debated principles and a comparison of the pros and cons of tidal theories, and then chosen on that basis by the standard-setting body. Second, there are definite conflicts of interests and needs among the entities concerned with accounting principles. Third, the development of accounting principles has been a chaotic one — first dominated by management, then regulated by the profession, and finally becoming a truly political exercise. Fourth, every form of standard setting — in the free market, the private sector, or the public sector — has its advantages and limitations; there is no clear-cut conceptual or practical winner. Fifth, the accounting standards-overload problem needs corrective solutions.

NOTES

[1] Baxter, W.T., "Accounting Standards — Boon or Curse?", in *The Emmanuel Saxe Distinguished Lectures in Accounting 1978–1979* (New York: The Bernard M. Baruch College, 1979), p. 30.
[2] Edey, H.C., "Accounting Standards in the British Isles," in *Studies in Accounting*, Third Edition, (eds) W.T. Baxter and Sydney Davidson (London: Institute of Chartered Accountants of England and Wales, 1977), pp. 295–8.
[3] George J. Benston refers to the types of standards, respectively, as *disclosure-content, specific-instruction-content*, and *conceptually-based-content* standards. See Benston, George

J., "Methods, Benefits, and Costs," *Accounting and Business Research* (Winter, 1980), p. 53.

[4] Edey, H.C., "Accounting Standards in the British Isles," op. cit., p. 57.

[5] Skinner, Ross M., *Accounting Standards in Evolution* (Toronto: Holt, Rinehart and Winston of Canada, Ltd., 1987), p. 622.

[6] Roland, Robert G., "Duty, Obligation, and Responsibility in Accounting Policy Making," *Journal of Accounting and Public Policy* (Fall, 1984), p. 225.

[7] Tinker, Anthony, "Towards a Political Economy of Accounting," *Accounting, Organizations and Society* (May, 1980), pp. 147–60.

[8] Tinker, Anthony, "Theories of the State and State Accounting: Economic Reduction and Political Voluntarism in Accounting Regulation Theory," *Journal of Accounting and Public Policy* (Spring, 1984), pp. 55–74.

[9] Cooper, David J. and Michael J. Sherer, "The Value of Corporate Accounting Reports: Arguments for a Political Economy of Accounting," *Accounting, Organizations and Society* (September, 1984), p. 184.

[10] Moonitz, Maurice, *The Basic Postulates of Accounting*, Accounting Research Study No. 1 (New York: American Institute of Certified Public Accountants, 1961); Sprouse, R.T., and Moonitz, Maurice, *A Tentative Set of Broad Accounting Principles for Business Enterprises*, Accounting Research Study No. 3 (New York: American Institute of Certified Public Accountants, 1962).

[11] For more information, see Ainsworth, Leroy, and Turner, Johnny S., Jr., *An Overview of the SEC with a Guide to Researching Accounting-Related SEC Problems* (Provo, Ut.: Brigham Young University Press, 1971), p. 11.

[12] Horngren, Charles T., "Accounting Principles: Private or Public Sector?," *Journal of Accountancy* (May, 1972), p. 38.

[13] The statement is from an interview with John C. Burton, "Paper Shuffling and Economic Reality," *Journal of Accountancy* (January, 1973), p. 26.

[14] Stigler, G.J., "The Theory of Economic Regulation," *Bell Journal of Economics* (Spring, 1971), pp. 3–21.

[15] Posner, R.A., "Theories of Economic Regulation," *Bell Journal of Economics* (Autumn, 1974), pp. 335–58.

[16] Ibid., p. 336.

[17] Peltzman, S., "Toward a More General Theory of Regulation," *The Journal of Law and Economics* (August, 1976), pp. 211–40.

[18] Benston, George J., "Accounting Standards in the U.S. and the U.K.: Their Nature, Causes, and Consequences," *Vanderbilt Law Review* (January, 1975), p. 255.

[19] Hussein, M.E., and Ketz, J.E., "Ruling Elites of the FASB: A Study of the Big Eight," *Journal of Accounting, Auditing, and Finance* (Summer, 1980), pp. 354–67.

[20] Gonedes, N.J., and Dopuch, N., "Capital-Market Equilibrium, Information Production, and Selecting Accounting Techniques: Theoretical Framework and Review of Empirical Work," *Studies on Financial Accounting Objectives*, supplement to *Journal of Accounting Research* (1974), pp. 48–129.

[21] Leftwich, R.W., "Market Failure Fallacies and Accounting Information," *Journal of Accounting and Economics* (December, 1980), p. 200.

[22] Ball, R., "Changes in Accounting Techniques and Stock Prices," *Empirical Studies in Accounting: Selected Studies, 1972*, supplement to *Journal of Accounting Research* (1972), p. 4.

[23] Leftwich, R.W., "Market Failure Fallacies and Accounting Information," op. cit., p. 208.

[24] Kripke, Homer, "World Market Forces Cause Adequate Disclosure Without SEC Mandate," in *Government Regulation of Accounting and Information*, (ed.) A.R. Abdel-Khalik (Gainesville: University Presses of Florida, 1980), p. 210.

[25] Brown, P.R., "FASB Responsiveness to Corporate Input," *Journal of Accounting, Auditing, and Finance* (Summer, 1982), p. 283.

[26] Kaplan, Robert S., "Should Accounting Standards Be Set in the Public or Private Sector?," in *Regulation and the Accounting Profession*, (eds) J.W. Buckley and J.F. Weston (Belmont, Ca.: Lifetime Learning Publications, 1980), p. 185.

[27] US Senate Committee on Government Operations, Subcommittee on Reports, Accounting, and Management, *Summary of the Accounting Establishment. A Staff Study* (New York: National Association of Accountants, December 1976).

[28] Kaplan, Robert S., "Should Accounting Standards Be Set in the Public or Private Sector?," op. cit., p. 183.

[29] Horngren, Charles T., "Accounting Principles: Private or Public Sector?," op. cit., p. 10.

[30] Elliot, R.K., and Schuetze, W., "Regulation of Accounting: A Practitioner's Viewpoint," in *Government Regulation of Accounting Information*, (ed.) A.R. Abdel-Khalik (Gainseville, Fl.: University Presses of Florida, 1980), pp. 109–10.

[31] Buckley, J.W., and O'Sullivan, P., "Regulation and the Accounting Profession: What Are The Issues?" in *Regulation and the Accounting Profession*, (eds) J.W. Buckley and J.F. Weston (Belmont, Ca: Lifetime Learning Publications, 1980), pp. 46–8.

[32] Burton, John C., "The SEC and Financial Reporting: The Sand in the Oyster," in *Government Regulation of Accounting Information*, (ed.) A.R. Abdel-Khalik (Gainesville, Fl.: University Presses of Florida, 1980), p. 74.

[33] Ibid., pp. 79–80.

[34] Ibid., p. 85.

[35] Ibid., p. 80.

[36] Kaplan, Robert S., "Should Accounting Standards Be Set in the Public or Private Sector?," op. cit., p. 187.

[37] Chetkovich, M.N., "The Accounting Profession Responds to the Challenge of Regulation," in *Regulation and the Accounting Profession*, (eds) J.W. Buckley and J.F. Weston (Belmont, Ca.: Lifetime Learning Publications, 1980), p. 148.

[38] Buchholz, R.A., "Corporate Cost for Compliance with Government Regulation of Information," in *Government Regulation of Accounting and Information*, (ed.) A.R. Abdel-Khalik (Gainesville, Fl.: University Presses of Florida, 1980), p. 26.

[39] Niskaven, W., *Bureaucracy and Representative Government* (Chicago: Aldine Atherton Press, 1971).

[40] Watts, R.L., "Beauty Is in the Eye of the Beholder: A Comment on John C. Burton's 'The SEC and Financial Reporting: The Sand in the Oyster'," in *Government Regulation of Accounting Information*, (ed.) A.R. Abdel-Khalik (Gainesville, Fl.: University Presses of Florida, 1980), pp. 99–100.

[41] This point was suggested to me by Professor Ronald Picur, University of Illinois at Chicago.

[42] Mosso, David, "Regulation and the Accounting Profession: An FASB Member's View," in *Regulation and the Accounting Profession*, (eds) J.W. Buckley and J.F. Weston (Belmont, Ca.: Lifetime Learning Publications, 1980), p. 137.

[43] Marshall, Ronald, "Determining an Optimal Accounting Information System for an Undefined User," *Journal of Accounting Research* (Fall, 1972), pp. 286–307.

[44] Arrow, K., *Social Choice and Individual Values* (New York: Wiley, 1963).

[45] Demski, Joel S., "The General Impossibility of Normative Accounting Standards," *The Accounting Review* (October, 1973), pp. 718–723.

[46] Ibid., pp. 721–2.

[47] Demski, Joel S., "Choice Among Financial Reporting Alternatives," *The Accounting Review* (April, 1974), pp. 221–32.

[48] Beaver, William H., and Deusli, Joel S., "The Nature of Financial Accounting Objectives: A Summary and Synthesis," *Studies on Financial Accounting Objectives: 1974,* Supplement to *Journal of Accounting Research* (1974), pp. 170–87.

[49] Cushing, Barry E., "On the Possibility of Optimal Accounting Principles," *The Accounting Review* (April, 1977), p. 310.

[50] Ibid., p. 313.

[51] Bromwich, Michael, "The Possibility of Partial Accounting Standards," *The Accounting Review* (April, 1980), pp. 288–300.

[52] Chambers, R.J., "The Possibility of a Normative Accounting Standard," *The Accounting Review* (July, 1976), pp. 646–56.

[53] Ibid., p. 651.

[54] Tullock, G., "The General Irrelevance of the General Impossibility Theorem," *Quarterly Journal of Economics* (August, 1967), pp. 256–70.

[55] Johnson, S.B., and Solomons, D., "Institutional Legitimacy and the FASB," *Journal of Accounting and Public Policy* (Fall, 1984), pp. 165–83.

[56] Buchanan, J., and Tullock, G., *The Calculus of Consent: Logical Foundations of Constitutional Democracy* (Ann Arbor, Mi.: University of Michigan Press, 1962).

[57] Johnson, S.B., and Solomons, D., "Institutional Legitimacy and the FASB," op. cit., p. 167.

[58] Ibid., pp. 175–9.

[59] Moss, David, "Standards Overload — No Simple Solution," *Journal of Accountancy* (November, 1983), p. 120.

REFERENCES

Goals of Standard Setting

Buckley, John W., "The FASB and Impact Analysis," *Management Accounting* (April, 1976), pp. 13–17.

Cooper, David J., and Sherer, Michael J., "The Value of Corporate Accounting Reports: Arguments for a Political Economy of Accounting," *Accounting, Organizations and Society* (September, 1984), pp. 207–32.

Gellein, Oscar S., "Neutrality has Consequences," *FASB Viewpoints* (Stamford, Ct.: FASB, 1978).

Kirk, Donald J., "Concepts, Consensus, Compromise and Consequences: Their Setting," *Journal of Accountancy* (April, 1981), pp. 83–6.

May, Robert G., and Sundem, Gary L., "Research in Accounting Policy: An Overview," *The Accounting Review* (October, 1976), pp. 747–63.

Ruland, Robert G., "Duty, Obligations and Responsibility in Accounting Policy Making," *Journal of Accounting and Public Policy* (Fall, 1984), pp. 223–38.

Solomons, David, "The Politicization of Accounting," *Journal of Accountancy* (November, 1978), pp. 65–72.

Tinker, Anthony, "Theories of the State and State Accounting: Economic Reduction and Political Voluntarism in Accounting Regulation Theory," *Journal of Accounting and Public Policy* (Spring, 1984), pp. 55–74.

Tinker, Anthony, "Towards a Political Economy of Accounting," *Accounting, Organizations and Society* (May, 1980), pp. 147–60.

Who Should Set Accounting Standards?

Armstrong, Marshall S., "The Politics of Establishing Accounting Standards," *Journal of Accountancy* (February, 1971), pp. 76–9.

Benston, George J., "The Market for Public Accounting Services: Demand, Supply, and Regulation," *Journal of Accounting and Public Policy* (Spring, 1985), pp. 33–80.

Bromwich, Michael, *The Economics of Accounting Standard Setting* (Prentice Hall/Institute of Chartered Accountants in England and Wales, 1985).

Brown, P.R., "FASB Responsiveness to Corporate Input," *Journal of Accounting, Auditing, and Finance* (Summer, 1982), pp. 282–90.

Chatov, Robert, *Corporate Financial Reporting: Public or Private Control* (The Free Press, 1975).

Committee, Bruce Edward, "The Delegation and Privatization of Financial Accounting Rulemaking Authority in the United States of America," *Critical Perspectives on Accounting* (June, 1990), pp. 145–66.

Chow, Chee W., "Empirical Studies of the Effects of Accounting Regulations on Security Prices: Findings, Problems, and Prospects," *Journal of Accounting Literature* (Spring, 1983), pp. 73–109.

Ellyson, R.C., and Van Reusselaer, W.H., "Sunset — Is the Profession Ready for It?" *Journal of Accountancy* (June, 1980), pp. 52–61.

Forster, George, "Externalities and Financial Reporting," *Journal of Finance* (May 1980), pp. 521–33.

Forster, George, "Accounting Policy Decisons and Capital Market Research," *Journal of Accounting and Economics* (June, 1980), pp. 29–62.

Haring, J.R., Jr., "Accounting Rules and 'The Accounting Establishment'," *Journal of Business* (October, 1979), pp. 507–19.

Holthausen, Robert W. and Leftwich, Richard W., "The Economic Consequences of Accounting Choice: Implications of Costly Contracting and Monitoring." *Journal of Accounting and Economics* (August, 1983), pp. 77–117.

Horngren, Charles T., "Accounting Principles: Private or Public Sector?" *Journal of Accountancy* (May, 1972), pp. 37–41.

Horngren, Charles T., "Accounting Principles: Private or Public Sector?" *Journal of Accountancy* (May, 1972), pp. 38–42.

Hussein, M.E., and Ketz, J.E. "Ruling Elites of the FASB: A Study of the Big Eight," *Journal of Accounting, Auditing, and Finance* (Summer, 1980), pp. 357–67.

Ingram, Robert W., and Chewning, Eugene G., "The Effect of Financial Disclosure Regulation on Security Market Behavior," *The Accounting Review* (July, 1983), pp. 562–80.

Johnson, S.B., and Messier, W.F., Jr., "The Nature of Accounting Standards Setting: An Alternative Explanation," *Journal of Accounting, Auditing, and Finance* (Spring, 1982), pp. 195–213.

Kelly-Newton, L., *Accounting, Policy Formulation: The Role of Corporate Management* (Reading, Ma.: Addison-Wesley, 1980).

Kirk, Donald J., "How to Keep Politics Out of Standard Setting: Making Private Sector Rule-Making Work," *Journal of Accountancy* (September, 1978), pp. 92–4.

Leftwich, Richard W., "Market Failure Fallacies and Accounting Information," *Journal of Accounting Economics* (December, 1980). pp. 193–211.

Lindahl, Frederick W., "Accounting Standards and Olson's Theory of Collective Action," *Journal of Accounting and Public Policy* (Spring, 1987), pp. 59–72.

Miller, Paul B.W., and Redding, Rodney, *The FASB: The People, the Process and the Politics* (Richard D. Irwin, 1986).

Moonitz, Maurice, "Obtaining Agreement on Standards in the Accounting Profession," *Studies in Accounting Research No. 8* (American Accounting Association, 1974).

Nerino, Barbara Dubois, and Neimark, Marilyn Dale, "Disclosure Regulation and Public Policy: A Sociohistorical Reappraisal," *Journal of Accounting and Public Policy* (Fall, 1982), pp. 33–57.

O'Leary, Ted, "Observations on Corporate Financial Reporting in the Name of Politics," *Accounting, Organizations and Society* 10 (1985, no. 1), pp. 87–102.

Olson, W.E., "Self-Regulation — What's Ahead?" *Journal of Accountancy* (March, 1980), pp. 46–9.

Peltzman, S., "Toward a More General Theory of Regulation," *The Journal of Law and Economics* (August, 1976), pp. 211–40.

Phillips, Susan M., and Zecher, J. Richard, *The SEC and the Public Interest* (MIT Press, 1981).

Posner, R.A., "Theories of Economic Regulation," *Bell Journal of Economics* (Autumn, 1974), pp. 335–58.

Puro, Marsha, "Audit Firm Lobbying Before the Financial Accounting Standards Board: An Empirical Study," *Journal of Accounting Research* (Autumn, 1984), pp. 624–46.

Puxty, A.G., Wilmott, Hugh C., Cooper, David J. and Lowe, Tony, "Modes of Regulation in Advanced Capitalism: Locating Accountancy in Four Countries," *Accounting, Organizations and Society* 12 (1987, no. 3), pp. 273–91.

Sterling, Robert R. (ed.), *Institutional Issues in Public Accounting* (Scholars Book Company, 1974).

Stigler, G.J., "Theory of Economic Regulation," *Bell Journal of Economics* (Spring, 1971), pp. 3–21.

Solomons, David, *Making Accounting Policy: The Quest for Credibility in Financial Reporting* (Oxford University Press, 1986).

U.S. Senate Committee on Government Operations, Subcommittee on Reports, Accounting, and Management, *Summary of The Accounting Establishment, A Staff Study* (New York: National Association of Accountants, December 1976).

Watts, Ross L., "Corporate Financial Statements: Product of the Market and Political Processes," *Australian Journal of Management* (April, 1977), pp. 53–75.

Watts, Ross L., "Can Optimal Information Be Determined by Regulation?" in *Regulation and the Accounting Profession*, (eds) John W. Buckley and Fred Weston (Lifetime Learning Publication, 1980), pp. 153–62.

Legitimacy of the Standard-Setting Process

Beaver, W.H. and Demski, Joel S., "The Nature of Financial Accounting Objectives: A Summary and Synthesis," *Studies in Financial Accounting Objectives*, 1974, Supplement to *Journal of Accounting Research* (1974), pp. 170–87.

Bromwich, Michael, "The Possibility of Partial Accounting Standards," *The Accounting Review* (April, 1980), pp. 288–300.

Chambers, R.J., "The Possibility of a Normative Accounting Standard," *The Accounting Review* (July, 1976), pp. 646–56.

Cushing, Barry E., "On the Possibility of Optimal Accounting Principles," *The Accounting Review* (April, 1977).

Demski, Joel S., "The General Impossibility of Normative Accounting Standards," *The Accounting Review* (October, 1973), pp. 718–23.

Demski, Joel S., "Choice Among Financial Reporting Alternatives," *The Accounting Review* (April, 1974), pp. 221–32.

Johnson, S.B., and Solomons, D.,"Institutional Legitimacy and the FASB," *Journal of Accounting and Public Policy* (Fall, 1984), pp. 165–83.

Marshall, Ronald, "Determining an Optimal Accounting Information System for an Unidentified User," *Journal of Accounting Research* (Fall, 1978), pp. 286–307.

Accounting Standards Overload

Alderman, C.W., Gary, D.M. and Meals, D.R., "Other Comprehensive Bases of Accounting: Alternative to GAAP?" *Journal of Accountancy* (August, 1982), pp. 52–62.

Chazen, C. and Benson, B., "Fitting GAAP to Smaller Businesses," *Journal of Accountancy* (February, 1978), pp. 46–51.

Hepp, G.W. and McRae, T.W., "Accounting Standards Overload: Relief is Needed," *Journal of Accountancy* (May, 1988), pp. 52–62.

Larson, R.E., and Kelly, T.P., "Differential Measurement in Accounting Standards: The Concept Makes Sense," *Journal of Accountancy* (November, 1984), pp. 78–90.

Lee, B.Z., Larson, R.E., and Chenok, P.B., "Issues Confronting the Accounting Profession," *Journal of Accountancy* (November, 1983), pp. 78–85.

APPENDIX 4.A

Members of the International Accounting Standards Committee

Australia	Australian Society of Accountants
	The Institute of Chartered Accountants in Australia
Austria	Institut Österreichischer Wirtschaftsprüfer
Bahamas	The Bahamas Institute of Chartered Accountants
Bahrain	The Bahrain Society of Accountants and Auditors
Bangladesh	The Institute of Chartered Accountants of Bangladesh
	The Institute of Cost and Management Accountants of Bangladesh
Barbados	The Institute of Chartered Accountants of Barbados
Belgium	L'Institut des Experts Comptables
	Institut des Reviseurs d'Entreprises
Botswana	The Association of Accountants in Botswana
Brazil	Instituto Brasileiro de Contadores
Canada	The Canadian Institute of Chartered Accountants
	Certified General Accountants' Association of Canada
	The Society of Management Accountants of Canada
Chile	Colegio de Contadores de Chile A.G.
Colombia	Instituto Nacional de Contadores Publicos de Colombia
Cyprus	The Institute of Certified Public Accountants of Cyprus
Denmark	Foreningen af Statsautoriserede Revisorer (FSR)

	Foreningen af Registrerede Revisorer (FRR)
Dominican Republic	Instituto de Contadores Publicos Autorizados de la Republica Dominicana
Ecuador	Federacion Nacional de Contadores del Ecuador
Egypt	The Egyptian Society of Accountants and Auditors
Federal Republic of Germany	Institut der Wirtschaftsprüfer in Deutschland e.V. Wirtschaftsprüferkammer
Fiji	The Institute of Accountants
Finland	KHT − Yhidstys Foreningen CGR
France	Compagnie Nationale des Commissaires Aux Comptes Ordre des Experts Comptables et des Comptables Agrées
Ghana	The Institute of Chartered Accountants (Ghana)
Greece	Association of Certified Accountants and Auditors of Greece Institute of Certified Public Accountants of Greece
Hong Kong	Hong Kong Society of Accountants
Iceland	Felag Loggiltra Endurskooenda
India	The Institute of Chartered Accountants of India The Institute of Cost and Works Accountants of India
Indonesia	Indonesian Institute of Accountants
Iraq	The Association of Public Accountants and Auditors
Ireland	The Institute of Certified Public Accountants of Ireland The Institute of Chartered Accountants in Ireland
Israel	The Institute of Certified Public Accountants in Israel
Italy	Consiglio Nazionale dei Dottori Commercialisti
Jamaica	The Institute of Chartered Accountants of Jamaica
Japan	The Japanese Institute of Certified Public Accountants
Jordan	Arab Society of Certified Accountants
Kenya	Institute of Certified Public Accountants of Kenya
Korea	Korean Institute of Certified Public Accountants
Lebanon	The Lebanese Association of Certified Public Accountants The Middle East Society of Associated Accountants
Lesotho	Lesotho Institute of Accountants
Liberia	The Liberian Institute of Certified Public Accountants
Luxemburg	Ordre des Experts Comptables Luxembourgeois
Malawi	The Society of Accountants in Malawi
Malaysia	The Malaysian Association of Certified Public Accountants Institut Akauntan Malaysia
Malta	The Institute of Accountants
Mexico	Instituto Mexicano de Contadores Publicos A.C.
Morocco	Compagnie des Experts Comptables du Maroc
Netherlands	Nederlands Institut van Registeraccountants
New Zealand	New Zealand Society of Accountants
Nigeria	The Institute of Chartered Accountants of Nigeria
Norway	Norges statsautoriserte Revisorers Forening Norges Registrerte Revisorers Forening

Pakistan	Institute of Chartered Accountants of Pakistan
	Institute of Cost and Management Accountants of Pakistan
Paraguay	Colegio de Contadores del Paraguay
Philippines	Philippine Institute of Certified Public Accountants
Portugal	Camara dos Revisores Oficiais de Contas
Republic of Panama	Colegio de Contadores Publicos Autorizados de Panama
	Associacion de Mujeres Contadores de Panama
Singapore	Singapore Society of Accountants
South Africa	The South African Institute of Chartered Accountants
Spain	Instituto de Censores Jurados de Cuentas de Espana
Sri Lanka	Institute of Chartered Accountants of Sri Lanka
Swaziland	The Swaziland Institute of Accountants
Sweden	Foreningen Auktoriserade Revisorer FAR
Switzerland	Schweizerische Treuhand-und Revisionskammer
Syria	Association des Experts Comptables Syrienne
Taiwan	National Federation of Certified Public Accountants
	Associations of the Republic of China
Tanzania	Tanzania Association of Accountants
	The National Board of Accountants and Auditors, Tanzania
Thailand	The Institute of Certified Accountants and Auditors of Thailand
Trinidad and Tobago	The Institute of Chartered Accountants of Trinidad and Tobago
Tunisia	Ordre des Experts Comptables et des Commissaires aux Comptes de Sociétés de Tunisie
Turkey	Expert Accountants' Association of Turkey
United Kingdom	The Chartered Association of Certified Accountants
	The Chartered Institute of Management Accountants
	The Chartered Institute of Public Finance and Accountancy
	The Institute of Chartered Accountants in England and Wales
	The Institute of Chartered Accountants in Ireland
	The Institute of Chartered Accountants in Scotland
United States of America	American Institute of Certified Public Accountants
	National Association of State Boards of Accountancy
	National Association of Accountants
	Institute of Internal Auditors
Uruguay	Colegio de Doctores en Ciencias Economicas y Contadores del Uruguay
Yugoslavia	The Social Accountancy Service of Yugoslavia
Zambia	The Zambia Institute of Certified Accountants
Zimbabwe	The Institute of Chartered Accountants of Zimbabwe

QUESTIONS

4.1 Name the main standard-setting bodies in the private sector during the past 50 years.

4.2 Identify the accounting organizations that issue the following types of documents:

a. *Financial Accounting Standards*   b. *Technical Bulletins*
c. *Financial Accounting Concepts*   d. *Invitations to Comment*
e. *Accounting Research Bulletins*   f. *Issue Papers*
g. *Financial Reporting Releases*   h. *Statements of Position*
i. *Discussion Memoranda*   j. *Opinions*

4.3 A press release announcing the appointment of the trustees of the new Financial Accounting Foundation stated that the Financial Accounting Standards Board (to be appointed by the trustees) "... will become the established authority for setting accounting principles under which corporations report to the shareholders and others" (AICPA news release, July 20, 1972).

Required

a. No mention is made of the Securities and Exchange Commission in the press release. What role does the SEC play in setting accounting principles?
b. How have accounting principles been set in the past ten years? In your answer, identify the body performing this function, the sponsoring organization, and the method by which the body arrived at its decisions.
c. What methods have management and management accountants used to influence the development of accounting principles in the past ten years?

(CMA adapted)

4.4 Some accountants have said that politicization in the development and acceptance of general accounting principles (standard setting) is taking place. Some use the term "politicization" in a narrow sense to mean the influence of governmental agencies, particularly the SEC, on the development of generally accepted accounting principles. Others use it more broadly to mean the compromising that occurs within the bodies that are responsible for developing generally accepted accounting principles due to the influence and pressure of special-interest groups (the SEC, the American Accounting Association, businesses, the National Association of Accountants, financial analysts, bankers, lawyers, and so on).

Required

a. The Committee on Accounting procedures (CAP) of the AICPA was established in the mid-to-late 1930s and functioned until 1959, at which time the Accounting Principles Board (APB) came into existence. In 1973, the Financial Accounting Standards Board (FASB) was formed and the APB ceased to exist. Do the reasons why these groups were formed, their methods of operations while they were/are in existence, and the reasons for the demise of the first two groups indicate an increasing "politicization" (as the term is used in the broad sense) of accounting standard setting? Explain your answer by indicating how the CAP, the APB, and the FASB operated or now operate. Cite specific developments that tend to support your answer.
b. What arguments can be raised to support the "politicization" of accounting standard setting?
c. What arguments can be raised in opposition to the "politicization" of accounting standard setting?   *(CMA adapted)*

4.5 What is the main objective behind the issuance of the "Statement of Financial Position" by the Accounting Standards Executive Committee?

4.6 What is the SEC's role in financial disclosure?

4.7 What are the differences between public regulation and self-regulation? Present some of the advantages of self-regulation in the accounting profession. Finally, what is the main mechanism for self-regulation?

4.8 The following statements were made by George J. Benston in *Corporate Financial Disclosure in the U.K. and the U.S.A.* (Lexington, Ma.: Lexington Books, D. C. Heath, 1976), p. 150:

In a fine society, government ought not to require private companies or persons to do anything unless, at the very least, the requirement resulted in a net benefit to society. Why, then, should financial disclosure be required from privately owned companies?

What might be some of the possible benefits to society of financial disclosure?

4.9 The following statements were made by R. Chatov in "Should the Public Sector Take Over the Function of Determining Generally Accepted Accounting Principles?," *The Accounting Journal* (Spring, 1977), p. 119:

I suggest that what is needed is a national commission to develop a comprehensive accounting code for industrial corporations within the United States. You may shudder with horror at my assertion that this accounting code ought to provide several things: (1) it ought to provide for uniformity in accounting treatment; (2) it ought to provide for the elimination of alternative treatments of accounting; (3) it ought to provide for comparability among the financial reports of different corporations, which should result if the first two objectives are met. Only in this way will investors be able to rely on corporate financial reports and on making comparisons between them. Only in this way will the government have reliable financial information that it will be able to appraise on the basis of knowing specifically what is in the reports and their aggregations. And only in this way can we look forward to intelligent and meaningful public-policy decisions to be made by government, based on consistent, aggregatable corporate financial data.

Do you think that accounting standard setting should be transferred to the public sector? Explain.

CHAPTER 5

THE EVENTS, BEHAVIORAL, AND HUMAN INFORMATION PROCESSING APPROACHES

In previous chapters, we stated that accounting theory arises from the need to provide a rationale for what accountants are expected to do and that, to be complete, the construction of an accounting theory should be followed by theory verification. We also presented the traditional and regulatory approaches to the formulation of an accounting theory as approaches aimed at developing an accounting framework but characterized, in general, by a rigorous process of verification. Because an accounting theory should result from both processes, new approaches have been developed or revised recently, the aims of which are not yet generally accepted by the various interest groups or by the accounting profession in particular. They represent new streams of accounting research that use both conceptual and empirical reasoning to formulate and verify a conceptual accounting framework. Among the new approaches, we may distinguish the events approach; the behavioral approach; the human information processing approach; the predictive approach; and the positive approach.

Each of these approaches has generated new methodologies and interest and has employed unique ways of looking at accounting problems. Because the interests and the methodologies are unique, each approach has acquired the attributes of a distinct paradigm, causing accounting to become a multiparadigmatic science in a constant state of crisis. Each theorist, dissatisfied with competing paradigms, will use a particular approach to provide a theoretical framework for the accounting field.

Our purpose in this chapter and the following chapter is first to elaborate on each of the new approaches, emphasizing the contribution of each approach to accounting theory construction, and then to explain the resulting paradigmatic status of accounting. This chapter will examine the events, behavioral and human information processing approaches; the following chapter will cover the predictive and positive approaches.

5.1   THE EVENTS APPROACH

5.1.1   The Nature of the Events Approach

The events approach was first explicitly stated after a divergence of opinion among the members of the Committee of the American Accounting Association, which issued *A Statement of Basic Accounting Theory* in 1966. The majority of the Committee members favored the *value approach* to accounting. Only one member, George Sorter, favored the events approach.[1]

The Value School

The value school, also called the user-need school, considers that needs of users to be known sufficiently to allow the deduction of an accounting theory that provides optimal input to the specified decision models. Input values cannot be optimal for all uses, and an exhaustive list of all normative and descriptive models is lacking. Furthermore, the conventional accounting model, based on the value approach, suffers from the following weaknesses:

- Its dimensions are limited. Most accounting measurements are expressed in monetary terms — a practice that precludes maintenance and use of productivity, performance, reliability, and other multidimensional data.
- Its classification schemes are not always appropriate. The chart of accountants for a particular enterprise represents all of the categories into which information concerning economic affairs may be placed. This will often lead to data being left out, or classified in a manner that hides its nature from nonaccountants.
- Its aggregation level for information is too high. Accounting data is used by a wide variety of decision makers, each needing different degrees of quantity, aggregation, and focus, depending on their personalities, decision styles, and conceptual structures. Therefore, information concerning economic events and objects should be kept in as elementary a form as possible to be aggregated by the eventual user.
- Its degree of integration with the other functional areas of an enterprise is too restricted. Information concerning the same set of phenomena will often be maintained separately by acountants and nonaccountants, thus leading to inconsistency as well as information gaps and overlaps.[2]

The Events Approach

The events approach, on the contrary, suggests that the purpose of accounting is "to provide information about relevant economic events that might be useful in a variety of decision models."[3] *It is up to the accountant to provide information about the events and leave to the user the task of fitting the events to their decision models. It is up to the user to aggregate and assign weights and values to the data generated by the event in conformity with his or her own utility function.* The user, rather than the accountant, transforms the event into accounting information suitable to the user's own individual decision model. As a result, the contents of the accounting reports reflect observations of the real world, rather than the "wishful inferences of devious managers whose 'use' of alternative accounting techniques is manipulative rather than informative."[4]

"Event" refers to any action that may be portrayed by one or more basic dimensions or attributes. According to Johnson, "event" means "feasible observations of specified characteristics of an action in regard to which a reporter could say 'I foresaw that and saw it happen myself.' "[5]

Thus, the characteristics of an event may be directly observed and are of economic significance to the user. Given the number of characteristics and the number of events susceptible to observation that might be relevant to the decision models of all types of users, the events approach suggests a tremendous expansion of the accounting data presented in financial reports. Characteristics of an event other than monetary values may have to be disclosed. The events approach also assumes that the level of aggregation and evaluation of accounting data are decided by the user, given the user's *loss function*. If the user aggregates and evaluates data on events at this time, then measurement errors, biases, and information losses generated by the accountant's attempt to match, assign weights, generate values, and aggregate information into the financial statements can be avoided.

5.1.2 Financial Statements and the Events Approach

What would be the consequence of the events approach to conventional annual reports?

In the value approach, the balance sheet is perceived as an indicator of the financial position of the firm at a given point in time. In the events approach, the balance sheet is perceived as an *indirect* communication of all accounting events relevant to the firm since its inception. Sorter proposes the following operational definition for the construction of a balance sheet when the events approach is employed: "A balance sheet should be constructed [in such a way] as to maximize the reconstructibility of the events to be aggregated."[6] Sorter's definition implies that all aggregated figures in the balance sheet may be disaggregated to show all the events that have occurred since the inception of the firm.

In the value approach, the income statement is perceived as an indicator of the financial performance of the firm for a given period. In the events approach, the balance sheet is perceived as a *direct* communication of the operating events that occur during a given period. Sorter proposes the following operational rule when the events approach is employed: "Each event should be described in a manner facilitating the forecasting of the same event in a future time period given exogeneous changes."[7]

In the value approach, the funds statement is perceived as an expression of the changes in working capital. In the events approach, however, the funds statement is better perceived as an expression of financial and investment events. In other words, an event's relevance, rather than its impact on the working capital, determines the reporting of an event in the funds statement.

5.1.3   The Normative Events Theory of Accounting

The normative events theory of accounting has been tentatively summarized as follows:

> In order for interested persons (shareholders, employees, managers, suppliers, customers, government agencies, and charitable institutions) to better forecast the future of social organizations (households, businesses, governments, and philanthropies), the most relevant attributes (characteristics) of the crucial events (internal, environmental, and transactional) which affect the organization are aggregated (temporally and sectionally) for periodic publication free of inferential bias.[8]

Thus, the objective of the normative events theory of accounting is to maximize the forecasting accuracy of accounting reports by focusing on the most *relevant* attributes of events *crucial* to the users. The theory calls for:

1 An explicit taxonomy of real events, which the accountant is to report.
2 More effective classification schemes, with particular reference to labels that make it possible to associate observations of particular events with other related events.[9]
3 The structuring of an events-based accounting information system.

5.1.4   Events-Based Accounting Information Systems

One way to meet the objective of the normative events theory of accounting is to integrate the events approach with *data-base approaches* to information management that assume that an enterprise creates a centrally-managed data base to be shared among a wide range of users with highly diverse needs. Such accounting systems included *hierarchical* models,[10] *network* models,[11] *relational* models,[12] *entity-relationship* models,[13] and *REA accounting* models.[14]

1 The hierarchical model is based on the idea of an events-accounting information system that allows users to make inquiries of a data base. The components of such a system include:
   a. A *mass data base* that contains a record of all events in some generalized format.
   b. A *user-defined structure* that provides each user with his or her own conceptual structure (and aggregation levels) of the events.
   c. *User-defined functions*, or operations, for manipulating the data.[15]
2. The network model is based on the concept of multidimensional accounting presented by Ijiri[16] and Charnes, Colontini, and Cooper.[17] It uses as input the initially unstructured data base and a collection of queries or data requests to develop a hierarchical data structure that will minimize the number of records to be accessed to answer the desired set of queries.[18]
3. The relational model is founded on the mathematical theory of *relations*. Basically, a data base is considered to be a collection of time-varying relations of assorted degrees. Users interact with the model via a language meaningful to the particular user. Substantial work remains to be done to improve the applicability of the relational approach to accounting models.[19]
4. The entity-relationship model assumes that an accounting system is most naturally modeled in a data-base environment as a collection of real-world *entities* and *relationships* among these entities.[20] This model basically replaces the tradi-

tional chart of accounts and double-entry bookkeeping procedures by viewing entity-relationship in the form of entity tables and relationship tables. To construct such an accounting data model, the following steps are suggested:

a. Identify (1) the *entity sets*, such as classes of objects, agents, and events that exist in the conceptual world, and (2) the *relationship sets* that connect these entities.

b. Construct an entity-relationship (E-R) diagram that will exhibit the semantic nature of identified relationships.

c. Define the characteristics of entity sets and relationship sets that will be of interest to users of particular systems, and specify mapping that will identify those characteristics.

d. Organize the results of Steps (a), (b), and (c) into entity-relationship tables, and identify a key (unique) characteristic for each entity-relationship set.[21]

5. The REA accounting model is a generalized entity-relationship representation of accounting phenomena with components that consist of sets representing economic resources, economic events, and economic agents.[22]

5.1.5   Evaluation of the Events Approach

The events approach offers certain advantages and certain limitations. The advantages predominantly take the form of efforts to provide information about relevant economic events that might be useful to a variety of decision models. As a result, more information may be available to users who can then use their own utility function to determine the nature and level of aggregation of the information they need to make their particular decisions. The usefulness of the events approach may depend, however, on one of more of the following arguments:

1 The usefulness of the events approach may depend on the psychological type of the decision maker.[23] It has been shown, for example, that structured/aggregate reports are preferable for high-analytic decision makers, but that data-base inquiry systems (the events approach) are preferable for low-analytic decision makers.[24]

2 Information overload may result from the attempt to measure the relevant characteristics of all crucial events affecting the firm.

3 An adequate criterion for the choice of the crucial events has not been developed.

4 Measuring all the characteristics of an events approach may prove to be difficult, given the state of the art in accounting.

5 More research may be needed to examine the impact of different design approaches to the events approach theory, such as the hierarchical, network, relational, entity-relationship, and REA models.

5.2   THE BEHAVIORAL APPROACH

5.2.1   The Nature of the Behavioral Approach

Most traditional approaches to the construction of an accounting theory have failed to take into consideration user behavior in particular, and behavioral assumptions in general. In 1960, Devine made the following critical remark:

> Let us now turn to ... the psychological reactions of those who consume accounting output or are caught in its threads of control. On balance, it seems fair to conclude that accountants seem to have waded through their relationships to the intricate psychological network of human activity with a heavy-handed crudity that is beyond belief. Some degree of crudity may be excused in a new discipline, but failure to recognize that much of what passes as accounting theory is hopelessly entwined with unsupported behavior assumptions is unforgivable.[25]

The behavioral approach to the formulation of accounting theory emphasizes the relevance to decision making of the information being communicated (*communication-decision orientation*) and the individual and group behavior caused by the communication of the information (*decision-maker orientation*). Accounting is assumed to be action-oriented; its purpose is to influence action (behavior) directly through the informational content of the message conveyed and indirectly through the behavior of accountants. Because accounting is considered to be a behavioral process,[26] the behavioral approach to the formulation of an accounting theory applies behavioral science to accounting. The overall objective of this approach is similar to that of behavioral science. The American Accounting Association's Committee on Behavioral Science Content of the Accounting Curriculum provides the following view of the objective of behavioral science, which may also apply to behavioral accounting:

> The objective of behavioral science is to understand, explain, and predict human behavior — that is, to establish generalizations about human behavior that are supported by empirical evidence collected in an impersonal way by procedures that are completely open to review and replication and capable of verification by other interested scholars. Behavioral science thus represents the systematic observation of man's behavior for the purpose of experimentally confirming specific hypotheses by reference to observable changes in behavior.[27]

The behavioral approach to the formulation of an accounting theory is concerned with human behavior, as it relates to accounting information and problems. In this context, the choice of an accounting technique must be evaluated with reference to the objectives and behavior of the users of financial information.

Although relatively new, the behavioral approach has generated an enthusiasm and a new impetus in accounting research that focuses on the behavioral structure within which accountants function. A new multidisciplinary area in the field of accounting has been conveniently labeled *behavioral accounting*. The basic objective of behavioral accounting is to explain and predict human behavior in all possible accounting contexts. Research studies in behavioral accounting have relied on experimental, field, or correlational techniques. Most studies have made little attempt to formulate a theoretical framework that would support the problems or hypotheses to be tested. Instead, the studies generally have focused on the behavioral effects of accounting information or on the problems of human information processing. The results of these kinds of studies may provide an understanding of the behavioral environment of accounting that may serve as a guide in formulating an accounting theory. We will examine each group of studies and then evaluate the behavioral accounting approach.

5.2.2   Behavioral Effects of Accounting Information

That accounting information, in terms of its content and format, may have an impact on individual decision making, although evident and easily accepted, suggests avenues of research for the improvement of accounting and reporting systems. Accordingly, research studies in this area have examined alternative reporting models and disclosure practices to assess the available choices in terms of relevance and impact on behavior. Because a general theoretical framework has not been established, however, it is difficult to classify these studies. Several writers have attempted to provide classification schemes.[28] A more recent and exhaustive attempt by Dyckman, Gibbins, and Swieringa[29] will be used in this section to illustrate the nature of studies of the behavioral effects of accounting information.

We may divide these studies into five general classes: (1) the adequacy of disclosure, (2) the usefulness of financial statement data, (3) attitudes about corporate reporting practices, (4) materiality judgments, and (5) the decision effects of alternative accounting procedures.[30]

Three approaches were used to examine the *adequacy of disclosure*. The first approach examined the patterns of use of data from the viewpoint of resolving controversial issues concerning the inclusion of certain information.[31] The second approach examined the perceptions and attitudes of different interest groups.[32] The third approach examined the extent to which different information items were disclosed in annual reports and the determinants of any significant differences in the adequacy of financial disclosure among companies.[33] The research on disclosure adequacy and use showed a general acceptance of the adequacy of available financial statements, a general understanding and comprehension of these financial statements, and a recognition that the differences in disclosure adequacy among the financial statements are due to such variables as company size, profitability, and size and listing status of the auditing firm.

Three approaches were used to examine the *usefulness of financial statement data*. The first approach examined the relative importance of the investment analysis of different information items to both users and preparers of financial information.[34] The second approach examined the relevance of financial statements to decision making, based on laboratory communication of financial statement data in terms of readability and meaning to users in general.[35,36] The overall conclusions of these studies were that (1) some consensus exists between users and preparers regarding the relative importance of the information items disclosed in financial statements, and (2) users do not rely solely on financial statements when making their decisions.

Two approaches were used to examine attitudes about *corporate reporting practices*. The first approach examined preferences for alternative accounting techniques.[37] The second approach examined attitudes about general reporting issues, such as how much information should be available, how much information is available, and the importance of certain items.[38] These research studies showed the extent to which some accounting techniques proposed by the authoritative bodies are accepted, and brought to light some attitudinal differences among professional groups concerning reporting issues.

Two approaches were used to examine *materiality judgments*. The first approach examined the main factors that determine the collection, classification, and summarization of accounting data.[39] The second approach focused on what items people consider to be material and sought to determine that degree of difference in accounting data that is required before the difference is perceived as material.[40] These studies indicated that several factors appear to affect materiality judgments and that these judgments differ among individuals.

Finally, the *decision effects of alternative accounting procedures* were examined, primarily in the context of the use of different inventory techniques, price-level information, and nonaccounting information.[41] The results indicated that alternative accounting techniques may influence individual decisions, and that the extent of the influence may depend on the nature of the task, the characteristics of the users, and the nature of the experimental environment.

5.2.3   Linguistic Effects of Accounting Data and Techniques

Linguistics and accounting have a great number of similarities. Jain, for example, considers accounting rules to be analogous to financial grammar and, based on this analogy, uses the effect of grammatical structure on the perceptions of listeners to support the hypothesis that accounting methods affect decision making.[42] More formally, Belkaoui argues that accounting is a language and that according to the "Sapir–Whorf hypothesis" its lexical characteristics and grammatical rules will affect both the linguistic and the nonlinguistic behavior of users.[43] Four propositions are introduced, derived from the linguistic relativity paradigm to conceptually integrate the research findings on the impact of accounting information on the user's behavior:

- The users that make certain lexical distinctions in accounting are enabled to talk and/or solve problems that cannot be solved by users who do not.
- The users that make certain lexical distinctions in accounting are enabled to perform (nonlinguistic) tasks more rapidly or more completely than those users who do not.
- The users that possess the accounting (grammatical) rules are more predisposed to different managerial styles or emphases than those who do not.
- The accounting techniques may tend to facilitate or render more difficult various (nonlinguistic) managerial behaviors on the part of users.[44]

These propositions have been empirically tested and verified in two studies that emphasize the importance of linguistic considerations in the use of accounting information and in international standard-setting.[45,46]

Within the *linguistic relativism thesis*, the role of language is emphasized as a mediator and shaper of the environment; this would imply that accounting language may predispose "users" to a given method of perception and behavior. Furthermore, the affiliation of users with different professional organizations or communities that have distinct interaction networks may create different accounting language repertoires. Accountants from different professional groups may use different organizational constraints and objectives. At worst, a confounding lack of communication may emerge. Using the *sociolinguistic thesis*, Belkaoui empirically shows that various affiliations in accounting create different linguistic repertoires or codes for intragroup communications and/or intergroup communications.[47] The sociolinguistic construct is used to justify the possible lack of consensus on the meaning of the accounting concepts. As a result, specific issues identified as in need of further research include: (1) the presence and nature of the "institutional language" within each accounting professional group; (2) the presence of a profession-linked linguistic code in the accounting field that is composed of a "formal language" and a "public language"; and (3) the construction of a test to determine whether or not the public language is understood by users of public data (such as financial analysis) and whether or not the formal language is understood by users of formal data (such as students).[48]

Other studies have investigated the linguistic effects of accounting data and techniques without relying on the linguistic relativism thesis or the sociolinguistic thesis. Instead, these studies have focused on the differences between the intragroup and intergroup communication of accounting data and/or techniques among users and producers of accounting data. To prove that these differences exist, accounting researchers have relied on various techniques, including: (1) the semantic differential technique,[49,50,51] the antecedent-consequent technique,[52] multidimensional scaling techniques,[53] and the Cloze procedure.[54]

5.2.4   Functional Fixation

In psychology, functional fixation refers to a phenomenon of most human behavior: the individual attaches a meaning to a title or an object and is unable to see alternative meanings or uses. In short, the individual *fixates* on only one function of that object. The application of functional fixation to accounting begins with Ijiri, Jaedicke, and Knight's discussion of the conditions under which a decision maker may be unable to change the decision-making process in response to a change in the underlying accounting process that provided him or her with the data.[55] They attribute the failure of decision makers to change their decision-making processes in response to a change in accounting methods to the phenomenon of functional fixation:

> Psychologists have found that there appears to be "functional fixation" in most human behavior in which the person attaches a meaning to a title or an object (for example, manufacturing cost) and is unable to see alternative meanings or uses. People intuitively associate a value with an item through past experience and often do not recognize that the value of the item depends, in fact, on the particular moment in time and may be significantly different from what it was in the past. Therefore, when a person is placed in a new situation, he or she views the object or term as it was used previously.[56]

In applying this concept to accounting, they extrapolated that:

> . . . if the outputs from different accounting methods are called by the same name, such as profit, cost, etc., people who do not understand accounting well tend to neglect the fact that alternative methods may have been used to prepare the outputs. In such a case, a change in the accounting process clearly influences the decisions.[57]

Following Ijiri, Jaedicke, and Knight's suggestions, various accounting researchers explained the impact of alternative accounting techniques using functional fixation. These include Jensen's study of the effect of alternative depreciation and inventory-costing methods in decision making,[58] Livingstone's empirical study of the effects of alternative methods of interperiod income-tax allocation on regulatory rate-of-return decisions affecting electric utilities,[59] and Mlyanarczyk's study of the effect of alternative tax accounting methods on common stock prices of electric utility companies.[60] These studies, however, have given functional fixation a cross-sectional orientation by applying it to alternative accounting methods rather than to changes in accounting methods over time. The exception has been provided by Ashton, whose study is concerned with the extent to which individual decision makers change their decision processes after the occurrence of an accounting change, evidenced by the effect of this cognitive change on subsequent decisions.[61] Ashton's results provided additional evidence of the existence of functional fixation in an accounting context.

5.2.5   Information Inductance

The behavior of an individual is influenced by information in two ways: (1) through information use when acting as a recipient, and (2) through information inductance when acting as a sender. Although the impact on information use is generally known and accepted as part of the stimulus-response paradigm, the more recent phenomenon of *information inductance* or simple *inductance*, introduced in accounting by Prakash and Rappaport,[62] is intended to refer to the complex process whereby the behavior of an individual is affected by the information he or she is required to communicate. Information inductance results from the sender's tendencies to anticipate the possible use of information, the consequences of such use, and his or her reactions to these consequences. As stated by Prakash and Rappaport:

> An individual's anticipating the consequences of his or her communication might lead him or her — before any information is communicated and, hence, even before any consequences arise — to choose to alter the information, or his or her behavior, or even his or her objectives. This is the process of information inductance.[63]

Time factors seem to govern inductance as follows:

> First, communication of information that is either in fact a description of the sender's behavior, or is regarded as such by the information sender, or concerning which the information sender has some apprehension that it could be so regarded by the information recipient, will be strongly conducive to information inductance. Secondly, consequences that represent possible feedback effects on the information sender will be strongly conducive to information inductance. We go on to classify broadly the feedback effects to an information sender as arising from (1) external evaluation of performance, (2) regulation and control of operations, (3) interaction with the decisions of other behavioral units, and (4) changes in the set of choices open to the information sender.[64]

Information inductance may be integrated to information use to provide an integrated theory of the impact of information involving both senders and users.

5.3   THE HUMAN INFORMATION PROCESSING APPROACH

Interest in the human information processing approach arose from a desire to improve both the information set presented to users of financial data and the ability of users to use the information. Theories and models from human information processing in psychology provide a tool for transforming accounting issues into generic information processing issues. There are three main components of an information processing model — input, process, and output. Studies of the information set *input* (or *cues*) focus on the variables that are likely to affect the way people process information for decision making. The variables examined are (1) the scaling characteristics of individual cues (level of measurement, discrete or continuous, deterministic or probabilistic), (2) the statistical properties of the information set (number of cues, distributional characteristics, inter-relationship of cues, underlying dimensionality), (3) the informational content or predictive significance (bias, reliability or form of relationship to criterion), (4) the method of presentation (format, sequence, level of aggregation), and (5) the context (physical viewing conditions, instructions, task characteristics and feedback).[65]

Studies of the process component focus on the variables affecting the decision maker, such as (1) characteristics of judgment (personal, task-related, human or mechanical, number of judges), and (2) characteristics of decision rules (form, cue usage, stability, and heuristics).[66]

Studies of the output component focus on variables related to the judgment, prediction, or decision that are likely to affect the way the user processes the information. The variables examined include (1) the qualities of the judgment (accuracy, speed, reliability in terms of consistency, consensus, and convergence, response biases, and predictability), and (2) self-insight (subjective cue usage, perceived decision quality, and perceptions of characteristics of information sets).[67]

The varying emphasis on any of the three components of an information processing model led to the use of four different approaches: (1) the lens model approach, (2) probabilistic judgment, (3) predecisional behavior, and (4) the cognitive style approach. Each approach will be examined next.

5.3.1 The Lens Model

Brunswick's Lens Model allows explicit recognition of the interdependence of environmental and individual-specific variables.[68] It is used primarily to assess human judgmental situations — situations in which people make judgments on the basis of a set of explicit cues from the environment. The model emphasizes the similarities between the environment and the subject response. As seen in Exhibit 5.1, the right side of the model describes the relationships between the subject responses or judgments (Y_s) and the level of cues (X_i) in terms of their correlation (r_i). The left side of the model describes the relationships between the actual criterion or event (Y_e) and the level of cues (X_i). The analysis relies on a *regression model* when the cues are continuous and on an *analaysis of variance (ANOVA) model* when the cues take on categorical values. Other methods include conjoint measurement, multidimensional scaling techniques, and discriminant analysis.

Most accounting research using the lens model has been motivated by the need "(1) to build mathematical models that represent the relative importance of different information cues (often called 'policy capturing'), and (2) to measure the accuracy of judgment and its consistency, consensus, and predictability."[69] Various accounting decision problems have been examined using the lens model. These include (1) *policy-capturing* studies, which examine the relative importance of different cues in the judgment process and consensus among decision makers, (2) *accuracy of judgments* made on the basis of accounting cues, and (3) *effects of task characteristics on achievement and learning.*[70]

The policy-capturing research focused on issues related to between-judge *consensus*, the relative *importance of cues*, the *functional form* of the decision rule, and the judges' *self-insight*. Decision problems examined in the policy-capturing research included materiality judgments, internal control evaluation, reasonableness of forecasts, uncertainty disclosures, policy making, and loan classification.

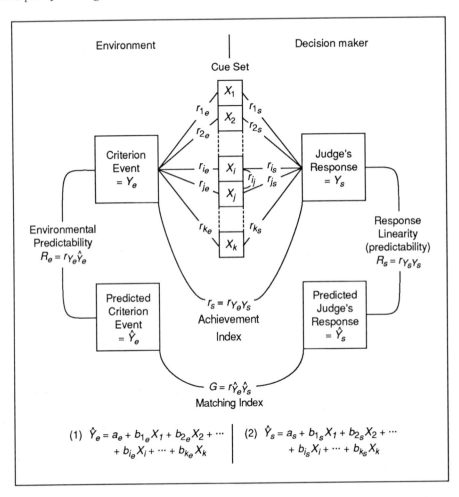

EXHIBIT 5.1

The accuracy of judgments is very important to accountants. The research focused not only on *judgmental accuracy* but also on *judgmental consistency, consensus,* and *predictability*. The decision problems examined in the accuracy of judgment research included bankruptcy prediction and stock recommendations and price predictions.

The effects of task characteristics on achievement and learning were examined in both the psychological and the accounting literature. In psychology, the problems examined included task predictability, the functional form of cue criterion relationships, the number of cues, cue validity distributions and intercorrelations, and feedback type. In accounting, the problems examined included the impact of accounting changes, feedback methods, the report format, and cue presentation.

5.3.2 Probabilistic Judgment

The probabilistic judgment approach, sometimes known as the *Bayesian approach*, focuses first on a comparison of intuitive probability judgments and the normative model. The *normative* model for probability revision, known as *Bayes' Theorem*, is used as the *descriptive* model of human information processing. Basically, the a posteriori probability form of Bayes' Theorem states that

$$\underbrace{\frac{P(H_1/D)}{P(H_2/D)}}_{\substack{\text{A posteriori} \\ \text{probability}}} = \underbrace{\frac{P(D/H_1)}{P(D/H_2)}}_{\substack{\text{Likelihood} \\ \text{ratio}}} \times \underbrace{\frac{P(H_1)}{P(H_2)}}_{\substack{\text{A priori} \\ \text{probability}}}$$

where H_1 and H_2 are the alternative hypotheses and D is the datum.

The basic question examined in the early research in probabilistic judgment is whether probabilities are revised in the direction indicated by Bayes' Theorem.[71] The findings suggest that this occurs to a lesser extent than Bayes' Theorem would suggest. The phenomenon has been labeled *conservatism*. This shifted the focus of the research to finding the sources of the observed human information processing biases. Tversky and Kahneman reported that people rely on a number of heuristics to reduce the complex tasks of assessing probabilities and predicting values to simpler judgmental operations.[72] These heuristics include *representativeness, availability, and adjustment and anchoring.*

Representativeness refers to the heuristic people use when they assess the probability of an event on the basis of its degree of similarity, or representativeness, to the category of which it is perceived to be an example. *Availability* refers to the heuristic people use when they assess the probability of an event on the basis of the case with which it comes to mind. Finally, *adjustment* and *anchoring* refer to the heuristic people use when they make estimates by starting with an initial value (anchoring) and then adjusting the value to yield the final answer.

The early literature of probabilistic judgment in accounting reached the same conclusion concerning the decision makers' use of simplifying heuristics in their processing of information, with the difference that such use may be sensitive to task and situation variables. More current research has examined the choice of techniques used to elicit subjective probabilities and the departures from normative decision-making behavior.

Research on probability elicitation has attempted to assess the convergent validity of different elicitation techniques in auditing as well as their accuracy and their effect on audit decisions. No general conclusions can be derived at this stage of the research.

Research on the departures from normative decision-making behavior has focused on heuristics and biases — basically, representativeness in auditing, anchoring in auditing, anchoring in management control, and anchoring in financial analysis — and on the ability of decision makers to perform the role of information evaluators. Little, however, is known about how the information processing capabilities of individuals interact with task structure to produce heuristics and biases.

5.3.3 Predecisional Behavior

Most of the experiments based on the lens model or on probabilistic judgment involve highly repetitive situations in which the task is well-defined, the subject is exposed to the right cues, and the possible responses are prespecified. These experiments fail to deal with the dynamics of problem definition, hypothesis formation, and information search in less structured environments. In brief, they fail to explore the stages of predecisional behavior.

Predecisional behavior is generally examined using *process-tracing methods*. The process-tracing method evolved from the theory of problem solving developed by Newell and Simon,[73] who argue that humans have a limited capacity to process information. They also suggest that humans have short-term memory with limited capacity and virtually unlimited long-term memory. As a result, humans tend to display satisficing rather than optimal responses, leading them to be adaptive. This adaptiveness, in turn, implies that the cognitive representation (nature and complexity) of the task determines the way in which the problems are solved, since the tasks tend to elicit and therefore control the behavioral responses of decision makers.

Process tracers tend to rely on four methods: (1) eye movements, (2) information search behavior, (3) information cue attending or response time, and (4) verbal "think aloud" introspective protocols.[74] Verbal protocol, the most frequently used technique in accounting, consists of asking subjects to "think aloud" into an audio or video recorder while performing a task. The protocols are then analyzed, using a particular coding strategy. Given the potential reasonableness of the verbal protocol coding strategy employed by the researchers, Payne suggests the additional use of other data-collection methods so that the results of several methods can be compared to determine their convergence.[75] Joyce and Libby add the following disadvantages:

> Among the disadvantages are (1) the sheer volume of data collected in such studies, which limits the number of subjects than can be studied, and (2) the lack of objective coding techniques. This makes the analysis arduous and the communication of the results quite difficult. Reports of verbal protocol studies are usually quite long to read, even when the results from just a few subjects are presented.[76]

Very few accounting studies have relied on process tracing methods. Issues examined include the modeling of expert financial analysts, the general strategies used by managers in performance report evaluation, and audit decision making. Although they are in the early stages of development, the accounting applications of the process tracing approaches are promising. Some of these potentials follow:

> For example, research examining the memory of experts might indicate explanations for differences between experts and novices demonstrated in prior research and might lead to the development of training aids. The role of cognitive representation in the choice of decision heuristics may provide insights into methods for redesigning management

reports or audit programs to lead to proper heuristic choice. Studies of the interaction of memory and information search may lead to the development of decision aids to be used at these important stages in less structured accounting situations such as variance investigation and audit client screening.[77]

5.3.4 The Cognitive Style Approach

The cognitive style approach focuses on the variables that are likely to have an impact on the quality of the judgments made by the decision makers. "Cognitive style" is a hypothetical construct that is used to explain the mediation process between stimuli and responses. Five approaches to the study of cognitive style in psychology have been reported: authoritarianism, dogmatism, cognitive complexity, integrative complexity, and field dependence:[78]

1. *Authoritarianism* arose from the focus by Adorno and others on the relationship between personality, anti-democratic attitudes, and behavior.[79] These researchers were primarily interested in individuals whose way of thinking made them susceptible to anti-democratic propaganda. Two of the behavioral correlates of authoritarianism — rigidity and intolerance of ambiguity — were reflections of an underlying cognitive style.

2. *Dogmatism* arose from Rokeach's efforts to develop a structurally-based measure of authoritarianism to replace the content-based measure developed by Adorno and his colleagues.[80] Their interest was in developing a measure of cognitive style that would be independent of the content of thought.

3. *Cognitive complexity*, as introduced by Kelly[81] and Bieri,[82] focuses on the psychological dimensions that individuals use to structure their environments and to differentiate the behavior of others. More cognitively complex individuals are assumed to have a greater number of available dimensions with which to construe the behavior of others than less cognitively complex persons. Decision makers are also classified in terms of two cognitive styles: *heuristic* and *analytic*. Based on terms used by Huysman,[83] they may be defined as follows:

   a. *Analytic decision makers* reduce problem situations to a more or less explicit, often quantitative, model on which they base decisions.

   b. *Heuristic decision makers* refer instead to common sense, intuition, and unquantified feelings about future development as applied to the totality of the situation as an organic whole rather than to clearly identifiable parts.

4. *Integrative complexity*, as presented by Harvey and others,[84] and later expanded by Schroeder and others,[85] results from the view that people engage in two activities in processing sensory input: differentiation and integration. *Differentiation* refers to the individual's ability to place stimuli along dimensions. *Integration* refers to the individual's ability to employ complex rules to combine these dimensions. A person engaging in less of both activities is said to be *concrete*; a person engaging in more of both activities is said to be *abstract*. The continuum from concrete to abstract is referred to as *integrative or conceptual complexity*.

   To the concept of integrative complexity is usually added the concept of environmental complexity and the level of information processing, as expressed by the *U-curve Hypothesis* depicted in Exhibit 5.2. As the level of environmental complexity increases, the level of information processing increases and reaches a maximum level at an optimal level of environmental complexity beyond which it begins to decrease.[86] Schroeder and others extended the concept of the inverted U-shaped curve to the study of integrative complexity. The differences between the concrete and the abstract individual are also shown in Exhibit 5.2. The more abstract the individual, the higher the maximum level of information processing.

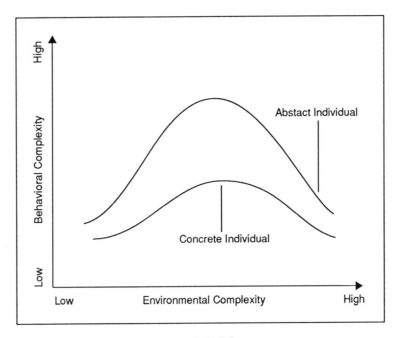

EXHIBIT 5.2

5 Finally, *field dependence*, as presented by Witkin and his associates, is a measure of the extent of differentiation in the area of perception.[87] *Field-dependent* individuals tend to perceive the overall organization of a field and are relatively unable to perceive parts of the field as discrete. *Field-independent* individuals, however, tend to perceive parts of the field as discrete from the overall organization of the field, rather than as fused with it.

Accounting studies based on these five approaches to cognitive style have focused on classifying users of information by their cognitive structure and on designing information systems that are best suited to the cognitive style of the decision maker. Evidence to support a tailor-made information system is, however, rather mixed, due mainly to the failure to account for and control a host of unmeasured, intervening variables. Similarly, evidence on the impact of "information overload" on the quality of the decision is also mixed and suffers from the failure to arrive at an adequate operational definition of accounting information overload.

5.4   EVALUATION OF THE BEHAVIORAL APPROACH

Most of the behavioral accounting research discussed in the preceding sections has attempted to establish generalizations about human behavior in relation to accounting information. The implicit objective of all these studies is to develop and verify the behavioral hypotheses relevant to accounting theory — hypotheses on the adequacy of disclosure, the usefulness of financial statement data, attitudes about corporate reporting practices, materiality judgments, the decision effects of alternative accounting procedures, and the components of an information processing model (input, process, and output). This implicit objective has not yet been reached, however, because most of the experimental and survey research in behavioral accounting suffers from a lack of theoretical and methodological rigor. Studies have examined the use of surrogates in behavioral accounting research without any conclusive results.[88]

Similarly, viewing the experiment as a social contract implies a relationship between the subject and the experimenter. Some aspects of this relationship may threaten the validity of the experiment.

5.5   CONCLUSIONS

This chapter has elaborated on the meanings and important findings of event, behavioral, and human information processing to the formulation of an accounting theory. Each of these approaches relies on different assumptions and on new methodologies and unique ways of looking at accounting problems and research questions. Each approach is beginning to take on the attributes of a distinctive paradigm, thereby causing accounting to become a multiparadigmatic science in which competing paradigms strive for dominance. In the next chapter, we will explain the impact of the predictive and positive approaches to the formulation of an accounting theory.

NOTES

[1] Sorter, G.H., "An 'Events' Approach to Basic Accounting Theory," *The Accounting Review* (January, 1969), pp. 12–19.

[2] McCarthy, W.E., "Construction and Use of Integrated Accounting Systems with Entity-Relationship Modeling," in *Entity-Relationship Approach to Systems Analysis and Design* (ed.) P. Chen (New York: North Holland Publishing Company, 1980), p. 628.

[3] Sorter, G.H., "An 'Events' Approach to Basic Accounting Theory,"op. cit., p. 13.

[4] Johnson, O., "Towards an 'Events' Theory of Accounting," *The Accounting Review* (October, 1970), p. 649.

[5] Ibid., pp. 643–44.

[6] Sorter, G.H., "An 'Events' Approach to Basic Accounting Theory," op. cit., p. 15.

[7] Ibid., p. 17.

[8] Johnson, O., "Towards an 'Events' Theory of Accounting," op. cit., p. 650.

[9] Wheeler, J.T., "Accounting Theory and Research in Perspective," *The Accounting Review* (January, 1970), p. 7.

[10] Colantoni, C.S., Manes, R.P., and Whinston, A.B., "A Unified Approach to the Theory of Accounting and Information Systems," *The Accounting Review* (January, 1971), pp. 90–102; Lieberman, A.Z., and Whinston, A.B., "A Structuring of an Events-Accounting Information System," *The Accounting Review* (April, 1975), pp. 246–57.

[11] Haseman, W.D., and Whinston, A.B., "Design of a Multidimensional Accounting System," *The Accounting Review* (January, 1976), pp. 65–79.

[12] Everest, G.C., and Weber, R., "A Relational Approach to Accounting Models," *The Accounting Review* (April, 1977), pp. 340–59.

[13] McCarthy, W.E., "An Entity-Relationship View of Accounting Models," *The Accounting Review* (October, 1979), pp. 667–86.

[14] McCarthy, W.E., "The REA Accounting Model: A Generalized Framework for Accounting Systems in a Shared Data Environment," *The Accounting Review* (July, 1982), pp. 554–78.

[15] Lieberman, A.Z., and Whinston, A.B., "A Structuring of an Events-Accounting Information System," op. cit., p. 249.

[16] Ijiri, Yuji, *The Foundations of Accounting Measurements* (Englewood Cliffs, N. J.: Prentice-Hall, 1967), p. 110.

[17] Charnes, A., Colantoni, C.S., and Cooper, W.W., "A Futorological Justification for Historical Cost and Multidimensional Accounting" (Pittsburgh: Carnegie Mellon University, School of Urban and Public Affairs, November, 1974).

[18] Haseman, W.D., and Whinston, A.B., "Design of a Multidimensional Accounting System," op. cit., p. 79.

[19] Everest, G.C., and Weber, R., "A Relational Approach to Accounting Models," op. cit., p. 359.

[20] McCarthy, W.E., "An Entity-Relationship View of Accounting Models," op. cit., p. 667.

[21] Chen, P., "The Entity-Relationship Model — Toward a Unified View of Data," *ACM Transactions on Data-Base Systems* (March, 1976), pp. 9–36.

[22] McCarthy, W.E., "The REA Accounting Model: A Generalized Framework for Accounting Systems in a Shared Data Environment," op. cit., p. 556.

[23] Benbasat, I., and Dexter, A.S., "Value and Events Approaches to Accounting: An Experimental Evaluation," *The Accounting Review* (October, 1979), pp. 735–45.

[24] The low/high analytic dimension is a psychological type variable whereby low-analytic decision makers tend to use hypothetical testing, feedback, and trial-and-error approaches to reach solutions, and high-analytic decision makers tend to approach a problem by structuring it in terms of a planned method that may produce a likely solution. For more information, see Huysmans, J.H.B., "The Effectiveness of Cognitive Style Constraint in Implementing Operations Research Proposals," *Management Science* (September, 1970), pp. 92–104.

[25] Devine, C.T., "Research Methodology and Accounting Theory Formation," *The Accounting Review* (July, 1960), pp. 387–99.

[26] Report of The Committee on Behavioral Science Content of the Accounting Curriculum," *The Accounting Review* (supplement, 1971), p. 247.

[27] Ibid., p. 394.

[28] Birnberg, J.G., and Nath, R., "Implications of Behavioral Science for Managerial Accounting," *The Accounting Review* (January, 1975), pp. 81–98; Hofstedt, T.R., "Some Behavioral Parameters of Financial Analysis," *The Accounting Review* (October, 1972), pp. 679–92; Rhode, J.G., "Behavioral Science Methodologies with Application for Accounting Research: References and Source Materials," Chapter 7 of "Report of the Committee on Research Methodology in Accounting," *The Accounting Review* (supplement, 1972), pp. 454–504.

[29] Dyckman, T.R., Gibbins, M., and Swieringa, R.J., "Experimental and Survey Research in Financial Accounting: A Review and Evaluation," in *The Impact of Accounting Research in Financial Accounting and Disclosure on Accounting Practice*, (eds) A.R. Abdel-Khalik and T.F. Keller (Durham, N.C.: Duke University Press, 1978), pp. 48–89.

[30] We will present a brief overview of the studies included in each class to provide an overview of the research topics and methodologies behavioral accountant researchers employ to conduct their inquiry. For a full examination of these studies, see Dyckman, Gibbins, and Swieringa's survey.

[31] Horngren, Charles T., "Security Analysis and the Price Level," *The Accounting Review* (October, 1955), pp. 575–81, and "The Funds Statement and Its Use by Analysts," *Journal of Accountancy* (January, 1956), pp. 55–9.

[32] Bradish, R.D., "Corporate Reporting and the Financial Analyst," *The Accounting Review* (October, 1965), pp. 757–66; Ecton, W.W., "Communication Through Accounting — Bankers' Views," *Journal of Accountancy* (August, 1969), pp. 79–81.

[33] Cerf, A.R., *Corporate Reporting and Investment Decisions* (Berkeley, Ca.: Institute of Business and Economic Research, 1961); Singhvi, S.S., and Desai, H.B., "An Empirical Analysis of the Quality of Corporate Financial Disclosure," *The Accounting Review* (January, 1971), pp. 129–38; Buzby, S.L., "Selected Items for Information and their Disclosure in Annual Reports," *The Accounting Review* (July, 1974), pp. 423–35; Belkaoui, A., and Kahl, A., "Corporate Financial Disclosure in Canada," *CCGAA Research Monograph No. 1* (Vancouver: Canadian Certified General Accountants Association, 1978).

[34] Baker, H.K., and Haslem, J.A., "Information Needs of Individual Investors," *Journal of Accountancy* (November, 1973), pp. 64–9; Chandra, G., "A Study of the Consensus on Disclosure Among Public Accountants and Security Analysts," *The Accounting Review* (October, 1974), pp. 733–42; Belkaoui, A., Kahl, A., and Peyrard, J., "Information Needs of Financial Analysts: An International Comparison," *Journal of International Education and Research in Accounting* (Fall, 1977), pp. 19–27; Belkaoui, A., "Consensus on Disclosure," *The Canadian Chartered Accountant Magazine* (June 1979), pp. 44–6.

[35] Falk, H., and Ophir, T., "The Effect of Risk on the Use of Financial Statements by Investment Decision Makers: A Case Study," *The Accounting Review* (April, 1973), pp. 323–8, and "The Influence of Differences in Accounting Policies on Investment Decision," *Journal of Accounting Research* (Spring, 1973), pp. 108–16; Libby, R., "Accounting Ratios and the Prediction of Failure: Some Behavioral Evidence," *Journal of Accounting Research* (Spring, 1975), pp. 150–61, and "The Use of Simulated Decision Makers in Information Evaluation," *The Accounting Review* (July, 1975), pp. 475–89.

[36] Soper, F.J., and Dolphin, R., Jr., "Readability and Corporate Annual Reports," *The Accounting Review* (April, 1964), pp. 358–62; Smith, J.E., and Smith, N.P., "Readability: A Measure of the Performance of the Communication Function of Financial Reporting,"

The Accounting Review (July, 1971), pp. 552–61; Haried, A.A., "The Semantic Dimensions of Financial Statements," *Journal of Accounting Research* (Autumn, 1972), pp. 376–91, and "Measurement of Meaning in Financial Reports," *Journal of Accounting Research* (Spring, 1973), pp. 117–45; Oliver, B.L., "The Semantic Differential: A Device for Measuring the Interprofessional Communication of Selected Accounting Concepts," *Journal of Accounting Research* (Autumn, 1974), pp. 299–316; Belkaoui, A., "The Interprofessional Linguistic Communication of Accounting Concepts: An Experiment in Sociolinguistics," *Journal of Accounting Research* (Autumn, 1980), pp. 362–74.

[37] Nelson, K., and Strawser, R.H., "A Note on APB Opinion No. 16," *Journal of Accounting Research* (Autumn, 1970), pp. 284–9; Brenner, V., and Shuey, R., "An Empirical Study of Support for APB Opinion No. 16," *Journal of Accounting Research* (Spring, 1972), pp. 200–208.

[38] Copeland, R.M., Francia, A.J., and Strawser, R.H., "Students as Subjects in Behavioral Business Research," *The Accounting Review* (April, 1973), pp. 365–74; Godurn, L.B., "CPA and User Opinions on Increased Corporate Disclosure," *The CPA Journal* (July, 1975), pp. 31–5.

[39] Woolsey, S.M., "Materiality Survey," *Journal of Accountancy* (September, 1973), pp. 91–2; Patillo, James W., and Siebel, J.D., "Materiality in Financial Reporting," *Financial Executive* (October, 1973), pp. 27–8; Dyer, J., "A Search for Objective Materiality Norms in Accounting and Auditing," Dissertation, University of Kentucky, 1973; Boatsman, J.A., and Robertson, J.C., "Policy-Capturing on Selected Materiality Judgments," *The Accounting Review* (April, 1974), pp. 342–52.

[40] Rose, J., Beaver, W.H., Becker, S., and Sorter, G.H., "Toward an Empirical Measure of Materiality," supplement to Vol. 8, *Journal of Accounting Research* (1970), pp. 138–56; Dickhaut, J.W., and Eggleton, I.R.C., "An Examination of the Processes Underlying Comparative Judgments of Numerical Stimuli," *Journal of Accounting Research* (Spring, 1975), pp. 38–72.

[41] Horngren, Charles T., "Security Analysts and the Price Level," *The Accounting Review* (October, 1955), pp. 575–81; Jensen, R.E., "An Experimental Design for the Study of Effects of Accounting Variations in Decision Making," *Journal of Accounting Research* (Autumn, 1966), pp. 224–38; Livingstone, John L., "A Behavioral Study of Tax Allocation in Electric Utility Regulations," *The Accounting Review* (July, 1967), pp. 544–52; Khemakhem, Adbellatif, "A Simulation of Management-Decision Behavior: 'Funds' and Income," *The Accounting Review* (July, 1968), pp. 522–34; Dyckman, T.R., *Accounting Research Study No. 1*, "Investment Analysis and General Price-Level Adjustments: A Behavioral Study" (Sarasota, Fl.: American Accounting Association, 1969), and "On the Investment Decision," *The Accounting Review* (April, 1976), pp. 258–95; Barrett, M.E., "Accounting for Intercorporate Investments: A Behavioral Field Experiment," supplement to Vol. 9, *Journal of Accounting Research* (1971), pp. 50–92; Elias, N., "The Effects of Human Asset Statements on the Investment Decision: An Experiment," supplement to Vol. 10, *Journal of Accounting Research* (1972), pp. 215–40; Hofstedt, T.R., "Some Behavioral Parameters of Financial Analysis," pp. 679–92; Belkaoui, A., and Cousineau, A., "Accounting Information, Nonaccounting Information, and Common Stock Perception," *Journal of Business* (July, 1977), pp. 334–42.

[42] Jain, Tribhowan, N., "Alternative Methods of Accounting and Decision Making: A Psycholinguistic Analysis," *The Accounting Review* (January, 1973), pp. 95–104.

[43] Belkaoui, A., "Linguistic Relativity in Accounting," *Accounting, Organizations, and Society* (October, 1978), pp. 97–104.

44 Ibid., p. 103.

45 Belkaoui, A., "The Impact of Socioeconomic Accounting Statements on the Investment Decision: An Empirical Study," *Accounting, Organizations, and Society* (September, 1980), pp. 263–84.

46 Belkaoui, Janice, and Belkaoui, A., "Bilingualism and the Perception of Professional Concepts," *Journal of Psycholinguistic Research*, Vol. 12, No. 12 (1983), pp. 111–27.

47 Belkaoui, A., "The Interprofessional Linguistic Communication of Accounting Concepts: An Experiment in Sociolinguistics," op. cit., pp. 362–74.

48 Ibid., p. 371.

49 Haried, A.A., "The Semantic Dimensions of Financial Statements," op. cit., pp. 376–91.

50 Oliver, B.L., "The Semantic Differential: A Device for Measuring the Interprofessional Communication of Selected Accounting Concepts," op. cit., pp. 299–316.

51 Flamholtz, E., and Cook, E., "Connotative Meaning and its Role in Accounting Change: A Field Study," *Accounting, Organizations, and Society* (October, 1978), pp. 115–39.

52 Haried, A.A., "Measurement of Meaning in Financial Reports," *Journal of Accounting Research* (Spring, 1973), pp. 117–45.

53 Libby, R., "Bankers' and Auditors' Perceptions of the Message Communicated by the Audit Report," *Journal of Accounting Research* (Autumn, 1979), pp. 99–122.

54 Adelberg, A.H., "A Methodology for Measuring the Understandability of Financial Report Messages," *Journal of Accounting Research* (Autumn, 1979), pp. 565–92.

55 Ijiri, Yuji, Jaedicke, R.K., and Knight, K.E., "The Effects of Accounting Alternatives on Management Decisions," in *Research of Accounting Measurement* (eds) R.K. Jaedicke, Yuji Ijiri, and O. Nielsen (New York: American Accounting Association, 1966), pp. 186–99.

56 Ibid., p. 194.

57 Ibid., p. 194.

58 Jensen, R.E., "An Experimental Design for the Study of Effects of Accounting Variations in Decision Making," op. cit., pp. 224–38.

59 Livingstone, John L., "A Behavioral Study of Tax Allocation in Electric Utility Regulations," op. cit., pp. 544–52.

60 Mlyanarczyk, F.A., "An Empirical Study of Accounting Methods and Stock Prices," *Empirical Research in Accounting: Selected Studies*, supplement to Vol. 7, *Journal of Accounting Research* (1969), pp. 63–81.

61 Ashton, R.H., "Cognitive Changes Induced by Accounting Changes: Experimental Evidence on the Functional Fixation Hypothesis," *Studies on Human Information Processing in Accounting*, supplement to Vol. 14, *Journal of Accounting Research* (1976), pp. 1–17.

62 Prakash, P., and Rappaport, A., "Information Inductance and Its Significance for Accounting," *Accounting, Organizations, and Society* (February, 1977), pp. 29–38.

63 Ibid., p. 38.

64 Ibid., p. 38.

65 Libby, R., and Lewis, B.L., "Human Information Processing Research in Accounting: The State of the Art in 1982," *Accounting, Organizations, and Society* (December, 1982), p. 233.

66 Ibid., p. 233.

67 Ibid., p. 233.

68 Brunswick, E., *The Conceptual Framework of Psychology* (Chicago: University of Chicago Press, 1952).

[69] Libby, R., and Lewis, B.L., "Human Information Processing Research in Accounting: The State of the Art in 1982," op. cit., p. 233.

[70] Ibid., p. 234.

[71] Edwards, W., "Conservatism in Human Information Processing," in *Formal Representations of Human Judgment*, (ed.) B. Kleinmutz (New York: John Wiley & Sons, 1968).

[72] Tversky, 'A., and Kahneman, D., "Judgment Under Uncertainty: Heuristics and Biases," *Science*, Vol. 185 (1974), pp. 1125–31.

[73] Newell, A., and Simon, H.A., *Human Problem Solving* (Englewood Cliffs, N.J.: Prentice-Hall, 1972).

[74] Payne, J.N., Braunstein, M.L., and Caroll, J.S., "Exploring Predecisional Behavior: An Alternative Approach to Decision Research," *Organizational Behavior and Human Performance* (February, 1978), pp. 17–44.

[75] Ibid., pp. 17–44.

[76] Joyce, E.J., and Libby, R., "Behavioral Studies of Audit Decision Making," *Journal of Accounting Literature* (Spring, 1982), p. 115.

[77] Libby, R., and Lewis, B.L., "Human Information Processing Research in Accounting: The State of the Art in 1982," op. cit., p. 279.

[78] Goldstein, K.R., and Blackman, S., *Cognitive Style: Five Approaches and Relevant Research* (New York: John Wiley & Sons, 1978), pp. 12–13.

[79] Adorno, T.W., Frenkel-Brunswick, E., Levinston, D.J., and Sanford, R.N., *The Authoritarian Personality* (New York: Harper & Row, 1950).

[80] Rokeach, M., *The Open and Closed Mind* (New York: Basic Books, 1960).

[81] Kelly, G.A., *The Psychology of Personal Constructs* (New York: W.W. Norton, 1955).

[82] Bieri, J., "Cognitive Complexity and Personality Development," in *Experience, Structure, and Adaptability*, (ed.) O.J. Harvey (New York: Springer Publishing, 1966).

[83] Huysman, J.H.B., "The Effectiveness of the Cognitive Style Constraint in Implementing Operations Research Proposals," *Management Science* (September, 1970), pp. 94–5.

[84] Harvey, O.J., Hunt, D.E., and Schroeder, H.M., *Conceptual Systems and Personality Organizations* (New York: John Wiley & Sons, 1961).

[85] Schroeder, H.M., Driver, M.J., and Streufert, S., *Human Information Processing* (New York: Holt, Rinehart & Winston, 1967).

[86] Ibid., p. 37.

[87] Witkin, H.A., Dyks, R.B., Faterson, H.F., Goodenough, D.R., and Karyn, S.A., *Psychological Differentiation* (New York: John Wiley & Sons, 1962).

[88] Dickhaut, J.W., Livingstone, John L., and Watson, D.J., "On the Use of Surrogates in Behavioral Experimentation," in *Report of the Committee on Research Methodology in Accounting*, supplement to Vol. 48, *The Accounting Review* (1972), pp. 455–70; Abdel-Khalik, R.A., "On the Efficiency of Subject Surrogation in Accounting Research," *The Accounting Review* (October, 1974), pp. 443–50.

REFERENCES

The Events Approach to Accounting

Benbasat, I., and Dexter, A.S., "Value and Events Approaches to Accounting: An Experimental Evaluation," *The Accounting Review* (October, 1979), pp. 735–49.

Calantoni, C.S., Manes, R.P., and Whinston, A.B., "A Unified Approach to the Theory of Accounting and Information Systems." *The Accounting Review* (January, 1971), pp. 90–102.

Chen, P. (ed.), *Entity-Relationship Approach to Information Modeling and Analysis* (ER Institute, 1981).

Chen, P. (ed.), *Entity-Relationship Approach to Systems Analysis and Design* (New York: North Holland Publishing Company, 1980).

Everest, G.C., and Weber, R., "A Relational Approach to Accounting Models," *The Accounting Review* (April, 1977), pp. 340–59.

Haseman, W.D., and Whinston, A.B., "Design of a Multidimensional Accounting System," *The Accounting Review* (January, 1976), pp. 65–79.

Johnson, O., "Toward an 'Events' Theory of Accounting," *The Accounting Review* (October, 1970), pp. 641–53.

Lieberman, A.Z., and Whinston, A.B., "A Structuring of an Events-Accounting Information System," *The Accounting Review* (April, 1975), pp. 246–58.

McCarthy, W.E. "An Entity-Relationship View of Accounting Models," *The Accounting Review* (October, 1979), pp. 667–86.

McCarthy, W.E., "The REA Accounting Model: A Generalized Framework for Accounting Systems in a Shared Data Environment," *The Accounting Review* (July, 1982), pp. 554–78.

McCarthy, W.E., "A Relational Model for Events-Based Accounting Systems," Dissertation, University of Massachusetts, 1978.

Sorter, G.H., "An 'Events' Approach to Basic Accounting Theory," *The Accounting Review* (January, 1969), pp. 12–19.

Behavioral Effects of Accounting Information

Dyckman, T.R., Gibbins, M., and Swieringa, R.J. "Experimental and Survey Research in Financial Accounting: A Review and Evaluation," In *The Impact of Accounting Research in Financial Accounting and Disclosure on Accounting Practice*, (eds) A.R. Abdel-Khalik and T.F. Keller (Durham, N.C.: Duke University Press, 1978), pp. 48–89.

Rhode, J.G. "Behavioral Science Methodologies with Application for Accounting Research: References and Source Materials," chapter 7 of "Report of the Committee on Research Methodology in Accounting," *The Accounting Review* (supplement 1972), pp. 454–504.

Linguistic Effects of Accounting Data and Techniques

Adelberg, A.H., "An Empirical Evaluation of the Communication of Authoritative Pronouncements in Accounting," *Accounting and Finance* (November, 1982), pp. 73–94.

Adelberg, A.H., "A Methodology for Measuring the Understandability of Financial Report Messages," *Journal of Accounting Research* (Autumn, 1979), pp. 565–92.

Belkaoui, A., "The Impact of Socioeconomic Accounting Statements on the Investment Decision: An Empirical Study," *Accounting, Organizations, and Society* (September, 1980), pp. 263–84.

Belkaoui, A., "The Interprofessional Linguistic Communication of Accounting Concepts: An Experiment in Sociolinguistics," *Journal of Accounting Research* (Autumn, 1980), pp. 362–74.

Belkaoui, A., "Linguistic Relativity in Accounting," *Accounting, Organizations, and Society* (October, 1978), pp. 97–104.

Belkaoui, Janice, and Belkaoui, A. "Bilingualism and the Perception of Professional Concepts," *Journal of Psycholinguistic Research*, Vol. 12, No. 12 (1983), pp. 111–27.

Belkaoui, A., and Cousineau, A., "Accounting Information, Nonaccounting Information, and Common Stock Perception," *Journal of Business* (July, 1977), pp. 334–42.

Flamholtz, E., and Cook, E., "Connotative Meaning and its Role in Accounting Change: A Field Study," *Accounting Organizations, and Society* (October 1978), pp. 115–39.

Haried, A.A., "Measurement of Meaning in Financial Reports," *Journal of Accounting Research* (Spring, 1973), pp. 117–45.

Haried, A.A., "The Semantic Dimensions of Financial Statements," *Journal of Accounting Research* (Autumn, 1972), pp. 376–91.

Jain, Tribhowan N., "Alternative Methods of Accounting and Decision Making: A Psycholinguistic Analysis," *The Accounting Review* (January, 1973), pp. 95–104.

Li, D., "The Semantic Aspect of Communication Theory and Accounting," *Journal of Accounting Research* (Autumn, 1963), pp. 102–107.

Libby, R., "Bankers' and Auditors' Perceptions of the Message Communicated by the Audit Report," *Journal of Accounting Research* (Spring, 1979), pp. 99–122.

Oliver, B.L., "The Semantic Differential: A Device for Measuring the Interprofessional Communication of Selected Accounting Concepts," *Journal of Accounting Research* (Autumn, 1974), pp. 299–316.

Functional Fixation Hypothesis

Ashton, R.H., "Cognitive Changes Induced by Accounting Changes: Experimental Evidence on the Functional Fixation Hypothesis," *Studies on Human Information Processing in Accounting 1976,* supplement to Vol. 14, *Journal of Accounting Research* (1976), pp. 1–17.

Ijiri, Yuji, Jaedicke, R.K., and Knight, K.E., "The Effects of Accounting Alternatives of Management Decisions," in *Research in Accounting Measurement,* (eds) R.K. Jaedicke, Yuji Ijiri, and O. Nielsen (New York: American Accounting Association, 1966), pp. 186–99.

Information Inductance

Prakash, P., and Rappaport, A., "Information Inductance and its Significance for Accounting," *Accounting, Organizations, and Society* (February, 1977), pp. 29–38.

Human Information Processing

Belkaoui, A., "Judgment Related Issues in Performance Evaluation," *Journal of Business Finance and Accounting* (Winter, 1982), pp. 489–500.

Brunswick, E., *The Conceptual Framework of Psychology* (Chicago: University of Chicago Press, 1952).

Einhorn, H.J., "A Synthesis: Accounting and Behavioral Science," *Studies on Human Information Processing in Accounting,* supplement to Vol. 14, *Journal of Accounting Research* (1976), pp. 196–206.

Einhorn, H.J., and Hogarth, R.M., "Behavioral Decision Theory: Processes of Judgment and Choice," *Journal of Accounting Research* (Spring, 1981), pp. 1–31.

Joyce, E.J., and Libby, R., "Behavioral Studies of Audit Decision Making," *Journal of Accounting Literature* (Spring, 1982), pp. 103–23.

Libby, R., *Accounting and Human Information Processing: Theory and Applications* (Englewood Cliffs, N.J.: Prentice-Hall, 1981).

Libby, R., and Lewis, B.L., "Human Information Processing Research in Accounting: The State of the Art," *Accounting, Organizations, and Society* (September, 1977), pp. 245–68.

Libby, R., and Lewis, B.L., "Human Information Processing Research in Accounting: The State of the Art in 1982," *Accounting, Organizations, and Society* (December, 1982), pp. 231–86.

Schroeder, H.M., Driver, M.J., and Streufert, S., *Human Information Processing* (New York: Holt, Rinehart & Winston, 1967).

Snowball, D., "On the Integration of Accounting Research on Human Information Processing," *Accounting and Business Research* (Summer, 1980), pp. 307–18.

Wright, W.F., "Comparison of the Lens and Subjective Probability Paradigms for Financial Research Purposes," *Accounting, Organizations and Society* (February, 1982), pp. 65–75.

The Lens Model in Accounting Research

Abdel-Khalik, A.R., and El-Sheshai, K., "Information Choice and Utilization in an Experiment on Default Prediction," *Journal of Accounting Research* (Autumn, 1980), pp. 325–42.

Ashton, R.H., "A Descriptive Study of Information Evaluation," *Journal of Accounting Research* (Spring, 1981), pp. 42–61.

Ashton, R.H., and Brown, P.R., "Descriptive Modeling of Auditor's Internal Control Judgments: Replication and Extensions," *Journal of Accounting Research* (Spring, 1980), pp. 1–15.

Belkaoui, A., "Diagnostic and Redundant Information: The Effects on the Quality of Loan Officers' Predictions of Bankruptcy in Terms of Accuracy, Calibration, and Decision Time," *Accounting and Business Research* (forthcoming).

Brown, P.R., "A Descriptive Analysis of Select Input Bases of the Financial Accounting Standards Board," *Journal of Accounting Research* (Spring, 1981), pp. 62–85.

Danos, P., and Imhoff, E.A., "Auditor Review of Financial Forecasts: An Analysis of Factors Affecting Reasonableness of Judgments," *The Accounting Review* (January, 1982), pp. 39–54.

Ebert, R.J., and Kruse, T.E., "Bootstrapping the Security Analyst," *Journal of Applied Psychology* (February, 1978), pp. 110–19.

Gibbs, T.E., and Schroeder, R.G., "Evaluating the Competence of Internal Audit Departments," in *Symposium on Audit Research III* (Urbana, Ill.: University of Illinois, 1979).

Hamilton, R.E., and Wright, W.F., "The Evaluation of Internal Controls Over Payroll" (unpublished manuscript, University of Minnesota, 1977).

Harrell, A.M., "The Decision-Making Behavior of Air Force Officers and the Management Control Process," *The Accounting Review* (October, 1977), pp. 833–41.

Harrell, A.M., and Klick, H.D., "Comparing the Impact of Monetary and Nonmonetary Human Asset Measures on Executive Decision Making," *Accounting, Organizations, and Society* (December, 1980), pp. 393–400.

Holt, R.N., and Carroll, R.J. "Classification of Commercial Bank Loans Through Policy Capturing," *Accounting, Organizations, and Society* (September, 1980), pp. 285–96.

Kessler, L., and Ashton, R.H., "Feedback and Prediction Achievement in Financial Analysis," *Journal of Accounting Research* (Spring, 1981), pp. 146–62.

Libby, R., "Bankers' and Auditors' Perceptions of the Message Communicated by the Audit Report," *Journal of Accounting Research* (Spring, 1979), pp. 99–122.

Libby, R., "The Impact of Uncertainty Reporting on the Loan Decision," *Studies in Auditing — Selections from the Research Opportunities in Auditing Program*, supplement to *Journal of Accounting Research* (1979), pp. 35–57.

Mock, T.J., and Turner, J.L., "The Effect of Changes in Internal Controls on Audit Programs," in *Behavioral Experiments in Accounting*, Vol. II, (ed.) T.J. Burns (Columbus: Ohio State University, 1979).

Moriarity, S., "Communicating Financial Information Through Multidimensional Graphics," *Journal of Accounting Research* (Spring, 1979), pp. 205–23.

Moriarity, S., and Barron, F.H., "Modeling the Materiality Judgments of Audit Partners," *Journal of Accounting Research* (Autumn, 1976), pp. 320–41.

Rockness, H.O., and Nikolai, L.A., "An Assessment of APB Voting Patterns," *Journal of Accounting Research* (Spring, 1977), pp. 154–67;.

Schultz, J.J., and Gustavson, S.G., "Actuaries' Perceptions of Variables Affecting the Independent Auditor's Legal Liability," *The Accounting Review* (July, 1978), pp. 626–41.

Swieringa, R.J., Dyckman, T.R., and Hoskin, R.E., "Empirical Evidence About the Effects of an Accounting Change on Information Processing," in *Behavior Experients in Accounting*, Vol. II, (ed.) T.J. Burns (Columbus: Ohio State University, 1979).

Zimmer, I., "A Lens Study of the Prediction of Corporate Failure by Bank Loan Officers," *Journal of Accounting Research* (Autumn, 1980), pp. 629–36.

The Probabilistic Judgment Model in Accounting Research

Biddle, G.C., and Joyce, E.J., "Heuristics and Biases: Some Implications for Probabilistic Inference in Auditing," in *Symposium on Auditing Research*, Vol. IV (Urbana: University of Illinois, 1981).

Chesley, G.R., "Subjective Probability Elicitation: Congruity of Datum and Response Mode," *Journal of Accounting Research* (Spring, 1977), pp. 1–11.

Chesley, G.R., "Subjective Probability Elicitation Techniques: A Performance Comparison," *Journal of Accounting Research* (Autumn, 1978), pp. 225–41.

Corless, J., "Assessing Prior Distributions for Applying Bayesian Statistics in Auditing," *The Accounting Review* (July, 1972), pp. 556–66.

Crosby, M., "Bayesian Statistics in Auditing: A Comparison of Probability Elicitation Techniques," *The Accounting Review* (April, 1981), pp. 355–65.

Crosby, M., "Implications of Prior Probability Elicitation on Auditor Sample Size Decisions," *Journal of Accounting Research* (Autumn, 1980), pp. 585–93.

Felix, W.L., "Evidence on Alternative Means of Assessing Prior Probability Distributions for Audit Decision Making," *The Accounting Review* (October, 1976), pp. 800–807.

Hirsch, M., "Disaggregated Probabilistic Accounting Information: The Effect of Sequential Events on Expected Value Maximization Decisions," *Journal of Accounting Research* (Autumn, 1978), pp. 256–69.

Joyce, E.J., and Biddle, G.C. "Anchoring and Adjustment in Probabilistic Inference in Auditing," *Journal of Accounting Research* (Spring, 1981), pp. 120–45.

Joyce, E.J., and Biddle, G.C., "Are Auditors' Judgments Sufficiently Regressive?" *Journal of Accounting Research* (Autumn, 1981), pp. 323–49.

Lewis, B.L., "Expert Judgment in Auditing: An Expected Utility Approach," *Journal of Accounting Research* (Autumn, 1980), pp. 594–602.

Magee, R.P., and Dickhaut, J.W., "Effect of Compensation Plans on Heuristics in Cost Variance Investigations," *Journal of Accounting Research* (Autumn, 1978), pp. 294–314.

Newton, L.K., "The Risk Factor in Materiality Decisions," *The Accounting Review* (January, 1977), pp. 97–108.

Snowball, D., and Brown, C., "Decision Making Involving Sequential Events: Some Effects of Disaggregated Data and Disposition Toward Risk," *Decision Sciences* (October, 1979), pp. 527–46.

Uecker, W.C., "The Effects of Knowledge of the User's Decision Model in Simplified Information Evaluation," *Journal of Accounting Research* (Spring, 1980), pp. 191–213.

Ward, B.H., "An Investigation of the Materiality Construct in Auditing," *Journal of Accounting Research* (Spring, 1976), pp. 138–52.

Wright, W.F., "Accuracy of Subjective Probabilities for a Financial Variable," in *Behavioral Experiments in Accounting*, Vol. II, (ed.) T.J. Burns (Columbus: Ohio State University, 1979).

Predecisional Behavior Approach in Accounting Research

Biggs, S.F., "An Empirical Investigation of the Information Process Underlying Four Models of Choice Behavior," in *Behavioral Experiments in Accounting*, Vol II, (ed.) T.J. Burns (Columbus: Ohio State University, 1979).

Shields, M.D., "Effects of Information Supply and Demand on Judgment Accuracy: Evidence from Corporate Managers," *The Accounting Review* (April, 1983), pp. 284–303.

Shields, M.D., "Some Effects of Information Load on Search Patterns Used to Analyze Performance Reports," *Accounting, Organizations, and Society* (December, 1980), pp. 429–42.

Stephens, R.G., "Accounting Disclosures for User Decision Processes," in *Quantitative Planning and Control*, (eds) Yuji Ijiri and A.B. Whinston (New York: Academic Press, 1979) pp. 291–309.

Weber, R., "Some Characteristics of the Free Recall of Computer Controls by EDP Auditors," *Journal of Accounting Research* (Spring, 1980), pp. 214–41.

The Cognitive Style Model in Accounting Research

Belkaoui, A., "How Receptive Are Accountants to Innovation? Personality Can Hinder Progress," *The Canadian Chartered Accountant Magazine* (May, 1982), pp. 46–9.

Belkaoui, A., "Relationship Between Self-Disclosure Style and Responsibility Accounting," *Accounting, Organizations and Society* (December, 1981), pp. 281–90.

Benbasat, I., and Dexter, A.S., "Value and Events Approaches to Accounting: An Experimental Evaluation," *The Accounting Review* (October, 1979), pp. 735–49.

Casey, C.J., "Variation in Accounting Information Load: the Effect on Loan Officer's Prediction of Bankruptcy," *The Accounting Review* (January, 1980), pp. 36–49.

Vasarhelyi, M., "Man-Machine Planning systems: A Cognitive Style Examination of Interactive Decision Making," *Journal of Accounting Research* (Spring, 1977), pp. 138–53.

Weber, R., "Some Characteristics of the Free Recall of Computer Controls by EDP Auditors," *Journal of Accounting Research* (Spring, 1980), pp. 214–41.

Wisk, E.J., "A Test of Differential Performance Peaking for a Disembedding Task," *Journal of Accounting Research* (Spring, 1979), pp. 286–94.

QUESTIONS

5.1 Define and explain the *events* approach to accounting theory construction and verification.

5.2 Define and explain the *behavioral* approach to accounting theory construction and verification.

5.3 What are some of the basic criticisms of the *value* approach to accounting theory?

5.4 Compare the role of the accountant and the role of the user according to the events approach to basic accounting theory.

5.5 What type of accounting reports are appropriate when the events approach is employed?

5.6 What do we mean by the word *event*?

5.7 Orace Johnson made the following statement in "Toward an 'Events' Theory of Accounting," *The Accounting Review* (October, 1970), p. 653:

The major issue between the events observation approach and the value inference approach to accounting theory is whether the receivers are better served by the limited range of forecasts possible with inferences, or by the wider range possible with observation.

Do you agree? Why or why not?

5.8 A.Z. Lieberman and A.B. Whinston made the following statement in "A Structuring of an Events-Accounting Information System," *The Accounting Review* (April, 1975), pp. 247–48:

A problem that too often is not recognized is that each figure on the financial statements represents the aggregation of many events. For example, the revenue derived by selling a company's many products is summed into the Sales account balance. A computer accounting system designed around the value approach would report only a total dollar value of sales on an income statement. Hence, the meaning of the figure is lost; the information concerning the many events that took place to create the total is not saved by the system, and breaking down these aggregated figures could be a very difficult process. The value system will aggregate events as deemed necessary to achieve predetermined goals of reporting and not take into consideration that another accounting function — perhaps in the future — will need the data broken down differently. (If the sales department of the firm desires a sales analysis, it is often required to keep its own set of data corresponding to individual sales; data are generally shared by users.)

Do you agree with this defense of an events accounting information system? Why or why not?

5.9 A. Belkaoui made the following statement in "Linguistic Relativity in Accounting," *Accounting, Organizations, and Society* (October, 1978), p. 102:

Given the existence of the components identified — symbols and grammatical rules — accounting may be defined *a priori* as a language. Consequently, according to the "Sapir–Whorf Hypothesis," both its lexical and grammatical characteristics will shape the world view held by users of accounting; that accounting influences thinking may be supported by the "linguistic relativity" paradigm.

What are the implications of the "Linguistic relativity" paradigm for the construction of an accounting theory?

5.10 T.R. Hofstedt and J.C. Kinard asked the following questions in "A Strategy for Behavioral Accounting Research," *The Accounting Review* (January, 1970), pp. 38–54:

Is it "proper" for accountants to conduct research on human behavior?. . . is it an issue worthy of research?

Answer each of these questions.

5.11 In their review article on behavioral accounting research "Experimental and Survey Research in Financial Accounting: A Review and Evaluation." in *The Impact of Accounting Research in Financial Accounting and Disclosure on Accounting Practice*, (eds.) A.R. Abdel-Khalik, and T.F. Keller (Durham, N.C.: Duke University Press, 1978), p. 87, T.R. Dyckman, M. Gibbins, and R.J. Swieringa reached the following conclusions:

The impact of behavioral research on accounting practice has been almost nonexistent. While the pronouncements of the APB and now the FASB may have reflected behavioral considerations, there is no clear tie-in to the behavioral research we have examined. The changes we have seen in recent years and those being considered by policymakers at this time do not reflect the findings of behavioral research nor do the official pronouncements indicate any reliance on the existing behavioral literature. The thinking of senior and influential practitioners as expressed in their writings and speeches gives little evidence of a behavioral research impact. Operating rules and requirements of major government bureaus and organizations involved with accounting reports also do not appear to reflect any behavioral research findings.

What are the reasons for this situation?

5.12 Yuji Ijiri, R.K. Jaedicke, and K.E. Knight were the first to suggest that the reason for a decision maker's inability to adjust the decision process to a change in the accounting process was "functional fixation." These researchers made the following statements in "The Effects of Accounting Alternatives on Management Decisions," in *Research in Accounting Measurement*, (eds.) R.K. Jaedicke, Yuji Ijiri, and O. Nielsen (New York: American Accounting Association, 1966), p. 194:

Psychologists have found that there appears to be "functional fixation in most human behavior in which the person attaches a meaning to a title or object (for example, manufacturing cost) and is unable to see alternative meanings or uses. People intuitively associate value with an item through past experience and often do not recognize that the value of the item depends, in fact, on the particular moment in time and may be significantly different from what it was in the past. Therefore, when a person is placed in a new situation, he or she views the object or term as used previously ... If the outputs from different accounting methods are called by the same name, such as profit, cost, etc., people who do understand accounting well tend to neglect the fact that alternative methods may have been used to prepare the outputs. In such cases, a change in the accounting process clearly influences the decision.

What are the implications of "functional fixation" for the construction of an accounting theory?

5.13 What are some of the problems associated with the behavioral approach to the construction verification of an accounting theory?

THE PREDICTIVE AND POSITIVE APPROACHES TO THE FORMULATION OF AN ACCOUNTING THEORY

Chapter 6 presents the predictive and positive approaches to the formulation of an accounting theory. Both of these approaches are emerging and popular paradigms striving for dominance in the accounting literature. In what follows, the contributions and findings of each approach, as well as the limitations recognized in the literature, will be examined.

6.1 THE NATURE OF THE PREDICTIVE APPROACH

The predictive approach arose from the need to solve the difficult problem of evaluating alternative methods of accounting measurement and from the search for a criterion on which to base the choice between measurement alternatives. The predictive approach to the formulation of an accounting theory utilizes the criterion of predictive ability, in which the choice among different accounting options depends on the ability of a particular method to predict events that are of interest to users. More specifically, "the measure with the greatest predictive power with respect to a given event is considered to be the 'best' method for that particular purpose."[1]

The criterion of predictive ability follows from the emphasis on relevance as the primary criterion of financial reporting.[2] Relevance connotes a concern with information about future events. Relevant data, therefore, are characterized by an ability to predict future events.

The criterion of predictive ability is also well accepted in the natural and physical sciences as a method of choosing among competing hypotheses. Beaver and others,[3] by showing that alternative accounting measures have the properties of competing hypotheses, have rationalized the use of predictive ability in accounting. An obvious advantage of the predictive approach is that it allows us to evaluate alternative accounting measurements empirically and to make a clear choice on the basis of a discriminatory criterion.

Predictive ability is also a purposive criterion that can easily be related to one purpose of gathering accounting data — the facilitation of decision making. The accounting literature has always held that accounting data must facilitate decision making. As soon as the "facilitation of decision making" is introduced, however, two problems arise. First, it is difficult to identify and define all the decision models employed by accounting information users, because most of the models are descriptive rather than normative. Second, even when the decision model is well-defined, a criterion for the choice of relevant information is missing. Intended to resolve this second problem, the criterion of predictive ability allows us to determine which accounting measure produces the better decisions. Let us note here the fundamental distinction between prediction and decision. It is possible to predict without making a decision, but it is not possible to make a decision without a prediction.

It appears then that the predictive method may suffer from a failure to identify and define the decision models of users and types of events that ought to be predicted. Even if a given theoretical structure were developed to identify items or events that ought to be predicted, the problem remains of specifying a theory that will link those events to the accounting measures in terms of an explanatory and predictive relationship.

A growing body of empirical accounting research has evolved from the predictive approach. Two streams may be identified. One is concerned with the ability of accounting data to explain and predict economic events; the other is concerned with the ability of accounting data to explain and predict market reaction to disclosure.

6.2 PREDICTION OF AN ECONOMIC EVENT

One general objective of accounting is to provide information that can be used to predict business events. In the perspective of the predictive approach to the formulation of an accounting theory, alternative accounting measurements should be evaluated on the basis of their ability to predict economic or business events. In general, the predictive value criterion is a probability relationship between economic events of interest to the decision maker and relevant predictor variables derived in part from accounting information.

6.2.1   Time-Series Analysis

Time-series analysis is a structural methodological approach by which temporal statistical dependencies in a data set may be examined.[4] Past values of a single data set are used to give clues regarding future realizations of the same data set. Time-series analysis research focuses mainly in (1) time-series properties of reported earnings, and (2) prediction issues in time-series analysis. Each is examined next.

Time-Series Properties of Reported Earnings

Knowledge of the properties of reported earnings may enhance their information content, predictive ability and feedback value. The application of statistical procedures to the study of the time-series properties of accounting variables stems from the thesis that accounting variables can best be described as random variables. The research has examined both the behavior of reported earnings and models that describe quarterly earnings:[5]

1 With respect to the *annual-earnings series*, findings present a *moving-average process*, a *submartingale*, or one of two processes: *Martingale* or *moving average regressive*. What results is a continuous debate over which time-series model(s) should be applied to observed accounting numbers. Fortunately, a new line of research may provide some closure on the debate. It consists of first modeling the observed time series, and then using the method to test the fit of the derived models.[6,7] In any case, this type of research would be of more use and more interest to policymakers if it was applied to determine the effect of accounting policy changes on probabilistic models of earnings behavior.[8]

2 With respect to the *quarterly-earnings series*, findings seem to show that the quarterly-earnings process is not totally random in character. It appears to follow an *autoregressive process* characterized by seasonal and quarter-to-quarter components.[9,10]

Predicting Future Accounting Earnings

The reported earning number is an aggregate number in two dimensions: one dimension is temporal, in that annual earnings are an aggregate of four individual quarterly earnings; one dimension is compositional, in that annual earnings are an aggregate of time-equivalent subseries, much as sales and cost of goods sold.[11] Accounting time-series-based research has considered the predictive ability of past annual earnings, past quarterly earnings, and earnings components:

1 With respect to the use of *past annual earnings* to predict future earnings, studies show that sophisticated autoregressive (or moving average) processes developed using Box and Jenkins' procedures do not appear to forecast significantly better than the random-walk model.[12,13]

2 With respect to the use of *past quarterly earnings* to predict future earnings, studies show a better predictive ability of the models of quarterly earnings compared with annual models and more comprehensive Box and Jenkins' "individually identified" models.[14]

3 With respect to the use of *earnings components* to predict future earnings, evidence is in favor of good forecasting ability of disaggregated sales and earnings data,[15] but this is not demonstrated for models based on components such as interest expense, depreciation expense, and operating income before depreciation.[16] More work needs to be done before closure on the subject.

6.2.2   Relevance of Earnings Forecasts

Earnings forecasts are becoming increasingly popular and important to an efficient functioning of capital markets. These forecasts are assumed to be particularly useful to users of accounting information. Earnings forecasts may be provided by analysts, management, or statistical models. The relevance of these forecasts rests to a great extent on their reasonable accuracy; the investors in particular and the capital markets in general would have no confidence in inaccurate earnings forecasts, and consequently would not utilize them. An important question centers then on the predictive accuracy of each type of forecast. Given that both analysts and managers use more information in forecasting earnings per share than historically-based mechanical models, the question centers more specifically on comparing the accuracy of each of the three types of forecasts. Accordingly, various studies have examined the research question, "Are forecasts of earnings by analysts or management superior to statistical models?"

At this stage of the research, there seems to be a disagreement as to whether earnings forecasts made by analysts and/or management are more accurate than forecasts based on a statistical analysis of the pattern in historical annual-earnings and quarterly-earnings time-series models. In addition, industry variables seem to make "a difference" in the ability to forecast a firm's earnings. It is too early to have closure on the subject. Various issues remain unanswered, and the research to date suffers from various limitations. Abdel-Khalik and Thompson identify the following unanswered issues:

> ... the relevance of forecasted data, the value of nonaccounting information in forecasting, the randomness of earnings time series, the cost of alternative forecasting procedures, and the respective motives of management and security analysts in making forecasts.[17]

Similarly, Griffin identifies the following caveats of the research:

> First, the results are typically based on an "average" firm or a firm at the median position in a cross section. Such average results may have application in specific contexts. Second, analysis by industry, size, risk, and other possible explanatory variables has received only scant attention so far in developing statistical models. Third, most studies use rather naive models and thus do not recognize recent research on the properties of accounting earnings. This suggests that they are potentially biased in favor of the superiority of the published forecasts.
>
> Finally, the finding that managers and analysts have about the same degree of forecasting success is probably not unreasonable given the present institutional setting. Company investor-relations programs and analysts' periodic meetings with management suggest that, insofar as the earnings forecast is concerned, the overlap of information accessible to management and analysts is considerable.[18]

6.2.3   Distress Prediction

The most relevant applications of the predictive approach are attempts made to seek empirically-validated characteristics that distinguish financially distressed from non-distressed firms. Both univariate and multivariate models have been used to help an auditor determine when a firm is approaching default. Scott provides the following brief overview of the process:

> Most bankruptcy-prediction models are derived using a paired-sample technique. Part of the sample contains data from firms that eventually failed; the other part contains contemporaneous data from firms that did not fail. A number of plausible and traditional financial ratios are calculated from financial statements that were published before failure. Next, the researcher searches for a formula based either on a single ratio or a combination of ratios, that best discriminates between firms that eventually failed and firms that remained solvent. A careful researcher also tests the resulting formula both on the original sample and a holdout sample that was not used to derive the formula.[19]

In Beaver's univariate study,[20] which tested a set of accounting ratios to predict corporate failure, the most noticeable result was the superior predictive ability of cash flow to total debt ratios, followed by net income to total assets. Among the multivariate studies, Altman's use of a multiple discriminant analysis for the prediction of corporate failure[21] resulted in a discriminant model that contained five variables: (1) working capital/total assets (liquidity), (2) retained earnings/total assets (age of firm and cumulative profitability), (3) earnings before interest and taxes/total assets (profitability), (4) market value of equity/book value of debt (financial structure), and (5) sales/total assets (capital turnover). Altman was able to classify more than 90 per cent of the firms in his sample correctly. The discriminant analysis technique for the prediction of distress has been used successfully in other studies to demonstrate the information value of various types of accounting data. The results of this research have led to the acceptance of the ZETA discriminant analysis model of Altman, Haldeman, and Narayanan[22] by over three dozen financial institutions.[23]

The major limitation of the research and distress prediction arises from the absence of an articulated economic theory of financial distress. Witness the following statement made by Ohlson:

> This paper presents some empirical results of a study predicting corporate failure as evidenced by the event of bankruptcy . . . . One might ask a basic and possibly embarrassing question: Why forecast bankruptcy? This is a difficult question, and no answer or justification is given here . . . . Most of the analysis should simply be viewed as descriptive statistics — which may, to some extent, include estimated prediction error-rates—and no "theories" of bankruptcy or usefulness of financial ratios are tested.[24]

Despite the absence of economic theory of distress, the discriminant analysis based models can be very helpful in a variety of practical decision contexts. For example, "(i) they can process information quicker and at a lower cost than do individual loan officers and bank examiners, (ii) they can process information in a more consistent manner, and (iii) they can facilitate decisions about loss function being made at more senior levels of management."[25]

Various limitations are associated with research on corporate distress prediction.[26] The first limitation arises from the absence of a general economic theory of financial distress that can be used to specify the variables to be included in the models.

A second limitation relates to the different definition of the event of interest. All of the studies examined observable events, such as legal bankruptcy, loan default, and omission of preferred dividend rather than financial distress *per se*. Finally, the results of the superior predictive ability of some accounting ratios may not be generalized to permit the formulation of an accounting theory based on consistent predictors of corporate failure.

6.2.4   Prediction of Bond Premiums and Bond Ratings

The following four factors are assumed to create bond risks and consequently to affect the yields to maturity of bonds:

1 Default risk: the inability of a firm to meet part or all bond interest and principal payments.
2 Marketability risk: the possibility of learning to dispose of the bonds at a loss.
3 Purchasing-power risk: the loss incurred by bondholders due to changes in the general price level.
4 Interest-rate risk: the effect of unexpected changes in the interest rates on the market value of bonds.

Fisher examined the power of a four-factor model to explain differences in the risk premiums of industrial corporate bonds.[27] The following four variables are included in the model:

1 Earnings variability, measured as the coefficient of variation on after-tax earnings of the most recent nine years.
2 Solvency, or reliability in meeting obligations, measured as the length of time since the latest of the following events occurred: the firm was founded, the firm emerged from bankruptcy, or a compromise was made in which creditors settled for less than 100 percent of their claims.
3 Capital structure, measured by the market value of the firm's equity/par value of its debt.
4 Total value of the market value of the firm's bonds.

The first three variables represent different proxies for default risk; the fourth variable represents a proxy for marketable risk. The four variables account for 75 percent of the variation in the risk premiums on bonds.

The bonds ratings issued by the three rating agencies in the United States (Fitch Investors' Service, Moody's Investors' Service, and Standard & Poor's Corporation) are judgments about the investment quality of long-term obligations. Each rating is an aggregation of default probability. Despite the claims by these agencies that their ratings cannot be empirically explained and predicted, various studies have attempted to develop models to predict the rating categories assigned to industrial bonds,[28] electric utility bonds,[29] and general-obligation municipal bonds.[30]

All of these studies tried in the first stage to develop a bond-ratings model from an experimental sample of bond ratings on the basis of a selected list of accounting and financial variables, using either regression, dichotomous probability function, or multiple discriminant or multivariate probit analysis. In the second stage, the obtained model was applied to a holdout sample to test the predictive ability of the model. Despite the general success of such models, some unresolved problems may limit their usefulness:

1 With one exception, these models suffer from the lack of an explicit and testable statement of what a bond rating represents and the absence of an "economic rationale" for the variables to be included.
2 None of these models accounts for possible differences in the accounting treatments used by individual companies.
3 The studies among the regression models treat the dependent variable as if it were on an interval scale. In other words, the assumption is that the risk differential between an AAA and an AA bond is the same as the risk differential between a BB and a B bond.
4 With one exception, all of the studies confused ex-ante predictive power with ex-post discrimination. When a given discriminant model is developed on the basis of a sample A_1 and tested on a timecoincident sample A_2, the authors claim predictive success but actually only demonstrate ex-post discriminant success. Testing on A_2 implies only that the inference about the importance of the independent variables in the discriminant function is warranted. Prediction requires intertemporal validation. Ex-ante prediction means using the discriminant model developed on the basis of A_1 from time dimension t_1 on a sample B from time dimension $t + 1$.[31]

6.2.5   Predictive Ability of Information Decomposition Measures

Information theory is concerned with the problem of measuring changes in knowledge.[32] Theil applied information theory and the related entropy concept to the development of a set of measures for financial statement analysis.[33] These information decomposition measures are assumed to express the degree of stability over time in financial statement decomposition. In studies investigating their predictive ability, information decomposition measures have been associated with corporate bankruptcy[34] and corporate takeover.[35] Initial results point to the usefulness of the entropy concept in financial analysis and suggest opportunities for future research.

6.2.6   Explaining Corporate Restructuring Behavior

Corporate restructuring behavior includes such mechanisms as mergers, consolidations, acquisitions, divestitures, going private, leverage buyouts (LBOs) and spinoffs. They are undertaken to either a) maximize the market value of equities held by existing shareholders, or b) maximize the welfare of existing management.[36] Research focused on the characteristics of acquired and nonacquired firms, and covered two areas a) ex-post classificatory analysis and b) ex-ante predictive analysis, using either univariate or multivariate models.[37] All the studies point to the relevance of various accounting ratios in classifying or predicting takeovers. The limitations of these studies are similar to those advanced in the case of distress prediction.

6.2.7   Credit and Bank-Lending Decisions

Trade and bank-lending decisions constitute another example of economic events that may be explained and/or predicted on the basis of accounting and other financial information.

Various organizations, such as Dun & Bradstreet, Inc., the National Credit Office, the National Association of Credit Management, The Robert Morris Associates, and various industry trade associations, engage in some form of trade-credit analysis. From the perspective of the predictive approach, the research consists of replicating or predicting the credit evaluation or change therein on the basis of accounting and other financial information. For example, Ewert evaluates, with some success, the extent to which financial ratios can be used to differentiate good from bad accounts, where bad accounts are either placed in collection or written off as uncollectable.[38] On the other hand, Backer and Gosman have had less success in predicting the firms that would be likely to be downgraded by Dun & Bradstreet on the basis of financial ratios.[39]

The bank-lending decision has also been the subject of empirical and predictive research. Three areas of research may be identified:

1 The first area deals with efforts to simulate aspects of a bank's investment and lending processes. The investment decision is the subject of simulation analysis by Clarkson[40] and Cohen, Gilmore, and Singer.[41] The results imply that financial information plays a major role in the decision.

2 The second area deals with a prediction of the loan-classification decision. Orgler uses, with minor success, a multiple regression model to replicate the Federal Deposit Insurance Corporation's classification of bank loans into "criticized" and "uncriticized" categories.[42] However, Dietrich and Kaplan have been more successful in using a statistical "logit" model to explain and predict four classes of loans from "current/in good standing" to "doubtful".[43]

3 The third area deals with the estimation and prediction of commercial bank financial distress. The studies have examined the feasibility of predicting bank financial distress on the basis of accounting data. Sinkey has been able to predict a large proportion of failures based on a model that includes two variables: (a) operating expenses to operating income, and (b) investments to assets.[44] Similarly, Pettaway and Sinkey have continued the same line of research using both market- and accounting-based screening models.[45] The accounting screen has been found to provide valuable lead time that regulators can use to carry out their statutory responsibilities more effectively.

6.3   PREDICTION OF MARKET REACTION: MARKET-BASED RESEARCH IN ACCOUNTING

6.3.1   Capital Markets and External Accounting

According to one interpretation of the predictive approach, the observations of capital-market reaction may be used as a guide for evaluating and choosing among various accounting measurements. For example, Gonedes contends that:

Observations of market reactions of recipients of accounting outputs should govern evaluations of the actual information content of accounting numbers produced via a given set of procedures and the informational content of accounting numbers produced via an alternative set of accounting procedures.[46]

Beaver and Dukes favor the predictive approach when they state that:

The method which produces earnings numbers having the highest association with security prices is the most consistent with the information that results in an efficient determination of security prices.... It is the method that ought to be reported.[47]

In other words, the predictive approach favors the adoption of the accounting numbers that have the highest association with market prices. It calls for an evaluation of the usefulness of accounting numbers that are transmitted to capital-market transactors viewed as an aggregate. In this case, "aggregate" means the focus is on the reaction of the securities market rather than on the individual investors making up the market.

The roles of the securities market and of information in the securities market justify the use of the prediction of market reaction in the formulation of an accounting theory. The role of the securities market is to provide an orderly exchange market whereby investors may exchange claims to present and future consumption on a continuous basis. The role of the information is twofold: "(1) to aid in establishing a set of security prices, such that there exists an optimal allocation of securities among investors, and (2) to aid the individual investor, who faces a given set of prices, in the selection of an optimal portfolio of securites."[48] Thus, the relevance of accounting information and the choice of accounting measurement procedures may be examined in terms of market reactions. The predictive approach is based on the theory and evidence of the efficient market model.

6.3.2   The Efficient Market Model

It is generally assumed that the securities market is efficient. A perfectly efficient market is in continuous equilibrium, so that the intrinsic values of securities vibrate randomly and market prices always equal underlying intrinsic values at every instant in time.[49] "Intrinsic value" is generally regarded as what the price ought to be and what price would be given by other individuals who possessed the same information and competence as the person making the estimate.[50]

Various definitions of market efficiency need to be examined:

1   One definition, suggests Fama, is that in an efficient market, prices "fully reflect" the information available and, by implication, prices react instantaneously and without bias to new information.[51] A mathematical formulation of this definition, called the expected-return model or fair-game model, is also suggested by Fama:

$$Z_{j,t+1} = r_{j,t+1} - E(r_{j,t+1} \, \varphi_t)$$
$$E(Z_{j,t+1} \, \varphi_t) = 0$$

where:

$r_{j,t+1}$ = the realized return on security j in period $t+1$ (where "return" is defined as percentage change in security price adjusted for dividends received).

$E(r_{j,t+1} \, \varphi_t)$ = the expected return on security j in period $t+1$, conditional on φ_t.

φ_t = the information set assumed to be fully reflected in prices in period t.

$Z_{j,t+1}$ = abnormal return on security j in period $t + 1$.

In other words, the rate-of-return series $(r_{j,t+1})$ is "a fair game" relative to the information series (φ_t).

Fama's definition has been criticized for being tautological (in that it merely implies that the expected deviation of a realization from its expected value is zero), for not being empirically testable unless some equilibrium model of security returns is specified, for failing to give a clear meaning to the term "information set," and for requiring prices to exist in an imaginary "as if" economy and the information set to be available in that "as if" economy.[52,53]

2 The second definition is based on some form of a model derived from the theory of rational expectations, whereby correct expectations are formed on the basis of all the available information, including prices. A behavioral process is generated whereby more informed individuals reveal information to less informed individuals through their trading actions or exchange of information. As a result, the rational expectations model that is derived produces prices that do not fully reveal everything.[54] Information is not free, and efficiency, in the strong sense, does not exist unless there is a decrease in the cost of information.

3 A third definition, proposed by Beaver, makes the distinction between market efficiency with respect to a signal (such as a particular type of accounting change) and with respect to an information system (such as all published accounting information).[55] Signal efficiency (or y-efficiency) and information system efficiency (or η-efficiency), respectively, are defined as follows:

y-efficiency:
A securities market is efficient with respect to a signal y_t' if and only if the configuration of security prices $\{P_{jt}\}$ is the same as it would be in an otherwise identical economy (with an identical configuration of preferences and endowments), except that every individual receives y_t' as well as y_{it}.

η-efficiency:
A securities market is efficient with respect to η_t' if y-efficiency holds for every signal (y_t') from η_t'.[56]

6.3.3   The Efficient Market Hypothesis

By defining the information set (φ_t) in three different ways, Fama distinguishes three levels of market efficiency: the weak, the semi-strong, and the strong forms.[57]

The Weak Form of the Efficient Market Hypothesis

The weak form of the efficient market hypothesis states that the equilibrium expected returns (prices) "fully reflect" the sequence of past returns (prices). In other words, historical price and volume data for securities contain no information that may be used to earn a profit superior to a simple "buy-and-hold" strategy. The weak form of the hypothesis began with the theory that price changes follow a true "random walk" (with an expected value of zero). This school of thought is challenged by "technical analysts" or "chartists," who believe that their rules, based on past information, can earn greater-than-normal profits. Filter rules, serial correlation, and run tests have tested the weak efficient market hypothesis. The results support the hypothesis, particularly for returns longer than a day.

The Semi-Strong Form of the Efficient Market Hypothesis

The semi-strong form of the efficient market hypothesis states that the equilibrium expected return (prices) "fully reflect" all publicly-available information. In other words, no trading rule based on available information may be used to earn an excess return. The semi-strong form of the hypothesis is relevant to accounting because publicly-available information includes financial statements. Tests of the semi-strong hypothesis have been concerned with the speed with which prices adjust to specific kinds of events. Some of the events examined have been stock splits, announcements of annual earnings, large secondary offerings of common stocks, new issues of stocks, announcements of changes in the discount rate, and stock dividends.

The results again support the efficient market hypothesis in so far as prices adjust rather quickly after the first public announcement of information. The list of events examined is not exhaustive, and further empirical research is warranted to prove this hypothesis, which is of extreme importance to accounting.

The Strong Form of the Efficient Market Hypothesis

The strong form of the efficient market hypothesis states that the equilibrium expected returns (prices) "fully reflect" all information (not just publicly available information). In other words, no trading rule based on any information, including inside information, may be used to earn an excess return.

Evidence on the strong form of the efficient market hypothesis is not conclusive. Although Jensen[58] has been able to show that mutual funds do not exhibit any consistent superior performance over time (given presumed access to special information), Nieder-hoffer and Osborne[59] argue that superior returns are possible (given access to the specialists' books).

6.3.4   The Capital-Asset Pricing Model and the Market Model

The efficient market hypothesis requires the use of "expected returns" and assumes that securities are properly priced. A theory is needed to specify the relationship between the expected returns and the prices of the individual stock in question. One such theory is Sharpe, Lintner, and Mossin's capital-asset pricing model,[60] which relates asset returns to asset risk as follows:

$$E(R_{it}) = R_{ft} + [E(E(R_{mt}) - R_{ft}]\beta$$

where:

$$E(R_{it}) = \text{the expected return of security } i \text{ in period } t.$$
$$R_{ft} = \text{the return on a riskless asset in period } t.$$

$E(R_{mt})$ = the expected return on the market portfolio in period t.

$\sigma(R_{it}, R_{mt})$ = the covariance between R_{it} and R_{mt}.

$\sigma^2(R_{mt})$ = the variance of the return on the market portfolio.

$$\beta = \frac{\sigma(R_{it}, R_{mt})}{\sigma^2(R_{mt})} = \text{risk coefficient.}$$

Given certain assumptions, the capital-assets pricing model asserts that there is a linear relationship between an individual security and its systematic risk.

The capital-asset pricing model does not lend itself to an easy test of the efficient market hypothesis. Instead, Markovitz and Sharpe's[61] market model is used for the purpose. This model defines the stochastic process generating security price as:

$$R_{it} = a_i + \beta_i R'_{mt} + \mu_{it}$$

where:

$E(\mu_{it})$ = 0

$\sigma(R'_{mt}, \mu_{it})$ = 0

$\sigma(\mu_{mt}, \mu_{jt})$ = 0

R_{it} = the return of security i in period t.

a_i, β_i = the intercept and the slope of linear relationship between R_{it} and R_{mt}.

R'_{mt} = the market factor in period t.

μ_{it} = the stochastic portion of the individualistic component of R_{it}.

The market model asserts that the return of each security is linearly related to the market return. More specifically, it states that the total return R_{it} can be separated into a systematic component $\beta_i R'_{mt}$, which reflects the extent of common movement of the return of security i in conjunction with the average return on all other securities in the market. The systematic risk β_i reflects the response of security i to economy-wide events reflected in the market factor, and μ_{it} reflects the response to the class of events having an impact on security i only. Thus, the isolation of the individualistic component of a security i, or μ_{it}, allows an evaluation of the effect of specific information items or measurements. This model has been used in most studies that evaluate the announcement effect of several types of information items and measurements.

6.3.5   Evaluation of the Market-Based Research in Accounting

Using theory and evidence regarding the efficient market hypothesis and the methodologies provided mainly by the capital-asset pricing model, portfolio theory and the market model, the predictive approach proceeds with the evaluation of accounting numbers and techniques on the basis of capital market reactions. The available evidence for market-based research in accounting has generally been classified in the following form categories:

1 Information content studies.
2 Difference in discretionary accounting techniques.
3 Consequences of regulation.
4 Impact on related disciplines.[62]

Information Content Studies

The interest in these studies is with the marginal information contribution of accounting signals to the determination of security-return behavior. The approach used is to examine whether the announcement of some event results in a change in the characteristics of the stock-return distributions (i.e., mean or variance). The impetus was created by the famous Ball and Brown study,[63] in which unexpected earning changes (with a form only in the sign of the change) were found to be correlated with residual stock returns. These results are consistent with the hypothesis that accounting information — especially earnings — convey information in the sense of leading to changes in equilibrium prices held with the following situations: a) changes in the earnings-expectation models from a random-walk generating process to more complex models, b) examining both the magnitude and the sign of the unexpected earnings, c) using a methodology focusing on another property of the return distribution — the variance of residual returns, d) analyzing trading rather than price changes, and e) examining the impact of some nonearnings financial variables.

Voluntary Differences and Changes in Accounting Techniques

The interest in these studies is in the impact of the differences and changes on investors. The issue is whether the market is "sophisticated enough" not to be "fooled" by cosmetic accounting differences or accounting changes. If the investors are not able to "see through" the veil of accounting practices, the phenomenon is labeled as a *functional fixation* or *naive investor* hypothesis. The functional fixation or naive investor hypothesis assumes that a sufficient number of investors are unable to perceive the cosmetic nature of certain accounting changes, or are "fixated" on the bottom figure of net income. The efficient market hypothesis stipulates instead that rational investors should see through the veil of accounting practices, packaging of information and forms of disclosure. In addition, an *extended functional fixation* hypothesis assumes that when responding to accounting data, sometimes the price of a firm's stock is set by a sophisticated marginal investor, and sometimes it is set by an unsophisticated marginal investor.[64]

Research on the subject has distinguished between accounting differences or changes having cash flow consequences and those having no cash flow consequences.

1 Research on the impact of accounting cross-sectional differences having no direct cash-flow effects, whose investors' ability to adjust for the differences in a few well-known and clearly-disclosed accounting techniques.
2 Research on the impact of accounting changes having no direct cash-flow (tax) effects, show both cases where a) investors reacted rationally to changes in accounting techniques and b) investors did not "see through" the veil of accounting practices.
3 Research on the impact of accounting changes having substantive direct cash-flow effects showed results that are generally inconsistent with investor rationality. For

example, with respect to the market reaction to the adoption of LIFO, most of the studies, with the exception of Sunder's,[65] show a negative market reaction. In this case, it is also very tempting to rely on a naive investor hypothesis or a functional fixation hypothesis as an explanation. As will be suggested later, various method-ological limitations need to be corrected, and future research may be needed to provide additional insights into the nature of the market response to LIFO adoption.

The Market Impact of Accounting Regulation

The interest in these studies is with the market effects of accounting regulation. Concerted research effects in this area have focused on line-of-business, oil and gas accounting, and replacement costs, to name only a few. The main evidence is that concerted and direct research effects in this area seem to create convergent results. For example a) mandated line-of-buisness information has affected investor assessment of the return distributions of multiproduct firms; b) the FASB and SEC regulation on the "full cost"/"successful-effects" issue are associated with statistically significant stock-price reactions of oil and gas stocks; c) price-adjusted estimates of earnings as well as replacement cost data did not generate any noticeable market reaction. One consequence of this research is the increased demand for these studies by policy makers, aware of the relevance of research to the consequences of their decisions. The research, however, has failed to answer fundamental questions:

> The cynic is still tempted to say "so what?" to the many identified consequences of regulations. The key question still open can be stated as follows: How do we identify a successful or effective regulation? A corollary is: what market variables are potentially relevant and why? . . . Formal theoretical analysis has the advantage of guiding research toward variables that bear directly on the impact of regulation. This is not to suggest that the identification of such variables would lead to a direct or easy resolution of policy issues—just that the variables researched would be more relevant.[66]

Impact on Related Disciplines

The interest is with the contribution of market-based research in accounting to accounting and related disciplines. We will evaluate the research in terms of the implications of the evidence for financial reporting and in terms of the adequacy of the methodology used.

a.   Implications of the evidence for financial reporting The findings identified earlier are not trivial. They have important implication for corporate financial reporting and planning. For example, Copeland uses the empirical evidence on the effect of various accounting changes in efficient capital markets to suggest the following implications for corporate financial reporting and planning:

1 Relevant new information, which will affect the future cash flows of the firm, should be announced as soon as it becomes available, so that shareholders can use it without the (presumably greater) expense of discovering it from alternative resources.
2 The most important information is forward-looking. Old news is no news. Shareholders are interested in information that can be presented in the President's

letter or in an unaudited section of the annual report—information such as how much new investment is planned; what is the expected rate of return; how long will the expected rate be favorable; how much new equity will be issued; what is the firm's target capital structure; what are its plans and policies with respect to repurchasing its own common stock; and what is its dividend policy?

3 It does not matter whether cash-flow effects are reported in the balance sheet, in the income statement, or in footnotes; the market can evaluate the news as long as it is publicly available, whatever form it may take.

4 The market reacts to the cash-flow impact of management decisions, not to the effect on reported earnings per share. Companies should never seek to increase earnings per share if cash flow will decline as a result.

5 The Securities and Exchange Commission (SEC) should conduct a thorough cost-benefit analysis of all proposed changes in disclosure requirements. It can be aided in its efforts by academic studies, which, in some cases, have already demonstrated that certain types of disclosure are irrelevant.[67]

Above all, most of the evidence cited earlier seems to imply that capital markets are reasonably efficient handlers of accounting information and may be used to evaluate published numbers. This optimism is not, however, generally shared.

First, the efficient market hypothesis has been contested by Gonedes and Dopuch on the grounds that stock-price associations are not sufficient grounds on which to evaluate alternative information systems, and that social-welfare considerations are needed.[68] More specifically, Gonedes and Dopuch have identified two assertions used in the predictive approach for the evaluation of alternative accounting procedures:

1 Capital-market efficiency, taken by itself, provides justification for using prices of (or rates of return on) firms' ownership shares in assessing the desirability of alternative accounting procedures or regulations.

2 Capital-market efficiency, taken by itself, provides justification for using prices of (or rates of return on) firms' ownership shares in assessing the effects of alternative accounting procedures or regulations.[69]

Gonedes and Dopuch argue that the contemporary institutional setting allows a "free-rider" effect that makes the desirability assertion (1) logically invalid, although they consider the effects assertion (2) to be valid.

Second, the efficient market hypothesis and the empirical evidence suporting it are silent concerning the "optimal" amount of information. This point in particular is recognized in the SEC's Sommer Report (after its chairman, Al Sommer, Jr.) as follows:

The "efficient market hypothesis" — which asserts that the current price of a security reflects all publicly available information — even if valid, does not negate the necessity of a mandatory disclosure system. This theory is concerned with how the market reacts to disclosed information and is silent as to the optimum amount of information required or whether that optimum should be achieved on a mandatory or voluntary basis; market forces alone are insufficient to cause all material information to be disclosed . . . .[70]

Third, a qualifier has been omitted in all of the studies cited earlier. The qualifier is whether the firm's decision-making is unchanged as a result of the accounting change, because market efficiency may be implied only if both no change in stock prices and the firm's decision-making are observed. This point is emphasized as follows:

> If the accounting change triggered a revision of the decision making process which would, if extrapolated, alter the anticipated performance of the entity, and if the stock price remained unchanged, then market inefficiency would be the conclusion.[71]

Fourth, finding what information is used and should be provided to investors may be difficult. Published numbers are not the only source of information in terms of content and quality, and the task may be too complex for regulators and researchers to solve.[72]

Fifth, most of the empirical research cited suffers from the absence of a theory "to predict who should be better or worse off by accounting policy changes and which changes, if any, might include changes in management behavior to offset the effect of an accounting policy change."[73]

Sixth, some major arguments exist against the use of the predictive approach with capital markets. For example, it has been argued that users individually or in aggregate react because they have been conditioned to react to accounting data, rather than because the data have any informational content. Accordingly, observations of users' reaction should not guide the formulation of an accounting theory. Sterling contends that:

> If the response of receivers to accounting stimuli is to be taken as evidence that certain kinds of accounting practices are justified, then we must not overlook the possibility that those responses were conditioned. Accounting reports have been issued for a long time, and their issuance has been accompanied by a rather impressive ceremony performed by the managers and accountants who issue them. The receivers are likely to have gained the impression that they ought to react and have noted that others react, and thereby have become conditioned to react.[74]

It may also be argued that the recipients of accounting information react when they should not react or do not react the way they should.

b.   Adequacy of the methodology used Most of the empirical evidence on the information content of financial accounting numbers rests on research designs and methodological assumptions, which are frequently the subject of critical assessment.[75]

1 *Anomalous evidence regarding market efficiency:* there are a number of scattered pieces of anomalous evidence regarding market efficiency. Ball, who examined evidence showing that post-announcement, risk-adjusted abnormal returns are systematically nonzero in the period following earnings announcements, argues that the anomalous evidence is due to inadequacies in the two-parameter, capital-asset pricing model used to adjust for risk differentials and to market inefficiencies.[76]

Watts, however, examined evidence on systematic abnormal returns after quarterly earnings announcements to determine whether they emanate from market inefficiencies or deficiencies in the asset-pricing model.[77] The results show the abnormal returns to be due to market inefficiencies, and not to asset-pricing model inefficiencies. As a result, some accounting studies were based on dependent variables other than the change in security price, or some variant such as yield, volatility, or security beta. An analysis of trading volume is recommended when the theory suggests that the disclosure change may cause a change in the level of consensus.

Other suggested dependent variables are a change in the variance–covariance structure, when it is deemed that the disclosure changes affect the risk levels of firms, and the use of systematic risk. Newer methodologies have also been proposed; these include the use of option prices and the use of intraday stock prices.[78]

2 *Self-selection bias and omitted variables:* one objective of the research design in capital-market studies is to determine whether the observed market reaction is due to the variables being examined and to ensure that the reaction is caused by the variable of interest, and not by some other variable. This is basically a control problem. Hence, most studies evaluating the impact of accounting changes have shown an earnings bias, meaning that the changes in reported earnings of the firms are negatively related to the income effect of the accounting change.[79] This creates a systematic self-selection bias, given that a systematic characteristic of all these firms also affects market performance. This self-selection bias is in fact the result of a failure to account for other omitted variables that have an impact on market reaction. The impact of omitted variables should be thoroughly addressed in capital-market studies.

3 *Confounding effects:* a confounding effect arises with the release of other unrelated and relevant informational items by some of the test firms during the time period of interest. This effect can pose a serious threat to the internal validity of the study. Five alternative approaches to controlling for unrelated information events have been proposed:
   a. Alternative 1: retain all firms in the sample, and partition the firms into various event combination categories.
   b. Alternative 2: delete firms experiencing other events in the time period from the sample.
   c. Alternative 3: retain all firms in the sample, but delete an "appropriate" time-period for each announcement.
   d. Alternative 4: retain all firms in the sample, explicitly estimate the capital-market efficiency of other events, and subtract this estimate from the observed return for the sample.
   e. Alternative 5: retain all firms in the sample, and assume that the net position of other events is minimal.[80]

4 *The timing of capital-market impact:* the choice of the most appropriate time to investigate the market reaction to an event is crucial to the interpretation of the results of a study. Although the date of public disclosure is the most evident and popular, the problem remains that the reaction may be anticipated or delayed, depending on the nature of the accounting issue being investigated. For instance, Foster refers to the fact that a policy process occurs in conjunction with many accounting issues, during which the following information can be disseminated to the market:
   a. Information relating to the policy decision itself.
   b. Information relating to the information that firms will release in compliance with a specific decision.
   c. Information relating to the actions that management will take in response to a specific decision.[81]

Given this complex situation, the researcher must determine which event or set of events is the relevant one to examine.

5 *The choice of a control group:* the most effective research design used in capital-market studies of accounting policy decision is the pre-test/post-test control-group design, in which

$$\text{Group A: } O_1 \; \chi \; O_2$$
$$\text{Group B: } O_3 \quad O_4$$

where O_i is the capital-market reaction observation at point i and χ is the experimental effect expressed as either (1) the announcement of a policy decision by a standard-setting body, or (2) the firm's disclosure of the "mandated" informational items. Although laboratory experimentation dictates a random assignment of firms to O_2 and O_4 samples, capital-market studies rely on self-selection, given the impossibility of random assignment. A self-selection bias is created in that the differences between O_2 and O_4 may not be due to the impact of χ but to differences between the samples. To alleviate the self-selection problem, Foster provided the two tests as interval validity checks:

a. A firm profile analysis.
b. A nontreatment period, security-return analysis[82]

6.4 THE POSITIVE APPROACH

6.4.1 Nature of the Positive Approach

The positive approach to accounting is generally drawn from a well-known essay in which Friedman argues "for distinguishing positive economics sharply from normative economics".[83] In fact, Friedman credits his distinction between "positive" and "normative" science to Keynes, who wrote:

> [A] positive science may be defined as a body of systematized knowledge concerning what is; a normative or regulative science as a body of systematized knowledge relating to criteria of what ought to be, and concerned, therefore, with the ideal as distinguished from the actual.[84]

The call for a positive approach to accounting came when Jensen charged that:

> ... research in accounting has been (with one or two notable exceptions) unscientific ... because the focus of this research has been overwhelmingly normative and definitional.[85]

Jensen then called for:

> ... the development of a positive theory of accounting which will explain why accounting is what it is, why accountants do what they do, and what effects these phenomena have on people and resource utilization.[86]

The basic message, later to become known as "the Rochester School of Accounting," is that most accounting theories are "unscientific" because they are "normative" and should be replaced by "positive" theories that explain actual accounting practices in terms of management's voluntary choice of accounting procedures and how the regulated standards have changed over time.

The major thrust of the positive approach to accounting is to explain and predict management's choice of standards by analyzing the costs and benefits of particular financial disclosures in relation to various individuals and to the allocation of resources within the economy. The positive theory is based on the propositions that managers, shareholders, and regulators/politicians are rational and that they attempt to maximize their utility, which is directly related to their compensation and, hence, to their wealth. The choice of an accounting policy by any of these groups rests on a comparison of the relative costs and benefits of the alternative accounting procedures in such a way as to maximize their utility. For example, it is hypothesized that management considers the effects of the reported accounting of numbers on taxes, regulation, political costs, management compensation, information product costs, and restrictions found in bond-indenture provisions. Similar hypotheses may be related to standard-setters, academicians, auditors, and others. In fact, the central ideal of the positive approach is to develop hypotheses about factors that influence the world of accounting practices and to test empirically the validity of these hypotheses.

6.4.2   Findings of Positive Research in Accounting

The findings of positive research in accounting will be divided between research on the income-smoothing hypothesis and research on positive theories because different assumptions underlie each type of research.

The Income-Smoothing Hypothesis

As far back as 1953, Hepworth argued that management's objectives may not necessarily be to report maximum profits, but rather to smooth the firm's income over the years.[87] Gordon was, however, the first to analyze seriously the economic motives that managers might have in choosing accounting principles; he concluded that managers will choose accounting principles that smooth the net-income series.[88]

Income smoothing may be defined as the intentional dampening of fluctuations about some level of earnings that is currently considered to be normal for a firm. The various empirical studies assumed various smoothing objects (operating income or ordinary income), various smoothing instruments (operating expenses, ordinary expenses, or extraordinary items), and various smoothing dimensions (accounting smoothing or "real" smoothing). Accounting smoothing affects income through accounting dimensions — namely, smoothing through the occurrence and/or recognition of events, smoothing through allocation over time, and smoothing through classification. Real smoothing affects income through the intentional changing of the operating decisions and their timing.

In general, two main motivations for smoothing are speculated in the literature:

1 To enhance the reliability of prediction based on the observed smoothed series of accounting numbers along a trend considered best or normal by management.
2 To reduce the uncertainty resulting from the fluctuations of income numbers in general and the reduction of systematic risk in particular by reducing the covariance of the firm's returns with the market returns.

Both reasons of motivation result from the need felt by management to neutralize environmental uncertainty and dampen the wide fluctuations in the operating performance of the firm subject to an intermittent cycle of good and bad times. To do so, management may resort to organizational slack behavior, budgetary slack behavior,[89] or risk-avoiding behavior.[90] Each of these behaviors necessitates decisions that affect the incurrence and/or allocation of discretionary expenses (costs) and result in income smoothing.

In addition to these behaviors intended to neutralize environmental uncertainty, it is also possible to identify organizational characterizations that differentiate among the extent of smoothing in different firms. Kamin and Ronen have examined the effects of the separation of ownership and control on income smoothing on the basis of the hypothesis that management-controlled firms are more likely to be engaged in smoothing as a manifestation of managerial discretion and budgetary slack.[91] Their results confirm that a majority of the firms examined behave as if they were smoothers; a particularly strong majority is included among management-controlled firms with high barriers to entry.

Other organizational characterizations may exist that differentiate among firms according to the dimension of the attempt to smooth. One such characterization derived from theories of economic dualism divides the industrial sector into two distinct core and periphery sectors. Belkaoui and Picur hypothesize that a higher degree of smoothing of income numbers will be exhibited by firms in the periphery sector than by firms in the core sector, due to a reaction to different opportunity structures and experiences.[92] The results indicate that a majority of firms may be resorting to income smoothing and that a greater number of these income smoothers are firms in the periphery sector.

Positive Theories of the Choices of Accounting Procedures

Unlike the income-smoothing hypothesis, positive theories in accounting assume that the stock price depends on cash flows rather than on reported earnings. Furthermore, given an efficient market, two firms with identical cash-flow distributions are valued the same way, despite the use of different accounting procedures. The central problem in positive theories is to determine how accounting procedures affect cash flows and, therefore, management's utility functions to obtain an insight into the factors that influence a manager's choices of accounting procedures. Resolution of the problem is guided by the following theoretical assumptions:

1 *Agency theory:* the agency theory may have originated with Coase's emphasis on voluntary contracts that arise among various organizational parties as the efficient solution to these conflicts of interest.[93] The theory evolves to a view of the firm as a "nexus of contracts" with the statement by Jensen and Meckling that firms are "legal fictions which serve as a nexus for a set of contracting relationships among individuals."[94] Fama expands this "nexus of contracts" view to include both capital markets and markets for managerial labor.[95]

2 *Contracting cost theory:* given this "nexus of contracts" perspective of the firm, the contracting cost theory views the role of accounting information as the monitoring and enforcing of these contracts to reduce the agency costs of certain conflicts of interest. One possible conflict may be the conflict of interest between bondholders and stockholders of firms with debts outstanding; in such instances, decisions

favorable to stockholders are not necessarily in the best interests of bondholders. This may require that lending agreements define the measurement rules used to calculate accounting numbers for the purposes of restrictive covenants. Other possible agreements that may require the use of accounting numbers from audited financial settlements to monitor the covenants of the agreements inlcude management compensation contracts and corporate bylaws.

Thus, the contracting cost theory assumes that accounting methods are selected as part of the wealth-maximizing process:

> The firm's choice of accounting method is viewed as being embedded in the overall choice problem of maximizing share price subject to investment and financial opportunity to loci. Management is assumed to face an opportunity set of vectors of investment/financing/accounting method possibilities and to select an investment/financing cum accounting method mix so as to maximize shareholder wealth.[96]

Both propositions imply that management is selecting the choice of the optimal accounting procedure for a given purpose. The central problem of the positive approach rests in determining what factors are likely to affect this optimum choice, guided by the assumptions of agency and contracting cost theories.

The empirical findings of the positive approach to accounting may be presented in terms of managers', the auditors', or the regulators' choices of accounting procedures:

1 With regard to the findings on managers' choices of accounting procedures, various relevant factors are beginning to emerge. Watts and Zimmerman argue that the following factors will increase management wealth:
   a. Decreased or delayed tax payments.
   b. Favorable governmental regulations.
   c. Decreased political costs (for example, threats of nationalization, expropriation, or antitrust suits).
   d. Decreased information production costs.
   e. Increases in the income measure used as the base for incentive bonus plans.[97]

Watts and Zimmerman tested their idea by examining the lobbying position of the firms that made submissions to FASB about the proposed General Price-Level Accounting (GPLA) standard and its relationship to (1) size and market share, used as proxy variables for political costs, (2) the existence of a management profit-sharing plan, (3) two proxy variables for possible tax effects, and (4) whether or not the firm was regulated. Size was found to be the only significant variable for the larger firms lobbying to lower earnings.

This effort was continued by Hagerman and Zmijewski[98] and Zmijewski and Hagerman,[99] who derived and tested cross-selectional models of managers' choice of four accounting policies (depreciation, inventory, pension amortization, and investment tax credit). Both political costs and the existence of management-compensation plans were found to be significant, thereby providing further evidence to support the researcher's theory that firms adopt an "income strategy" approach when they have to choose from among several competing accounting policies.

The impact of the choice of accounting policies on debt indentures and management-compensation plans was examined by Holthausen for voluntary switch-back to straight-line depreciation for financial reporting purposes,[100] by

Leftwich for mandatory changes in accounting for business combinations,[101] and by Collins, Rozeff, and Dhaliwal for the proposed elimination of full costing.[102] With the exception of Holthausen, the results were consistent with the hypothesis.

As stated earlier, the conflict between stockholders and bondholders led to the addition of restrictions on the financing of borrowing firms and to the addition of investment decisions to lending agreements. Activities subject to restrictive covenants include:

a. Payment of dividends.
b. Incurrence of additional debt.
c. Maintenance of working capital.
d. Merger activity.
e. Disposal of all or part of the assets of the firm.
f. The purchase of certain securities.[103]

This may require the use of accounting numbers to monitor these covenants. Leftwich presents evidence that indicates that parties to lending agreements select accounting measurement rules that differ from generally accepted accounting principles and that restrict management's ability to choose accounting rules that favor stockholders at the expense of bondholders.[104]

2 With regard to auditors' and regulators' choices of accounting procedures, various relevant factors are also emerging. Haring examined the possible correlation between the FASB's support for particular accounting standards and the preferences expressed by academics, business executives, large accounting firms, and FASB sponsors.[105] The correlation is significant only with sponsors and large accounting firms.

Watts and Zimmerman present evidence consistent with the hypothesis that auditing arose not as a result of governmental requirements but rather for the purpose of reducing the agency costs from conflicts of interest among parties to the firm.[106]

The incentives offered to auditors and regulators to participate in the process by which accounting standards are determined should be investigated to develop a rigorous positive theory of accounting that incorporates auditors and regulators.

The positive approach has also been used to determine the factors that influence the development of accounting theory. Some interesting hypotheses have been presented.[107] It is suggested that accounting theory is an economic good and that its supply and demand are determined by market forces. The demand for accounting theories is really a demand for "excuses" — that is to say, for special concessions to vested interest groups lobbying for accounting standards that will promote wealth transfers favorable to them. The supply of accounting theories rises to meet the demand and supplies "excuses" that satisfy the demand created by political processes. As a result, all accounting theories may be based on self-interest:

No other theory, no normative theory currently in the accounting literature (for example, current value theories) can explain or will be used to justify all accounting standards, because

■ accounting standards are justified using the theory (excuse) of the vested interest group, which is benefited by the standard;

- vested interest groups use different theories (excuses) for different issues; and
- different vested interest groups prevail on different issues.[108]

6.4.3   Evaluation of the Positive Approach

The positive approach looks into "why" accounting practices and/or theories have developed in the way they have in order to explain and/or predict accounting events. As such, the positive approach seeks to determine the various factors that may influence rational factors in the accounting field. It basically attempts to determine a theory that explains observed phenomena. The positive approach is generally differentiated from the normative approach, which seeks to determine a theory that explains "what should be" rather than "what is." Right now, the positive approach is part of an emerging paradigm and seems to generate considerable optimism among its advocates, as the following statement attests:

> There is virtually an unlimited supply of interesting positive research questions that can be addressed with our existing methodology due to the rate at which the SEC and FASB continue to promulgate standards. Furthermore, this research is of interest not only to academics in accounting, finance, and economics, but to our students and the accounting profession (even though the profession may find some of the results disturbing).[109]

This optimism is not naturally shared by everybody. One striking criticism of the positive approach was based on four points:[110]

- The Rochester School's assertion that the kind of "positive" research they are undertaking is a prerequisite for normative accounting theory is based on a confusion of phenomenal domains at the different levels (accounting entities versus accountants), and is mistaken.
- The concept of "positive theory" is drawn from an obsolete philosophy of science and is, in any case, a misnomer, because the theories of empirical science make no positive statement of "what is."
- Although a theory may be used merely for prediction even if it is known to be false, an explanatory theory of the type sought by the Rochester School, or one that is to be used to test normative proposals, ought not to be known to be false. The method of analysis, which reasons backward from the phenomena to the premises which are acceptable on the basis of independent evidence, is the appropriate method for constructing explanatory theories.
- Contrary to the empirical method of subjecting theories to severe attempts to falsify them, the Rochester School introduces ad hoc arguments to excuse the failure of their theories.[111]

Another criticism is based on the argument that positive or "empirical" theories are also normative and value-laden because they usually mark a conservative ideology in their accounting-policy implications.[112]

The most striking criticism of positive accounting theory (PAT) comes from Sterling, with his comments that a) the two pillars of value-free study and accounting practices are insubstantial, b) the economic and scientific support of the theory is mistaken and c) the accomplishments have been nil.[113] His conclusion is not to be missed; he states:

...I recommend that accountants adopt the weaker, shamelessly stolen, "Sterling's scalpel" which is that any accounting concept that does not have a common-sense core that you can explain to *Yourself* should be discarded. I am confident that a careful application of that criterion in accounting will result in PAT becoming a cottage industry and displace it as the current dominant fad, as well as provide protection from future fads.[114]

6.5 THE PARADIGMATIC STATUS OF ACCOUNTING

6.5.1 Evolution or Revolution in Accounting?

In these first chapters, we have presented an array of approaches used to formulate an accounting theory. Given the advantages and flaws of each approach, we may expect that the situation will lead to a fruitful debate and a unified theory of accounting. This view may be advanced by anyone who believes that progress in accounting will proceed through the accumulation of ideas or evolution. Such a view requires the acceptance of most proposed approaches as potential contributors to a final, unified, or comprehensive theory of accounting.

The prevailing and more logical view, however, is that accounting, like most social and natural sciences, progresses through revolution rather than evolution. The notion of revolution in accounting is taken from Kuhn's "The Structure of Scientific Revolutions"[115] and proposed, successively, and in the American Accounting Association's Statement of Accounting Theory and Theory Acceptance.[116] Kuhn's model of revolution comprises the following steps:

1 A science at any given time is dominated by a specific paradigm.
2 The science goes through a period of accumulation of knowledge, during which researchers work on and expand the dominant paradigm; during this period, it is known as a normal science.
3 Anomalies may develop that cannot be explained by the existing paradigm.
4 A crisis stage is reached, beginning with the search for new paradigms and ending with a revolution and the overthrow of the dominant paradigm by a new reigning paradigm.

After using the term "paradigm" in at least twenty-one different ways and being criticized for vagueness, Kuhn offered the following definition:

Paradigm: The concrete puzzle solutions which, when employed as models or examples, can replace explicit rules as a basis for the solution of the remaining puzzles of normal science.[117]

Given this narrow definition, Ritzer, in a pioneering article in sociology, offered a more operational definition:

A Paradigm is a fundamental image of the subject matter within a science. It serves to define what should be studied, what questions should be asked, how they should be asked, and what rules should be followed in interpreting the answers obtained. The paradigm is the broadest unit of consensus within a science and serves to differentiate one scientific community (or subcommunity) from another. It assumes, defines, and interrelates the exemplars, theories, methods, and instruments that exist within it.[118]

A paradigm, therefore, may be identified by three basic components: (1) a major article explicating the idea or exemplar, (2) theories, and (3) methods and techniques.

We may easily argue that accounting is currently in the crisis stage, given the general dissatisfaction with the old matching–attaching approach to the specification of the content of the annual reports.

6.5.2   Accounting: A Multiparadigmatic Science

If accounting is in the crisis stage, then it may be possible to identify competing paradigms. In other words, accounting is a multiparadigmatic science, with each of its paradigms competing for hegemony within the discipline. Following Ritzer's definition of paradigm, each existing accounting paradigm will contain its own exemplar, theories, and methods. In other words, the approaches to the formulation of an accounting theory presented in the first chapters result from the attempt of each of the accounting paradigms to resolve accounting questions. More specifically, "Each of the currently competing accounting paradigms tends to specify a different empirical domain over which an accounting theory ought to apply."[119]

An examination of the existing accounting literature allows us to identify the following basic accounting paradigms:

1 The anthropological paradigm, which specifies accounting practices as the domain of accounting.
2 The behavior-of-the-markets paradigm, which specifies the capital-market reaction as the domain of accounting.
3 The economic-event paradigm, which specifies the prediction of economic events as the domain of accounting.
4 The decision-process paradigm, which specifies the decision theories and the decision processes of individuals as the domain of accounting.
5 The ideal-income paradigm, which specifies the measurement of performance as the domain of accounting.
6 The information-economics paradigm, which specifies the evaluation of information as the domain of accounting.
7 The user' behavior paradigm, which specifies the information recipients' behavior as the domain of accounting.

We will examine each of these paradigms in Chapter 16.

6.6   CONCLUSIONS

The new approaches to the formulation of an accounting theory differ from the traditional approaches in terms of their novelty, their less general acceptance, and their reliance on verification. They present innovative and more empirically oriented methods of resolving accounting issues. The influence of the new approaches is manifested in the accounting literature of the last decade.

Both the new and the traditional approaches to the formulation of an accounting theory may be perceived as emanating from different accounting paradigms competing in a period of crisis for the domination of accounting thought. It may be assumed that some of the approaches to the formulation of an accounting theory and their respective paradigms will probably be replaced in the future by other paradigms. The attempts for theoretical closure may lead to "infinite regress," caused by a continuous appraisal of the nature and scope of the field of accounting.

NOTES

[1] Beaver, W.H., Kennelly, J.W., and Voss, W.M., "Predictive Ability as a Criterion for the Evaluation of Accounting Data," *The Accounting Review* (October, 1968), p. 675.

[2] *A Statement of Basic Accounting Theory*, Chapter 3 (New York: American Accounting Association, 1966).

[3] Beaver, W.H., Kennelly, J.W., and Voss, W.M., "Predictive Ability as a Criterion for the Evalution of Accounting Data," p. 676.

[4] Nelson, Charles R., *Applied Time Series Analysis for Managerial Forecasting* (New York: Holden-Day, 1973).

[5] Surveys of the literature include Abdel-Khalik, A.R., "Three Generations of Research on Quarterly Reports: Some Thoughts on the Research Process," in Nair, R.D., and Williams, T.H., *Perspectives on Research* (Madison: University of Wisconsin, 1980); Lorek, K.S., Kee, R., and Van, W. H. "Time-Series Properties of Annual Earnings Data: The State of the Art," *Quarterly Review of Economics and Business* (Spring, 1981), pp. 97–113.

[6] Cogger, K., "A Time-Series Analytic Approach to Aggregation Issues in Accounting Data, "*Journal of Accounting Research* (Autumn, 1981), pp. 285–98.

[7] Dharan, B.C., "Identification and Estimation Issues for a Causal Earnings Model," *Journal of Accounting Research* (Spring, 1983), pp. 18–41.

[8] Dopuch, N., and Watts, R.L., "Using Time-Series Models to Assess the Significance of Accounting Changes," *Journal of Accounting Research* (Spring, 1972), pp. 180–94.

[9] Foster, G., "Quarterly Accounting Data: Time-Series Properties and Predictive Ability Results," *The Accounting Review* (January, 1977), pp. 1–21.

[10] Griffin, P.A., "The Time-Series Behavior of Quarterly Earnings: Preliminary Evidence," *Journal of Accounting Research* (Spring, 1977), pp. 71–83.

[11] Ball, Ray, and Foster, George, "Corporate Financing Reporting: A Methodological Review of Empirical Research," *Journal of Accounting Research, Studies on Current Research Methodologies in Accounting: A Critical Evaluation*, Vol. 20, Supplement 1982, p. 209.

[12] Watts, R.L., and Leftwich, R.W., "The Time-Series of Annual Accounting Earnings," *Journal of Accounting Research* (Autumn, 1977), pp. 253–71.

[13] Albrecht, W.S., Lookabill, L.L., and McKeown, J.C., "The Time-Series Properties of Annual Accounting Earnings," *Journal of Accounting Research* (Autumn, 1977), pp. 226–44.

[14] Collins, W.A., and Hopwood, W.S., "A Multivariate Analysis of Annual Earnings Forecasts Generated from Quarterly Forecasts of Financial Analysts and Univariate Time-Series Models," *Journal of Accounting Research* (Autumn, 1980), pp. 390–406.

[15] Collins, D.W., "Predicting Earnings with Subentity Data: Some Further Evidence," *Journal of Accounting Research* (Spring, 1976), pp. 163–77.

[16] Manegold, J.G., "Time-Series Properties of Earnings: A Comparison of Extrapolative and Component Models," *Journal of Accounting Research* (Autumn, 1981), pp. 360–73.

[17] Abdel-Khalik, A.R., and Thompson, R.B. "Research on Earnings Forecasts: The State of the Art," *The Accounting Journal* (Winter, 1977–8), p. 192.

[18] Griffin, P.A., "Usefulness to Investors and Creditors of Information Provided by Financial Reporting: A Review of Empirical Accounting Research," *Research Report* (Stamford, Ct.: Financial Accounting Standards Board, 1982), p. 83.

[19] Scott, J., "The Probability of Bankruptcy: A Comparison of Empirical Predictions and Theoretical Models," *Journal of Banking and Finance* (September, 1981), p. 320.

[20] Beaver, W.H., "Financial Ratios and Predictors of Failure," *Empirical Research in Accounting: Selected Studies,* supplement to Vol. 4, *Journal of Accounting Research* (1966), pp. 71–111.

[21] Altman, E.I., "Predicting Railroad Bankruptcies in America," *Bell Journal of Economics and Management Science* (Spring, 1973), pp. 184–211.

[22] Altman, E., Haldeman, R., and Narayanan, P., "Zeta Analysis," *Journal of Banking and Finance* (June, 1977), pp. 29–54.

[23] Altman, E., *Corporate Financial Distress* (New York, NY: John Wiley & Sons, 1983).

[24] Ohlson, J.A., "Financial Ratios and Probabilistic Prediction of Bankruptcy," *Journal of Accounting Research* (Spring, 1980), pp. 109–31.

[25] Ball, R., and Foster, G., "Corporate Financial Reporting: A Methodological Review of Empirical Research," *Journal of Accounting Research* (Vol. 20, Supplement 1982), p. 218.

[26] Jones, Frederick L., "Current Techniques in Bankruptcy Predictions," *Journal of Accounting Literature* (Vol. 6, 1987), pp. 131–64.

[27] Fisher, L., "Determinants of Risk Premium on Corporate Bonds," *Journal of Political Economy* (June, 1959), pp. 217–37.

[28] Horrigan, J.O., "The Determination of Long-Term Credit Standing with Financial Ratios," *Empirical Research in Accounting: Selected Studies,* supplement to Vol. 4, *Journal of Accounting Research* (1966), pp. 44–62; Pinches, G.E., and Mingo, K.A., "A Multivariate Analysis of Industrial Bond Ratings," *Journal of Finance* (March, 1973), pp. 1–18; Belkaoui, A., "Industrial Bond Ratings: A Discriminant Analysis Approach," *Financial Management* (Autumn, 1980), pp. 44–51; Belkaoui, A., *Industrial Bonds and the Rating Process* (Westport, Ct.: Greenwood Press, 1984).

[29] Altman, E.I., and Katz, S., "Statistical Bond-Rating Classification Using Financial and Accounting Data," *Proceedings of the Conference on Topical Research in Accounting,* (eds) M. Schiff and G.H. Sorter (New York: New York University Press, 1976), pp. 205–39.

[30] Horton, J.J., "Statistical Classification of Municipal Bonds," *Journal of Bank Research* (Autumn, 1970), pp. 29–40.

[31] Belkaoui, A., *Industrial Bonds and the Rating Process* (Westport, Ct.: Greenwood Press, 1983).

[32] Kullback, S., *Information Theory and Statistics* (New York: John Wiley & Sons, 1959), p. 7.

[33] Theil, H., "On the Use of Information Theory Concepts in the Analysis of Financial Statements," *Management Science* (May, 1969), pp. 459–80.

[34] Lev, B., *Accounting and Information Theory,* Accounting Research Study No. 2 (Evanston, Ill.: American Accounting Association, 1969), pp. 18–34.

[35] Belkaoui, A., "The Entropy Law, Information Decomposition Measures, and Corporate Takeover," *Journal of Business Finance and Accounting* (Autumn, 1976), pp. 41–52.

[36] Foster, George, *Financial Statement Analysis*, Second Edition (Englewood Cliffs, N.J.: Prentice-Hall, 1986), p. 461.

[37] Examples of studies include Palepu, K.G., "Predicting Takeover Targets: A Methodological and Empirical Analysis," *Journal of Accounting and Economics* (March, 1986), pp. 3–36; Belkaoui, A, "Financial Ratios as Predictors of Canadian Takeovers," *Journal of Business Finance and Accounting* (Spring, 1978), pp. 93–107; and Rege, U.P., "Accounting Ratios to Locate Takeover Targets," *Journal of Business Finance and Accounting* (Autumn, 1984), pp. 301–11.

[38] Ewert, D.C., "Trade Credit Management: Selection of Accounts Receivable Using a Statistical Model," Research Monograph, No. 79 (Atlanta: Georgia State University, 1980).

[39] Backer, Morton, and Gosman, M.L., *Financial Reporting and Business Liquidity* (New York: National Association of Accountants, 1978).

[40] Clarkson, G.P.E., *Portfolio Selection: A Simulation of Trust Investment* (Englewood Cliffs, N.J.: Prentice-Hall, 1962).

[41] Cohen, K.J., Gilmore, T.C., and Singer, F.A., "Bank Procedures for Analyzing Business-Loan Applications," in *Analytical Methods in Banking*, (eds) K.J. Cohen and F.S. Hammer (Homewood, Ill.: Richard D. Irwin, 1966).

[42] Orgler, Yuir E., "A Credit-Scoring Model for Commercial Loans," *Journal of Money, Credit and Banking*, Vol. 2 (November, 1970), pp. 435–45.

[43] Dietrich, J.R., and Kaplan, Robert S., "Empirical Analysis of Commercial-Loan Classification Decisions," *The Accounting Review* (January, 1982), pp. 18–38.

[44] Sinkey, J.F., Jr., "A Multivariate Statistical Analysis of the Characteristics of Problem Banks," *Journal of Finance* (March, 1975), pp. 21–36.

[45] Pettaway, R.H., and Sinkey, J.F., Jr., "Establishing On-Site Bank Examination Priorities: An Early-Warning System Using Accounting and Market Information," *Journal of Finance* (March, 1980), pp. 137–50.

[46] Gonedes, N.J., "Efficient Capital Markets and External Accounting," *The Accounting Review* (January, 1972), p. 12.

[47] Beaver, W.H., and Dukes, R.E., "Interperiod Tax Allocation, Earnings Expectations, and the Behavior of Security Prices," *The Accounting Review* (April, 1972), p. 321.

[48] Beaver, W.H., "The Behavior of Security Prices and Its Implications for Accounting Research (Methods)," *The Accounting Review* (April, 1972), p. 408.

[49] Samuelson, P., "Proof That Properly Discounted Present Values of Assets Vibrate Randomly," *Bell Journal of Economics and Management Science* (Autumn, 1973), pp. 369–74.

[50] Lorie, J., and Hamilton, M., *The Stock Market: Theories and Evidence* (Homewood, Ill.: Richard D. Irwin, 1973).

[51] Fama, E.F., "Efficient Capital Markets: A Review of Theory and Empirical Work," *Journal of Finance* (May, 1970), pp. 383–417.

[52] Verrecchia, R.E., "Consensus Beliefs, Information Acquisition, and Market Information Efficiency," *The American Economic Review* (December, 1980), pp. 874–84.

[53] Rubinstein, M., "Securities Market Efficiency in an Arrow-Debreu Economy," *American Economic Review* (December, 1975), pp. 812–24.

[54] Grossman, S.J., and Stiglitz, J.E., "Information and Competitive Price Systems," *The American Economic Review* (May, 1976), pp. 246–53.

[55] Beaver, W.H., "Market Efficiency," *The Accounting Review* (January, 1981), p. 28.

[56] Ibid.

[57] Fama, E.F., "Efficient Capital Markets: A Review of Theory and Empirical Work," op. cit., p. 383.

[58] Jensen, M.C., "Risk, the Pricing of Capital Assets, and the Evaluation of Investment Portfolios," *Journal of Business* (April, 1969), p. 170.

[59] Niederhoffer, V., and Osborne, M.F.M. "Market Making and Reversal on the Stock Exchange," *Journal of the American Statistical Association* (December, 1966), pp. 897–916.

[60] Sharpe, W.F., "Capital-Asset Prices: A Theory of Market Equilibrium Under Conditions of Risk," *Journal of Finance* (September, 1974), pp. 425–42; Lintner, J., "The Valuation of Risky Assets and the Selection of Risky Investment in Stock Portfolios and Capital Budgets," *Review of Economics and Statistics* (February, 1965), pp. 13–37; Mossin, J., "Equilibrium in a Capital-Asset Market," *Economica* (October, 1966), pp. 768–83.

[61] Markovitz, H., "Portfolio Selection," *Journal of Finance* (March, 1952), pp. 77–91; Sharpe, W.F., "A Simplified Model of Portfolio Analysis," *Management Science* (January, 1963), pp. 277–93.

[62] Lev, B. and Ohlson, J.A., "Market-Based Empirical Research in Accounting: A Review, Interpretation, and Extension," *Studies on Current Research Methodologies in Accounting: A Critical Evaluation*, Supplement to *Journal of Accounting Research*, 1982, p. 257.

[63] Ball, R.J., and Brown, P., "An Empirical Evaluation of Accounting Income Numbers," *Journal of Accounting Research* (Autumn, 1968), pp. 103–26.

[64] Hand, John R.M., "A Test of the Extended Functional Fixation Hypothesis," *Accounting Review* (October, 1990), pp. 740–63.

[65] Sunder, S., "Stock Price and Risk Related to Accounting Changes in Inventory Valuation," *The Accounting Review* (April, 1975), pp. 305–15.

[66] Lev, B., and Ohlson, J.A., "Market-Based Empirical Research in Accounting: A Review, Interpretation, and Extension," op. cit., p. 283.

[67] Copeland, R.M., "Efficient Capital Markets: Evidence and Implications for Financial Reporting," *Journal of Accounting, Auditing, and Finance* (Winter, 1981), p. 47.

[68] Gonedes, N.J., and Dopuch, N., "Capital-Market Equilibrium Information, Production, and Selecting Accounting Techniques: Theoretical Framework and Review of Empirical Work," *Studies on Financial Accounting Objectives: 1974*, supplement to Vol. 12, *Journal of Accounting Research* (1974), pp. 48–129.

[69] Ibid., p. 50.

[70] *Report of the Advisory Committee on Corporate Disclosure to the Securities and Exchange Commission* (Washington, D.C.: US Government Printing Office, November, 1977), D-6.

[71] Greer, W.R., Jr., and Morrissey, L.E., Jr., "Accounting Rule-Making in a World of Efficient Markets," *Journal of Accounting, Auditing and Finance* (Winter, 1981), p. 56.

[72] Benston, George J., "Investors' Use of Financial Accounting Statement Number: A Review of Evidence from Stock Market Research," *Arthur Young Lecture No. 2* (Glasgow: University of Glasgow Press, 1981), p. 37.

[73] Griffin, P.A., *Usefulness to Investors and Creditors of Information Provided by Financial Reporting: A Review of Empirical Accounting Research* (Stamford, Ct.: Financial Accounting Standards Board, 1982), p. 15.

[74] Sterling, Robert R., "On Theory Construction and Verification," *The Accounting Review* (July, 1970), p. 453.

[75] Many of the methodological issues covered in this section are also discussed in the following manuscripts:

Abdel-Khalik, A.R., and Ayjinka, Bipin B., *Empirical Research in Accounting: A Methodological Viewpoint* (Sarasota, Fl.: American Accounting Association, 1979).

Foster, G., "Accounting Policy Decisions and Capital-Market Research," *Journal of Accounting and Economics* (March, 1980), pp. 29–62.

Ricks, W., "Market Assessment of Alternative Accounting Methods: A Review of the Empirical Evidence," *Journal of Accounting Literature* (Spring, 1982), pp. 59–99.

[76] Ball, R., "Anomalies in Relationships Between Securities' Yields and Yield-Surrogates," *Journal of Financial Economics* (June/September, 1978), pp. 103–26.

[77] Watts, R.L., "Systematic 'Abnormal' Returns After Quarterly-Earnings Announcements," *Journal of Financial Economics* (June/September, 1978), pp. 127–50.

[78] Patell, J.M., and Wolfson, M.A., "Anticipated Information Releases Reflected in Call-Option Prices," *Journal of Accounting and Economics* (August, 1979), pp. 117–40.

[79] Bremster, W.G., "The Earnings Characteristics of Firms Reporting Discretionary Accounting Changes," *The Accounting Review* (July, 1975), pp. 563–73.

[80] Foster, G., "Accounting Policy Decisions and Capital-Market Research," op. cit., pp. 55–6.

[81] Ibid., p. 39.

[82] Ibid, pp. 47–8.

[83] Friedman, Milton, "The Methodology of Positive Economics," in *Essays in Positive Economics* (Chicago: University of Chicago Press, 1953), pp. 6–7.

[84] Keynes, John Maynard, *The Scope and Method of Political Economy* (Macmillan, 1981), pp. 34–5.

[85] Jensen, M.C., "Reflections on the State of Accounting Research and the Regulation of Accounting," *Stanford Lectures in Accounting* (Stanford, Ca.: Stanford University, 1976), p. 11.

[86] Ibid., p. 13.

[87] Hepworth, S.R., "Smoothing Periodic Income," *The Accounting Review* (January, 1953), p. 34.

[88] Gordon, M.J., "Postulates, Principles, and Research in Accounting," *The Accounting Review* (April, 1964), pp. 251–63.

[89] Schiff, M., and Lewin, A.Y., "Where Traditional Budgeting Fails," *Financial Executive* (May, 1968), pp. 57–62.

[90] Thompson, J.D., *Organizations in Action* (New York: McGraw-Hill, 1967).

[91] Kamin, J.Y., and Ronen, J., "The Smoothing of Income Numbers: Some Empirical Evidence on Systematic Differences Among Management-Controlled and Owner-Controlled Firms," *Accounting, Organizations, and Society* (October, 1978), pp. 141–53.

[92] Belkaoui, A., and Picur, R.D., "The Smoothing of Income Numbers: Some Empirical Evidence on Systematic Differences Between Core and Periphery Industrial Sectors," *Journal of Business Finance and Accounting* (forthcoming).

[93] Coase, R., "The Nature of the Firm," *Economica* (November, 1937), pp. 386–405.

[94] Jensen, M.C., and Meckling, W.H., "Theory of the Firm: Managerial Behavior, Agency Costs, and Ownership Structure," *Journal of Financial Economics* (October, 1976), p. 31.

[95] Fama, E.F., "Agency Problems and Theory of the Firm," *Journal of Political Economy* (April, 1980), pp. 288–307.

[96] Collins, D.W., Rozeff, M.S., and Dhaliwal, D.S., "The Economic Determinants of the

Market Reaction to Proposed Mandatory Accounting Changes in the Oil and Gas Industry: A Cross-Sectional Analysis," *Journal of Accounting and Economics* (March, 1981), p. 43.

[97] Watts, R.L., and Zimmerman, J.L., "Toward a Positive Theory of Determination of Accounting Standards," *The Accounting Review* (January, 1978), pp. 112–34.

[98] Hagerman, R.L., and Zmijewski, M.E., "Some Economic Determinants of Accounting Policy Choice," *Journal of Accounting and Economics* (August, 1979), pp. 141–61.

[99] Zmijewski, M.E., and Hagerman, R.L., "An Income Strategy Approach to the Positive Theory of Accounting Standard Setting/Choice," *Journal of Accounting and Economics* (August, 1981), pp. 129–50.

[100] Holthausen, R.W., "Evidence on the Effect of Bond Covenants and Management Compensation Contracts on the Choice of Accounting Techniques: The Case of the Depreciation Switch-Back," *Journal of Accounting and Economics* (March, 1981), pp. 73–109.

[101] Leftwich, R.W., "Evidence of the Impact of Mandatory Changes in Accounting Principles on Corporate Loan Agreements," *Journal of Accounting and Economics* (March, 1981), pp. 3–36.

[102] Collins, D.W., Rozeff, M.S., and Dhaliwal, D.S., "The Economic Determinants of the Market Reaction to Proposed Mandatory Accounting Changes in the Oil and Gas Industry: A Cross-Sectional Analysis," op. cit., pp. 37–72.

[103] Leftwich, R.W., "Accounting Information in Private Markets: Evidence from Private Lending Agreements," *The Accounting Review* (January, 1983), pp. 23–42.

[104] Ibid.

[105] Haring, J.R., Jr., "Accounting Rules and 'The Accounting Establishment'," *Journal of Business* (January, 1979), pp. 507–19.

[106] Watts, R.L., and Zimmerman, J.L., "Auditors and Determination of Accounting Standards," Unpublished Working Paper GPB78-06 (Univesity of Rochester, New York, 1980).

[107] Watts, R.L., and Zimmerman, J.L., "The Demand for and Supply of Accounting Theories: The Market for Excuses," *The Accounting Review* (April, 1979), pp. 273–305.

[108] Ibid., p. 301.

[109] Zimmerman, J.L., "Positive Research in Accounting," in *Perspectives on Research: 1980 Beyer Consortium*, (eds) R.D. Nair and T.H. Williams (Madison: University of Wisconsin, 1980), pp. 107–28.

[110] Christenson, C., "The Methodology of Positive Accounting," *The Accounting Review* (January, 1983), pp. 1–22.

[111] Ibid., pp. 19–20.

[112] Tinker, A.M., Merion, B.D., and Neimark, M.D., "The Normative Origins of Positive Theories: Ideology and Accounting Thought," *Accounting, Organizations, and Society* (May, 1982), pp. 167–200.

[113] Sterling, Robert, R., "Positive Accounting: An Assessment," *Abacus* (26,2,1990), pp. 97–135.

[114] Ibid., p. 133.

[115] Kuhn, Thomas S., "The Structure of Scientific Revolutions," *International Encyclopedia of Unified Science*, Second enlarged edition (Chicago: University of Chicago Press, 1970).

[116] Committee on Concepts and Standards for External Financial Reports, *Statement on Accounting Theory and Theory Acceptance* (Sarasota, Fl.: American Accounting Association, 1977).

[117] Kuhn, Thomas S., "The Structure of Scientific Revolutions," op. cit., p. 105.

[118] Ritzer, G., "Sociology: A Multiparadigm Science," *The American Sociologist* (August, 1975), p. 157.

[119] *Statement on Accounting Theory and Theory Acceptance*, op. cit., p. 47.

REFERENCES

The Predictive Approach to Accounting

Ashton, R.H., "The Predictive Ability Criterion and User-Prediction Models," *The Accounting Review* (October, 1974), pp. 719–32.

Beaver, W.H., "The Behavior of Security Prices and Its Implications for Accounting Research (Methods)," *The Accounting Review* (April, 1972), pp. 407–37.

Beaver, W.H., Kennelly, J.W., and Voss, W.M., "Predictive Ability as a Criterion for the Evaluation of Accounting Data," *The Accounting Review* (October, 1968), pp. 675–83.

Buck, R.C., "Reflexive Predictions," *Philosophy of Science* (October, 1963), pp. 359–69.

Greenball, M.N., "The Predictive Ability Criterion: Its Relevance in Evaluating Accounting Data," *Abacus* (June, 1971), pp. 1–7.

Williams, P.F., "The Predictive Ability Paradox in Behavioral Accounting Research," *Accounting, Organization, and Society* (December, 1982), pp. 405–10.

Time-Series Properties of Reported Earnings

Ball, R., and Watts, R.L., "Some Time-Series Properties of Accounting Income Numbers," *Journal of Finance* (June, 1972), pp. 663–81.

Beaver, W.H., "The Time-Series Properties of Earnings," *Empirical Research in Accounting: Selected Studies*, supplement to *Journal of Accounting Research* (Autumn, 1970), pp. 67–99.

Brooks, L.D., and Buckmaster, D.A., "Further Evidence on the Time-Series Properties of Accounting Income," *Journal of Finance* (December, 1976), pp. 1359–72.

Time-Series Analysis

Abdel-Khalik, A.R., "Three Generations of Research on Quarterly Reports: Some Thoughts on the Research Process," in Nair, R.D., and William, T.H., *Perspectives on Research* (Madison: University of Wisconsin, 1980).

Brown, L.D., and Rozeff, M.S., "Univariate Time-Series Models of Quarterly Earnings Per Share: A Proposed Model," *Journal of Accounting Research* (Spring, 1979), pp. 179–89.

Cogger, K., "A Time-Series Analytic Approach to Aggregation Issues in Accounting Data," *Journal of Accounting Research* (Spring, 1981), pp. 285–98.

Dharan, B.C., "Identification and Estimation Issues for a Causal Earnings Model," *Journal of Accounting Research* (Spring, 1983).

Dopuch, N., and Watts, R.L., "Using Time-Series Models to Assess the Significance of Accounting Changes," *Journal of Accounting Research* (Spring, 1972), pp. 180–94.

Foster, G., "Quarterly Accounting Data: Time-Series Properties and Predictive Ability Results," *The Accounting Review* (January, 1977), pp. 1–21.

Griffin, P.A., "The Time-Series Behavior of Quarterly Earnings: Preliminary Evidence, "*Journal of Accounting Research* (Spring, 1977), pp. 71–83.

Lookabill, L.L., "Some Additional Evidence on the Time-Series Properties of Accounting Earnings," *The Accounting Review* (October, 1976), pp. 724–38.

Lorek, K.S., Kee, R. and Vass, W.H., "Time-Series Projection of Annual Earnings Data: The State of the Art," *Quarterly Review of Economics and Business* (Spring, 1981), pp. 97–113.

Predicting Future Accounting Earnings

Albrecht, W.S., Lookabill, L.L., and McKeown, J.C., "The Time-Series Properties of Annual Earnings," *Journal of Accounting Research* (Autumn, 1977), pp. 226–44.

Ball, R., and Watts, R.L., "Some Time-Series Properties of Accounting Income Numbers," *Journal of Fianance* (June, 1972), pp. 663–81.

Brown, L.D., and Rozeff, M.S., "Univariate Time-Series Models of Quarterly Earnings Per Share: A Proposed Model," *Journal of Accounting Research* (Spring, 1979), pp. 179–89.

Collins, D.W., "Predicting Earnings with Subentity Data: Some Future Evidence," *Journal of Accounting Research* (Spring, 1976), pp. 163–77.

Collins, W.A., and Hopwood, W.S., "A Multivariate Analysis of Annual Earnings Forecasts Generated from Quarterly Forecasts of Financial Analysts and Univariate Time-Series Models," *Journal of Accounting Research* (Autumn, 1980), pp. 390–406.

Kinney, W.R., Jr. "Predicting Earnings: Entity Versus Subentity Data," *Journal of Accounting Research* (Spring, 1971), pp. 127–36.

Lorek, K.S., "Predating Annual Net Earnings with Quarterly-Earnings Time-Series Models," *Journal of Accounting Research* (Spring, 1979), pp. 190–204.

Manegold, J.G., "Time-Series Properties of Earnings: a Comparison of Extrapolative and Component Models," *Journal of Accounting Research* (May, 1973), pp. 389–96.

Salamon, G.L., and Smith, E.D., "Additional Evidence on the Time-Series Properties of Reported Earnings Per Share: Comment," *Journal of Finance* (December, 1977), pp. 1795–1801.

Watts, R.L., and Leftwich, R.W., "The Time-Series of Annual Accounting Earnings," *Journal of Accounting Research* (Autumn, 1977), pp. 253–71.

The Information Content of Earnings Forecasts

Abdel-Khalik, A.R., and Espejo, J., "Expectations Data and the Predictive Value of Interim Reporting," *Journal of Accounting Research* (Autumn, 1977), pp. 226–44.

Abdel-Khalik, A.R., and Thompson, R.B., "Research on Earnings Forecasts: 'The State of the Art," *The Accounting Journal* (Winter, 1977–8), pp. 180–209.

Basi, B.A., Carey, K.J., and Twark, R.D., "A Comparison of the Accuracy of the Corporate and Security Analysts' Forecasts of Earnings," *The Accounting Review* (April, 1976), pp. 244–54.

Brown, L.D., Hughes, J.S., Rozeff, M.S., and Vanderweide, J.H., "Expectations Data and the Predictive Value of Interim Reporting," *Journal of Accounting Research* (Spring, 1980), pp. 278–88.

Copeland, R.M., and Marioni, R.J., "Executives' Forecasts of Earnings Per Share Versus Forecasts of Naive Models," *Journal of Business* (October, 1972), pp. 497–512.

Cragg, J.G., and Malkiel, B.G., "The Consensus and Accuracy of Some Predictions of the Growth of Corporate Earnings," *Journal of Finance* (March, 1968), pp. 67–84.

Crichfield, T., Dyckman, T., and Lakonishok, J., "An Evaluation of Security Analysts' Forecasts," *The Accounting Review* (July, 1978), pp. 651–68.

Elton, E.J., and Gruber, M.J., "Earnings Estimate and the Accuracy of Expectational Data," *Management Science* (April, 1972), pp. 409–24.

Gray, W.S., "The Role of Forecast Information in Investment Decisions," *Public Reporting of Corporate Financial Forecasts*, (eds) P. Prakash and A. Rappaport (Chicago: Commerce Clearing House, 1974), pp. 47–79.

Imhoff, E.A., Jr., "The Representatives of Management Earnings Forecasts," *The Accounting Review* (October, 1978), pp. 836–50.

Jaggi, Bikki, "Further Evidence on the Accuracy of Management Forecasts *vis-à-vis* Analysts' Forecasts," *The Accounting Review* (January, 1980), pp. 96–101.

Lorek, K.S., McDonald, C.L., and Patz, D.H., "A Comparative Examination of Management Forecasts and Box Jenkins Forecasts of Earnings," *The Accounting Review* (April, 1976), pp. 321–30.

Ruland, W., "The Accuracy of Forecasts by Management and Financial Analysts," *The Accounting Review* (April, 1978), pp. 439–47.

Corporate Failure Prediction

Altman, E.I., "Financial Ratios, Discriminant Analysis and the Prediction of Corporate Bankruptcy," *Journal of Finance* (September, 1968), pp. 585–609.

Altman, E.I., Haldeman, R.G., and Narayanan, P., "ZETA Analysis: A New Model to Identify Bankruptcy Risk of Corporations," *Journal of Banking and Finance* (June, 1977), pp. 29–54.

Beaver, W.H., "Alternative Accounting Measures as Predictors of Failure," *The Accounting Review* (January, 1968), pp. 113–22.

Beaver, W.H., "Financial Ratios and Predictors of Failure," *Journal of Accounting Research*, supplement, *Empirical Research in Accounting: Selected Studies* (1966), pp. 71–111.

Beaver, W.H., "Market Prices, Financial Ratios, and Prediction of Failure," *Journal of Accounting Research* (Autumn, 1968), pp. 179–92.

Blum, M.P., "Failing Company Discriminant Analysis," *Journal of Accounting Research* (Spring, 1974), pp. 1–25.

Deakin, E.B., "A Discriminant Analysis of Predictors of Business Failure," *Journal of Accounting Research* (Spring, 1972), pp. 167–79.

Elam, R., "The Effect of Lease Data on the Predictive Ability of Financial Ratios," *The Accounting Review* (January, 1975), pp. 25–43.

Ketz, J.E., "The Effect of General Price-Level Adjustments on the Predictive Ability of Financial Ratios," *Journal of Accounting Research*, supplement, *Studies in Accounting for Changes in General and Specific Prices: Empirical Research and Public Policy Issues* (1978), pp. 273–84.

Norton, C.L., and Smith, R.E., "A Comparison of General Price-Level and Historical-Cost Financial Statements in the Prediction of Bankruptcy," *The Accounting Review* (January, 1979), pp. 72–87.

Ohlson, J.A., "Financial Ratios and the Probabilistic Prediction of Bankruptcy," *Journal of Accounting Research* (Spring, 1980), pp. 109–31.

Wilcox, Jarrod W., "A Prediction of Business Failure Using Accounting Data," *Journal of Accounting Research*, supplement, *Empirical Research in Accounting: Selected Studies* (1973), pp. 163–79.

Wilcox, Jarrod W., "A Simple Theory of Financial Ratios as Predictors of Failure," *Journal of Accounting Research* (Autumn, 1971), pp. 385–95.

The Prediction of Bond Premiums and Bond Ratings

Altman, E.I., "Financial Ratios, Discriminant Analysis, and the Prediction of Corporate Bankruptcy," *Journal of Finance* (September, 1968), pp. 589–609.

Altman, E.I., and Katz, S., "Statistical Bond-Rating Classification Using Financial and Accounting

Data," in *Proceedings of the Conference on Topical Research in Accounting*, (eds) M. Schiff and G.H. Sorter (New York: New York University Press, 1976), pp. 205–39.

Ang, James S., and Patel, Kiritkumar A., "Bond-Rating Methods: Comparison and Validation," *Journal of Finance* (May, 1978), pp. 631–40.

Atkinson, Thomas A., and Simpson, Elizabeth T., *Trends in Corporate Bond Quality* (New York: National Bureau of Economic Research, 1967).

Belkaoui, A., "Industrial Bond Ratings: A Discriminant Analysis Approach," *Financial Management* (Autumn, 1980), pp. 44–51.

Belkaoui, A., *Industrial Bonds and the Rating Process* (Westport, Ct.: Greenwood Press, 1984).

Fisher, L., "Determinants of Risk Premium on Corporate Bonds," *Journal of Political Economy* (June, 1959), pp. 217–37.

Frank, R.E., Massey, W.F., and Morrison, G.D., "Bias in Multiple Discriminant Analysis," *Journal of Marketing Research* (August, 1965), pp. 250–58.

Harold, Gilbert, *Bond Ratings as Investment Guide* (New York: Ronald Press, 1938).

Hickman, W. Braddock, *Corporate Bonds, Quality, and Investment Performance* (Princeton: Princeton University Press, 1958).

Horrigan, J.O., "The Determination of Long-Term Credit Standing with Financial Ratios," *Journal of Accounting Research*, supplement, Empirical Research in Accounting: Selected Studies (1966), pp. 44–62.

Joy, O. Maurice, and Toffelson, John O., "On the Financial Application of Discriminant Analysis," *Journal of Financial and Quantitative Analysis* (December, 1975), pp. 723–38.

Kaplan, Robert S., and Urwitz, Gabriel, "Statistical Models of Bond Ratings: A Methodological Inquiry," *Journal of Business* (April, 1979), pp. 231–61.

McKelvey, R., and Zovoina, W., "A Statistical Model for the Analysis of Ordinal-level Dependent Variables," *Journal of Mathematical Sociology* (Summer, 1975), pp. 103–20.

Pinches, G.E., and Mingo, K.A., "A Multivariate Analysis of Industrial Bond Ratings," *Journal of Finance* (March, 1973), pp. 1–18.

Pinches, G.E., and Mingo, K.A., "The Role Subordination and Industrial Bond Ratings," *Journal of Finance* (March, 1975), pp. 201–206.

Pogue, Thomas, F., and Soldovsky, Robert M., "What is in A Bond Rating?" *Journal of Financial and Quantitative Analysis* (June, 1969), pp. 201–28.

West, Richard R., "An Alternative Approach to Predicting Corporate Bond Ratings," *Journal of Accounting Research* (Spring, 1970), pp. 118–27.

The Prediction of Mergers and Takeovers

Belkaoui, A., "Financial Ratios as Predictors of Canadian Takeovers," *Journal of Business Finance and Accounting* (Spring, 1978), pp. 93–107.

Simkovitz, M., and Moroe, R.J., "A Discriminant Analysis Function for Conglomerate Targets," *The Southern Journal of Business* (November, 1971), pp. 1–16.

Stevens, D.L., "Financial Characteristics of Merged Firms: A Multivariate Analysis," *Journal of Financial and Quantitative Analysis* (March, 1973), pp. 149–58.

Tausig, R.A., and Hayes, Amuel, L., III, "Cash Takeovers and Accounting Valuation," *The Accounting Review* (January, 1968), pp. 68–72.

Tzoannos, J., and Samuels, J.M., "Mergers and Takeovers: The Financial Characteristics of Companies Involved, "*Journal of Business Finance and Accounting* (Spring, 1972), pp. 5–16.

The Predictive Ability of Information Decomposition Measures

Belkaoui, A., "The Entropy Law, Information Decomposition Measures, and Corporate Takeover," *Journal of Business Finance and Accounting* (Autumn, 1976), pp. 41–52.

Lev, B., *Accounting and Information Theory*, Accounting Research Study No. 2 (Evanston, Ill.: American Accounting Association, 1969), pp. 18–34.

Theil, H., *Information Theory and Statistics* (New York: John Wiley & Sons, 1959).

Theil, H., "On the Use of Information Theory Concepts in the Analysis of Financial Statements," *Management Science* (May, 1969), pp. 459–80.

Credit and Bank-Lending Decisions

Backer, Morton, and Gosman, M.L., *Financial Reporting and Business Liquidity* (New York: National Association of Accountants, 1978).

Clarkson, G.P.E., *Portfolio Selection: A Simulation of Trust Investment* (Englewood Cliffs, N.J.: Prentice-Hall), 1962.

Cohen, K.J., Gilmore, T.C., and Singer, F.A., "Bank Procedures for Analyzing Business-Loan Applications," in *Analytical Methods in Banking*, (eds) K.J. Cohen and F.S. Hammer (Homewood, Ill.: Richard D. Irwin, 1966).

Dietrich, J.R., and Kaplan, Robert S., "Empirical Analysis of the Commercial-Loan Classification Decision," *The Accounting Review* (January, 1982), pp. 18–38.

Ewert, D.C., *Trade Credit Management: Selection of Accounts Receivable Using a Statistical Model*, Research Monograph No. 79 (Atlanta: Georgia State University, 1980).

Orgler, Yuir E., "A Credit-Scoring for Commercial Loans," *Journal of Money, Credit, and Banking*, Vol. 2 (November, 1970), pp. 435–45.

Pettaway, R.H., and Sinkey, J.F., Jr., "Establishing On-Site Bank Examination Priorities: An Early-Warning System Using Accounting and Market Information," *Journal of Finance* (March, 1980), pp. 137–50.

Sinkey, J.F., Jr., "A Multivariate Statistical Analysis of the Characteristics of Problem Banks," *Journal of Finance* (March, 1975), pp. 21–36.

Predictions of Market Reactions

Ball, R.J., and Brown, P., "An Empirical Evaluation of Accounting Income Numbers," *Journal of Accounting Research* (Autumn, 1968), pp. 159–78.

Beaver, W.H., "The Behavior of Security Prices and Its Implications for Accounting Research (Methods)," *Committee Reports*, supplement to *The Accounting Review* (1972), pp. 402–37.

Belkaoui, A., "The Impact of the Disclosure of the Environmental Effects of Organizational Behavior on the Market," *Financial Management* (Winter, 1976), pp. 26–31.

Fama, E.F., "Efficient Capital Markets: A Review of Theory and Empirical Evidence," *Journal of Finance* (May, 1970), pp. 383–417.

Gonedes, N.J., and Dopuch, N., "Capital Market Equilibrium, Information Production, and Selecting Accounting Techniques: Theoretical Framework and Review of Empirical Work," *Studies on Financial Accounting Objectives: 1974*, supplement to *Journal of Accounting Research*, pp. 48–129.

Lev, B., and Ohlson, James A., "Market-Based Empirical Research in Accounting: A Review, Interpretation and Extension," in *Studies on Current Research Methodologies in Accounting: A Critical Evaluation*, Supplement to *The Journal of Accounting Research*, 1982, pp. 249–322.

The Income-Smoothing Hypothesis

Barefield, R.M., and Comiskey, E.E., "The Smoothing Hypothesis: An Alternative Test," *The Accounting Review* (April, 1972), pp. 291–8.

Barnea, A., Ronen, J., and Sadan, S., "Classificatory Smoothing of Income with Extraordinary Items," *The Accounting Review* (January, 1976), pp. 110–22.

Beidleman, C.R., "Income Smoothing: The Role of Management," *The Accounting Review* (October, 1973), pp. 653–67.

Copeland, R.M., "Income Smoothing," *Empirical Research in Accounting: Selected Studies* (1968), supplement, *Journal of Accounting Research* (1968), pp. 101–16.

Copeland, R.M., and Licostro, R.E., "A Note on Income Smoothing," *The Accounting Review* (July, 1968), pp. 540–46.

Dasher, B.E., and Malcom, R.E., "A Note on Income Smoothing in the Chemical Industry," *Journal of Accounting Research* (Autumn, 1970), pp. 253–59.

Gordon, M.J., "Postulates, and Research in Accounting," *The Accounting Review* (April, 1964), pp. 251–63.

Gordon, M.J., and Meyers, E.T., "Accounting Measurements and Normal Growth of the Firm," *Research and Accounting Measurement*, (eds) R.K. Jaedicke, Yuji Ijiri, and O. Nielsen (New York: American Accounting Association, 1966), pp. 221–31.

Hepworth, S.R., "Smoothing Periodic Income," *The Accounting Review* (January, 1953), pp. 32–9.

Kamin, J.Y., and Ronen, J., "The Smoothing of Income Numbers: Some Empirical Evidence On Systematic Differences Among Management-Controlled and Owner-Controlled Firms," *Accounting, Organizations, and Society* (October, 1978), pp. 141–53.

Lev, B., and Kunitzky, S., "On the Association Between Smoothing Reasons and the Risk of Common Stock," *The Accounting Review* (April, 1974), pp. 259–70.

Ronen, J., and Sadan, S., *Smoothing Income Numbers: Objectives, Reasons, and Implications* (Reading, Ma.: Addison-Wesley, 1981).

Schiff, M., and Lewin, A.Y., "Where Traditional Budgeting Fails," *Financial Executive* (May, 1968), pp. 57–62.

White, C.E., "Discretionary Accounting Decisions and Income Normalization," *Journal of Accounting Research* (Autumn, 1970), pp. 260–73.

The Positive Approach to Accounting

Bowen, Robert M., Noreen, E.W., and Lacey, J.M., "Determinants of the Corporate Decision to Capitalize Interest," *Journal of Accounting and Economics* (August, 1981), pp. 151–79.

Christenson, D., "The Methodology of Positive Accounting," *The Accounting Review* (January, 1983), pp. 1–22.

Collins, D.W., Rozeff, M.S., and Dhaliwal, D.S., "The Economic Determinants of the Market Reaction to Proposed Mandatory Accounting Changes in the Oil and Gas Industry: A Cross-Sectional Analysis," *Journal of Accounting and Economics* (March, 1981), pp. 37–72.

Dhaliwal, D.S., "The Effect of the Firm's Capital Structure on the Choice of Accounting Methods," *The Accounting Review* (January, 1980), pp. 141–3.

Felton, Sandra, "Positive Thinking in Accounting Research," *The Chartered Accounting Magazine* (March, 1982), pp. 60–64.

Hagerman, R.L., and Senbet, L., "A Test of Accounting Bias and Market Structure," *Journal of Business* (January, 1976), pp. 509–14.

Hagerman, R.L., and Zmijewski, M.E., "Some Economic Determinants of Accounting Policy Choice," *Journal of Accounting and Economics* (August, 1979), pp. 141–61.

Haring, J.R., Jr., "Accounting Rules and 'The Accounting Establishment'." *Journal of Business* (January, 1979), pp. 507–19.

Holthausen, R.W., "Evidence on the Effect of Bond Covenants and Management Compensation Contracts on the Choice of Accounting Techniques: The Case of the Depreciation Switch-Back," *Journal of Accounting and Economics* (March, 1981), pp. 73–109.

Jensen, M.C., "Reflections on the State of Accounting Research and Regulation of Accounting," *Stanford Lectures in Accounting* (Stanford, Ca.: Stanford University, 1976).

Leftwich, R.W., "Accounting Information in Private Markets: Evidence from Private Lending Agreements," *The Accounting Review* (January, 1983), pp. 23–42.

Leftwich, R.W., "Evidence of the Impact of Mandatory Changes in Accounting Principles on Corporate Loan Agreements," *Journal of Accounting and Economics* (March, 1981), pp. 3–37.

Smith, C., and Warner, J., "Financial Contracting: An Analysis of Bond Covenants," *Journal of Financial Economics* (June, 1979), pp. 117–62.

Sterling, Robert, R., "Positive Accounting: An Assessment," *Abacus* (September, 1990), pp. 97–135.

Tinker, A.M., Merino, B.D., and Neimark, M.D., "The Normative Origins of Positive Theories: Ideology and Accounting Thought," *Accounting, Organizations, and Society* (May, 1982), pp. 167–200.

Watts, R.L., "Corporate Financial Statements: A Product of the Market and Political Processes," *Australian Journal of Management* (January, 1977), pp. 53–75.

Watts, R.L., and Zimmerman, J.L., *The Accounting Review* (April, 1979), pp. 273–305.

Watts, R.L., and Zimmerman, J.L., "Toward a Positive Theory of the Determination of Accounting Standards," *The Accounting Review* (January, 1978), pp. 112–34.

Zimmerman, J.L., "Positive Research in Accounting," in *Perspectives on Research: 1980 Beyer Consortium*, (eds) R.D. Nair and T.H. Williams (Madison: University of Wisconsin, 1980), pp. 107–28.

QUESTIONS

6.1 Define and explain the *predictive approach* to accounting theory construction and verification.

6.2 What are the similarities between SPR (security price research) and BAR (behavioral accounting research)?

6.3 W.H. Beaver, J.W. Kennelly, and W.M. Voss made the following statement in "Predictive Ability as a Criterion for the Evaluation of Accounting Data," *The Accounting Review* (October, 1968), p. 680:

Because predictions are an inherent part of the decision process, knowledge of the predictive ability of alternative measures is a prerequisite to the use of the decision making criterion. At the same time, it permits tentative conclusions regarding alternative measures, subject to subsequent confirmation when the decision models eventually become specified. The use of predictive ability as a purpose criterion is more than merely consistent with accounting's decision-making orientation. It can provide a body of research that will bring accounting closer to its goal of evaluation in terms of a decision-making criterion.

Do you agree with this evaluation of the predictive approach to the formulation of an accounting theory? Why or why not?

6.4 What economic events may be predicted by accounting data? Support your answer by empirical results from the literature.

6.5 N.J. Gonedes made the following statement in "Efficient Capital Markets and External Accounting," *The Accounting Review* (January, 1972), p. 19:

The market reactions (for example, anticipatory price reactions) to accounting numbers provide reliable indicants of accounting numbers' informational content. It might be added that one who seeks a market-based evaluation of accounting numbers' informational content need not use only direct reactions to particular accounting numbers, with respect to income numbers. One might also attempt to evaluate the informational content of accounting numbers by examining their predictive ability in regard to accounting numbers from which market reactions have been documented.

Do you agree with this evaluation of the predictive approach to the formulation of an accounting theory? Why or why not?

6.6 W.H. Beaver made the following statement on the findings of security-price research in "The Behavior of Security Prices and Its Implications for Accounting Research (Methods)," *The Accounting Review* (April, 1972), p. 407:

The nature of the findings is twofold: (1) evidence is provided regarding the efficiency of the market in processing accounting information: (2) the evidence indicates an association exists between accounting data and security prices both in the contexts of returns and risk measures. The implication is that the market acts as if it uses accounting data in setting equilibrium prices. Alternatively stated, accounting data are consistent in many respects with the underlying information set used by the market. The consistency reflects either or both of two possible states of the world. The market literally uses accounting data, or the market uses other sources or information where these sources and accounting data reflect the same underlying relationships.

In what ways are the implications of these findings related to the formulation of an accounting theory?

6.7 What is a *fair-game model*?

6.8 Explain the various degrees of *market efficiency*.

6.9 Does *functional fixation* imply market inefficiency?

6.10 Briefly explain the market model and the capital-asset pricing model.

6.11 E.H. Caplan made the following statement in an article titled "Accounting Research as an Information Source for Theory Construction," *The Accounting Review* (April, 1972), p. 443:

We have an abundance of opinions in accounting. Unfortunately, these opinions are often called theories, and so we may tend to mistakenly believe that we have an abundance of theories. This does not mean that opinions are unimportant to theory formulation. Indeed, the first step in developing theory is to have an idea or opinion on the subject. But meaningful progress in theory construction relationship between such phenomena and behavior and various accounting valid and for selecting the appropriate opinion from among views on a particular issue. Because accounting is pragmatic and can be justified only in terms of its usefulness in the real world, the test of what is valid and appropriate in accounting must relate to real-world phenomena and behavior. In turn, the relationship between such phenomena and behavior and various accounting concepts and procedures can only be determined by empirical research.

Do you agree with this view of accounting theory construction? Why or why not?

6.12 What is meant by the term *paradigm*?

6.13 Do you think Thomas S. Kuhn's notion of a revolution can be applied to accounting? Why or why not?

6.14 Identify the existing basic paradigms.

6.15 Thomas S. Kuhn made the following statement in "The Structure of Scientific Revolutions," *International Encyclopedia of Unified Science*, 2nd enlarged ed. (Chicago: University of Chicago Press, 1970), p. 150:

Practicing in different worlds, the two groups of scientists see different things when they look from the same point in the same direction. Again, that is not to say that they can see anything they please. Both are looking at the world, and what they look at has not changed. But in some areas they see different things, and they see them in different relations one to the other. That is why a law that cannot even be demonstrated to one group of scientists may occasionally seem intuitively obvious to another.

How does this statement apply to the different approaches to the construction of an accounting theory?

CHAPTER 7

A CONCEPTUAL FRAMEWORK FOR FINANCIAL ACCOUNTING AND REPORTING

In Chapter 3, we established that accounting theory constitutes the frame of the reference on which the development of accounting techniques is based. This frame of reference, in turn, is based primarily on the establishment of accounting concepts and principles. Of vital importance to the accounting discipline is that the accounting profession and other interest groups accept these concepts and principles. To guarantee such a consensus, a statement of the reasons or objectives that motivate the establishment of the concepts and principles must be the first step in the formulation of an accounting theory.

A statement of the objectives of financial statement has always been recognized as urgent and essential if debate over alternative standards and reporting techniques is to be resolved by reason and logic. For example, in 1960, Devine argued that:

... the first order of business in constructing a theoretical system for a service function is to establish the purpose and the objectives of the function. The objectives and purposes may shift through time, but for any period, they must be specified or specifiable.[1]

Watts and Zimmerman note that financial accounting theory has had little substantive, direct impact on accounting theory and practice and offer the following explanation:

Often the lack of impact is attributed to basic methodological weaknesses in the research. Or, the prescriptions offered are based on explicit or implicit objectives that frequently differ from writers. Not only are the researchers unable to agree on the objectives of financial statements, but they also disagree over the methods of deriving the prescriptions from the objectives.[2]

Aware of the importance of objectives, the accounting professions in the United States, the United Kingdom, and Canada have made various attempts to formulate the objectives of financial statements. In the United States, the importance of the development of financial statements objectives was first expressed by the report of the Study Group on the Objectives of Financial Statements[3] and emphasized the FASB attempts to develop a conceptual framework or constitution.[4] In the United Kingdom, the importance of these objectives was highlighted by the publication of *The Corporate Report*[5] by the Institute of Chartered Accountants in England and Wales. In Canada, interest in the subject resulted in the publication of *Corporate Reporting*.[6] Although relatively recent, all of these efforts are directly influenced to a great extent by Chapter 4 of APB Statement No. 4.[7]

In this chapter, we will elaborate on the various attempts to formulate the objectives of financial statements and a conceptual framework for financial accounting and reporting in the United States, United Kingdom, and Canada.

7.1 CLASSIFICATION AND CONFLICTS OF INTERESTS

Formulating the objectives of accounting depends on resolving the conflicts of interests that exist in the information market. More specifically, financial statements result from the interaction of three groups: firms, users, and the accounting profession.[8]

Firms comprise the main party engaged in the accounting process. By their operational, financial, and extraordinary (that is, nonoperational) activities, they justify the production of financial statements. Their existence and behavior produce financial results that are partly measurable by the accounting process. Firms are also the preparers of accounting information.

Users comprise the second group. The production of accounting information is influenced by their interests and needs. Although it is not possible to compile a complete list of users, the list would include shareholders, financial analysts, creditors, and governmental agencies.

The *accounting profession* constitutes the third group that may affect the information to be included in financial statements. Accountants act principally as "auditors" in charge of verifying that financial statements conform to generally accepted accounting principles.

Following Cyert and Ijiri's analysis, the interaction between these three groups may be represented by a Venn diagram, as shown in Exhibit 7.1, where circle U represents the interests of the users in the information deemed useful for their economic decision making, circle C represents the set of information that the corporation publishes and discloses (whether or not it is within the boundaries of generally accepted accounting principles), and circle P represents the set of information that the accounting profession is capable of producing and verifying. The area labeled I represents the set of information that is acceptable to all three groups. In other words, these data are disclosed by the firm, accountants are capable of producing and verifying them, and they are perceived as relevant by users. Areas II–VII represent areas of conflicts of interest.

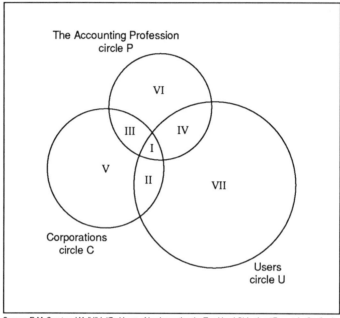

Source: R.M. Cyert and Yuji Ijiri, "Problems of Implementing the Trueblood Objectives"Report, in *Studies in Financial Accounting Objectives; 1974,* supplement to Vol. 12, *Journal of Accounting Research, pp. 29-42.*

EXHIBIT 7.1

Given these conflicts, Cyert and Ijiri examine three possible approaches to the formulation of accounting objectives. The first approach considers the set of information that the firm is ready to disclose and attempts to find the best means of *measuring* and *verifying* it. (In other words, circle C is kept fixed, and circles P and U are moved toward it.) The second approach considers the information that the profession is capable of measuring and verifying and attempts to accommodate users and firms through various accounting options. (In other words, circle P is kept fixed and circles C and U are moved toward it.) The third approach views the set of information deemed relevant by users as central and encourages the profession and the firms to produce and verify that information. (In other words, circle U is kept fixed and circles P and C are moved toward it.)

Stated simply, the first approach is *firm-oriented*, the second approach is *profession-oriented*, and the third approach is *user-oriented*. Needless to say, given the dominance of the political and legislative approaches to the formulation of an accounting theory, as we saw in Chapter 3, the user-oriented approach will prevail when future objectives of financial statements are formulated. In fact, the user-oriented approach is employed both by the study group on the objectives of financial statements in the United States and by *The Corporate Report* in the United Kingdom; other approaches have been utilized for APB Statement No. 4.

7.2 TOWARD A FORMULATION OF THE OBJECTIVES OF FINANCIAL STATEMENTS

7.2.1 The Objectives of Financial Statements as Stated in APB Statement No. 4

The Accounting Research Division of the Accounting Principles Board was created to motivate research on the basic postulates and principles of accounting. Accounting Research Statements (ARS) Nos. 1 and 3 were rejected, however, and although ARS No. 7 was accepted, it did not lead to a statement of broad principles of accounting. Subsequently, the Accounting Principles Board recommended that the objectives of accounting be defined and that the basic concepts, principles, and terminology known as "generally accepted accounting principles" be enumerated and described. This recommendation resulted in the publication of APB Statement No. 4, *Basic Concepts and Accounting Principles Underlying Financial Statements of Business Enterprises*. Although it was basically descriptive, which diminished its chances of providing the first accounting conceptual framework, the statement did influence most subsequent attempts to formulate the objectives of financial statements and to develop a basic conceptual framework for the field of accounting. Chapter 4 of APB Statement No. 4 classifies objectives as particular, general, and qualitative, and places them under a set of constraints. These objectives may be summarized as follows:

1. The *particular* objectives of financial statements are to present fairly, and in conformity with generally accepted accounting principles, financial position, results of operations, and other changes in financial position.
2. The *general* objectives of financial statements are:
   a. To provide reliable information about the economic resources and obligations of a business enterprise in order to:
      (1) evaluate its strengths and weaknesses;
      (2) show its financing and investments;
      (3) evaluate its ability to meet its commitments;
      (4) show its resource base for growth.
   b. To provide reliable information about changes in net resources resulting from a business enterprise's profit-directed activities in order to:
      (1) show expected dividend return to investors;
      (2) demonstrate the operation's ability to pay creditors and suppliers, provide jobs for employees, pay taxes, and generate funds for expansion;
      (3) provide management with information for planning and control;
      (4) show its long-term profitability.

   c. To provide financial information that can be used to estimate the earnings potential of the firm.
   d. To provide other needed information about changes in economic resources and obligations.
   e. To disclose other information relevant to statement users' needs.
 3 The *qualitative* objectives of financial accounting are the following:
   a. *Relevance*, which means selecting the information most likely to aid users in their economic decisions.
   b. *Understandability*, which implies not only that selected information must be intelligible, but also that the users can understand it.
   c. *Verifiability*, which implies that the accounting results may be corroborated by independent measures, using the same measurement methods.
   d. *Neutrality*, which implies that the accounting information is directed toward the common needs of users, rather than the particular needs of specific users.
   e. *Timeliness*, which implies an early communication of information, to avoid delays in economic decision making.
   f. *Comparability*, which implies that differences should not be the result of different financial accounting treatments.
   g. *Completeness*, which implies that all the information that "reasonably" fulfills the requirements of the other qualitative objectives should be reported.

The objectives expressed by APB Statement No. 4 appear to provide a rationale for the form and the content of conventional financial reports. The statement even admits that the particular objectives are stated in terms of accounting principles that are generally accepted at the time the financial statements are prepared. The general objectives fail to identify the informational needs of users. The statement implicitly recognizes these limitations when it admits that "the objectives of financial accounting and financial statements are at least partially achieved at present." Despite these limitations, APB Statement No. 4 has been a necessary step toward the development of a more consistent and comprehensive structure of financial accounting and of more useful financial information. As we will see, it has directly influenced both the *"Trueblood Report"* (discussed in the following sections) and *The Corporate Report* in their search for the objectives of financial statements as well as the FASB's attempts to develop a conceptual framework for financial accounting and reporting.

7.2.2 Report of the Study Group on the Objectives of Financial Statements

Methodology Used

In response to the criticism of corporate financial reporting and the realization that a conceptual framework of accounting is urgently needed, the Board of Directors of the American Institute of Certified Public Accountants announced the formation of two study groups in April 1971. The study group on the establishment of accounting principles, known as the "Wheat Committee," was charged with the task of improving the standard-setting process. Its report resulted in the formation of the Financial Accounting Standards Board (FASB). A second study group, known as the "Trueblood Committee," was charged with the development of the objectives of financial statements; that is, with determining:

1 Who needs financial statements.
2 What information they need.
3 How much of the needed information can be provided through accounting.
4 What framework is required to provide the needed information.

The Trueblood Committee was composed of nine members, representing the accounting profession, the academic world, industry, and the Financial Analysts Federation. A team of academics, practitioners, and consultants served as advisers. The Committee conducted meetings and interviews to assess the informational needs of various interested groups from all sectors of government and the business and professional communities. Relevant literature in accounting, economics, and finance provided the basic conceptual foundations. On the basis of the empirical and conceptual data gathered, the study group issued two reports. The first and more important, *Report of the Study Group on the Objectives of Financial Statements*, contains the principal conclusions and the stated objectives of financial statements. The second report contains a selection of articles by the team of advisers that the study group considered when forming the conclusions and objectives in the first report.[9]

The Objectives of Financial Statements as Expressed in the "Trueblood Report"

Although the twelve objectives in the study group's report were intended to be equal, there is a justifiable tendency to distinguish a definite hierarchical structure to the objectives.[10] Differences in emphasis and the relative dependency among the objectives justify such a hierarchy. Accordingly, Exhibit 7.2 illustrates a hierarchical structure of the objectives of accounting; the basic objective appears at the top, and specific recommendations are arranged below it. The following six objective levels may be derived from the "Trueblood Report:"

1 The basic objective (No. 1).
2 Four objectives (Nos. 2, 3, 11, and 12) that specify the diverse users and uses of accounting information.
3 Two objectives (Nos. 4 and 5) that specify enterprise earning power and management ability (accountability) as the type of information needed.
4 One objective (No. 6) that specifies the nature of the needed information as factual and interpretive.
5 Four objectives (Nos. 7, 8, 9, and 10) that describe the financial statements required to meet objective No. 6.
6 A number of specific recommendations for the financial statements are made in order to meet each of the preceding objectives (Nos. 7, 8, 9, and 10).

We will analyze each of the objectives:

No. 1: The basic objective of financial statements is to provide information on which to base economic decisions

The first objective clearly and directly links accounting to decision making. The emphasis again is directed to the *usefulness* of accounting information. Decisions are characterized as "economic" in the sense that they refer to resource allocation. In other words, there is a direct link between the relevance of accounting information and the efficient allocation of resources.

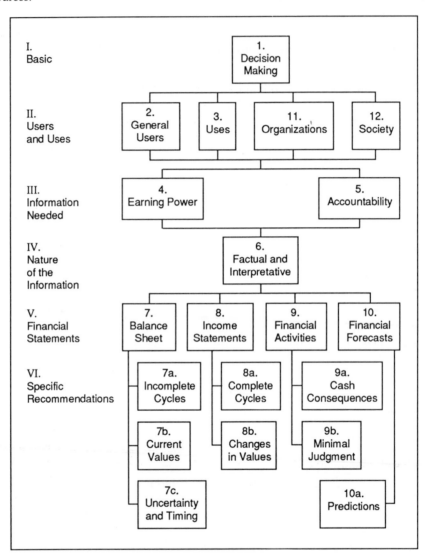

EXHIBIT 7.2

No. 2   An objective of financial statements is to serve primarily those users who have limited authority, ability, or resources to obtain information and who rely on financial statements as their principal source of information about an enterprise's activity

Objective No. 2 seems to designate a "primary audience" for financial statements. This audience consists of those who have limited access to the information and therefore must rely on accounting reports. If we interpret the objective literally, the primary users of accounting information are shareholders who depend on financial statements for information about a firm's financial position, performance, and changes in financial position. It may appear, therefore, that accountants should present a set of financial statements that, standing alone, contain relevant information for shareholders.

> *No. 3: An objective of financial statements is to provide information useful to investors and creditors for predicting, comparing, and evaluating potential cash flows to them in terms of amount, timing, and related uncertainty.*

Objective No. 3 identifies two important users: investors and creditors. The basis of their interest in financial statements is the cash flow from the enterprise; no mention is made of net income. The decision models of both investors and creditors involve the tasks of prediction, comparison, and evaluation of cash flows. The characteristics of cash flows of interest to investors and creditors pertain to amount, timing, and degree of uncertainty. We may perceive an emphasis on the stochastic nature of accounting information in general and cash flow in particular.

> *No. 4: An objective of financial statements is to provide users with information for predicting, comparing, and evaluating enterprise earning power.*

Although the third objective specifies the information and the decision model of investors and creditors, the fourth objective accomplishes the same task for all users. The decision model is still expressed in terms of the activities of prediction, comparison, and evaluation, but the information needed is specified in terms of "earnings power." This objective is important because it designates earning power rather than accounting income as the information primarily needed by users. Earning power is perceived as the ability to bring in cash, rather than as the ability to produce earnings. The emphasis on earning power, and consequently on *cash flow*, is a shift in emphasis from traditional accounting objectives.

> *No. 5: An objective of financial statements is to supply information useful in judging management's ability to utilize enterprise resources effectively in achieving the primary enterprise goal.*

To cash flows and earning power, specified by the third and fourth as the information needed, the fifth objective adds *management ability*. This implies that accounting data may be used to evaluate the economic behavior of management. This economic behavior includes the fiduciary stewardship function, or safekeeping of assets to prevent their loss. It goes beyond the stewardship function, however, to include all of management's decisons regarding the use of assets. Objective No. 5 assumes that accounting data can measure management's ability to use resources effectively to achieve the primary enterprise goal.

> *No. 6: An objective of financial statements is to provide factual and interpretive information about transactions and other events that is useful for predicting, comparing, and evaluating enterprise earning power. Basic underlying assumptions with respect to matters subject to interpretation, evaluation, prediction, or estimation should be disclosed.*

Objective No. 6 expands the scope of accounting measurement to include not only factual or objective information but also *interpretive* or *subjective* information. The prediction, comparison, and evaluation of enterprise earning power rest not only on objective and verifiable information, but also subjective information, which may be subject to interpretation. Such factual and interpretive information is the result of both transactions and events. We may interpret the sixth objective as an application of the events approach, which was presented in Chapter 2. Because information may be interpretive rather than factual, and because it may result from events rather than transactions, the sixth objective specifically recommends that the accountant discloses the assumptions from which the information was derived. Such disclosure facilitates the interpretation, evaluation, prediction, or estimation on the basis of factual and inter- pretive information about transactions and events.

> *No. 7: An objective is to provide a statement of financial position that is useful for predicting, comparing, and evaluating enterprise earning power. This statement should provide information concerning enterprise transactions and other events that are part of incomplete earnings cycles. Current values should also be reported when they differ significantly from historical cost. Assets and liabilities should be grouped or segregated by the relative uncertainty of the amount and timing of prospective realization or liquidation.*

Objective No. 7 refers to a concept of a balance sheet or a statement of financial position. The objective specifically recommends that the *balance sheet* or *statement of financial position* include transactions and events of incomplete earning cycles, the possible reporting of current values, and the criteria for grouping or segregating assets and liabilities. The seventh objective distinguishes between a *completed* earnings cycle (a chain of events with an impact on earning power that lies in the past), an *incomplete* cycle (a chain of events that has commenced but is not yet complete), and a *prospective* cycle (a chain of events that lies wholly in the future). Thus, a statement of financial position reports on the transactions and events that are not yet complete. More specifically,

[an] earnings cycle is defined as incomplete when:
(i)   a realized sacrifice or a benefit has occurred, but the related benefit or sacrifice has not been realized;
(ii) both sacrifice and benefit are not realized; or
(iii) the effort has not taken place.[11]

Given this objective, a timid step is made toward the disclosure of current values. The uncertainty of the amount and timing of prospective realization or liquidation seems to call for probabilistic values.

> *No. 8: An objective is to provide a statement of periodic earnings useful for predicting, comparing, and evaluating enterprise earning power. The net result of completed earnings cycles and enterprise activities resulting in recognizable progress toward completion of incomplete cycles should be reported. Changes in the values reflected in successive statements of financial position should also be reported, but separately, since they differ in terms of their certainty of realization.*

Objective No. 8 refers to a concept of a profit-and-loss statement or a statement of periodic earnings. The objective recommends that the profit-and-loss statements or the statement of periodic earnings include transactions and events of completed earnings cycles, results of the progress of incomplete cycles, and changes in values. Specifically, the reporting of transactions and events that are complete and the progress of incomplete cycles is recommended:

For an earnings cycle to be defined as completed, three conditions should be fulfilled:
(1) a realized sacrifice (an actual or high disbursement of cash),
(2) a related realized benefit (an actual or high probable receipt of cash),
(3) no further related substantive effort.[12]

The eighth objective states that the inclusion of unrealized value changes in earnings is both desirable and practical as long as they are disclosed separately to emphasize the uncertainty of their realization.

No. 9: An objective is to provide a statement of financial activities useful for predicting, comparing, and evaluating enterprise earning power. This statement should report mainly on factual aspects of enterprise transactions having or expected to have significant cash consequences. This statement should report data that require minimal judgment and interpretation by the preparer.

The statement refers to a *concept of funds statement*, or a *statement of financial activities*. Objective No. 9 specifically recommends reporting transactions that establish highly probable receipts and disbursements of cash, and factual information with minimal intervention by the preparer. The statement of earnings shows *progress* and *results* and the statement of financial position shows *status*, but the statement of financial activities shows *conduct*. The statement of earnings reports the relationship between sacrifices and benefits during different periods through matching and allocation procedures. The statement of financial activities reports only the enterprise's financial transactions (the benefits and sacrifices) made during the period that are presumed to have cash consequences.

No. 10: An objective of financial statements is to provide information useful for the predictive process. Financial forecasts should be provided when they will enhance the reliability of users' predictions.

Again, the objective emphasizes the importance of predicting and forecasting in the economic decision-making process. Publication of explicit forecasts of enterprise activities is deemed an important objective of financial statements. Specifically, Objective No. 10 recommends that, in order to be published, these forecasts must enhance the relative accuracy of users' predictions.

No. 11: An objective of a financial statement for governmental and not-for-profit organizations is to provide information useful for evaluating the effectiveness of the management of resources in achieving the organization's goals. Performance measures should be quantified in terms of identified goals.

Objective No. 11 expansion of the scope of financial accounting to the measurement of the performance and goal attainment of governmental and not-for-profit organizations is rather difficult, and because the goals of such organizations are primarily nonmonetary, performance measures should be expressed in terms of the not-for-profit organization's goals.

No. 12: An objective of financial statements is to report on those activities of the enterprise affecting society which can be determined and described or measured and which are important to the enterprise in its social environment.

Objective No. 12 adds a socioeconomic dimension to the scope of financial accounting. It recognizes the possible interactions between the private goals of the enterprise and its social goals. There may be *reciprocal* or *direct* interactions when the enterprise derives social benefits, such as fire and police protection, in exchange for tax payments or private costs. In the case of direct protection, in exchange for tax payments or private costs. In the case of direct and reciprocal interactions, therefore, the firm enjoys benefits and incurs costs. Interactions may also be *nonreciprocal* or *indirect*. Examples are situations in which a firm contributes to the social welfare, which is a social cost. Objective No. 12 seems to call for reporting both the sacrifices and the benefits accruing to a firm that result from direct and reciprocal interactions and indirect and nonreciprocal interactions. The stewardship function may be perceived not only as the safeguarding of assets of the firm but also the safeguarding of the social welfare.

Qualitative Characteristics of Reporting

To satisfy users' needs, information contained in financial statements must possess certain characteristics. The "Trueblood Report" mentions seven qualitative characteristics of reporting:

1 relevance and materiality
2 form and substance
3 reliability
4 freedom from bias
5 comparability
6 consistency, and
7 understandability.

In the Report's words:

> The qualitative characteristics of financial statements should be based largely on the needs of users of the statements. Information should be free as possible from any bias of the preparer. In making decisions, users should not only understand the information presented, but also should be able to assess its reliability and compare it with information about alternative opportunities and previous experience. In all cases, information is more useful if it stresses economic substance rather than technical form.[13]

7.3　TOWARD A CONCEPTUAL FRAMEWORK

7.3.1　The Nature of a Conceptual Framework

The "Trueblood Report" specified twelve objectives and seven qualitative characteristics of financial reporting. Since its inscription, the FASB has recognized the importance of the objectives of financial statements in the adoption of financial standards. The FASB has also realized that the whole problem of standard setting rests not only on the objectives, but also on an established body of concepts and objectives. In fact, the Board has acknowledged the erosion of the credibility of financial reporting in recent years, and has criticized the following situations:

- Two or more methods of accounting are accepted for the same facts.
- Less conservative accounting methods are being used rather than the earlier, more conservative methods.

- Reserves are used to artificially smooth earning fluctuations.
- Financial statements fail to warn of impending liquidity crunches.
- Deferrals are followed by "big bath" write-offs.
- Unadjusted optimism exists in estimates of recoverability.
- Off balance-sheet financing (that is, disclosure in the notes to the financial statements) is common.
- An unwarranted assertion of immateriality has been used to justify nondisclosure of unfavorable information or departures from standards.
- Form is relevant over substance.[14]

To correct some of these situations and to provide a more rigorous way of setting standards and increasing financial statement users' understanding and confidence in financial reporting, the FASB instituted a conceptual-framework project. The Board described this project as follows:

> A conceptual framework is a constitution, a coherent system of interrelated objectives and fundamentals that can lead to consistent standards and that prescribes the nature, function, and limits of financial accounting and financial statements. The objectives identify the goals and the purposes of accounting. The fundamentals are the underlying concepts of accounting—concepts that guide the selection of events to be accounted for, the measurement of those events and the means of summarizing and communicating to interested parties. Concepts of that type are fundamental in the sense that other concepts flow from them and repeated references to them will be necessary in establishing, interpreting, and applying accounting and reporting standards.[15]

The conceptual framework, therefore, is intended to act as a constitution for the standard-setting process. Its purpose is to guide in resolving disputes that arise during the standard-setting process by narrowing the question to whether or not specific standards conform to the conceptual framework. In fact, the FASB has identified five specific benefits that will result from a conceptual framework. A conceptual framework, when completed, will:

- Guide the FASB in establishing accounting standards.
- Provide a frame of reference for resolving accounting questions in the absence of specific promulgated standards.
- Determine the bounds of judgment in preparing financial statements.
- Enhance comparability by decreasing the number of alternative accounting methods.[16]

7.3.2   Conceptual Framework Issues

Before starting effective work on the conceptual framework, the FASB attempted to identify the most important conceptual issues of concern to standard setting. Nine issues were presented for discussion and resolution.

Issue 1: Which View of Earnings Should be Adopted?

Three distinct views about measuring earnings are identified:

- the asset/liability view;

- the revenue/expense view;
- the nonarticulated view.

For both the asset/liability view and the revenue/expense view, the statement of earnings "articulates" with the statement of financial position, in the sense that they are both part of the same measurement process. The difference between revenues and expenses are also equivalent to the increase in net capital.

The asset/liability view, also called the balance-sheet or capital-maintenance view, holds that revenues and expenses result only from changes in assets and liabilities. Revenues are increases in assets and decreases in liabilities; expenses are decreases in assets and increases in liabilities. Some increases and decreases in net assets are excluded from the definition of earnings — namely, capital contributions, capital withdrawals, corrections of earnings of prior periods, and holding gains and losses. The asset/liability view should not be interpreted as an abandonment of the matching principle. In fact, matching revenues and expenses result from clear definitions of assets and liabilities.

The revenue/expense view, also called the income statement or matching view, holds that revenues and expenses result from the need for a proper matching. Earnings are merely the differences between revenues in a period and the expenses incurred earning those revenues. Matching, the fundamental measurement process in accounting, is comprised of two steps:

1 Revenue recognition or timing through the realization principle.
2 Expense recognition in three possible ways:
   a. Associating cause and effect, such as for cost of goods sold.
   b. Systematic and rational allocation, such as for depreciation.
   c. Immediate recognition, such as for selling and administrative costs.

Thus, contrary to the asset/liability view, the revenue/expense view primarily emphasizes measuring the earnings of the firm, and not the increase or decrease in net capital. Assets and liabilities, including deferred charges and credits, are considered residuals that must be carried to future periods in order to ensure proper matching and avoid distortion of earnings.

The nonarticulated view is based on the belief that articulation leads to redundancy, "since all events reported in the income statement are also reported in the balance sheet, although from a different perspective."[17] According to this view, the definitions of assets and liabilities may be critical in the presentation of financial position and the definitions of revenues and expenses may dominate the measurement of earnings. The two financial statements have independent existence and meanings; therefore, different measurement schemes may be used for them. An example of the nonarticulated view would be the use of LIFO in the income statement and of FIFO in the balance sheet. The nonarticulated view has gained some ground recently. In fact, the American Accounting Association's *Statement of Basic Accounting Theory* criticizes articulation:

> We find no logical reason why external financial reports should be expected to "balance" or articulate with each other. In fact, we find that forced balancing and articulation have frequently restricted the presentation of relevant information. The important guide should be the disclosure of all relevant information with measurement procedures that meet the other standards suggested in ASOBAT [*A Statement of Basic Accounting Theory*].[18]

Which view of earnings should be adopted as the basis of a conceptual framework for financial accounting and reporting? If articulation can be proved not only to be necessary but also to be advantageous, then the choice is between the asset/liability view and the revenue/expense view. The choice between these two views rests on which view constitutes the fundamental measurement process:

1 measurement of the attributes of assets and liabilities and changes in them; or
2 the matching process.

If measurement of the attributes of assets and liabilities and changes in them is deemed the fundamental measurement process (as in the asset/liability view), then earnings are only the consequences and the result of certain changes in assets and liabilities. On the other hand, if the matching process is deemed the fundamental measurement process (as in the revenue/expense view), then changes in assets and liabilities are merely the consequences and results of revenues and expenses. This latter view has led to the recognition in the statement of financial position of such items as "deferred charges," "deferred credits," and "reserves," which do not represent economic resources and obligations but which are necessary to ensure a proper matching and income determination. The asset/liability view would reject the deferral method of intraperiod tax allocation in favor of either the liability method or the net-of-tax method. By rejecting these new items in the balance sheet, the asset/liability view faces a major criticism, which concerns its unwillingness to recognize as revenues and expenses anything except current changes in economic resources and obligations to transfer resources, making it incapable of dealing with the complexities of the modern business world.

A choice between these views would provide not only an underlying basis for a conceptual framework for financial accounting and reporting but also definitions of the elements of financial statements.

Issues 2–7: Definitions

Definitions of each element of financial statements may be provided by both the asset/liability view and the revenue/expense view.

According to the asset/liability view, assets are the economic resources of a firm; they represent future benefits that are expected to result directly or indirectly in a net cash inflow. Alternatively, we may exclude from the definition of "assets" economic resources that do not have the characteristics of exchangeability or severability. In either case, based on the asset/liability view, assets are restricted to representations of economic resources of the firm. The economic resources of the firm are:

1 productive resources of the enterprise,
2 contractual rights to productive resources,
3 products,
4 money,
5 claims to receive money,
6 ownership interests in other enterprises.[19]

According to the revenue/expense view, assets include not only the assets defined from the asset/liability viewpoint, but also all items that do not represent economic resources but are required for proper matching and income determination.

A third view of assets arises from the perception of the balance sheet not as a statement of financial position, but as "a statement of the sources and composition of company capital." According to this view, assets constitute the "present composition of invested capital."[20]

If we exclude the problem of the element of "deferred charges" on the statement of financial position, the definitions of assets presented in these three different views have the following characteristics in common:

1 An asset represents potential cash flow to a firm.
2 Potential benefits are obtainable by the firm.
3 The legal concept of property may affect the accounting definition of assets.
4 The way an asset is acquired may be part of the definitions. It may have been acquired in a past or current transaction or event; the event includes either an exchange transaction, a nonreciprocal transfer from owners or nonowners, or a windfall, and may exclude executory contracts.
5 Exchangeability may be an essential characteristic of assets.

Which of these definitions or modifications of these definitions should comprise the substance of a definition of "assets" for a conceptual framework for financial accounting and reporting? What is needed is a definition that lends itself to the generality of application required for a conceptual framework. Such a definition should take into account the following characteristics:

1 An asset represents only economic resources and does not include "deferred charges."
2 An asset represents potential cash flows to a firm.
3 Potential benefits are obtainable by the firm.
4 An asset represents the legal binding right to a particular benefit, results from a past or current transaction, and includes all commitments, as in wholly executory contracts.
5 Exchangeability is not an essential characteristic of assets except for "deferred charges," in order to keep most intangibles as assets and exclude "deferred charges."

The second element to be defined is liabilities. According to the asset/liability view, liabilities are the obligations of the firm to transfer economic resources to other entities in the future. We may expand this definition to exclude items that do not represent binding obligations to transfer economic resources to other entities in the future.

According to the revenue/expense view, liabilities comprise not only the liabilities defined from the asset/liability viewpoint but also certain deferred credits and reserves that do not represent obligations to transfer economic resources but that are required for proper matching and income determination.

A third view of liabilities arises from the perception of the balance sheet as "a statement of the sources and composition of company capital." According to this view, liabilities constitute sources of capital and include certain deferred credits and reserves that do not represent obligations to transfer economic resources.

If we disregard the element of "deferred credits," the definitions of liabilities presented in these three different views have the following characteristics in common:

1 A liability is a future sacrifice of economic resources.
2 A liability represents an obligation of a particular enterprise.

3 A liability may be restricted to legal debt.

4 A liability results from past or current transaction or events.

APB Statement No. 4 summarizes these characteristics of liabilities in paragraph 58:

> The economic obligations of an enterprise at any time are its present responsibilities to transfer economic resources or provide services to other entities in the future. Obligations usually arise because the enterprise has received resources from other entities through purchases or borrowing. Some obligations, however, arise by other means (for example, through the imposition of taxes or through legal action). Obligations are general claims against the enterprise, rather than claims to specific resources of the enterprise, unless the terms of the obligation or applicable legal rules provide otherwise.

Which of these definitions or modifications of these definitions should comprise the substance of a definition of "liabilities" for a conceptual framework for financial accounting and reporting? As in the case of assets, what is needed is a definition of liabilities that lends itself to the generality of application required for a conceptual framework.

The third element to be defined is earnings. According to the asset/liability view, earnings are the net assets of the firm except for "capital" changes.

According to the revenue/expense view, earnings result from the matching of revenues and expenses and, perhaps, from the gains and losses. Gains and losses, therefore, may be distinguished from the revenues and expenses, or they may be considered part of them. Each possible component of earnings (revenues, expenses, gains, and losses) may be defined as follows:

1 *Revenues and expenses:* according to the asset/liability view, revenues, which encompass gains and losses, are defined as increases in the assets or decreases in the liabilities that do not affect capital. Similarly, expenses, which encompass gains and losses, are defined as decreases in the assets or increases in the liabilities arising from the use of economic resources and services during a given period.

   According to the revenue/expense view, revenues, which encompass gains and losses, result from the sale of goods and services and include gains from the sale and exchange of assets other than inventories, interests and dividends earned on investments, and other increases in owners' equity during a period other than capital contributions and adjustments. Similarly, expenses comprise all of the expired costs that correspond to the revenues of the period. If gains and losses are defined as a separate element of earnings, however, revenues are defined as measures of enterprise outputs that result from the production or delivery of goods and the rendering of services during a period. Similarly, expenses are the expired costs corresponding to the revenues of the period.

   Which of these definitions of earnings should comprise the substance of "revenues" and "expenses" for a conceptual framework for financial accounting and reporting? In other words, which definition lends itself to the generality of application needed for a conceptual framework?

   The definitions generated by the revenue/expense viewpoint rely on a listing of all items that may be perceived as revenues or expenses. First, such a list is not necessarily exhaustive, and second, the items in the list may change. As a result, the revenue/expense view of earnings and the ensuing definitions of revenues and expenses lack the generality of application needed for a conceptual framework.

2 *Gains and losses:* according to the asset/liability view, gains are defined as increases in net assets other than increases from revenues or from changes in capital. Similarly, losses are defined as decreases in net assets other than decreases from expenses or from changes in capital. Thus, gains and losses constitute that part of earnings not explained by revenues and expenses.

According to the revenue/expense view, gains are defined as the excess of proceeds over the cost of assets sold, or as windfalls and other benefits obtained at no cost or sacrifice. Similarly, losses are defined as the excess over the related proceeds, if any, of all or an appropriate portion of the costs of assets sold, abandoned, or wholly or partially destroyed by casualty (or otherwise written off), or as costs that expire without producing revenues. Thus, according to the revenue/expense view, gains and losses are independent from the definitions of other elements of financial statements.

Which of these definitions of gains and losses contains the generality of application required for a conceptual framework? According to the revenue/expense view, the definitions are independent of the definitions of the other elements and may, for that reason, be viewed as lacking generality of application. According to the asset/liability view, the definitions are derived from the other definitions and emphasize the incidental nature of gains and losses; they appear to contain the generality of application required for a conceptual framework.

In any case, gains and losses may be either gains and losses from exchanges, "holding" gains and losses resulting from a change in the value of assets and liabilities held by the firm, or gains and losses from nonreciprocal transfers.

3 *Relationships between earnings and the component of earnings:* Three major relationships exist between earnings and the component of earnings:

a. Earnings = Revenues − Expenses + Gains − Losses

b. Earnings = Revenues − Expenses

c. Earnings = Revenues (including gains) − Expenses (including losses)

In the first relationship, each component is separate and essential to a definition of earnings. The different sources of earnings are distinguished, thereby providing greater flexibility in the classification and analysis of a firm's performance.

In the second relationship, gains and losses are not separate and are not essential to the definition of earnings. All increases and decreases are treated similarly as either revenues or expenses. Such a definition does not fit all the gains and losses from nonreciprocal transfers, windfalls, casualties, and holding gains and losses.

In the third relationship, although gains and losses are separate concepts, they are part of revenues and expenses. Such a definition has the same advantages as the first relationship, and avoids the disadvantages of the second relationship. The definitions of revenues and expenses, however, must mix different items and may require a complete identification and listing of the items that comprise revenues, expenses, gains, and losses.

The first relationship appears to present the least disadvantage according to both the asset/liability view and the revenue/expense view. It allows identification and disclosure of the three kinds of gains and losses: gains and losses from exchanges, holding gains and losses, and gains and losses from nonreciprocal transfers, windfalls, and casualties.

4 *Accrual accounting:* the elements of financial statements are accounted for and included in financial statements through the use of accrual accounting procedures. Accrual accounting rests on the concepts of accrual, deferral, allocation, amortization, realization, and recognition. The FASB opted for the following definitions of these concepts:

> Accrual is the accounting process of recognizing noncash events and circumstances as they occur; specifically, accrual entails recognizing revenues and related increases in assets and expenses and related increases in liabilities for amounts expected to be received or paid, usually in cash, in the future . . . .
>
> Deferral is the accounting process of recognizing a liability for a current cash receipt or an asset for a current cash payment (or current incurrence of a liability) with an expected future impact on revenues and expenses . . . .
>
> Allocation is the accounting process of assigning or distributing an amount according to a plan or a formula. It is a broader term than "amortization;" that is, amortization is an allocation process . . . .
>
> Amortization is the accounting process of systematically reducing an amount by periodic payments, or write-downs . . . .
>
> Realization is the process of converting noncash resources and rights into money; it is most precisely used in accounting and financial reporting to refer to sales of assets for cash or claims of cash. The related terms, "realized" and "unrealized," therefore identify revenues or gains and losses on assets sold and unsold, respectively . . . .
>
> Recognition is the process of formally recording or incorporating an item in the accounts and financial statements of an enterprise. Thus, an element may be recognized (recorded) or unrecognized (unrecorded). "Realization" and "recognition" are not used synonymously, as they sometimes are in the accounting and financial literature.[21]

Issue 8: Which Capital-Maintenance or Cost-Recovery Concepts Should be Adopted?

The concept of capital maintenance allows us to make a distinction between the return *on* capital, or earnings, and the return *of* capital, or cost recovery. Earnings follow from recovery or maintenance of capital. Two concepts of capital maintenance exist: the financial capital concept, and the physical capital concept. Both concepts use measurements in terms of units of money or units of the same general purchasing power, resulting in four possible concepts of capital maintenance:

1 Financial capital measured in units of money.
2 Financial capital measured in units of the same general purchasing power.
3 Physical capital measured in units of money.
4 Physical capital measured in units of the same general purchasing power.

We will examine the conceptual and operational differences among these concepts in Chapters 12–14. Note, however, that the comprehensive income is a return on financial capital, as distinguished from a return on physical capital. The essential difference between the two concepts is that "holding gains and losses" are included in income under the financial capital concept, but are treated as "capital maintenance adjustments" under the physical capital concept.

Issue 9: Which Measurement Method Should be Adopted?

The issue of measurement method concerns the determination of both the unit of measure and the attribute to be measured. As far as the unit of measure is concerned, the choice is between actual dollars and general purchasing power adjusted dollars. As far as the particular attribute to be measured is concerned, we have five options:

1 historical cost method
2 current cost
3 current exit value
4 expected exit value, and
5 present value of expected cash flows.

Issue 9 will also be the subject of Chapters 9–11.

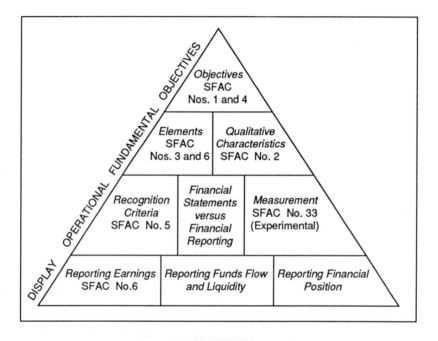

EXHIBIT 7.3

7.3.3   Development of a Conceptual Framework

Exhibit 7.3 illustrates the overall scope of the conceptual framework and lists the related documents issued thus far by the FASB.[22]

At the first level, the objectives identify the goals and purposes of accounting. Statement of Financial Accounting Concepts No. 1 (*Objectives of Reporting by Business Enterprises*) presents the goals and purposes of accounting for business enterprises. Statement of Financial Accounting Concepts No. 2 (*Objectives of Financial Reporting by Nonbusiness Organizations*) presents the goals and purposes of accounting for business organizations.

At the second level, the fundamentals include the qualitative characteristics of accounting information (Statement of Financial Accounting Concepts No. 2) and the definitions of the elements of financial statements (Statement of Financial Accounting Concepts No. 3).

At the third level, the operational guidelines that the accountant uses in establishing and applying accounting standards include the recognition criteria, financial statements versus financial reporting, and measurement (Statement of Financial Accounting Standards No. 33).

At the fourth level, the display mechanisms that accounting uses to convey accounting information include reporting earnings, reporting funds flow and liquidity, and reporting financial position.

Each of these levels and components will be examined in the next section.

7.3.4 The Objectives of Financial Reporting

The Objectives of Financial Reporting by Business Enterprises

The FASB began its efforts to develop a constitution for financial accounting and reporting in November 1978 when it issued authoritative, broadly-based guidelines spelling out the objectives of financial reporting in Statement of Financial Accounting Concepts No. 1, *Objectives of Financial Reporting by Business Enterprises*. The statement was not limited to the contents of financial statements:

> Financial reporting includes not only financial statements but also other means of communicating information that relates, directly or indirectly, to the information provided by the accounting system — that is, information about an enterprise's resources, obligations, earnings, etc.[23]

The objectives of financial reporting are summarized in the following excerpts from the statement:

> Financial reporting should provide information that is useful to present and potential investors and creditors and other users in making rational investment, credit, and similar decisions. The information should be comprehensible to those who have a reasonable understanding of business and economic activities and are willing to study the information with reasonable diligence. [Paragraph 34]
>
> Financial reporting should provide information to help present and potential investors and creditors and other users in assessing the amounts, timing, and uncertainty of prospective cash receipts from dividends or interests and the proceeds from the sale, redemption, or maturity of securities or loan. The prospects for those cash receipts are affected by an enterprise's ability to generate enough cash to meet its obligations when due and its other cash operating needs, to reinvest in operations, and to pay cash dividends, and may also be affected by perceptions of investors and creditors generally about that ability, which affect market prices of the enterprise's securities. Thus, financial reporting should provide information to help investors, creditors, and others assess the amount, timing, and uncertainty of prospective net cash inflows to the related enterprise. [Paragraph 37]
>
> Financial reporting should provide information about the economic resources of an enterprise, the claims to those resources (obligations of the enterprise to transfer resources to other entities and owners' equity), and the effects of transactions, events, and circumstances that change resources and claims to those resources. [Paragraph 40]

Financial reporting should provide information about an enterprise's financial performance during a period. Investors and creditors often use information about the past to help in assessing the prospects of an enterprise. Thus, although investment and credit decisions reflect investors' and creditors' expectations about the future enterprise performance, those expectations are commonly based at least partly on evaluations of past enterprise performance. [Paragraph 42]

The primary focus of financial reporting is information about an enterprise's performance provided by measures of earnings and its components. [Paragraph 43]

Financial reporting should provide information about how an enterprise obtains and spends cash, about its borowing and repayment of borrowing, about its capital transactions, including cash dividends and other distributions of enterprise resource to owners, and about other factors that may affect an enterprise's liquidity or solvency. [Paragraph 49]

Financial reporting should provide information about how management of an enterprise has discharged its stewardship responsibility to owners (stockholders) for the use of enterprise resources entrusted to it. [Paragraph 50]

Financial reporting should provide information that is useful to managers and directors in making decisions in the interests of owners. [Paragraph 52]

The statement also points out that:

Financial reporting is not an end in itself, but is intended to provide information that is useful in making business and economic decisions.

The objectives of financial reporting are not immutable—they are affected by the economic, legal, political, and social environment in which financial reporting takes place.

The objectives are also affected by the characteristics and limitations of the kind of information that financial reporting can provide.

The objectives in this statement are those of general-purpose external financial reporting by business enterprises.

The terms "investor" and "creditor" are used broadly, and apply not only to those who have or contemplate having a claim to enterprise resources, but also those who advise or represent them.

Although investment and credit decisions reflect investors' and creditors' expectations about future enterprise performance, such expectations are commonly based, at least partly, on evaluations of past enterprise performance.

The primary focus of financial reporting is information about earnings and its components.

Information about enterprise earnings based on accrual accounting generally provides a better indication of an enterprise's present and continuing ability to generate favorable cash flows than information limited to the financial effects of cash receipts and payments.

Financial reporting is expected to provide information about an enterprise's financial performance during a period and about how management of an enterprise has discharged its stewardship responsibility to owners.

Financial accounting is not designed to measure directly the value of a business enterprise, but the information it provides may be helpful to those who wish to estimate its value.

Investors, creditors, and others may use reported earnings and information about the elements of financial statements in various ways to assess the prospects for cash flows.

They may wish, for example, to evaluate management's performance, estimate "earning power," predict future earnings, assess risk, or to confirm, change, or reject earlier predictions or assessments. Although financial reporting should provide basic information to aid them, users do their own evaluating, estimating, predicting, assessing, confirming, changing, and rejecting.

Management knows more about the enterprise and its affairs than investors, creditors, or other "outsiders" and, accordingly, many often increase the usefulness of financial information by identifying certain events and circumstances and explaining their financial effects on the enterprise.

After issuing this statement on the objectives of financial reporting, the FASB is in a better position to evaluate existing standards that are inconsistent with the stated objectives and to complete the remaining phases of the conceptual framework project.

The Objectives of Financial Reporting by Nonbusiness Organizations

Nonbusiness organizations differ from business organizations in at least two respects. Nonbusiness organizations:

1 have no indicator of performance comparable to a business enterprise's profit;
2 generally are not subject to the test of competition in markets.

Three major distinguishing characteristics of nonbusiness organizations are:

1 Significant amounts of resources are received from resource providers, who do not expect to receive either repayment or economic benefits proportionate to the resources they provide.
2 The business operates primarily for purposes other than the provision of goods or services at a profit or a profit equivalent.
3 There are no defined ownership interests that can be sold, transferred, or redeemed, or that would convey entitlement to a share of a residual distribution of the resources in the event of liquidation of the organization.

On the basis of this definition, the FASB exposure draft on the "Objectives of Financial Reporting by Nonbusiness Organizations," issued September 15, 1980, cites examples of nonbusiness organizations, which include private, nonprofit, and philanthropic organizations, such as colleges and universities, hospitals, health and welfare agencies, churches, and foundations; state and local governmental units; and such membership organizations as trade and professional associations. Examples of organizations that do not possess all of the distinguishing characteristics of nonbusiness organizations are membership clubs in transferable equity interests, investor-owned hospitals and educational institutions, mutual insurance companies, and types of mutual and cooperative organizations that provide dividends, lower costs, or economic benefits directly to their owners, members, or participants.

Four particular groups are especially interested in the information provided by the financial reporting of nonbusiness organizations:

1 The resource providers: lenders, suppliers, employees, taxpayers, members, and contributors.

2 The constituents who use and benefit from the services rendered by the organization.
3 The governing and overseeing bodies responsible for setting policies and overseeing and appraising the managers of nonbusiness organizations.
4 The managers of nonbusiness organizations.

To meet the needs of these particular users of information provided by nonbusiness organization, the FASB exposure draft presents the following objectives:

Information useful in making resource allocation decisions: financial reporting by nonbusiness organizations should provide information that is useful to resource providers in making rational decisions about the allocation of resources in those organizations.

Information useful in assessing services and the ability to provide services: financial reporting by nonbusiness organizations should provide information that is useful to present and potential resource providers in assessing the services that a nonbusiness organization provides and its ability to continue to provide those services.

Information useful in assessing management stewardship and performance: financial reporting by nonbusiness organizations should provide information that is useful to present and potential resource providers in assessing how managers of a nonbusiness organization have discharged their stewardship responsibilities and other aspects of their performance. Information about an organization's performance should be the focus for assessing the stewardship, or accountability, of managers. Information about departures from such spending mandates as formal budgets and donor restrictions on the use of resources that may impinge on an organization's financial performance or on its ability to provide a satisfactory level of services is also important in assessing how well managers have discharged their stewardship responsibilities.

Information about economic resources, obligations, net resources, and charges on them: financial reporting by nonbusiness organizations about interest in those resources.

Organizational performance: financial reporting by nonbusiness organizations should provide information about the performance of an organization during a given period. Periodic measurement of the changes in the amount and nature of the net resources of a nonbusiness organization and information about the service's efforts and accomplishments of an organization, taken together, represent the information most useful in assessing organizational performance.

Liquidity: financial reporting by nonbusiness organizations should provide information about how a nonbusiness organization obtains and spends cash, about its borrowing and repayment of borrowing, and about other factors that may affect an organization's liquidity.

Managers' explanations and interpretations: financial reporting by nonbusiness organizations should include explanations and interpretations to help resource providers and other users understand the financial information they receive. Because managers usually know more about an organization and its affairs than resource providers or others outside the organization, managers can often increase the usefulness of financial reporting information by identifying certain transactions, events, and circumstances that affect the organization, and by explaining their financial impact.

7.3.5   Fundamental Concepts

The fundamental concepts include both the qualitative characteristics of accounting information and the definitions of the elements of financial statements.

The Qualitative Characteristics of Accounting Information

The FASB issued Statement of Financial Accounting Concepts No. 2, *Qualitative Characteristics of Accounting Information*, to provide criteria for choosing between:

1 alternative accounting and reporting methods; or
2 disclosure requirements.[24]

Basically, these criteria indicate which information is better (more useful) for decision-making purposes. The characteristics may be viewed as a hierarchy — see Exhibit 7.4. Usefulness of decision making is presented as the most important informational quality. Relevance and reliability are the two primary qualities, with related ingredients. Comparability and consistency are presented as secondary and interactive qualities. Finally, the concepts of cost-benefit considerations and materiality are recognized, respectively, as a pervasive constraint and a threshold for recognition. Each of these qualitative characteristics of accounting information will now be examined.

Relevance Relevance has been approximately defined as follows:

> For information to meet the standard of relevance, it must bear on or be usefully associated with the action it is designed to facilitate or the result it is desired to produce. This requires that either the information or the act of communicating exert influence . . . on the designated actions.[25]

Relevance therefore refers to the ability of the information to influence the managers' decisions by changing or confirming their expectations about the results or consequences of actions or events.

There can be degrees of relevance. The relevance of particular information will vary among users and will depend on their needs and on the particular context in which the decisions are made. In the concept of the conceptual framework, the relevant information helps investors, creditors, and other users to evaluate the past, present, and future events (predictive value) or to confirm or correct prior expectations (feedback value). To be relevant, the information must also be available to a decision maker before it loses its capacity to influence decisions (timeliness).

In short, to be relevant, information must have predictive value and feedback value and, at the same time, must be conveyed on a timely basis.

Reliability Reliability refers to the "quality which permits users of data to depend on it with confidence as representative of what it proposes to present."[26] Thus, the reliability of information depends on its degree of faithfulness in the representation of an event. Reliability will differ between users, depending on the extent of their knowledge of the rules used to prepare information. Similarly, different users may seek information with different degrees of reliability. In the context of the conceptual framework, to be reliable, information must be verifiable, neutral, and faithfully presented.

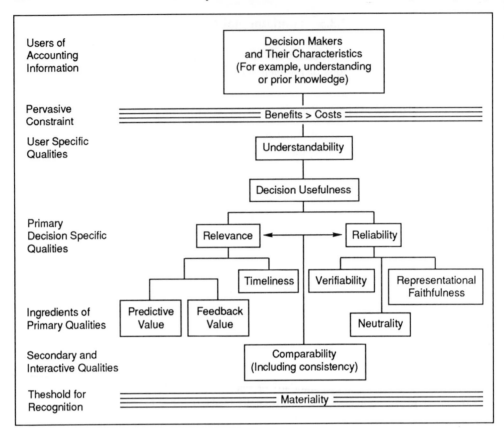

EXHIBIT 7.4

Verifiability is the "attribute ... which allows qualified individuals working independently of one another to develop essentially similar measures or conclusions from an examination of the same evidence, data, or records."[27] It implies consensus and absence of measure bias. Verifiable information can be substantially reproduced by independent measurers using the same measurement methods. Notice that verifiability refers only to the correctness of the resulting information, not to the appropriateness of the measurement methods used.

Representational faithfulness and completeness refer to the correspondence between accounting data and the events those data are supposed to represent. If the measure portrays what it is supposed to represent, it is considered to be free of measurement and measurer bias.

Neutrality refers to the absence of bias in the presentation of accounting reports or information. Thus, neutral information is free from bias toward attaining some desired result or inducing a particular mode of behavior. This is not to imply that the preparers of information do not have a purpose in mind when preparing the reports; it only means that the purpose should not influence a predetermined result.

Secondary qualities Comparability and consistency are the secondary qualities suggested by the FASB Statement of Financial Accounting Concepts No. 2.

Comparability describes the use of the same method over time by a given firm. The consistency principle does not, however, mean that a particular method of accounting cannot be changed once it is adopted. Environmental circumstances may dictate a more desirable change in accounting policy or technique if properly justified. APB Opinion No. 2, *Accounting Changes*, states that

> The presumption that an entity should not change an accounting principle may be overcome only if the enterprise justifies the use of an alternative acceptable accounting principle on the basis that it is preferable. . . . The nature and justification for a change in accounting principle and its effect on income should be disclosed . . . . The justification for the change should explain why the newly adopted accounting principle is preferable.[28]

Cost-Benefit Considerations Cost-benefit considerations are recognized as one pervasive constraint. Financial accounting information will be sought if the benefit to be derived from the information exceeds its cost. Thus, before preparing and disseminating financial information, the benefits and costs of providing the information must be compared. The FASB emphasizes the importance of cost-benefit considerations:

> Before a decision is made to develop a standard, the Board needs to satisfy itself that the matter to be ruled on represents a significant problem, and that a standard that is promulgated will not impose costs on the many for the benefit of the few. If the proposal passes that first test, a second test may subsequently be useful. There are usually alternative ways of handling an issue. Is one of them less costly and only slightly less effective? Even if absolute magnitudes cannot be attached to costs and benefits, a comparison between alternatives may yet be possible and useful.[29]

Materiality Materiality is regarded as a threshold for recognition. Materiality is a state of relative importance. Basically, consideration must be given to whether or not the information is likely to have a significant, or material, impact on decisions. The question of crucial importance is who should determine the materiality rules, and how? (This question will be fully examined in Chapter 8.) The FASB's position on the subject is best illustrated by the following statement:

> The Board's present position is that no general standards of materiality could be formulated to take into account all the considerations that enter into an experienced human judgment. However, that position is not intended to imply either that the Board may not in the future review that conclusion or that quantitative guidance on materiality of specific items may not approximately be written into the Board's standards from time to time. That has been done on occasion already (for example, in the statement on financial reporting by segments of a business enterprise), and the Board recognizes that quantitative materiality guidance is sometimes needed . . . . However, whenever the Board or any other authoritative body imposes materiality rules, it is substituting generalized collective judgment for specific individual judgments, and there is no reason to suppose that the collective judgments are always superior.[30]

The Basic Elements of Financial Statements of Business Enterprises

Statements of Financial Accounting Concepts No. 3, *Elements of Financial Statements of Business Enterprises*, defines ten interrelated elements that are directly related to measuring the performance and status of an enterprise: assets, liabilities, equity, investments by owners, distributions to owners, comprehensive income, revenues, expenses, gains, and losses.[31] These elements are defined as follows:

Assets: probable future economic benefits obtained or controlled by a particular entity as a result of past transactions or events.

Liabilities: probable future sacrifices of economic benefits arising from the present obligations of a particular entity to transfer assets or provide services to other entities in the future as a result of past transactions or events.

Equity: residual interests in the assets of an entity that remains after deducting its liabilities. In a business enterprise, the equity is the ownership interest.

Investments by owners: increases in the net asset of a particular enterprise that result from transfers to it from other entities of something of value to obtain or increase ownership interests (or equity) in the enterprise. Assets are most commonly received as investments by owners, but may also include services or satisfaction or conversion of liabilities of the enterprise.

Distributions to owners: decreases in the net assets of a particular enterprise that result from transferring assets, rendering services, or incurring liabilities by the enterprise to owners. Distributions to owners decrease ownership interests (or equity) in the enterprise.

Comprehensive income: the change in the equity (net assets) of an entity during a given period that results from transactions and other events and circumstances from nonowner sources. Comprehensive income includes all changes in equity during a period except those that result from investments by owners and distribution to owners.

Revenues: inflows or other enhancements of the assets of an entity or settlement of the liabilities of an entity (or a combination of both) during a given period that result from delivering or producing goods, rendering services, or carrying out other activities that constitute the entity's ongoing major or central operations.

Expenses: outflows or other using-up of the assets of an entity or incurrences of the liabilities of an entity (or a combination of both) during a given period that result from delivering or producing goods, rendering services, or carrying out other activities that constitute the entity's ongoing major or central operations.

Gains: increases in equity (net assets) from the peripheral or incidental transactions of an entity and from all other transactions and other events and circumstances affecting the entity during a given period except those resulting from revenues or investments by owners.

Losses: decreases in equity (net assets) from the peripheral or incidental transactions of an entity and from all other transactions and other events and circumstances affecting the entity during a given period except those resulting from expenses or distributions to owners.[32]

These definitions provide a significant first screening method for determining the content of financial statements. They describe the essential characteristics to be met before events and circumstances are considered to be any element of financial statements. Three points are worth noting:

First, the concept of comprehensive income is more inclusive than the traditional concept of accounting income.

Second, the definitions of assets, liabilities, and equities relate to amounts of resources and claims to resources at a given point in time, whereas the definitions of revenues, expenses, gains, and losses relate to the impact of transactions, events, and circumstances over a period of time.

Third, the values of assets, liabilities, and equities are assumed to change as a result of revenues, expenses, gains, and losses, which imply "articulation." In other words, the financial statements are assumed to interact and to interrelate.

Statement of Financial Accounting Concept No. 3 was later replaced by Statement of Financial Accounting Concept No. 6. The definitions of the elements are virtually identical to those in Statement No. 3, except that they are now applicable to nonbusiness organizations also.

7.3.6 Recognition and Measurement

Statement of Financial Accounting Concept No. 5 was intended to tackle the problems of recognition and measurement.

With regards to recognition, the statement was a cop-out as it stated at the outset that recognition and guidance criteria are generally consistent with current accounting practice and do not imply radical change. In addition, it states that disclosure by other means than the financial statements is not recognition.

The statement made a useful distinction between income, earnings, and comprehensive income. Basically, earnings differed from income by excluding certain accounting adjustments of earlier periods that are not recognized in the current period, like the cumulative effects of a change in accounting principle. An example of the difference between present net income and earnings is shown in Exhibit 7.5.

The difference between earnings and comprehensive income is shown in Exhibit 7.6. Basically comprehensive income recognizes two classes of items that are excluded from earnings; these are the effects of certain accounting adjustments of earlier periods that are recognized in the current period, and certain other changes in net assets (principally certain holding gains and losses) that are recognized in the period but excluded from earnings, such as some changes in market value of investments in marketable securities classified as noncurrent assets, some changes in market values of investments in industries having specialized accounting practices for marketable securities, and foreign currency translation adjustments.

The recognition criteria include:

- *Definition:* the item meets the definition of an element of financial statements.
- *Measurability:* it has a relevant attribute measurable with sufficient reliability.
- *Relevance:* the information about it is capable of making a difference in user decisions.
- *Reliability:* the information is representationally faithful, verifiable, and neutral.

With regard to measurement, the statement recognizes the five different attributes of assets and liabilities presented in the discussion memorandum, namely:

1 historical cost;
2 current replacement cost;
3 current market value;

4 net realizable (settlement) value;

5 present (or discounted) value of future cash flows.

EXHIBIT 7.5
Income Versus Earnings

	Present Net Income	Earnings
Revenues	200	200
Expenses	140	140
Gain from unusual source	(10)	(10)
Income from continuing operations	70	70
Losses on discontinued operations		
Income from operating discontinued segment		
Loss on disposal of discontinued segment	10	10
Income before extraordinary items and effect of a change in accounting principle	60	60
Extraordinary loss		10
Cumulative effect on years of a change in accounting principle	30	
Earnings		50
Net Income	30	

EXHIBIT 7.6
Earnings and Comprehensive Income

+	Revenues	200	+	Earnings	50
−	Expenses	140	−	Cumulative Accounting adjustments	20
+	Gains	10	+	Other nonowner changes in equity	10
−	Losses	20			
=	Earnings	50	=	Comprehensive Income	40

7.4 THE OTHER REPORTS

7.4.1 The Corporate Report

In July 1976, the Accounting Standards Steering Committee of the Institute of Chartered Accountants in England and Wales published *The Corporate Report* — a discussion paper intended as a first step toward a major review of users, purposes and methods of modern financial reporting in the United Kingdom. The report presented the efforts of an eleven-member party, working within the following frame of reference:

> The purpose of this study is to reexamine the scope and aims of published financial reports in the light of modern needs and conditions.
>
>   It will be concerned with the public accountability of economic entities of all kinds, but especially of business enterprises.
>
>   It will seek to establish a set of working concepts as a basis for financial reporting. Its aims will be to identify the persons or groups for whom published financial reports should be prepared, and the information appropriate to their interests.
>
>   It will consider the most suitable means of measuring and reporting the economic position, performance, and prospects of undertakings for the purposes and persons identified above.[33]

How well the report lives up to its stated aims is evidenced by its major findings and recommendations.

First, the basic philosophy and starting point of *The Corporate Report* is that financial statements should be appropriate to their expected use by potential users. In other words, financial statements should attempt to satisfy the informational needs of their users.

Second, the report assigns responsibility for reporting to the "economic entity" having an impact on society through its activities. The economic entities are itemized as limited companies, listed and unlisted; pension schemes, charitable and other trusts, and not-for-profit organizations; noncommercially oriented central government departments and agencies; partnerships and other forms of unincorporated business enterprises; trade unions and trade and professional associations; local authorities; and nationalized industries and other commercially oriented public sector bodies.[34]

Third, the report defined users as those having a reasonable right to information whose information needs should be recognized by corporate reports. The users are identified as the equity investor group, the loan creditor group, the employee group, the analyst-advisor group, the business contract group, the government, and the public.[35]

Fourth, to satisfy the fundamental objectives of annual reports established by the basic philosophy, seven desirable characteristics are cited — namely, that the corporate report be relevant, understandable, reliable, complete, objective, timely, and comparable.

Fifth, after documenting the limitations of current reporting practices, the report suggests the need for the following additional statements:

1 A statement of value added, showing how the benefits of the efforts of an enterprise are shared among employees, providers of capital, the state, and reinvestment. Exhibit 7.7 is an example of a statement of value added.
2 An employment report, showing the size and composition of the work force relying on the enterprise for its livelihood, the work contribution of employees, and the benefits earned.

3 A statement of money exchange with government, showing the financial relationship between the enterprise and the state.
4 A statement of transactions in foreign currency, showing the direct cash dealings
between Great Britain and other countries.
5 A statement of future prospects, showing likely future profit, employment, and
investment levels.
6 A statement of corporate objectives, showing management policy and medium-term
strategic targets.

EXHIBIT 7.7
A Manufacturing Company Statement of Value

			Year to December 31, 1984
			$
Turnover			100
Brought-in material and services			60
Value Added			40
Applied the following way:			
To Pay Employees			
Wages, pensions, and fringe benefits			19
To Pay Providers of Capital:			
Interests on loans		0.1	
Dividends to shareholders		0.9	
			1
To Pay Government			
Corporation tax payable			5
To Provide for Maintenance and Expansion of Assets			
Depreciation		5	
Retained profits		10	
			15
Value Added			40

Finally, after assessing six measurement bases (historical cost, purchasing power,
replacement cost, net realizable value, value to the firm, and net present value) against
three criteria (theoretical acceptability, utility, and practicality), the report rejected the use
of historical cost in favor of current values accompanied by the use of general index
adjustment.

In conclusion, a comparison of the principal findings and recommendations of *The
Corporate Report* and the "Trueblood Report" cannot be made without considering the

different economic and political environments in Great Britain and the United States. In general, *The Corporate Report* expresses a more pronounced concern for statements that can be used to improve both the social and economic welfare of society.

7.4.2   The "Stamp Report"

The Canadian Institute of Chartered Accountants (CICA) published a research study in June 1980 entitled *Corporate Reporting: Its Future Evolution*, written by Professor Edward Stamp and hereafter referred to as the "Stamp Report."[36] The main motivations behind this effort are that, first, the FASB conceptual framework is not suitable for Canada, given the environmental, historical, political, and legal differences between the United States and Canada and, second, the framework will provide a Canadian solution to the problem of improving the quality of corporate financial accounting standards.

The approach advocated in the "Stamp Report" is evolutionary. It identifies problems and conceptual issues and provides solutions in terms of the identification of the objectives of corporate financial reporting, the users of corporate reports, the nature of the users' needs, and the criteria for the assessment of the quality of standards and of corporate accountability as the possible components of a Canadian conceptual framework. Each of these components will be examined later.

Problems Faced by Standard Setters

The "Stamp Report" begins with an examination of some of the problems accounting standard-setters have to face:

- How is economic reality to be measured in an unambiguous manner?
- What is the nature of accounting, since the question of how best to develop accounting standards rests on it?
- Are there permanent and universal concepts on which financial reporting and accounting standards rest?
- Who are the users, what kind of decisions are they apt to make as the result of reading an annual report, and what kind of information will they be looking for in the report on which to base these decisions?
- What criteria do standard setters, preparers, and users need to judge the quality of accounting standards, to choose between the possible alternative standards on any given subject, and to assess the utility of published accounting reports?
- How can the costs and benefits be estimated when deciding what action to take in the area of standard setting?
- Can standards resolve the conflicts of interests between preparers and users and between different users by achieving neutrality?
- How useful is a published accounting report in the light of the "efficient market" evidence? Is the report predictive? Is it too concise, and does it include too much information?
- Should there be extensions to disclosure? Should these extensions include disclosure?
- Given that the process of accounting standardization is to narrow the areas of difference, is the resulting increase in uniformity possible? How can stifling the

process of legitimate innovation in accounting measurement be avoided and the trend toward the "book of rules" be accelerated?

- Should information be made available regarding the size of the margins of error in preparing accounts, or should the illusion of precision be presented?
- Are general-purpose reports enough? If not, should additional information be published in the form of supplementary statements or by adding further columns to the present financial reports?
- How should standards be enforced? (It is, however, noted that since 1975 the Canada Business Corporation Act specified that the operational definition of generally accepted accounting principles is the set of accounting pronouncements in the Canadian Institute of Chartered Accountants Handbook.)

Conceptual Issues in Standard Setting

In addition to the problems just outlined, Stamp has identified some complex conceptual issues that accountants must face in formulating their standards:

- *Allocation problems:* accountants must make periodic measurements of the financial position and performance of an enterprise and, in the process, develop systematic and rational methods of allocation. Unfortunately, these allocations are generally arbitrary and incorrigible.
- *Income problems:* should income be regarded and defined as the result of matching costs against revenues, or as the change in the net assets of the entity during a period?
- *Reporting focus:* should the proprietary concept (which looks at the financial affairs of an enterprise through the eyes of its owners) or the entity concept (which looks at the financial affairs of the enterprise from within, as it were) be used?
- *Capital-maintenance concepts:* which capital-maintenance concept is most suitable?
- *Asset-valuation base:* which asset-valuation base is to be used — historical cost, replacement cost, net realizable value, or value to the firm?
- *Economic reality:* what is economic reality? Can the balance sheet measure the current worth of an enterprise? As an example, the goodwill problem is presented as insolvable. As Stamp states:

> The problem of how to account for goodwill, especially internally generated goodwill, is probably the most perplexing problem in accounting, and one that is almost certainly irresolvable. Human talent, technical and other know-how, and many other largely unquantifiable assets are involved, making the measurement task virtually insoluble... many of the perplexing problems of accounting are indeed irresolvable in the sense that a unique solution is neither possible nor necessary.[37]

The Objectives of Corporate Financial Reporting

Now that we have outlined the problems and conceptual issues of — and the need for — accounting standards, we will examine the objectives of financial reporting. These objectives are assumed to apply to all legitimate users of published corporate financial reports.

The first major objective concerns accountability:

One of the primary objectives of published corporate financial reports is to provide an accounting by management exercise of its stewardship function but also of its success (or otherwise) in achieving the goal of producing a satisfactory economic performance by the enterprise and maintaining it in a strong and healthy financial position.[38]

The objective is then extended to all types of users:

In short, an important objective of financial reporting is the provision of useful information to all of the potential users of such information in a form and in a time frame that is relevant to their various needs.[39]

The second major objective concerns uncertainty and risk. Although it is impossible to eliminate uncertainty and risk,

. . . it is an objective of good financial reporting to provide such information in such a form as to minimize uncertainty about the validity of the information, and to enable the user to make his or her own assessment of the risks associated with the enterprise.[40]

The third major objective concerns change and innovation:

It is therefore necessary that the standards governing financial reporting should have ample scope for innovation and evolution as improvements become feasible.[41]

The fourth major objective concerns complexity and the unsophisticated user. The objectives of financial reporting

. . . should be taken to be directed towards the needs of users who are capable of comprehending a complete (and necessarily sophisticated) set of financial statements or, alternatively, to the needs of experts who will be called on by unsophisticated users to advise them.[42]

Users of Corporate Reports

Attention now shifts to the users. Users demand accountability, but a major issue must be resolved to strike the right balance between accountability and the right to privacy. Because accountability is a broader concept in Canada than it is in the United States, the range of users is broader in Canada than the range of users considered by the FASB's conceptual-framework project. The range of Canadian users includes the following fifteen categories:

- Shareholders (present and potential);
- long-term creditors (present and potential);
- short-term creditors (present and potential);
- analysts and advisers serving the above (present);
- employees (past, present, and potential);
- nonexecutive directors (present and potential);
- customers (past, present, and potential);
- suppliers (present and potential);
- industry groups (present);
- labor unions (present);
- governmental departments and ministers (present);

- the public (present);
- regulatory agencies (present);
- other companies, both domestic and foreign (present); and
- standard setters and academic researchers (present).[43]

Users' Needs

After the types of users are determined, the next step is to determine their informational needs. This task is complicated by the difficulties of determining the users' decision models. The "Stamp Report" emphasized that "one of the most difficult problems in developing accounting standards arises from our ignorace about the nature of users' decision-making processes" and "about the rational (and often irrational) mental processes that users go through in reaching their decisions."[44] In any case, the following thirteen categories of user needs are proposed:

- assessing performance;
- assessing management quality;
- estimating future prospects;
- assessing financial strength and stability;
- assessing solvency;
- assessing liquidity;
- assessing risk and uncertainty;
- aiding resource allocation;
- making comparisons;
- making valuation decisions;
- assessing adaptability;
- determining compliance with the law or regulations; and
- assessing contributions to society.

Criteria for Assessment of the Quality of Standards and of Corporate Accountability

The next step is to define the criteria for assessment that are "the yardsticks whereby standard setters, as well as preparers and users of published financial statements, can decide whether . . . published financial statements are indeed meeting the needs of users and the objectives of financial reporting."[45] These criteria are to be used to decide which information can and ought to be excluded from financial statements. They included objectivity, comparability, full disclosure, freedom from bias, uniformity, materiality and cost-benefit effectiveness, flexibility, consistency, and conservatism.

Toward a Canadian Conceptual Framework

A conceptual framework project for Canada (and elsewhere), based on an evolutionary approach and resting on the concepts (objectives and criteria for assessment), is offered at the end of the "Stamp Report." Unlike the FASB's conceptual framework, which it deemed too normative (if not axiomatic) and too narrow in its scope (its primary concern is with the investors), the Canadian conceptual framework is based on an evolutionary (rather than revolutionary) approach and would be less narrow in its scope (its primary concern is with the reasonable needs of the legitimate users of published financial reports). Furthermore, a public justification and explanation of the standards is suggested, to win general acceptance of the Canadian conceptual framework.

It is now up to the Canadian Institute of Chartered Accountants to evaluate the recommendations of the "Stamp Report" and to develop a truly Canadian conceptual framework. The report is successful in listing the major conceptual problems encountered in developing any framework and also provides a basis or background so that more and more research can be conducted.

Reactions to the "Stamp Report" have been mixed. It has been rightfully perceived as an opinion document:

> In the final analysis, *Corporate Reporting* is an opinion document. It is not, nor do I believe it attempts to be, a classic inquiry-type research study. Rather, it is based on the informed opinion of a group of experienced and capable accountants.[46]

The Report has also been characterized as confusing, before it finally opts for a socioeconomic-political world view:

> We might conclude that the "Stamp Report," though arriving at many blind alleys, going through several iterations, and making several detours, does arrive at a position on a world view that might prove to be very fruitful in the development of public accounting theory and standards — the socioeconomic-political world view.[47]

Finally, practitioners found the Report's recommendations either far from practical,[48] or too costly to implement.[49]

7.5   DISCUSSIONS AND CONCLUSIONS

Logically, the formulation of an accounting theory entails a sequential process that begins with the development of the objectives of financial statements and ends with the derivation of a conceptual framework or constitution to be used as a guide to accounting techniques. Such a process was initiated and is manifested by:

APB Statement No. 4

The "Trueblood Report"

The Corporate Report

The "Stamp Report"

The FASB's conceptual-framework project.

The FASB's conceptual framework is by far the most advanced project in the creation of an accounting constitution. Its major benefit is that it will facilitate the resolution of conceptual disputes in the standard-setting process. To be effective, this constitution must gain general acceptance, represent collective behavior, and protect the public interest in areas in which it is affected by financial reporting. Can this be achieved? Several issues must be resolved before this question can be adequately answered.

The conceptual framework may not be sufficient to resolve certain standard-setting problems. Some of these problems are related to the social-choice aspect of accounting standard setting. One prevailing idea is that it is impossible to develop a set of accounting standards that can be applied to accounting alternatives in a way that will satisfy everybody.[50] In response to this pessimistic view, Cushing suggests that those who reject the possibility of finding an unobjectionable social-welfare function may be overstating the problem.[51] A partial, piecemeal approach is recommended by Cushing as a way of tackling accounting problems. Bromwich, however, feels that the conditions for successful use of the partial approach are fairly restrictive.[52] His analysis suggests that:

> Cushing's approach of seeking the best out of a set of mutually exclusive standards for a given accounting problem, while holding all other standards constant, will be successful only where interdependence of the utility, attached to the outcomes addressed by that standard, from all the outcomes affected by other standards can be assumed.[53]

The conceptual framework must be workable and acceptable to all interested parties. The workability of the conceptual framework may be hampered by the level of abstractness of some of the qualitative characteristics and other recommendations. The acceptability of the conceptual framework may be hampered by the difficulty of resolving the conflicts of interest of all users and by the fear that the framework may be calling for radical changes in business reporting. One way of determining acceptability is to reaffirm the soundness of the reasoning underlying the elements of the framework. As Horngren states:

> A major role of the conceptual framework is ultimately to enhance the likelihood of acceptability of specific statements to be proposed or already in place. The more plausible the assumptions and the more compelling the analysis of the facts, the greater the chance of winning the support of diverse interests — and retaining and enhancing the Board's power.[54]

The ultimate test of the conceptual framework is its implementation and survival. In substance, the framework should exist in more than form. A view that the conceptual framework may be forgotten presents the following argument:

> Our initial guess is that the objectives selected by the board will be ignored in future rule-making activities, just as were those from previous authoritative attempts. Following the publication of these objectives, the Board will probably feel obligated to pay lip service to them in future pronouncements, but these pronouncements will not be affected in any substantive way by what is contained in the present documents.[55]

One way of dismissing this view is to ensure that the conceptual framework be used to resolve controversial accounting issues. But will the conceptual framework guide the FASB in correcting some of these accounting problems? Dopuch and Sunder make a strong argument that the framework is unlikely to help resolve major accounting issues or to set standards.[56] They illustrate their point by analyzing three much-debated accounting techniques:

> The FASB's definition of liabilities is so general that at this stage we cannot predict the Board's position on deferred taxes. However, those who favor the recognition of deferred taxes can adopt a somewhat broad interpretation of the FASB's definition of liabilities to justify the inclusion of deferred taxes as an element of financial statements, particularly at the individual asset level. In contrast, those who do could take the FASB's statements literally and just as easily argue against the inclusion of deferred taxes.[57]

The conceptual framework is also shown to support either a full-cost or a successful-efforts method for oil and gas accounting. The only explicit statement bearing on this problem is that "information about enterprise earnings and its components measured by accrual accounting generally provides a better indication of enterprise performance than information about current cash receipts and payments." However, both full-cost and successful-efforts accounting are forms of accrual accounting, so that proponents of the former (for example, the Federal Trade Commission) have the same support for their position as do the proponents of the latter (for example, the FASB).[58]

Finally, with regard to the asset-valuation debate, Dopuch and Sunder conclude that:

> no conceptual framework, however logically conceived, can counter practical issues regarding the reliability of estimates of, say, replacement costs. So the issue is not whether costs are useful in making economic decisions;" rather, the issue is what criteria may be used to determine alternative estimates of unknown parameters.[59]

Three other issues concern the conceptual framework:

First, the conceptual framework has often been referred to as a kind of constitution. Yet there may be great differences that make the analogy an imperfect one, and at the same time a strong case for the conceptual framework. Solomons, for example, cites the following three differences:

> 1. A constitution has the force of law. A conceptual framework has no authority except that which flows from its intellectual pervasiveness.
> 2. Constitutions contain many arbitrary elements, for example, the number of senators each state is to have, the length of the interval between elections, and so forth. There is no room for arbitrariness in a conceptual framework.
> 3. There are significant differences among the nations of the world in their constitutional arrangements. There could be important national differences among conceptual frameworks — this is mere speculation because no country other than the United States has yet made any attempt to construct one.[60]

Second, Miller points to eight myths about conceptual frameworks:

> The myth that the Accounting Principles Board failed because it did not have a conceptual framework.
> FASB cannot succeed unless it has a conceptual framework.
> A conceptual framework will lead to consistent standards.
> That a conceptual framework will eliminate the problem of standard overload.
> That the FASB's conceptual framework captures only the status quo of accounting practice.
> That the conceptual framework project has cost more than it should have.
> That the FASB will revise the existing standards to make them consistent with the conceptual framework.
> That the FASB has abandoned the conceptual framework project.[61]

The realities are that the framework is a political document that is not the ultimate authority for resolving issues; it is neither a complete description of existing practice nor a blueprint for the future. It is a point of departure for future debates.[62]

Third, the conceptual framework is not going to provide all the answers, but at least it will provide a direction for setting standards and reduce the influence of personal biases and political pressures in making accounting judgments.[63]

Various scenarios await the conceptual framework project. Sterling offers his views of the future as follows:

The most pessimistic one is that the Board meets so much resistance that it fails to complete the task and reverts to "ad hocery." The most optimistic scenario, indeed widely optimistic, is that I can convince everyone that it is possible for accounting to become a scientific discipline and thereby rely more on the method of science — empirical and logical testing — and less on the method of authority. The most likely scenario is that the Board will complete this task, albeit faced with increasing resistance, and will therefore be forced to slow it down or water it down or both. Thus, the most likely scenario is that the Board will continue to make progress, continue to improve accounting, but that this will occur by inching along and not by quantum leap.[64]

It is very hard not to agree with the most likely scenario as described, as the Board continue to improve gradually through a "muddling through" process created by the political quagmire that characterizes the accounting environment and its interests groups. The Board, however, ought to consider the useful suggestions offered in the literature. The best suggestions for improvement, offered by Agrawal, are as follows:

The need to make an explicit distinction between what the FASB considers to be the basic concepts and policy issues. Only the basic concepts should be the subject matter of the conceptual framework. Policy issues are those that depend upon the particular circumstance of each case and may need to be changed with changes in circumstances over time. These issues should be addressed by FASB's standard-setting function. The primary accounting model will be the connecting link between the two categories. This, in turn, would involve specification of:
  (a) the attribute to be measured;
  (b) the capital maintenance concept;
  (c) timing of recognition (particularly of revenues/gains and expenses/losses);
  (d) relative importance to be placed on the Income Statement and Balance Sheet; and
  (e) the unit of measurement.

FASB should indicate the primary model it implies in its standards currently, with a proviso that exceptions may be made for dominant, but specific, reasons. The justification must be based upon the objectives of financial reporting, qualitative characteristics of information, definitions of elements and the recognition criteria. FASB should also state that it might experiment with other models under appropriate circumstances and that a different model might be adopted as the primary model when considered appropriate.
  The need to specify a temporal hierarchy of objectives and needs. The first tier should consist of those the fulfillment of which is sought currently (or in the near future). Subsequent tiers should be aimed for achievement in a more distant future when
  (a) there is a better understanding of information needed, and
  (b) means are available to provide such information.
The ideas of "freedom from error" and "precision" that have been used rather ambiguously should be integrated properly in the qualitative characteristics. This will require consideration of several related concepts that have been considered only briefly in the network, including:
  (a) accuracy;
  (b) truth or truthfulness; and
  (c) evenhandedness or fairness.
The need to provide criteria for the disclosure of items that are not formally "recognized." These criteria may be the same as for formal recognition but might also provide for:

(a) disclosure of attribute(s) in addition to those under the primary accounting model; and

(b) explanation or further details of items that are formally recognized.[65]

NOTES

[1] Devine, C.T., "Research Methodology and Accounting Theory Formulation," *The Accounting Review* (July, 1960), p. 399.

[2] Watts, R.L., and Zimmerman, J.L., "The Demand for and Supply of Accounting Theories: The Market for Excuses," *The Accounting Review* (April, 1979), pp. 273–305.

[3] *Objectives of Financial Statements* (New York: American Institute of Certified Public Accountants, 1973).

[4] FASB Discussion Memorandum, *Conceptual Framework for Financial Accounting and Reporting: Elements of Financial Statements and Their Measurement* (Stamford, Ct.: Financial Accounting Standards Board, 1976).

[5] The Accounting Standards Steering Committee, *The Corporate Report* (London: The Institute of Chartered Accountants, 1980).

[6] Stamp, Edward, *Corporate Reporting: Its Future Evolution* (Toronto: Canadian Institute of Chartered Accountants, 1980).

[7] APB Statement No. 4, *Basic Concepts and Accounting Principles Underlying Financial Statements of Business Enterprises* (New York: American Institute of Certified Public Accountants, 1970).

[8] Cyert, R.M., and Ijiri, Yuji, "Problems of Implementing the Trueblood Objectives Report," in *Studies on Financial Accounting Objectives*, supplement to Vol. 12, *Journal of Accounting Research* (1974), p. 29.

[9] Cramer, J.J., Jr., and Sorter, G.H. (eds), *Objectives of Financial Statements: Selected Papers*, Vol. 2 (New York; American Institute of Certified Public Accountants, 1973).

[10] Sorter, G.H., and Gans, M.S., "Opportunities and Implications of the Report on Objectives of Financial Statements," in *Studies on Financial Accounting Objectives*, supplement to Vol. 12, *Journal of Accounting Research* (1974), pp. 1–12.

[11] *Objectives of Financial Statements: Selected Papers*, op. cit., p. 29.

[12] Ibid., p. 29.

[13] Ibid., p. 60.

[14] *The Conceptual Framework for Financial Accounting and Reporting: Elements of Financial Statements and Their Measurement* (Stamford, Ct.: Financial Accounting Standards Board, 1976), p. 4.

[15] Ibid., p. 2.

[16] *Scope and Implications of the Conceptual Framework Project* (Stamford, Ct.: Financial Accounting Standards Board, 1976), pp. 7–8.

[17] Sorter, G.H., "The Partitioning Dilemma," *Objectives of Financial Statements: Selected Papers*, Vol. 2, (eds) J.J. Cramer, Jr., and G.H. Sorter (New York: American Institute of Certified Public Accountants, 1974), p. 117.

[18] *A Statement of Basic Accounting Theory* (Evanston, Ill.: American Accounting Association, 1966), p. 118.

[19] APB Statement No. 4, op. cit., paragraph 57.

[20] Marple, R.P., "The Balance Sheet: Capital Sources and Composition," *Journal of Accountancy* (November, 1962), p. 57. Reprinted in R.P. Marple (ed.), *Toward a Basic Accounting Philosophy* (New York: National Association of Accountants, 1964), p. 69.

[21] Ibid., pp. 35–7.

[22] Norby, W.C., *The Financial Analysts Journal* (March/April, 1982), p. 22.

[23] Statement of Financial Accounting Concepts No. 1, *Objectives of Financial Reporting by Business Enterprises* (Stamford, Ct.: Financial Accounting Standards Board, 1980).

[24] Statement of Financial Accounting Concepts No. 2, *Qualitative Characteristics of Accounting Information* (Stamford, Ct.: Financial Accounting Standards Board, 1980).

[25] *A Statement of Basic Accounting Theory* (Evanston, Ill.: American Accounting Association, 1966), p. 9.

[26] *Statement of Accounting Theory and Theory Acceptance* (Sarasota, Florida: American Accounting Association, 1977), p. 16.

[27] *A Statement of Basic Accounting Theory*, op. cit., p. 10.

[28] APB Opinion No. 21, *Accounting Changes* (New York: American Institute of Certified Public Accountants, 1971), p. 391.

[29] Statement of Financial Accounting Concepts No. 2, op. cit., p. 58.

[30] Ibid., p. 53.

[31] Statement of Financial Accounting Concepts No. 3, *Elements of Financial Statements of Business Enterprises* (Stamford, Ct.: Financial Accounting Standards Board, 1980).

[32] Ibid., pp. xi–xii.

[33] *The Corporate Report*, op. cit., p. 10.

[34] Ibid., p. 16.

[35] Ibid., p. 17.

[36] Stamp, Edward, *Corporate Reporting: Its Future Evolution*, op. cit.

[37] Ibid., p. 19.

[38] Ibid., p. 33.

[39] Ibid., p. 34.

[40] Ibid., p. 35.

[41] Ibid., p. 36.

[42] Ibid., p. 38.

[43] Ibid., p. 44.

[44] Ibid., p. 48.

[45] Ibid., p. 52.

[46] Archibald, T. Ross, "A Research Perspective on *Corporate Reporting: Its Future Evolution*," in *Research to Support Standard Setting in Financial Accounting: A Canadian Perspective*, (eds) S. Basu and J. Alex Milburn (Toronto: The Clarkson Gordon Foundation, 1982), p. 229.

[47] Derhirst, John F., "An Evaluation of Corporate Reporting: Its Future Evolution Based on Different 'World Views,' " in *Research to Support Standard Setting in Financial Accounting: A Canadian Perspective*, op. cit., p. 244.

[48] Fowler, G.C., "A Public Practitioner's View of Corporate Reporting: Its Future Evolution," in *Research to Support Standard Setting in Financial Accounting: A Canadian Perspective*, op. cit., p. 253.

[49] Park, R.W., "Is *Corporate Reporting* Asking Too Much?," *The Canadian Chartered Accountant Magazine* (December, 1981), pp. 34–7.

[50] Demski, Joel S., "The Choice Among Financial Reporting Alternatives," *The Accounting Review* (April, 1974), pp. 718–83.

[51] Cushing, B.E., "On the Possibility of Optimal Accounting Principles," *The Accounting Review* (April, 1977), pp. 380–421.

[52] Bromwich, M., "The Possibility of Partial Accounting Standards," *The Accounting Review* (April, 1980), pp. 288–300.

[53] Ibid., p. 299.

[54] Horngren, Charles T., "Uses and Limitations of a Conceptual Framework," *Journal of Accountancy* (April, 1981), p. 90.

[55] Dopuch N., and Sunder, S., "FASB's Statements on Objectives and Elements of Financial Accounting: A Review," *The Accounting Review* (January, 1980), p. 8.

[56] Ibid., p. 8.

[57] Ibid., pp. 6–7.

[58] Ibid., p. 7.

[59] Ibid., pp. 7–8.

[60] Solomons, David, "The FASB's Conceptual Framework: An Evaluation," *Journal of Accountancy* (June, 1986), p. 115.

[61] Miller, Paul B., "The Conceptual Framework: Myths and Realities," *Journal of Accountancy* (March, 1985), pp. 62–71.

[62] Ibid.

[63] Pacter, Paul A., "The Conceptual Framework: Make no Mystique About it," *Journal of Accountancy* (July, 1983), p. 88.

[64] Sterling, Robert R., "The Conceptual Framework: An Assessment," *The Journal of Accountancy* (November, 1982), p. 108.

[65] Agrawal, Surendra P., "On the Conceptual Framework of Accounting," *Journal of Accounting Literature* (June, 1987), pp. 176–7.

REFERENCES

The "Trueblood Report"

Anton, H.R. "Objectives of Financial Accounting: Review and Analysis," *Journal of Accountancy* (January, 1976), pp. 40–51.

Beaver, W.H., "What Should Be the FASB's Objectives?" *Journal of Accountancy* (August, 1973), pp. 49–56.

Beaver, W.H., and Demski, Joel S., "The Nature of Financial Objectives: A Summary and Synthesis," in *Studies in Financial Accounting Objectives: 1974*, supplement to Vol. 12, *Journal of Accounting Research* (1974), pp. 170–87.

Bird, P., "Objectives and Methods of Financial Reporting: A Generalized Search Procedure," *Accounting and Business Research* (Summer, 1975), pp. 23–32.

Carlsberg, B., Hope, A., and Scapens, R.W., "The Objectives of Published Accounting Reports," *Accounting and Business Research* (Summer, 1974), pp. 34–50.

Chastain, C.E., "Accounting Objectives and User Needs: A Behavioral View," *National Public Accountant* (May, 1974), pp. 24–7.

Chastain, C.E., "Accounting Objectives and User Needs: A Behavioral View," *National Public Accountant* (June, 1974), pp. 26–31.

Chen, R.S., "Social and Financial Stewardship," *The Accounting Review* (July, 1975), pp. 533–43.

Clinton, R.P., "Objectives of Financial Statements," *Journal of Accountancy* (November, 1972), pp. 56–68.

Cramer, J.J., Jr., and Sorter, G.H. (eds), *Objectives of Financial Statements: Selected Papers*, Vol. 2 (New York: American Institute of Certified Public Accountants, 1973).

Cyert, R.M., and Ijiri, Yuji, "Problems of Implementing the Trueblood Objectives Report," in *Studies on Financial Accounting Objectives*, supplement to Vol. 12, *Journal of Accounting Research* (1974), pp. 29–42.

Mautz, R.K., "Accounting Objectives — The Conservative View," *CPA Journal* (September, 1973), pp. 771, 774–7.

Most, K.S., and Winters, A.L., "Focus on Standard Setting: From Trueblood to the FASB," *Journal of Accountancy* (February, 1977), pp. 67–75.

Scott, G., and Decelles, M., "United States: Objectives of Financial Reporting Revisited," *Accountant's Magazine* (February, 1980), pp. 16–23.

Sorter, G.H., and Gans, M.S., "Opportunities and Implications of the Report on Objectives of Financial Statements," in *Studies on Financial Accounting Objectives*, supplement to Vol. 12, *Journal of Accounting Research (1974)*, pp. 1–12.

Williams, R.J., "Differing Opinions on Accounting Objectives," *CPA Journal* (August, 1973), pp. 651–6.

The Conceptual Framework

Agrawal, Surendra, P., "On the Conceptual Framework of Accounting," *Journal of Accounting Literature* (Vol. 6, 1987), pp. 165–78.

Brown, W.W., "Industry and Conceptual Framework," *Journal of Accountancy* (August, 1980), pp. 20–25.

Depree, C.M., Jr., "Testing and Evaluating a Conceptual Framework of Accounting," *Abacus* (September, 1989), pp. 61–73.

Edwards, J.D., Wyatt, A.R., and Defliese, P.L., "Conceptual Framework for Accounting Standards," in *Contemporary Issues in Accounting*, (eds) D.D. Alhasim and J.W. Robertson (Indianapolis: Bobbs-Merrill Educational Publishing, 1975), pp. 1–54.

Gerboth, Dale, "The Conceptual Framework: Not Definitions, But Professional Values," *Accounting Horizons* (September, 1987), pp. 1–9.

Heath, Lloyd C., "The Conceptual Framework as Literature," *Accounting Horizons* (June, 1988), pp. 100–104.

Holder, W.W., and Hanendy, K., "A Framework for Building an Accounting Constitution," *Journal of Accounting, Auditing, and Finance* (Winter, 1982), pp. 110–25.

Horngren, Charles T., "Uses and Limitations of a Conceptual Framework," *Journal of Accountancy* (April, 1981), pp. 86–95.

Ijiri, Yuji, "Critique of the APB Fundamentals Statement," *Journal of Accountancy* (November, 1971), pp. 43–50.

Kirk, D.J., "Concepts, Consensus, Compromise, and Consequence: Their Roles in Standard Setting," *Journal of Accountancy* (April, 1981), pp. 85–6.

Koepper, David R., "Using the FASB's Conceptual Framework: Fitting the Pieces Together," *Business Horizons* (June, 1988), pp. 18–26.

Langenderfer, H.Q., "Conceptual Framework for Financial Reporting." *Journal of Accountancy* (July, 1973), pp. 46–55.

Miller, Paul B.W., "The Conceptual Framework as Reformation and Counterreformation," *Business Horizons* (June, 1990), pp. 23–32.

Murray, Dennis and Raymond Johnson, "Differential GAAP and the FASB's Conceptual Framework," *Journal of Accounting, Auditing and Finance* (Fall, 1983), pp. 4–16.

Peasnell, K.V., "The Function of a Conceptual Framework for Corporate Financial Reporting," *Accounting and Business Research* (Autumn, 1982), pp. 243–56.

Practer, Paul A., "The Conceptual Framework: Make No Mystique About it," *Journal of Accountancy* (July, 1983), pp. 76–88.

Schattke, R.W., "An Analysis of APB Statement No. 4," *The Accounting Review* (April, 1972), pp. 233–44.

Shultis, R.L., "Opinion: FASB — The Only 'Game' in Town," *Management Accounting* (March, 1981), pp. 6,47.

Sprouse, Robert T., "The Importance of Earnings in the Conceptual Framework," *Journal of Accountancy* (January, 1978), pp. 64–71.

Solomons, David, "The FASB's Conceptual Framework: An Evaluation," *Journal of Accountancy* (June, 1986), pp. 114–25.

Statement of Financial Accounting Concepts No. 1, *The Objectives of Financial Reporting by Business Enterprises* (Stamford, Ct.: Financial Accounting Standards Board, 1978).

Statement of Financial Accounting Concepts No. 2, *Qualitative Characteristics of Accounting Information* (Stamford, Ct.: Financial Accounting Standards Board, 1980).

Statement of Financial Accounting Concepts No. 3, *Elements of Financial Statements of Business Enterprises* (Stamford, Ct.: Financial Accounting Standards Board, 1980).

Statement of Financial Accounting Concepts No. 4, *Objectives of Financial Reporting by Nonbusiness Organizations* (Stamford, Ct.: Financial Accounting Standards Board, 1975).

Statement of Financial Accounting Concepts No. 5, *Recognition and Measurement in Financial Statement of Business Enterprises* (Stamford, Ct.: Financial Accounting Standards Board, 1984).

Statement of Financial Accounting Concepts No. 6, *Elements of Financial Statements: A Replacement of FASB Concepts Statement No. 3* (Stamford, Ct.: Financial Accounting Standards Board, 1985).

Storey, R.K., "Conditions Necessary for Developing a Conceptual Framework," *FASB Viewpoints* (March 3, 1981), pp. 1–6.

Storey, R.K., "Conditions Necessary for Developing a Conceptual Framework," *Journal of Accountancy* (June, 1981), pp. 84–96.

Walter, H.E., II, and Sale, J.T., "Financial Reporting: A Two-Perspective Issue," *Management Accounting* (June, 1981), pp. 33–37.

The Corporate Report

The Accounting Standards Steering Committee, *The Corporate Report* (London: The Institute of Chartered Accountants in England and Wales, 1975).

Climo, Tom, "What's Happening in Britain?" *Journal of Accountancy* (February, 1976), pp. 55–9.

Harrison, R.B., "Corporate Report: A Critique," *The Chartered Accountant Magazine* (December–January, 1976), pp. 27–33.

The "Stamp Report"

Archibald, T. Ross., "A Research Perspective on *Corporate Reporting: Its Future Revolution*," in *Research to Support Standard Setting in Financial Accounting: A Canadian Perspective*, (eds) S. Basu and J. Alex Milburn (Toronto: The Clarkson Gordon Foundation, 1982), pp. 218–30.

Denman, J.H., "Corporate Reporting and the Conceptual Framework Issue," *The Chartered Accountant Magazine* (April, 1981), pp. 74, 76–8.

Dewhirst, John F., "An Evaluation in Corporate Reporting: Its Future Evolution," Based on *Different 'World Views'*, in *Research to Support Standard Setting in Financial Accounting: A Canadian Perspective*, op. cit., pp. 231–46.

Falk, H., "Do We Really Need Accounting and Auditing Standards?" *The Chartered Accountant Magazine* (October, 1980), pp. 40–5.

Fowler, G.C., "A Public Practitioner's View of Corporate Reporting; Its Future Evolution," in *Research to Support Standard Setting in Financial Accounting: A Canadian Perspective*, op. cit., pp. 247–53.

Park, R.W., "Is *Corporate Reporting* Asking Too Much?" *The Chartered Accountant Magazine* (December, 1981), pp. 34–7.

Stamp, Edward, "Accounting Standard Setting — A New Beginning," *The Chartered Accountant Magazine* (September, 1980), pp. 38–42.

Stamp, Edward, *Corporate Reporting: Its Future Evolution* (Toronto: Canadian Institute of Chartered Accountants, 1980).

Stephen, Elliot, "Accounting and Canada," *Arthur Anderson Chronicle* (July, 1974), pp. 78–82.

QUESTIONS

7.1 Why is it important to know the objectives of accounting in order to construct an accounting theory?

7.2 List the various attempts to develop the objectives of accounting in the United States, Canada, and the United Kingdom.

7.3 Describe the conflicts of interest in the information market and the impact of such conflicts on the methodology for the development of accounting objectives.

7.4 Evaluate the methodology used by the Trueblood Committee.

7.5 List and Discuss the twelve objectives of financial statements contained in the "Trueblood Report".

7.6 List and discuss the seven qualitative characteristics of reporting contained in the "Trueblood Report".

7.7 What economic entities are identified in *The Corporate Report*?

7.8 List and explain the different financial statements advocated by *The Corporate Report*.

7.9 What is meant by an "accounting constitution?"

7.10 Explain the different views about measuring earnings.

7.11 Recently, the accounting profession has shown substantial interest in delineating the objectives and principles of accounting. For example, APB Statement No. 4, *Basic Concepts and Accounting Principles Underlying Financial Statements of Business Enterprises*, (1) discuss the nature of financial accounting, the environmental forces that influence it, and the potential and limitations of financial accounting in providing useful information, (2) sets forth the objectives of financial accounting and financial statements, and (3) presents a description of present generally accepted accounting principles.

Required

a. Discuss the basic purpose of financial accounting and financial statements.

b. Identify and discuss each of the general and each of the qualitative objectives of financial accounting and financial statements.   (*AICPA adapted*)

7.12 In "Opportunities and Implications of the Report on Objectives of Financial Statements" (in *Studies on Financial Accounting Objectives*, supplement to Vol. 12, *Journal of Accounting Research* (1974), pp. 1–2.) G.H. Sorter and M.S. Gans made the following statement concerning the importance of the "*Trueblood Report*" and the objectives suggested:

The Report's mere existence and acknowledgement can have profound implications for the development of accounting standards and the resolution of accounting problems. No longer should it be possible to legislate accounting standards by fiat; no longer should it be possible to thunder "Thou shalt" without continuing with "because." If the existence of explicit objectives is acknowledged, then each proposed accounting standard should be evaluated in terms of how the standard relates to and furthers the objectives. Disagreement relating to alternative standards should be analyzed and resolved in terms of what standard relates to and furthers the objectives. In other words, for something to be a part of the recognized body of generally accepted accounting principles, it should be demonstrated to be right because it is the best available means for executing the objectives.

In your opinion, how valid is this implication?

7.13 What are the differences between *complete* and *incomplete* earnings cycles?

7.14 What is meant by *earning power*?

7.15 Explain the differences among the three distinct views of measuring earnings: the *asset/liability view*, the *revenue/expense view*, and the *nonarticulated view*.

7.16 Should the asset/liability view, the revenue/expense view or the nonarticulated view be adopted as the basis for a conceptual framework for financial accounting and reporting? Discuss your answer.

7.17 Explain the differences between the definitions of *assets, liabilities, revenues, expenses, gains*, and *losses* according to the asset/liability view and the revenue/expense view. Which alternative definition should make up the substance of a definition of assets, liabilities, revenues, expenses, gains, and losses for a conceptual framework for financial accounting and reporting?

7.18 What are the arguments to support *articulation*? What are the arguments to support *nonarticulation*?

7.19 Evaluate the three different formulations of the relationship between earnings and its components.

7.20 List the different concepts of *capital maintenance*. How do they differ?

7.21 Discuss the *objectives* of financial reporting by business enterprises.

7.22 Discuss the nature and purpose of the *qualitative criteria* for selecting and evaluating financial accounting and reporting policies.

7.23 In "Recommendations and Accounting Theory" (in *Studies in Accounting Theory*, (eds) W.T. Baxter and Sidney Davidson, London: Sweet and Maxwell, 1962. p. 427), Baxter makes the following statement:

Recommendations by authority on matters of accounting theory may in the short run seem unmixed blessings. In the end, however, they will probably do harm. They are likely to yield little fresh knowledge . . . . They are likely to weaken the education of accountants: the conversion of the subject into cut-and-dried rules, approved by authority and not to be lightly questioned, threatens to reduce its value as a subject of liberal education almost to *nil*. They are likely to narrow the scope of individual thought and judgment: and a group of men who resign their hard problems to others must eventually give up all claim to be a learned profession.

Does this statement apply to the FASB's effort to develop a conceptual framework? Explain your answer.

7.24 The Financial Accounting Standards Board (FASB) has been developing a conceptual framework for financial accounting and reporting. The FASB has issued four Statements of Financial Accounting Concepts, intended to set forth objectives and fundamentals that will provide the basis for developing financial accounting and reporting standards. The *objectives* identify the goals and purposes of financial reporting. The *fundamentals* are the underlying concepts of financial accounting — concepts that guide the selection of transactions, events, and circumstances to be accounted for; their recognition and measurement; and the means of summarizing and communicating them to interested parties.

The purpose of Statement of Financial Accounting Concepts No. 2. *Qualitative Characteristics of Accounting Information* is to examine the characteristics that make accounting information useful. The characteristics or qualities of information discussed in this statement are the ingredients that make information useful and the qualities to be sought when accounting choices must be made.

Required

a. Identify and discuss the benefits that can be expected to be derived from the FASB's conceptual-framework project.
b. What is the most important quality of accounting information identified in Statement of Financial Accounting Concepts No. 2? Explain why this is the most important quality.
c. Statement of Financial Accounting Concepts No. 2 describes a number of key characteristics or qualities of accounting information. Briefly discuss the importance of any three of these qualities for financial reporting purposes.

(CMA adapted)

7.25 Characteristics of Useful Information

Financial accounting and reporting provide information that is used in decision making regarding the allocation of resources. In Statement of Financial Accounting Concepts No. 1, *Objectives of Financial Reporting by Business Enterprises*, the Financial Accounting Standards Board (FASB) defined the following basic objectives of financial reporting.

Financial reporting should provide understandable information to present and potential users:

That is useful in making rational decisions.

That facilitates assessing the amounts, timing, and uncertainty related to the enterprise's cash flows.

About the enterprise's economic resources, its claims to those resources, and the changes in its resources and obligations occurring from earnings and other operating activities.

The qualitative characteristics of useful accounting information were identified in the FASB's Statement of Financial Concepts No. 2, *Qualitative Characteristics of Accounting Information*. These characteristics distinguish better information (more useful) from inferior information (less useful).

Required

1 For the primary quality relevance,
  a. define relevance
  b. explain the meaning and importance of each of the three ingredients of relevance
2 For the primary quality reliability,
  a. define reliability
  b. explain the meaning and importance of each of the three ingredients of reliability
3 Explain the concepts of
  a. comparability
  b. consistency
  c. materiality   (*CMA adapted*)

7.26 Standard Setting

When the Accounting Principles Board was founded in 1959, it planned to establish financial accounting standards using empirical research and logical reasoning only; the role of political action was little recognized at this time. Today, there is wide acceptance of the view that political action is as much an ingredient of the standard-setting process as is research evidence. Considerable political and social influence is wielded by user groups, those parties who are most interested in or affected by accounting standards.

Two basic premises of the Financial Accounting Standards Board (FASB) are that (1) it should be responsive to the needs and viewpoints of the entire economic community and (2) it should operate in full view of the public, affording interested parties ample opportunity to make their views known. The extensive procedural steps employed by the FASB in the standard-setting process support these premises.

Required

Describe why financial accounting standards inspire or encourage political action and social involvement during the standard-setting process.   (*CMA adapted*)

7.27 Conceptual Framework

The Financial Accounting Standards Board (FASB) has been working on a conceptual framework for financial accounting and reporting. The FASB has issued 6 Statements of Financial Accounting Concepts. These statements are intended to set forth objectives and fundamentals that will be the basis for developing financial accounting and reporting standards. The objectives identify the goals and purposes of financial reporting. The fundamentals are the underlying concepts of financial accounting — concepts that guide the selection of transactions, events, and circumstances to be accounted for; their recognition and measurement; and the means of summarizing and communicating them to interested parties.

The purpose of Statement of Financial Accounting Concepts No. 2, *Qualitative Characteristics of Accounting Information,* is to examine the characteristics that make accounting information useful. The characteristics or qualities of information discussed in Concepts No. 2 are the ingredients that make information useful and are the qualities to be sought when accounting choices are made.

Required

1. Identify and discuss the benefits which can be expected to be derived from the FASB's conceptual framework study.
2. What is the most important quality for accounting information as identified in Statement of Financial Accounting Concepts No. 2 and explain why it is the most important.
3. Statement of Financial Accounting Concepts No. 2 describes a number of key characteristics or qualities for accounting information. Briefly discuss the importance of understandability, relevance, and reliability for financial reporting.

(*CMA adapted*)

7.28 Objectives, Users, and Stewardship

The owners of CSC Inc., a privately held company, are considering a public offering of the company's common stock as a means of acquiring additional funding. Preparatory to making a decision about a public offering, the owners had a lengthy conversation with John Duncan, CSC's Chief Financial Officer. Duncan informed the owners of the reporting requirements of the Securities and Exchange Commission, including the necessity for audited financial statements. At the request of the owners, Duncan also discussed the objectives of financial reporting, the sophistication of users of financial information, and the stewardship responsibilities of management, all of which are addressed in Statement of Financial Accounting Concepts No. 1, *Objectives of Financial Reporting by Business Enterprises.*

Required

1. Discuss the primary objectives of financial reporting.
2. Describe the level of sophistication that can be expected of the users of financial information.
3. Explain the stewardship responsibilities of management.   (*CMA adapted*)

CHAPTER 8

THE STRUCTURE OF ACCOUNTING THEORY

The general boundaries of accounting theory have previously been defined to be the measurement and communication of data revealing economic activity consisting of three elements:

1 data revealing economic activity
2 the measurement of data revealing economic activity and
3 communication of data revealing economic activity.[1]

A full appreciation of the current and future scope of accounting depends, however, on an understanding not only of accounting techniques but also of the *structure* of accounting theory from which the techniques are derived. The development of a structure of accounting theory to better justify the existing rules and techniques began with Paton's examination of the basic foundations of accounting.[2] The effort was continued by a number of accounting theorists who used either a deductive approach[3] or an inductive approach.[4] Their primary objectives were to codify the postulates and principles of accounting and to formulate a coherent accounting theory to enable accountants to improve the quality of financial reporting.

Although the resulting theories differ in terms of who uses accounting information, what constitutes the "use" of accounting data, and the nature of the environment assumed by users and preparers of the accounting data, all of these theories provide a frame of reference, or a structure of accounting theory, within which the adequacy of specific methods may be judged. Although the elements of the structure may differ according to the methodologies used and the assumptions made, a consensus exists in the literature and in practice regarding the primacy of certain elements as essential foundations of accounting theory. Accordingly, in this chapter, we will discuss the principal elements of the broad structure of accounting theory.

8.1   THE NATURE OF THE STRUCTURE OF AN ACCOUNTING THEORY

Whatever approaches and methodologies are used in the formulation of an accounting theory (deductive or inductive, normative or descriptive), the resultant frame of reference is based on a set of elements and relationships that govern the development of accounting techniques. As shown in Exhibit 8.1, the structure of an accounting theory contains the following elements:

1 A statement of the objectives of financial statements.
2 A statement of the postulates and the theoretical concepts of accounting concerned with the environmental assumptions and the nature of the accounting unit. These postulates and theoretical concepts are derived from the stated objectives.
3 A statement of basic accounting principles based on both the postulates and the theoretical concepts.
4 A body of accounting techniques derived from the accounting principles.

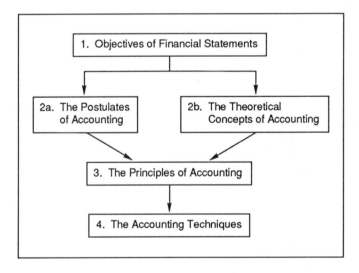

EXHIBIT 8.1

We discussed the first element — the formulation of the objectives of financial state-ments — in Chapter 7. Recall the importance of the objectives in the development of a structure of accounting theory. The fourth element — a body of knowledge or techniques for accountants — is the subject of other technique-oriented courses, and will not be covered here. In this chapter, we will discuss the remaining three elements of an accounting theory:

1 the postulates of accounting;
2 the theoretical concepts of accounting;
3 the principles of accounting.

8.2 THE NATURE OF ACCOUNTING POSTULATES, THEORETICAL CONCEPTS, AND PRINCIPLES

The development of the postulates, theoretical concepts, and principles of accounting has always been one of the most challenging and difficult tasks in accounting. The lack of a precise terminology, which has been recognized by most theorists, has compounded the problem. Littleton refers to this problem when he states that

> Each book usually contains a mixture of axioms, conventions, generalizations, methods, rules, postulates, practices, procedures, principles, and standards. These terms cannot all be synonymous.[5]

Such confusion may be avoided by considering the formulation of the structure of accounting theory as a deductive, interactive process in which the objectives of accounting provide the basis for both the postulates and the theoretical concepts from which the techniques are derived. We begin with the following definitions.

1 The *accounting postulates* are self-evident statements or axioms, generally accepted by virtue of their conformity to the objectives of financial statements, that portray the economic, political, sociological, and legal environments in which accounting must operate.
2 The *theoretical concepts* of accounting are also self-evident statements or axioms, also generally accepted by virtue of their conformity to the objectives of financial statements, that portray the nature of accounting entities operating in a free economy characterized by private ownership of property.
3 The *accounting principles* are general decision rules, derived from both the objectives and the theoretical concepts of accounting, that govern the development of accounting techniques.
4 The *accounting techniques* are specific rules derived from the accounting principles that account for specific transactions and events faced by the accounting entity.

8.3 THE ACCOUNTING POSTULATES

8.3.1 The Entity Postulate

Accounting measures the results of the operations of specific *entities*, which are separate and distinct from owners of entities. The entity postulate holds that each enterprise is an accounting unit separate and distinct from its owners and other firms. The postulate defines the accountant's area of interest and limits the number of objects, events, and events attributes that are to be included in financial statements. The postulate enables the accountant to distinguish between business and personal transactions: the accountant is to report the transactions of the enterprise, rather than the transactions of the enterprise's owners. The postulate also recognizes the fiduciary responsibility of management to stockholders. The entity concept applies to partnerships, sole proprietorships, corporations (incorporated and unincorporated), and small and large enterprises. It may also apply to a segment of a firm (such as a division) or to several firms (such as a consolidation of interrelated firms).

One way to define an *accounting entity* is to define the economic unit responsible for the economic activities and the administrative control of the unit. Postulate A.2 of Accounting Research Study No. 1 states that the "economic activity is carried on through specific units or entities."[6] This approach is better exemplified by the consolidated reporting of different entities as a single economic unit, regardless of their legal differences.

Another way to define an accounting entity is in terms of the economic interests of various users, instead of the economic activities and administrative control of the unit. This approach is user-oriented rather than firm-oriented. The interests of the users, not of the economic activities of the firm, define the boundaries of the accounting entity and the information to be included in the financial statements. The American Accounting Association's 1964 Concepts and Standards Research Study Committee on the Business Entity Concept supported this view, stating "the boundaries of such an economic entity are identifiable

1 by determining the interested individual or group, and
2 by determining the nature of that individual's or that group's interest."[7]

This second approach justified the possible data expansion that may result from the new scope of accounting as it attempts to meet the potential informational needs of all users. For example, information generated by the possible adoption of human-resource accounting, socioeconomic accounting, accounting for the cost of capital, and the reporting of financial forecasts may be more easily included in financial reports that are based on the user approach rather than on the firm approach to the definition of an accounting entity.

8.3.2   The Going-Concern Postulate

The going-concern postulate, or continuity postulate, holds that the business entity will continue its operations long enough to realize its projects, commitments, and ongoing activities. The postulate assumes either that the entity is not expected to be liquidated in the foreseeable future or that the entity will continue for an indefinite period of time. Such a hypothesis of stability reflects the expectations of all parties interested in the entity. Thus, the financial statements provide a tentative view of the financial situation of the firm and are only part of a series of continuous reports. Except for the case of liquidation, the user will interpret the information as computed on the basis of the assumption of the continuity of the firm. Accordingly, if an entity has a limited life, the corresponding reports will specify the terminal data and the nature of the liquidation.

The going-concern postulate justifies the valuation of assets on a nonliquidation basis and provides the basis for depreciation accounting. First, because neither current values nor liquidation values are appropriate for asset valuation, the going-concern postulate calls for the use of historical cost for many valuations. Second, the fixed assets and intangibles are amortized over their useful life, rather than over a shorter period in expectation of early liquidation.

The going-concern postulate may also be employed to support the *benefit theory*. Expectations of future benefits encourage managers to be forward looking and motivate investors to commit capital to an enterprise. The going concern (that is, an indefinite continuance of the accounting entity) is essential for the justification of the benefit theory.

Many accounting theorists consider the going-concern postulate to be a necessary and essential accounting convention. Paton and Littleton simply state that "the possibility of abrupt cessation of activity cannot afford a foundation for accounting."[8]

All accounting theorists do not share this interpretation of the going-concern postulate. Storey and Sterling separately argue that the going-concern postulate does not provide justification for valuing inventories at cost.[9] Storey argues that "it is the realization convention and not the going-concern convention which requires valuation of inventories at cost."[10] Sterling argues that assuming that an accounting entity has an indefinite life does not justify the use of liquidation value, but also that his assumption is not a sufficient reason for using historical cost when other relevant valuation alternatives exist. Furthermore, if the going-concern postulate is to be retained, it should be perceived as a *prediction*.

Some accounting theorists prefer not to include the going-concern postulate in the structure of accounting theory. Chambers views a going concern as an entity that is in a continuous state of orderly liquidation, rather than in forced liquidation.[11] This interpretation of a going concern conforms with the use of the "current cash equivalent" Chambers proposes as a valuation base. Other theorists do not include the going-concern postulate, because they assume it is irrelevant to a structure of accounting theory.[12]

All these objections point to the necessity of reinterpreting the going-concern postulate. The postulate may be viewed as a judgment on continuity based on actual evidence to that effect. Fremgen offers a definition consistent with the view that the going-concern postulate is a conclusion or a judgment, rather than an assumption, when he states that "the entity is viewed as remaining in operation indefinitely" *in recognition of evidence to that effect*, not "in the absence of evidence to the contrary."[13]

8.3.3   The Unit-of-Measure Postulate

A unit of exchange and of measurement is necessary to account for the transactions of firms in a uniform manner. The common denominator chosen in accounting is the *monetary unit*. The exchangeability of goods, services, and capital is measured in terms of money. The unit-of-measure postulate holds that accounting is a measurement and communication process of the activities of the firm that are measureable in monetary terms.

The unit-of-measure postulate, or the monetary-unit postulate, implies two principal limitations of accounting. First, accounting is limited to the prediction of information expressed in terms of a monetary unit; it does not record and communicate other relevant but nonmonetary information. Accounting information is perceived as essentially monetary and quantified; nonaccounting information is perceived as nonmonetary and nonquantified. This view leads us to define accounting information as "quantitative, formal, structured, audited, numerical, and past-oriented" and to define nonaccounting information as "qualitative, informal, narrative, unaudited, and future-oriented,"[14] These definitions show, however, that although accounting is a discipline concerned with the measurement and communication of monetary activities, it has been expanding into areas previously viewed as qualitative in nature. In fact, a number of empirical studies refer to the relevance of nonaccounting information compared with accounting information.[15]

The limitation implied by the unit-of-measure postulate concerns the monetary unit itself as a unit of measure. The primary characteristic of the *monetary-unit purchasing power*, or the quantity of goods or services that money can acquire, is of concern. Unlike the meter, which is invariably 100 centimeters long, the purchasing power of the monetary unit, which is the dollar, is subject to change. Conventional accounting theory deals with this problem by stating that the unit-of-measure postulate is also a "stable monetary postulate" in the sense that the postulate assumes that the purchasing power of the dollar is either stable over time or changes insignificantly. Although it is still employed in current financial reporting, the *stable monetary postulate* is the object of continuous and persistent criticism. The accounting profession faces the challenge of choosing between units of money and units of general purchasing power as the unit of accounting measurement.

8.3.4 The Accounting-Period Postulate

Although the going-concern postulate holds that the firm will exist for an indefinite period of time, users require a variety of information about the financial position and performance of a firm to make short-term decisions. In response to this constraint imposed by the user environment, the accounting-period postulate holds that financial reports depicting changes in the wealth of a firm should be disclosed periodically. The duration of the period may vary, but income-tax laws, which require income determination on an annual basis, and traditional business practices, result in a normal period of a year. Although most companies use an accounting period that corresponds to the calendar year, some companies use a fiscal or a "natural" business year. When the business cycle does not correspond to the calendar year, it is more meaningful to end the accounting period when the business activity has reached its lowest point. Due to the need for more timely, relevant, and frequent information, most companies also issue interim reports that provide financial information on a quarterly or a monthly basis. Empirical studies on stock market reactions to the issuance of interim reports and their impact on users' investment decisions indicate the usefulness of interim reports. To ensure the credibility of interim reports, the Accounting Principles Board issued APB Opinion No. 28, which requires interim reports to be based on the same accounting principles and practices employed in the preparation of annual reports.

By requiring the entity to provide periodic, short-term financial reports, the accounting-period postulate imposes *accruals* and *deferrals*, the application of which is the principal difference between *accrual accounting* and *cash accounting*. Each period, the use of accruals and deferrals is required in the preparation of the financial position of the firm in terms of prepaid expenses, uncollected revenues, unpaid wages, and depreciation expense. The accountant may have to rely on experience and judgment to reconcile the postulate of continuity with the necessity for accruals and deferrals. Although short-term financial reports may be arbitrary and imprecise, such drawbacks are overridden by their significance to users, thereby dictating that the accounting process continue to produce them.

8.4 THE THEORETICAL CONCEPTS OF ACCOUNTING

8.4.1 The Proprietary Theory

According to the proprietary theory, the entity is the "agent, representative or arrangement through which the individual entrepreneurs or shareholders operate."[16] That is the viewpoint of the proprietor group is the center of interest is reflected in the ways in which accounting records are kept and financial statements are prepared. The primary objective of the proprietary theory is the determination and analysis of the proprietor's *net worth*. Accordingly, the accounting equation is

$$\text{Assets} - \text{Liabilities} = \text{Proprietor's Equity}$$

In other words, the proprietor owns the assets and the liabilities. If the liabilities may be considered negative assets, the proprietary theory may be said to be "centered" and, consequently, balance-sheet oriented. Assets are valued and balance sheets are prepared to measure the changes in the proprietary interest or wealth. Revenues and expenses are considered to be increases or decreases, respectively, in proprietorship that do not result from proprietary investments or capital withdrawals by the proprietor. Thus, net income on debt and corporate income taxes are expenses; dividends are withdrawals of capital.

Although the proprietary theory is generally viewed as primarily adaptable to such closely-held corporations as proprietorships and partnerships, the influence of the proprietary theory may be found in some of the accounting techniques and terminology used by widely-held corporations. For example, the corporate concept of income, which is arrived at after treating interest and income taxes as expenses, represents "net income to the stockholders" rather than to all providers of capital. Similarly, terms such as "earnings per share," and "dividend per share" connote a proprietary emphasis. The equity method of accounting for nonconsolidated investments in subsidiaries and recommends that the firm's share of the unconsolidated subsidiary net income be included in the net income. Thus practice also implies a proprietary concept.

The proprietary theory can assume at least two forms, which differ on the basis of who is included in the proprietary group. In the first form, only the common stockholders are part of the proprietary group, and preferred stockholders are excluded.[17] Thus, preferred dividends are deducted when calculating the earnings of the proprietor. This narrow form of the proprietary theory is identical to the *residual equity concept* set forth by Staubus.[18] Consistent with this form of the proprietary theory, the net income is extended to deduct preferred dividends to arrive at a net income to the residual equity on which the computation of earnings per share will be based. In the second form of the proprietary theory, both common stock and preferred stock are included in the proprietor's equity.[19] This wider view of the theory focuses attention on the shareholders' equity section of the balance sheet and the amount to be credited to all shareholders on the income statement.

8.4.2   The Entity Theory

The entity theory views the entity as something separate and distinct from those who provide capital to the entity. Simply stated, the business unit, rather than the proprietor, is the center of accounting interest. The business unit owns the resources of the enterprise and is liable to both the claims of the owners and the claims of the creditors. Accordingly, the accounting equation is

$$\text{Assets} = \text{Equities}$$

or

$$\text{Assets} = \text{Liabilities} + \text{Stockholders' Equity}$$

Assets are rights accruing to the entity; equities represent sources of the assets and consist of liabilities and the stockholders' equity. Both the creditors and the stockholders are equity holders, although they have different rights with respect to income, risk control, and liquidation. Thus, income earned is the property of the entity until it is distributed as dividends to the shareholders. Because the business unit is held responsible for meeting the claims of the equity holders, the entity theory is said to be "income-centered" and, consequently, income-statement oriented. Accountability to the equity holders is accomplished by measuring the operating and financial performances of the firm. Accordingly, income is an increase in the stockholders' equity after the claims of other equity holders (for example, interest on long-term debt and income taxes) are met. The increase in the stockholders' equity is considered income to the stockholders only if a dividend is declared. Similarly, undistributed profits remain the property of the entity because they represent the "corporation's proprietary equity in itself."[20] Note that strict adherence to the entity theory dictates that income taxes and interest on debt be considered distributions of income rather than expenses. The general belief and the interpretation of the entity theory, however, is that interest and income taxes are expenses.

The entity theory is most applicable to the corporate form of business enterprise, which is separate and distinct from its owners. The impact of the entity theory may be found in some of the accounting techniques of terminology used in practice. First, the entity theory favors the adoption of LIFO rather than FIFO inventory valuation, because LIFO valuation achieves a better income determination, due to its application under the proprietary theory. Second, the common definitions of revenues as products of an enterprise and expenses as goods and services consumed to obtain these revenues are consistent with the entity theory's preoccupation with an index of performance and accountability to equity holders. Third, the preparation of consolidated statements and the recognition of a class of minority interests as additional equity holders are also consistent with the entity theory. Finally, both the entity theory, with its emphasis on the proper determination of income to equity holders, and the proprietary theory, with its emphasis on proper asset valuation, may be perceived to favor the adoption of current values, or valuation bases other than historical costs.

8.4.3   The Fund Theory

Under the fund theory, the basis of accounting is neither the proprietor nor the entity, but a group of assets and related obligations and restrictions, called a *fund*, that governs the use of the assets.[21] Thus, the fund theory views the business unit as consisting of economic resources (funds) and related obligations and restrictions regarding the use of these resources. The accounting equation is

$$\text{Assets} = \text{Restrictions of Assets}$$

The accounting unit is defined in terms of assets and the uses to which these assets are committed. Liabilities represent a series of legal and economic restrictions on the use of the assets. The fund theory is therefore "asset-centered" in the sense that its primary focus is on the administration and the appropriate use of assets. Instead of the balance sheet or the financial statement, the statement of sources and uses of funds is the primary objective of financial reporting. This statement reflects the conduct of the operations of the firm in terms of sources and dispositions of funds.

The fund theory is useful primarily to government and nonprofit organizations. Hospitals, universities, cities and governmental units, for example, are engaged in multifaceted operations that warrant separate funds. Each self-balanced fund produces separate reports through a separate accounting system and a proper set of accounts. A fund may be defined as:

> . . . an independent fiscal and accounting entity with a self-balancing set of accounts recording cash and/or other resources together with all related liabilities, obligations, reserves, and equities which are segregated for the purpose of carrying on specific activities or attaining certain objectives in accordance with special regulations, restrictions, or limitations.[22]

The number of funds employed by any nonprofit institution depends on the number and type of activities on which legal restrictions are imposed regarding the use of the assets entrusted to the organization. For instance, the following eight major funds are recommended for the sound financial administration of a governmental unit:

1 The General Fund to account for all financial transactions not properly accounted for in another fund.
2 Special Revenue Funds to account for the proceeds of specific revenue sources (other than special assessments) or to finance specified activities as required by law or adminstrative regulation.
3 Debt Service Funds to account for the payment of interest and principal on long-term debts other than special assessment and revenue bonds.
4 Capital Projects Funds to account for the receipt and disbursement of moneys used

for the acquisition of capital facilities other than those financed by special assessment and enterprise funds.

5 Enterprise Funds to account for the financing of services to the general public, where all or most of the costs involved are paid in the form of charges by users of such services.

6 Trust and Agency Funds to account for assets held by a governmental unit as trustee or agent for individuals, private organizations, and other governmental units.

7 Intragovernmental Service Funds to account for the financing of special activities and services performed by a designated organizational unit within a government jurisdiction.

8 Special Assessment Funds to account for special assessments levied to finance public improvements or services deemed to benefit the properties against which the assessments are levied.[23]

The fund theory is also relevant to profit-oriented organizations, which use funds for such diverse activities as sinking funds, accounting for bankruptcies and estates and trusts, branch or divisional accounting, segregation of assets into current or fixed assets, and consolidation.

8.5   THE ACCOUNTING PRINCIPLES

8.5.1   The Cost Principle

According to the cost principle, the *acquisition cost*, or *historical cost*, is the appropriate valuation basis for recognition of the acquisition of all goods and services, expenses, costs, and equities. In other words, an item is valued at the exchange price at the date of acquisition and is recorded in the financial statements at that value or an amortized portion of that value. Accordingly, APB Statement No. 4 defines cost as follows:

> Cost is the amount, measured in money, of cash expended or other property transferred, capital stock issued, services performed, or a liability incurred, in consideration of goods or services received or to be received. Costs can be classified as unexpired or expired. Unexpired costs (assets) are those which are applicable to the production of future revenues . . . . Expired costs are not applicable to the production of future revenues, and for that reason are treated as deductions from current revenues or are charged against retained earnings.[24]

Cost represents the exchange price of or the monetary consideration given for the acquisition of goods or services. If the consideration comprises nonmonetary assets, the exchange price is the cash equivalent of the assets or services given up. The cost principle is equally applicable to the measurement of liabilities and capital transactions.

The cost principle may be justified in terms of both its objectivity and the going-concern postulate. First, acquisition cost is objective, verifiable information. Second, the going-concern postulate assumes that the entity will continue its activities indefinitely, thereby eliminating the necessity of using current values or liquidation values for asset valuation.

The precarious validity of the unit-of-measure postulate, which assumes that the purchasing power of the dollar is stable, is a major limitation to the application of the cost principle. Historical-cost valuation may produce erroneous figures if changes in the values of assets over time are ignored. Similarly, the values of assets acquired at different times over a period during which the purchasing power of the dolllar is changing cannot be added together in the balance sheet and provide meaningful results.

8.5.2   The Revenue Principle

The revenue principle specifies:

1 the nature of the components of revenue;
2 the measurement of revenue; and
3 the timing of revenue recognition.

Each fact of the revenue principle raises interesting and controversial issues in accounting theory.

The Nature and Components of Revenue

Revenue has been interpreted as:

1 an inflow of net assets resulting from the sale of goods or services;[25]
2 an outflow of goods or services from the firm to its customers;[26] and
3 a product of the firm resulting from the mere creation of goods or services by an enterprise during a given period of time.[27]

Hendriksen considers that:

1 the product concept is superior to the outflow concept, which is superior to the inflow concept; and
2 the product concept is neutral with respect to both the measurement (amount) and timing (date of recognition) of revenue, but the inflow concept confuses both measurement and timing with the revenue process.[28]

The different interpretations of the nature of revenue are compounded by different views on what should be included in revenue. Basically, there are two views of the components of revenue. The broad or comprehensive view of revenue includes all of the proceeds from business and investment activities. This view identifies as revenue all changes in the net assets resulting from the revenue-producing activities and other gains or losses resulting from the sale of fixed assets and investments. Applying this view, Accounting Terminology Bulletin No. 2 defines revenue as follows:

> Revenue results from the sale of goods and the rendering of services and is measured by the charge made to customers, clients or tenants for goods and services furnished to them. It also includes gains from the sale or exchange of assets (other than stock in trade) interest and dividends earned on investments, and other increases in the owners' equity except those arising from the capital contributions and capital adjustments.[29]

The narrower view of revenue includes only the results of the revenue-producing activities and excludes investment income and gains and losses on the disposal of fixed assets. This view requires that a clear distinction be made between revenue and gains and losses. Adopting the narrower view of revenue, the American Accounting Association in a 1957 statement defined *net income* as

> ...the excess of deficiency of revenue compared with related expired costs and other gains and losses to the enterprise from sales, exchanges, or other conversions of assets.[30]

The Measurement of Revenue

Revenue is measured in terms of the value of the products or services exchanged in an "arm's-length" transaction. This value represents either the net cash equivalent or the present discounted value of the money received or to be received in exchange for the products or services that the enterprise transfers to its customers. Two primary interpretations arise from this concept of revenue:

1 Cash discounts and any reductions in the fixed prices, such as bad debt losses, are adjustments necessary to compute the true net cash equivalent or the present discounted value of the money claims and consequently should be deducted when computing revenue. (This interpretation conflicts with the view that cash discounts and bad debt losses should be considered expenses.)
2 For noncash transactions, the exchange value is set equal to the fair market value of the consideration given or received, whichever is more easily and clearly computed.

The Timing of Revenue Recognition

It is generally admitted that revenue and income are earned throughout all stages of the operating cycle (that is, during order reception, production, sale, and collection). Given the difficulties of allocating revenue and income to the different stages of the operating cycle, accountants employ the realization principle to select a "critical event" in the cycle for the timing of revenue and recognition of income. The critical event is chosen to indicate when certain changes in assets and liabilities may be accounted for appropriately. An early definition of the realization principle is:

> The essential meaning of realization is that a change in asset or liability has become sufficiently definite and objective to warrant recognition in the accounts. This recognition may rest on an exchange transaction between independent parties, or on established trade practices, or on the terms of a contract performance which is considered to be virtually certain.[31]

The broad nature of this statement has led accountants to search for specific rules or considerations necessary to the recognition of certain asset and liability changes. Naturally, the realization principle and the corresponding criteria for the recognition of asset and liability changes have been subject to different interpretations.[32] As reported by the 1973–1974 American Accounting Association Committee on Concepts and Standards — External Reporting, the specific criteria for revenue and income recognition are:

1 Earned, in some sense or another.
2 In distributable form.
3 The result of a conversion brought about in a transaction between the enterprise and someone external to it.

4 The result of a legal sale or similar process.
5 Severed from capital.
6 In the form of liquid assets.
7 Both its gross and net effects on shareholder equity must be estimable with a high degree of reliability.[33]

The committee tied the realization principle to a concept of a *reliable income measurement*. The realization principle is an expression of the level of certainty of the profit impact of an event reported as revenue. More explicitly, the Committee defined realization as follows:

> Income must always be in existence before the question of realization can arise. Realization is not a determinant in the concept of income; it only serves as a guide in deciding when events, otherwise resolved as being within the concept of income, can be entered in the accounting records in objective terms; that is, when the uncertainty has been reduced to an acceptable level.[34]

Given these different interpretations of the realization principle and of the criteria to be used for the recognition of asset and liability changes, reliance on the realization principle may be misleading.[35] In general, revenue is recognized on an accrual basis or on a critical-event basis.

The *accrual basis* for revenue recognition may imply that revenue should be reported during production (in which case the profit may be computed proportionally to the work completed or the service performed), at the end of production, on sale of goods, or on collection of sale. Revenue is generally recognized during production in the following situations:

1 Rent, interest, and commission revenue are recognized as earned, given the existence of a prior agreement or a contract specifying the gradual increase in the claim against the customer.
2 An individual or a group rendering professional or similar services might better use an accrual basis for the recognition of revenue, given that the nature of the claim against the customer is a function of the proportion of services rendered.
3 Revenues on long-term contracts are recognized on the basis of the progress of construction or the "percentage of completion." The percentage of completion is computed as either:
   a. the engineering estimates of the work performed to date compared with the total work to be completed in terms of the contract, or
   b. the total costs incurred to date compared with the total costs estimated for the total project in the contract.
4 Revenues on "cost plus fixed-fee contracts" are better recognized on the accrual basis.
5 Asset changes due to accretion give rise to revenue (for example, when liquor or wines age, timber grows, or livestock matures). Although a transaction must occur before revenue is recognized in these examples, accretion revenue is based on comparative inventory valuations.

The *critical-event basis* for revenue recognition is triggered by a crucial event in the operating cycle. That event may be

1 the time of sale;
2 the completion of production: or
3 the receipt of payment subsequent to sale.

1 The *sales basis* for the recognition of revenue is justified because
   a. the price of the product is then known with certainty;
   b. the exchange has been finalized by delivery of goods, leading to an objective knowledge of the costs incurred; and
   c. in terms of realization, a sale constitutes a crucial event.
2 The *completion-of-production basis* for the recognition of revenue is justified when a stable market and a stable price exist for a standard commodity. The production process rather than the sale therefore constitutes the crucial event for the recognition of revenue. This rule is primarily applicable to "precious metals that have a fixed selling price and insignificant market prices."[36] The completion-of-production treatment is appropriate for gold, silver, and other precious metals and may also be appropriate for agricultural and mineral products that meet the required criteria.
3 The *payment basis* for the recognition of revenue is justified when the sale will be made and when a reasonably accurate valuation cannot be placed on the product to be transferred. This method, which amounts to a mere deferral of revenue, is primarily identified with the "installment method" of recognizing revenue.

8.5.3 The Matching Principle

The matching principle holds that expenses should be recognized in the same period as the associated revenues; that is, revenues are recognized in a given period according to the revenue principle, and the relatead expenses are then recognized. The association is best accomplished when it reflects the cause-and-effect relationship between costs and revenues. Operationally, it consists of a two-stage process for accounting for expenses. First, costs are capitalized as assets representing bundles of service potentials or benefits. Second, each asset is written off as an expense to recognize the proportion of the assets' service potential that has expired in the generation of the revenue during this period. Thus, accrual accounting rather than cash accounting is implied by the matching principle in terms of capitalization and allocation.

The association between revenues and expenses depends on one of four criteria:

1 Direct matching of expired costs with a revenue (for example, cost of goods sold matched with related sale).
2 Direct matching of expired cost with the period (for example, president's salary for the period).
3 Allocation of costs over periods benefitted (for example, depreciation).
4 Expensing all other costs in the period incurred, unless it can be shown that they have future benefit (for example, advertising expense).

Unexpired costs (that is, assets) not meeting one of these four criteria for expensing the current period are chargeable to future periods and may be classified under different categories according to their different uses in the firm. Such varying uses may justify differences in the application of the matching principle.

We will now examine the major asset and cost categories and the corresponding rule for the time of expenses.

Costs of Producing Finished Goods for Sale

The costs of producing finished goods for sale generally include raw materials, direct labor, and factory overhead. A two-stage process is employed to account for these costs:

1 inventory valuation, or the determination of the product costs attached to the product; and
2 income determination, or the matching of product costs with revenues.

When determining the amount of inventory valuation, the problem is to decide which costs are product costs (because they benefit future periods and should be inventoried) and which costs are period costs (because they benefit only the current period and should be charged against current income). The absorption (or full) costing method and the direct (or variable) costing method produce different answers.

The *absorption costing* method treats all production costs as product costs that are attached to the product, carried forward, and only released as period costs at the time of sale. The *direct costing* method treats only the variable production costs as product costs and all of the fixed manufacturing overhead costs as period costs. The choice between these two methods has posed a major controversy in the accounting literature for many years. Neither method has emerged as the primary victor.[37] It is generally admitted, however, that direct costing is more relevant to internal decision making. The separate reporting of fixed and variable costs is assumed to facilitate incremental profit analysis and to remove the impact of inventory changes from income.

Depreciable Operating Assets

Depreciable operating assets are also referred to as *wasting capital assets*. Because a depreciable operating asset is assumed to benefit more than one period, the asset is capitalized at its acquisition cost, which is then allocated on some logical basis over the asset's useful life. This allocation process is known as *depreciation* for such tangible assets as building, equipment, tools, and furniture, as *depletion* for assets represented by a natural resource (such as mineral deposits and timber tracts), and *amortization* for such intangible assets as special rights or benefits (examples are patents, copyrights, franchises, trademarks, goodwill, deferred charges, research and development costs, organizational costs, and leaseholds). Depreciation accounting has been defined as follows:

> *Depreciation accounting* is a system of accounting which aims to distribute the cost or other basic value of tangible capital assets, less salvage (if any), over the estimated useful life of the unit (which may be a group of assets) in a systematic and rational manner. It is a process of allocation, not of valuation. *Depreciation for the year* is the portion of the total charge under such a system that is allocated during the year. Although the allocation may properly take into account occurrences during the year, it is not intended to be a measurement of the effect of all such occurrences.[38]

A number of depreciation methods have been developed, each of which is based on a different pattern of depreciation charges over the life of the tangible asset. A depreciation method may be based on:

1 *Time,* such as the straight-line method.
2 *Output,* such as the service-hours and the unit-of-output method.
3 *Reducing depreciation charge,* such as the sum-of-the-years' digits method, the fixed percentage on declining base amount method, the declining rate on cost method, and the double-declining balance method.
4 *Investment and interest concepts,* such as the annuity method and the sinking-fund method.[39]

Nondepreciable Operating Assets

The third major asset and cost category consists of nondepreciable operating assets, which are also referred to as *permanent capital assets,* because it is assumed that they are not consumed while the operations of the business are being conducted. Their value is not affected by productive activities, and they have no impact on income determination until they are sold or revalued. Accordingly, the matching principle is not applicable to nondepreciable operating assets.

Costs of Selling and Administration

The costs of selling and administration are all of the nonmanufacturing costs necessary to maintain a basic selling and administrative organization. They are treated as period costs in the period in which they are incurred, under either the direct or absorption costing method.

8.5.4   The Objectivity Principle

The usefulness of financial information depends heavily on the *reliability* of the measurement procedure used. Because ensuring maximum reliability is frequently diffi-cult, accountants have employed the objectivity principle to justify the choice of a measurement or a measurement procedure. The principle of objectivity, however, has been subject to different interpretations:

1 An objective measurement is an "impersonal" measure, in the sense that it is free from the personal bias of the measurers. "In other words, objectivity refers to the external reality that is independent of the persons who perceive it."[40]
2 An objective measurement is a verifiable measurement, in the sense that it is based on an evidence.[41]
3 An objective measurement is the result of a "consensus among a given group of observers or measurers."[42] This view also implies that objectivity will depend on the given group of measurers.
4 The size of the dispersion of the measurement distribution may be used as an indicator of the degree of objectivity of a given measurement system.

Ijiri and Jaedicke employ the fourth interpretation of objectivity.[43] Specifically, they define objectivity V as

$$V = \frac{1}{n} \sum_{i=1}^{n} (x_i - \bar{x})^2$$

where:

n = the number of measures in the reference group
x_i = the quantity that the ith measurer reports
$\bar{x}$ = the average of x_is over all measurers in the reference group

In other words, when choosing between accounting measurement techniques that result in two measurement distributions, the technique that results in the smaller variance is the more objective. This concept is illustated in Exhibit 8.2 by two measurement techniques, which both yield the same average value.

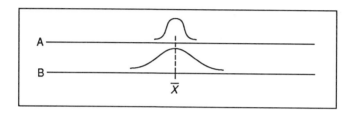

EXHIBIT 8.2 Results of two different measurement techniques

Measurement technique A is more objective than measurement technique B, because A exhibits a narrower dispersion of values around the mean. However, as we learned earlier, objectivity does not reflect *reliability*, which is a more useful concept for accountants. Ijiri and Jaedicke suggest the use of the mean square error as a measure of reliability.[44] Specifically, they define reliability R as:

$$R = \frac{1}{n} \sum_{i=1}^{n} (x_i - x^*)^2$$

where x^* is the alleged value, or

$$R = \frac{1}{n} \sum_{i=1}^{n} (x_i - \bar{x})^2 + (\bar{x} - x^*)^2$$

From the second expression of reliability, Ijiri and Jaedicke state that the degree of reliability is equal to the degree of objectivity (first term) plus a reliance bias (second term). Note that the *reliance bias* is equal to the differences between the mean value and the alleged value of the measurement.

The application of this reliability measure is illustrated in Exhibit 8.3 in two measurement procedures, which yield different average values, although they have similar alleged values.

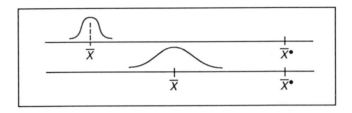

EXHIBIT 8.3   Application of the reliability measure

From this analysis, we may conclude that the accounting profession should define a trade-off point between objectivity and bias that leads to acceptable levels of reliability. This is only possible when a consensus exists as to the alleged values that should be measured.

8.5.5   The Consistency Principle

The consistency principle holds that similar economic events should be recorded and reported in a consistent manner from period to period. The principle implies that the same accounting procedures will be applied to similar items over time. Application of the consistency principle makes financial statements more comparable and more useful. Trends in accounting data and relationships with external factors are more accurately revealed when comparable measurement procedures are used. Similarly, the distortion of income and balance sheet amounts and the possible manipulation of financial statements are avoided by the consistent application of accounting procedures over time. Consistency is therefore a user constraint intended to facilitate the user's decision by ensuring the comparable presentation of the financial statements of a given firm over time, thereby enhancing the utility of the statements. Consistency is a major concern of accountants when auditing financial statements. In the standards opinion, the certified public accountant recognizes the consistency principle by noting whether or not the financial statements have been prepared in conformity with generally accepted accounting principles applied on a basis "consistent with that of the preceding year."

The consistency principle does not preclude a firm changing accounting procedures when this is justified by changing circumstances, or if the alternative procedure is preferable (*the rule of preferability*). According to APB Opinion No. 20, changes that justify a change in procedure are:

1 a change in accounting principle;
2 a change in accounting estimate;
3 a change in reporting entity.

These changes are to be reflected in the accounts and reported in the financial staements *retroactively* for a change in accounting entity, *prospectively* for a change in accounting estimate, and *generally* and *currently* for a change in accounting principle.

8.5.6 The Full-Disclosure Principle

There is a general consensus in accounting that there should be "full," "fair," and "adequate" disclosure of accounting data. *Full disclosure* requires that financial statements be designed and prepared to portray accurately the economic events that have affected the firm for the period and to contain sufficient information to make them useful and not misleading to the average investor. More explicitly, the full-disclosure principle implies that no information of substance or of interest to the average investor will be omitted or concealed.

The principle is further reinforced by the various disclosure requirements set forth by the APB Opinions, the FASB Statements, and the SEC Accounting Releases and requirements. Full disclosure is, however, a broad, open-ended construct that leaves several questions unanswered or open to different interpretations. First, what is meant by "full," "fair," and "adequate" disclosure? "Adequate" connotes a minimum set of information to be disclosed; "fair" implies an ethical constraint dictating an equitable treatment of users; and "full" refers to complete and comprehensive presentation of information. Another accepted position is to view "fairness" as the central objective and trade-off point between full and adequate disclosure. Hence, under the title *Fair Presentation in Conformity with Generally Accepted Accounting Principles*, APB Statement No. 4 states that "fair" presentation is met when;

> ... a proper balance has been achieved between the conflicting needs to disclose important aspects of financial positions and results of operations in accordance with conventional aspects and to summarize the voluminous underlying data into a limited number of financial statement captions and supporting notes.

Second, what data should be disclosed so that a "prudent, average investor" will not be misled? Should the data be essentially accounting information? Should the data include novel information and such additions as human-asset accounting, socioeconomic accounting, inflation accounting, and segment reporting?

The answers to these questions rest on proper determination of the users, their needs, their level of sophistication, and — more importantly — their information-processing capabilities, given the risks of information overload caused by data expension. Skinner draws attention to some matters that should be the subject of full disclosure:

1 Details of accounting policies and methods, particularly when judgment is required in the application of an accounting method, when the method is peculiar to the reporting entity, or when alternative accounting methods can be used.
2 Additional information to aid in investment analysis or to indicate the rights of various parties that have claims on the reporting entity.
3 Changes from the preceding year in accounting policies or methods of applying them, and the effects of such changes.
4 Assets, liabilities, costs, and revenues arising from transactions with parties that have controlling interests or with directors or officers that have special relationships to the reporting entity.
5 Contingent assets, liabilities, and commitments.
6 Financial or other nonoperating transactions occurring after the balance sheet date that have a material effect on the entity's financial position as indicated in the year-end statement.[45]

8.5.7   The Conservatism Principle

The conservatism principle is an exception or modifying principle in the sense that it acts as a constraint to the presentation of relevant and reliable accounting data. The conservatism principle holds that when choosing among two or more acceptable accounting techniques, some preference is shown for the option that has the least favorable impact on the stockholders' equity. More specifically, the principle implies that preferably the lowest values of assets and revenues and the highest values of liabilities and expenses should be reported. The conservatism principle therefore dictates that the accountant display a generally pessimistic attitude when choosing accounting tehniques for financial reporting. To accomplish the objectives of understanding current income and assets, the conservatism principle may lead to treatments that constitute a departure from acceptable or theoretical approaches. For example, the adoption of the "lower-of-cost-or-market" concept conflicts with the historical principle. Although the LIFO valuation and accelerated depreciation are generally perceived as counterinflationary measures, they may be viewed as resulting from the adoption of the conservatism principle. Thus Chatfield maintains that:

> Both [LIFO and accelerated depreciation] reinforced an older tradition of balance sheet conservatism, so much so that taxpayers are still not allowed to use LIFO together with lower-of-cost-or-market inventory valuation. Both gave precedence to management's need for cash retention and asset replacement, even at the expense of the accountant's desire for more precise asset valuation.[46]

In the past, conservatism has been employed when dealing with uncertainty in the environment, and the possible over-optimism of managers and owners and also when protecting creditors against an unwarranted distribution of the firm's assets as dividends. Conservatism was a more highly esteemed virtue in the past than it is today. It has led to arbitrary and inconsistent treatment in the form of rapid asset write-offs, or the creation of excessive provisions for liabilities, or both.

Sterling calls conservatism "the most ancient and probably the most pervasive principle of accounting valuation."[47] Today, the emphasis on objective and fair prensentation and the primacy of the investor as user has lessened the reliance on conservatism. It is now perceived more as a guide to be followed in extraordinary situations, than as a general rule to be rigidly applied to all circumstances. Conservatism is still employed in some situations that require the accountant's judgment, such as choosing the estimated useful life and residual value of an asset for depreciation accounting and the corollary rule of applying the "lower-of-cost-or-market" concept in valuing inventories and marketable equity securities. Because it is essentially the manifestation of the accountant's intervention that may result in the introduction of bias, errors, possible distortions, and misleading statements, the present view of conservatism as an accounting principle is bound to disappear.

8.5.8   The Materiality Principle

Like conservatism the materiality principle is an exception or modifying principle. The principle holds that transactions and events having insignificant economic effects may be handled in the most expeditious manner, whether or not they conform to generally accepted accounting principles, and need not be disclosed. Materiality serves as an implicit guide for the accountant in terms of what should be disclosed in the financial reports, enabling the accountant to decide what is not important or what does not matter on the basis of record-keeping cost, accuracy of financial statements, and relevance to the user.

In general, the accounting bodies have left the application of materiality to the accountant's judgment, at the same time stressing its importance. According to APB Statement No. 4, materiality implies that "financial reporting is only concerned with information that is significant enough to affect evaluations or decisions."[48] APB Opinion No. 30 relies on an undefined concept of materiality to describe extraordinary items. Similarly, APB Opinion No. 22 recommends the disclosure of all of the policies or principles that materially affect the financial position, results of operations, and changes in the financial position of the entity. More recently, the FASB issued a Discussion Memorandum on the materiality issue, stressing the importance of this principle.[49]

The materiality principle lacks an operational definition. Most definitions of materiality stress the accountant's role in interpreting what is and what is not material. For example, Frishkoff defines materiality as the "relative, quantitative importance of some piece of financial information to a user, in the context of a decision to be made."[50]

A recent study by the Accountants' International Study Group characterizes materiality as follows:

> Materiality is essentially a matter of professional judgment. An individual item should be judged material if the knowledge of that item could reasonably be deemed to have influence on the users of the financial statements.[51]

Guidelines or criteria to be used in determining materiality are urgently needed. Two basic criteria have been recommended. The first, referred to as the *size approach*, relates the size of the item to another relevant variable, such as net income. For example, Bernstein suggests a border zone of 10–15 percent of net income after taxes as the point of distinction between what is and what is not material.[52] Similarly, the FASB Discussion Memorandum on materiality suggests criteria based on the size approach:

> If the amount of its current or potential effect equals or exceeds 10 percent of a pertinent financial statement amount, the matter should be presumed to be material.
> If its amount or current or potential effect is between 5 and 10 percent of a pertinent financial statement amount, the materiality of the matter depends on the surrounding circumstances.[53]

The second criterion, referred to as the *change criterion approach*, evaluates the impact of an item on trends or changes between accounting periods. This approach is advocated primarily by Rappaport, who contends that materiality criteria can be stated in terms of financial averages, trends, and ratios that express significant analytic relationships in terms of accounting information.[54] The change criterion approach has influenced the Accountants' International Study Group, as the following excerpt from *Materiality in Accounting* indicates:

> An amount is not material solely by reason of its size; other factors including those set out below must be considered in making decisions as to materiality: The nature of the item; whether it is:
> - A factor entering into the determination of net income.
> - Unusual or extraordinary.

- Contingent on an event or condition.
- Determinable based on existing facts and circumstances.
- Required by statute or regulation.

The amount itself, in relationship to:

- The financial statements taken as a whole.
- The total of the accounts of which it forms, or should form, a part.
- Related items.
- The corresponding amount in previous years or the expected amount in future years.[55]

8.5.9   The Uniformity and Comparability Principles

The consistency principle refers to the use of the same procedures for related items by a given firm over time; the uniformity principle refers to the use of the same procedures by different firms. The desired objective is to achieve comparability of financial statements by reducing the diversity created by the use of different accounting procedures by different firms. In fact, a constant debate is taking place over whether flexibility or uniformity should prevail in accounting and financial reporting. The principal supports for *uniformity* are the claims that it would:

1 Reduce the diverse use of accounting procedures and the inadequacies of accounting practices.
2 Allow meaningful comparisons of the financial statements of different firms.
3 Restore the confidence of users in the financial statements.
4 Lead to governmental intervention and regulation of accounting practices.

The main supports for the *flexibility* are the claims that:

1 The use of uniform accounting procedures to represent the same item occurring in many cases poses the risk of concealing important differences among cases.
2 Comparability is a utopian goal; "it cannot be achieved by the adoption of firm rules that do not take adequate account of different factual situations."[56]
3 "Differences in circumstances" or "circumstantial variables" call for different treatments, so that corporate reporting can respond to circumstances in which transactions and events occur. The circumstantial variables are defined as:

    . . . environmental conditions which vary among companies and which influence
    a) the feasibility of accounting methods, and/or
    b) the objectivity of the measures resulting from applying the accounting methods.[57]

The implicit objective of both uniformity and flexibility is to protect the user and to present the user with meaningful data. Both principles fail due to their extreme positions on the issue of financial reporting. Uniformity does not lead to comparability — an admittedly unfeasible goal. Flexibility evidently leads to confusion and mistrust. A trade-off solution may be provided by encouraging uniformity by narrowing the diversity of accounting practices and, at the same time, allowing a proper recognition of market and economic events peculiar to a given firm and a given industry by a proper association of certain economic circumstances with related accounting techniques. This middle position calls for an operational definition of "differences in circumstances" and for better guidelines for relating differences in circumstances to various procedures.[58]

8.6 CONCLUSIONS

Existing accounting rules and techniques are based on foundations of accounting theory. These foundations are composed of hierarchical elements that function as a frame of reference or a theoretical structure. In this chapter, we have viewed the formulation of such a theoretical structure as a deductive, interactive process consisting of the successive formulation of the objectives, the postulates, the concepts, the principles, and the techniques of accounting. An understanding of these elements and relationships of accounting theory guarantees an understanding of the rationale behind actual and future practices. The financial statements presented in the formal accounting reports are merely reflections of the application of the theoretical structure of accounting. Improving the content and the format of financial statements is definitely linked to improving the theoretical structure of accounting. Foremost on the agenda of accounting bodies should be the formulation of the elements of accounting theory — namely the objectives of accounting, the environmental postulates, the theoretical concepts, and the principles of accounting.

NOTES

[1] Prince, Thomas R., *Extensions of the Boundaries of Accounting Theory* (Cincinatti: South Western Publishing Co., 1963), p. 4.

[2] Paton, W.A., *Accounting Theory* (New York: The Ronald Press, 1922).

[3] Canning, John B., *The Economics of Accountancy* (New York: The Ronald Press, 1929); Sweeney, Henry W., *Stabilized Accounting* (New York: Harper & Row, 1936); MacNeal, Kenneth, *Truth in Accounting* (Philadelphia: University of Pennsylvania Press, 1939); Alexander, Sidney S., "Income Measurement in a Dynamic Economy," *Five Monographs on Business Income* (New York: American Institute of Certified Public Accountants, 1950); Edwards, E.O., and Bell, P.W., *The Theory and Measurement of Business Income* (Berkeley: University of California Press, 1961); Moonitz, Maurice, Accounting Research Study No. 1, *The Basic Postulates of Accounting* (New York: American Institute of Certified Public Accountants, 1961); Sprouse, R.T., and Moonitz, Maurice, Accounting Research Study No. 3, *A Tentative Set of Broad Accounting Principles for Business Enterprises* (New York: American Institute of Certified Public Accountants, 1962).

[4] Hatfield, H.R., *Accounting: Its Principles and Problems* (New York: D. Appleton & Company, 1927); Gilman, Stephen, *Accounting Concepts of Profits* (New York: The Ronald Press, 1939); Paton, W.A., and Littleton, A.C., Monograph No. 3, *An Introduction to Corporate Accounting Standards* (Columbus, Oh.: American Accounting Association, 1940); Littleton, A.C., AAA Monograph No. 5, *Structure of Accounting Theory* (Iowa City: American Accounting Association, 1953); Ijiri, Yuji, Studies in Accounting Research No. 10, *Theory of Accounting Measurement* (Sarasota, Fl.: American Accounting

Association, 1975); Skinner, R.M., *Accounting Principles* (Toronto: Canadian Institute of Chartered Accountants, 1973).

[5] Littleton, A.C., "Tests for Principles," *The Accounting Review* (March, 1938), p. 16.

[6] Moonitz, Maurice, Accounting Research Study No. 1, op. cit., p. 22.

[7] Concepts and Standards Research Study Committee on the Business Entity Concept, "The Entity Concept," *The Accounting Review* (April, 1965), pp. 358–67.

[8] Paton, W.A., and Litteton, A.C., *An Introduction to Corporate Accounting Standards*, op. cit., p. 9.

[9] Storey, R.K., "Revenue Realization, Going Concern, and Measurement of Income," *The Accounting Review* (April, 1959), pp. 232–8; Sterling, Robert R., "The Going Concern: An Examination," *The Accounting Review* (July, 1968), pp. 481–502.

[10] Storey, R.K., "Revenue Realization, Going Concern, and Measurement of Income," op. cit., p. 238.

[11] Chambers, R.J., *Accounting, Evaluation, and Economic Behavior* (Englewood Cliffs, N.J.: Prentice-Hall, 1966), p. 218.

[12] Ijiri, Yuji, "Axioms and Structures of Conventional Accounting Measurement," *The Accounting Review* (January, 1965), pp. 36–53; Sterling, Robert R., "Elements of Pure Accounting Theory," *The Accounting Review* (January, 1967), pp. 62–73.

[13] Fremgen, James M., "The Going-Concern Assumption: A Critical Appraisal," *The Accounting Review* (October, 1968), pp. 649–56.

[14] Hofstedt, T.R., "Some Behavioral Parameters of Financial Analysis," *The Accounting Review* (October, 1972), pp. 680, 681.

[15] Ibid., pp. 679–92; Belkaoui, A., and Cousineau, A., "Accounting Information, Non-accounting Information, and Common Stock Perception," *Journal of Business* (July, 1977), pp. 334–42.

[16] Coughlan, J.W., *Guide to Contemporary Theory of Accounts* (Englewood Cliffs, N.J.: Prentice-Hall, 1965), p. 155.

[17] Husband, G.R., "The Entity Concept in Accounting," *The Accounting Review* (October, 1954), p. 561.

[18] Staubus, G.J., "The Residual Equity Point of View in Accounting," *The Accounting Review* (January, 1959), p. 12.

[19] Lorig, A.N., "Some Basic Concepts of Accounting and Their Implications," *Accounting Review* (July, 1964), p. 565.

[20] Husband, G.R., "The Entity Concept in Accounting," op. cit., p. 554.

[21] Vatter, W.J., *The Fund Theory of Accounting and Its Implications for Financial Reports* (Chicago: University of Chicago Press, 1947), p. 20.

[22] National Committee on Governmental Accounting, *Governmental Accounting, Auditing, and Financial Reporting* (Chicago: Municipal Finance Officers Association of the United States and Canada, 1968), pp. 6–7.

[23] Ibid., pp. 7–8.

[24] APB Statement No. 4 (New York: American Institute of Certified Public Accountants, 1970), p. 57.

[25] American Institute of Certified Public Accountants, *Professional Standards* (Chicago: Commerce Clearing House, 1975), p. 7248.

[26] Staubus, G.J., "Revenue and Revenue Accounts," *The Accounting Review* (July, 1956), pp. 284–94.

[27] Paton, W.A., and Littleton, A.C., "An Introduction to Corporate Accounting Standards," op. cit., p. 46.

[28] Hendriksen, W.S., *Accounting Theory* Third Edition (Homewood, Ill.: Richard D. Irwin, 1977), pp. 177–8.

[29] Accounting Terminology Bulletin No. 2, *Proceeds, Revenue, Income, Profit and Earnings* (New York: American Institute of Certified Public Accountants, 1955), p. 2.

[30] AAA Committee on Accounting Concepts and Standards, *Accounting and Reporting Standards for Corporate Financial Statements and Preceding Statements and Supplements* (Columbus, Oh.: American Accounting Association, 1957), p. 5.

[31] Ibid., p. 3.

[32] Myers, J.H., "The Critical Event and Recognition of New Profit," *The Accounting Review* (October 1959), pp. 528–32; Windal, F.W., Occasional Paper No. 5, *The Accounting Concept of Realization* (East Lansing: Bureau of Business and Economic Research, Michigan State University, 1961); AAA Committee on Concepts and Standards Research, "The Realization Concept," *The Accounting Review* (April, 1965), pp. 312–22.

[33] "Report of the 1973–1974 Committee on Concepts and Standards — External Reporting," supplement to Vol. 40, *The Accounting Review* (1974), pp. 207–208.

[34] Ibid., p. 209.

[35] Arnett, H.E., "Recognition as a Function of Measurement in the Realization Concept," *The Accounting Review* (October, 1963), pp. 733–41.

[36] American Institute of Certified Public Accountants, *Professional Standards*, op. cit., p. 7301.

[37] Green, David G., Jr., "A Moral to Direct-Costing Controversy?," *Journal of Business* (July, 1960), pp. 218–26; Staubus, G.J., "Direct, Relevant, or Absorption Costing?," *The Accounting Review* (January, 1963), pp. 64–75; Fremgen, James M., "The Direct-Costing Controversy: An Identification of Issues," *The Accounting Review* (January, 1964), pp. 43–51; Horngren, Charles T., and Sorter, G.H., "The Effects of Inventory Costing Methods on Full and Direct Costing," *Journal of Accounting Research* (Spring, 1965), pp. 63–74; Fekrat, A.M., "The Conceptual Foundation of Absorption Costing," *The Accounting Review* (April, 1972), pp. 351–5.

[38] Accounting Terminology Bulletin No. 1 (New York: American Institute of Certified Public Accountants, 1955), p. 100.

[39] Welsh, G.A., Zlatkovitch, C.T., and White, J.A., *Intermediate Accounting* (Homewood, Ill.: Richard D. Irwin, 1976), pp. 547–8.

[40] Ijiri, Yuji, and Jaedicke, R.K., "Reliability and Objectivity of Accounting Measurement," *The Accounting Review* (July, 1966), p. 476.

[41] Paton, W.A., and Littleton, A.C., "An Introduction to Corporate Accounting Standards," op. cit., p. 18.

[42] Ijiri, Yuji, and Jaedicke, R.K., "Reliability and Objectivity of Accounting Measurements," op. cit., p. 476.

[43] Ibid., p. 477.

[44] Ibid., p. 481.

[45] Skinner, R.M., *Accounting Principles*, op. cit., p. 234.

[46] Chatfield, M., *A History of Accounting Thought* (New York: Dryden Press, 1974), p. 244.

[47] Sterling, Robert R., "Conservatism: The Fundamental Principle of Valuation in Traditional Accounting," *Abacus* (December, 1967), p. 110.

[48] APB Statement No. 4, op. cit., p. 48.

[49] APB Opinion No. 22, *Disclosure of Accounting Policies*, (New York: American Institute of Certified Public Accountants, 1972), paragraph 12; APB Opinion No. 30, *Reporting the*

Results of Operations (New York: American Institute of Certified Public Accountants, 1973), paragraph 24; FASB Discussion Memorandum, *An Analysis of Issues Related to Criteria for Determining Materiality* (Stamford, Ct.: Financial Accounting Standards Board, March 21, 1975).
[50] Frishkoff, P., "An Empirical Investigation of the Concept of Materiality in Accounting," *Empirical Research in Accounting: Selected Studies*, supplement to Vol. 8, *Journal of Accounting Research* (1970), p. 116.
[51] Accountants' International Study Group, *Materiality in Accounting* (London: AISG, 1974), p. 30.
[52] Bernstein, L.A., "The Concept of Materiality," *The Accounting Review* (January, 1967), p. 93.
[53] FASB Discussion Memorandum, op. cit., p. 50.
[54] Rappaport, A., "Materiality," *The Journal of Accountancy* (April, 1964), p. 48.
[55] Accountants' International Study Group, *Materiality in Accounting*, op. cit., p. 30.
[56] Keller, T.F., "Uniformity Versus Flexibility: A Review of the Rhetoric," *Law and Contemporary Problems* (Autumn, 1965), p. 637.
[57] Cadenhead, G.M., "Differences in Circumstances: Fact or Fantasy?," *Abacus* (September, 1970), p. 72.
[58] Dewhirst, John F., "Is Accounting Too Principled?," *The Canadian Chartered Accountant Magazine* (July, 1976), pp. 44–9.

REFERENCES

Equity Theories

Bird, Francis A., Davidson, Lewis F., and Smith, Charles H., "Perceptions of External Accounting Transfers Under Entity and Proprietary Theory," *The Accounting Review* (April, 1974), pp. 233–44.

Goldberg, Louis, *An Inquiry Into the Nature of Accounting* (Evanston, Ill.: American Economic Association, 1965).

Gynther, Reginald S., "Accounting-Concepts and Behavioral Hypotheses," *The Accounting Review* (April, 1967), pp. 274–90.

Husband, G.R., "The Entity Concept in Accounting," *The Accounting Review* (October, 1954), p. 561.

Staubus, G.J., "The Residual Equity Point of View in Accounting," *The Accounting Review* (January, 1959).

Lorig, A.N., "Some Basic Concepts of Accounting and Their Implications," *The Accounting Review* (July, 1964).

Vatter, W.J., *The Fund Theory of Accounting and Its Implications for Financial Reporting* (Chicago: University of Chicago Press, 1947).

Moore, K., and Steadman, G., "The Comparative Viewpoints of Groups of Accountants: More on the Entity–Proprietary Debate," *Accounting, Organizations and Society* (February, 1986).

Ricchiute, David N., "Standard Setting and the Entity–Proprietary Debate," *Accounting, Organizations and Society* (January, 1980), pp. 67–76.

Postulates, Concepts, and Principles

American Accounting Association, *A Statement of Basic Accounting Theory* (New York: American Accounting Association, 1966).

Burton, John C., "Some General and Specific Thoughts on the Accounting Environment," *Journal of Accountancy* (October, 1973), pp. 40–46.

Byrne, Gilbert R., "To What Extent Can the Practice of Accounting Be Reduced to Rules and Standards?" *Journal of Accountancy* (November, 1937), pp. 364–79.

Carlson, Marvin L., and Lamb, James W., "Constructing a Theory of Accounting — An Axiomatic Approach," *The Accounting Review* (July, 1981), pp. 544–73.

Chambers, R.J., "The Anguish of Accountants," *Journal of Accountancy* (March, 1972), pp. 68–74.

Deinzer, Harvey T., *Development of Accounting Thought* (New York: Holt, Rinehart, & Winston, 1965), Chapters 8 and 9.

Grady, Paul, "Inventory of Generally Accepted Accounting Principles in the United States of America," *The Accounting Review* (January, 1965), pp. 21–30.

Hicks, E.L., "APB: The First 3600 Days," *Journal of Accountancy* (September, 1969), pp. 56–60.

Higgins, T.S., and Bevis, Herman, "Generally Accepted Accounting Principles — Their Definition and Authority," *The New York Certified Public Accountant* (February, 1964), pp. 93–4.

Horngren, Charles T., "Accounting Principles: Private or Public Sector?" *Journal of Accountancy* (May, 1972), pp. 37–41.

Husband, G.R., "The Entity Concept in Accounting," *The Accounting Review* (October, 1954), pp. 560–62.

Lambert, Samuel Josheph, III, "Basic Assumptions in Accounting Theory Construction," *Journal of Accountancy* (February, 1974), pp. 41–8.

Lorig, A.N., "Some Basic Concepts on Accounting and Their Implications," *The Accounting Review* (July, 1964), pp. 563–73.

Mautz, Robert K., "The Place of Postulates in Accounting," *Journal of Accountancy* (January, 1965), pp. 46–9.

May, George O., "Generally Accepted Principles of Accounting," *Journal of Accountancy* (January, 1958), p. 26.

Metcalf, Richard W., "The Basic Postulates in Perspective," *The Accounting Review* (January, 1964), pp. 16–21.

Murphy, George, "A Numerical Representation of Some Accounting Conventions," *The Accounting Review* (April, 1974), pp. 233–44.

Popoff, Boris, "Postulates, Principles and Rules," *Accounting and Business Research* (Summer, 1972), pp. 182–93.

Staubus, G.J., "The Residual Equity Point of View in Accounting," *The Accounting Review* (January, 1959), pp. 11–15.

Storey, R.K., *The Search for Accounting Principles — Today's Problems in Perspective* (New York: American Institute of Certified Public Accountants, 1964).

Vatter, W.J., *The Fund Theory of Accounting and Its Implications for Financial Reports* (Chicago: University of Chicago Press, 1947).

Zeff, Stephen A., *Forging Accounting Principles in Five Countries: A History and an Analysis of Trends* (Champaign, Ill.: Stipes Publishing, 1971).

The Going-Concern Postulate

Devine, C.T., "Entity, Continuity, Discount, and Exit Values," *Essays in Accounting Theory*, Vol. 3 (1971), pp. 111–35.

Fremgen, James M., "The Going-Concern Assumption: A Critical Appraisal," *The Accounting Review* (October, 1968), pp. 649–56.

Sterling, Robert R., "The Going Concern: An Examination," *The Accounting Review* (July, 1968), pp. 481–502.

Storey, R.K., "Revenue Realization, Going Concern, and Measurement of Income," *The Accounting Review* (April, 1959), pp. 232–8.

Van Seventer, A., "The Continuity Postulate in the Dutch Theory of Business Income," *International Journal of Accounting, Education, and Research* (Spring, 1969), pp. 1–9.

Yu, S.C. "A Reexamination of the Going-Concern Postulate," *International Journal of Accounting, Education, and Research* (Spring, 1971), pp. 37–58.

The Revenue Principle

AAA Committee on Concepts and Standards Research, "The Realization Concept," *The Accounting Review* (April, 1965), pp. 312–22.

Arnett, H.E., "Recognition as a Function of Measurement in the Realization Concept," *The Accounting Review* (October, 1963), pp. 733–41.

Horngren, Charles T., "How Should We Interpret the Realization Concept?" *The Accounting Review* (April, 1965), pp. 323–33.

Myers, J.H., "The Critical Event and the Recognition of Net Profit," *The Accounting Review* (October, 1959), pp. 528–32.

Staubus, G.J., "Revenue and Revenue Accounts," *The Accounting Review* (July, 1956), pp. 284–94.

The Matching Principle

Fekrat, A.M., "The Conceptual Foundations of Absorption Costing," *The Accounting Review* (April, 1972), pp. 351–5.

Fremgen, James M., "The Direct Costing Controversy: An Identification of Issues," *The Accounting Review* (January, 1964), pp. 43–51.

Green, David G., Jr., "A Moral to Direct-Costing Controversy?" *Journal of Business* (July, 1960), pp. 218–26.

Horngren, Charles T., and Sorter, G.H., "The Effects of Inventory Costing Methods on Full and Direct Costing," *Journal of Accounting Research* (Spring, 1965), pp. 63–74.

Staubus, G.J., "Direct Relevant or Absorption Costing?" *The Accounting Review* (January, 1963), pp. 64–75.

Materiality

Barlev, B., "On the Measurement of Materiality," *Accounting and Business Research* (Summer, 1972), pp. 194–7.

Barnes, D.P., "Materiality — An Illusive Concept," *Management Accounting* (October, 1976), pp. 19–20.

Bernstein, L.A., "The Concept of Materiality," *The Accounting Review* (January, 1967), pp. 86–95.

FASB Discussion Memorandum, *An Analysis of Issues Related to Criteria for Determining Materiality* (Stamford, Ct.: Financial Accounting Standards Board, March 22, 1975).

Financial Accounting Standards Board, *An Analysis of Issues Related to Criteria for Determining Materiality* (Stamford, Ct.: Financial Accounting Standards Board, March 22, 1975).

Frishkoff, P., "An Empirical Investigation of the Concept of Materiality in Accounting," *Journal of Accounting Research*, supplement, *Empirical Research in Accounting: Selected Studies* (1970), pp. 138–53.

Hicks, E.L., "Some Comments on Materiality," *The Arthur Young Journal* (April, 1958), pp. 15–18.

Holmes, W., "Materiality — Through the Looking Glass," *Journal of Accountancy* (February, 1972), pp. 44–9.

Leitch, R.A., and Williams, J.R., "Materiality in Financial Statement Disclosure," *The Canadian Chartered Accountant Magazine* (December, 1975/January, 1976), pp. 53–8.

O'Connor, Melvin, and Collins, Daniel W., "Toward Establishing User-Oriented Materiality Standards," *Journal of Accountancy* (December, 1974), pp. 171–9.

Rappaport, A., "Materiality," *Journal of Accountancy* (April, 1964), pp. 45–52.

Rose, J.W., and Sorter, G.H., "Toward an Empirical Measure of Materiality," *Journal of Accounting Research*, supplement, *Empirical Research in Accounting: Selected Studies* (1970), pp. 138–53.

Woolsey, S., "Approach to Solving the Materiality Problem," *Journal of Accountancy* (March, 1973), pp. 47–50.

Woolsey, S., "Materiality Survey," *Journal of Accountancy* (September, 1973), pp. 91–2.

Conservatism

Devine, C.T., "The Rule of Conservatism Reexamined," *Journal of Accounting Research* (Autumn, 1963), pp. 137–8.

Landry, M., "Le Conservatism en Compatibilité — Essai d'Explication," *The Canadian Chartered Accountant Magazine* (November, 1970), pp. 321–4; (January, 1970), pp. 44–9.

Sterling, Robert R., "Conservatism: The Fundamental Principle of Valuation in Traditional Accounting," *Abacus* (December, 1967), p. 110.

Reliability, Objectivity, and Freedom from Bias

Arnett, H.E., "What Does Objectivity Mean to Accountants?" *Journal of Accountancy* (May, 1961), pp. 65–70.

Ijiri, Yuji, and Jaedicke, R.K., "Reliability and Objectivity of Accounting Measurements," *The Accounting Review* (July, 1966), pp. 474–83.

McFarland, W. B., "Concept of Objectivity," *Journal of Accountancy* (September, 1961), pp. 25–32.

Murphy, G.J., "A Numerical Representation of Some Accounting Conventions," *The Accounting Review* (April, 1976), pp. 277–86.

Consistency, Uniformity, and Comparability Principles

Bedford, Norton, and Toshio, Iino, "Consistency Reexamined," *The Accounting Review* (July, 1968), pp. 453–8.

Cadenhead, G.M., "Differences in Circumstances: Fact or Fantasy?" *Abacus* (September, 1970), pp. 71–80.

Chasteen, L.G., "An Empirical Study of Differences in Economic Circumstances as a Justification for Alternative Inventory Pricing Methods," *The Accounting Review* (July, 1971), pp. 504–508.

Frishkoff, P., "Consistency in Auditing and APB Opinion No. 20," *Journal of Accountancy* (August, 1972), pp. 64–70.

Hendriksen, E.S., "Toward Greater Comparability Through Uniformity of Accounting Principles," *CPA Journal* (February, 1967), pp. 105–15.

Keller, T.F., "Uniformity Versus Flexibility: A Review of the Rhetoric," *Law and Contemporary Problems* (Autumn, 1965), pp. 637–51.

Mautz, R.K., "An Approach to the Uniformity-Flexibility Issues in Accounting," *Financial Executive* (February, 1971), pp. 14–19.

Revsine, Lawrence, "Toward Greater Comparability in Accounting Reports," *Financial Analysts Journal* (January/February, 1975), pp. 45–51.

Simmons, John K., "A Concept of Comparability in Financial Reporting," *The Accounting Review* (October, 1967), pp. 680–92.

Sterling, Robert, R., "A Test of the Uniformity Hypotheses," *Abacus* (September, 1969), pp. 37–47.

APPENDIX   8.A

The Basic Postulates of Accounting (ARS 1)

Postulates Stemming from the Economic and Political Environment

Postulate A.1: Quantification Quantitative data are helpful in making rational economic decisions, i.e., in making choices among alternatives so that actions are correctly related to consequences.

Postulate A.2: Exchange Most of the goods and services that are produced are distributed through exchange, and are not directly consumed by the producers.

Postulate A.3: Entities (including identification of the entity) Economic activity is carried on through specific units or entities. Any report on the activity must identify clearly the particular unit or entity involved.

Postulate A.4: Time period (including specification of the time period) Economic activity is carried on during specifiable periods of time. Any report on that activity must identify clearly the period of time involved.

Postulate A.5: Units of measure (including identification of the monetary unit) Money is the common denominator in terms of which goods and services, including labor, natural resources, and capital are measured. Any report must clearly indicate which money (e.g., dollars, francs, pounds) is being used.

Postulates Stemming from the Field of Accounting Itself

Postulate B.1: Financial statements (related to A.1) The results of the accounting process are expressed in a set of fundamentally related financial statements which articulate with each other and rest upon the same underlying data.

Postulate B.2: Market price (related to A.2) Accounting data are based on prices generated by past, present or future exchanges which have actually taken place or are expected to.

Postulate B.3: Entities (related to A.3) The results of the accounting process are expressed in terms of specific units or entities.

Postulate B.4: Tentativeness (related to A.4) The results of operations for relatively short periods of time are tentative whenever allocations between past, present, and future periods are required.

The Imperatives

Postulate C.1: Continuity (including the correlative concept of limited life) In the absence of evidence to the contrary, the entity should be viewed as remaining in operation indefinitely. In the presence of evidence that the entity has a limited life, it should not be viewed as remaining in operation indefinitely.

Postulate C.2: Objectivity Changes in assets and liabilities, and the related effects (if any) on revenues, expenses, retained earnings, and the like, should not be given formal recognition in the accounts earlier than the point of time at which they can be measured in objective terms.

Postulate C.3: Consistency The procedures used in accounting for a given entity should be appropriate for the measurement of its position and its activities and should be followed consistently from period to period.

Postulate C.4: Stable unit Accounting reports should be based on a stable measuring unit.

Postulate C.5: Disclosure Accounting reports should disclose that which is necessary to make them not misleading.

Appendices 8.A and 8.B are reprinted by permission of the American Institute of Certified Public Accountants.

APPENDIX 8.B

A Tentative Set of Broad Accounting Principles for Business Enterprises (ARS 3)

The principles summarized below are relevant primarily to formal financial statements made available to third parties as representations by the management of the business enterprise. The "basic postulates of accounting" developed in Accounting Research Study No. 1 are integral parts of this statement of principles.

Broad principles of accounting should not be formulated mainly for the purpose of validating policies (e.g., financial management, taxation, employee compensation) established in other fields, no matter how sound or desirable those policies may be in and of themselves. Accounting draws its real strength from its neutrality as among the demands of competing special interests. Its proper functions derive from the measurement of the resources of specific entities and of changes in these resources. Its principles should be aimed at the achievement of those functions.

The principles developed in this study are as follows:

A Profit is attributable to the whole process of business activity. Any rule or procedure, therefore, which assigns profit to a portion of the whole process should be continuously re-examined to determine the extent to which it introduces bias into the reporting of the amount of profit assigned to specific periods of time.

B Changes in resources should be classified among the amounts attributable to:
   1 Changes in the dollar (price-level changes) which lead to restatements of capital but not to revenues or expenses.
   2 Changes in replacement costs (above or below the effect of price-level changes) which lead to elements of gain or loss.
   3 Sale or other transfer, or recognition of net realizable value, or which lead to revenue or gain.
   4 Other causes, such as accretion or the discovery of previously unknown natural resources.

C All assets of the enterprise, whether obtained by investments of owners or of creditors, or by other means, should be recorded in the accounts and reported in the financial statements. The existence of an asset is independent of the means by which it was acquired.

D The problem of measuring (pricing, valuing) an asset is the problem of measuring the future services, and involves at least three steps:
   1 A determination if future services do in fact exist. For example, a building is capable of providing space for manufacturing activity.
   2 An estimate of the quantity of services. For example, a building is estimated to be usable for twenty more years, or for half of its estimated total life.
   3 The choice of a method or basis or formula for pricing (valuing) the quantity of services arrived at under (2) above. In general, the choice of a pricing basis is made from the following three exchange prices:
      a. A past exchange price, e.g., acquisition cost or other initial basis. When this basis is used, profit or loss, if any, on the asset being priced will not be recognized until the sale or other transfer out of the business entity.
      b. A current exchange price, e.g., replacement cost. When this basis is used, profit or loss on the asset being priced will be recognized in two stages. The first stage will recognize part of the gain or loss in the period or periods from time of acquisition to time of usage or other disposition; the second stage will recognize the remainder of the gain or loss at the time of the sale or other transfer out of the entity, measured by the difference between sale (transfer) price and replacement cost. This method is still a cost method; an asset priced on this basis is being treated as a cost factor awaiting disposition.
      c. A future exchange price, e.g., anticipated selling price. When this basis is used, profit or loss, if any, has already been recognized in the accounts. Any asset priced on this basis is therefore being treated as though it were a receivable, in that sale or other transfer out of the business (including conversion into cash) will result in no gain or loss, except for any interest (discount) arising from the passage of time.

The proper pricing (valuation) of assets and the allocation of profit to accounting periods are dependent in large part upon estimates of the existence of future benefits, regardless of the bases used to price the assets. The need for estimates is unavoidable and cannot be eliminated by the adoption of any formula as to pricing.

4 All assets in the form of money or claims to money should be shown at their discounted present value or the equivalent. The interest rate to be employed in the accounting process is the market (effective) rate at the date the asset was acquired.

The discounting process is not necessary in the case of short-term receivables where the force of interest is small. The carrying value of receivables should be reduced by allowance for uncollectable elements; estimated collection costs should be recorded in the accounts.

If the claims to money are uncertain as to time or amount of receipt, they should be recorded at their current market value. If the current market value is so uncertain as to be unreliable, these assets should be shown at cost.

5 Inventories which are readily saleable at known prices with readily predictable costs of disposal should be recorded at net realizable value, and the related revenue taken up at the same time. Other inventory items should be recorded at their current (replacement) cost, and the related gain or loss separately reported. Accounting for inventories on either basis will result in recording revenues, gains, or losses before they are validated by sale but they are nevertheless components of the net profit (loss) of the period in which they occur.

Acquisition costs may be used whenever they approximate current (replacement) costs, as would probably be the case when the unit prices of inventory components are reasonably stable and turnover is rapid. In all cases the basis of measurement actually employed should be "subject to verification by another competent investigator."

6 All items of plant and equipment in service, or held in stand-by status, should be recorded at cost of acquisition or construction, with appropriate modification for the effect of the changing dollar either in the primary statements or in supplementary statements. In the external reports, plant and equipment should be restated in terms of current replacement costs whenever some significant event occurs, such as reorganization of the business entity or its merger with another entity or when it becomes a subsidiary of a parent company. Even in the absence of a significant event, the accounts could be restated at periodic intervals, perhaps every five years. The development of satisfactory indexes of construction costs and of machinery and equipment prices would assist materially in making the calculation of replacement costs feasible, practical, and objective.

7 The investment (cost or other basis) in plant and equipment should be amortized over the estimated service life. The basis for adopting a particular method of amortization for a given asset should be its ability to produce an allocation reasonably consistent with the anticipated flow of benefits from the asset.

8 All "intangibles" such as patents, copyrights, research, and development, and goodwill should be recorded at cost, with appropriate modification for the effect of the changing dollar either in the primary statements or in supplementary statements. Limited-term items should be amortized as expenses over their estimated lives. Unlimited-term items should continue to be carried as assets, without amortization.

If the amount of the investment (cost or other basis) in plant and equipment or in the "intangibles" has been increased or decreased as the result of appraisal or the use of index-numbers, depreciation or other amortization should be based on the changed amount.

E All liabilities of the enterprise should be recorded in the accounts and reported in the financial statements. Those liabilities which call for settlement in cash should be measured by the present (discounted) value of the future payments or the equivalent. The yield (market, effective) rate of interest at date of incurrence of the liability is the pertinent rate to use in the discounting process and in the amortization of "discount" and "premium." "Discount" and "premium" are technical devices for relating the issue price to the principal amount and should therefore be closely associated with principal amount in financial statements.

F Those liabilities which call for settlement in goods or services (other than cash) should be measured by their agreed selling price. Profit accrues in these cases as the stipulated services are performed or the goods produced or delivered.

G In a corporation, stockholders' equity should be classified into invested capital and retained earnings (earned surplus). Invested capital should, in turn, be classified according to source, that is, according to the underlying nature of the transactions giving rise to invested capital.

   Retained earnings should include the cumulative amount of net profits and net losses, less dividend declarations, and less amounts transferred to invested capital.

   In an unincorporated business, the same plan may be followed, but the acceptable alternative is more widely followed of reporting the total interest of each owner or group of owners at the balance sheet date.

H A statement of the results of the operations should reveal the components of profit in sufficient detail to permit comparisons and interpretations to be made. To this end, the data should be classified at least into revenues, expenses, gains, and losses.

   1 In general, the revenue of an enterprise during an accounting period represents a measurement of the exchange value of the products (goods and services) of that enterprise during that period. The preceding discussion, under D3b, is also pertinent here.

   2 Broadly speaking, expenses measure the costs of the amount of revenue recognized. They may be directly associated with revenue-producing transactions themselves (e.g., so-called "product costs") or with the accounting period in which the revenues appear (e.g., so called "period costs").

   3 Gains include such items as the results of holding inventories through a price rise, the sale of assets (other than stock-in-trade) at more than book value, and the settlement of liabilities at less than book value. Losses include items such as the result of holding inventories through a price decline, the sale of assets (other than stock-in-trade) at less then book value or their retirement, the settlement of liabilities at more than book value, and the imposition of liabilities through a lawsuit.

QUESTIONS

8.1 Define the *structure of accounting theory*.

8.2 Briefly explain the following elements of the structure of accounting theory:
   a. Accounting objectives.
   b. Accounting postulates.
   c. Accounting theoretical concepts.
   d. Accounting principles.
   e. Accounting techniques.

8.3 Name the three theoretical accounting concepts and briefly explain each.

8.4 Name the four accounting postulates and briefly explain each.

8.5 Name the nine accounting principles and briefly explain each.

8.6 What are the primary sources of accounting techniques?

8.7 What is meant by the term *generally accepted accounting principles*?

8.8 Robert R. Sterling made the following statement in "The Going Concern: An Examination," *The Accounting Review* (July, 1968), p. 481:

Thus, the going concern is one of the most important concepts in accounting. Such status would lead one to believe that the concept would be well-defined, its necessity as an axiom thoroughly discussed, and its connection to historical cost demonstrated. Anyone with such expectations is due for disappointment.

Do you agree with Sterling's statement? Why or why not?

8.9 L.A. Bernstein made the following statement in "The Concept of Materiality." *The Accounting Review* (January, 1967), p. 90:

In a profession where objectivity is a consideration of cardinal importance, materiality seems to be its "Achilles' Heel." If materiality is really such an important concept, and it certainly does play a dominant role in a number of pronouncements, then how is the profession to attain any semblance of consistent or uniform treatment in this area? How are new entrants to the profession to be trained? What are they to be told about the judgment processes leading up to materiality decisions?

Suggest some solutions to these questions.

*8.10 The following problem consists of 22 alternative disclosures or treatments. In each case, specify whether the treatment is supported by the *proprietary theory* or the *entity theory*:

   1 A company maintains a qualified pension plan. In prior years, the related pension provision has been included in the determination of corporate net income. In accounting for the costs related to qualified pension plans, ignore pension-related activities in the accounts of the company that maintains the pension plan.

   2 For the same situation described in (1), record pension-related activities in the accounts of the company that maintains the pension plan.

   3 Report earnings per share in external financial statements.

   4 Do not report earnings per share in external financial statements.

---

* Adapted from David N. Ricchiute. "Standard Setting and the Entity–Proprietary Debate," *Accounting, Organizations, and Society* (January, 1980), pp. 67–76.

5 Report income-tax payments as distributions of income (that is, do not include them in the determination of net income).

6 Report income-tax payments as expenses in the determination of net income.

7 Two autonomous and independent entities effect a plan of business combination in which the voting equity securities are exchanged for substantially all the common-stock interest of each of the combining companies. The surviving company does not plan to dispose of a substantial part of the assets of the formerly separate companies within the next several years. Account for this combination as a purchase.

8 Account for the combination described in (7) as a pooling of interests.

9 A parent company holds all of the outstanding voting equity securities of another company. The products of each company are homogeneous, and it is reasonable to anticipate that the parent company will maintain continuity of control over the other company. The treatment is not to combine the accounts of the two companies.

10 Combine the accounts of the two companies described in (9).

11 An investor company purchases 25 percent of the outstanding voting equity securities of another company, the investee. The investor has the ability to exercise significant influence over the investee. In accounting for the income or loss of an investee in the accounts of the investor, record an appropriate amount of the investee's income or loss in the accounts of the investor.

12 For the situation described in (11), ignore the investee's income or loss in the accounts of the investor.

13 A company issues convertible debt securities that can be converted by the holder into voting equity securities at a specified price. Attached to the convertible securities are detachable warrants that may be traded separately from the debt instrument. In accounting for the proceeds from the sale of convertible debt securities that have detachable stock purchase warrants, assign all of the proceeds to debt.

14 For the situation described in (13), allocate the proceeds to debt and equity.

15 A company issues a stock dividend to common shareholders. The amount of the stock dividend is equal to the par value of the related common shares. In determining whether stock dividends at par represent net income to recipients, do not treat stock dividends at par as income to recipients.

16 For the situation described in (15), treat stock dividends at par as income to recipients.

17 No special standards of financial accounting and reporting should be applied to development-stage companies.

18 Special standards of financial accounting and reporting should be applied to development-stage companies.

19 A company has sustained heavy losses over a period of time, resulting in a significant deficit in Retained Earnings. Furthermore, the carrying values of certain assets are significantly overstated. In accounting for quasi-reorganizations, effect the quasi-reorganization.

20 For the situation described in (19), do not effect the quasi-reorganization.

21 A company reports its inventory or stock-in-trade at cost or market, whichever is lower. Departures from historical cost to reflect inventory prices in excess of

historical cost dictate to report inventory at the lower cost or market.

22 For the situation described in (21), report inventory at current values.

8.11 Inconsistent Statements on Accounting Principles

The following two statements have been taken directly or with some modification from the accounting literature. Each of them is either taken out of context, involves circular reasoning, and/or contains one or more fallacies, half-truths, erroneous comments, conclusions, or inconsistencies (internally or with generally accepted principles or practices).

Statement 1

Accounting is a service activity. Its function is to provide quantitative financial information that is intended to be useful in making economic decisions about and for economic entities. Thus the accounting function might be viewed primarily as being a tool or device for providing quantitative financial information to management to facilitate decision making.

Statement 2

Financial statements that were developed in accordance with generally accepted accounting principles, which apply the conservatism convention, can be free from bias (or can give a presentation that is fair with respect to continuing and prospective stockholders as well as to retiring stockholders).

Required

Evaluate each of the preceding numbered statements on separate appropriately numbered answer sheets as follows:

1 List the fallacies, half-truths, circular reasoning, erroneous comments or conclusions, and/or inconsistencies.

2 Explain by what authority and/or on what basis each item listed in (1) can be considered to be fallacious, circular, inconsistent, a half-truth, or an erroneous comment or conclusion. If the statement or a portion of it is merely out of context, indicate the context(s) in which the statement would be correct.

(AICPA adapted).

8.12 Accounting Entity

The concept of the accounting entity often is considered to be the most fundamental of accounting concepts, one that pervades all of accounting.

Required

1 a. What is an accounting entity? Explain.

b. Explain why the accounting entity concept is so fundamental that it pervades all of accounting.

2 For each of the following indicate whether the accounting concept of entity is applicable; discuss and give illustrations.

a. A unit created by or under law

    b. The product-line segment of an enterprise

    c. A combination of legal units and/or product-line segments

    d. All of the activities of an owner or a group of owners

    e. An industry

    f. The economy of the United States   *(AICPA adapted)*

CHAPTER 9

CURRENT-VALUE ACCOUNTING

The theory and measurement of *business income* occupy a central place in the literature of financial and managerial accounting. Despite the proliferation of articles on its merits and measurement methods, however, the *income concept* remains the subject of different interpretations and schools of thought, each claiming practical or conceptual superiority to the others. Basically, four schools of thought exist concerning the better measurement of business income.

The *classical school* is characterized primarily by adherence to the unit-of-measure postulate and the historical-cost principle. Generally known as *historical cost accounting* or *conventional accounting*, the classical school regards "accounting income" as business income.

The *neoclassical school* is characterized primarily by its abandonment of the unit-of-measure postulate, recognition of changes in the general price level, and adherence to the historical cost principle. Generally known as *general, price-level-adjusted historical cost-accounting*, the neoclassical school's concept of business income is the "general, price-level-adjusted accounting income."

The *radical school* is characterized by its choice of *current values* as the valuation base. This school is divided into two forms. In one form, the current value-based financial statements are not adjusted for changes in the general price level. Generally known as *current-value accounting*, this school's concept of business income is "current income." In the second form of the radical school, the current-value-based financial statements are adjusted for changes in the general price level. Generally known as *general, price-level-adjusted current-value accounting*, this school's concept of business income is "adjusted current income."

In this chapter, our purposes are (1) to rationalize the existence of these four schools of thought by examining some of the features of the income concept in accounting and economics and introducing the concept of *capital maintenance*, and (2) to elaborate on the conceptual and operational problems associated with the implementation of current-value accounting. We will examine the other schools of thought in subsequent chapters.

9.1   THE RELEVANCE OF THE INCOME CONCEPT

Arguments in favor of measuring income could be extended *ad infinitum*. Income is a basic and important item of financial statements that has various uses in various contexts. Income is generally perceived as a basis for taxation, a determinant of dividend-payment policies, an investment and decision-making guide, and an element of prediction.

First, income is a basis for the *taxation* and *redistribution of wealth* among individuals. A version of income known as *taxable income*, is computed according to rules specified by governmental fiscal legislation. However, two bases of taxation other than income have been suggested. The possession of *resources* may be a more equitable basis for taxing economic entities. It also may be argued that individuals should be taxed on the basis of their *expenditures* rather than on the basis of their income.[1]

Second, income is perceived as a guide to a firm's *dividend* and *retention policy*. The income that is recognized is an indicator of the maximum amounts to be distributed as dividends and retained for expansion or reinvested in the firm. Due to the differences between accrual accounting and cash accounting, however, a firm may recognize an amount of income and, at the same time, not possess the funds to pay dividends. Thus, the recognition of income per se does not guarantee that dividends will be paid. Liquidity and investment prospects are additional variables necessary for the determination of dividend policies.

Third, income is viewed as an *investment* and *decision-making guide* in general. It is generally hypothesized that investors seek to maximize the return on capital invested, commensurate with an acceptable degree of risk. For example, the American Accounting Association's Committee on External Reporting defined a normative stockholders' valuation model centering on (1) the future dividend-per-share flows to be derived from an investment, and (2) the risk associated with these flows.[2] The model is

$$V_{0k} = \sum_{i=1}^{m} \frac{(a_{ik})\,(D_{ik})\,(m_{ik})}{\displaystyle\prod_{i=1}^{m} [1 + \beta_j(m_{jk})]} + \frac{(I_{nk} - CG_{nk})\,(a_{nk})}{\displaystyle\prod_{i=1}^{m} [1 + \beta_j(m_{jk})]} - I_0$$

where

V_{0k} = the net subjective present value of the gain that can be obtained by an investor k at time period 0 from buying one share at the market price I_0.

D_{ik} = the expected value of cash flows (dividends per share) during each period i.

I_{nk} = the expected transaction price of the stock at period n as projected by investor k, less commission and other direct outlays.

CG_{nk} = the expected capital-gains tax to be paid by the investor k when the securities are sold in period n.

β_j = the before-tax opportunity rate for a riskless investment. The rate may change over time j.

n_k = the discrete time period used by the investor.

a_{ik} = a "certainty equivalent" factor that adjusts the expected cash flows to a value such that a given investor is indifferent between D_{ik} and a cash flow that is certain to be paid. This factor is determined by each investor's utility preference for risk.

$m_{ik}\,(m_{jk})$ = $1 -$ the expected marginal tax rate for each cash flow for each investor k and for each time period i or j.

I_0 = the transaction price at the time of decision.

The Committee on External Reporting also suggested that a firm's ability to pay dividends is a function of the following variables: (1) net cash flows from operations, (2) nonoperating cash flows, (3) cash flows from changes in the levels of investment by stockholders and creditors, (4) cash flows from investment in assets, (5) cash flows from priority claims, (6) cash flows from random events, (7) management attitudes regarding stocks of resources, and (8) cash dividend policy.[3] It is doubtful, however, that accounting income could be used to predict most of these variables. In addition, there has been a gradual shift of emphasis from the income concept to a cash-flow concept. For example, the "Trueblood Report" expresses the following objective:

> An objective of financial statements is to provide information useful to investors and creditors for predicting, comparing, and evaluating potential cash flows to them in terms of account, timing, and related uncertainty.[4]

Fourth, income is perceived as a *predictive* device that aids in the prediction of future incomes and future economic events. In fact, past values of income, based on historical cost and on current value, have been found to be useful in predicting future values of both versions of income.[5] Income consists of both *operational* results, or *ordinary income*, and *nonoperational* results, or *extraordinary gains and losses*, the sum of which is equal to net income. Ordinary income is assumed to be current and repetitive; extraordinary gains and losses are not. Research findings show that, as a predictor of future earnings, ordinary income is superior to net income.[6] Because such findings imply that the behaviour of net income may be erratic and of no use to investment decision making, there is some reason to use a measure of income that is conducive to accurate predictions. In others words, *income smoothing* may be justified by the need for sound predictive ability and may be intended by management to show plausible forms of trends over time to outside users of financial statements.[7] Income smoothing has been defined as the "intentional dampening of fluctuations about some level of earnings that is currently considered to be normal for a firm."[8] This definition implies that a choice must be made among a number of accounting procedures and measurements to minimize the cyclical behavior of accounting income. Income smoothing is motivated by the desire to enhance the reliability of prediction based on income and to reduce the risk surrounding the accounting numbers.[9]

A recent study focuses more precisely on the reduction of systematic risk through the impact of income smoothing on reducing the covariance of the firm's returns with market returns.[10] Three smoothing dimensions may be identified: (1) smoothing through the occurrence and/or recognition of events, (2) smoothing through allocation over time, and (3) smoothing through classification.[11]

The fifth way that income may be perceived is a measure of *efficiency*. Income is both a measure of management's stewardship of an entity's resources and of management's efficiency in conducting the affairs of a firm. This concern is well expressed in the FASB Report of the Study Group on the Objectives of Financial Statements, which maintains that "an objective of financial statements is to supply information useful in judging management's ability to utilize enterprise resources effectively in achieving the primary enterprise goal" and "the earning process consists of effort and performance directed at reaching the primary enterprise goal of returning, over time, the maximum amount of cash to its owners."[12] Management's primary goal is assumed to be to maximize earnings per share. In fact, the *stockholders' welfare-maximization* (SWM) model may be challenged by the *management welfare-maximization* (MWM) model. The management welfare-maximization model implies that managers may try to increase their remunerations by maximizing sales or assets, the firm's rate of growth, or managerial utility.[13] As a result, Findlay and Whitmore contend the following with respect to earnings:

> SWM assumes that earnings are objectively determined to reveal the time position of the business to its owners and the capital market.... MWM presumes management manipulation or avoidance within the legality of full disclosure in order to present the firm's operations in the most favorable light.[14]

Thus, management welfare-maximization casts doubt on income as a measure of efficiency.

In conclusion, income has a role to play in various areas, but its uesfulness may be subject to a number of limitations, as indicated by the five cases we have discussed here.

9.2   THE TRADITIONAL ACCOUNTING CONCEPT OF INCOME

9.2.1   A Description of Accounting Income

Accounting income is operationally defined as the difference between the *realized revenues* arising from the transactions of the *period* and the *corresponding historical costs*. This definition suggests *five* characteristics of accounting income:

1 Accounting income is based on the *actual transaction* entered into by the firm (primarily revenues arising from the sales of goods or services minus the costs necessary to achieve these sales). Conventionally, the accounting profession has employed a transaction approach to income measurement. The transactions may be external or internal. *Explicit* (external) *transactions* result from the acquisition by a firm of goods or services from other entities. *Implicit* (internal) *transactions* result from the use or allocation of assets within a firm. External transactions are explicit because they are based on objective evidence; internal transactions are implicit because they are based on less objective evidence, such as the use and passage of time.

2 Accounting income is based on the *period postulate* and refers to the financial performance of the firm during a given period.

3 Accounting income is based on the *revenue principle* and requires the definition, measurement, and recognition of revenues. In general, the *realization principle* is the test for the recognition of revenues and, consequently, for the recognition of income. Specific circumstances present exceptions, however, as suggested in Chapter 6.

4 Accounting income requires the measurement of expenses in terms of the *historical cost* to the enterprise, constituting a strict adherence to the cost principle. An asset is accounted for at its acquisition cost until a sale is realized, at which time any change in value is recognized. Thus, expenses are expired assets or expired acquisition costs.

5 Accounting income requires that the realized revenues of the period be related to appropriate or corresponding relevant costs. Accounting income, therefore, is based on the *matching principle*. Basically, certain costs or period costs are allocated to or matched with revenues and the other costs are reported and carried forward as assets. Costs allocated and matched with period revenues are assumed to have an expired service potential.

9.2.2 Advantages of Accounting Income

Among the important and most spirited defenders of accounting income are Ijiri, Kohler, Littleton, and Mautz.[15] We will discuss four of their principal arguments.

The first argument in favor of accounting income is that it has survived the test of time. Most users of accounting data believe that accounting income is useful and that it constitutes a determinant of the practices and thought patterns of decision makers. To support this argument, Mautz states that:

> Accounting is what it is today not so much because of the desire of accountants as because of the influence of businessmen. If those who make management and investment decisions had not found financial reports based on historical cost useful over the years, changes in accounting would long since have been made.[16]

Second, because it is based on actual, factual transactions, accounting income is measured and reported objectively and is therefore basically verifiable. Objectivity is generally reinforced by the belief of advocates of the use of accounting income that accounting should report facts rather than values. As Kohler states, "Accounting has never been a device for 'measuring (current) value,' 'changes in value' or the present worth of an asset or asset group."[17]

Third, by relying on the realization principle for the recognition of revenue, accounting income meets the criterion of conservatism. In other words, reasonable caution is taken in the measurement and reporting of income by ignoring value changes and recognizing only realized gains.

Fourth, accounting income is considered useful for control purposes, especially in reporting on stewardship (management's use of resources entrusted to it). Accounting income conveys the background of the story of the way in which management has met its responsibilities.

9.2.3   Disadvantages of Accounting Income

In addition to being strongly defended, accounting income has also been severely criticized in the literature for its various limitations. Basically, the arguments against the use of accounting income question its relevance to decision making. Let us examine some of these arguments.

One argument is that accounting income fails to recognize unrealized increases in values of assets held in a given period due to the application of the historical-cost and realization principles. This prevents useful information from being disclosed and permits the disclosure of a heterogeneous mix of gains from prior and current periods. The net result does not correspond effectively to the income of the current period.

A second argument is that the reliance of accounting income on the historical-cost principle makes comparability difficult, given the different acceptable methods of computing "cost" (for example, the different inventory costing methods) and the different acceptable methods of cost allocation deemed arbitrary and incorrigible.[18]

Third, reliance of accounting income on the realization principle, historical-cost principle, and conservatism may result in misleading and misunderstood data or data that is irrelevant to users. A case in point is the lack of usefulness of ratios based on financial statements prepared in conformity with these principles.

Reliance on the historical-cost principle may give users the impression that the balance sheet represents an approximation of value rather than merely a statement of unallocated cost balances. In addition, the emphasis on income determination has led to a resolution of controversial issues based on their impact on the income statement, thereby creating a mixture of items on the balance sheet that are quite hard to define (for example, deferred tax-allocation debits and credits).

9.3   THE NATURE OF THE ECONOMIC CONCEPT OF INCOME

The concept of *income* has always been an important point of interest to economists. Adam Smith was the first economist to define income as an *increase in wealth*.[19] Most classicists — Marshall, in particular — followed Smith's concept of income and linked its conceptualization to business practices.[20] For example, they separated *fixed* and *circulating* (working) *capital*, separated *physical capital* and *income*, and emphasized realization as a test of income recognition. Toward the end of the nineteenth century, the understanding that income is more than cash was expressed in Von Bohm Bawerk's theories on capital and income.[21] Von Bohm Bawerk attempted to develop a nonmonetary concept of income despite the monetary movement that dominated economic analysis at the time.[22]

At the beginning of the twentieth century, ideas concerning income advanced by Fisher, Lindahl, and Hicks provided a major, new outlook on the nature of the economic concept of income. Fisher defined economic income as a series of events that corresponds to different states: the enjoyment of psychic income, the real income, and the money income.[23] *Psychic income* is the actual personal consumption of goods and services that produces a psychic enjoyment and satisfaction of wants. Psychic income is a psychological concept that cannot be measured directly, but it can be approximated by real income. *Real income* is an expression of the events that give rise to psychic enjoyments. Real income is best measured by the *cost of living*. In other words, the satisfaction created by the psychic enjoyment of profit is measured by the money payments made for the acquisition of goods and services before or after consumption. Thus, psychic income, real income, and the cost of living are three different stages of income. Finally, *money income* represents all the money received and intended to be used for consumption to meet the cost of living. Although psychic income is the most fundamental income level and money income is that stage of income most often referred to as "income," Fisher perceived real income to be the most practical for accountants.

Lindahl introduced the concept of income as *interest*, referring to the continuous *appreciation* of capital goods over time.[23] The differences between the interest and the consumption anticipated for a given period are perceived as *saving*. This idea led to the generally accepted concept of economic income as consumption plus saving expected to take place during a certain period, the saving being equal to the change in economic capital. This may be expressed by the identity

$$Y_e = C + (K_t - K_{t-1})$$

where

Y_e = economic income.
C = consumption.
K_t = capital as of period t.
K_{t-1} = capital as of period $t-1$.

Hicks used the concepts introduced by Fisher and Lindahl to develop a general theory of *economic income*,[24] which defined a person's personal income as "the maximum amount he can consume during a week and still expect to be as well-off at the end of the week as he was at the beginning."[25] This definition has become the basis of many discussions on the concept of income. One problem raised by such a definition, however, is the lack of consensus on the interpretation of the term "as well-off," or "welloffness." The most accepted interpretation is that of capital maintenance, in which case the "Hicksian" income is the maximum amount that may be consumed in a given period and still maintain the capital intact.

9.4 CONCEPTS OF CAPITAL MAINTENANCE

The concept of *capital maintenance* implies that income is recognized after capital has been maintained or costs have been recovered. *Return on capital* (income) is distinguished from *return of capital* (cost recovery). Two principal concepts of capital maintenance or cost recovery may be expressed both in terms of units of money (*financial capital*) and in terms of units of the same general purchasing power (*physical capital*). Thus we are provided with four concepts of capital maintenance:

1 *Money maintenance:* financial capital measured in units of money.
2 *General purchasing-power money maintenance:* financial capital measured in units of the same purchasing power.

3 *Productive-capacity maintenance:* physical capital measured in units of money.
4 *General purchasing-power, productive-capacity maintenance:* physical capital measured in units of the same purchasing power.

The first concept implies that the financial capital invested or reinvested by the owners is maintained. Under the money-maintenance concept, income is equal to the change in net assets adjusted for capital transactions expressed in terms of dollars. Conventional accounting as it relies on historical cost for the valuation of assets and liabilitites, conforms to the money-maintenance concept.

The second concept implies that the purchasing power of the financial capital invested or reinvested by the owner is maintained. Under the general purchasing-power, money-maintenance concept, income is equal to the change in net assets adjusted for capital transactions expressed in units of the same purchasing-power money. General price-level adjusted, historical-cost financial statements conform to the general purchasing-power, money-maintenance concept.

The third concept implies that the physical productive capacity of the firm is maintained. Interpretations of the specific meaning of "productive capacity" differ. The *Sandilands Report* in the United Kingdom interprets productive capacity as follows:

> What is meant by a company's "productive capacity" and how is it to be maintained intact? We have received various suggestions as to how this calculation should be made, which may be classified into three alternative definitions of productive capacity:
>
> ■ Productive capacity should be defined as the *physical assets* possessed by the company, so that profit would be the amount that could be distributed after making sufficient provision to replace the physical assets held by the company as they are consumed or wear out.
> ■ Productive capacity should be defined as the capacity to produce the same *volume* of goods and services [output] in the following year as could be produced in the current year.
> ■ Productive capacity should be defined as the capacity to produce the same *value* of goods and services [output] in the following year as could be produced in the current year.[26]

Although the first definition of productive capacity in terms of same assets does not take into account technological improvements, the last two definitions in terms of "same volume of output" and "same value of output" do allow technological improvements to be made. Productive-capacity maintenance is the concept of capital maintenance used in current-value accounting that discloses assets and liabilities in the financial statements at their current values.

Finally, the fourth concept of capital maintenance implies the maintenance of the physical productive capacity of the firm measured in units of the same purchasing power. General purchasing-power, productive-capacity maintenance is the concept of capital maintenance used in general price-level-adjusted, current-value accounting.

The following example illustrates the impact of each of the four concepts of capital maintenance on the income statement. Suppose that a given firm has $2,000 in net assets at the beginning and $3,000 in net assets at the end of a given period. Also assume that $2,500 in net assets are required to maintain the firm's actual physical productive capacity and that the general price level increased 10 percent during the period. According to each of the concepts of capital maintenance, the firm's income would be:

1 Money maintenance:

$$\$3,000 - \$2,000 = \$1,000$$

2 General purchasing-power maintenance:

$$\$3,000 - [\$2,000 + (0.10 \times \$2,000)] = \$800$$

3 Productive-capacity maintenance:

$$\$3,000 - \$2,500 = \$500$$

4 General purchasing-power, productive-capacity maintenance:

$$\$3,000 - [\$2,500 + (0.10 \times \$2,500)] = \$250$$

The accounting income is therefore $1,000, the general price-level-adjusted accounting income is $800, the current-value-based income is $500, and the general price-level-adjusted, current-value-based income is $250. In the rest of this chapter, we will discuss current-value accounting; the other concepts will be presented in the following chapters.

9.5 CONCEPTS OF CURRENT VALUE

The productive-capacity maintenance concept requires that the assets and liabilities of a firm be represented in terms of current values. Current value can be calculated on the basis of (1) capitalization, or the present-value method, (2) current entry price, (3) current exit price, or (4) a combination of values derived from these three methods.

9.5.1 Capitalization

Under the *capitalization method* for calculating current value, the *capitalized value* or *present value* of an asset, group of assets, or total assets is the net amount of the discounted expected cash flows pertaining to the asset, group of assets, or total assets during their useful lives. To compute this capitalized value, four variables must be known: (1) the expected cash flows that may result from the use or disposal of the asset, (2) the timing of those expected cash flows, (3) the number of years of the asset's remaining life, and (4) the appropriate discount rate. If these variables can be determined in an accurate and objective manner, the capitalization or present-value method can be expressed by

$$P_0 = \sum_{j=2}^{n} \frac{R_j}{(1+i)^j}, \quad P_1 = \sum_{j=2}^{n} \frac{R_j}{(1+i)^{j-1}}, \text{ and } I_1 = (P_1 - P_0) + R_j$$

where

P_0 = the capitalized value or present value at time 0.
P_1 = the capitalized value or present value at time 1.
I_1 = income for the first year.

R_j = expected net cash flow in period j.
i = appropriate discount rate.
n = useful remaining life of the asset.

Whereas the accounting income based on historical data for a specified period may be labeled *ex post income*, or *periodic income*, the present-value income is the *total pure-profit income* expected to be accrued up to the firm's planning horizon. It is an *ex ante income*, or *economic income*, that reflects expectations about future cash flows. Such income may be computed when all the relevant variables are known with certainty as well as when all the relevant variables are probabilistic.

For example, assume that the following net cash flows are expected to result from the total assets of a firm with a remaining useful life of four years:

Year	0	1	2	3	4
Cash Flow	—	$7,000	$8,500	$10,000	$12,000

If the appropriate discount rate is assumed to be 5 percent, then the present value at the beginning of Year 1 will be $32,887, which (using present-value tables) is computed

Capitalized Value at Beginning of Year 1	Capitalized Value at End of Year 1
$ 7,000 × 0.9524 = $ 6,667	$ 8,500 × 0.9524 = $ 8,095
8,500 × 0.9070 = 7,710	10,000 × 0.9070 = 9,070
10,000 × 0.8638 = 8,638	12,000 × 0.8638 = 10,366
12,000 × 0.8227 = 9,872	$27,531
$32,887	

The income for the first year can then be computed

Expected cash flow from the use of the assets for Year 1	$ 7,000
+ Capitalized value of the total asset at the end of Year 1	27,531
= Total value of the firm at the end of Year 1	$34,531
− Capitalized value of the total assets at the beginning of Year 1	$32,887
= Income for the first year	$ 1,644

The present-value or economic income, of $1,644 represents the real increase in the value of the firm in the first year. This value is equivalent to 5 per cent of the starting capital of $32,887. Because most theorists define the discount rate as the *subjective rate of return*, Edwards and Bell call the present-value or economic income the *subjective profit*.[27] Several appropriate discount rates, however, may be used to compute capitalized value:

(1) the historical rate of discount, (2) the current rate of discount, (3) the average expected rate of discount, (4) the weighted-average cost of capital, and (5) the incremental borrowing rate. The FASB appropriately defines these rates as follows:

> The *historical rate* of discount is the rate of return that is implicit in the amount of cash (or other consideration) paid to acquire an asset. More specifically, it is the rate of discount that, at the date of acquisition, causes the present value of the expected cash flows from an asset to be equal to the asset's historical cost....
>
> The *current rate* of discount is the rate of return implicit in the amount of cash (or other consideration) that would have to be paid if the same asset were acquired currently....
>
> The *average expected rate* of discount is the average rate of return that is expected to be earned on similar assets during some (usually long-term) future period....
>
> The *weighted-average cost of capital* is based on a particular structure — that is, a particular ratio of long-term debt, preferred stockholders' equity, and common stockholders' equity....
>
> The *incremental borrowing rate* is the rate of interest that would have to be paid to obtain additional borrowed capital currently....[28]

The variables included in the capitalized-value formula are merely expectations that are subject to change. At the end of the first year, for example, suppose it is estimated that the expected cash flows will be $10,000 a year for the remaining three years, instead of $8,500, $10,000, and $12,000. The present-value income for the first year is found as follows:

Cash flow expected at the end of the first year	$ 7,000
+ Capitalized value at the end of Year 1 of expected cash flows of $10,000 a year for three years	27,232
= Total value of the firm at the end of Year 1	$34, 232
− Capitalized value of the total assets at the beginning of Year 1	$32,887
= Income for the year	$ 1,345

The new income for the year ($1,345) includes the following elements:

1	Anticipated economic income (0.05 × $32,887)	$1,644
2	Diminution in the capitalized value of the firm	(299)
3	Income for the year	$1,345

Although we consider the diminution in the capitalized value of the firm to be a loss in this analysis, another point of view considers it to be a mere adjustment of the original value of the firm due to changes in expectations. In other words, the capitalized value of the firm based on the new expectations would be $32,602, rather than $32,887. Consequently, the new income for the year ($1,345) would then include the following elements:

1 Economic income (0.05 × $32,602) $1,630
2 Changes in the original value
   of the firm ($32,887 − $32,602)   (285)
3 Decrease in the capitalized value $1,345

TABLE 9.1
Computation of Economic Income

Year	(1) Capitalized Value at the Beginning of the Year	(2) Capitalized Value at the End of the Year	(3) Expected Cash Flow for the Year	(4) Economic Profit (4) = (2) + (3) − (1)
1	$32,887	$27,531	$ 7,000	$1,644
2	27,531	20,408	8,500	1,377
3	20,408	11,428.8	10,000	1,020.8
4	11,428.8	—	12,000	571.2
Total economic profit				4,613
Total cash flow			37,500	
Total depreciation expense (assumed)			28,000	
Accounting income			9,500	9,500
Subjective goodwill				4,887

The next question that arises pertains to the nature of the differences between the present-value or economic income and the accounting income. The economic income is an *ex ante* income based on future cash-flow expectations; the accounting income is an *ex post* or *periodic* income based on historical values. Solomons, in his revision of a work by Alexander, proposes the following distinction between economic income and accounting income:

       Accounting income
    + Unrealized tangible asset changes
    − Realized tangible asset changes that occurred in prior periods
    + Changes in the value of intangible assets
    = Economic income[29]

Here, intangible assets refer not to the conventional intangible assets found on the balance sheet but to a concept called *subjective goodwill*, which arises from the use of expectations in the computation of economic income. Thus, in the previous example, the economic income for the four-year period is equal to $4,613, as shown in Table 9.1. Assuming an annual depreciation of $7,000, the accounting income is equal to $9,500. The difference between the economic income and the accounting income is $4,887, which is the subjective goodwill. A reconciliation is presented in Table 9.2.

TABLE 9.2
Reconciliation of the Economic and Accounting Incomes

Year	Depreciation Accounting	Subjective Goodwill	Difference
1	$ 7,000	$ 5,356	($1,644)
2	7,000	7,123	123
3	7,000	8,979.2	1,979.2
4	7,000	11,428.8	4,428.8
Total	$28,000	$32,887	$4,887

The capitalized-value method is deemed useful for such long-term operating decisions as capital budgeting and product development. The options yielding the highest positive capitalized values are deemed to be the best methods. Capitalized values of long-term receivables and long-term payables are also used in financial statements, as shown by APB Opinion No. 21, *Interest on Receivables and Payables.*[30] The capitalized value is generally considered to be an ideal attribute of assets and liabilities, although it presents some conceptual and practical limitations. From a practical view-point, capitalized value suffers from the subjective nature of the expectations used for its computation. From a conceptual viewpoint, capitalized value suffers from (1) the lack of an adequate adjustment for the risk preferences of all users, (2) the ignorance of the contribution of other factors than physical assets to the cash flows, (3) the difficulty of allocating total cash flows to the separate factors that comprised the contribution, and (4) the fact that the marginal present values of physical assets used jointly in operations cannot be added together to obtain the value of the firm.[31]

9.5.2   Current Entry Price

Interpretations of Current Entry Prices

Current entry price represents the amount of cash or other consideration that would be required to obtain the same asset or its equivalent. The following interpretations of current entry price have been used.

Replacement cost–used is equal to the amount of cash or other consideration that would be needed to obtain an *equivalent* asset on the second-hand market having the same remaining useful life.

Reproduction cost is equal to the amount of cash or other consideration that would be needed to obtain an *identical* asset to the existing asset. Edwards and Bell focus on the replacement of an existing asset with an *identical* asset:

> It must be remembered that it is not the current cost of equivalent services provided by fixed assets over some time period which we wish to measure, but the current cost of using the particular fixed asset which the entrepreneur chose to adopt and is still using. It is that particular decision that the entrepreneur wishes to evaluate on the basis of accounting data. It may well be that he then may wish to compare these data with

opportunity cost data relating to selling and/or replacing the fixed asset, but in order to make this decision about the future, he must have information about the actual, present, and past.[32]

Whereas both replacement cost–used and reproduction cost emphasize the replacement of existing assets, *replacement cost–new* emphasizes the replacement of the productive capacity of assets. Replacement cost–new is equal to the amount of cash or other consideration needed to replace or reproduce the productive capacity of an asset with a new asset that reflects changes in technology. For example, Paton and Paton consider the alternative of replacing an existing asset with an asset of equivalent capacity:

> It should be understood that the significant replacement cost is the cost of providing the existing capacity to produce in terms of the most up-to-date methods available. Thus, it is largely a waste of time to estimate the cost of replacing an obsolete or semi-obsolete plant unit literally in kind; such an estimate will never afford a basis for a sound appraisal of the property nor furnish a useful measure of current operating cost. The fact of interest is what it would cost to replace the capacity represented in the existing asset with a machine of modern design. To put the point in another way, cost of replacing in kind is a significant basis on which to measure the economic importance of property in use only in the case of standard, up-to-date facilities.[33]

The common characteristic of the three notions of current entry prices is that they all correspond to the costs of replacing or reproducing an asset held. The issue that remains to be solved is the choice of the method of measurement of current entry prices. The three most advocated methods use *quoted market prices*, *specific price indexes*, and *appraisals*, or management estimates. The American Accounting Association Committee on Concepts and Standards has expressed the following order of preference:

> The current cost of obtaining the same or equivalent services should be the basis for valuation subsequent to acquisition, as well as at the date of acquisition. Where there is an established market for assets of like kind and condition, quoted market prices provide the most objective evidence of current cost. Such prices may be readily available for land, buildings, and certain types of standard equipment. Where there is no established market for assets of like kind and condition, current cost may be estimated by reference to the purchase price of assets which provide equivalent service capacity. The purchase price of such substitute assets should be adjusted for differences in operating characteristics such as cost, capacity, and quality. In other cases, adjustment of historical cost by the use of specific price indexes may provide acceptable approximations of current cost. Appraisals are acceptable only if they are based on the above methods of estimating costs.[34]

Accounting for Holding Gains and Losses

The valuation of assets and liabilities at current entry prices gives rise to *holding gains and losses* as entry prices change during a period of time when they are held or owed by a firm. Holding gains and losses may be divided into two elements: (1) the realized holding gains and losses that correspond to the items sold or to the liabilities discharged, and (2) the nonrealized holding gains and losses that correspond to the items still held or to the liabilities owed at the end of the reporting period. These holding gains and losses may be classified as income when capital maintenance is viewed solely in money terms. They may also be classified as capital adjustments, because they measure the additional elements of income that must be retained to maintain the existing productive capacity. Thus, justification for the holding gains and losses on capital adjustment may be related to a particular definition of income.

Proponents of the capital-adjustment alternative favor a definition of income based on the preservation of physical capital. Such an approach would define the profit of an entity for a given period as the maximum amount that could be distributed and still maintain the operating capability at the level that existed at the beginning of the period. Because the changes in replacement cost cannot be distributed without impairing the operating capability of the entity, this approach dictates that replacement-cost changes be classified as capital adjustments.

Proponents of this alternative favor a definition of income based on the preservation of financial capital (the money-maintenance concept). Such an approach would define profit as the maximum amount that could be distributed and still maintain the financial capital invested at the level that existed at the beginning of the period. Such an approach dictates that replacement-cost changes be classified as holding gains and losses. The academic literature provides two alternative arguments in support of the holding-gains treatment. The first argument is that holding gains represent a "realizable cost savings" in the sense that the entity is better off because it would now cost more to acquire the asset. The second argument is that replacement-cost changes may be viewed as "surrogates" for changes in net realizable value or capitalized value. Thus, the holding gains represent increases in the expected net receipts from using or selling the asset in the future.

The following two examples demonstrate the accounting treatments of holding gains and losses for inventories and depreciable assets.

Example 1: The accounting treatment of inventories at the current entry price and the corresponding holding gains and losses.

Assume that a firm invests $6,000 in a new company on January 1. On the same date, it buys 1,000 pounds of coffee at $6.00 a pound. During the year, the firm sells 600 pounds of coffee at $10.00 per pound when the replacement cost is $8.00 per pound. The replacement cost of coffee at the end of the year is $9.00 per pound. The accounting entries are as follows:

Merchandise Inventory (1,000 × $6.00)	$6,000	
Cash		$6,000
(to record purchase of merchandise)		
Cash	6,000	
Cost of Goods Sold (600 × $8.00)	4,800	
Sale (600 × $10.00)		6,000
Merchandise Inventory (600 × $8.00)		4,800
(to record sale of merchandise)		
Merchandise Inventory	2,400	
Realized Holding Gain [600 × ($8 − $6)]		1,200
Unrealized Holding Gain [400 × ($9 − $6)]		1,200
(to record holding gains)		

Example 2: The accounting treatment of noncurrent assets at the current entry price and the corresponding holding gains and losses.

Assume that a firm purchases an asset with a four-year useful life for $2,000 and that its replacement cost increases $1,000 a year. The depreciation expenses must be determined on the basis of replacement cost. Most proponents of the replacement cost method agree on the need to include added amounts in current expenses as a "catch-up", "make-up," or "back-log" depreciation if the replacement costs continue to increase over the useful life of the asset. Determination of the "backlog" depreciation is shown in the following table:

Year	1	2	3	4
Year-end replacement cost	$3,000	$4,000	$5,000	$6,000
Depreciation expense based on replacement cost	750	1,000	1,250	1,500
Backlog depreciation	—	250	500	750
Opening accumulated depreciation		750	2,000	3,750
Adjusted accumulated depreciation	$ 750	$2,000	$3,750	$6,000

Thus, the accounting entries in each year would be:

Year 1:
Asset (replacement cost)	$1,000	
Depreciation	750	
Holding Gain		$1,000
Accumulated Depreciation		750

Year 2:
Asset (replacement cost)	1,000	
Depreciation	1,000	
Backlog Depreciation	250	
Holding Gain		1,000
Accumulated Depreciation		1,250

Year 3:
Asset (replacement cost)	1,000	
Depreciation	1,250	
Backlog Depreciation	500	
Holding Gain		1,000
Accumulated Depreciation		1,750

Year 4:
Asset (replacement cost)	1,000	
Depreciation	1,500	
Backlog Depreciation	750	
Holding Gain		1,000
Accumulation Depreciation		2,250

If, however, we assume that the value of the asset increases uniformly over the year, then the depreciation expense should be computed on the basis of the average current entry price for the year. The entries for the first year result from the fact that depreciation expense is $625 (25 percent of the average asset value of $2,500) and that the holding gain will be $875 ($1,000 less one-half-year depreciation on the $1,000 increase). Accordingly, the entries for each year would be:

Year 1:

Asset (replacement cost)	$1,000	
Depreciation	625	
Holding Gain		$ 875
Accumulated Depreciation		750

Year 2:

Asset (replacement cost)	1,000	
Depreciation (0.25 × $3,500	875	
Holding Gain		625
Accumulated Depreciation		1,250

Year 3:

Asset (replacement cost)	1,000	
Depreciation (0.25 × $4,500)	1,125	
Holding Gain		375
Accumulated Depreciation		1,750

Year 4:

Asset (replacement cost)	1,000	
Depreciation (0.25 × $5,500)	1,375	
Holding Gain		125
Accumulated Depreciation		2,250

Three methods have been suggested to account for *backlog depreciation*, (1) charge or credit to retained earnings, (2) charge or credit to current income, and (3) adjust holding gains and losses by the amount of backlog depreciation.

The first method treats backlog depreciation as a prior-period adjustment, given that it represents the amount that should have been charged in previous periods for the replacement of the asset.

The second method treats backlog depreciation as an expense of the current period, given that income should be charged with all of the estimated costs of replacing assets.

The third method argues that the true holding gain or loss should reflect the age of the asset.

In fact, the three methods result from two fundamentally different interpretations of depreciation. One view is that depreciation should provide a reserve for the future replacement of assets, so that backlog depreciation should be treated according to either of the first two methods. The second view is that depreciation is a current cost of operations, so that backlog depreciation should be treated according to the third method.

EXHIBIT 9.1
Reeves Corporation Balance Sheet

	December 31, 19X6		December 31, 19X7	
	Debit	Credit	Debit	Credit
Cash	$ 10,000		$ 30,000	
Accounts Receivable	20,000		30,000	
Inventories	30,000	(3,000 units)	20,000	(2,000 units)
Land	40,000		40,000	
Plant (five-year life)	50,000		50,000	
Less: Allowance for				
Depreciation		$ 10,000		$ 20,000
Bonds (10% interest rate)		50,000		50,000
Common Stock		50,000		50,000
Retained Earnings		40,000		50,000
Total	$150,000	$150,000	$170,000	$170,000

Replacement-Cost Techniques Applied

Exhibit 9.1 shows the Reeves Corporation balance sheet on December 31, 19X6, and December 31, 19X7. The Reeves Corporation's income statement appears in Exhibit 9.2. The following additional information is available:

1 The firm uses a LIFO inventory method.
2 During 19X7, the replacement cost was $70,000 for the land and $80,000 for the plant.
3 The sales were made at the end of 19X7, when the replacement cost of inventory was $20 per unit.

EXHIBIT 9.2
Reeves Corporation Income Statement

Sales (5,000 units @ $40 per unit)		$200,000
Cost of Goods Sold		
Beginning Inventory (3,000 units @ $10 per unit)	$ 30,000	
Purchases (4,000 units @ $12 per unit)	48,000	
Units Available	$ 78,000	
Ending Inventory (2,000 units @ $10 per unit)	20,000	58,000
Gross Margin		$142,000
Operational Expenses		
Depreciation	$ 10,000	
Interest	5,000	
Other Expenses	117,000	$132,000
Net Operating Profit		$ 10,000

The income statement of the Reeves Corporation for 19X7 under the current entry price is shown in Exhibit 9.3. Two items deserve explanation and further attention. First, the holding gain on plant was determined by the following entry:

Plant	$30,000	
Depreciation	13,000	
Accumulated Depreciation		22,000
Holding Gain		21,000

EXHIBIT 9.3
Reeves Corporation Income Statement for 19X7
Current Entry Price Basis

Sales (5,000 units @ $40)		$200,000
Cost of Goods Sold		
Beginning Inventory (3,000 units @ $20)	$ 60,000	
Purchases (4,000 units @ $20)	80,000	
Goods Available	$140,000	
Ending Inventory (2,000 units @ $20)	40,000	100,000
Gross Margin		$100,000
Depreciation $\left(0.20 \times \dfrac{80,000 + 50,000}{2}\right)$	$ 13,000	
Interest	5,000	
Other Expenses	117,000	$135,000
Operating Profit Before		
Holding Gains and Losses		$(35,000)
Realizable Holding Gains		
1 On Inventory		
a. Purchases:		
[4,000 units × ($20 − $12)]	$ 32,000	
b. Beginning Inventory:		
[1,000 units × ($20 − $10)]	10,000	
2 On Depreciation: ($13,000 − $10,000)	3,000	
		$ 45,000
Unrealized Holding Gains		
1 On Ending Inventory:		
($20 − $10) × (2,000 units)	$ 20,000	
2 On Plant	18,000	
3 On Land: ($70,000 − $40,000)	30,000	68,000
Net Profit		$ 78,000

In other words, if the $30,000 increase in plant value is accrued uniformly over the year, the depreciation expense should be $13,000 (20 percent of the average asset value of

$65,000). The holding gain is equal to $30,000 less the $1\frac{1}{2}$-year depreciation on the $30,000.

Second, the operating profit before holding gains and losses and the realized holding gains and losses are both based on the realization concept. Consequently, their sum is equal to the accounting profit. The added advantage of employing the current entry price is the dichotomy between the results of (1) the operational decisions involving the production and sales of goods and services, and (2) the holding decisions involving holding assets over time in expectation of an increase in their replacement cost.

The Reeves Corporation balance sheet for 19X7, based on the current entry price, appears in Exhibit 9.4.

EXHIBIT 9.4
Reeves Corporation Balance Sheet December 19X7
Current Entry Price Basis

Assets		
Cash		$ 30,000
Accounts Receivable		30,000
Inventories (2,000 units @ $20)		40,000
Land		70,000
Plant	$ 80,000	
Less: Accumulated Depreciation	(32,000)	48,000
Total Assets		$218,000
Equities		
Bonds		$ 50,000
Common Stock		50,000
Retained Earnings		
Beginning Balance		40,000
Operating Profit		(35,000)
Realized Holding Gain		45,000
Unrealized Holding Gain		68,000
Total Liabilities and Equities		$218,000

Evaluation of Current Entry-Price-Based Accounting

The primary advantage of *current-entry-price-based accounting* results from the breakdown and segregation of current-value income into current operating profit and holding gains and losses.

First, the dichotomy between current operating profit and holding gains and losses is useful in evaluating the past performance of managers. Current operating profit and holding gains and losses constitute the separate results of holding or investment decisions and production decisions, allowing a distinction to be made between the recurring and relatively controllable gains arising from production and the gains arising from factors that are independent of current and basic enterprise operations. Edwards and Bell state:

> These two kinds of gains are often the result of quite different sets of decisions. The business firm usually has considerable freedom in deciding what quantity of assets to

hold over time at any or all stages of the production process and what quantity of assets to commit to the production process itself . . . . The difference between the forces motivating the business firm to make profit by one means rather than by another and the difference between the events on which the two methods of making profits depend require that the two kinds of gain be carefully separated if the two types of decisions involved are to be meaningfully evaluated.[35]

Second, the dichotomy between current operating profit and holding gains and losses is useful in making business decisions. Such a dichotomy allows the long-run profitability of the firm to be assessed, assuming the continuation of existing conditions. Because it is recurring and relatively controllable, the current operating profit may be used for predictive purposes.

Third, current operating profit corresponds to the income that contributes to the maintenance of physical productive capacity — that is, the maximum amount that the firm can distribute and maintain its physical productive capacity. As such, current operating profit has been appropriately labeled *distributable* or *sustainable income*.

> An important characteristic of distributable income from operations is that it is sustainable. If the world does not change, the company maintains its physical capacity next year and will have the same amount of distributable income that it had this year.[36]

Fourth, the dichotomy between current operating profit and holding gains and losses provides important information that can be used to analyze and compare interperiod and intercompany performance gains.

Fifth, in addition to the dichotomy between current operating profit and holding gains and losses, the current-entry-price method allows the separation to be made between realized holding gains and losses and unrealized holding gains and losses. It represents an abandonment of the realization and conservatism principles, so that holding gains and losses are recognized as they are accrued rather than as they are realized.

The feasibility of financial statements based on replacement costs is apparently becoming more and more accepted. Revsine reports the results of efforts to prepare replacement-cost financial statements for an electronic equipment manufacturer:

> Very few implementation problems were encountered during the course of the study. In those cases where data were initially absent, it was usually possible to reconstruct the missing information or to develop some surrogate approach. One might reasonably expect that even these occasional problems would diminish were market-based measures widely adopted for reporting purposes.
>
> This study has indicated that the test company was already employing what is essentially a replacement-cost system for internal inventory accounting. This itself indicates the practicality of the replacement-cost inventory procedures more forcefully than any academic study ever could . . . .
>
> On the basis of these results, it would appear defensible to conclude that the data necessary to prepare replacement-cost financial statements were generally available. Thus, this case study did not disclose any obstacles which would impede the implementation of replacement-cost reports. Whether this conclusion can be generalized to other situations is a subject for future research.[37]

There are, however, some disadvantages to the current-entry-price system. Each claim about the benefits to be derived from dichotomizing current-value income into current operating profit and holding gains and losses has been contested.[38]

The current-entry-price system is based on the assumptions that the firm is a going concern and that realiable current-entry-price data may be easily obtained. Both assumptions have been called "invalid" and "unnecessary."[39]

The current-entry-price system recognizes current value as a basis of valuation but does not account for changes in the general price level and gains and losses on holding monetary assets and liabilities.

Finally, there is the difficulty of correctly specifying what is meant by "current entry price." Is an asset held for use or sale to be replaced by an equivalent, identical, or new asset? A defensible argument may be made for each of the interpretations of current entry price — namely, replacement cost–used, reproduction cost, and replacement cost–new.

9.5.3 Current Exit Price

Interpretations of Current Exit Prices

Current exit price represents the amount of cash for which an asset might be sold or a liability might be refinanced. The current exit price is generally agreed to correspond (1) to the selling price under conditions of orderly rather than forced liquidation, and (2) to the selling price at the time of measurement. In case the adjusted future selling price is of concern, the concept of *expected exit value*, or *net realizable value*, is employed instead. More specifically, expected exit value or net realizable value is the amount of cash for which an asset might be expected to be sold or a liability might be expected to be refinanced. Thus, expected exit value or net realizable value refers to the proceeds of expected future sales, whereas current exit price refers to the current selling price under conditions of orderly liquidation.

The concept of current exit price was introduced by MacNeal and was further developed by Sterling and Chambers.[40] In fact, another embracing term for current exit price — *current cash equivalent* — has been proposed by Chambers, who explains:

> At any *present* time, all past prices are simply a matter of history. Only present prices have any bearing on the choice of an action. The price of a good ten years ago has no more relation to this question than the hypothetical price 20 years hence. As individual prices may change even over an interval when the general purchasing power of money does not, and as the general purchasing power of money may change even though some individual prices do not, no useful inference may be drawn from past prices which has a necessary bearing on present capacity to operate in a market. Every measurement of a financial property for the purpose of choosing a course of action — to buy, to hold, or to sell — is a measurement at a point of time, in the circumstances of the time, and in the units of currency at that time, even if the measurement process itself takes some time.
>
> Excluding all past prices, there are two prices which could be used to measure the monetary equivalent of any nonmonetary good in possession: the buying price and the selling price. But the buying price, or replacement price, does not indicate capacity, on the basis of present holdings, to go into a market with cash for the purpose of adapting oneself to contemporary conditions, whereas the selling price does. We propose, therefore, that the single financial property which is uniformly relevant at a point of time for all possible future actions in markets is the market selling price or realizable

price of any or all goods held. Realizable price may be described as *current cash equivalent*. What men wish to know, for the purpose of adaptation, is the numerosity of the money tokens which could be substituted for particular objects and for collections of objects if money is required beyond the amount which one already holds.[41]

According to the current exit approach, all assets and liabilities are revalued at their net realizable values. Net realizable values are generally obtained from market quotations adjusted for estimated selling costs and therefore correspond to the quoted sales prices on the demand market, whereas current entry prices correspond to the quoted sales prices on the supply market. Whenever the net realizable value cannot be estimated directly from the demand market, two alternatives may be considered: (1) the use of specific sales price indices, computed either by external sources or internally by the firm, and (2) the use of appraisals by external appraisers or by management.

The primary characteristic of current-exit-price systems is the complete abandonment of the realization principle for the recognition of revenues. Valuing all nonmonetary assets at their current exit prices produces an immediate recognition of all gains. Thus, operating gains are recognized at the time of production, whereas holding gains and losses are recognized at the time of purchase — and, consequently, whenever prices change — rather than at the time of sale. The critical event in the accounting cycle becomes the point of purchase or production rather than the point of sale.

Net Realizable Value Techniques Applied

Assume the same data given in Example 1 (page 279), except that the current exit price of coffee at the end of the period is $12 per unit. The income statement, balance sheet, and relevant notes, based on the current exit price, are shown in Exhibits 9.5 and 9.6.

EXHIBIT 9.5
Income Statement
Current-Exit-Price Basis

Revenues		
Sales (600 lbs × $10)	$6,000	
Inventory (400 lbs × $12)	4,800	
Total		$10,800
Cost		
Cost of Sales (600 lbs × $8)	$4,800	
Inventory (400 lbs × $9)	3,600	$ 8,400
Operating Profit		$ 2,400
Realized Holding Gains on Sales [600 lbs × ($8 − $6)]		$ 1,200
Unrealized Holding Gains on Inventory		
[400 lbs × ($9 − $6)]		1,200
Current-Exit-Price Income		$ 4,800

EXHIBIT 9.6
Balance Sheet
Current-Exit-Price Basis

Assets		Liabilities and Stockholders' Equity	
Cash	$10,000	Share Capital	$10,000
Inventory[a]	4,800	Retained Earnings	
		Realized[b]	2,400
		Unrealized[c]	2,400
Current-Exit-Price			
Income	$14,800		$14,800

[a] Inventory at the end of the year is valued at the net realizable value at that time
(400 lbs × $12 = $4,800).
[b] Realized retained earnings include:
(1) Realized operating profit (sales − cost of goods sold = $6,000 − $4,800 = $1,200).
(2) Realized holding gains on sales ($1,200).
[c] Unrealized retained earnings include:
(1) Unrealized operating profit: revenues on inventory on hand − cost of inventories on hand =
$4,800 − $3,600 = $1,200.
(2) Unrealized holding gains on inventory ($1,200).

Evaluation of Current Exit-Price-Based Accounting

The use of current-value accounting based on current exit price presents advantages and disadvantages. First, we will discuss some of the advantages attributed to *current exit-price-based accounting.*

First the current exit price and the capitalized value of an asset provide different measures of the economic concept of *opportunity costs.* Thus, a firm's *opportunity cost* is either the cash value to be derived from the sale of the asset or the present value of the benefits to be derived from the use of the asset. Both values are relevant to making decisions concerning whether a firm should continue to use or to sell assets already in use and whether or not a firm should remain a going concern.

Second, current exit price provides relevant and necessary information on which to evaluate the financial adaptability and liquidity of a firm. Thus, a firm holding fairly liquid assets has a greater opportunity to adapt to changing economic conditions than a firm holding assets with little or no resale value.

Third, current exit price provides a better guide for the evaluation of managers in their stewardship function because it reflects current sacrifices and other choices. Chambers states:

> As financial statements include in general terms the disposition of assets and in-crements in assets from time to time, they are regarded as the basis on which the performance of a company and its management may be judged . . . . If the amounts of assets from time to time were stated on any basis other than their money equivalents, there would be no firm and satisfactory basis for determining the use and dispositions of assets. Since all uses and dispositions in a period entail movements of money and money equivalents, financial statements based on the money equivalents of assets provided information on which periodical performance may fairly be judged.[42]

Fourth, the use of current exit price eliminates the need for arbitrary cost allocation on the basis of the estimated useful life of the asset. More explicitly, depreciation expense for a given year is the difference between the current exit price of the asset at the beginning and at the end of the period.

Finally, the feasibility of exit-price-based financial statements is apparently becoming more accepted. For example, McKeown reports the results of efforts by an electronic manufacturer to prepare exit-price-based financial statements:

> Preparation of two exit-value balance sheets and an exit-value income statement for X Company demonstrated that, in this case, readily available market prices could be determined at very little cost for the land and building and most of the equipment. Market prices for the rest of the equipment (mainly metal furniture) were estimated — again, at nominal cost — by use of general guidelines suggested by used-furniture dealers. A more accurate estimate for these items might have been obtained by employing an appraiser. However, the cost of appraisal of these items would have been significant (5 percent of the appraised value) and would probably be incurred every three or five years, if at all. This procedure of relatively infrequent appraisals should yield accurate estimates because, according to the used-furniture dealers, the resale price is determined mainly by the type and quality of the asset rather than the age. Thus, barring major changes in the used-asset market, an appraisal of a particular item (possibly adjusted by a specific price index) should be valid for several years.
>
> Measurements of items other than fixed assets were readily computed at nominal cost. The only way management would have had any effect on the exit-value figures reported would have been solicitation of special offers for particular assets. Although this activity could be called manipulation, the economic fact remains that management could realize the offered amount. Further, the effect of these offers could easily be segregated. Other than the solicitation of special offers, management cannot manipulate exit-value figures because the measurements are taken from the markets rather than management estimates. This provides less opportunity for manipulation of profit figures than is available under conventional accounting procedures (alternative depreciation methods, sale of particular fixed assets to realize an available gain or loss, etc.).
>
> The conclusion must be reached that critics of exit value who based their opposition on lack of feasibility of implementation will find no evidence to support their position in this case. Preparation of exit-value statements for X Company was possible at a reasonable cost.[43]

There are, however, some significant disadvantages to the current exit-price-based system that need to be mentioned.

First, the current exit-price-based system is relevant only for assets that are expected to be sold for a determined market price. The current exit price may be easily determined for an asset for which a second-hand market exists. It may be more difficult to determine the current exit price of specialized, custom-designed plant and equipment that has little or no alternative use. Scrap values may be the only alternative measure for such assets.

Second, the current exit-price-based system is not relevant for assets that the firm expects to use. The disclosure of the amount of cash that would be available if the firm sold such assets to move out of its industry and move into another one is not likely to be relevant to any user interested in the actual profitability of the firm in its present industry.

Third, the valuation of certain assets and liabilities at the current exit price has not yet been adequately resolved. On one hand, there is the general problem of valuation of intangibles and the specific problem of valuation of goodwill. Also, the absence of marketable value makes the determination of realizable value difficult. McKeown, however, has shown that the realizable values may be known or imputed.[44] On the other hand, there is the problem of valuation of liabilities. Should they be valued at their contractual amounts or at the amounts required to fund the liabilities? Chambers makes a strong case for valuing liabilities at their contractual amounts, pointing out that "at a given time, the issuer owes the bondholders the contractual amount of the bonds, whatever the price at which the bonds are traded."[45]

Fourth, the abandonment of the realization principle at the point of sale and the consequent assumption of liquidation of the firm's resources contradict the established assumption that the firm is a going concern.

Finally, the current exit-price-based system does not take into account changes in the general price level.

9.5.4 Other Interpretations of Current Values

Other proposals for the implementation of current-value accounting have been made. In this section, we will examine these proposals. For convenience, they will be grouped into the following categories:

1 Essential versus nonessential assets
2 The value to the firm
3 SEC replacement-cost proposal
4 The combination of values
5 The concept of business income

Essential Versus Nonessential Assets

In October 1975, the Australian Institute of Chartered Accountants and the Australian Society of Accountants published an exposure draft advocating the disclosure of supplementary current-value-based financial statements by July 1, 1977. Although that deadline was postponed, the Australian Accounting Standards Committee published a preliminary exposure draft on *A Method of Current-Value Accounting* in June 1975. The exposure draft introduced a form of current-value accounting that uses different treatments for *essential assets* and *nonessential assets*. Essential assets are determined on the basis of "the expected role of particular assets in the entity's operations on the immediately foreseeable future — that is, broadly speaking, continuing use or termination of use."[46] A nonessential asset is valued at its current exit price; an essential asset is valued at its current entry price. The holding gains and losses on essential assets are credited or debited to a revaluation account; the holding gains and losses on nonessential assets are included in income. Liabilities are valued at their contractual amounts. This valuation of liabilities is also the position taken by Chambers, who contends that:

> No amount shall be shown as liability unless it represents an amount owed to and legally recoverable by a creditor. Whether the due date is near or distant is immaterial. Long-dated obligations may become due and payable if any circumstances threaten the security of creditors.[47]

The distinction between essential and nonessential assets represents a modification of the current entry-price-based system to reflect economic realities. In other words, exit price is a preferred alternative for an asset that has no future use.

The Value to the Firm

In the United Kingdom, the "Report of the Inflation Accounting Committee," chaired by F.E.P. Sandilands, was issued in September 1975.[48] The "Sandilands Report" concludes that the following developments are necessary for changes in the laws of corporations:

1 The same unit of measure should be employed for all users.
2 The operating profit should be disclosed separately from the holding gains and losses.
3 The financial statements should include relevant information for assessing the liquidity of the company.

The most important recommendation of the "Sandilands Report," however, is the use of the *value to the firm* as a valuation base. Accounting based on the value to the firm is also described as *current-cost accounting (CCA)*. According to this approach, assets are valued at an amount that represents the opportunity costs to the firm — that is, the maximum loss that might be incurred if the firm is deprived of these assets. Thus, the value to the firm in most cases will be measured by the replacement cost, given that the replacement cost represents the amount of cash necessary to obtain an equivalent or identical asset. If the replacement cost is greater than the net realizable value, the value to the firm will be: (1) the discounted cash-flow value if it is greater than net realizable value, given that it is preferable to use the asset than to sell it, and (2) the net realizable value if it is greater than the discounted cash flow, given that it is preferable to sell the asset than to use it.

The "Sandilands Report" also recommends that all holding gains and losses be excluded from current-cost profit, which leads to:

- All unrealized gains arising from the reevaluation of fixed assets (and stock, where applicable) should be shown in reevaluation reserves on the balance sheet.
- Realized holding gains arising on fixed assets should similarly be included in movements in balance sheet reserves.
- The cost of sales adjustment (where applicable) should be taken to a balance sheet "stock adjustment reserve," whether it is positive or negative.
- Extraordinary gains should be classed as "extraordinary items," which implies that they may be included in profit for the year, provided they are shown separately and distinguished from current-cost profit.
- Operating gains should be shown "above the line" in the profit-and-loss account (earnings statement) as current-cost profit for the year.[49]

The "Sandilands Report" also recommends that a "summary statement of total gains and losses for the year" appear immediately after the income statement. Such a summary statement might be

Current-Cost Profit After Tax (as shown in Proft-and-Loss Account)		£XXX
Extraordinary Items After Tax		XXX
Net Profit After Tax and Extraordinary Items		£XXX
Movements in Reevaluation Reserves Net of Tax		
Stock-Adjustment Reserve	£XXX	
Reevaluation Reserves		
Gain or Loss Due to Changes in the Asset-Valuation Bases	XXX	
Other Gains or Losses	XXX	XXX
Total Gain (Loss) for the Year After Tax		£XXX

SEC Replacement-Cost Proposal

As a first step toward correcting some of the limitations of historical-cost accounting, the Securities and Exchange Commission cited replacement cost as the mandatory method of disclosure for large corporations. In March 1976, the SEC issued Accounting Series Release No. 190, which calls for supplementary disclosure of replacement-cost information by all SEC registrants with inventories, gross property, plant, and equipment that aggregate more that $100 million and that make up more than 10 percent of total assets.[50] Replacement cost is defined as the lowest amount that would have to be paid in the normal course of business to obtain a new piece of equipment operating at productive capacity. The regulation requires the designated firms (1) to estimate the current replacement cost of inventories and productive capacity and (2) to restate cost of goods sold and services, depreciation, depletion, and amortization for the two most recent full fiscal years on the basis of the replacement cost of equivalent productive capacity.

The SEC proposal was a timid attempt to show the impact of inflation on fixed assets and inventory, rather than on all monetary and nonmonetary assets. The SEC explicity states its objectives in Regulation 210.3-17:

> The purpose of this rule is to provide information to investors which will assist them in obtaining an understanding of the current cost of operating the business, which cannot be obtained from historical-cost financial statements taken alone.... A secondary purpose is to provide information which will enable investors to determine the current cost of inventories and productive capacity as a measure of the current economic investment in these assets existing at the balance sheet date.[51]

The Combination of Values

The *combination-of-values* approach avoids some of the disadvantages of the current-exit-price, current-entry-price, and capitalization methods. The Canadian Accounting Research Committee's preliminary position favors a combined use of current entry and current exit prices.[52] More specifically, the following values are advocated:

- Monetary assets should be shown at discounted cash flow, except for short-term items where the time-value-of-money effect is small....
- Marketable securities should be valued at current exit prices with adjustments for selling costs....

- In general, inventory items should be valued at current entry prices ....
- Normally, longer-term intercorporate investments should be valued at current entry prices ....
- Fixed assets should normally be valued at replacement cost–new (less applicable depreciation calculated on the basis of the estimated useful life of the assets held) ....
- In general, intangible values should be valued at current value ....
- Liabilities should be shown at the discounted value of future payments, except for short-term items when the time-value-of-money effect is small .... [53]

A similar combination-of-values approach has been proposed by Sprouse and Moonitz, except that they advocate common-dollar current-value statements. [54]

Although the combination-of-values approach may appear to be based on arbitrary rules, advocates of this approach have suggested specific decisions rules for the choice of a valuation method based on the market opportunity costs of assets. [55]

The *opportunity cost of an action* is the value of the benefits foregone as a result of the choice of the proposed action rather than the best option.

The *opportunity cost of an asset* is indicated by one of the following decision rules:

1 If $C > \bar{R} > S^*$, use the asset until replacement is required.
2 If $C > S > \bar{R}$, use the asset until replacement is required.
3 If $R > C > \bar{S}$, use the asset but do not replace it.
4 If $S > C > \bar{R}$, sell the asset and replace it for resale rather than use.
5 If $S > \bar{R} > C^*$, sell the asset and replace it for resale rather than use.
6 If $R^* > \bar{S} > C$, sell the asset and do not replace it.

where

$$
\begin{aligned}
C &= \text{the capitalized value of the asset.} \\
R &= \text{the replacement cost of the asset (current entry price).} \\
S &= \text{the net realizable value (current exit price).} \\
^* &= \text{the opportunity cost.} \\
^- &= \text{the nonrelevant value in the comparison.} [56]
\end{aligned}
$$

From these rules, we can state the following valuation bases:

1 Use the replacement cost of the assets for all situations in which the assets need to be replaced, as in (1), (2), (4) and (5).
2 Use the net realizable value of the assets for all situations in which the assets should be used but should not be replaced, as in (3), and should be sold and should not be replaced, as in (6).

If we add to these two rules a decision rule advocating the valuation of monetary assets and liabilities at their capitalized values, the resulting combination-of-values approach may be easily justified conceptually and practically.

The combination-of-values approach is deemed relevant within a particular set of financial statements by the FASB Study Group on the Objectives of Financial Statements:

> The Study Group believes that the objectives of financial statements cannot be best served by the exclusive use of a single valuation basis. The objectives that prescribe

statements of earnings and financial position are based on users' needs to predict, compare, and evaluate earning power. To satisfy these informational requirements, the Study Group concludes that different valuation bases are preferable for different assets and liabilities. That means that financial statements might contain data based on a combination of valuation bases .... Current replacement cost may be the best substitute for measuring the benefits of long-term assets held for use rather than sale. Current replacement cost may be particularly appropriate when significant price changes or technological developments have occurred since the assets were acquired .... Exit value may be an appropriate substitute for measuring the potential benefit or sacrifice of assets and liabilities expected to be sold or discharged in a relatively short time.[57]

Edwards also argues for a combination-of-values approach:

A firm that values its assets at exit prices derived from markets in which the firm is normally a buyer reports unusual values — those which would obtain in a liquidation situation, at least so far as the assets being so valued are concerned. To employ such values when liquidation is not contemplated is surely misleading ....

I am not convinced of the merit of adopting, as a normal basis for asset valuations in the going concern, exit prices in buyer markets. These are unusual values suitable for unusual situations ....

The point at issue, of course, is not whether to value by current entry or exit prices, but when to shift from entry to exit values ....

The principle ... that all assets and liabilities of the going concern should be valued at current prices except for those that the firm normally sells ... would come close to a rule of "replacement cost or net realizable value, whichever is higher," [except for] a firm which is temporarily selling at a loss.[58]

The Concept of Business Income

Edwards and Bell have introduced the concept of *business income,* labeled *money income* by others.[59] To explain the components of business or money income, we will highlight the ways in which it differs from accounting income.

We have defined *accounting income* as the difference between the realized revenues arising from the transactions of the period and the corresponding historical costs. In presenting replacement-cost income, we also have showed that (1) the *current operating profit* (representing the difference between the realized revenues and the corresponding replacement costs) and (2) the *realized holding gains and losses* (representing the difference between the replacement costs of the units sold and the historical costs of the same units) constitute the two types of gains included in accounting income. The realized holding gains and losses also may be divided into two elements: (1) the holding gains and losses realized and accrued during the period, and (2) the holding gains and losses realized during the period but accrued during previous periods. More specifically, accounting income P_a may be expressed

$$P_a = x + y + z$$

where

x = current operating profit.
y = realized and accrued holding gains for the period.
z = realized holding gains for the period accrued during previous periods.

Business income differs from accounting income in two ways: (1) business income is based on replacement-cost valuation, and (2) business income recognizes only the gains accrued during the period. More specifically, business income comprises (1) the current operating profit x defined earlier, (2) the realized and accrued holding gains for the period y, and (3) the unrealized holding gains and losses accrued during the period. Business income P_b may be expressed

$$P_b = P_a - z + w$$

In other words, business income is equal to accounting income *less* realized holding gains for the period accrued during previous periods *plus* unrealized holding gains and losses. A reconciliation of business or money income with accounting income is provided in Exhibit 9.7.

This difference may be illustrated by the following example. Assume that 1,000 units of given product are acquired at a price of $1 per unit. At the end of t_1, the replacement cost is $2 per unit. The 1,000 units are sold during t_2 for $3 per unit when replacement cost is $2.50 per unit. Table 9.3 shows the differences between business income and accounting income for periods t_1 and t_2.

EXHIBIT 9.7
Reconciliation of Business Money Income with Accounting Income

	A.	Holding gains accrued and realized during the current period		MONEY INCOME $\downarrow$
plus		*plus*	*equals* →	*less*
	B.	Holding gains accrued but not realized during the current period	B.	Holding gains accrued but not realized during the current period
CURRENT OPERATING PROFIT				*plus*
	A.	Holding gains accrued and realized during the current period	C.	Holding gains realized during the current period but accrued during previous periods
plus		*plus*	*equals* →	*equals* $\downarrow$
	C.	Holding gains realized during the current period but accrued during previous periods		ACCOUNTING PROFIT

Source: Parker, R.H., and Harcourt, G.C. (eds), *Readings in the Concept and Measurement of Income* (New York: Cambridge University Press, 1969), p. 6.

TABLE 9.3
Accounting and Business Incomes

Period	X (1)	Y (2)	Z (3)	W (4)	P_a (1) + (2) + (3)	P_b (1) + (2) + (4)
t_{0-1}	—	—	—	$1,000	—	$1,000
t_{0-2}	$500	$500	$1,000	—	$2,000	1,000
Total	500	500	1,000	1,000	2,000	2,000

9.6 CONCLUSIONS

The accounting model for current-value accounting discussed in this chapter is based on the interpretation of the "Hicksian" concept of capital maintenance, or physical productive-capacity maintenance. Four different concepts of current value have been proposed in the literature and in practice — the capitalized value, the current entry price, the current exit price, and a combination of these values. Each method provides definite advantages compared with historical-cost accounting. The major disadvantage of any current-value method, as well as of historical-cost accounting, is that none of these methods recognizes changes in the purchasing power of the dollar. Accordingly, in Chapter 10, we will focus on general price-level-adjusted historical-cost accounting; in Chapter 11, we will focus on general price-level-adjusted current-value accounting.

NOTES

[1] Kaldor, N., *An Expenditure Tax* (London; Allen & Unwin, 1955), pp. 54–78.

[2] 1966–1968 Committee on External Reporting, *An Evaluation of External Reporting Practices* (Evanston, Ill.: American Accounting Association, 1969), p. 81.

[3] Ibid., pp. 83–8.

[4] Ibid., p. 81.

[5] Werner, Frank, "A Study of the Predictive Significance of Two Incomes Measures," *Journal of Accounting Research* (Spring, 1969), pp. 123–33.

[6] Ronen, J., and Sadan, S., "Extraordinary Items and the Predictive Ability of Income Number," Vincent C. Ross Institute of Accounting Research, *Working Paper 74-3* (New York: New York University, 1974).

[7] Beidleman, Carl R., "Income Smoothing: The Role of Management," *The Accounting Review* (October, 1973), pp. 653–67.

[8] Ibid., p. 654.

[9] Barnea, A., Ronen, J., and Sadan, S., "Classificatory Smoothing of Income with Extraordinary Items," *The Accounting Review* (January, 1976), pp. 110–22.

[10] Beidleman, Carl R., "Income Smoothing: The Role of Management," p. 654.

[11] Barnea, A., Ronen, J., and Sadan, S., "Classificatory Smoothing of Income with Extraordinary Items," p. 111.

[12] *Objectives of Financial Statements* (New York: American Institute of Certified Public Accountants, 1974), p. 26.

[13] Papandreou, A., "Some Basic Issues in the Theory of the Firm," in *Survey of Contemporary Economics*, (ed.) B. Haley (Homewood, Ill.: Richard D. Irwin, 1952), pp. 250–62; Baumol, W., *Business Behavior, Value, and Growth* (New York: Macmillan, 1959); Marris, R., *The Economic Theory of "Managerial Capitalism"* (London: Macmillan, 1964); Findlay, Chapman M., III, and Whitmore, G.A., "Beyond Shareholder Wealth Maximization," *Financial Management* (Winter, 1974), pp. 25–35.

[14] Ibid., p. 30.

[15] Littleton, A.C., "The Significance of Invested Cost," *The Accounting Review* (April, 1952), pp. 167–73; Kohler, E.L., "Why Not Retain Historical Cost?," *Journal of Accountancy* (October, 1963), pp. 35–41; Ijiri, Yuji, "A Defense of Historical-Cost Accounting," in *Asset Valuation and Income Determination*, (ed.) Robert R. Sterling (Lawrence, Kn.: Scholars Book Co., 1971), pp. 1–14; Mautz, R.K., "A Few Words for Historical Cost," *Financial Executive* (January, 1973), pp. 93–8.

[16] Kohler, E.L., "Why Not Retain Historical Cost?," op. cit., p. 36.

[17] Ibid., p. 32.

[18] Thomas, Arthur L., *Accounting Research Study No. 3*, "The Allocation Problem in Financial Accounting" (Evanston, Ill.: American Accounting Association, 1969), and Accounting Research Study No. 9, "The Allocation Problem: Part 2" (Sarasota, Fl.: American Accounting Association, 1974).

[19] Smith, Adam, *An Enquiry into the Nature and Causes of the Wealth of Nations* (London: George Routledge, 1890).

[20] Marshall, Alfred, *Principles of Economics*, 8th ed. (London: Macmillan, 1947), Book II, Chs. 2, 4, Appendix E.

[21] Von Bohm Bawerk, Eugene, *Positive Theory of Capital*, Vol. 88 of *Capital and Interest*, (South Holland, Ill.: Libertarian Press, 1959), pp. 16–66.

[22] Keynes, John Maynard, *The General Theory of Employment, Interest, and Money* (London: Macmillan, 1936), Ch. 6.

[23] Fisher, Irving, *The Nature of Capital and Income* (New York: Macmillan, 1912), p. 38; Lindahl, E., *Die Gerechtigkeit der Besteuerung* (Lund, 1919), translated in R.A. Musgrave and A. Peacock, *Classics in the Theory of Public Finance* (New York: Macmillan, 1958).

[24] Hicks, J.R., *Value and Capital*, 2nd ed. (Oxford: Clarendon Press, 1946).

[25] Ibid., p. 122.

[26] Sandilands, F.E.P., *Inflation Accounting: Report of the Inflation Accounting Committee* (London: Her Majesty's Stationery Office, Cmmd, 6225, September 1975), p. 35.

[27] Edwards, E.O., and Bell, P.W., *The Theory and Measurement of Business Income* (Berkeley and Los Angeles: University of California Press, 1961), pp. 38–44.

[28] FASB Discussion Memorandum, *An Analysis of Issues Related to Conceptual Framework for Financial Accounting and Reporting: Elements of Financial Statements and Their Measurement* (Stamford, Ct.: Financial Accounting Standards Board, December 2, 1976), pp. 206–8.

[29] Alexander, Sidney S., "Income Measurement in a Dynamic Economy," rev. by David Solomons, in *Studies in Accounting Theory*, (eds) W.T. Baxter and Sidney Davidson (Homewood, Ill.: Richard D. Irwin, 1962), pp. 126–7.

[30] APB Opinion No. 21., *Interest on Receivables and Payables* (New York: American Institute of Certified Public Accountants, 1972).

[31] Thomas, Arthur L., "Discounted Services Again: The Homogeneity Problem," *The Accounting Review* (January, 1964), pp. 1–11; A.D. Barton, *An Analysis of Business Income Concepts*, International Center for Research in Accounting, *Occasional Paper No. 7* (Lancaster, England: University of Lancaster, 1975), p. 50.

[32] Edwards, E.O., and Bell, P.W., *The Theory and Measurement of Business Income*, p. 286.

[33] Paton, W.A., and Paton, W.A., Jr., *Asset Accounting* (New York: Macmillan, 1952), p. 325.

[34] "Accounting for Land, Buildings, and Equipment," *The Accounting Review* (July, 1964), p. 696.

[35] Edwards, E.O., and Bell, P.W., *The Theory and Measurement of Business Income*, p. 73.

[36] Vancil, Richard, F., and Weil, Roman L., "Current Replacement-Cost Accounting, Depreciable Assets, and Distributable Income," in *Replacement-Cost Accounting: Readings on Concepts, Uses, and Methods* (Glen Ridge, N.J.: Thomas Horton and Daughters, 1976), p. 58.

[37] Revsine, L., "Replacement-Cost Accounting: A Theoretical Foundation," in *Objectives of Financial Statements: Selected Papers*, Vol. 2, (eds) J.J. Cramer, Jr., and G.H. Sorter (New York: American Institute of Certified Public Accountants, 1974), pp. 241–4.

[38] Drake, D.F., and Dopuch, N., "On the Case of Dichotomizing Income," *Journal of Accounting Research* (Autumn, 1965), pp. 192–205; Prakash, P., and Sunder, S., "The Case Against Separation of Current Operating Profit and Holding Gain," *The Accounting Review* (January, 1979), pp. 1–22.

[39] Sterling, Robert R., "The Going Concern: An Examination," *The Accounting Review* (July, 1968), pp. 481–502.

[40] Chambers, R.J., *Accounting, Evaluation, and Economic Behavior* (Englewood Cliffs, N.J.: Prentice-Hall, 1966); MacNeal, Kenneth, *Truth in Accounting* (Lawrence, Kn.: Scholars Book Co., 1970); Sterling, Robert R., *Theory of the Measurement of Enterprise Income* (Lawrence: University of Kansas Press, 1970).

[41] Ibid., pp. 91–2.

[42] Chambers, R.J., *Accounting for Inflation, Exposure Draft* (Sydney, Australia: University of of Sydney, September, 1975), paragraph 20.

[43] McKeown, James C., "Usefulness of Exit-Value Accounting Statements in Satisfying Accounting Objectives," in *Objectives of Financial Statements: Selected Papers*, Vol. 2, (eds) J.J. Cramer, Jr., and G.H. Sorter (New York: American Institute of Certified Public Accountants, 1973), p. 227.

[44] McKeown, James C., "An Empirical Test of a Model Proposed by Chambers," *The Accounting Review* (January, 1971), pp. 12–29.

[45] Chambers, R.J., "Continuously Contemporary Accounting," *Abacus* (September, 1970), pp. 643–7.

[46] Australian Accounting Standards Committee, *A Method of Current-Value Accounting* (Sydney: Australian Institute of Chartered Accountants and Australian Society of Accountants, June, 1975), paragraph 16.

[47] Chambers, R.J., *Accounting for Inflation*, paragraph 30.

[48] Sandilands, F.E.P., *Inflation Accounting: Report of the Inflation Accounting Committee*.

[49] Ibid., paragraph 621.

[50] Accounting Series Release No. 190, *Notice of Adoption and Amendments to Regulation S-X Requiring Disclosure of Certain Replacement-Cost Data* (Washington, D.C.: Securities and Exchange Commission, 1976).

[51] *SEC Regulation 210.3-17,* "Current Replacement-Cost Information, Statement of Objectives" (Washington, D.C.: Securities and Exchange Commission, 1976).

[52] Accounting Research Committee Discussion Paper, *Current-Value Accounting* (Toronto: Canadian Institute of Chartered Accountants, August, 1976), p. 28.

[53] Ibid., pp. 66–8.

[54] Sprouse, R.T., and Moonitz, Maurice, *Accounting Research Study No. 3,* "A Tentative Set of Accounting Principles for Business Enterprises" (New York: American Institute of Certified Public Accountants, 1962).

[55] Barton, Allan, *An Analysis of Business Income Concepts,* pp. 45–6.

[56] Ibid., p. 46.

[57] *Objectives of Financial Statements,* op. cit., pp. 41–3.

[58] Edwards, E.O., "The State of Current-Value Accounting," *The Accounting Review* (April, 1975), pp. 235–45.

[59] Edwards, E.O., and Bell, P.W., *The Theory and Measurement of Business Income;* Parker, R.H., and Harcourt, G.C. (eds), *Readings in the Concept and Measurement of Income* (New York: Cambridge University Press, 1969), pp. 17–18.

REFERENCES

Historical Cost

Anthony, R.N. "Case for Historical Costs," *Harvard Business Review* (November/December, 1976), pp. 69–79.

Ijiri, Yuji. "The Significance of Historical-Cost Valuation." In *The Foundation of Accounting Measurement.* Englewood Cliffs, N.J.: Prentice-Hall, 1967, pp. 64–7.

Ijiri, Yuji, "A Defense of Historical-Cost Accounting." In *Asset Valuation and Income Determination,* (ed.) Robert R. Sterling, Lawrence, Kn.: Scholars Book Co., 1971, pp. 1–14.

Ijiri, Yuji. *Research Monograph Report No. 1.* "Historical-cost Accounting and Its Rationality." Vancouver: Canadian Certified General Accountants' Research Foundation, 1981.

Kohler, E.L. "Why Not Retain Historical Cost?" *Journal of Accountancy* (October, 1963), pp. 35–41.

Littleton, A.C. "The Significance of Invested Cost." *The Accounting Review* (April, 1952), pp. 167–73.

Mautz, R.K. "A Few Words for Historical Cost." *Financial Executive* (January, 1973), pp. 23–7, 93–8.

Capitalization

Alexander, Sidney S. "Income Measurement in a Dynamic Economy." Rev. by David Solomons in *Studies in Accounting Theory,* (eds) W.T. Baxter and Sidney Davidson. Homewood, Ill.: Richard D. Irwin, 1962), pp. 126–200.

Barton, A.D. "Expectations and Achievements in Income Theory." *The Accounting Review* (October, 1974), pp. 664–81.

Bierman, H., Jr., and Davidson, Sidney. "The Income Concept — Value Increment or Earnings Predictor?" *The Accounting Review* (April, 1969), pp. 239–46.

Bromwich, M. "The Use of Present Valuation Models in Published Accounting Reports." *The Accounting Review* (July, 1977), pp. 587–96.

Mattessich, R. "On the Perennial Misunderstanding of Asset Reassessment by Means of 'Present Values'." *Cost and Management* (March/April, 1970), pp. 29–31.

Parker, R.H., and Harcourt, G.C. (eds). *Readings in the Concept and Measurement of Income.* New York: Cambridge University Press, 1969.

Schwader, K. "A Critique of Economic Income in an Accounting Concept." *Abacus* (August, 1967), pp. 23–35.

Shwayder, K. "The Capital-Maintenance Rule and the New Asset Valuation Rule" *The Accounting Review* (April, 1969), pp. 3–16.

Sterling, Robert R., and Lemke, K.W. (eds). *Maintenance of Capital: Financial Versus Physical.* Lawrence, Kn.: Scholars Book Company, 1982.

Current Entry Price

Drake, D.F., and Dopuch, N. "On the Case of Dichotomizing Income." *Journal of Accounting Research* (Autumn, 1965), pp. 192–205.

Prakash, P., and Sunder, S. "The Case Against Separation of Current Operating Profit and Holding Gain." *The Accounting Review* (January, 1979), pp. 1–22.

Revsine, L. "Replacement-Cost Accounting." *Contemporary Topics in Accounting Series.* Englewood Cliffs, N.J.: Prentice-Hall, 1973.

Rosenfield, P. "Current Replacement Value Accounting — A Dead-End." *Journal of Accountancy* (September, 1975), pp. 63–73.

Rosenfield, P. "Reporting Subjective Gains and Losses." *The Accounting Review* (October, 1969), pp. 788–97.

Stamp, Edward. "The Valuation of Assets." *The Chartered Accountant Magazine* (November, 1975), pp. 67–9.

Current Exit Price

Bedford, N.M., and McKeown, James C. "Net Realizable Value and Replacement Cost." *The Accounting Review* (April, 1972), pp. 333–8.

Chambers, R.J. *Accounting, Evaluation, and Economic Behavior,* Englewood Cliffs, N.J.: Prentice-Hall, 1966; *reprinted* Houston, Tx.: Scholars Book Co., 1974.

Chambers, R.J. *Accounting for Inflation: Exposure Draft.* Sydney, Australia: University of Sydney, August, 1975.

Chambers, R.J. *Accounting for Inflation: Methods and Problems.* Sydney, Australia: University of Sydney, August, 1975.

Chambers, R.J. "NOD, COG, and PUPU See How Inflation Teases." *Journal of Accountancy* (February, 1975), pp. 56–62.

Staubus, G.J. "Current Cash Equivalent for Assets: A Dissent." *The Accounting Review* (October, 1967), pp. 650–61.

Sterling, Robert R. *Theory of the Measurement of Enterprise Income.* Lawrence: University of Kansas Press, 1970.

QUESTIONS

9.1 Provide a definition for each of the following terms:
   a. Concepts of capital maintenence
   b. General purchasing-power maintenance

c. Money maintenance
d. Productive-capacity maintenance
e. Current-value accounting
f. Deflation
g. Discounted cash flow
h. Entry price
i. Exit price
j. General purchasing power
k. Holding gains and losses
l. Inflation
m. Measuring unit
n. Operating profit (loss)

9.2 Are *discounted cash-flow techniques*, where feasible, the preferable valuation basis for obtaining "current values"?

9.3 What are some advantages and disadvantages of *accounting income*?

9.4 Discuss the evolution of the *economic* concept of *income*.

9.5 Describe the different concepts of *capital maintenance*.

9.6 List and describe the different concepts of *current value*.

9.7 Evaluate *current entry-price-based accounting*.

9.8 Evaluate the *combination-of-values* approach.

9.9 Evaluate *current exit-price-based accounting*.

9.10 Explain Edwards and Bell's concept of *business income*.

9.11 The following data are presented for Propulsion Inc.:

Propulsion, Inc.
Balance Sheet
May 31, 19X4

Assets		
Cash		$ 50,000
Inventory, FIFO cost (6,000 units @ $5.00)		30,000
Land		15,000
Building	$220,000	
Less: Accumulated Depreciation	55,00	165,000
Equipment	$ 90,000	
Less: Accumulated Depreciation	45,000	45,000
Total		$305,000
Liabilities and Shareholders' Equity		
Income Taxes Payable		$ 30,000
Mortgage Payable		65,000
Capital Stock		150,000
Retained Earnings		60,000
Total		$305,000

Transaction data during the year ending May 31, 19X5, included:
(1) Cash sales for the year total 50,000 × $12.00 = $600,000.
(2) Purchases for the year total 52,000 × $7.00 = $364,000.

(3) Other expenses, including depreciation, total $175,000.

(4) The building has an estimated useful life of 20 years and the equipment has an estimated useful life of 10 years. Neither asset is expected to have any salvage value at the end of its useful life. The building and the equipment were purchased five years ago.

(5) The income-tax rate is 50 percent of reported income, including realized holding gains and losses.

(6) The year-end replacement cost of inventory is $8.00 per unit.

(7) The land has an appraised value of $20,000 at the end of the year.

(8) The replacement cost of the building is $250,000 and the replacement cost of the equipment is $120,000, which represent year-end gross values.

(9) All transactions are assumed to have been uniformly incurred over the year.

Required

Prepare a comparative balance sheet and income statement for 1975, based on generally accepted accounting principles and replacement cost.

(*Society of Management Accountants, adapted 1975*)

9.12 A.D. Barton made the following statement in "Expectations and Achievements in Income Theory" in *The Accounting Review* (October, 1974), pp. 664–5:

The case for dominant position of *ex-ante* present-value income rests on the needs of investors for information about the future income prospects of the firm. Investors in business enterprises (that is, owners), are interested in the prospects of future income from investments, and it is differences in these future prospects which determine the allocation of their investment funds. Ideally, they require information on the expected income to be earned in each form of investment so that they can select those promising the highest returns. The appropriate measures for this are present-value income and its corollary, the present value of assets. They do not invest money in firms just because of past financial performances.

Do you agree with this evaluation of present-value accounting? Why or why not?

9.13 N.M. Bedford and James C. McKeown made the following statement in "Net Realizable Value and Replacement Cost" in *The Accounting Review* (April, 1972), p. 338:

On balance, it seems to the authors that advantages accrue to both net realizable value and current replacement-cost valuations. It is our conclusion that the complexities of modern economic life require both calculations. We contend that attempts to find simple unequivocal answers to complex problems are bound to fail. Complex problems require complex solutions. Clearly, the accounting profession must start presenting multiple valuations and make multiple disclosures in their annual report. Simple income statements and balance sheets of the past were designed for a much simpler society. This analysis of the nontrivial valuation issue (net realizable value versus current replacement cost) indicates that multiple and complex, but precise, annual reports are now required if the accounting profession is to comply with its ethical requirements to provide useful information.

Do you agree with the authors' conclusion? Why or why not?

9.14 The controller of the Robinson Company is discussing a comment you made in the course of presenting your audit report.

Frankly, I agree that we, too, are responsible for finding ways to produce more relevant financial statements that are as reliable as the ones we now produce.

For example, suppose that the company acquires a finished item for inventory for $40 when the general price-level index is 110. Later, the item is sold for $75 when the general price-level index is 121 and the current replacement cost is $54. We could calculate a "holding gain."

Required

a. Explain to what extent and how current replacement costs already are used to value inventories within generally accepted accounting principles.
b. Calculate in good form the amount of the holding gain in the controller's example.
c. Why is the use of current replacement costs for both inventories and cost of goods sold preferred by some accounting authorities over the generally accepted use of FIFO or LIFO?   (*AICPA adapted*)

9.15 An asset with a three-year life span is purchased for $3,000; its replacement cost (new) increases $1,000 per year.

Required

a. Complete a depreciation schedule based on replacement-cost values that includes "backlog" values.
b. Describe the alternative treatments to deal with "backlog depreciation."

9.16 The Clancy James Company invested $100 in a new company on January 1. The same day, management bought 100 pounds of sugar at $1 per pound. On January 15, it sold 60 pounds of sugar at $2 per pound. The current replacement cost of sugar is $1.30 per pound on January 15 and $1.60 per pound on January 31.

Required

a. Prepare the company's income statement and balance sheet for the month of January, using current-entry-price based accounting.
b. What are the advantages and disadvantages of the company's financial statements when prepared on a current-entry-price basis?
c. Assuming that the current exit price of sugar is $2.50 per pound on January 31, prepare the company's income statement and balance sheet using current-exit-price based accounting.
d. What are the advantages and disadvantages of the company's financial statements when prepared on a current-exit-price basis?

9.17 The Clancy James Company (introduced in Question 9.16) wishes to prepare income statements and balance sheets for the month of February. Additional data are as follows:
a. The remaining 40 pounds of sugar are sold on February 15 at $3 per pound.
b. The current entry price of sugar on February 15 is $3 per pound.
c. No additional inventory was purchased in February.

Required

Prepare the company's income statement and balance sheet for the month of February using (1) historical-cost accounting, (2) current-entry-price based accounting, and (3) current-exit-price based accounting.

9.18 Current Costs

The controller of the Robinson Company is discussing a comment you made in the course of presenting your audit report.

" . . . and frankly," Mr. Fisher continued, "I agree that we, too, are responsible for finding ways to produce more relevant financial statements which are as realiable as the ones we now produce."

"For example, suppose the company acquired a finished item for inventory for $40 when the general price-level index was 110. And, later, the item was sold for $75 when the general price-level index was 121 and the current replacement cost was $54. We could calculate a 'holding gain'."

Required

1 Explain to what extent and how current replacement costs already are used within generally accepted accounting principles to value inventories.
2 Calculate in good form the amount of the holding gain in Fisher's example.
3 Why is the use of current replacement cost for both inventories and cost of goods sold preferred by some accounting authorities to the generally accepted use of FIFO or LIFO?   (*AICPA adapted*)

CHAPTER 10

GENERAL PRICE-LEVEL ACCOUNTING

In Chapter 9, we introduced the radical school of thought associated with the adoption of current-value accounting. We also established that a neoclassical school exists as a middle ground between the classical school of historical-cost accounting and the radical school of current-value accounting. This option consists of the restatement of historical-cost financial statements prepared in accordance with general purchasing power. Known as *general price-level accounting,* or *general price-level-adjusted, historical-cost accounting,* this school differs from current-value accounting and historical-cost accounting in its complete renunciation of the stable monetary unit postulate. Also, it should be emphasized at the outset that *general price-level accounting and current-value accounting are competing alternative measures for dealing with problems created by inflation.* General price-level accounting reflects changes in the *general* price level; current-value accounting reflects changes in the *specific* price level. In general price-level accounting, the *change* in the unit of measure is measured.

In this chapter, we will analyze the conceptual and operational features of general price-level accounting information and the means of providing such information.

10.1 GENERAL PRICE-LEVEL RESTATEMENT OF HISTORICAL-COST FINANCIAL STATEMENTS

Historical-cost accounting assumes either that the monetary unit is stable or that the changes in the value of the monetary unit are not material. It is well recognized, however, that the general purchasing power of the dollar has been continually declining. *General purchasing power*, which refers to the ability of the monetary unit to purchase goods or services, is inversely related to the price of the goods or services for which it may be exchanged. When the price of goods or services increases, the movement is referred to as *inflation*, which is also a decrease in the general purchasing power of money. When the price of goods or service decreases, the movement is referred to as *deflation*, which is also an increase in the general purchasing power of money. Because historical-cost accounting does not recognize these changes in the general purchasing power of money, the balance sheet contains diverse kinds of assets and liabilities that refer to different dates and that are expressed in changes in the purchasing power of the dollar. General price-level accounting corrects this situation by completely restating the historical-cost financial statements in a way that reflects changes in the purchasing power of the dollar.

Changes in the purchasing power of the dollar are measured by means of *index numbers*. A *price index* is the ratio of the average price of a group of goods or services on a given date and the average price of a similar group of goods or services on another given date, known as the *base year*, when the price index is equal to 100. Price indices that measure the changes in prices on a general basis reflect the purchasing power of the dollar. Such indices are used to restate the historical-cost based amounts on the financial statements in terms of units of purchasing power at a base year or at the end of the current period. So that intercompany comparisons will be meaningful, the established common date to which dollars are to be restated in terms of general purchasing power is the end of the current period.

To introduce the steps required in the preparation of general price-level statements, we will use a simplified model drawn from the discussion introduced by Chambers.[1] Assume that a firm's balance sheet may be divided into *monetary* items and *nonmonetary* items. At this level, *monetary items* may be defined as items for which amounts are fixed in terms of number of dollars by contract or otherwise, regardless of changes in price levels. For the period t_0, the balance sheet equation, expressed in dollars at time 0, is

$$M_0 + N_0 = R_0$$

where

M_0 = net monetary items.
N_0 = net nonmonetary items.
R_0 = residual equity.

Let us also assume that there is a change in the general price level p. By definition, $p = (P_1 / P_0) - 1$, where P_0 is the price index at time 0 and P_1 is the price index at time 1. The balance sheet equation at t_2, restated for the changes in the general price level, is

$$M_0(1 + p) + N_0(1 + p) = R_0(1 + p)$$

which is equivalent to

$$M_0 + M_{0p} + N_0 + N_{0p} = R_0 + R_{0p}$$

Given that, by definition, net monetary assets are expressed in fixed amounts of dollars, it is appropriate to remove M_{Op} from each side of the equation and to replace M_0 from each side of the equation and to replace M_0 with M_1:

$$M_1 + (N_0 + N_{Op}) = (R_0 + R_{Op}) - M_{Op}$$

The last equation may be interpreted as follows:

1 M_1 represents the net monetary assets at t_1.
2 $N_0 + N_{Op}$ represents the general price-level restated monetary assets at t_1.
3 $R_0 + R_{Op}$ represents the general price-level restated residual equity at t_1.
4 M_{Op} represents the gains or losses on monetary items. By definition, M_0 is equal to net monetary assets C_0 less monetary liabilities L_0.
The balance sheet equation at t_2 may be restated

$$C_1 + (N_0 + N_{Op}) - L_1 = (R_0 + R_{Op}) - (C_{Op} - L_{Op})$$

or

$$C_1 + (N_0 + N_{Op}) - L_1 = (R_0 + R_{Op}) - C_{Op} + L_{Op}$$

Consequently, L_{Op} represents the gain from the outstanding liabilities during the period, and C_{Op} represents the loss resulting from holding monetary assets from t_0 to t_1.

From this simplified model, we can develop the methodology required for the restatement of historical-cost amounts in traditional financial statements into units of general purchasing power. The following steps are necessary:

1 Obtain the complete set of historical-cost financial statements.
2 Determine and obtain an acceptable general price-level index on which data on the index numbers are available to cover the life of the oldest item on the balance sheet.
3 Classify each item on the balance sheet as a monetary or a nonmonetary item.
4 Adjust the nonmonetary items by a conversion factor to reflect the current general purchasing power.
5 Calculate the general purchasing power (general price-level) gains or losses arising from holding monetary items.

With the exception of the first step, we will discuss each of these steps in the remainder of Chapter 10.

10.2 ADJUSTING SPECIFIC ITEMS FOR GENERAL PRICE-LEVEL CHANGES

10.2.1 Treatment of Monetary Items

Calculation of the General Price-Level Gain or Loss

As previously stated, the amounts of monetary items are fixed in terms of number of dollars, by contract or otherwise, regardless of changes in the general or specific price levels. Although these amounts are fixed, the values of the monetary items in terms of purchasing power change. Holders of monetary items, therefore, gain or lose purchasing power because the general level of prices changes. Such gains and losses are called *general purchasing-power gains or losses*, or *general price-level gains or losses on monetary items*. More specifically, during periods of rising prices, (1) monetary assets lose purchasing power, which is recognized by a general price-level loss, and (2) monetary liabilities gain purchasing power, which is recognized by a general price-level gain. During periods of decreasing prices, (1) monetary assets gain purchasing power, which is recognized by a general price-level gain, and (2) monetary liabilities lose purchasing power, which is recognized by a general price-level loss.

The general price-level gain or loss is calculated by:

1 Computing the net monetary asset position at the beginning of the period. For example, if cash and payables at the beginning of the period are $30,000 and $20,000, respectively, net monetary assets will be $10,000.

2 Restating the net monetary asset position at the beginning of the period in terms of the purchasing power of the dollar at the end of the period. If, for example, the general price-level index is 120 at the beginning of the period and 180 at the end of the period, then the net monetary asset position at the beginning of the period ($10,000) is restated as $15,000 [$10,000 × (180/120)].

3 Restating all of the monetary receipts for the year on a year-end basis and adding the result to the restated net monetary position at the beginning of the period (found in Step 2). Assuming that sales of $20,000 occur evenly during the year and that the average general price index is 150, the adjusted monetary receipts are restated as $24,000 [$20,000 × (180/150)]. This result is added to the $15,000 found in Step 2 to arrive at a total restated net increase in monetary items of $39,000.

4 Restating all of the monetary payments of the year on a year-end basis and deducting the result from the total restated net increase in monetary items found in Step 4. Assume that purchases and expenses of $15,000 also occur evenly during the year. The adjusted monetary payments are then restated as $18,000 [$15,000 × (180/150)]. This result is deducted from the $39,000 found in Step 3 to yield the adjusted, computed net monetary asset position of $21,000 at the end of the period.

5 Deducting the actual net monetary assets at the end of the period from the computed net monetary assets at the end of the period found in Step 4 to obtain a purchasing power gain of $6,000.

Using our example, these five steps may be summarized as follows:

| | Monetary Items | |
	Unadjusted	Adjusted
Steps 1 and 2	$10,000	$15,000
Step 3	20,000	24,000
Total	$30,000	$39,000
Step 4	$15,000	$18,000
Total	$15,000	$21,000

Step 5 $15,000
  Purchasing power gain (or loss) $ 6,000

To summarize, general price-level gains or losses are computed by restating the net monetary position at the beginning of the period and the net monetary transactions during the period as units of general purchasing power at the end of the period. The result is compared with actual net monetary position, and the difference is the general price-level gain or loss.

Treatment of the General Price-Level Gain or Loss

A lack of agreement exists on the nature of the general price-level gain or loss and its relevant accounting treatment. The following approaches have been suggested:

1 Accounting Research Study No. 6, APB Statement No. 3, and the FASB and the CICA Exposure Drafts on general price-level accounting take the position that the general price-level gain or loss should be included in current income.[2]
2 Only the general price-level loss should be included in current income; the general price-level gain should be treated as a capital item.
3 Both the general price-level gain and loss should be treated as capital items.
4 Both the general price-level gain and loss should be included in current income, with the exception of gains and losses related to long-term debt, which should not appear until they are realized through the redemption of the bonds.[3]
5 All price-level gains and losses should be included in current income, with the exception of gains and losses that arise from including monetary items in shareholders' equity (for example, preferred shares having monetary characteristics).

Despite the controversy generated by each of these different viewpoints, pronouncements of the various accounting bodies predominantly favor the first treatment. The AICPA first expressed this viewpoint in 1969 in APB Statement No. 3:

41. General price-level gains and losses on monetary items arise from changes in the general price level and are not related to subsequent events, such as the receipt or payment of money. Consequently, the Board has concluded that these gains and losses should be recognized as part of the net income of the period in which the general price level changes.
42. A different viewpoint than that expressed in paragraph 41, held by a Board member, is that all of a monetary gain should not be recognized in the period of general price-level increase. Under this view, a portion of the gain on net monetary liabilities in a period of general price-level increase should be deferred to future periods as a reduction of the cost of nonmonetary assets, since the liabilities represent a source of funds for the financing of these assets. The proponent of this view believes that the gain from holding net monetary liabilities during inflation is not realized until the assets acquired from the funds borrowed are sold or consumed in operations. The Board does not agree with this view, however, because it believes that the gain accrues during the period of the general price-level increase and is unrelated to the cost of nonmonetary assets.[4]

The conclusion reached by the APB was sustained by the FASB Exposure Draft on the subject, which stated:

48. The net gain or loss of general purchasing power that results from holding monetary assets and liabilities shall be included in determining net income in units of general purchasing power. No portion of the general purchasing-power gain or loss shall be deferred to future periods.

77. General purchasing-power gains or losses on monetary assets and liabilities arise from changes in the general price level while the assets are held or the liabilities are owned. They are not related to subsequent events, such as the receipt or payment of money. Consequently, the Board concludes (paragraph 48) that those gains and losses should be recognized in determining general purchasing-power income in the period in which general price level changes.[5]

The same position was also reached by the Accounting Standards Steering Committee in the United Kingdom, which published a Provisional Statement of Standard Accounting Practice No. 7 in May 1974. The Committee justified its position as follows:

16. It has been argued that the gain on long-term borrowing should not be shown as profit in the supplementary statement because it might not be possible to distribute it without raising additional finance. This argument, however, confuses the measurement of profitability with the measurement of liquidity. Even in the absence of inflation, the whole of a company's profit may not be distributable without raising additional finance, for example, because it has been invested in, or earmarked for investment in nonliquid assets.

17. Moreover, it is inconsistent to exclude such gains when profit has been debited with the cost of borrowing (which must be assumed to reflect anticipation of inflation by the lender during the currency of the loan) and with depreciation on the converted cost of fixed assets.[6]

The Accounting Research Committee in Canada took a similar position.[7]

Thus, as a general rule, all price-level gains or losses are recognized in the general price-level income statement. The only exception, recommended in both the FASB and the Canadian positions, concerns gains or losses attributable to preferred shares (monetary preference shares) carried at an amount equal to their fixed redemption or liquidation price, which should be credited or charged to common shareholders' equity on the general price-level balance sheet.

10.2.2   Treatment of Nonmonetary Items and Stockholders' Equity

Nonmonetary items are restated in terms of the current general purchasing power by multiplying the cost of the item reported on the historical-cost-based financial statements by the following conversion factor:

$$\frac{\text{Current Year Index}}{\text{Index When Nonmonetary Item Was Acquired}}$$

For example, assume that a piece of equipment is acquired for $100,000 on December 31, 19X0, when the general price-level index is 120. The estimated useful life of the asset is four years. Further assume that the financial statements at the end of 19X2 are restated in terms of units of general purchasing power. If the current price index on December 31, 19X3 is 180, the adjustment of the equipment account will then be

	Unadjusted Amount	Conversion Factor	Adjusted Amount
Equipment	$100,000	180/120	$150,000
Accumulated Depreciation	50,000	180/120	75,000
Net Equipment	$ 50,000		$ 75,000

The restatement of stockholders' equity, with the exception of retained earnings, is similar to the restatement of nonmonetary items. The original invested capital is multiplied by the following conversion factor:

$$\frac{\text{Current Year Index}}{\text{Index When Capital Was Invested}}$$

Retained earnings, which cannot be adjusted by a single conversion factor, represent net income after dividends accumulated since the creation of the going concern. Retained earnings may be restated as follows:

1 The first time historical-cost financial statements are restated in terms of units of current general purchasing power, retained earnings may be determined simply as the residual after all other items in the balance sheet have been restated.
2 In the following periods, the end-of-period retained earnings in units of current general purchasing power may be determined by:
   a. Net income in units of current general purchasing power reported in the general price-level statement (including general price-level gains and losses on monetary items).
   b. Adjustments resulting from general price-level gains or losses on monetary shareholders' equity items.

An important difference is not apparent between general price-level accounting and current-value accounting. Under current-value accounting, an increase in the price of a nonmonetary item results in a holding gain. Under general price-level accounting, the adjustment of historical cost is simply a restatement of a nonmonetary item in terms of the current general purchasing power, and no gain or loss is recognized.

10.3 THE MONETARY–NONMONETARY DISTINCTION

It is important to distinguish between monetary and nonmonetary items, because different treatments are applied to the two types of items. *Nonmonetary items* must be translated into dollars of the same purchasing power at the end of the current period. *Monetary items,* on the other hand, are already stated in end-of-current-period dollars and gain or lose purchasing power as a result of changes in the general price level.

The distinction between monetary and nonmonetary items seems apparent. Monetary items gain or lose purchasing power; nonmonetary items do not. This line of reasoning is used in APB Statement No. 3 and reported by different researchers.[8] Determining monetary items according to expected effect (gain or loss of purchasing power) and then calculating the gain or loss is, however, circular reasoning. As Hendriksen points out, it "bases the classification on the assumed effect, rather than determining the effect from the classification and a change in the price level."[9]

What definition will allow monetary assets to be identified apart from their expected effects? Accounting Research Study No. 6 defined a monetary item in terms of *fixed claims* as an item "the amount of which is fixed by statute or contract and is therefore not affected by a change in the general price level."[10]

Because it does not specify *how* the amount is to be fixed, however, this definition is inadequate. Thus, to correct for this misspecification, the official definition adopted in the various pronouncements of the accounting bodies considers monetary items to be items the amounts of which *are fixed by contracts or otherwise fixed in terms of dollars* (or whatever is the domestic currency), *regardless of changes in specific prices or in the general price level.* This definition is general and applies to assets, liabilities, and shareholders' equities that have the specified characteristics. Accordingly, monetary and nonmonetary items are identified and segregated as shown in Exhibit 10.1. Problem areas exist, however, because some assets and liabilities may exhibit characteristics of both monetary and nonmonetary items. Thus, various degrees of *fixity* are possible, as implied by the word "fixed" in the definition of a monetary item. Must a monetary item be a monetary item permanently? Because conditions may change, the price of a monetary item need not be fixed permanently. But what degree of fixity justifies classifying an item as monetary? The decision remains a matter of professional judgment, as the following problem areas indicate.

EXHIBIT 10.1
Classification of Items as Monetary or Nonmonetary

Assets	Monetary Item	Nonmonetary Item
Cash on hand and demand bank deposits (US dollars)	X	
Time deposits (US dollars)	X	
Foreign currency on hand and claims to foreign currency	X	
Marketable securities		
Stocks		X
Bonds (other than convertibles)	X	
Convertible bonds (until converted, these represent		
an entitlement to receive a fixed number of dollars)	X	
Accounts and notes receivable	X	
Allowance for doubtful accounts and notes receivable	X	
Inventories		
Produced under fixed contracts and accounted for at		
the contract price	X	
Other inventories		X
Loans to employees	X	

Prepaid insurance, advertising, rent, and other prepayments		X
Long-term receivables	X	
Refundable deposits	X	
Advances to unconsolidated subsidiaries	X	
Equity investment in unconsolidated subsidiaries or other investees		X
Pension, sinking, and other funds under an enterprise's control	X	X
Property, plant, and equipment		X
Accumulated depreciation of property, plant, and equipment		X
Cash-surrender value of life insurance	X	
Purchase commitments (portion paid on fixed-price contracts)		X
Advances to a supplier (not on contract)	X	
Patents, trademarks, licenses, formulas		X
Goodwill		X
Other intangible assets and deferred charges		X

Liabilities

Accounts and notes payable	X	
Accrued expenses payable (for example, wages)	X	
Accrued vacation pay (if it is to be paid at the wage rates as of the vacation dates and if those rates may vary)		X
Cash dividends payable	X	
Obligations payable in foreign currency	X	
Sales commitments (portion collected on fixed-price contracts)		X
Advances from customers (not on contract)	X	
Accrued losses of firm purchase commitments	X	
Deferred income		X
Refundable deposits	X	
Bonds payable and other long-term debts	X	
Unamortized premiums or discounts and prepaid interest on bonds and notes payable	X	
Convertible bonds	X	
Accrued pension obligations	X	X
Obligations under warranties		X
Deferred income-tax credits	X	
Deferred investment-tax credits		X
Preferred stock		
Carried at an amount equal to a fixed liquidation or redemption price	X	
Carried at an amount less than fixed liquidation or redemption price		X
Common stockholders' equity		X

First, *preferred shares* are classified as nonmonetary items in APB Statement No. 3. The FASB Exposure Draft considers that

...preferred stock carried at an amount equal to its fixed liquidation or redemption price is monetary because the claim of the preferred stockholders on the assets of the enterprise is in a fixed number of dollars; preferred stock carried at less than its fixed liquidation or redemption price is nonmonetary, but becomes monetary when restated to an amount equal to its fixed liquidation or redemption price.[11]

The FASB Exposure Draft also recommends that

...gains or losses of general purchasing power that result from monetary stockholders' equity items (for example, preferred stock that is carried...at...fixed liquidation or redemption price) shall be charged or credited directly to common stockholders' equity in the general purchasing-power financial statements.[12]

Second, *deferred income taxes* are classified as nonmonetary items in APB Statement No. 3 on the basis that they are a cost-saving and are deferred as reductions of expenses in future periods. A similar classification is retained in the FASB Exposure Draft. The argument is that tax-allocation credits are classified as liabilities under the accrual method, whereas under the deferred method, these are credits simply treated as deferred credits representing savings to be amortized to income in future periods. It follows that deferred income taxes would be classified as nonmonetary items, given the adoption of the deferred method in the United States. On the other hand, the Canadian Institute of Chartered Accountants recommends that deferred income taxes be treated as monetary items, even though the deferred method is required in Canada. The *CICA Handbook* indicates that the deferral should be computed at current tax rates without subsequent adjustment of the accumulated tax-allocation debit or credit balances to reflect changes in the tax rates.[13] Consequently, deferred income taxes refer to fixed amounts of money and can be defined as monetary units.

The FASB Exposure Draft *Constant Dollar Accounting* changed the classification of deferred income-tax items to monetary items. The FASB states its position as follows:

Again, although the nonmonetary classification may be technically preferable, the monetary classification provides a more practical solution and identifies the effect of inflation with the period the inflation occurs, rather than with the period the deferred income tax item is reversed.[14]

Third, *foreign currency on hand, claims to foreign currency,* and *obligations payable in foreign currency* may be interpreted as either monetary or nonmonetary items. If they are perceived as commodities, they are nonmonetary items, because the prices of commodities may fluctuate. If they are perceived as similar to domestic-currency items, they are monetary items. A more logical viewpoint is to classify foreign-currency items as monetary if they are stated at the *closing* rate of exchange in the historical-cost financial statements and as nonmonetary if they are stated at the *historical* rate of exchange in the historical-cost financial statements. The FASB Exposure Draft *Constant Dollar Accounting* classifies foreign currencies on hand, claims to foreign currency, and obligations payable in foreign currency as monetary items. The FASB states its position as follows:

Although the nonmonetary classification may be technically preferable and result in somewhat different disclosures, as a practical matter, the monetary classification produces essentially the same net effect on aggregate disclosure as restating those foreign-currency items as nonmonetary and then reducing them to their net realizable value. The monetary classification obviates that two-step procedure and is more understandable.[15]

Fourth, *long-term debts in foreign currency* also may be interpreted as either monetary or nonmonetary. Again, a logical alternative is to classify long-term debt in a foreign currency as monetary if it is stated at the closing rate of exchange and as nonmonetary if it is stated at the historical rate of exchange.

Fifth, *convertible debt* is perceived to have monetary and nonmonetary characteristics. Accounting Research Study No. 6 proposes that convertible debt be treated as monetary when the market price of shares is below the conversion price and as nonmonetary when the market price of shares is at or above the conversion price. Another, more accepted position is that convertible bonds should be treated as monetary debts — obligations to pay a fixed number of dollars — until they are converted.

10.4   PRICE-LEVEL INDICES

A *price-level index* compares general or specific changes in price from one period to another. A *general price-level index* can be defined as a series of measurements, expressed as percentages, of the relationship between the average price of a group of goods and services on a succession of dates and the average price of a similar group of goods and services on a common date. The components of the series are called *price-index numbers*. A price index does not, however, measure the movement of the individual component prices, some of which move in one direction and some of which move in the opposite direction. Thus, the general price-level index is based on a large range of goods and services, whereas the specific price-level index refers to a particular good or industry. Because general price-level accounting reflects changes in the purchasing power of the dollar, a general price-level index must be employed to restate the historical-cost statements in terms of dollars of constant purchasing power.

10.4.1   Index Formulas

The computations of a general price-level index differ according to the formula used to assign weights to prices. We will use the following symbols to represent the four basic formulas:

p = the price of the commodity or service.
q = the quantity of the commodity or service.
p_0, q_0 = the price and quantity of the commodity in the base period.
p_n, q_n = the price and quantity of the commodity in the current period.
p_a, q_a = the price and quantity of the commodity in some average period.

The *Laspeyres formula* assumes that the price index is a weighted sum of current-period prices divided by a weighted sum of base-period prices, where the weights are *base-period* quantities of commodities. Such an index, called a *Laspeyres index*, is computed

$$I = \frac{\Sigma p_n q_0}{\Sigma p_0 q_0}$$

The *Paasche formula* assumes that the price index is a weighted sum of current-period prices divided by a weighted sum of base-period prices, where the weights are *current-period* quantities of commodities. Such an index, called a *Paasche index*, is computed

$$I = \frac{\Sigma p_n q_n}{\Sigma p_0 q_n}$$

The *fixed-weighted formula* assumes that the price index is a weighted sum of current-period prices divided by a weighted sum of base-period prices, where the weights are *average-period* quantities of commodities. Such an index, called a *fixed-weighted index*, is computed

$$I = \frac{\Sigma p_n q_a}{\Sigma p_0 q_a}$$

The *Fisher formula* assumes that the price index is a geometric average of Laspeyres and Paasche formulas. The *Fisher index* is computed

$$I = \sqrt{\frac{\Sigma p_n q_n}{\Sigma p_0 q_n} = \frac{\Sigma p_n q_a}{\Sigma p_0 q_a}}$$

10.4.2 Choice of a General Price-Level Index

General price-level accounting employs a conversion factor based on changes in the general price-level index to convert dollars on one date to the number of dollars having the same purchasing power on another date. An appropriate concept of purchasing power and an appropriate general price-level index must be chosen. Hendriksen presents different concepts of purchasing power — namely, general purchasing power of the dollar, purchasing power of the stockholders, investment purchasing power of the firm, and specific replacement purchasing power.[16] The general purchasing power measured by a general price-level index reflects changes in the value of money and, consequently, is deemed most relevant for general price-level accounting. For example, APB Statement No. 3 states:

> The purpose of the general price-level restatement procedures is to restate historical-dollar financial statements for changes in the general purchasing power of the dollar, and this purpose can only be accomplished by using a general price-level index.[17]

Thus, the concept of general purchasing power implies the use of a general price-level index. In the United States, the Department of Commerce and the Department of Labor regularly maintain and publish general price indices. Among the most important are:

1 *The Consumer Price Index*, prepared by the Bureau of Labor Statistics of the US Department of Labor.
2 *The Wholesale Price Index*, prepared by the Bureau of Labor Statistics of the US Department of Labor.

3 *The Composite Construction-Cost Index*, prepared by the Construction Industry Division of the Business and Defense Service Administration of the US Department of Commerce.

4 *The GNP (Gross National Product) Implicit Price Deflator*, prepared by the Office of Business Economics of the US Department of Commerce.

The two price indices most commonly suggested for general price-level accounting are the *Consumer Price Index* (CPI) and the GNP *(Implicit Price Deflator* (IPI). The CPI is a *base-weighted* index designed to measure price changes in a *basket* of retail goods and services acquired by middle-income families of specific size living in urban centers. The GNP Implicit Price Deflator is a *currently weighted* index designed to measure price changes in all goods and services produced in a given year. Both the CPI and the IPI have limitations. The base-weighted CPI fails to account for the substitution of relatively lower-priced goods that takes place when relative prices change. In other words, the CPI has an *upward bias*; it *overstates* the effect of changes in prices on the cost of living. On the other hand, the currently weighted IPI has a *downward bias*; it *understates* the price increase in the cost of living. For example, Rosen says that:

> In summary, when prices are rising, currently weighted indices may have a downward bias (that is, they tend to understate the percentage price increase) and base-weighted indices may have an upward bias (that is, they tend to overstate a percentage price increase).[18]

The IPI is considered to be a better currently compiled, general price-level index than the CPI. The IPI covers all goods and services produced in the economy, whereas the CPI covers only goods and services purchased by a "typical consumer." Thus, in terms of measuring the extent of overall price changes, the IPI is probably more relevant. Annual estimates are available from 1919, and quarterly estimates are available from 1947.

However, the FASB Exposure Draft *Constant-Dollar Accounting* designates the *Consumer Price Index for All Urban Consumers* (CPI-U) rather than the GNP Implicit Price Deflator as an index of general purchasing power for two reasons. First, the CPI-U has two practical advantages: (1) It is calculated more frequently (monthly instead of quarterly), and (2) it is not revised after its initial publication. Second, the rates of change in the CPI-U and the GNP Implicit Price Deflator tend to be similar and, therefore, use of the CPI-U tends to produce a comparable result.[19]

10.5 A SIMPLIFIED ILLUSTRATION OF GENERAL PRICE-LEVEL INDEXING

The following simplified example briefly illustrates how general price-level, historical-cost financial statements can be prepared from historical-cost financial statements.

The Picur Company began business operations on December 31, 19X5, when the price level was 100 (base period). The comparative balance sheets for 19X5 and 19X6 are shown in Exhibit 10.2. The 19X6 income statement appears in Exhibit 10.3.

In addition to the balance sheets and the income statement, the following supplementary information is available:

1 The price deflator is
            December 31, 19X5   100
            December 31, 19X6   180
            Average price index for 19X6   120
2 All revenues and costs were incurred evenly throughout the year, with the exception of the cost of goods sold and the depreciation expense.
3 The inventory purchases were made on a date when the price-level index was at 150.
4 A LIFO flow is assumed.
5 Depreciation for plant and equipment was accumulated by the straight-line method over a five-year life span.

EXHIBIT 10.2
The Picur Company
Comparative Balance Sheets as of December 31

	December 31, 19X5		December 31, 19X6	
	Debit	Credit	Debit	Credit
Monetary Assets	$ 30,000		$ 60,000	
Inventories	30,000	(3,000 units)	20,000	(2,000 units)
Land	40,000		40,000	
Plant and Equipment	50,000		50,000	
Accumulated Depreciation				$ 10,000
Liabilities (1%)		$ 50,000		50,000
Capital Stock		100,000		100,000
Retained Earnings				10,000
Total	$150,000	$150,000	$170,000	$170,000

EXHIBIT 10.3
The Picur Company
Income Statement For the Year Ended December 31, 19X6

Sales (5,000 units @ $40)		$200,000
Cost of Goods Sold		
Beginning Inventory (3,000 units @ $10)	$ 30,000	
Purchases (4,000 units @ $12)	48,000	
Units Available	$ 78,000	
Ending Inventory (2,000 units @ $10)	20,000	58,000
Gross Margin		$142,000
Operational Expenses		
Depreciation	$ 10,000	
Interest	5,000	
Selling and Administrative Expenses	117,000	$132,000
Net Operating Profit		$ 10,000

EXHIBIT 10.4
The Picur Company
Balance Sheet December 31, 19X5

Assets	Unadjusted Amount	Conversion Factor	Adjusted Amount
Monetary Assets	$ 30,000	180/100	$ 54,000
Inventories	30,000	180/100	54,000
Land	40,000	180/100	72,000
Plant and Equipment	50,000	180/100	90,000
Accumulated Depreciation	—		—
Total	$150,000		$270,000
Equities			
Liabilities (10%)	$ 50,000	180/100	$ 90,000
Capital	100,000	180/100	180,000
Retained Earnings	—	—	—
Total	$150,000		$270,000

EXHIBIT 10.5
The Picur Company
Balance Sheet December 31, 19X6

Assets	Unadjusted Amount	Conversion Factor	Adjusted Amount
Monetary Assets	$ 60,000	180/180	$ 60,000
Inventories	20,000	180/100	36,000
Land	40,000	180/100	72,000
Plant and Equipment	50,000	180/100	90,000
Accumulated Depreciation	(10,000)		(18,000)
Total	$160,000		$240,000
Equities			
Liabilities (10%)	$ 50,000	180/180	$ 50,000
Capital	100,000	180/100	180,000
Retained Earnings	10,000	—	10,000
Total	$160,000		$240,000

EXHIBIT 10.6
The Picur Company December 31, 19X6 Income Statement Adjusted to 19X6 Price Levels

	Unadjusted Amount	Conversion Factor	Adjusted Amount
Sales (5,000 units @ $40)	$200,000	180/120	$300,000
Cost of Goods Sold			
Beginning Inventory (3000 units @ $10)	$ 30,000	180/100	$ 54,000
Purchases (4,000 units @ $12)	48,000	180/150	57,600
Units Available			$111,600
Ending Inventory (2,000 units @ $10)	20,000		36,000
Cost of Goods Sold	$ 58,000		$ 75,600
Gross Margin	$142,000		$224,400
Operational Expenses			
Depreciation	$ 10,000	180/100	$ 18,000
Interest	5,000	180/120	7,500
Selling and Administrative Expenses	117,000	180/120	175,500
Net Operating Profit	$ 10,000		$ 23,400

EXHIBIT 10.7
Monetary Gains or Losses on Monetary Items

	Unadjusted Amount	Conversion Factor	Adjusted Amount
Net Monetary Assets on			
January 1, 19X6	$ (20,000)	180/100	$ (36,000)
Add: Monetary Receipts			
During 19X6 Sales	200,000	180/120	300,000
Net Monetary Items	$180,000		$264,000
Less: Monetary Payments			
Purchases	$ 48,000	180/150	$ 57,600
Interest	5,000	180/120	7,500
Selling and Administrative			
Expenses	117,000	180/120	175,500
Total			$240,600
Computed Net Monetary Assets,			
December 31, 19X6			$ 23,400
Actual Net Monetary Assets,			
December 31, 19X6			(10,000)
Loss on Monetary Assets			$ 13,400

The procedure for restating the historical-cost financial statements is:

1 Restate the 19X5 balance sheet to 19X6 price levels. (The 19X5 balance sheet for the Picur Company adjusted to 19X6 price levels is shown in Exhibit 10.4).
2 Restate the 19X6 balance sheet to current 19X6 price levels. (The 19X6 adjusted balance sheet for Picur appears in Exhibit 10.5). At this stage, there is no direct conversion factor for retained earnings. It is simply the amount required to achieve a balance between assets and equities.
3 Restate the 19X6 income statement to 19X6 price levels. (The 19X6 adjusted income statement for Picur is illustrated in Exhibit 10.6).
4 Calculate the monetary gains or losses that result from changes in the general price level. (This computation is shown in Exhibit 10.7 for Picur.)
5 Prepare a reconciliation of retained earnings as follows:

Retained earnings, January 1, 19X6	$ 0
Add: Net profit	23,400
Less: General price-level loss	(13,000)
Retained earnings, January 1, 19X6	$10,000

10.6 EVALUATION OF GENERAL PRICE-LEVEL ACCOUNTING

The controversy concerning the relevance of general price-level accounting has been an ongoing one. Some of the arguments in favor of and against general price-level accounting will be presented here as a reflection of the positions taken in the literature and in practice. The number and order of these presentations do not reflect on their relative merits.

10.6.1 Arguments in Favor of General Price-Level Accounting

A number of arguments have been advanced in favor of general price-level accounting. First, financial statements that are not adjusted for general price-level changes include diverse kinds of assets and claims expressed in dollars of different purchasing power. General price-level accounting is designed to express the level of changes in the price of these assets and in the purchasing power of the claims. General price-level statements present data expressed on the basis of a common denominator — the purchasing power of the dollar at the end of the period. Such statements facilitate comparisons between firms because a common unit of measure is used. The FASB states that:

Changes in the purchasing power of the dollar affect individual enterprises differently, depending on the amount of the change and the age and composition of the enterprise's assets and equities. For example, during periods of inflation, those who hold monetary assets (cash and receivables in fixed dollar amounts) suffer a loss in purchasing power represented by those monetary assets. On the other hand, in periods of inflation, debtors gain because their liabilities are able to be repaid in dollars having less purchasing power. In periods of deflation, the reverse is true. Conventional financial statements do not report the effects of inflation or deflation on individual enterprises.[20]

The second argument in favor of general price-level accounting is that conventional historical-cost accounting does not measure income properly as a result of the matching of dollars of different "size" on the income statement. Expenses incurred in previous periods are set off against revenues that are usually expressed in current dollars. General price-level accounting provides a better matching of revenues and expenses because common dollars are used. A more realistic income relationship is therefore possible through the development of more logical dividend policies. The FASB states that:

> Investors and others often look to the income statement, or to ratios that are based in part on measures of income, for information about the ability of an enterprise to earn a return on its invested capital. In the conventional income statement, revenues are measured in dollars of current, or at least very recent, purchasing power, whereas certain significant expense items are measured in dollars of different purchasing power of earlier periods. Depreciation and cost of goods sold are two of the most commonly cited examples, although the problem arises whenever amounts in the income statement represent expenditure of dollars of different purchasing power. In periods of inflation, depreciation and cost of goods sold tend to be understated in terms of the purchasing power sacrificed to acquire depreciable assets and inventory. Further, information stated in terms of current general purchasing power may indicate that an enterprise's income-tax and dividend payout rates are significantly different in terms of units of money and in units of general purchasing power.[21]

The third argument in favor of general price-level accounting is that it is relatively easy to apply. It merely replaced a "rubber dollar" with a "dated dollar."[22] General price-level accounting represents the least departure from generally accepted accounting principles. As a result, it may be relatively objective and verifiable. These characteristics may make it more acceptable to many firms than current-value accounting.

Fourth, general price-level accounting provides relevant information for management evaluation and use. Thus, the general price-level gains and losses resulting from holding monetary items reflect management's response to inflation. The restated nonmonetary items approximate the purchasing power needed to replace the assets. Finally, general price-level accounting presents the impact of general inflation on profit and provides more realistic returns on investment rates.

The staff of the Accounting Research Division of the AICPA argues the case for the preparation of price-level statements as a means for financial analysis as follows:

> If price-level changes can be measured in some satisfactory manner and if the effects of those changes can be properly disclosed, the inferences that can be drawn from accounting data will be statistically more reliable. Specifically, for example, all the revenues and expenses in the earnings statement for any one year will be expressed in dollars of the same size and not in a mixture of dollars from different years. Similarly, the various balance sheet items will all be expressed in terms of a common dollar. Since both the results of operations and financial position will be stated in terms of the same "common dollar," a calculation of a rate of return on invested capital can be made in which both numerator and denominator are expressed in the same units.
>
> Some inferences can be drawn in terms of the various groups interested in business activity. Investors and their representatives (for example, management, including the

board of directors) can tell whether the capital invested in the business has been increased or decreased as the result of all the policies followed and all the financial events that have taken place bearing on the business entity. More specifically, management and owners can tell if the dividend policy actually followed in the past has resulted in distributions out of economic or business capital, and if not, what proportion of the earnings (adjusted for price-level changes) has in fact been distributed. With price-level adjusted data before them, the directors can tell if a proposed dividend will equal, exceed, or fall short of current earnings, or any other norm or standard they wish to use.

Owners, management, and government can tell if taxes levied on income were less than pre-tax earnings, and if so, to what extent, and if not, how much they exceeded pre-tax earnings. Creditors will be better informed as to the buffer or cushion behind their claims. In addition, employees, as well as investors, and management will have a more reliable gauge of the rate of return to date on the capital employed and will be able to use the information more intelligently to decide if the business entity has been profitable or not.

Financial statements fully adjusted for the effect of price-level changes will also reveal the losses or gains from holding or owning monetary items. All interested groups then have one important measure of the effect of a changing dollar on their positions as debtors or creditors.

Financial data adjusted for price-level effects provide a basis for a more intelligent, better informed allocation of resources, whether those resources are in the hands of individuals, of business entities, or of government.[23]

10.6.2 Arguments Against General Price-Level Accounting

A case against general price-level accounting may be based on the following arguments. First, most empirical studies indicate that the relevance of general price-level information is either weak[24] or not accepted.[25] Further research is warranted before any definite conclusions can be reached regarding the relevance of general price-level information and the ability to interpret it meaningfully.

Second, general price-level changes account only for changes in the general price level and do not account for changes in the specific price level. Thus, holding gains and losses on nonmonetary assets are not recognized. In addition, users of general price-level-adjusted data may believe that the restated values correspond to current values.

Third, the impact of inflation differs among firms. Capital-intensive firms may be affected by inflation more than firms that rely heavily on short-term assets. Similarly, high-leverage firms stand to gain from inflation. As a result, general price-level accounting may distort normal income. High-leverage companies will "look good" by showing high general price-level gains. Some of the general price-level gains and losses on monetary items, however, are unrealized and should be excluded from the financial statements and deferred to later periods.

Fourth, the costs of implementing general price-level accounting may exceed the benefits. Miller presents the following arguments:

- Companies may lose the ability to use LIFO for tax purposes.
- GPP [general purchasing power] may result in higher property tax assessments.
- Companies must roll forward (restate) prior years each time comparative statements are prepared.

- Companies must also provide replacement-cost information to the Securities and Exchange Commission (SEC).
- Investors may not attempt to understand the statements.
- There are better ways to disclose the effect of inflation on a specific company, its assets, its operations, and its future.[26]

Finally, some technical problems beset general price-level accounting. The first problem is related to the choice of an appropriate general price-level index. Of the two general indices suggested for use in price-level accounting — the Consumer Price Index and the GNP Implicit Price Deflator — it has been suggested that if price-level restatements are to be made, only the GNP Price Deflator is sufficiently representative of the entire economy. For this reason, this index is more appropriate for measuring fluctuations in the exchange value of the dollar. There is, however, a problem of timeliness. The GNP Implicit Price Deflator is only available quarterly; the Consumer Price Index is available monthly. If the GNP Implicit Price Deflator were adopted, it might be necessary to approximate its effects with the Consumer Price Index for periods when the GNP Implicit Price Deflator is not available. The FASB's decision to adopt the Consumer Price Index for All Urban Consumers has resolved this problem.

The second problem is that general price-level accounting requires assets and liabilities to be identified and classified as monetary or nonmonetary items. Although there is general agreement on how most items should be classified, some items are subject to different interpretations. Examples are deferred income taxes, preferred shares, foreign-currency items, and convertible debt.

The third technical problem is that general price-level accounting applies the accounting principles employed in conventional accounting. Only the unit of measurement is changed. Therefore, the restated cost of nonmonetary assets should not exceed the current value. For example, the lower-of-cost-or-market rule is applied, just as it is applied in historical-cost accounting. Inventories should not be restated at more than net realizable value. Paragraph 37 of APB Statement No. 3 recommends a write down of restated cost to replacement cost only for nonmonetary assets that are stated at lower-of-cost-or-market, such as inventories or other current assets. It does not consider, however, the write down of noncurrent assets to replacement costs. Accordingly, the FASB Discussion Memorandum on general price-level accounting poses the following questions:

> If the cost of a nonmonetary asset is to be restated upward for a decrease in the general purchasing power of the dollar and the restated amount would exceed replacement cost or some other defined amount, should the restated amount be limited to such a defined amount in general price-level financial statements? Further, if such a limit to restatement is required, should it be required for all nonmonetary assets or only for certain assets (for example only for inventory)?[27]

10.7   CONCLUSIONS

In this chapter and in Chapter 9, we have established that all the profit concepts are based on different notions of capital maintenance. Conventional accounting, because it relies on historical-cost accounting for the valuation of assets and liabilities, conforms to the money-maintenance concept. Current-value accounting, in which assets and liabilities are brought into the financial statements at their current value, conforms to the physical productive-capacity maintenance concept. Finally, general price-level accounting, because it relies on a general price-level restatement of historically based assets and liabilities, conforms to the general purchasing-power, money-maintenance concept.

Each of these accounting methods is based on certain principles and rules. Conventional accounting is based on generally accepted accounting principles in general and the historical-cost principle and stable monetary-unit postulate in particular. Conventional accounting recognizes neither changes in the general price level nor changes in the specific price level. Current-value accounting is characterized by the complete abandonment of the historical-cost principle and recognizes only changes in the specific price-level. General price-level accounting is characterized by the abandonment of the stable monetary-unit postulate and recognizes only changes in the general price level. Each of these methods apparently attempts to correct some of the deficiencies of conventional historical-cost accounting — but not all of them. Consequently, in Chapter 11, we will introduce another accounting valuation method based on a recognition of changes in both the general and the specific price levels.

NOTES

[1] Chambers, R.J., *Toward a General Theory of Accounting* (Adelaide, Australia: University of Adelaide, 1961), and *Accounting, Evolution, and Economic Behavior* (Englewood Cliffs, N.J.: Prentice-Hall, 1965), pp. 223–7.

[2] Accounting Research Study No. 6, *Reporting the Financial Effects of Price-Level Changes* (New York: American Institute of Certified Public Accountants, 1963), p. 13; APB Statement No. 3, *Financial Statements Restated for General Price-Level Changes* (New York: American Institute of Certified Public Accountants, June 1969), p. 8; FASB Exposure Draft, *Financial Reporting in Units of General Purchasing Power* (New York: Financial Accounting Standards Board, December 31, 1974), paragraph 30; FASB Exposure Draft, *Constant-Dollar Accounting* (New York: Financial Accounting Standards Board, March 2, 1979), p. 3; Accounting Research Committee, *Accounting for Changes in the General Purchasing Power of Money* (Toronto: Canadian Institute of Chartered Accountants, July, 1975), p. 12.

[3] Mason, Perry, *Price-Level Changes and Financial Statements — Basic Concepts and Methods* (Columbus, Oh.: American Accounting Association, 1956), pp. 23–4.

[4] APB Statement No. 3, op. cit., paragraphs 41, 42.

[5] FASB Exposure Draft, *Financial Reporting in Units of General Purchasing Power*, op. cit., paragraphs 48, 77.

[6] Accounting Standards Steering Committee, Provisional Statement of Standard Accounting Practice No. 7, *Accounting for Changes in the Purchasing Power of Money* (London: Her Majesty's Stationery Office, May, 1974), paragraphs 16, 17.

[7] Accounting Research Committee, *Accounting for Changes in the General Purchasing Power of Money*.

[8] Johnson, G.L., "The Monetary and Nonmonetary Distinction," *The Accounting Review* (October, 1965), pp. 281–3: Heath, L.C., "Distinguishing Between Monetary and Nonmonetary Assets and Liabilities in General Price-Level Accounting," *The Accounting Review* (July, 1972), pp. 458–68; Boersema, J.M., "The Monetary–Nonmonetary Distinction in Accounting for Inflation," *Cost and Management* (May/June, 1975), pp. 6–11.

[9] Hendriksen, E.S., *Accounting Theory* (Homewood, Ill.: Richard D. Irwin, 1970), p. 207.

[10] Accounting Research Study No. 6, op. cit., p. 38.

[11] FASB Exposure Draft, *Financial Reporting in Units of General Purchasing Power*, op. cit., p. 13.

[12] Ibid., p. 14.

[13] *CICA Handbook* (Toronto: Canadian Institute of Chartered Accountants, 1980), Section 3470.19.

[14] FASB Exposure Draft, *Constant Dollar Accounting*, p. 5.

[15] Ibid., p. 2.

[16] Hendriksen, E.S., *Accounting Theory*, 3rd ed. (Homewood, Ill.: Richard D. Irwin, 1977), pp. 231–36.

[17] APB Statement No. 3, op. cit., p. 13.

[18] Rosen, L.S., *Current-Value Accounting and Price-Level Restatements* (Toronto: Canadian Institute of Chartered Accountants, 1972), p. 40.

[19] FASB Exposure Draft, *Constant-Dollar Accounting*, op. cit., p. 2.

[20] FASB Discussion Memorandum, *Reporting the Effects of General Price-Level Changes in Financial Statements* (Stamford, Ct.: Financial Accounting Standards Board, 1977), p. 8.

[21] Ibid.

[22] Miller, Elwood, L., "What's Wrong with Price-Level Accounting?," *Harvard Business Review* (November/December, 1978), p. 113.

[23] Accounting Research Study No. 6, op. cit., pp. 14–16.

[24] Dyckman, T.R., *Studies in Accounting Research No. 1*, "Investment Analysis and General Price-Level Adjustments" (Evanston, Ill.: American Accounting Association, 1969), p. 17; Morris, R.C., "Evidence of the Impact of Inflation Accounting on Share Prices," *Accounting and Business Research* (Spring, 1975), p. 90; Peterson, Russel J., "A Portfolio Analysis of General Price-Level Restatement," *The Accounting Review* (July, 1975), p. 532.

[25] Horngren, Charles T., "Security Analysts and the Price Level," *The Accounting Review* (October, 1955), pp. 575–81; Baker, M., *Financial Reporting for Security and Investment Decisions* (New York: National Association of Accountants, 1970).

[26] Miller, Elwood, L., "What's Wrong with Price-Level Accounting?," op. cit., p. 114.

[27] FASB Discussion Memorandum, *Reporting the Effects of General Price-Level Changes in Financial Statements*, p. 11.

REFERENCES

APB Statement No. 3, *Financial Statements Restated for General Price-Level Changes* (New York: American Institute of Certified Public Accountants, June, 1969).

Accounting Research Committee: *Accounting for Changes in the General Purchasing Power of Money* (Toronto: Canadian Institute of Chartered Accountants, July, 1975).

Accounting Research Study No. 6, *Reporting the Financial Effects of Price-Level Changes* (New York: American Institute of Certified Public Accountants, 1963).

Baker, M., *Financial Reporting for Security and Investment Decisions* (New York: National Association of Accountants, 1970).

Boersema, J.M., "The Monetary–Nonmonetary Distinction in Accounting for Inflation," *Cost and Management* (May/June, 1975), pp. 6–11.

Davidson, Sidney, Stickney, Clyde P., and Weil, Roman L., *Inflation Accounting: A Guide for the Accountant and the Financial Analyst* (New York: McGraw-Hill, 1976).

Davidson, Sidney, and Weil, Roman L., "Inflation Accounting." *Financial Analysts Journal* (January/February, 1975), pp. 27–31, 70–84.

Dyckman, T.R., *Studies in Accounting Research No. 1.* "Investment Analysis and General Price-Level Adjustments" (Evanston, Ill.: American Accounting Association, 1969).

FASB Exposure Draft, *Financial Reporting in Units of General Purchasing Power* (Stamford, Ct.: Financial Accounting Standards Board, December 31, 1974).

Heath, L.C., "Distinguishing Between Monetary and Nonmonetary Assets and Liabilities in General Price-Level Accounting," *The Accounting Review* (July, 1972), pp. 458–68.

Horngren, Charles T., "Security Analysts and the Price Level," *The Accounting Review* (October, 1955), pp. 575–81.

Johnson, G.L., "The Monetary and Nonmonetary Distinction," *The Accounting Review* (October, 1965), pp. 821–3.

Largay, James, A., III, and Livingstone, John L., *Accounting for Changing Prices* (New York: John Wiley & Sons, 1976).

Mason, Perry, *Price-Level Changes and Financial Statements — Basic Concepts and Methods* (Columbus, Oh.: American Accounting Association, 1956).

Miller, Elwood L., "What's Wrong with Price-Level Accounting?," *Harvard Business Review* (November/December, 1978), pp. 111–18.

Morris, R.C., "Evidence of the Impact of Inflation Accounting on Share Prices," *Accounting and Business Research* (Spring, 1975), pp. 87–95.

Peterson, Russel J., "A Portfolio Analysis of General Price-Level Restatement," *The Accounting Review* (July, 1975), pp. 525–32.

Rosen, L.S., *Current-Value Accounting and Price-Level Restatements* (Toronto: The Canadian Institute of Chartered Accountants, 1972).

Short, Daniel G., "The Impact of Price-Level Adjustment in the Context of Risk Assessment," *Journal of Accounting Research.* Supplement, *Studies for Changes in General and Specific Prices: Empirical Research and Public Policy Issues* (1978), pp. 259–72.

Stickney, Clyde P., "Adjustments for Changing Prices," *Handbook of Modern Accounting*, 2nd ed., (eds) Sidney Davidson and Roman L. Weil (New York: McGraw-Hill, 1977).

QUESTIONS

10.1 Define *general price-level accounting*.

10.2 Explain the differences among historical-cost accounting, current-value accounting, and general price-level accounting.

10.3 Define and present the procedures for computing a general price-level gain or loss.

10.4 What accounting treatments are suggested for a general price-level gain or loss?

10.5 Distinguish between *monetary* assets and liabilities and *nonmonetary* assets and liabilities.

10.6 Give some examples of *monetary* assets and liabilities.

10.7 Give some examples of *nonmonetary* assets and liabilities.

10.8 List and discuss the arguments in favor of and against general price-level accounting.

10.9 The president of Selectronics, Limited, is concerned about the effect of inflation on his company's financial statements and return on investment during the last ten years. He purchased Selectronics at the end of 1975, and the net profit of the company had increased each year from $34,975 in 1976 to $68,200 in 1984. On this basis, the president has established that return on shareholders' equity has increased from 7.4 percent to 12.4 percent during this period. The 1976 and 1984 financial statements for Selectronics, Limited, are given here.

Selectronics, Limited
Comparative Balance Sheet
December 31

	1984	1976
Assets		
Liabilities	$300,000	$125,000
Common Stock	350,000	350,000
Retained Earnings	200,000	125,000
Total Assets	$850,000	$600,000

Selectronics, Limited
Comparative Income Statements
for the Year Ended December 31

	1984	1976
Sales	$1,200,000	$600,000
Cost of Goods Sold		
Beginning Inventory	$ 150,000	$110,000
Purchases	985,000	470,000
	$1,135,000	$580,000
Ending Inventory	180,000	100,000
	$ 955,000	$480,000
Gross Profit	$ 245,000	$120,000
Expenses		
Selling and Administrative Expenses	$ 93,000	$ 56,025
Depreciation	15,000	9,000
	$ 108,000	$ 65,025
Profit Before Income Taxes	$ 136,200	$ 54,975
Income Taxes	68,000	20,000
Net Profit for the Year	$ 68,200	$ 34,975

Additional data

(1) All revenue and expenses, except depreciation, are earned or incurred evenly throughout each year.
(2) The beginning inventory for 1984 was acquired when the price-level index was 60.
(3) Common stock was issued when the price-level index was 70. Retained earnings amounted to $132,000 in 1976 and $247,000 in 1984, on the basis of constant dollars for December 31, 1984.
(4) Fixed assets of the company were purchased in 1968, when the price-level index was 75. Some additions were made in 1980, when the price-level index was 125. No other transactions affected fixed assets.
(5) The index of general purchasing power of the dollar was

	1984
Beginning of year	170
Average for year	180
End of year	185

Required

a. Prepare an income statement for Selectronics, Limited, for the year ended December 31, 1984, stating all dollar aggregates in terms of dollars of uniform purchasing power.
b. If the 1977 net income in constant 1984 dollars is $11,000, calculate the return on shareholders' equity on the same basis for 1976 and 1984. (Round all of your calculations to the nearest $1,000.)

10.10 The directors of Hemmings & Hemmings, Ltd., have adopted a firm policy to convert all financial-statement items into common dollars beginning on January 1, 19X4. The treasurer of the company has prepared comparative financial statements for 19X3 and 19X4, but the directors do not understand the meanings and the calculations of some items in these financial statements. The unadjusted comparative balance sheets are summarized here:

Hemmings & Hemmings, Ltd.
Comparative Balance Sheet
as of December 31

	19X3	19X4
Monetary Assets	$110,000	$125,000
Inventories	50,000	60,000
Land	70,000	70,000
Buildings and Equipment	100,000	95,000
Total	$330,000	$350,000

Liabilities	$ 60,000	$ 65,000
Capital Stock	200,000	200,000
Retained Earnings	70,000	85,000
Total	$330,000	$350,000

The 19X4 income statement follows:

Revenues		$180,000
Cost of Sales	$98,000	
Wages	25,000	
Depreciation	5,000	
Taxes	35,000	
Other	2,000	165,000
Net income		$ 15,000

On the basis of the general price-level index, the treasurer makes all of the necessary adjustments and presents the following statements to the directors:

Balance Sheet
December 31, 19X3

	Unadjusted Amount	Conversion Factor	Adjusted Amount
Monetary Assets	$110,000	125/100	$137,500
Inventories	50,000	125/100	62,500
Land	70,000	125/80	109,375
Buildings and Equipment	100,000	125/80	156,250
Total	$330,000		$465,625

Balance Sheet
December 31, 19X4

	Unadjusted Amount	Conversion Factor	Adjusted Amount
Monetary Assets	$125,000	125/125	$125,000
Inventories	60,000	125/116	64,655
Land	70,000	125/80	109,375
Buildings and Equipment	95,000	125/80	148,438
Total	$350,000		$447,468
Liabilities	$ 65,000	125/125	$ 65,000
Capital Stock	200,000	125/70	357,143
Retained Earnings	85,000		25,325
Total	$350,000		$447,468

Income Statement
For the Year Ended December 31, 19X4

	Unadjusted Amount	Conversion Factor	Adjusted Amount
Revenues	$180,000	125/110	$204,545
Cost of Goods Sold from Stock	50,000	125/100	62,500
Cost of Goods Sold from Purchases	48,000	125/114	52,632
Wages	25,000	125/110	28,410
Depreciation	5,000	125/80	7,812
Taxes	35,000	125/110	39,772
Other	2,000	125/110	2,272
	$165,000		$193,398
Net Income	$ 15,000		$ 11,147

Required

a. Briefly distinguish between monetary and nonmonetary assets and liabilities.
b. Prepare a schedule to establish the loss incurred during the year on monetary items.
c. Prepare a schedule to reconcile the adjusted retained earnings as of December 31, 19X4.   (Society of Management Accountants adapted)

10.11 Constant Purchasing Power Adjustments

Part a. Price-level adjusted financial statements are prepared in an effort to eliminate the effects of inflation or deflation. An integral part of determining restated amounts and applicable gain or loss from restatement is the segregation of all assets and liabilities into monetary and nonmonetary classifications. One reason for this classification is that price-level gains and losses for monetary items are currently matched against earnings.

Required

What are the factors that determine whether an asset or liability is classified as monetary or nonmonetary? Include in your response the justification for recognizing gains and losses from monetary items and not for nonmonetary items.

Part b. Proponents of price-level restatement of financial statements state that a basic weakness of financial statements not adjusted for price-level changes is that they are made up of "mixed dollars."

Required

1 What is meant by the term mixed dollars and why is this a weakness of unadjusted financial statements?

2 Explain how financial statements restated for price-level changes eliminate this weakness. Use property, plant, and equipment as your example in this discussion.   (*AICPA adapted*)

10.12 Constant Purchasing Power Adjustments

Barden Corp., a manufacturer with large investments in plant and equipment, began operations in 1938. The company's history has been one of expansion in sales, production, and physical facilities. Recently, some concern has been expressed that the conventional financial statements do not provide sufficient information for decisions by investors. After consideration of proposals for various types of supplementary financial statements to be included in the 1992 annual report, management has decided to present a balance sheet as of December 31, 1992, and a statement of income and retained earnings for 1992, both restated for changes in the general price level.

Required

1 On what basis can it be contended that Barden's conventional statements should be restated for changes in the general price level?

2 Distinguish between historical cost/constant purchasing power financial statements and current value financial statements.

3 Distinguish between monetary and nonmonetary assets and liabilities, as the terms are used in general price-level accounting. Give examples of each.

4 Outline the procedures the Barden Corp. should follow in preparing the proposed supplementary statements.

5 Indicate the major similarities and differences between the proposed supplementary statements and the corresponding conventional statements.

6 Assuming that in the future Barden will want to present comparative supplementary statements, can the 1992 supplementary statements be presented in 1993 without adjustment? Explain.   (*AICPA adapted*)

10.13 Constant Purchasing Power Adjustment

Published financial statements of United States companies are currently prepared on a stable dollar assumption, even though the general purchasing power of the dollar has declined because of inflation in recent years. To account for this changing value of the dollar, many accountants suggest that financial statements should be adjusted for general price-level changes. Three independent, unrelated statements regarding constant purchasing power financial statements follow. Each statement contains some fallacious reasoning.

Statement I

The accounting profession has not seriously considered constant purchasing power financial statements before, because the rate of inflation usually has been so small from year to year that the adjustments would have been immaterial in amount. Constant purchasing power financial statements represent a departure from the historical cost basis of accounting. Financial statements should be prepared from facts, not estimates.

Statement II

If financial statements were adjusted for general price-level changes, depreciation charges in the earnings statement would permit the recovery of dollars of current purchasing power and, thereby, equal the cost of new assets to replace the old ones. General price-level adjusted data would yield statement-of-financial-position amounts closely approximating current values. Furthermore, management can make better decisions if constant purchasing power financial statements are published.

Statement III

When adjusting financial data for general price-level changes, a distinction must be made between monetary and nonmonetary assets and liabilities, which, under the historical cost basis of accounting, have been identified as "current" and "noncurrent." When using the historical cost basis of accounting, no purchasing power gain or loss is recognized in the accounting process, but when financial statements are adjusted for general price-level changes, a purchasing-power gain or loss will be recognized on monetary and nonmonetary items.

Required

Evaluate each of the independent statements and identify the areas of fallacious reasoning in each and explain why the reasoning is incorrect. Complete your discussion of each statement before proceeding to the next statement.

(AICPA adapted)

CHAPTER 11

ALTERNATIVE ASSET-VALUATION AND INCOME-DETERMINATION MODELS

In Chapters 9 and 10, we established that income may be recognized only after "capital" has been kept intact. Consequently, income measurement depends on the particular concept of capital maintenance that is chosen. The various concepts of capital mainten- ance imply different ways of evaluating and measuring the elements of financial statements. Thus, both income determination and capital maintenance are defined in terms of the *asset-valuation base* used. A given asset-valuation base determines a particular concept of capital maintenance and a particular income concept. An asset-valuation base is a method of measuring the elements of financial statements, based on the selection of both an attribute of the elements to be measured and the unit of measure to be used in measuring that attribute. As we discussed in Chapters 9 and 10 four attributes may be measured and two units of measure may be used. The four attributes of all classes of assets and liabilities that may be measured are: (1) historical cost, (2) current entry price (for example, replacement cost), (3) current exit price (for example, net realizable value), and (4) capitalized or present value of expected cash flows. The two units of measure that may be used are units of *money* and units of *purchasing power*. Combining the four attributes and the two units of measure yields the following eight alternative asset- valuation and income-determination models:

1 *Historical-cost accounting* measures historical cost in units of money.
2 *Replacement-cost accounting* measures replacement cost (that is, current and entry price) in units of money.

3 *Net-realizable-value accounting* measures net realizable value (that is, current exit price) in units of money.
4 *Present-value accounting* measures present value in units of money.
5 *General price-level accounting* measures historical cost in units of purchasing power.
6 *General price-level replacement-cost accounting* measures replacement cost in units of purchasing power.
7 *General price-level net-realizable-value accounting* measures net realizable value in units of purchasing power.
8 *General price-level present-value accounting* measures present value in units of purchasing power.

Each of these alternatives yields a different financial statement that imparts a different meaning and relevance to its users. In this chapter, we will evaluate these alternatives using a simplified example to enhance conceptual clarity and comparability among the approaches. The nature of the differences and the basis of comparison among the results of the various alternatives will also be highlighted.

11.1   THE NATURE OF THE DIFFERENCES

The differences among the alternative asset-valuation and income-determination models arise from the different attributes to be measured and the units of measure to be used. We will examine each characteristic of the elements of the financial statements in the following sections.

11.1.1   Attributes to Be Measured

The attributes of assets and liabilities refer to what is being measured. First we will define the four attributes to be measured:

1 *Historical cost* refers to the amount of cash or cash-equivalent paid to acquire an asset, or the amount of cash-equivalent liability.
2 *Replacement cost* refers to the amount of cash or cash-equivalent that would be paid to acquire an equivalent or the same asset currently, or that would be received to incur the same liability currently.
3 *Net realizable value* refers to the amount of cash or cash-equivalent that would be obtained by selling the asset currently, or that would be paid to redeem the liability currently.
4 *Present* or *capitalized value* refers to the present value of net cash flows expected to be received from the use of the asset, or the net outflows expected to be disbursed to redeem the liability.

We may classify these attributes in three ways:

1 These measures may be classified with respect to whether they focus on the past, present, or future. Historical-cost focuses on the past, replacement cost and net realizable value focus on the present, and present value focuses on the future.

2 These measures may be classified with respect to the kind of transactions from which they are derived. Historical cost and replacement cost concern the acquisition of assets, or the incurrence of liabilities; net realizable value and present value concern the disposition of assets, or the redemption of liabilities.
3 The third classification is with respect to the nature of the event that originates the measure. Historical cost is based on an actual event, present value is based on an expected event, and replacement cost and net realizable value are based on hypothetical events.

One question that we will examine in this chapter is: What attribute or attributes of the elements of financial statements should be measured in financial accounting or reporting?

11.1.2   Units of Measure

Financial accounting measurements can be made in one of two units of measure: (1) units of money, or (2) units of general purchasing power. Similarly, each of the four attributes we have defined is measurable in either units of money or units of general purchasing power. In the United States and in most other countries, conventional financial statements are expressed in units of money. Given the continuous decline of the purchasing power of the dollar, however, another unit of measure — the unit of purchasing power — is frequently presented as a preferable alternative, because it recognizes changes in the general price level.

Do not confuse the general price level with either the specific price level or the relative price level. A change in the general price level refers to changes in the prices of *all* goods and services throughout the economy; the reciprocal of such changes would be a change in the general purchasing power of the monetary unit. A change in the specific price level refers to a change in the price of a particular product or service. Current-value accounting differs from historical-cost accounting in that the former recognizes changes in the specific price level on the basis of either replacement cost or net realizable value.

Finally, a change in the relative price level of a commodity refers to the part of the specific price change that remains after the effects of the general price-level change have been eliminated. Thus, if all prices increase by 32 percent and the price of a specific good increases by 10 percent, the relative price change is only 20 percent, or $(132/110) - 1$.

All three types of price changes may be incorporated in the asset-valuation and income-determination models. Note that both historical cost and current value are expressed in units of money and that general price-level restatements may be made for both.

Another question that we will examine in this chapter is: What unit of measure should be used to measure any particular attribute of the elements of financial statements?

11.2   BASIS FOR COMPARISON AND EVALUATION

We have established that the alternative accounting models (historical-cost accounting, general price-level accounting, replacement-cost accounting, general price-level-adjusted replacement-cost accounting, net-realizable-value accounting, present-value accounting, and general price-level-adjusted present-value accounting) are based on a choice of one of four available attributes (historical cost, replacement cost, net realizable value, and present value) and one of two available units of measure (units of money and units of general purchasing power). Now, we will compare the models on the basis of whether they *avoid timing errors* and *avoid measuring-unit errors*, and we will evaluate them in terms of interpretability[1] and relevance.

Although theoretically considered the best accounting models, the present-value models will not be included in our comparison and evaluation due to their recognized practical deficiences. First, present-value models require the estimation of future net cash receipts and the timing of those receipts, as well as the selection of the appropriate discount rates. Second, when applied to the valuation of individual assets, these models require the arbitrary allocation of estimated future net cash receipts and the timing of those receipts, as well as the selection of the appropriate discount rates. Third, when applied to the valuation of individual assets, present-value models require the arbitrary allocation of estimated future net cash receipts among the individual assets.[2] Due to this lack of objectivity, present-value models have been largely rejected as impractical. In this chapter, we will compare and evaluate the remaining accounting models. The criteria for comparison and evaluation will be examined next.

11.2.1   Timing Errors

The criteria for determining what attribute or attributes of the elements of financial statements should be measured in financial accounting and reporting should favor the attribute that avoids *timing errors*. Timing errors result when changes in value occur in a given period but are accounted for and reported in another period. A preferable attribute would be the recognition of changes in value in the same period that the changes occur. Ideally, "profit is attributable to the whole process of business activity."[3]

11.2.2   Measuring-Unit Errors

The criteria for determining what unit of measure should be applied to attributes of the elements of financial statements should favor the unit of measure that avoids *measuring-unit errors*. Measuring-unit errors occur when financial statements are not expressed in units of general purchasing power. A preferred measuring unit would recognize the general price-level changes in the financial statements.

11.2.3   Interpretability

Our first criterion for evaluation is the *interpretability* of the accounting model. In other words, the resulting statements should be understandable in terms of both meaning and use. According to Sterling

When an attribute involves an arithmetical calculation, the "empirical interpretation" of that attribute requires that it be placed in an "if . . . then . . . " statement.[4]

Thus, for an accounting model to be interpretable, it must be placed in an "if ... then ..." statement to convey to the user an understanding of its meaning as well as to demonstrate one of its uses. Given that we have two possible units of measure, the interpretation of the accounting models, by definition, will be one of the following:

1 If the accounting model measures any of the attributes in units of money, its results are expressed in the *number of dollars* (NOD) or, as Chambers refers to it, the *number of odd dollars* (NOOD).[5]
2 If the accounting model measures historical cost in units of general purchasing power, its results still are expressed in NOD.
3 If the accounting model measures current values in units of general purchasing power, its results are expressed in the *command of goods* (COG) or, as Chambers refers to it, the *command of goods in general* (COGG).[6]

11.2.4 Relevance

The second criterion for evaluation is the *relevance* of the accounting model. In other words, the resulting financial statements should be useful. Sterling defines relevance as follows:

> If a decision model specifies an attribute as an input or as a calculation, then that attribute is relevant to that decision model.[7]

Because decision models are not available or are not well specified, relevance focuses on what ought to be measured. For our purposes, the problem is to decide whether NOD or COG constitutes the relevant measure. From a normative point of view, the answer is straightforward. Because COG expresses changes in both the specific and general price levels, it should be considered the most relevant attribute. COG expresses the goods that could be commanded in either the input or the output market. Thus, COG can be defined, in terms of the input market, as price-level-adjusted replacement-cost or, in terms of the output market, as a price-level-adjusted net realizable value.

11.3 ILLUSTRATION OF THE DIFFERENT ACCOUNTING MODELS

To illustrate the different accounting models, we will consider the simplified case of the DeCooning Company, which was formed January 1, 19X6, to distribute a new product called "Omega." Capital is composed of $3,000 equity and $3,000 liabilities that carry a 10-percent interest. On January 1, the DeCooning Company began operations by purchasing 600 units of Omega at $10 per unit. On May 1, the company sold 500 units at $15 per unit. Changes in the general and specific price levels for the year 19X6 are

	January 1	May 1	December 31
Replacement cost	$ 10	$ 12	$ 13
Net realizable value	—	15	17
General price-level index	100	130	156

A brief description of each accounting model follows, accompanied by illustrations using the given data.

11.3.1 Alternative Accounting Models Expressed in Units of Money

To illustrate and isolate only the timing difference, first we will present the alternative accounting models that do *not* reflect changes in the general price level. These models are (1) historical-cost accounting, (2) replacement-cost accounting, and (3) net-realizable-value accounting. The income statements and the balance sheets for 19X6, under the three accounting models are shown in Exhibits 11.1 and 11.2, respectively.

Historical-Cost Accounting

Historical-cost accounting, or *conventional accounting,* is characterized primarily by (1) the use of historical cost as the attribute of the elements of financial statements, (2) the assumption of a stable monetary unit, (3) the matching principle, and (4) the realization principle.

EXHIBIT 11.1
DeCooning Company
Income Statements for the Year Ended December 31, 19X6

	Historical Cost	Replacement Cost	Net Realizable Value
Revenues	$7,500[a]	$7,500	$9,200[b]
Cost of Goods Sold	5,000[c]	6,000[d]	7,300[e]
Gross Margin	$2,500	$1,500	$1,900
Interest (10%)	300	300	300
Operating Income	$2,200	$1,200	$1,600
Realized Holding Gains and Losses	(included above)	1,000[f]	1,000
Unrealized Holding Gains and Losses	(not applicable)	300[g]	300
General Price-Level Gains and Losses	(not applicable)	(not applicable)	(not applicable)
Net Income	$2,000	$2,500	$2,900

[a] 500 × $15 = $7,500
[b] 7,500 + ($17 × 100) = $9,200
[c] 500 × $10 = $5,000
[d] 500 × $12 = $6,000
[e] 6,000 + ($13 × 100) = $7,300
[f] 500($12 − $10) = $1,000
[g] 100($13 − $10) = $300

EXHIBIT 11.2
DeCooning Company
Balance Sheet for the Year Ended December 31, 19X6

	Historical Cost	Replacement Cost	Net Realizable Value
Assets			
Cash	$7,200	$7,200	$7,200
Inventory	1,000	1,300[a]	1,700[b]
Total Assets	$8,200	$8,500	$8,900
Equities			
Bonds (10%)	$3,000	$3,000	$3,000
Capital	3,000	3,000	3,000
Retained Earnings			
Realized	2,200	2,200[c]	2,200[c]
Unrealized	(not applicable)	300	700[d]
Total Equities	$8,200	$8,500	$8,900

[a] 100 × $13 = $1,300
[b] 100 × $17 = $1,700
[c] May be divided into Current Operating Profit ($1,200) and Realized Holding Gains and Losses ($1000)
[d] Unrealized Operating Gain $400 ($1,700 − $1,300) + Unrealized Holding Gain $300

Accordingly, *historical-cost income,* or *accounting income,* is the difference between realized revenues and their corresponding historical costs. As shown in Exhibit 11.1, accounting income is equal to $2,200. What does this figure represent to the DeCooning Company? Generally, it is perceived as a basis for the computation of taxes and dividends and for the evaluation of performance. Its possible use in various decision models results from the unconditional and long-standing acceptance of this version of income by the accounting profession and the business world. This attachment to accounting income may be explained primarily by the fact that it is objective, verifiable, practical, and easy to understand. Accountants and business people may prefer accounting income over other measures of income due to its practical advantages and the concern that confusion could result from the adoption of another accounting model.

Despite these practical advantages, both timing and measuring-unit errors are reflected in DeCooning's accounting income figure of $2,200. First, the accounting income contains timing errors because this single figure (1) includes operating income and holding gains and losses that are recognized in the current period and that occurred in previous periods, and (2) omits the operating profit and holding gains and losses that occurred in the current period but that are recognizable in future periods. Second, the accounting income contains measuring-unit errors because (1) it does not take into account changes in the general price level that would have resulted in amounts expressed in units of general purchasing power, and (2) it does not take into account changes in the specific price level, because it relies on historical cost (rather than replacement cost of net realizable value) as the attribute of the elements of financial statements.

Then how should we evaluate historical-cost financial statements? First, they are *interpretable*. Historical-cost financial statements are based on the concept of money maintenance, and the attribute being expressed is the *number of dollars* (NOD). The balance sheet reports the stocks in NOD as of December 31, 19X6, and the income statement reports the change in NOD during the year.

Second, historical-cost financial statements are *not relevant* because the *command of goods* (COG) is not measured. A measure of COG reflects changes in both the specific price level and the general price level, and, as such, represents the ability to buy the amount of goods necessary for capital maintenance.

In summary, historical-cost financial statements (1) contain timing errors, (2) contain measuring-unit errors, (3) are interpretable, and (4) are not relevant.

Replacement-Cost Accounting

Replacement-cost accounting, as a particular case of current-entry-price based accounting, is characterized primarily by (1) the use of replacement cost as the attribute of the elements of financial statements, (2) the assumption of a stable monetary unit, (3) the realization principle, (4) the dichotomization of operating income and holding gains and losses, and (5) the dichotomization of realized and unrealized holding gains and losses.

Accordingly, *replacement-cost net income* is equal to the sum of replacement-cost operating income and holding gains and losses. *Replacement-cost operating income* is equal to the difference between realized revenues and their corresponding replacement costs. From Exhibit 11.1, the DeCooning Company's replacement-cost income of $2,500 is composed of (1) replacement-cost operating income of $1,200, (2) realized holding gains and losses of $1,000, and (3) unrealized holding gains and losses of $300.

What do these figures represent for DeCooning? The replacement-cost operating income of $1,200 represents the "distributable" income, or the maximum amount of dividends that DeCooning can pay and maintain its productive capacity. The realized holding gains and losses of $1,000 are an indicator of the efficiency of holding resources up to the point of sale. The realized holding gains and losses are an indicator of the efficiency of holding resources after the point of sale and may act as a predictor of future operating and holding performances.

In addition to these practical advantages, replacement-cost net income contains timing errors only on operating profit. It does, however, contain measuring-unit errors. First the replacement-cost net income contains timing errors because (1) it omits the operating profit that occurred in the current period but that is realizable in future periods, (2) it includes the operating profit that is recognized in the current period but that occurred in previous periods, and (3) it includes holding gains and losses in the same period in which they occur. Second, the replacement-cost net income contains measuring-unit errors because (1) it does not take into account changes in the general price level that would have resulted in amounts expressed in units of general purchasing power and (2) it does take into account changes in the specific price level, because it relies on replacement-cost as the attribute of the elements of financial statements.

We may evaluate replacement-cost financial statements as follows. First, they are *interpretable*. Replacement-cost financial statements are based on the concept of productive-capacity maintenance, and the attribute being expressed is the number of dollars (NOD) in the income statement. The asset figures, however, are interpretable as measures of the command of goods (COG). The asset figures shown in Exhibit 11.2 are expressed in terms of the purchasing power of the dollar at the end of the year. They reflect changes in both the specific price level and the general price level and therefore represent the COG required for capital maintenance. Second, because COG is the relevant attribute, the replacement-cost net income is not relevant, even though the asset figures are relevant.

In summary, replacement-cost financial statements (1) contain timing errors in operating profit, (2) contain measuring-unit errors, (3) are interpretable as NOD for income-statement figures and as COG for asset figures, and (4) provide relevant measures of COG only for asset figures.

Net-Realizable-Value Accounting

Net-realizable-value accounting, as a particular case of current-exit-price based accounting, is characterized primarily by (1) the use of net realizable value as the attribute of the elements of financial statements, (2) the assumption of a stable monetary unit, (3) the abandonment of the realization principle, and (4) the dichotomization of operating income and holding gains and losses.

Accordingly, *net-realizable-value net income* is equal to the sum of net-realizable-value operating income and holding gains and losses. *Net-realizable-value operating income* is equal to the operating income on sales and the net operating income on inventory. Operating income on sales is equal to the difference between realized revenues and their corresponding replacement costs of the items sold. In Exhibit 11.1, the DeCooning Company's net-realizable-value net income of $2,900 is composed of (1) net-realizable-value operating income of $1,600, (2) realized holding gains and losses of $1,000, and (3) unrealized holding gains and losses of $300.

Note that the net-realizable-value operating income of $1,600 is composed of operating income on sales of $1,200 and operating income on inventory of $400. Thus, in Exhibit 11.2, unrealized retained earnings equal the sum of unrealized holding gains and losses of $300 and operating income on inventory of $400.

What do these figures represent for DeCooning? They are similar to the figures obtained with replacement-cost accounting, except for the operating income on inventory, which results from the abandonment of the realization principle and the recognition of revenues at the time of production and at the time of sale. Net-realizable-value net income is an indicator of the ability of the firm to liquidate and to adapt to new economic situations.

To these practical advantages, we may add that net-realizable-value net income contains no timing errors, but it does contain measuring-unit errors. First, the net-realizable-value net income does not contain any timing errors (as shown in Exhibit 11.3) because (1) it reports all operating profit and holding gains and losses in the same period in which they occur, and (2) it excludes all operating and holding gains and losses that occurred in previous periods. Second, the net-realizable-value net income contains measuring-unit errors because (1) it does not take into account changes in the general price level (if it had, it would have resulted in amounts expressed in units of general purchasing power), and (2) it does take into account changes in the specific price level, because it relies on net realizable value as the attribute of the elements of financial statements.

EXHIBIT 11.3
DeCooning Company
Timing-Error Analysis for the Year Ended December 31, 19X6

	Historical Cost		Replacement Cost		Net Realizable Value	
Total Operating and Holding Gains	Reported Income	Error	Reported Income	Error	Reported Income	Error
$2,900	$2,200	$700	$2,500	$400	$2,900	0

We may evaluate net-realizable-value financial statements as follows. First, they are *interpretable*. Net-realizable-value financial statements are based on the concept of productive-capacity maintenance. The attribute being measured is expressed in NOD on the income statement and in COG on the balance sheet. Unlike replacement-cost accounting, under net-realizable-value accounting, asset figures are expressed as measures of COG in the ouput market rather than in the input market.

Second, because COG is the relevant attribute, net-realizable-value income is *not relevant*, although the asset figures are relevant.

In summary, net-realizable-value financial statements (1) contain no timing errors, (2) contain measuring-unit errors, (3) are interpretable as NOD for net income and as COG for asset figures, and (4) provide relevant measures of COG only for asset figures.

11.3.2 Alternative Accounting Models Expressed in Units of General Purchasing Power

To illustrate both timing and measuring-unit errors in this section, we will present accounting models that reflect changes in the general price level. These models are (1) general price-level-adjusted, historical-cost accounting, (2) general price-level-adjusted, replacement-cost accounting, and (3) general price-level-adjusted, net-realizable-value accounting. Continuing with our example of the DeCooning Company, the income statement and the balance sheet for 19X6, under the three accounting models, appear in Exhibits 11.4 and 11.5, respectively. The general price-level gain or loss is shown in Exhibit 11.6.

General Price-Level-Adjusted, Historical-Cost Accounting

General price-level-adjusted, historical-cost accounting is characterized primarily by (1) the use of historical cost as the attribute of the elements of financial statements, (2) the use of general purchasing power as the unit of measure, (3) the matching principle, and (4) the realization principle.

EXHIBIT 11.4
DeCooning Company
General Price-Level Income Statements for the Year Ended December 31, 19X6

	Historical Cost	Replacement Cost	Net Realizable Value
Revenues	$9,000[a]	$9,000	$10,700[b]
Cost of Goods Sold	7,800[c]	7,200[d]	8,500[e]
Gross Margin	$1,200	$1,800	$ 2,200
Interest (10%)	300	300	300
Operating Income	$ 900	$1,500	$1,900
Real Realized Holding Gains and Losses	(included above)	(600)[f]	(600)
Real Unrealized Holding Gains and Losses	(not applicable)	(260)[g]	(260)
General Price-Level Gain or Loss	180[h]	180	180
Net Income	$1,080	$ 820	$1,220

[a] $7,500 $\times \dfrac{156}{130} = $9,000$

[b] $9,000 + ($17 \times 100$ units$) = $10,700$

[c] $5,000 $\times \dfrac{156}{100} = $7,800$

[d] $6,000 $\times \dfrac{156}{130} = $7,200$

[e] $7,200 + ($13 \times 100$ units$) = $8,500$

[f] $\left[\left($12 \times \dfrac{156}{130} \right) - \left($10 \times \dfrac{156}{100} \right) \right] \times 500 = ($600)$

[g] $\left[$13 - \left($10 \times \dfrac{156}{100} \right) \right] \times 100$ units $= ($260)$

[h] See Exhibit 11.6.

Accordingly, *general price-level-adjusted, historical-cost income* is the difference between realized revenues and their corresponding historical costs, both expressed in units of general purchasing power. In Exhibit 11.4, general price-level-adjusted, historical-cost income is equal to $1,080. Included in the $1,080 historical-cost income figure is a $180 general price-level gain, computed as shown in Exhibit 11.5. Again, what does the $1,080 figure represent to the DeCooning Company? It represents accounting income expressed in dollars that have the purchasing power of dollars at the end of 19X6. In addition to the practical advantages listed for accounting income, general price-level-adjusted, historical-cost income is expressed in units of general purchasing power. For these reasons, the use of such an accounting model may constitute a less radical change for those used to historical-cost income than any current-value accounting model.

EXHIBIT 11.5
DeCooning Company
General Price-Level Balance Sheets for the Year Ended December 31, 19X6

	Historical Cost	Replacement Cost	Net Realizable Value
Assets			
Cash	$7,200	$7,200	$7,200
Inventory	1,560[a]	1,300	1,700
Total Assets	$8,760	$8,500	$8,900
Equities			
Bonds (10%)	$3,000	$3,000	$3,000
Capital	4,680[b]	4,680	4,680
Retained Earnings			
Realized	900	900	900
Unrealized	(not applicable)	(260)	140[c]
General Price-Level			
Gain or Loss	180	180	180
Total Equities	$8,760	$8,500	$8,900

[a] $1,000 \times \dfrac{156}{100} = \$1,560$

[b] $3,000 \times \dfrac{156}{100} = \$4,680$

[c] Unrealized Operating Gain $400 ($1,700 − $1,300) + Unrealized Holding Gain $260

Despite these practical advantages, the general price-level-adjusted, historical-cost income of $1,080 contains the same timing errors that historical-cost income contains. However, general price-level-adjusted, historical-cost income contains no measuring-unit errors, because it takes into account changes in the general price level. It does not, however, take into account changes in the specific price level, because it relies on historical cost, rather than replacement cost or net realizable value, as the attribute of the elements of financial statements.

How should we evaluate the general price-level-adjusted, historical-cost financial statements presented in Exhibits 11.4 and 11.5? First, they are *interpretable*. General price-level-adjusted, historical-cost financial statements are based on the concept of purchasing-power money maintenance. The attribute being measured is NOD in some cases and COG in other cases. Hence, general price-level-adjusted, historical-cost income and all balance sheet figures, with the exception of cash (and monetary assets and liabilities), may be interpreted as NOD measures. Only the cash figures (and monetary assets and liabilities) may be interpreted as COG measures. Second, only the cash figures (and monetary assets and liabilities) are *relevant*, because they are expressed as COG measures.

In summary, general price-level-adjusted, historical-cost financial statements (1) contain timing errors, (2) contain no measuring-unit errors, (3) are interpretable, and (4) provide relevant measures of COG only for cash figures (and monetary assets and liabilities).

EXHIBIT 11.6
DeCooning Company
General Price Level Gain or Loss for the Year Ended December 31, 19X6

	Unadjusted Amount	Conversion Factor	Adjusted Amount
Net Monetary Assets on January 1, 19X5	$ 3,000	156/100	$ 4,680
Add: Monetary Receipts During 19X6			
Sales	7,500	156/130	9,000
Net Monetary Items	$10,500		$13,680
Less: Monetary Payments			
Purchases	$ 6,000	156/100	$ 9,360
Interest (10%)	300	156/156	300
Total	$ 6,300		$ 9,660
Computed Net Monetary Assets, December 31, 19X6			$ 4,020
Actual Net Monetary Assets, December 31, 19X6			4,200
General Price-Level Gain			$ 180

General Price-Level-Adjusted, Replacement-Cost Accounting

General price-level-adjusted, replacement-cost accounting is characterized primarily by (1) the use of replacement cost as the attribute of the elements of financial statements, (2) the use of general purchasing power as the unit measure, (3) the realization principle, (4) the dichotomization of operating income and real realized holding gains and losses, and (5) the dichotomization of real realized and real unrealized holding gains and losses.

Accordingly, *general price-level-adjusted, replacement-cost income* is equal to the difference between realized revenues and their corresponding replacement costs, both expressed in units of general purchasing power. Similarly, general price-level-adjusted, replacement-cost financial statements eliminate "fictitious holding gains and losses" to arrive at "real holding gains and losses." *Fictitious holding gains and losses* represent the general price-level restatement that is required to maintain the general purchasing power of non-monetary items. We can see from Exhibit 11.4 that general price-level, replacement-cost income is equal to $820. Included in the $820 income figure is a $180 general price-level gain, computed as shown in Exhibit 11.5. The $820 figure represents DeCooning's replacement-cost net income, expressed in units of general purchasing power at the end of 19X7. Such a measure of income has all of the advantages of replacement-cost accounting income and the added advantage of being expressed in units of general purchasing power. For these reasons, general price-level-adjusted, replacement-cost accounting constitutes a net improvement over replacement-cost accounting, because this accounting model not only adopts replacement cost as the attribute of the elements of financial statements but also employs a general purchasing power as the unit of measure. Despite these improvements, however, general price-level-adjusted, replacement-cost income contains the same timing errors that replacement-cost income contains. Second, general price-level-adjusted, replacement-cost income contains no measuring-unit errors, because it takes into account changes in the general price level. In addition, this measure of income takes into account changes in the specific price level, because it adopts replacement cost as the attribute of the element of financial statements.

How should we evaluate the general price-level-adjusted, replacement-cost financial statements presented in Exhibits 11.4 and 11.5? First, they are *interpretable*. General price-level-adjusted, replacement-cost financial statements are based on the concept of purchasing-power, productive-capacity maintenance. The figures on both the income statement and the balance sheet are expressed as COG measures. Second, general price-level-adjusted, replacement-cost financial statements are *relevant*, because they are expressed as COG measures. Note, however, that COG is in the *input* market, rather than the output market.

In summary, general price-level-adjusted, replacement-cost financial statements (1) contain timing errors, (2) contain no measuring-unit errors, (3) are interpretable, and (4) provide relevant measures of COG in the input market.

General Price-Level-Adjusted, Net-Realizable-Value Accounting

General price-level-adjusted, net-realizable-value accounting is characterized primarily by (1) the use of net realizable value as the attribute of the elements of financial statements, (2) the use of general purchasing power as the unit of measure, (3) the abandonment of the realization principle, (4) the dichotomization of operating income and real holding gains and losses, and (5) the dichotomization of real realized and real unrealized gains and losses.

Accordingly, general price-level-adjusted, net-realizable-value net income is equal to the sum of net-realizable-value operating income and holding gains and losses, both expressed in units of general purchasing power. The general price-level-adjusted, net-realizable-value operating income is equal to the sum of operating income arising from sale and operating income on inventory, both expressed in units of general purchasing power. From Exhibit 11.4 the general price-level-adjusted, net-realizable-value net income of $1,220 is composed of (1) general price-level-adjusted, net-realizable-value operating income of $1,900, (2) real realized holding losses of ($600), (3) real unrealized holding losses of ($200), and (4) a general price-level gain of $180.

EXHIBIT 11.7
Error-Type Analysis

Accounting Model	Timing Error		Measuring-Unit Error	Interpretation		
	Operating Profit	Holding Gains		NOD	COG	Relevance
1. Historical-cost accounting	Yes	Yes	Yes	Yes	No	No
2. Replacement-cost accounting	Yes	Eliminated	Yes	Yes (income statement)	Yes (asset figures)	Yes (asset figures)
3. Net-realizable-value accounting	Eliminated	Eliminated	Yes	Yes (income statement)	Yes (monetary assets and liabilities)	Yes (monetary assets and liabilities)
4. General price-level-adjusted historical-cost accounting	Yes	Yes	Eliminated	Yes	Yes	Yes
5. General price-level-adjusted replacement-cost accounting	Yes	Eliminated	Eliminated	Eliminated	Yes	Yes
6. General price-level-adjusted net-realizable-value accounting	Eliminated	Eliminated	Eliminated	Eliminated	Yes	Yes

Again, the general price-level-adjusted, net-realizable-value operating income of $1,900 is composed of general price-level-adjusted, net-realizable-value operating income on sales of $1,500 and general price-level-adjusted, net-realizable-value operating income on inventory of $400.

In addition to the advantages of net-realizable-value net income, general price-level-adjusted, net-realizable-value net income is expressed in units of general purchasing power. For these reasons, general price-level-adjusted, net-realizable-value accounting represents a net improvement on net-realizable-value accounting, because it not only adopts net realizable value as an attribute of the elements of financial statements but also employs general purchasing power as the unit of measure.

Thus, general price-level-adjusted, net-realizable-value income contains *no* timing errors (as explained in the discussion of net-realizable-value accounting on page 342) and *no* measuring-unit errors, because it is expressed in units of general purchasing power.

How should we evaluate the general price-level-adjusted, net-realizable-value financial statements presented in Exhibits 11.4 and 11.5? FIrst, they are *interpretable*. General price-level-adjusted, net-realizable-value financial statements are based on the concept of purchasing-power, productive-capacity maintenance. The figures on both the income statement and the balance sheet are expressed as COG measures. Second, these financial statements are *relevant*, because they are expressed as COG measures. Note, however, that COG is in the *output market*, rather than the input market.

In summary, general price-level-adjusted, net-realizable-value financial statements (1) contain no timing errors, (2) contain no measuring-unit errors, (3) are interpretable, and (4) provide relevant measures of COG in the output market.

Such statements, therefore, meet all of the criteria established for the comparison and evaluation of the alternative accounting models, as shown in Exhibit 11.7.

11.4 TOWARD A SOLUTION TO THE PROBLEM OF FINANCIAL REPORTING AND CHANGING PRICES

11.4.1 Early Attempts

Long recognized as a problem in the accounting literature, the issue of accounting for changing prices has been extensively studied by the various accounting standard-setting bodies. The AICPA Committee on Accounting Procedures in 1947, 1948, and 1953[8] and APB Opinion No. 6 entitled *Status of Accounting Research Bulletins*, all examined the problems related to changes in the general price level without success. These attempts were followed by the AICPA's publication of Accounting Research Study No. 6, *Reporting the Financial Effects of Price-Level Changes*, in 1963, and by APB Statement No. 3 *Financial Statements Restated for General Price-Level Changes*, in June 1969. Both documents recommended the supplemental disclosure of general price-level information without success. The Financial Accounting Standards Board approached the price-level issue at a time when inflation was a major concern in the economy. After issuing a Discussion Memorandum (*Reporting the Effects of General Price-Level Changes in Financial Statements*) on February 15, 1974, an Exposure Draft (*Financial Reporting in Units of General Purchasing Power*) on December 31, 1974, a Research Report (*Field Tests of Financial Reporting in Units of General Purchasing Power*) in May 1977, another Exposure Draft (*Financial Reporting and Changing Prices*) on December 28, 1978, and a supplemental Exposure Draft to the 1974 proposed statement on general purchasing-power adjustments (*Constant-Dollar Accounting*) on March 2, 1979, the Board issued FASB Statement No. 33, *Financial Reporting and Changing Prices*, in September 1979, calling for information on the effects of both general inflation and specific price changes.

11.4.2   Financial Reporting and Changing Prices: A Step Forward

FASB Statement No. 33 is the result of years of attempts by the diverse standard-setting bodies to develop methods of reporting the effects of inflation on earnings and assets. In its deliberations, the FASB considered a variety of accounting systems,[9] which can be grouped under the following headings:

1 Measuring of inventory and property, plant, and equipment
   a. Historical cost
   b. Current reproduction cost
   c. Current replacement cost
   d. Net realizable value
   e. Net present value of expected future cash flows (value in use)
   f. Recoverable amount
   g. Current cost
   h. Value of business (current cost of lower recoverable amount)
2 Concepts of capital maintenance
   a. Financial capital maintenance
   b. Physical capital maintenance (the maintenance of operating capacity)
3 Measuring units
   a. Measurements in nominal dollars
   b. Measurements in constant dollars

This list suggests that the FASB examined all of the alternative asset-valuation and income-determination models presented in this chapter. The Board concluded, however, that supplementary information should be presented according to historical-cost/constant-dollar accounting and current-cost accounting. More specifically, the FASB now requires major companies to disclose the effects of both general inflation and specific price changes as supplementary information in their published annual reports. Major companies are defined as companies with assets or more than $1 billion (after deducting accumulated depreciation) or with inventory and property, plant, and equipment (before deducting accumulated depreciation) or more than $125 million.

Specifically, FASB Statement No. 33 requires major firms to report:

1 *Constant-dollar disclosures (current year)*
   a. Information on income from continuing operations for the current fiscal year, on a historical-cost/constant-dollar basis.
   b. The general purchasing-power gain or loss on net monetary items for the current fiscal year. The general purchasing-power gain or loss on net monetary items shall *not* be included in income from continuing operations.

2 *Current-cost disclosures (current-year)*
An enterprise is required to disclose:
  a. Information on income from continuing operations for the current fiscal year, on a current-cost basis.
  b. The current-cost amounts of inventory and property, plant, and equipment at the end of the current fiscal year.
  c. Increases or decreases for the current fiscal year in the current-cost amounts of inventory and property, plant, and equipment, net of inflation. The increases or decreases in current-cost amounts shall *not* be included in income from continuing operations.

3 *Five-year summary data*
  a. Net sales and other operating revenues.
  b. Historical-cost/constant-dollar information:
    (1) Income from continuing operations.
    (2) Income per common share from continuing operations.
    (3) Net assets at fiscal year-end.
  c. Current-cost information (except for individual years in which the information was excluded from the current-year disclosures):
    (1) Income from continuing operations.
    (2) Income per common share from continuing operations.
    (3) Net assets at fiscal year-end.
    (4) Increases or decreases for the current fiscal year in the current-cost amounts of inventory and property, plant, and equipment net of inflation.
  d. Other information:
    (1) General purchasing-power gain or loss on net monetary items.
    (2) Cash dividends declared per common share.
    (3) Market price per common share at fiscal year-end.

4 *Limitation*
Whenever the recoverable amount of an asset is less than either the constant-dollar value or the current-cost value, the recoverable amount should be used to value the asset. "Recoverable amount" means the current value of the net cash flow expected to be realized from the use or sale of the asset.

5 *Methodology*
  a. The constant-dollar method should use the Consumer Price Index for All Urban Consumers.
  b. The current-cost method may use internally or externally developed specific-price indices or evidence such as vendor invoice prices or price lists to determine the current cost of an asset. The method selected should be based on availability and cost, and should be applied consistently.
  c. The constant-dollar amounts should be based on average-for-the-year indices.
  d. The current costs should be based on average current costs of the period for the restatement of items required to compute operating income (cost of goods sold, depreciation, and depletion), and should be restated at end-of-period current costs, net of general inflation, for the measurement of increases or decreases in inventory, plant, property, and equipment. The latter statement requires the use of year-end current costs restated in average-for-the-period constant dollars.[10]

FASB Statement No. 33 also provides the following information to explain the minimum disclosure requirements for constant-dollar and current-cost data:

1 *Income from continuing operations* is income after applicable income taxes, excluding the results of discontinued operations, extraordinary items, and the cumulative effects of accounting changes. If none of the foregoing is present for a business enterprise, income from continuing operations is identical to *net income*.

2 The general purchasing-power gain or loss on net monetary items and the increase or decrease in current-cost amounts are excluded from income from continuing operations.

3 Current-cost information need not be disclosed if it is not materially different from constant-dollar information. The reasons for the omission of current-cost information must be disclosed in notes to the supplemental information.

4 Information relating to income from continuing operations may be presented either in the format of a conventional income statement or in a reconcilation format that discloses adjustments to income from continuing operations in the historical-cost/nominal-dollar income statement.

5 The *average* Consumer Price Index for All Urban Consumers (CPI-U) is used by business enterprises that present only the minimum constant-dollar data for a fiscal year. If an enterprise presents comprehensive financial statements on a constant-dollar basis, either the *average* or the *year-end* CPI-U may be used.

6 An enterprise that presents only the minimum data required by FASB Statement No. 33 need not restate any financial statement amounts other than inventories, plant assets, cost of goods sold, and depreciation, depletion, and amortization expense.

7 If the historical-cost/constant-dollar amounts or the current-cost amounts of inventories and plant assets exceed the recoverable amounts of those assets, all data required by FASB Statement No. 33 must be presented on the basis of the lower recoverable amounts. The recoverable amount of an asset *expected to be sold* is the net realizable value of the asset (expected sales proceeds *less* costs of completion and disposal). The recoverable amount of an asset *in continuing use* is its value in use (net present value of future cash inflows, including ultimate proceeds on disposal). Thus, *value in use* is synonymous with *direct valuation*.

8 The current costs of inventories, plant assets, cost of goods sold, and depreciation, depletion, and amortization expense may be determined by one of the following methods:
   a. Indexation by use of either externally or internally developed specific-price indices.
   b. Direct pricing by use of current invoice prices; vendor price lists, quotations, or estimates; or standard manufacturing costs that reflect current costs.[11]

Exhibits 11.8, 11.9 and 11.10 illustrate these FASB requirements. Thus, FASB Statement No. 33 requires two supplemental income computations — one dealing with the effects of general inflation, and the other dealing with specific price changes. Both types of information are intended to help users make decisions about investment, lending, and other matters in the following specific ways:

1 *Assessment of future cash flows:* Present financial statements include measurements of expenses and assets at historical prices. When prices are changing, measurements

that reflect current prices are likely to provide useful information for the assessment of future cash flows.

2 *Assessment of enterprise performance*: The worth of an enterprise can be increased as a result of the prudent timing of asset purchases when prices are changing. That increase is one aspect of performance, even though it may be distinguished from operating performance. Measurements that reflect current prices can provide a basis for assessing the extent to which past decisions about the acquisition of assets have created opportunities for earning cash flows.

EXHIBIT 11.8
Statement of Income from Continuing Operations
Adjusted for Changing Prices for the Year Ended December 31, 19X6
(in thousands of average 19X5 dollars)

	As Reported in the Primary Statements	Adjusted for General Inflation	Adjusted for Changes in Specific Prices (current costs)
Net sales and other operating revenues	$500,000	$500,000	$500,000
Cost of goods sold	$400,000	$450,000	$455,000
Depreciation and amortization expense	20,000	25,000	26,000
Other operating expenses	40,000	40,000	40,000
Interest expense	15,000	15,000	15,000
Provision for income taxes	20,000	20,000	20,000
Total Expenses	$495,000	$550,000	$556,000
Income (loss) from continuing operations	$ 5,000	$(50,000)	$(56,000)
Gain from decline in general purchasing power of net amounts owned		$ 5,000	$ 5,000
Increase in specific prices (current costs) of inventories and property, plant, and equipment held during the year[a]			$ 30,000
Effect of increase in general price level			20,000
Excess of increase in specific prices over increase in general price level			$ 10,000

[a] As of December 31, 19X5, current cost of inventory is $55,000 and current cost of property, plant, and equipment, net of accumulated depreciation, is $80,000

EXHIBIT 11.9

Five-Year Comparison of Selected Supplemental Financial Data Adjusted for Changing Prices
(in thousands of average 19X5 dollars)

	Year Ended December 31				
	19X1	19X2	19X3	19X4	19X5
Net sales and other operating revenues	$350,000	$400,000	$420,000	$450,000	$500,000
Historical-cost information adjusted for general inflation					
Income (loss) from continuing operations				(29,000)	(20,000)
Income (loss) from continuing operations per common share				(2.0)	(2.0)
Net assets at year-end				100,000	120,000
Current-cost information					
Income (loss) from continuing operations				(10,000)	(26,000)
Income (loss) from continuing operations per common share				(1.00)	(2.6)
Net assets at year-end				120,000	130,000
Excess of increase in specific prices over increase in general price-level				5,000	10,000
Gain from decline in general purchasing power of net amounts owed				4,500	5,000
Cash dividends declared per common share	2.00	2.05	2.10	2.15	2.20
Market price per common share at year-end	40	30	45	40	39
Average consumer price	170.5	181.5	195.4	205.0	220.9

EXHIBIT 11.10
Statement of Income from Continuing Operations
Adjusted for Changing Prices for the Year Ended December 31, 19X6
(in thousands of average 19X5 dollars)

Income from continuing operations, as reported on the income statement		$ 5,000
Adjustments to restate costs for the effect of general inflation		
Cost of goods sold	$(50,000)	
Depreciation and amortization expense	(5,000)	(55,000)
Loss from continuing operations adjusted for general inflation		$(50,000)
Adjustments to reflect the difference between general inflation and changes in specific prices (current costs)		
Cost of goods sold	$ (5,000)	
	(1,000)	(6,000)
Loss from continuing operations adjusted for changes in specific prices		$(56,000)
Gain from decline in general purchasing power of net amounts owed		$ 5,000
Increase in specific prices (current costs) of inventories and property, plant, and equipment held during the year[a]		$ 30,000
Effect of increase in general price level		20,000
Excess of increase in specific prices over increase in general price level		$ 10,000

[a] As of December 31, 19X5, current cost of inventory is $55,000 and current cost of property, plant, and equipment, net of accumulated depreciation, is $80,000.

3 *Assessment of the erosion of operating capability:* An enterprise typically must hold minimum quantities of inventory, property, plant, equipment, and other assets to maintain its ability to provide goods and services. When the prices of those assets are increasing, larger amounts of money must be invested to maintain the previous levels of output. Information on the current prices of resources that are used to generate revenues can help users assess the extent to which and the manner in which operating capability has been maintained.

4 *Assessment of the erosion of general purchasing power:* When general price levels are increasing, larger amounts of money are required to maintain a fixed amount of purchasing power. Investors typically are concerned with assessing whether or not an enterprise has maintained the purchasing power of its capital. Financial information that reflects changes in general purchasing power can help investors make that assessment.[12]

Obviously, because it requires the presentation of both general price-level and specific price-level information, FASB Statement No. 33 is a step forward. It falls short, however, of a total solution, which would require the use of general price-level-restated, current-cost accounting in conjunction with general price-level-restated, replacement-cost accounting or with general price-level-restated, net-realizable-value accounting. Moreover, some of the specific requirements discussed in FASB Statement No. 33 do not pertain to most situations.[13]

11.5   CONCLUSIONS

Given the existence of four measurable attributes of the elements of financial statements and two units of measure in which to express these attributes, eight alternative asset-valuation and income-determination models exist:

1 Historical-cost accounting
2 Replacement-cost accounting
3 Net-realizable-value accounting
4 Present-value accounting
5 General price-level-adjusted, historical-cost accounting
6 General price-level-adjusted, replacement-cost accounting
7 General price-level-adjusted, net-realizable-value accounting
8 General price-level-adjusted, present-value accounting

In this chapter, we have compared and evaluated six of these models on the basis of four criteria: (1) the avoidance of timing errors, (2) the avoidance of measuring-unit errors, (3) their interpretability, and (4) their relevance as measures of command of goods (COG).

Although the present-value models are conceptually preferable, they were not included in our comparison and evaluation because their subjectivity and the uncertainty surrounding their use make their implementation currently impractical.

Our comparison of the remaining models revealed that general price-level-adjusted, net-realizable-value accounting is the only model to meet each of the four criteria set forth in the chapter and therefore most closely represents a preferred-income position. FASB Statement No. 33, *Financial Reporting and Changing Prices*, falls short of adopting this solution and, instead, requires the disclosure of supplemental information on the effects of both inflation and specific-price changes.

NOTES

[1] Sterling, Robert R., "Relevant Financial Reporting in an Age of Price Changes," *Journal of Accountancy* (February, 1975), pp. 42–51; Basu, S., and Hanna, J.R., *Inflation Accounting: Alternatives, Implementation Issues, and Some Empirical Evidence* (Hamilton, Ontario: The Society of Management Accountants of Canada, 1977).

[2] Thomas, A.L., *The Allocation Problem in Accounting* (Sarasota, Fl.: American Accounting Association, 1969).

[3] Sprouse, R.T., and Moonitz, Maurice, *A Tentative Set of Broad Accounting Principles for Business Enterprises*, Accounting Research Study No. 3 (New York: American Institute of Certified Public Accountants, 1962), p. 55.

[4] Sterling, Robert R., "Relevant Financial Reporting in an Age of Price Changes," op. cit., p. 44.

[5] Chambers, R.J., "NOD, COG, and PuPu: See How Inflation Teases!," *Journal of Accountancy* (September, 1975), p. 61.

[6] Ibid., p. 61.

[7] Sterling, Robert R., "Relevant Financial Reporting in an Age of Price Changes," op. cit., p. 46.

[8] AICPA Committee on Accounting Procedures, Accounting Research Bulletin No. 33, *Depreciation and High Costs* (New York: American Institute of Certified Public Accountants, December, 1944); AICPA Committee on Accounting Procedures, Accounting Research Bulletin No. 43, *Restatement and Revision of Accounting Research Bulletins*, Ch. 9, Section A (New York: American Institute of Certified Public Accountants, June, 1953).

[9] FASB Statement No. 33, *Financial Reporting and Changing Prices* (Stamford, Ct.: Financial Accounting Standards Board, September, 1979), pp. 47–48.

[10] Ibid., paragraphs 29, 30, 35, 51, and 52.

[11] Ibid., paragraphs 9, 11, 12, 14, 17, 20, and 22.

[12] Ibid., paragraphs 1–2.

[13] Several FASB pronouncements dealing with specific situations have been issued subsequent to FASB Statement No. 33. These include FASB Statement No. 39, *Financial Reporting and Changing Prices: Specialized Assets — Mining and Oil and Gas* (October, 1980); FASB Statement No. 40, *Financial Reporting and Changing Prices: Specialized Assets — Timberlands and Growing Timber* (November, 1980); FASB Statement No. 41, *Financial Reporting and Changing Prices: Specialized Assets — Income-Producing Real Estate* (November, 1980); and FASB No. 46, *Financial Reporting and Changing Prices: Specialized Assets — Motion Picture Films* (March, 1981).

REFERENCES

Basu, S., and Hanna, J.R., *Inflation Accounting: Alternatives, Implementation Issues, and Some Empirical Evidence* (Hamilton, Ontario: The Society of Management Accountants of Canada, 1977).

Chambers, R.J., *Accounting, Evaluation, and Economic Behavior* (Englewood Cliffs, N.J.: Prentice-Hall, 1966).

Chambers, R.J., "NOD, COG, and PuPu: See How Inflation Teases!," *Journal of Accountancy* (September, 1975), pp. 56–62.

Edwards, E.O., and Bell, P.W., *The Theory and Measurement of Business Income* (Berkeley: University of California Press, 1961).

Gynther, R.S., "Capital Maintenance, Price Changes, and Profit Determination," *The Accounting Review* (October, 1970), pp. 712–30.

Hanna, J.R., *Accounting-Income Models: An Application and Evaluation*, Special Study No. 8 (Toronto: The Society of Management Accountants of Canada, July, 1974).

Kerr, Jean St. G., "Three Concepts of Business Income." In *An Income Approach to Accounting Theory*, (ed.) Sidney Davidson et al. (Englewood Cliffs, N.J.: Prentice-Hall, 1964), pp. 40–48.

Louderback, J.G., "Projectability as a Criterion for Income Determination Methods," *The Accounting Review* (April, 1971), pp. 298–305.

Parker, P.W., and Gibbs, P.M.D., "Accounting for Inflation: Recent Proposals and Their Effects," *Journal of the Institute of Actuaries* (December, 1974), pp. 1–10.

Revsine, L., and Weygandt, J.J., "Accounting for Inflation: The Controversy," *Journal of Accountancy* (October, 1974), pp. 72–8.

Rosen, L.S., *Current-Value Accounting and Price-Level Restatements* (Toronto: Canadian Institute of Chartered Accountants, 1972).

Rosenfield, Paul, "Accounting for Inflation: A Field Test," *Journal of Accountancy* (June, 1969), pp. 45–50.

Rosenfield, Paul, "CPP Accounting: Relevance and Interpretability," *Journal of Accountancy* (August, 1975), pp. 52–60.

Rosenfield, Paul, "The Confusion Between General Price-Level Restatement and Current-Value Accounting," *Journal of Accountancy* (October, 1972), pp. 63–8.

Sterling, Robert R., "Relevant Financial Reporting in an Age of Price Changes," *Journal of Accountancy* (February, 1975), pp. 42–51.

Sterling, Robert R., *Theory of Measurement of Enterprise Income* (Lawrence: University Press of Kansas, 1970).

Wolk, H.I., "An Illustration of Four Price-Level Approaches to Income Measurement," in *Accounting Education: Problems and Prospects*, (ed.) J. Don Edwards (Sarasota, Fl.: American Accounting Association, 1974), pp. 415–23.

Zeff, S.A., "Replacement Cost: Member of the Family, Welcome Guest, or Intruder?," *The Accounting Review* (October, 1962), pp. 611–25.

QUESTIONS

11.1 List and discuss the differences among the *attributes* of the elements of financial statements to be measured.

11.2 List and discuss the differences between the *units of measure* that may be used to measure the attributes of the elements of financial statements.

11.3 Define and explain *timing errors*.

11.4 Define and explain *measuring-unit errors*.

11.5 List and discuss the bases of evaluation of the alternative *asset-valuation* and *income-determination models*.

11.6 List the principal assumptions and characteristics of the following asset-valuation and income-determination models:
  a. Historical-cost accounting
  b. Replacement-cost accounting
  c. Net-realizable-value accounting

11.7 List the principal assumptions and characteristics of the following asset-valuation and income-determination models:
  a. General price-level-adjusted, historical-cost accounting
  b. General price-level-adjusted, replacement-cost accounting
  c. General price-level-adjusted, net-realizable accounting

11.8 What problems are associated with the implementation of the *present-value accounting models*?

11.9 Define each of the following concepts:
   a. Realized holding gains and losses
   b. Realizable or unrealized holding gains and losses
   c. Fictitious holding gains and losses
   d. General price-level gains and losses
   e. Specific price level
   f. Relative price level
   g. Number of dollars (or number of odd dollars)
   h. Command of goods
   i. Distributable income

11.10 An accountant has prepared four sets of financial statements for Wembley, Inc., on four different bases: (1) historical cost, (2) current value, (3) historical cost adjusted for general price-level fluctuations, and (4) current value adjusted for general price-level fluctuations. These four sets of statements are presented here in a comparative format. Wembley was incorporated on January 1, 19X4, and began operations on February 1, 19X4.

Additional information

(1) The general price-level index at the beginning of the year is 110.
(2) Land and building are acquired on February 15, 19X4. The general price-level index is 140 as of December 31, 19X4, and the average price-level index for 19X4 is 120. Assume that the price-level index applicable to Wembley's sales during the year is 125, because more sales are made during the last part of the year. Also assume that the average price-level index of 120 applies to merchandise remaining unsold at the end of the year.
(3) As of January 1, 19X4, monetary assets amount to $1,100,000. This amount represents the capital invested by Wembley's shareholders. There are no monetary liabilities as of January 1, 19X4.

Required

a. What is the primary advantage of each of the bases on which these sets of financial statements are prepared?
b. Analyze the following items, and explain how they are determined (include actual computations):
   (1) General price-level loss
   (2) Unrealized holding gain or loss
   (3) Realized holding gain
c. Compare and comment on the remaining items shown in the four sets of financial statements.
d. List the difficulties that an accountant might have encountered in preparing each set of financial statements, with the exception of the historical-cost financial statements.
e. Make recommendations, with supporting comments, concerning which set or sets of these financial statements should be presented to Wembley's shareholders.

EXHIBIT A

Wembley, Inc.
Cost of Goods Sold for the Year Ended December 31, 19X4

	Historical Cost	Current Value	Historical Cost Adjusted for General Price-Level Fluctuations	Current Value Adjusted for General Price-Level Fluctuations
Inventories on January 1, 19X4	—	—	—	—
Purchases (12,000 units)	$120,000	$168,000	$140,000	$168,000
	$120,000	$168,000	$140,000	$168,000
Less: Inventories on December 31, 19X4 (2,000 units)	20,000	28,000	23,334	28,000
Cost of Goods Sold	$100,000	$140,000	$116,666	$140,000

Wembley, Inc.
Balance Sheets for the Year Ended December 31, 19X4

	Historical Cost	Current Value	Historical Cost Adjusted for General Price-Level Fluctuations	Current Value Adjusted for General Price-Level Fluctuations
Assets	$ 778,000	$ 778,000	$ 778,000	$ 778,000
Cash	40,000	40,000	40,000	40,000
Accounts Receivable	20,000	28,000	23,334	28,000
Inventory	75,000	80,000	91,306	80,000
Land and Building	225,000	300,000	273,912	300,000
Less: Accumulated Depreciation	(9,000)	(12,000)	(10,956)	(12,000)
Machinery and Equipment	250,000	236,000	280,000	236,000
Less: Accumulated Depreciation	(25,000)	(23,600)	(28,000)	(23,600)
Total Assets	$1,354,000	$1,426,400	$1,447,596	$1,426,400

Liabilities				
and Shareholders' Equity				
Accounts Payable	$ 20,000	$ 20,000	$ 20,000	$ 20,000
Mortgage Payable	190,000	190,000	190,000	190,000
Share Capital	1,100,000	1,100,000	1,400,000	1,400,000
Unrealized Holding				
Gain or (Loss)	—	72,000	—	(21,196)
Retained Earnings	44,000	44,000	(162,404)	(162,404)
Total Liabilities				
and Equities	$1,354,000	$1,426,000	$1,447,596	$1,426,400

Wembley, Inc.
Income Statements for the Year Ended December 31, 19X4

	Historical Cost	Current Value	Historical Cost Adjusted for General Price-Level Fluctuations	Current Value Adjusted for General Price-Level Fluctuations
Sales	$250,000	$250,000	$280,000	$280,000
Cost of Goods Sold				
(see Exhibit A)	100,000	140,000	116,666	140,000
Gross Profit on Sales	$150,000	$110,000	$163,334	$140,000
Out-of-Pocket Expenses	$ 60,000	$ 70,000	$ 70,000	$ 70,000
Depreciation				
Building	9,000	12,000	10,956	12,000
Equipment	25,000	23,600	28,000	23,600
Interest Expense				
Paid on December 31, 19X4	12,000	12,000	12,000	12,000
Total Expenses	$106,000	$117,600	$120,956	$117,600
Operating Income or (Loss)	$ 44,000	$ (7,600)	$ 42,378	$ 22,400
General Price-Level Loss	—	—	(204,782)	(204,782)
Realized Holding Gain	—	51,600	—	19,978
Net Income or (Loss)[a]	$ 44,000	$ 44,000	$(162,404)	$(162,404)

[a] Income taxes are ignored.

11.11 Valley Limited was incorporated in 1975 to manufacture a tool for a rapidly expanding Canadian market. At that time, production of the tool, although relatively simple, was highly automated and required heavy capital investments. The capacity of the manufacturing equipment installed in 1975 did meet production demands until 1984, when an unexpected maintenance cost indicated the need for replacement.

The firm's depreciation policy had been to write off fixed assets on a straight-line basis over their expected useful lives. The estimated ten-year life of the manufacturing equipment was accurate, and any scrap value would approximately equal the removal costs.

Replacing the manufacturing equipment was discussed at a recent directors' meeting, held to review Valley's 1981 financial statements. The controller was asked to explain why, despite the fact that the equipment was fully depreciated, Valley lacked sufficient funds to purchase replacement equipment. The controller explained that over the ten-year period, the value of money had declined by one-third. It was apparent that the firm would need to solicit outside financing to replace the equipment. Discussion then centered on the adequacy of Valley's reporting system in terms of internal management decisions as well as outside reporting to shareholders and potential sources of financing.

Although no significant technological changes have been made in the replacement equipment, the supplier quoted 60 percent in excess of the cost of the existing equipment. The sales manager pointed out that he would have to increase sales $1,500,000 to produce an after-tax profit of $300,000 to cover the excess replacement cost. He asked whether or not the annual net profits reported each year were realistic. He had heard about price-level accounting and replacement-cost accounting, and he now wondered whether these methods might not be beneficial to Valley Limited.

It soon became apparent that none of the directors understood the implications of price-level and replacement-cost accounting. The controller then consulted the company's auditor and requested a report in a week's time on these accounting methods.

Required

a. Write a short description of price-level accounting and replacement-cost accounting, outlining the relationship of each method to generally accepted accounting principles.

b. Prepare a general outline of the advantages and disadvantages of each of the two methods, and describe how the two methods may be effectively combined.

c. Explain the benefits to Valley Limited of the use of a combination of price-level accounting and replacement-cost accounting. Call attention to any problems that might arise in implementing these methods.   (CICA adapted)

11.12 R.S. Gynther makes the following statements in "Capital Maintenance. Price Changes, and Profit Determination." *The Accounting Review* (October, 1970), p. 716:

Under the operating-capacity concept, profit is not recognized for each firm until its specific operating capacity has been maintained. The concept requires *all* long-term capital to be restated (for example, through a Capital Maintenance Adjustment Account), and this is done in accordance with market buying-price changes relating to individual assets held. Total Net Assets = Operating Capacity, and the price changes for individual assets have to be accounted for separately, because they change in different ways. (To the extent that individual price changes might not be available, specific price indices are used.)

a. List and explain the different kinds of operating capacity.

b. Explain the meaning of this statement.

11.13 Robert R. Sterling makes the following statement in "Relevant Financial Reporting in an Age of Price Changes," *Journal of Accountancy* (February, 1975), pp. 50–1:

We should not be arguing that one set of figures is right and another is wrong; instead, we should be arguing about which attribute we ought to measure and report. Selection of the attribute that ought to be measured requires precise criteria, rigorously applied.

Discuss the validity of this statement.

11.14 R.J. Chambers makes the following statement in "NOD, COG, and PuPu: See How Inflation Teases!," *Journal of Accountancy* (September, 1975), p. 60:

These two things — changes in specific prices and changes in the general level of prices — occur concurrently in inflation. But they do not arise from the same causes, and they are not the same in effect on any person or firm. Their effects on any firm depend on its assets and debt composition and on the sources of its income. If we are to account for what occurs in an inflationary period, therefore, we must take account of both things concurrently, period by period. If we do not account for both, we do not represent the effects of inflation.

Discuss the validity of this statement.

11.15 R.J. Chambers also makes the following statement in the article just mentioned (p. 60), with reference to what is conveniently called "PuPu" (purchasing-power units):

It is easy to see that this is what PuPu accounting entails. The financial statements it yields are expressed in dollars — not in some other kind of PuPus. The dollars are admitted to be different from time to time; there is not a PuPu that is invariant through time, even in PuPu accounting. Unquestionably, a PuPu is a dated dollar, having the general purchasing power of a dollar at the date that identifies it — in particular, on a balance sheet, the date of the balance sheet.

Discuss the validity of this statement.

11.16 Gerald Margolin has asked you to explain the effect of inflation on his business. You have taken the following transactions from his records to prepare comparative statements and to isolate some variations in price level.

The general price-level index for 19X4 indicates the following changes in the purchasing power of the dollar:

January 1, 19X4	200
July 1, 19X4	205
December 31, 19X4	210

Margolin made the following purchases:

January 1, 19X4 (1,000 items @ $3.00 per unit)
July 1, 19X4 (500 items @ $3.30 per unit)
December 31, 19X4 (500 items @ $3.50 per unit)
January 15, 19X5 (500 items @ $3.70 per unit)

The year-end inventories are valued according to the first-in, first-out (FIFO) method. Margolin's company year ends on December 31.

Required

a. Assuming that no sales were made during 19X4, determine the valuation of the year-end inventories for balance sheet presentation using the following methods:
(1) Historical cost
(2) Adjusted cost on the basis of the general price index
(3) Replacement cost
State the basis of each of your valuations, and explain why the amounts differ.

b. Assuming that the company sold 50 percent of its inventory on December 31, 19X4, at a selling price of $4.20 per unit, prepare a comparative income statement using the following methods:
(1) Historical cost
(2) Adjusted cost on the basis of the general price index
(3) Replacement cost

c. Use the comparative income statement you prepared in part (b) to explain the composition of the net-income figure under the historical-cost method. Clearly indicate the impact of the general price-level increase, timing of purchases, and profit from sales. (*Society of Management Accountants adapted*)

11.17 After the issuance of FASB Statement No. 33,"Financial Reporting and Changing Prices," in September, 1979, no changes have been made in the basic financial statements. However, information required by FASB Statement No. 33 must now be presented in supplemental statements, schedules, or notes in the financial reports.

Required

a. A number of terms are defined and used in FASB Statement No. 33.
(1) Differentiate between the terms *constant dollar* and *current cost*.
(2) Explain what is meant by *current-cost, constant-dollar accounting*. How does it differ from *historical-cost, nominal-dollar accounting*?

b. Identify the accounts for which an enterprise must measure the effects of changing prices in order to present the supplemental information required by FASB Statement No. 33.

c. FASB Statement No. 33 is based on FASB Statement of Financial Concepts No. 1, *Objectives of Financial Reporting by Business Enterprises*, which concludes that financial reporting should provide information to help investors, creditors, and other financial statement users assess the amounts, timing, and uncertainty of prospective net cash inflows to the enterprise.
(1) Explain how FASB Statement No. 33 can help to attain this objective.
(2) Identify and discuss two ways in which the information required by FASB Statement No. 33 may be useful for internal management decisions.
(*CMA adapted*)

11.18 Financial reporting for both external and internal purposes is affected by generally accepted accounting principles. One of these principles (or assumptions) has been that dollar amounts on financial statements are based on unadjusted historical costs. This assumption implies that inflation does not affect the amounts presented on the financial statements. Financial reports prepared on the basis of this assumption are therefore at variance with economic reality. This has troubled financial managers, the accounting profession, and government, and all of these parties have been seeking a solution.

Required

a. When financial reports are based on unadjusted historical costs, explain what effect inflation has on a firm's:
   (1) Statement of financial position
   (2) Statement of income
b. Given your answers in part (a), explain what erroneous conclusions you could draw about a firm's financial performance if you based your analysis on financial statements that were prepared with no consideration for the effects of inflation.
c. Discuss the steps that a firm could take to reflect the effects of inflation in its internal reports.   (CMA adapted)

11.19 FASB Statement No. 33, *Financial Reporting and Changing Prices*, is applicable only to larger businesses, and two tests of size determine which businesses must comply with this statement.

1. The first dollar-size test is that the dollar amount of the firm's inventory and of property, plant, and equipment (before deducting accumulated depreciation) be greater than:
   a. $75 million
   b. $100 million
   c. $125 million
   d. $150 million
   e. $200 million
2. The second dollar-size test is that the dollar amount of the firm's total assets (after deducting accumulated depreciation) be greater than:
   a. $1 billion
   b. $1.5 billion
   c. $2 billion
   d. $500 million
   e. $750 million
3. FASB Statement No. 33 adopts a price-level index for the conversion of historical-cost figures to constant-dollar figures. The price-level index to be used is the:
   a. Capital-Equipment Price Index
   b. Consumer Price Index for All Urban Consumers
   c. Gross National Product (GNP) Deflator
   d. Retail Price Index
   e. Wholesale Price Index
4. Which one of the following is *not* a monetary item?
   a. accounts receivable

    b. wages payable

    c. long-term notes payable

    d. common stock outstanding

    e. none of the above

5. Which one of the following is not reported on a constant-dollar basis under minimum FASB disclosures?

    a. inventory

    b. land

    c. temporary investments

    d. equipment

    e. capital leases   *(CMA adapted)*

11.20 Four Alternative Accounting Methods

Part a. Advocates of current value accounting propose several methods for determining the valuation of assets to approximate current values. Two of the methods proposed are replacement cost and present value of future cash flows.

Required

Describe each of the two previously cited methods and discuss the pros and cons of the various procedures used to arrive at the valuation for each method.

Part b. The financial statements of a business entity could be prepared by using historical cost or current value as a basis. In addition, the basis could be stated in terms of unadjusted dollars or dollars restated for changes in purchasing power. The various permutations of these two separate and distinct areas are shown in the following matrix:

	Unadjusted Dollars	Dollars Restated for Changes in Purchasing Power
Historical cost	1	2
Current value	3	4

Block number 1 of the matrix represents the traditional method of accounting for transactions in accounting today, wherein the absolute (unadjusted) amount of dollars given up or received is recorded for the asset or liability obtained (relationship between resources). Amounts recorded in the method described in block 1 reflect the original cost of the asset or liability and do not give effect to any change in value of the unit of measure (standard of comparison). This method assumes the validity of the accounting concepts of going concern and stable monetary unit. Any gain or loss (including holding and purchasing power gains or losses) resulting from the sale or satisfaction of amounts recorded under this method is deferred in its entirety until sale or satisfaction.

Required

For each of the remaining matrix blocks (2, 3, and 4) respond to the following questions. Limit your discussion to nonmonetary assets only.

1 How will this method of recording assets affect the relationship between resources and the standard of comparison?

2 What is the theoretic justification for using each method?

3 How will each method of asset valuation affect the recognition of gain or loss during the life of the asset and ultimately from the sale or abandonment of the asset? Your response should include a discussion of the timing and magnitude of the gain or loss and conceptual reasons for any difference from the gain or loss computed using the traditional method.   (*AICPA adapted*)

11.21 Constant Dollar and Current Cost

Financial reporting should provide information to help investors, creditors, and other users of financial statements. Statement of Financial Accounting Standards No. 89 encourages companies to disclose certain supplementary information.

Required

1 Describe the historical cost/constant purchasing power method of accounting. Include in your discussion how historical cost amounts are used to make historical cost/constant purchasing power measurements.

2 Describe the principal advantage of the historical cost/constant purchasing power method of accounting over the historical cost method of accounting.

3 Describe the current cost method of accounting.

4 Why would depreciation expense for a given year differ using the current cost method of accounting instead of the historical cost method of accounting? Include in your discussion whether depreciation expense is likely to be higher or lower using the current cost method of accounting instead of the historical cost method of accounting in a period of rising prices, and why.

                                                                    (*AICPA adapted*)

CHAPTER 12

THE INCOME STATEMENT

12.1 INTRODUCTION

The income statement reports the results of a firm's operations for the accounting period. Other labels used include a *statement of income, statement of earnings,* or *statement of operations.* Two concepts of income exist:

1 the capital maintenance concept;
2 the transactional approach.

According to the *capital maintenance concept,* income is earned after capital (physical or financial) is maintained. The capital maintenance concept to income was fully explored in Chapters 9–11. A more useful approach to the determination of income is the transactional approach. The *transactional approach* relies on accrual accounting where the financial impacts of transactions and events on a firm are recorded for the period in which they occur, rather than when cash is received or paid. This chapter examines the theoretical and practical issues underlying the determination and preparations of the income statement under accrual accounting.

12.2   VIEWS OF ARTICULATION AND EARNINGS

12.2.1   Articulation

As seen in Chapter 7 the relation between balance sheet, income statement, and statement of cash flows is based on a principle of articulation, in the sense that they are all part of the same measurement process.

The FASB conceptual framework views articulation as an important feature of financial statements. Consider the following statements from Statement of Financial Accounting Concepts No. 5:

> The financial statements of an entity are a fundamentally related set that articulate with each other and derive from the same underlying data . . . .[1]

> A fully articulated set of several financial statements that provide those various kinds of information about an entity's financial position and changes in its financial position is necessary to satisfy the broad purposes of financial reporting.[2]

> Financial statements interrelate (articulate) because they reflect different aspects of the same transactions or other events affecting an entity.[3]

Sterling suggests the following articulation test:

> Articulation requires that the sum of the separate effects of all events during a fiscal period equal the change in magnitude of the pertinent economic resources and obligations from the beginning to the end of the period. If the sum of the separate effects recognized does not equal the change in magnitude, it is conclusive evidence that there were additional events that occurred during the period that have not yet been recognized. The difference between the sum of the separate effects recognized and the change in magnitude is the combined effects of the additional previously unrecognized events. The difference must be recognized prior to the issuance of financial statements.[4]

Sterling again argues that articulation is a matter of the additivity of the selected attribute and provides the following example:

> The quantity of cash, for example, is additive and therefore a cash flow statement *must* articulate with a cash position statement if *both* statements are faithful representations. If the cash flow statement shows a net cash increase of X dollars while the cash position shows a difference between the beginning and ending amount that is different from X dollars, then at least one of the statements is not a faithful representation. Articulation is not a convention to be decided by the FASB but rather a factual question about the behavior of the phenomena. The cash flow statement must articulate with the cash position statement for the straight-forward reason that the phenomena articulate.[5]

Within the articulation principle, there are two alternative views of earnings:

1 the revenue-expense approach;
2 the asset-liability approach.

12.2.2   Views of Earnings

As seen in Chapter 7, the asset-liability view (also called the balance sheet or capital maintenance view) holds that revenues and expenses result from changes in assets and liabilities. Revenues are increases in assets and decreases in liabilities; expenses are decreases in assets and increases in liabilities. The focus under the asset-liability view is in the measurement and reporting of assets and liabilities. The income statement is reduced to reporting and measuring the changes in net assets.

The revenue/expense view, also called the income statement or matching view, holds that revenues and expenses result from the need for a proper matching. The view focuses primarily on the measurement of the earnings of the firm, rather than the increase or decrease in net capital. As a result the balance sheet contains not only assets and liabilities, but also deferred charges and credits that are residuals to be carried to future periods in order to ensure proper matching and avoid distortion of earnings.

12.3   REVENUES AND GAINS

12.3.1   Nature of Revenues and Gains

The literature distinguishes between two approaches to the nature of revenues:

1 an *inflow concept*;
2 an *outflow concept*.

The inflow concept of revenue defines revenue as an inflow of assets or an increase in assets arising from the operational activities of the firm. It represents an asset-liability approach. It is also consistent with the following APB and FASB definition of revenue:

> Revenue — gross increases in assets and gross decreases in liabilities measured in conformity with generally accepted accounting principles that result from those types of profit-directed activities . . . .[6]

> Revenues are the inflows or other enhancements of assets of an entity or settlements of its liabilities (or a combination of both) during a period from delivering or producing goods, rendering services, or other activities that constitute the entity's ongoing major or central operations.[7]

The outflow concept of revenue defines revenue as an outflow of goods and services, a result of selling products, rendering services, and disposing of services. It represents a revenue-expense approach. Witness the following depiction of revenue:

> Revenue results from the sale of goods and rendering of services and is measured by the charge made to customers, clients, or tenants for goods furnished to them.[8]

In both concepts, revenue does not include gains in their definitions. They are nonrecurring income to be displayed separately in the financial statements under the current operating income concept, and under the all-inclusive income concept. They have been defined as follows:

> Gains are increases in net assets from peripheral or incidental transactions of an entity and from all other transactions and other events and circumstances affecting the entity during a period except those that result from revenues or investments by owners.[9]

12.3.2 Revenue Recognition

Sprouse and Moonitz stated that:

> ... revenues should be identified with the period during which the major economic activities necessary to the creation and disposition of goods and services have been accomplished provided objective measurements of the results of those activities are available. The two conditions, i.e., accomplishments of major economic activity and objectivity of measurement, are fulfilled at different stages of activity in different cases, sometimes as late as time of delivery of product or the performance of a service, in other cases, at an earlier point in time.[10]

What the definition implies is that the accomplishment of the major economic activities can take place at different times and periods, which makes it an awkward method. One alternative to the reporting of revenue at the time of accomplishment of the major economic activities is the *critical event approach*. Under the critical event approach, the revenue from the sale of a product or service is recognized in full at a critical event date when the most critical decision is made or where the most difficult task is performed. The events or points in time for recognizing revenue are as follows:

1 during production;
2 at the completion of production;
3 at the time of sale;
4 when cash is collected;
5 until a future event occurs.

Revenue Recognition During Production

The accretion approach suggests the recognition of revenue during production. The best example is furnished by accounting for long-term contracts. Because the construction can take place for a long period and the firm needs to show income every year, the question of revenue recognition is crucial. Two approaches exist:

1 the percentage-of-completion method;
2 the completed contract method.

The *completed contract method* recognizes profit only when the contract is completed.

The *percentage-of-completion* method recognizes the profit each period during the life of the contract in proportion to the accomplishment, in terms of either *input measures* or *ouput measures*. The input measures include either: a) the *cost-to-cost method*, where the percentage of completion is measured by a comparison of the costs incurred to date with the expected contractual total costs; or b) *the efforts-expended method*, where the percentage of completion is measured by a comparison of the work performed to date, as measured by labor hours, labor dollars, machine hours or material quantities, to the expected amount on the contract. The ouput measures rely on key indicators of accomplishment of the contract that reflect the results achieved to date, such as units produced, units delivered, value added or units of works accomplished.

Revenue Recognition at Completion of Production

Revenue is recognized at the completion of production for certain agricultural and mining operations. For those operations, not only is the production process a crucial part of the firm's operations, but also a) the products have an immediate marketability at quoted prices, given the existence of a determinable selling price, and b) there is an interchangeability of units, or c) the producer is unable to determine costs. This method of revenue recognition is, however, rare.

Revenue Recognition at Time of Sale

Revenue is recognized most often at the time of sale, when legal title is transferred and the amount of revenue can be estimated with reasonable certainty. This approach is best expressed in Chapter 1 of ARB 43:

> Profit (revenue) is deemed to be realized when a sale in the ordinary course of a business is effected, unless the circumstances are such that collection of the sales price is not reasonably assumed.[11]

Revenue Recognition where Cash is Collected

The measurement of revenue subsequent to sale represents a revenue-allocation approach. It takes place when:

1 the accurate measurement of the asset received in exchange in the transaction is impossible to measure; or
2 there is a likelihood of additional material expenses related to the transaction and that cannot be estimated with a reasonable degree of accuracy; or
3 there is no reliable basis for estimating the collectibility.

Two methods are generally used for deferring revenue recognition:

1 the installment method;
2 the cost-recovery method.

Under the *installment method* revenue is recognized at the time of cash collection and a portion of gross profit is recognized in proportion to the cash received. The *cost-recovery method* is similar to the installment method, except that no gross profit is recognized until the cost of the product sold has been recovered.

Revenue Recognition Delayed Until a Future Event Occurs

When there is insignificant transfer of risk and benefits of ownership, revenue is deferred until an event occurs that corrects the situation and transfers sufficient risks and benefits to the purchasers. Generally, the "deposit" method is used to defer the recognition of revenue, until exact determination is made of the event that transfers the sufficient risks and benefits to the purchasers.

12.4   EXPENSES AND LOSSES

12.4.1   Nature of Expenses and Losses

In introducing expenses and losses, a distinction has to be made of costs as well. They are conceptually related. The term *cost* has different meanings to accountants, economists, engineers and others facing managerial problems. Consider the following definitions from the cost accounting literature:

> The term cost would seem to refer to some type of measured sacrifice evolving from an operational sequence of events and centering upon a particular activity or product.[12]

> Cost is a foregoing, measured in monetary terms, incurred or potentially to be incurred to achieve a specific objective.[13]

> The amount, measured in money, of cash expended or other property transferred, capital stock issued, services performed, or a liability incurred, in consideration of goods and services received or to be received. Costs can be classified as unexpired or expired costs. Unexpired costs (assets) are those which are applicable to the production of future revenues .... Expired costs are those which are not applicable to the production of future revenues, and for that reason are treated as deductions from current revenues, or charged against retained earnings.[14]

The following from case analyses of costs may help avoid the confusion between cost, expense, loss, and asset:

Case 1: The acquisition of resources with potential benefits results in the creation of assets or unexpired costs.

Case 2: The use of the assets in the manufacturing process results in the cost of a product that is inventoried. The eventual selling of the product transforms this product cost into an expense to be matched with sales. This is consistent with the following definitions of expense:

> Expense in the broadest sense includes all expired costs which are deductible from revenues ....[15]

> Expenses — gross decreases in assets or gross increases in liabilities recognized and measured in conformity with generally accepted accounting principles that result from those types of profit directed activities of an enterprise.[16]

Both definitions represent the traditional revenue-expense orientation.

Case 3: The use of the assets in the selling and administrative processes results in an expense to be recognized for the period. This is consistent with the following definition of expense:

> Expenses are outflows or other using up of assets or incurrences of liabilities (or a combination of both) during a period from delivering or producing goods, rendering services, or carrying out other activities that constitute the entity's major or central operations.[17]

The FASB definition represents a strong asset-liability approach.

Case 4: The decrease of the assets from peripheral or incidental transactions and events that are beyond the control of the firm result in a loss. This is consistent with the FASB definition of a loss:

> Losses are decreases in equity (net assets) from peripheral or incidental transactions of an entity and from all other transactions and other events and circumstances affecting the entity except those that result from expenses or distributions to owners.[18]

What appears from the above definitions is that cost corresponds to a sacrifice resulting from the use of assets. A basic distinction should be made between unexpired cost (asset) and expired cost (cost), as well as between cost and expense. According to the third definition, cost results from the use of assets towards the creation of revenues. "Cost" also must be distinguished from the term "expense." The AICPA Accounting Research Study No. 3 defines expense as follows:

> The decrease in net assets as a result of the use of economic services in the creation of revenues or the imposition of taxes by government units.
> Expense is measured by the amount of the decrease in assets or the increase in liabilities related to the production and delivery of goods and the rendering of services . . . . In its broadest sense expense includes all expired costs which are deductible from revenues. In income statements, distinctions are made between various types of expired costs by captions or titles including such terms as cost, expense, or loss: e.g. cost of goods or services sold, operating expenses, marketing and administrative expenses, and loss on sale of property.[19]

The four cases indicate that events occur in the following sequences:

1 acquisition creates an asset;
2 manufacturing creates a cost of a product or activity;
3 equation-matching or allocation creates an expense;
4 misuse creates a loss.

The three central accounting techniques to create an expense are matching, allocation, and expiration. Basically, there are three possible cases:[20]

1 Costs that are directly associated with the revenue of the period and are matched against revenue.

2 Costs that are associated with period in some basis other than a direct relationship with revenue and are allocated to the period.

3 Costs that cannot, as a practical matter, be associated to any period and are expired and expensed immediately.

While the third case is straightforward, the first two cases require the use of two important accounting techniques: matching and allocation.

12.4.2 Matching and Allocation

Matching is an accounting procedure that requires first a determination of revenues, and second a matching with expenses that represent the effort needed for the generation of the revenues:

> The problem of properly matching revenues and costs is primarily one of finding satisfactory bases of association — clues to relationships which unite revenue deductions and revenue .... Observable physical connections often afford a means of tracing and assigning. It should be emphasized, however, that the essential test is reasonableness, in the light of all the pertinent conditions, rather than physical measurements.[21]

The problem is corrected by a reliance on three basic principles of matching: (1) association of cause and effect, (2) systematic and rational allocation, and (3) immediate recognition.

The association of cause and effect requires that matching be made on the basis of some discernible positive correlation of costs with revenues. One expression of this principle is the *"cost attach concept."* As stated by Paton and Littleton:

> Ideally, all costs should be viewed as ultimately clinging to definite items of goods sold or services rendered. If this conception could be effectively realized in practice, the net accomplishment of the enterprise could be measured in terms of units of output rather than intervals of time .... In the more typical situation the degree of continuity of activity obtaining tends to prevent the basis of affinity which will permit convincing assignments, of all classes of costs incurred, to particular operations, departments, and — finally — items of product. Not all costs attach in a discernible manner, and this fact forces the accountant to fall back upon a time-period as the unit for associating certain expenses with certain revenues.[22]

As the statement indicates, the association of cause and effect constitutes a difficult principle, if not an impossible one.

The allocation of costs over time is another way of implementing the matching principle. It is a partitioning process to separate classifications or periods of time, so that the periods receive the correct benefits or services of the asset, and in the process bear their share of the costs of the benefits received. A systematic and rational allocation is presumed to be used so that "the allocation method used should appear reasonable to an unbiased observer and should be followed systematically."[23]

To be theoretically justified, allocations are expected to meet the following three criteria:

1 *Additivity*: the total amount is allocated, so that the sum of the allocated amounts is equal to the whole.
2 *Unambiguity*: the allocation method should result in a unique allocation, i.e., should result in only one set of parts.
3 *Deferribility*: the allocation method selected is clearly superior to other methods on the basis of convincing arguments.[24]

The three criteria are generally difficult to meet, which renders most allocations arbitrary and impossible. They are incorrigible because they can't be verified or refuted by objective, empirical means. They do not correspond to anything in the real world. As Thomas states:

> Conventional allocation assertions do not refer to real-world partitioning; when an incorrigible allocation divides an accounting total, there is no reason to believe that this reflects the division of an external total into dependent parts .... Conventional

allocation assertions do not refer to real-world economic phenomena, but only to things in asserter's and readers' minds.[25]

One solution to this dilemma is to use allocation-free financial statements such as based on cash-flow statements, exit-price systems, and certain types of replacement-cost systems. In spite of these criticisms and limitations, in practice costs continue to be allocated to serve a variety of needs, such as inventory value determination, income determination, pricing and production determination, and meeting regulatory requirements.

The immediate recognition of expenses is used for costs viewed in the current period or in previous periods that are assumed to no longer provide future benefits, or because there is a high degree of uncertainty about the existence of future benefits.

12.5   CURRENT OPERATING VERSUS ALL-INCLUSIVE INCOME

Income is generally measured for short periods of time, to provide users with useful information about the financial performance of the firm. What is to be included in the income figure has led, however, to two basic concepts of income — the *current operating concept* and *the all-inclusive concept* of income.

The *current operating concept* of income includes in the income statement only the results of decisions of the current period and arising from normal operations and reports in the retained earnings statement nonoperating items. The focus on the operating items in the current operating concept of income derives from their characteristics as recurring, regular and predictable features of the operations of the firm. The advocates of the current operating concept of income argue that the end result is more meaningful and useful for interperiod and interfirm companies and for predicting possible future income and dividend flows if items extraneous to operating decisions are excluded. There is less risk of the financial statement users being misled or confused if the irregular, nonoperating items are excluded from the income statement.

The *all-inclusive concept* of income includes all the components of comprehensive income in the income statement, i.e., all the items that affected the net increase or decrease in stockholders' equity during the period, with the exception of capital transactions. The advocates of the all-inclusive concept of income argue that the concept is viable because:

1 net income of the firm for the life of the firm should be equal to the sum of the annual report net incomes:
2 income smoothing may be checked by the inclusion of all income charges and credits;
3 a better picture of the total performance of the firm is conveyed, especially when both recurring and unusual, infrequently occurring items are displayed separately in the same income statement.

The official position in this issue has varied over time. Prior to the issuance of APB 9, the AICPA favored the current operating concept of income. With the issuance of APB 9, *Reporting the Results of Operations*, the trend went toward the all-inclusive concept of income, with the opinions' conclusion that income should include all items of profit or loss during the period, with the exception of certain material prior-period adjustments that should be reflected as adjustments of the beginning retained earnings balance. The tilt toward the all-inclusive concept of income continued with the issuance of APB Opinions Nos 15, 20 and 30, requiring disclosure of the earnings per share, cumulative effects of changes in accounting principles, extraordinary items, and results from discontinued operations on the income statement. The FASB has definitely adopted an all-inclusive concept of income in its definition of "comprehensive income" as part of its conceptual framework. FASB Statement of Concepts No. 6 defines "comprehensive income" as follows:

> Comprehensive income is the change in equity of a business entity during a period from transactions and other events and circumstances from nonowner sources. It includes all changes in equity during a period except those resulting from investments by owners and distributions to owners.[26]

12.6   FORMAT APPROACHES

The display of the operating section of the income statement differs from one firm to another, using variations of two basic forms, the *single-step format* and the *multiple-step format*.

The single-step income statement includes two broad groups, revenues and expenses. The total revenues include operating revenues, other revenues and gains not meeting the criteria of being extraordinary. The total expenses include the cost of goods sold, operating expenses, other expenses and income tax expenses. The difference between the total revenues and total expenses is the income from continued operations. An example of a single-step format is shown in Exhibit 12.1. The single-step format is favored because of its simplicity and flexibility in reporting.

The multiple-step format proceeds through several steps to arrive at income from continuing operations. In the first step the cost of goods sold is deducted from net sales, to produce gross profit or gross margin on sales. In the second step, the operating expenses are deducted from gross profit to arrive at operating income. The "other revenues and expenses," the nonoperating items, are then deducted (or added) to operating income to derive the pretax income from continuing operations. In the final step, income tax expenses are deducted from the pretax income from continuing operations to arrive at income before continuing operations. An example of a multiple-set income statement is shown in Exhibit 12.2.

These additional sub-classifications on the multiple-step income statement are deemed more informative and useful to investors, creditors, and other users. The multiple-step income statement is becoming more popular, in spite of two potential limitations. The first limitation pertains to the potential different classifications of operating and non-operating items by different firms, leading to noncomparable income statements. The second limitation pertains to the potential misleading inference from the multiple-step income statement that the recovery of expenses is essential.[27]

EXHIBIT 12.1
KARABATSOS CORPORATION
Single-Step Income Statement For the Year Ended Dec. 31, 1991

Revenues

Sales revenue (net of $5,000 discounts and $2,000 returns and allowances)	153,000	
Interest Revenue	2,000	
Dividend Revenue	1,000	
Total Revenues		156,000

Expenses

Cost of Goods Sold (Exhibit 4-3)	80,000	
Selling Expenses (Exhibit 4-5)	10,000	
General and Administrative Expenses	15,000	
Depreciation Expense (Exhibit 4-5)	7,000	
Loss on Sale of Equipment	5,000	
Interest Expense	2,000	
Income Tax Expense	7,000	
		126,000

Income from Continuing Operations		30,000
Results from Discontinued Operations		
Income from operations of discontinued segment A (net of $2 000 income taxes)	4,500	
Loss on disposal of segment A (net of $3 000 income tax credit)	(2,000)	(2,500)
Income before extraordinary items		27,500
Extraordinary Loss from explosion (net of $700 income tax credit)		(2,000)
Cumulative Effect on prior years' income of change in depreciation method (net of $800 income taxes)		2,400
Net Income		27,900

Components of Income	*Earnings per Share*
Income from continuing operations	(0.00)
Results from discontinued operations	(0.50)
Extraordinary Loss from explosion	(0.40)
Cumulative effect of prior years' income of change in depreciation method	0.48
Net Income	5.58

EXHIBIT 12.2
KARABATSOS CORPORATION
Multiple-Step Income Statements For the Year Ended Dec. 31, 1991

Sales Revenue		160,000
Less: Sales returns and allowances	5,000	
sales discounts	2,000	7,000
Net Sales		153,000
Cost of Goods Sold		80,000
Gross Profit		73,000
Operating Expenses		
Selling Expenses	10,000	
General and Administrative Expenses	15,000	
Depreciation Expense	7,000	32,000
Operating Income		41,000
Other Revenues and Expenses		
Interest Revenue	2,000	
Dividend Income	1,000	
Loss on Sale of equipment	(5,000)	
Interest Expense	(2,000)	(4,000)
Pretax Income from continuing operations		37,000
Income tax expense		7,000
Income from continuing operations		30,000
Results from discontinued operations		
Income from operations of discontinued segment A		
(net of $2 000 income taxes)		4,500
Loss on disposal of segment A		
(net of $3 000 income tax credit)		(2,000)
Income before extraordinary items		27,500
Extraordinary loss from explosion		
(net of $700 income tax credit)		(2,000)
Cumulative effect on prior years' income of change in		
depreciation method (net of $800 income taxes)		2,400
Net Income		27,900

	Earnings per Share
Components of Income	
Income from continuing operations	6.00
Results from discontinued operations	(0.50)
Extraordinary loss from explosion	(0.40)
Cumulative effect on prior years' income of	
change in depreciation method	0.48
Net income	5.58

12.7   EXTRAORDINARY ITEMS

The ability to distinguish between normal recurring components of comprehensive income and nonrecurring items is essential to a sound evaluation of the results of current and past activities and the prediction of future results. And there lies the importance of extraordinary items, as they may affect that ability. The first explicit guidance on accounting for extraordinary items came in APB No. 9, that required the explicit display in a specifically designated section of the income statement.[28] The following definition of "extraordinary items" was provided:

> ...events and transactions of material effect which would not be expected to recur frequently and which would not be considered as recurring factors in any evaluation of the ordinary operating processes of the business.[29]

The ambiguity of the definition, as well as the need to ensure a more uniform interpretation of the provisions, led the Accounting Principles Board to issue APB No. 30, *Reporting the Results of Operations*, where extraordinary items were characterized as both unusual in nature and infrequent in occurrence.[30] These characteristics were defined as follows:

> *Unusual in nature* — The underlying event or transaction should possess a high degree of abnormality and be of a type clearly unrelated to, or only incidentally related to, the ordinary and typical activities of the entity, taking into account the environment in which the entity operates.

> *Infrequency of occurrence* — The underlying event or transaction should be of a type that would not reasonably be expected to recur in the foreseeable future, taking into account the environment in which the entity operates.[31]

Items and transactions defined as not meeting this definition included write-downs and write-offs of receivables, inventories, equipment leased to others, deferred research and development costs, or other intangible assets; gains or losses in foreign currency transactions or devaluations; gains or losses on disposal of segments of a business; other gains or losses on the sale or abandonment of property, plant, and equipment used in business; effects of strikes; and adjustments of accruals on long-term contracts. The new criteria for extraordinary items made such items rare for a while. However, some FASB pronouncements are bringing them back. Examples include:

1. *FASB Statement No. 4* requirement that a gain or loss on the extinguishment of debt be shown separately as an extraordinary item;
2. *FASB Statement No. 15* requirement that a gain on restructuring debt be reported as an extraordinary item by the debtor;
3. *FASB Statement No. 44* requirement that the initial write-off of unamortized costs of interstate operating rights impaired by the Motor Carrier Act of 1980 be reported as an extraordinary item.

12.8   RESULTS FROM DISCONTINUED OPERATIONS

A segment of a business refers to a component of an entity whose activities represent a separate major line of business or class of customers. By discontinued operations, it is meant the operations of a segment that has been sold, abandoned, spun off, or otherwise disposed of. A gain or loss is expected to be made from the discontinued operations at the measurement date. It includes two factors:

1 the income (or loss) from operations of discontinued segment from the measurement date until disposal date;
2 the loss (or gain) on the disposal.

APB No. 30 requires that the results from discontinued operations be reported net of tax on the income statement after the income from continuing operations, but before extraordinary items. The timing of the recognition of the deferrals is dependent upon whether the results are a gain or a loss. If a loss is expected, it is recognized at the measurement date, whereas a gain is deferred and recognized on the disposal date, which is in accordance with the general principle of conservatism.

12.9 PRIOR PERIOD ADJUSTMENTS

To be classified as prior period adjustments, APB Opinion No. 9 required events and transactions to be:

(a) specifically identified and directly related to the business activities of particular prior periods,
(b) not attributable to economic events occurring subsequent to the date of the financial statements for the prior period,
(c) dependent primarily on determination by persons other than management,
(d) not susceptible of reasonable estimation prior to such determinations.[32]

In response to the restrictive nature of these requirements, the Securities and Exchange Commission (SEC) released on June 8, 1976 Staff Bulletin No. 8, which excluded charges or credits resulting from litigation from being treated as prior period adjustments. Subsequently, the FASB issued its Statement No. 16, *Prior Period Adjustments*, in which it limited prior period adjustments to the following:

a. Correction of an error in the financial statements of a prior period.
b. Adjustments that result from the realization of income tax benefits of preacquisition operating loss carry-forwards of purchased subsidiaries.[33]

With regard to certain changes in accounting principles, prior period restatement (adjustment) is required, instead of a cumulative effect of adjustment, for the following cases:

1 change from the LIFO inventory cost flow method to another method;
2 a change in the method of accounting for long-term construction-type contracts;
3 a change to or from the "full cost" method of accounting used in the oil and gas industry;
4 a change from retirement-replacement-betterment accounting to depreciation accounting from railroad track structures;
5 a change from the cost method to the equity method for investments in common stock.

12.10   ACCOUNTING CHANGES

Three types of accounting changes and errors are identified in APB Opinion No. 20, as follows:

1 *Change in accounting principle*: this type of change occurs when a firm adopts a generally accepted accounting principle that differs from the one previously used for reporting purposes. Examples include a change from FIFO to LIFO inventory cost flow assumptions, or a change from straight line to accelerated depreciation.
2 *Change in accounting estimate*: these changes are a result of the periodic presentation. The preparation of financial statements requires estimation of future events, and such estimates are subject to periodic review. Examples of such change include the changes in the life of depreciable assets and the estimated collectibility of receivables.
3 *Change in reporting entity*: this type of change is caused by changes in the reporting units, which may be the result of consolidations, changes in specific subsidiaries, or a change in the number of companies consolidated.
4 *Errors*: errors are not accounting changes. They are the results of mistakes or oversights such as the use of incorrect accounting methods or mathematical miscalculations.[34]

All changes in accounting principles, except those specifically excluded by APB Opinion 20, and other APB Opinions and FASB statements, are accounted for as a cumulative effect change in the comprehensive income on the income statement of the period of change, in a separate section entitled "accounting changes." The effect of adopting the new accounting principle on income before extraordinary items and on net income (and on related per share amounts) of the period of change are disclosed in the notes to the financial statements. Furthermore, income before extraordinary items and net income computed on a pro forma basis is shown in the income statements of all periods presented as if the newly adopted accounting principles were applied during all periods affected.[35]

A change in accounting estimates is accounted for in the period of change if the change affects that period only, or in the period of change and future periods if the change affects both.[36]

A change in accounting entity is accounted for retroactively by prior period restatement of all financial statements as if the new reporting entity had existed for all periods. A description of the change, the reason for it, as well as the effect of the change on income before extraordinary items, net income, and related earnings per share is disclosed for all periods presented.[37]

An error is accounted for retroactively as prior period adjustments and therefore is excluded from the determination of net income for the period, under the provisions of FASB Statement No. 16.[38]

12.11   EARNINGS PER SHARE

Earnings per share is a summary indicator that can assuredly communicate considerable information about a firm's performance. To establish consistency in earnings per share computations and promote comparability of accounting information, APB Opinion No. 15 was issued to require the disclosure of earnings per share and provide guidelines for computation.[39] The calculations are examples that the AICPA published shortly after a 189-page document that contains unofficial accounting interpretations for the computation of earnings per share.[40]

The computation of earnings per share is different for two types of capital structures — the simple and the complex. A simple capital structure is one that consists of "only common stocks or includes no potentially dilutive convertible securities, options, warrants, or other rights that upon conversion or exercise could in the aggregate dilute earnings per share."[41] In the case of the simple capital structure, the earnings per share is computed by dividing the actual earnings applicable to the common shares by the weighted average number of shares outstanding.

A complex capital structure includes in addition to comon stocks such items as convertible preferred stocks and bonds, stock options and warrants, participating securities and two-class stocks, and contingent shares, that are potentially a common stock equivalent. In the case of the complex capital structure, two earnings per share figures are required:

1 A primary earnings per share that is based on the outstanding common shares and the common stock equivalents that have a dilutive effect.
2 A fully diluted earnings per share that reflects the dilution of earnings per share that would have occurred if all contingent issuances of common stock that would have individually reduced earnings per share had taken place.[42] The primary earnings per share is computed by dividing the earnings applicable to the common shares by weighted average number of shares of common stock and common stock equivalents (convertibles that met a yield test plus warrants and stock options). The fully diluted earnings per share are equivalent to the earnings that would result if all potential dilution took place.[43]

Earnings per share is not, however, the only summary indicator that can be provided to users. An FASB report identified the potential for other summary indicators that can communicate considerable information about both a firm's performance and its financial position. Examples include return on investment and cash flow per share.

12.12   CONCLUSIONS

This chapter covered the conceptual and practical issues associated with the income statement prepared on the basis of a transactional approach. Although the FASB seems to be bringing a lot of refinement of the document towards a clear determination of comprehensive income, a lot remains to be done, with a steady move towards an asset–liability approach to the financial statements.

NOTES

[1] Financial Accounting Standards Board, Statement of Financial Accounting Concepts No. 5, *Recognition and Measurement in Financial Statements of Business Enterprises* (Stamford, Ct: FASB, 1984), para. 5.

[2] Ibid., para. 12.

[3] Ibid., para. 23.

[4] Sterling, Robert R., *An Essay on Recognition*, R.J. Chambers Research Lecture 1985 (Sydney: The University of Sydney, Accounting Research Center, 1987), p. 82.

[5] Ibid., pp. 57–8.

[6] Accounting Principles Board Statement No. 4, *Basic Concepts and Accounting Principles Underlying Financial Statements of Business Enterprises* (New York, NY: AICPA, 1970), para. 34.

[7] Financial Accounting Standards Board, Statement of Financial Accounting Concept No. 6, *Elements of Financial Statements* (Stamford, Ct.:, 1985), para. 78.

[8] Committee on Terminology, Accounting Terminology Bulletin No. 2, *Proceeds, Revenue, Income, Profit and Earnings* (New York: AICPA, 1955), para. 5.

[9] Financial Accounting Standards Board, *Elements of Financial Statements*, op. cit., para. 88.

[10] Sprouse, Robert T., and Moonitz, Maurice, Accounting Research Study No. 3. *A Tentative Set of Broad Accounting Principles for Business Enterprises* (New York: AICPA, 1968), p. 47.

[11] Committee on Accounting Procedure, ARB No. 43, *Restatement and Revision of Accounting Research Bulletin* (AICPA, 1953), Chapter 1, para. 1.

[12] Haseman, Wilber E., "An Interpretive Framework of Cost," *The Accounting Review* (October, 1968), pp. 738–52.

[13] American Accounting Association, Committee on Cost Concepts and Standards, "Report of the Committee on Cost Concepts and Standards," *The Accounting Review* (April, 1952), p. 176.

[14] Accounting Principles Board, Statement No. 4, *Basic Concepts and Accounting Principles Underlying Financial Statements of Business Enterprises* (New York: AICPA, 1970).

[15] Committee on Terminology, Accounting Terminology Bulletin No. 4, *Proceeds, Revenue, Income, Profit, and Earnings* (New York: AICPA, 1955), para. 31.

[16] Accounting Principles Board, Statement No. 4, op. cit., para. 134.

[17] Financial Accounting Standards Board, Statement of Financial Accounting Concepts No. 6, *Elements of Financial Statements* (Stamford, Ct.: FASB, 1985), para. 80.

[18] Ibid.

[19] Sprouse, R.T., and Moonitz, M., Accounting Research Study No. 3, *A Tentative Set of Broad Accounting Principles for Business Enterprises* (New York: AICPA, 1962), p. 25.

[20] Accounting Principles Board, Statement No. 4, op. cit., para. 155.

[21] Paton, William and Littleton, A.C., *An Introduction to Corporate Accounting Standards* (American Accounting Association, 1940), p. 71.

[22] Ibid., p. 15.

[23] Accounting Principles Board, Statement No. 4, op. cit., para. 19.

[24] Thomas, Arthur, L., "The Allocation Problem in Financial Accounting Theory," *Studies in Accounting Research No. 3* (Sarasota, Fla: AAA, 1969), pp. 6–15.

[25] Thomas, Arthur, L., "The Allocation Problem: Part Two," *Studies in Accounting Research No. 9* (Sarasota, Fla.: AAA, 1974), p. 3.

[26] Financial Accounting Standards Board, Statement of Financial Accounting Concepts No. 1, *Elements of Financial Statements* (Stamford, Ct.: FASB, 1978), para. 45.

[27] Ibid.

[28] Accounting Principles Board, Opinion No. 9, *Reporting the Results of Operations* (American Institute of Certified Public Accountants, 1966).

[29] Ibid., para. 21.

[30] Accounting Principles Board, Opinion No. 30, *Reporting the Results of Operations* (New York: AICPA, 1973).

[31] Ibid., paras. 19–20.

[32] Accounting Principles Board Opinion No. 9, op. cit., para. 23.

[33] Financial Accounting Standards Board, Statement No. 16, *Prior Period Adjustments* (Stamford, Ct.: FASB, 1977), para. 11.

[34] Accounting Principles Board Opinion No. 20, *Accounting Changes* (New York: AICPA, 1971).

[35] Ibid., paras 18–22.

[36] Ibid., para. 31.

[37] Ibid., paras 34–5.

[38] Financial Accounting Standards Board, Statement No. 16, op. cit.

[39] Accounting Principles Board Opinion No. 15, *Earnings Per Share* (New York: AICPA, 1969).

[40] Ball, J.T., "Computing Earnings Per Share," *Unofficial Accounting Interpretations of APB Opinion No. 15* (New York: AICPA, 1970).

[41] Accounting Principles Board Opinion No. 15, op. cit., para. 14.

[42] Ibid., para. 15.

[43] Boyer, P.A., and Gibson, C.H., "How About Earnings Per Share?," *The CPA Journal* (1979).

REFERENCES

"The Matching Concept," *The Accounting Review* (April, 1965), pp. 368–72.

"The Realization Concept," *The Accounting Review* (April, 1965) pp. 312–22.

Accounting Terminology Bulletin No. 4, *Cost, Expense and Loss* (AICPA, 1957).

American Accounting Association, *A Tentative Statement of Accounting Principles Underlying Corporate Financial Statements* (AAA, 1936).

APB Opinion No. 9, *Reporting the Results of Operations* (AICPA, 1966).

APB Opinion No. 17, *Intangible Assets* (AICPA, 1970).

APB Opinion No. 20, *Accounting Changes* (AICPA, 1971).

APB Opinion No. 30, *Reporting The Results of Operations* (AICPA, 1973).

APB Statement No. 4, *Basic Concepts and Accounting Principles Underlying Financial Statements of Business Enterprises* (AICPA, 1970).

Committee on Accounting Procedure, *Restatement and Revision of Accounting Research Bulletins*, ARB No. 43 (AICPA, 1953).

Committee on Terminology, Accounting Terminology Bulletin No. 2, *Proceeds, Revenue, Income, Profit, and Earnings* (AICPA, 1955).

FASB Discussion Memorandum: *An Analysis of Issues Related to the Conceptual Framework of Financial Reporting: Elements of Financial Statements and Their Measurement* (Stamford, Ct.: FASB, 1976).

Financial Accounting Standards Board, Statement of Financial Accounting Concepts No. 6, *Elements of Financial Statements* (Stamford, Ct.: FASB).

Financial Accounting Standards Board, Statement of Financial Accounting Standards No. 2, *Accounting For Research and Development Costs* (Stamford, Ct.: FASB, 1974).

Financial Accounting Standards Board, Statement of Financial Accounting Standards No. 7, *Accounting and Reporting by Development Stage Enterprises* (Stamford, Ct.: FASB, 1975).

Financial Accounting Standards Board, Statement of Financial Accounting Standards No. 12, *Accounting for Certain Marketable Securities* (Stamford, Ct.: FASB, 1975).

Financial Accounting Standards Board, Statement of Financial Accounting Standards No. 96, *Accounting for Income Taxes* (Stamford, Ct.: FASB).

Frishkoff, Paul (1981). *Reporting of Summary Indicators: An Investigation of Research and Practice* (FASB).

Horngren, Charles T., "How Should We Interpret the Realization Concept?," *The Accounting Review* (April, 1965), pp. 323–33.

Jaenicke, Henry R. (1981). *Survey of Present Practices in Recognizing Revenues, Expenses, Gains, and Losses* (FASB).

Mobley, Sybil C., "The Concept of Realization: A Useful Device," *The Accounting Review* (April, 1966), pp. 292–6.

Myers, John H., "Revenue Realization, Going-Concern and Measurement of Income," *The Accounting Review* (April, 1959), pp. 232–8.

Philips, G. Edwards, "The Accretion Concept of Income," *The Accounting Review* (January, 1963), pp. 14–25.

Sprouse, R.T., and Moonitz, M., Accounting Research Study No. 3, *A Tentative Set of Broad Accounting Principles for Business Enterprises* (New York: AICPA, 1962).

Thomas, Arthur L., Michigan Business Reports No. 49, *Revenue Recognition* (Bureau of Business Research, Graduate School of Business Administration, University of Michigan, 1966).

Thomas, Arthur L., Studies in Accounting Research No. 3, *The Allocation Problem* (Sarasota, Fl.: American Accounting Association, 1974).

QUESTIONS

12.1 Discuss the various views of articulation and earnings.

12.2 Discuss the revenue recognition problem.

12.3 Discuss the matching and allocation problems.

12.4 Elaborate on the controversy of current versus all-inclusive approaches.

12.5 Timing of Revenue Recognition

Revenue is usually recognized at the point of sale. Under special circumstances, however, bases other than the point of sale are used for the timing of revenue recognition.

Required

1 Why is the point of sale usually used as the basis for the timing of revenue recognition?

2 Disregarding the special circumstances when bases other than the point of sale are used, discuss the merits of each of the following objections to the sales basis of revenue recognition:

    a. It is too conservative because revenue is earned throughout the entire process of production.

    b. It is not conservative enough because accounts receivable do not represent disposable funds; sales returns and allowances may be made; and collection and bad debt expenses may be incurred in a later period.

3 Revenue may also be recognized (a) during production and (b) when cash is received. For each of these two bases of timing revenue recognition, give an

example of the circumstances in which it is properly used and discuss the accounting merits of its use in lieu of the sales basis.   (*AICPA adapted*)

12.6 Cost and Expense Recognition

An accountant must be familiar with the concepts involved in determining earnings of a business entity. The amount of earnings reported for a business entity is dependent on the proper recognition, in general, of revenue and expense for a given time period. In some situations costs are recognized as expenses at the time of product sale; in other situations guidelines have been developed for recognizing costs as expenses or losses by other criteria.

Required

1 Explain the rationale for recognizing costs as expenses at the time of product sale.

2 What is the rationale underlying the appropriateness of treating costs as expenses of a period instead of assigning the costs to an asset? Explain.

3 Some expenses are assigned to specific accounting periods on the basis of systematic and rational allocation of asset cost. Explain the underlying rationale for recognizing expenses on this basis.   (*AICPA adapted*)

12.7 Income Statement Deficiencies. David Company's Statements of Income for the year ended December 31, 1993, and December 31, 1992 are presented here:

Additional facts are as follows:

(a) On January 1, 1992, David Company changed its depreciation method for previously recorded plant machinery from the double-declining-balance method to the straight-line method. The effect of applying the straight-line method for the year of and the year after the change is included in David Company's Statements of Income for the year ended December 31, 1993, and December 31, 1992, in "cost of goods sold."

(b) The loss from operations of the discontinued Dex Division from January 1, 1993, to September 30, 1993 (the portion of the year prior to the measurement date) and from January 1, 1992, to December 31, 1992, is included in David Company's Statements of Income for the year ended December 31, 1993, and December 31, 1992, respectively, in "other, net."

(c) David Company has a simple capital structure with only common stock outstanding and the net income per share of common stock was based on the weighted average number of common shares outstanding during each year.

(d) David Company common stock is listed on the New York Stock Exchange and closed at $13 per share on December 31, 1993, and $15 per share on December 31, 1992.

Required

Determine from the additional facts listed whether the presentation of those facts in David Company's Statements of Income is appropriate. If the presentation is appropriate, discuss the theoretical rationale for the presentation. If the presentation is not appropriate, specify the appropriate presentation and discuss its theoretical rationale. Do *not* discuss disclosure requirements for the Notes to the Financial Statements.   (*AICPA adapted*)

DAVID COMPANY
Statements of Income

	Year Ended December 31	
	1993	1992
Net sales	$900,000	$750,000
Costs and expenses:		
Cost of goods sold	$720,000	$600,000
Selling, general and administrative expenses	112,000	90,000
Other, net	11,000	9,000
Total costs and expenses	$843,000	$699,000
Income from continuing operations before income taxes	$ 57,000	$ 51,000
Income taxes	23,000	24,000
Income from continuing operations	$ 34,000	$ 27,000
Loss on disposal of Dex Division, including provision of $1,500 for operating losses during phase-out period, less applicable income taxes of $8,000	8,000	—
Cumulative effect on prior years of change in depreciation method, less applicable income taxes of $1,500	—	3,000
Net income	$ 26,000	$ 30,000
Earnings per share of common stock:		
Income before cumulative effect of change in depreciation method	$2.60	$2.70
Cumulative effect on prior years of change in depreciation method, less applicable income taxes	—	.30
Net income	$2.60	$3.00

12.8 Criteria for Revenue Recognition

The earning of revenue by a business enterprise is recognized for accounting purposes when the transaction is recorded. In some situations, revenue is recognized approximately as it is earned in the economic sense: in others, accountants have developed guidelines for recognizing revenue by other criteria, for example, at the point of sale.

Required (*ignore income taxes*)

1 Explain and justify why revenue is often recognized as earned at the time of sale.

2 Explain in what situations it would be appropriate to recognize revenue as the productive activity takes place.

3 At what times, other than those included in items (1) and (2), may it be appropriate to recognize revenue? Explain.   (*AICPA adapted*)

12.9 Revenue Recognition

Bonanza Trading Stamps, Inc., was formed early this year to sell trading stamps throughout the Southwest to retailers who distribute them gratuitously to their customers. Books for accumulating the stamps and catalogs illustrating the merchandise for which the stamps may be exchanged are given free to retailers for distribution to stamp recipients. Centers with inventories for merchandise premiums have been established for redemption of the stamps. Retailers may not return unused stamps to Bonanza.

The following schedule expresses Bonanza's expectations of the percentages of a normal month's activity that will be attained. For this purpose a normal month's activity is defined as the level of operations expected when expansion of activities ceases or tapers off to a stable rate. The company expects that this level will be attained in the third year, and that sales of stamps will average $2,000,000 per month throughout the third year.

Month	Actual Stamp Sales Percentage	Merchandise Premium Purchases Percentage	Stamp Redemptions Percentage
6	30%	40%	10%
12	60	60	45
18	80	80	70
24	90	90	80
30	100	100	95

Required

1 Discuss the factors to be considered in determining when revenue should be recognized in measuring the income of a business enterprise.

2 Discuss the accounting alternatives that should be considered by Bonanza Trading Stamps, Inc., for the recognition of its revenues and related expenses.

3 For each accounting alternative discussed in (2), give balance sheet accounts that should be used and indicate how each should be classified.   (*AICPA adapted*)

12.10 Construction Contracts

Village Company is accounting for a long-term construction contract using the percentage-of-completion method. It is a three-year-fixed-fee contract that is presently in its first year. The latest reasonable estimates of total contract costs indicate that the contract will be completed at a profit. Village will submit progress billings to the customer and has reasonable assurance that collections on these billings will be received in each year of the contract.

Required

1 a. What is the justification for the percentage-of-completion method for long-term construction contracts?

   b. What facts in the preceding situation indicate that Village should account for this long-term construction contract using the percentage-of-completion method?

2 How would the income recognized in each year of this long-term construction contract be determined using the cost-to-cost method of determining percentage of completion?

3 What is the effect on income, if any, of the progress billings and the collections on these billings?   (*AICPA adapted*)

CHAPTER 13

THE BALANCE SHEET

While the profit statement measures the performance of a firm over a period of time, the balance sheet measures the financial position at a point in time.

Each of the approaches to the financial statements presented in Chapters 7 and 12, namely:

1 the revenue-expense approach;
2 the asset-liability approach; and
3 the nonarticulated approach

has influenced the present state of the balance sheet. In addition various transactions are not yet recognized in the balance sheet, and are known as off-balance sheet transactions. A good example of the off-balance sheet transactions relates to new financial instruments; the general classification scheme used in balance sheet presentation goes as follows:

Current assets
- Investments
- Property, plant and equipment
- Intangible assets
- Other assets

Liabilities
- Current liabilities
- Long-term liabilities
- Other liabilities

Stockholders' equity
- Capital stock
- Additional paid-in capital
- Retained earnings

This chapter reviews the definition, the principles of recognition as well as the measurement rules for these components of the balance sheet.

13.1   MEASURING THE ELEMENTS OF THE BALANCE SHEET

The balance sheet measures the financial position or the revenue structure (i.e., major classes and amounts of assets) and the claims against the resources or financial structure (i.e., major classes and amount of liabilities and equity). It is best expressed by the following equation:

$$\text{Assets} = \text{Liabilities} + \text{Stockholders' Equity}$$

The measurement of each of the three elements of the balance sheet is an important task for any standard setting bodies. As seen in Chapters 9 and 11, five alternatives have been identified for measuring these elements. The list includes:

1 historical cost/historical proceeds;
2 current cost/current proceeds;
3 current exit value;
4 net realized value; and
5 present value.

These alternative valuation techniques are shown in Exhibit 13.1. They are each used in certain circumstances for selected elements of the balance sheet. As will be seen in the remainder of this chapter, the end result is that the balance sheet is the combined application of various valuation techniques, raising doubt about

1 the additivity of the resulting measures and
2 the overall significance of the whole document as a measure of the wealth of the firm.

13.2   ASSETS

13.2.1   Definition

The importance of the definition of assets lies in the fact that it identifies the economic events to be recognized, measured, and reported in the balance sheet. Most definitions focus on some of the characteristics that are common to all assets. These characteristics include the following.

1 Identification of a future benefit characteristic (including similar notions such as "service potential," of value to the reporting entity, and "economic resources").
2 Identification of a cost sacrifice, acquisition at a cost or unexpired cost as being relevant.
3 Delineation in terms of accounting process.

4 Specification of the connection with a specific entity.
5 Specification of the time dimension (exclusion of "future assets") other than by reference to cost.
6 Inclusion of measurability characteristic in definition other than by references to cost.
7 Inclusion of measurability characteristic.[1]

Assets are probable future economic benefits, or are controlled by a particular entity as a result of past transaction or events. An asset has three essential characteristics:

1 It embodies a potential, alone or in combination with other assets, to contribute directly or indirectly to future net cash inflows;
2 A particular enterprise can obtain the benefit and control others' access to an asset.
3 The transaction or other event giving rise to the enterprise's right to or control of the benefit has already occurred.[2]

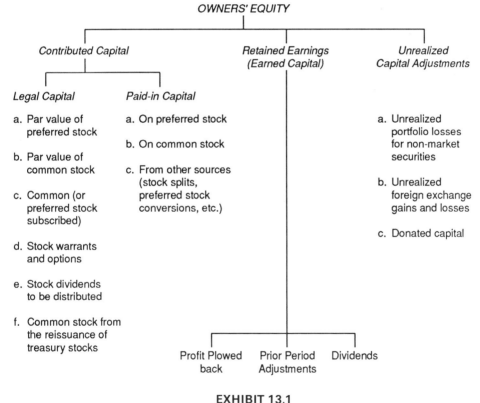

EXHIBIT 13.1

The focus in the FASB definition is:

1 the presence of probable future economic benefits that characterize the asset as providing an economic revenue;

2 the fact that these benefits accrue to the particular entity to be considered and asset of the entity; and

3 the specification of a past time-dimension.

Missing from the FASB definition is the condition of exchangeability or severability. The condition has been advocated as critical for the definition of assets and the exclusion of goodwill as an asset. According to MacNeal:

> A good that lacks exchangeability must lack economic value because its purchase or sale must forever remain impossible and thus no market price for it can ever exist.[3]

Chambers also argued for severability in his definition of asset, and for excluding goodwill as an asset. His reasons are as follows:

> ... the definition arose from the necessity of considering the capacity of an entity to adapt itself to changes in its state and its environment. Adaptive behavior implies that the goodwill subsisting in any collection of assets and liabilities is so susceptible to variation as to have no enduring quality.[4]

The FASB, however, rejected the idea of severability as being important for the definition of an asset. Basically, the benefits of assets are not restricted to their exchangeability. As Moonitz correctly states: "exchange does not make values, it merely reveals them."[5] Severability reduces value to the dimension of market prices and denotes a conservative approach that restricts the types of assets to be included in the balance sheet.

13.2.2   Recognition and Measurement of Assets

When it comes to recognition and measurement of assets, options abound, differing for each component of the balance sheet. In the case of recognition, various attempts have been made to identify criteria or tests of recognition. Sterling has suggested the following mix of tests to provide necessary and sufficient conditions for the recognition of a thing as an asset:[6]

1 First, the *detection of existence test* requires the detection of events that may be candidates for recognition.

2 Second, *the economic resources and obligations test* requires that the kind of things that are to be recognized are economic resources that are characterized by being a) scarce, b) desirable, c) commanding a price.

3 Third, *the entity association test* requires that the entity controls the resource.

4 Fourth, *the non-zero magnitude test* requires that the thing must have a non-zero magnitude.

5 Fifth, *the temporal association test* requires that the thing satisfies all tests at the balance sheet date.

6 Sixth, *the verification test* requires that there must be assurance of the representational faithfulness of

   a. the existence of the thing,

   b. that it is an economic resource and obligation,

   c. that it is under the control of or obligates the entity under consideration,

   d. that the magnitude of the yet-to-be-selected attribute has been reasonably measured or estimated, and

e. that all of those tests are satisfied at the date of the statement of financial position.[7]

The official FASB pronouncement of the general principles of recognition was included in Statement of Financial Accounting Concepts No. 5, *Recognition and Measurement in Financial Statements of Business Enterprises.*[8] The statement provides the following four "fundamental" recognition criteria:

Definition — The item meets the definition of an element of financial statements.
Measurability — It has a relevant attribute measurable with sufficient reliability.
Relevance — The information about it is capable of making a difference in user decisions.
Reliability — The information is representationally faithful, verifiable, and neutral.[9]

Both Sterling's and the FASB's tests are too elaborate and vague to be practical. That is why various pervasive principles are stated for the initial recognition and measurement of both assets and liabilities. A first example provided by Miller and Islam is as follows:

It is proposed in this monograph that an item satisfying the definition of an asset be recognized in the financial statements when, and only when:
(a) it is probable that the future economic benefits embodied in the asset will eventuate; and
(b) it possesses a relevant attribute that can be quantified in units of money with sufficient reliability.[10]

A more practical example provided by the APB is as follows:

Assets and liabilities generally are initially recorded on the basis of events in which the enterprise acquires the resources from other entities. The assets and liabilities are measured by the exchange prices at which the transfers take place.[11]

The APB principle points to recognition when control effectively occurs and to measurement at the market value (exchange price) of the consideration exchanged or sacrificed. Miller and Islam's definition ties measurement to the specification of an attribute that can be quantified in units of money. As will be seen later, various attributes are generally measured in the balance sheet in violation of the additive principle of measurement theory. The attributes considered in the balance sheet include original acquisition cost (historical cost), net book value, and various forms of current costs which contribute to the lack of additivity of the balance sheet.

13.2.3   Current Assets

The Committee on Accounting Procedure defined current assets as cash and other assets or resources commonly identified as those which are reasonably expected to be realized in cash or sold or consumed during the normal operating cycle of the business or one year, whichever is longer.[12] By "operating cycle" is meant the average time intervening between the acquisition of materials or services and the final cash realization. These current assets are classified in the balance sheet in order of their decreasing liquidity. They include cash, marketable securities, receivables, inventories, and prepaid expenses. The recognition and measurement of each of these components of current assets differ.

Receivables, consisting of claims against customers and other parties arising from the operations of the business enterprise, are valued at historical cost, adjusted by the estimate of uncollectible amounts. The attribute to be measured is an approximation of the net realization value.

Inventory is valued at acquisition at cost, which has been generally defined as the price paid or consideration given to acquire it.[13]

When inventory is manufactured, Accounting Research Bulletin No. 43 holds that inventory costs include acquisition and direct and indirect production costs, whereas "general and administrative expenses should be included as period changes, except for the portion of such expenses that may be clearly related to production and thus constitute a part of inventory. Selling expenses constitute no part of inventory costs."[14] Both the costs of purchase and the costs of production added to the beginning inventory constitute the cost of goods available to sale. Thus total cost needs to be allocated to the cost of goods sold and the ending inventory by means of a cost flow assumption. Major alternative flow assumptions include specific identification, first-in, first-out (FIFO), average cost, and last-in, first-out (LIFO). The choice of a flow method is intended to provide a proper determination of income through the process of matching appropriate costs and revenues.[15] The choice, as with any allocation technique, is arbitrary and incorrigible. However, the valuation at this historical cost, as determined by the cost flow assumption, is modified by the lower of cost or market rule, requiring that the inventory be written down to its market value when its utility is due. Accounting Research Bulletin No. 43 states:

> A departure from the cost basis of pricing the inventory is required when the utility of the goods is no longer as great as its cost. Where there is evidence that the utility of goods, in their disposal in the ordinary course of business, will be less than cost, whether due to physical deterioration, obsolescence, changes in price levels or other causes, the difference should be recognized as a loss of the current period. This is generally accomplished by stating such goods at a lower level commonly designated as market.[16]

Market value is defined as the current replacement cost, and not the selling price, where a) the upper constraint is that the market values should not exceed the net realizable value, and b) the lower constraint is that the market value should not be below the net realizable value, reduced by an allowance for a normal profit margin.

Prepaid expenses include such items as office and factory supplies, prepaid rent, unexpired insurance, prepaid interest and prepaid taxes. They represent resources committed for the current operating cycle. They are valued at their unexpired historical cost.

Temporary rather than long-term investments are classified as current assets, as they are expected to be converted into cash within the current operating cycle or a year, whichever is longer. The valuation of temporary securities can be made using:

1 the historical cost method;
2 the market value method; or
3 the lower of cost or market method.

The position taken in FASB Statement No. 12, *Accounting for Certain Marketable Securities*, favors a lower of cost or market method for equity securities where the difference between aggregate cost and market value is disclosed by means of a valuation allowance account offset against the original cost of the temporary investment account.[17]

13.2.4   Investments

Investments that are readily salable and do not meet the expectation that they will be converted into cash within one year or by the end of the operating cycle, are classified as long-term investments. The percentage of common stock ownership determines the valuation procedure to be used. Basically the lower of cost or market is used for ownership of less than 20 percent of the outstanding voting stock of the investee. Ownership of more than 20 percent requires the use of the equity method.[18,19] Ownership of more than 50 percent requires a consolidation with the investor's own accounts.

Investments in bonds or notes are valued at their acquisition cost, adjusted for the amortization of any purchase premium or discount.

13.2.5   Property, Plant, and Equipment

Property, plant, and equipment, also called fixed assets or plant assets, constitute tangible noncurrent assets. Some of these assets are subject to depreciation or depletion. The acquisition of property, plant, and equipment may occur either:

1 singly or by a lump-sum purchase,
2 with deferred payments,
3 through the issuance of securities,
4 in exchange for another asset,
5 by self-construction,
6 by donation, or
7 through a lease.

The acquisition of the asset singly is valued at the invoice price less any applicable cash or trade discounts, plus freight, assembly, installation, and testing costs. In addition the costs incidental to the transaction and necessary for making the asset useful are accounted for. In the case of land, these costs include

1 the costs of closing the transaction and obtaining title, including commissions, options, legal fees, title search, insurance and past due taxes;
2 the land survey costs;
3 the costs of preparing the land for its particular use.

The acquisition of different assets for a single lump-sum purchase price is followed by an allocation of the acquisition price proportionally to the relative market values of the individual assets.

The acquisition of the asset on a deferred payment basis is valued at its fair value or the fair value of the liability at the date of the transaction. In those cases where both valuation bases are not easily determined, the acquisition is valued at the present value of the deferred payments at the stated interest rate if it is not materially different from the market rate, or at the market rate.

The acquisition of the asset by issuance of securities is valued at the fair value of the asset or the stock, whichever is more verifiable.

The acquisition of the asset by exchange of other assets, known as a nonmonetary exchange a) is valued at the fair value of the asset(s) surrendered and b) a gain or loss is recognized on the exchange for dissimilar assets.[20]

The acquisition of the asset through self-construction or manufacturing leads to two problems:

1 the determination of production costs; and
2 the treatment of interest costs.

With regard to the determination of production costs, the two debated methods of absorption costing and variable costing agree that all variable manufacturing costs are product costs and hence inventoriable. The controversy lies in the treatment of fixed manufacturing overhead, with a) the absorption costing method treatment as an inventoriable product cost and b) the variable costing method treating it as a period cost. The absorption costing alternative is the most employed in practice. With regard to the treatment of interest costs FASB Statement No. 34 requires the capitalization of interest in certain situations, namely for the assets that are either constructed for a firm's own use or constructed as discrete projects for sale or lease to others, but not for routine inventory production.[21] The amount of interest to be capitalized is "intended to be that portion of the interest cost incurred during the assets' acquisition periods that theoretically could have been avoided."[22]

Assets acquired through donation are valued at their fair market value and any conditions imposed on the firm through the donation should be disclosed in the footnotes.

The valuation of assets acquired through a lease depends on the type of lease. In the case of the lessee, an operating lease is accounted for by the expensing procedure of the operating method; a capital lease is accounted for by the capitalization procedure of the capital lease method. Basically, FASB Statement No 13 asserts that a lease that transfers substantially all the ownership privileges of an asset — the risks and benefits of property ownership — represents in substance a purchase by the lessee and a sale by the lessor.[23] Accordingly, in such a case an asset — lease equipment under capital leases — and a liability—obligation under capital leases — are created and valued at the lower of the following two options:

1 The sum of the present value at the beginning of the lease term of the minimum lease payments during the lease term, excluding that portion of the payments representing executory costs such as insurance, maintenance, and taxes paid by the lessor, together with any profit thereon.
2 The fair value of the leased property at the inception of the lease.[24]

In the case of the lessor, an operating lease is valued by the revenue procedure of the operating method, while a sales-type lease and a direct financing lease are valued by the capitalization procedure of respectively the sales financing method and the financing method.

In the case of oil and gas properties, the debate centers on whether to use the successful-efforts method, which requires the capitalization of costs associated with successful wells and the expensing of costs associated with unsuccessful or dry wells, or the full-costing method which requires the capitalization associated with all costs, whether or not the wells were successful. FASB Statement No. 19, issued in 1978, required the use of the successful-efforts method.[25] It was suspended after the SEC objected, however, and required the use of *Reserve Recognition Accounting* (RRA). Subsequently the SEC rescinded the RRA and allowed the use of either the successful-efforts method or the full-costing method.

13.2.6   Intangible Assets

Intangible assets lack a physical substance, but result from legal or contractual rights. A distinction is generally made between a) *identifiable intangible assets* such as patents, franchises, organization costs, computer software costs, leases and leasehold improvements, deferred charges, and trademarks, and b) *unidentifiable intangible assets* such as goodwill. The valuation of intangibles as required by APB Opinion No. 17 requires:

1 externally acquired identifiable intangibles to be capitalized;
2 externally acquired unidentifiable intangibles to be expensed;
3 internally developed identifiable intangibles to be capitalized, with the exception of research and development; and
4 internally developed unidentifiable intangibles to be expensed.[26]

The Opinion also required the amortization of intangibles, stating that:

> The value of intangible assets at any one date disappears and . . . the recorded costs of intangible assets should be amortized by systematic charges to income over the periods estimated to be benefitted.[27]

The exception made for the capitalization of internally developed identifiable intangibles was for research and development. FASB No. 2 requires that all research and development costs be expensed as incurred, given the uncertainty surrounding the realization of benefits from probable future patents or products having economic value.

13.3   LIABILITIES

13.3.1   Definition

An early and exhaustive definition of liabilities that include deferred credits is contained in Accounting Terminology Bulletin No. 1 as follows:

> Something represented by a credit balance that is or would be properly carried forward upon a closing of books of account according to the rules or principles of accounting, provided such credit balance is not in effect a negative balance applicable to an asset. Thus the word is used broadly to comprise not only items which constitute liabilities in the popular sense of debts or obligations (including provision for those that are unascertained), but also credit balances to be accounted for which do not involve a

debtor and creditor relation. For example, capital stock and related or similar elements of proprietorship are balance sheet liabilities in that they represent balances to be accounted for, though these are not liabilities in the ordinary sense of debt owed to legal creditors.[28]

The reference to deferred credits was dropped, however, by FASB Statement No. 6, as follows:

Liabilities are probable future sacrifices of economic benefits arising from present obligations of a particular entity to transfer assets or provide services to other entities in the future as a result of past transactions or events.[29]

Three essential characteristics of a liability appear:

1 It embodies a present duty or responsibility to one or more other entities that entails settlement by probable future transfer or use of the assets at a specified or determinable date, on occurrence of a specific event, or on demand.
2 The duty or responsibility obligates a particular entity, leaving it little or no discretion to avoid the future sacrifice.
3 The transaction or other event obligating the entity has already happened.[30]

Types of liabilities include *contractual, constructive, equitable*, and *contingent* liabilities, and *deferred credits*. Contractual liabilities are based on written or oral agreements to pay cash or to provide goods and services to specified or determinable entities.

Constructive obligations are created, inferred or construed from the facts in a particular situation rather than contracted by agreement with another entity or imposed by government, such as in the case of vacation pay or year-end bonuses.[31] Equitable obligations arise from ethical or moral constraints rather than from rules of common or statute law, such as in the case of the obligation to complete and deliver a product to a customer that has no other source of supply.[32] Finally, contingent liabilities have been expanded in Statement of Financial Accounting Concept No. 6 to include:

... an existing condition, situation, or set of circumstances involving uncertainty as to possible gain (hereafter a "gain contingency") or loss (hereafter a "loss contingency") to an enterprise that will ultimately be resolved when one or more future events occur or fail to occur. Resolution of the uncertainty may confirm the acquisition of an asset or the reduction of a liability or the loss or impairment of an asset or the incurrence of a liability.[33]

Owing to conservatism, examples of loss contingencies to be recognized include noncollectibility, product defects, premium offers, risk of loss or damage of enterprise property by fire, explosion, or other hazards, threat of expropriation of assets, pending or threatened litigation, actual or possible claims and assessments, guarantees of indebtedness of others and agreement to repurchase receivables that have been sold.[34]

Finally, deferred credits are of two types: type 1 includes prepaid revenues that create a contractual duty to provide goods or services; type 2 results from a deferral and income statement recognition of an item to future periods, such as in the cases of investment tax credits[35] and deferred gains on sale-leaseback transactions.[36] Type 2 do not constitute a liability. This is reflected in the following FASB position:

Deposits and prepayments received for goods or services to be provided — "unearned revenues," such as subscriptions or rent collected in advance — likewise qualify as liabilities under the definition because an entity is required to provide goods or services to those who have paid in advance. They are mentioned separately from other liabilities only because they have commonly been described in the accounting literature and financial statements as "deferred credits" or reserves.[37]

13.3.2   Recognition and Measurement of Liabilities

The general principle for the measurement of liabilities is the use of the amount established in the exchange. In general, for current liabilities the amount is the face value of the obligation to be settled in the future. In long-term liabilities the general rule is to recognize the true value of money; the discounting calculation used goes as follows:

$$PV = F (1 + r)^{-t}$$

where:

F   is a future cash flow occurring t periods from the valuation date.
PV   is the present value on the valuation date after discontinuing F at the interest rate r.

Theoretically, an item should be discounted if the item satisfies the following criteria:

1 The item represents a claim to or an obligation to pay, an amount the firm can estimate with reasonable precision.
2 The firm will collect or pay the amount more than one year after the balance sheet date.
3 a. The claim or obligation arises from other than an executory contract; or
  b. the firm has revalued the balance sheet item because of new information.[38]

There are, however, cases meeting the above conditions for which discounting is not allowed in GAAP. Examples include:

1 deferred income taxes;
2 convertible bond debt;
3 liabilities for amounts received for goods or services the firm will provide in the future;
4 contractual payments made or rents collected under trouble debt restructuring.[39]

For some of these cases the excuse used is the immateriality of the present value from the nondiscounted future value. Another, more plausible, reason is stated as follows:

I believe that the current state of accounting for the time value of money is due to exceptional lobbying power on the part of banks and other financial institutions and the apparent discomfort of many accountants with compound interest arithmetic. The savings and loan crisis seems to be reducing the clout of the banking industry while the accounting profession is becoming more comfortable with compound interest.[40]

13.4   EQUITY

FASB Statement of Concepts No. 6 defines equity as "the residual interest in the assets of an entity that remains after deducting its liabilities."[41] A proprietary theory of the firm characterizes the FASB decision in the sense that equity is the ownership interest, ranking after liabilities as a claim to or interest in the assets of the firm. Another characteristic of the equity is that it may change as a result of activities from owner and nonowner sources. Both characteristics of equity are stated as follows:

1 Equity is the same as net assets, the difference between the enterprise's assets and its liabilities.
2 Equity is enhanced or burdened by increases and decreases in net assets from nonowner sources as well as investments by owners and distribution to owners.[42]

The basic framework of stockholders' equity was shown in Exhibit 13.1. It shows the legal distinction given in the corporate form of ownership between contributed capital, earned capital or retained earnings and unrealized capital adjustments.

1 The contributed capital includes both legal capital and other contributed capital. The legal capital as measured by the par value of stocks represents the amount of net assets that cannot be distributed to stockholders. The excess of par value received for shares is classified as additional paid-in capital. Other sources of contributed capital include, for example:
   a. conversion of convertible debt;
   b. issuance of detachable stock warrants with debt;
   c. common stock from the reissuance of treasury stock;
   d. common stock from the reissuance of employee stock options.
2 Unrealized capital includes, for example:
   a. donated capital;
   b. unrealized losses on long-term investments in equity securities;
   c. any excess of additional pension liability over unrecognized prior service cost as a negative compound;
   d. unrealized foreign exchange gains or losses from the translation of foreign net assets into dollars.
3 Retained earnings represent the cumulative net profit of a firm that has not been distributed as dividends. It changes through income-related transactions, dividend distributions and prior period adjustments.

This threefold segregation in shareholders' equity rests in state legal capital requirements for the protection of creditors. A minimum capital equal to the par value of common stock is used to buffer the claims of creditors against bankruptcy.[43] Five judicial theories are generally used for stockholders' liability for stocks issued at less than par value:

1 A *trust fund theory*, where stockholders hold the contributed capital in trust for creditors, retaining a residual interest upon liquidation,
2 A *fraud theory*, where capital contributions are required to avoid a fraud upon other investors such as creditors,
3 A *statutory obligation theory*, where stockholders are held liable on the basis of state statutory requirements for the maintenance of minimum capital,
4 A *contract by subscription theory*, where the stockholders' liability is based on their subscription contract,
5 A *balance sheet misrepresentation theory*, which is a classic tort misrepresentation that shares were fully paid when, in fact, they were not.[44,45]

It is, however, a fact that the recent wave of restructuring has diluted the importance of legal capital in those cases where the distributions to stockholders exceeded the net book value of the firm's assets. Witness the following comment:

> In this century, restrictions on corporate distributions based on legal capital have had little impact because the practice of using nominal accounts for par or stated values of capital stock has evolved, thereby giving corporate directors much latitude in declaring distributions to stockholders. In addition, although corporate boards of directors were statutorily bound to preserve paid-in capital in excess of par, they often were given the ability under state law to make transfers from paid-in capital in excess of par value to retained earnings by resolution. The recent wave of corporate restructuring has resulted in distributions in which the impairment of capital, at least as measured by GAAP, is clear-cut. Given the large number of restructuring transactions that have occurred, and the fact that many of these have been possible only because of the new flexibility of corporate laws, the relevance of the traditional accounting disclosures about a corporation's compliance in the state law and the corporation's capacity for making distributions to stockholders merit reconsideration.[46]

What has happened has been a gradual reliance, in these restructurings, on fair valuation of the assets, contributing to the erosion of the outmoded concepts of stated capital and par value. This was reinforced by the Committee's report on the 1980 revisions to the Model Business Corporation Act, which specifically authorizes departures for historical cost accounting, and sanctions the utilization of appraisal methods for the purposes of determining the funds available for distributions.[47] What this position implies is that the notion of par or stated value will no longer have the importance they once had as a legal capital.

13.5 FINANCIAL INSTRUMENTS AND OFF-BALANCE SHEET TRANSACTIONS

The new, complex reality of today's markets, with increased interest rate volatility, frequency of tax and regulatory changes, deregulation of the financial services industry and increased investment banking competition, demands a lot of financial innovation. It is the objective of financial engineering to provide such innovations. As defined by Finnerty: "financial engineering involves the design, the development, and the implementation of the innovative financial instruments and processes, and the formation of creative solutions to problems in finance."[48]

The following factors have been identified as being primarily responsible for these new financial instruments:

1 Tax advantages.
2 Reduced transaction costs.
3 Reduced agency costs.
4 Risk reallocation.
5 Increased liquidity.
6 Regulatory or legislative factors.
7 Level and volatility of interest rates.
8 Level and volatility of prices.

9 Academic work.
10 Accounting benefits.
11 Technological developments and other factors.[49]

These innovations can be classified as debt innovations, preferred stock innovations, convertible debt or preferred stock innovations, and common equity innovations. Those instruments do not necessarily fit the conventional definitions of debt, equity and hedging instruments. They are hybrids of the conventional instruments. The challenge to the accounting profession is now to create special or different accounting for these instruments.

To deal with these issues the FASB issued in November 1987 an exposure draft, *Disclosures about Financial Instruments*, that would have required for all financial instruments disclosures about credit risks, contractual futures, cash receipts and payments, interest rates and current market values. Because of the response of the constituents, the FASB decided to focus first on off-balance sheet risk and concentration of credit risk. In July of 1989 it issued a revised exposure draft, *Disclosures of Information about Financial Instruments with Off-Balance Sheet Risk and Financial Instruments with Concentration of Credit Risk*.

The project's intention is to provide an answer to such questions as:

- Should financial assets by considered *sold* if there is recourse or other continuing involvement with them? Should financial liabilities be considered *settled* when assets are dedicated to settle them? Under what other circumstances should related assets and liabilities be derecognized, not recognized, or offset?
- What should be the accounting treatment for financial instruments and transactions that seek to transfer market and credit risk — for example, futures contracts, interest rate swaps, options, forward commitments, nonrecourse arrangements, and financial guarantees — and for the underlying assets or liabilities to which the risk-transferring items are related?
- How should financial instruments be measured — for example at market value, at amortized original cost, or at the lower of cost or market?[50]

Effective with the 1989 calendar year reporting, firms have needed to include the extent nature and terms of financial instruments with off-balance sheet credit risk. The disclosure of information about collateral and concentrations of credit risk has had to be disclosed for financial statements for fiscal years ending after June 15, 1990.

Basically the statement requires all entries to disclose information about the following, for financial instruments with off-balance sheet risk:

- The face, contract, or notational principal amount and the amount recognized in the statement of financial position.
- The nature and terms of the instruments and a discussion of the credit, market and liquidity risk and related accounting policies.
- The accounting loss the entity would incur if any counterparty to the financial instrument failed to perform.
- The entity's policy for requiring collateral or other security on financial instruments it accepts, and a description of collateral on instruments presently held.[51]

The accounting loss from a financial instrument includes four risks, as follows:

1 *A credit risk*, or the possibility of loss, from the failure of another party to perform according to the terms of a contract.
2 *A market risk*, or the possibility that future changes in market prices may make a financial instrument less valuable or more onerous.
3 *A liquidity risk*, or the possibility that an entity may be obligated to pay cash that it may not have available.
4 *A risk of theft or physical loss.*

Which financial instruments have off-balance sheet risk, which refers to the risk of accounting loss (credit, market, or liquidity risk) that exceeds the amount recognized, if any, in the statement of financial position, remains to be determined.

In the 1989 exposure draft, FASB also provided a definition of a financial instrument that distinguishes between instruments that entail one party's right to receive and another party's obligation to deliver, and those that entail rights and obligation to exchange. It defined a financial instrument as cash, evidence of an ownership interest in an equity, or contract, that is both:

1 a (recognized or unrecognized) contractual *right* of one entity to (a) receive cash or another financial instrument from another entity or (b) exchange other financial instruments on potentially favorable terms with another entity; or
2 a (recognized or unrecognized) contractual *obligation* of another entity to (a) deliver cash or another financial instrument from another entity or (b) exchange other financial instruments on potentially favorable terms with another entity.

This definition results in six tentatively identified instruments:

1 unconditional receivable (payable);
2 conditional receivable (payable);
3 forward contract;
4 option;
5 guarantee or conditional exchange;
6 equity instrument.

These instruments need to be broken down to determine their economic substance and thoroughly develop consistent accounting standards:

> The approach is based on the premise that all financial instruments are made up of a few different "building blocks" — fundamental financial instruments — and that determining how to recognize and measure those fundamental instruments is the key to reaching consistent solutions for the accounting issues raised by other, more complex instruments and by various relationships between instruments.[52]

13.6   CONCLUSIONS

It is apparent that a lot remains to be done. The valuation bases for liabilities, assets and equities are at best eclectic and sometimes lack conceptual validation. In addition the financial instruments, created by the financial engineering drive, need more than the piecemeal adopted by the FASB. All their problems need to be corrected to make the balance sheet a more relevant source of information.

NOTES

[1] Miller, Malcolm C., and Islam, A. Atiqul, *The Definition and Recognition of Assets* (Gaufield, Vic.: Australian Accounting Research Foundation, 1988), pp. 34–6.

[2] FASB Concepts Statement No. 3, *Elements of Financial Statements of Business Enterprises* (December, 1980), para. 19.

[3] MacNeal, Kenneth, *Truth in Accounting* (University of Pennsylvania, 1939), p. 90.

[4] Chambers, Raymond, *Accounting, Evaluation and Economic Behavior* (Englewood Cliffs, N.J.: Prentice-Hall, 1966), pp. 209–10.

[5] Moonitz, Maurice, Accounting Research Study No. 1, *The Basic Postulates of Accounting* (New York: AICPA, 1961), p. 18.

[6] Sterling, Robert R., *An Essay on Recognition* (Accounting Research Center, The University of Sydney, 1985), pp. 69–71.

[7] Ibid., p. 69.

[8] Financial Accounting Standards Board, Statement No. 5, *Recognition and Measurement in Financial Statement of Business Enterprises* (Stamford, Ct.: FASB, 1984).

[9] Ibid., para. 63.

[10] Miller, Malcolm C., and Islam, A. Atiqul, *The Definition and Recognition of Assets*, op. cit., p. 59.

[11] Accounting Principles Board, APB Statement No. 4, *Basic Concepts and Accounting Principles Underlying Financial Statements of Business Enterprises* (American Institute of Certified Public Accountants, 1970), para. 145.

[12] Accounting Research Bulletin No. 43, *Restatement and Revision of Accounting Research Bulletins* (New York: American Institute of Certified Public Accountants, 1953), Chapter 3A.

[13] Ibid., Chapter 4, para. 4.

[14] Ibid.

[15] Ibid.

[16] Ibid., Ch. 4, para. 7.

[17] Financial Accounting Standards Board, Statement of Financial Accounting Standards No. 12, *Accounting for Certain Marketable Securities* (Stamford, Ct.: FASB, 1975).

[18] Accounting Principles Board, APB Opinion No. 18, *The Equity Method of Accounting for Investments in Common Stock* (New York: AICPA, 1971).

[19] FASB interpretation No. 35, however, presents various facts and circumstances that preclude an investor from using the equity method to account for its investment of 20 percent or more in the investee.

[20] American Institute of Certified Public Accountants, APB Opinion No. 25, *Accounting for Nonmonetary Transactions* (New York: AICPA, 1973), para. 18

[21] Financial Accounting Standards Board, Statement of Financial Accounting Standards No. 34, *Capitalization of Interest Cost* (Stamford, Ct.: FASB, 1979), para. 10.

[22] Ibid., para. 12.

[23] Financial Accounting Standards Board, Statement No. 13 as Amended and Interpreted through May 1980, *Accounting for Leases* (Stamford, Ct.: FASB, 1980).

[24] Ibid., para. 10.

[25] Financial Accounting Standards Board, Statement of Financial Accounting Standards No. 19, *Financial Accounting and Reporting by Oil and Gas Producing Companies* (Stamford, CT.: FASB, 1978).

[26] Accounting Principles Board, APB Opinion No. 17, *Accounting for Intangible Assets* (New York: AICPA, 1970).

[27] Ibid., para. 27.

[28] Committee on Terminology, Accounting Terminology Bulletin No. 1, *Review and Resume* (New York: AICPA, 1953), para. 27.

[29] Financial Accounting Standards Board, Statement of Financial Accounting Concepts No. 6, *Elements of Financial Reporting of Business Enterprises* (Stamford, Ct.: FASB, Dec. 1985), para. 28.

[30] Ibid., para. 36.

[31] Ibid., para. 40.

[32] Ibid.

[33] Financial Accounting Standards Board, Statement of Financial Accounting Standards No. 5, *Accounting for Contingencies* (Stamford, Ct.: FASB, 1975), para. 1.

[34] Ibid., para. 40.

[35] Accounting Principles Board, APB Opinion No. 2, *Accounting for the Investment Credit* (New York: AICPA, 1962).

[36] Financial Accounting Standards Board, Statement of Financial Accounting Standards No. 13, *Accounting for Leases* (Stamford, Ct.: FASB, 1976).

[37] Financial Accounting Standards Board, *Elements of Financial Reporting of Business Enterprises*, op. cit., para. 197.

[38] Weil, Roman L., "Role of Time Value of Money in Financial Reporting," *Accounting Horizons* (December, 1990), p. 50.

[39] Ibid., p. 48.

[40] Ibid., p. 61.

[41] Financial Accounting Standards Board, Statement of Concepts No. 6, *Elements of Financial Statements of Business Enterprises* (Stamford, Ct.: FASB, 1985), para. 49.

[42] Ibid., para. 60.

[43] Miller, M.A., *Miller Comprehensive GAAP Guide 1990* (New York: Harcourt Brace Jovanovich, 1989), p. 38.01.

[44] Manning, B., *A Concise Textbook on Legal Capital*, Second Edition (Mineola, N.Y.: Foundation Press, 1981)

[45] Roberts, Michael L., Samson, William D., and Dugan, Michael T., "The Stockholders' Equity Section: Form Without Substance," *Accounting Horizons* (December, 1990), pp. 37–8.

[46] Ibid., pp. 38–9.

[47] "The Report of the Committee on Corporate Laws," *The Business Lawyer* (July, 1979) pp. 1867–89.

[48] Finnerty, John D., "Financial Engineering in Corporate Finance: An Overview," *Financial Management* (Winter, 1988), p. 19.

[49] Ibid.

[50] Woods, III, Clifford, C., "An Overview of the FASB's Financial Instruments Project," *Journal of Accountancy* (November, 1989), p. 44.

[51] Bullen, H.G., Wilkins, R.C., and Woods, III, C.C., "The Fundamental Financial Instrument Approach," *Journal of Accountancy* (November, 1989), p. 72.

[52] Ibid., p. 71.

REFERENCES

Measurement of Assets and Liabilities in General

American Accounting Association, "Report of the Committee on Accounting Valuation Bases," *The Accounting Review* (1972, supplement to Volume 47), pp. 535–73.

Henderson, M. Scott, "Nature of Liabilities," *The Australian Accountant* (July, 1974), pp. 329–34.

Kulkarni, Deepak, "The Valuation of Liabilities," *Accounting and Business Research* (Summer, 1980), pp. 291-7.

Ma, Ronald, and Miller, Malcolm C., "Conceptualizing the Liability," *Accounting and Business Research* (Autumn, 1978), pp. 258–65.

Miller, Malcolm C. and Islam, A. Atiqul, *The Definition and Recognition of Assets* (Gaufield, Vic.: Australian Accounting Research Foundation, 1988) pp. 34–6.

Moonitz, Maurice, "The Changing Concept of Liabilities," *Journal of Accountancy* (May, 1960), pp. 41–6.

Sprouse, Robert T., "Balance Sheet-Embodiment of the Most Fundamental Elements of Accounting Theory," in *Foundations of Accounting Theory*, Willard E. Stone (ed.) (University of Florida Press), pp. 90–104.

Staubus, George J., "Measurement of Assets and Liabilities," *Accounting and Business Research* (Autumn, 1973), pp. 243–62.

Sterling, Robert R. (ed.) *Asset Valuation and Income Determination* (Scholars Book Company, 1971).

Walker, Robert G., "Asset Classification and Asset Valuation," *Accounting and Business Research* (Autumn, 1974), pp. 286–96.

Warrell, C.J., "The Enterprise Value Concept of Asset Valuations," *Accounting and Business Research* (Summer, 1974), pp. 220–6.

Weil, Roman L., "Role of Time Value of Money in Financial Reporting," *Accounting Horizons* (December, 1990), pp. 47–67.

Measurement of Specific Assets and Liabilities

Anthony, Robert N., *Accounting for the Cost of Interest* (Lexington Books, 1975).

Barden, Horace G., Accounting Research Study No. 13, *The Accounting Basis of Inventories* (AICPA, 1973).

Beidelman, Carl R., Accounting Research Study No. 7, *Valuation of Used Capital Assets* (American Accounting Association, 1973).

Chasteen, Lanny G., "Economic Circumstances and Inventory Method Selection," *Abacus* (June, 1973) pp. 22–7.

Clancy, Donald K., "What is a Convertible Debenture? A Review of the Literature in the USA," *Abacus* (December, 1978), pp. 171–9.

O'Connor, Melvin C., and Hamre, James C., "Alternative Methods of Accounting for Long-Term Nonsubsidiary Intercorporate Investments in Common Stock," *The Accounting Review* (April, 1972), pp. 308–19.

Sterling, Robert R., *An Essay on Recognition* (Accounting Research Center, The University of Sydney, 1985).

Measurement of Owner's Equity

American Accounting Association, "The Entity Concept — Report of the 1964 Concepts and Standards Research Committee," *The Accounting Review* (April, 1965), pp. 358–69.

Birnberg, Jacob G., "An Information-Oriented Approach to the Presentation of Common Shareholders' Equity," *The Accounting Review* (October, 1964), pp. 963–71.

Manning, B., *A Concise Textbook on Legal Capital*, Second Edition (Mineola, N.Y.: Foundation Press, 1981).

Melcher, Beatrice, Accounting Research Study No. 15, *Stockholders' Equity* (AICPA, 1973).

Roberts, Michael, Samson, William D., and Dugan, Michael T., "The Shareholders' Equity Section: Form Without Substance," *Accounting Horizons* (December, 1990), pp. 37–8.

Scott, Richard A., "Owners' Equity, the Anachronistic Element," *The Accounting Review* (October, 1979), pp. 750–63.

Smith, Ralph E., and Imdieke, Leroy F., "Accounting for Stock Issued to Employees," *Journal of Accountancy* (November, 1974), pp. 68–75.

QUESTIONS

13.1 Describe the recognition and measurement of assets.

13.2 Describe the recognition and measurement of liabilities.

13.3 Discuss the equity account.

13.4 Elaborate on the problems related to financial instruments and off-balance sheet transactions.

13.5 Capitalization and Depreciation

At the beginning of the year, Patrick Company acquired a computer to be used in its operations. The computer was delivered by the supplier, installed by Patrick, and placed into operation. The estimated useful life of the computer is five years, and its estimated residual (salvage) value is significant.

During the year, Patrick received cash in exchange for an automobile that was purchased in a prior year.

Required

1 a. What costs should Patrick capitalize for the computer?
 b. What is the objective of depreciation accounting? (Do not discuss specific methods of depreciation.)
2 What is the rationale for using accelerated depreciation methods?
3 How should Patrick account for and report the disposal of the automobile?

(AICPA adapted)

13.6 Revenue and Capital Expenditures

Property, plant, and equipment (plant assets) generally represent a material portion of the total assets of most companies. Accounting for the acquisition and usage of such assets is, therefore, an important part of the financial reporting process.

Required

1 Distinguish between revenue and capital expenditures and explain why this distinction is important.
2 Briefly define depreciation as used in accounting.

3 Identify the factors that are relevant in determining the annual depreciation and explain whether these factors are determined objectively or whether they are based on judgment.

4 Explain why depreciation is usually shown in the net cash flow from operating activities section of the statement of cash flows. (*AICPA adapted*)

13.7 Depreciation Concepts

Depreciation continues to be one of the most controversial, difficult, and important problem areas in accounting.

Required

1 a. Explain the conventional accounting concept of depreciation accounting, and

   b. Discuss its conceptual merit with respect to (1) the value of the asset, (2) the charge(s) to expense, and (3) the discretion of management in selecting the method.

2 a. Explain the factors that should be considered when applying the conventional concept of depreciation to the determination of how the value of a newly acquired computer system should be assigned to expense for financial reporting purposes. (Income tax considerations should be ignored for this case.)

   b. What depreciation methods might be used for the computer system?

(*AICPA adapted*)

13.8 Research and Development Costs

The Gratwick Company is in the process of developing a revolutionary new product. A new division of the company was formed to develop, manufacture, and market this new product. As of year-end (December 31, 1991) the new product has not been manufactured for resale; however, a prototype unit was built and is in operation.

Throughout 1992 the new division incurred certain costs. These costs include design and engineering studies, prototype manufacturing costs, administrative expenses (including salaries of administrative personnel), and market research costs. In addition, approximately $500,000 in equipment (estimated useful life, 10 years) was purchased for use in developing and manufacturing the new product. Approximately $200,000 of this equipment was built specifically for the design and development of the new product; the remaining $300,000 of equipment was used to manufacture the preproduction prototype and will be used to manufacture the new product once it is in commercial production.

Required

1 What is the definition of *research* and of *development* as defined in FASB Statement No. 2?

2 Briefly indicate the practical and conceptual reasons for the conclusion reached by the FASB on accounting practices for research and development costs.

3 In accordance with FASB Statement No. 2, how should the various costs of Gratwick described be recorded in the financial statements for the year ended December 31, 1992? (*AICPA adapted*)

13.9 Goodwill

Elson Corporation, a retail fuel oil distributor, has increased its annual sales volume to a level three times greater than the annual sales of a dealer it purchased in 1988 in order to begin operations.

The board of directors recently received an offer to negotiate the sale of Elson Corporation to a large competitor. As a result the majority of the board wants to increase the stated value of goodwill on the balance sheet to reflect the larger sales volume developed through intensive promotion and the current market price of sales gallonage. A few of the board members, however, would prefer to eliminate goodwill altogether from the balance sheet in order to prevent "possible misinterpretations." Goodwill was recorded properly in 1988.

Required

1. Discuss the meaning of the term *goodwill*.
2. List the techniques used to calculate the tentative value of goodwill in negotiations to purchase a going concern.
3. Why are the book and market values of the goodwill of Elson Corporation different?
4. Discuss the propriety of (a) increasing the stated value of goodwill prior to the negotiations and (b) eliminating goodwill completely from the balance sheet prior to negotiations.   (*AICPA adapted*)

13.10 Goodwill

After extended negotiations Rothman Corporation bought from Felzar Company most of the latter's assets on June 30, 1992. At the time of the sale Felzar's accounts (adjusted to June 30, 1992) reflected the following descriptions and amounts for the assets transferred:

	Cost	Contra (Valuation) Account	Book Value
Receivables	$ 83,600	$ 3,000	$ 80,600
Inventory	107,000	5,200	101,800
Land	20,000	—	20,000
Buildings	207,500	73,000	134,500
Fixtures and equipment	205,000	41,700	163,300
Goodwill	50,000	—	50,000
	$673,100	$122,900	$550,200

You ascertain that the contra (valuation) accounts were allowance for doubtful accounts, allowance to reduce inventory to market, and accumulated depreciation. During the extended negotiations Felzar held out for a consideration of approximately $600,000 (depending on the level of the receivables and inventory). As of

June 30, 1992, however, Felzar agreed to accept Rothman's offer of $450,000 cash plus 1% of the net sales (as defined in the contract) of the next 5 years with payments at the end of each year. Felzar expects that Rothman's total net sales during this period will exceed $15 million.

Required

1 How should Rothman Corporation record this transaction? Explain.
2 Discuss the propriety of recording goodwill in the accounts of Rothman Corporation for this transaction.   (*AICPA adapted*)

13.11 Various Liability Issues

Angela Company is a manufacturer of toys. During the year, the following situations arose:

a. A safety hazard related to one of its toy products was discovered. It is considered probable that liabilities have been incurred. Based on past experience, a reasonable estimate of the amount of loss can be made.

b. One of its small warehouses is located on the bank of a river and could no longer be insured against flood losses. No flood losses have occurred after the date that the insurance became unavailable.

c. This year, Angela began promoting a new toy by including a coupon, redeemable for a movie ticket, in each toy's carton. The movie ticket, which cost Angela $2, is purchased in advance and then mailed to the customer when the coupon is received by Angela. Angela estimated, based on past experience, that 60% of the coupons would be redeemed. Forty percent of the coupons were actually redeemed this year, and the remaining 20% of the coupons are expected to be redeemed next year.

Required

1 How should Angela report the safety hazard? Why? Do not discuss deferred income tax implications.
2 How should Angela report the noninsurable flood risk? Why?
3 How should Angela account for the toy promotion campaign in this year?
                                                                      (*AICPA adapted*)

13.12 Loss Contingencies

Part a. The two basic requirements for the accrual of a loss contingency are supported by several basic concepts of accounting. Three of these concepts are: periodicity (time periods), measurement, and objectivity.

Required

Discuss how the two basic requirements for the accrual of a loss contingency relate to the three concepts listed previously.

Part b. The following three independent sets of facts relate to (1) the possible accrual of (2) the possible disclosure by other means of a loss contingency.

Situation I

A company offers a one-year warranty for the product that it manufactures. A history of warranty claims has been compiled and the probable amount of claims related to sales for a given period can be determined.

Situation II

Subsequent to the date of a set of financial statements, but prior to the issuance of the financial statements, a company enters into a contract that will probably result in a significant loss to the company. The amount of the loss can be reasonably estimated.

Situation III

A company has adopted a policy of recording self-insurance for any possible losses resulting from injury to others by the company's vehicles. The premium for an insurance policy for the same risk from an independent insurance company would have an annual cost of $2,000. During the period covered by the financial statements, there were no accidents involving the company's vehicles that resulted in injury to others.

Required

Discuss the accrual and/or type of disclosure necessary (if any) and the reason(s) why such disclosure is appropriate for each of the three independent sets of facts in the situations described here. Complete your response to each situation before proceeding to the next situation.   (*AICPA adapted*)

13.13 Various Contingency Issues

Skinner Company has the following contingencies:

1 Potential costs due to the discovery of a possible defect related to one of its products. These costs are probable and can be reasonably estimated.

2 A potential claim for damages to be received from a lawsuit filed this year against another company. It is probable that proceeds from the claim will be received by Skinner next year.

3 Potential costs due to a promotion campaign whereby a cash refund is sent to customers when coupons are redeemed. Skinner estimated, based on past experience, that 70 percent of the coupons would be redeemed. Forty percent of the coupons were actually redeemed and the cash refunds sent this year. The remaining 30 percent of the coupons are expected to be redeemed next year.

Required

1 How should Skinner report the potential costs due to the discovery of a possible product defect? Why?

2 How should Skinner report this year the potential claim for damages that may be received next year? Why?

This year, how should Skinner account for the potential costs and obligations due to the promotion campaign?   (*AICPA adapted*)

13.14 Contingency Conditions and Disclosure

Loss contingencies may exist for companies.

Required

1. What conditions should be met for an estimated loss from a loss contingency to be accrued by a charge to income?
2. When is disclosure required, and what disclosure should be made for an estimated loss from a loss contingency that need not be accrued by a charge to income?   (*AICPA adapted*)

13.15 Marketable Equity Securities

The following are four *unrelated* situations involving marketable equity securities:

Situation I

A noncurrent portfolio with an aggregate market value in excess of cost includes one particular security whose market value has declined to less than one-half of the original cost. The decline in value is considered to be other than temporary.

Situation II

The statement of financial position of a company does not classify assets and liabilities as current and noncurrent. The portfolio of marketable equity securities includes securities normally considered current that have a net cost in excess of market value of $2,000. The remainder of the portfolio has a net market value in excess of cost of $5,000.

Situation III

A marketable equity security, whose market value is currently less than cost, is classified as noncurrent but is to be reclassified as current.

Situation IV

A company's noncurrent portfolio of marketable equity securities consists of the common stock of one company. At the end of the prior year the market value of the security was 50% of original cost, and the effect was properly reflected in a valuation allowance account. However, at the end of the current year the market value of the security had appreciated to twice the original cost. The security is still considered noncurrent at year-end.

Required

What is the effect upon classification, carrying value, and earnings for each of the preceding situations?   (*AICPA adapted*)

13.16 Definitions
In dealing with the various equity securities of a corporate entity it is important to understand certain related terminology.

Required

Define the following terms:
1 Treasury stock
2 Legal capital
3 Stock right
4 Stock warrant   (*AICPA adapted*)

13.17 Categories of Capital
A corporation's capital (stockholders' equity) is a very important part of its statement of financial position.

Required

Identify and discuss the general categories of capital (stockholders' equity) for a corporation. Be sure to enumerate specific sources included in each category.
(*AICPA adapted*)

CHAPTER 14

THE STATEMENT OF CASH FLOWS

14.1   INTRODUCTION

The balance sheet reflects the financial structure of the firm at a point in time. The profit and loss statement reflects the financial performance of a firm over a period of time. What is missing is a statement reflecting the financial conduct of the firm in managing the funds available. The concern gave rise to various calls and pronouncements for some form of funds statement, resulting in the mandatory disclosure of a statement of cash flows. This new statement provides a view of the financial conduct of the firm and is a step toward a form of cash flow accounting. Accordingly, this chapter explores both the nature of the statement of cash flows and the nature of cash flow accounting.

14.2   THE STATEMENT OF CASH FLOWS

14.2.1   Historical Development

The first recommendation of the funds statement as an important component of the annual reports was made by Perry Mason in Accounting Research Study No. 2.[1] Following Mason's recommendation, the APB issued APB Opinion No. 3 that recommended that a statement of source and application of funds be presented as supplementary information in financial reports.[2] An all-financial resources concept of fund was suggested to be used in this statement, so that "the statement will include the financial aspects of all significant transactions, e.g., 'non-fund' transactions such as the acquisition of property through the issue of securities."[3] The reaction to the issuing of Opinion No. 3 was favorable, as evidenced by a) the combined endorsement of the New York Stock Exchange and the Directors of the Financial Analysts Federation, b) the inclusion of a funds statement in the annual reports of many US companies between 1964 and 1971, and c) a 1970 SEC requirement that an audited funds statement be included in the annual reports filed with the Commission. That was a signal strong enough to make the AICPA act, publishing in 1971 APB Opinion No. 19, *Reporting Changes in Financial Position*.[41] It required that a "Statement of Changes in Financial Position" be presented for each period for which an income statement is included in the annual reports. An all-resources concept of funds was suggested in order to include interfirm transactions not affecting working capital, such as the acquisition of long-term assets through the issuance of securities. The Opinion called for flexibility in form, content, and terminology, leading to a variety of applications and a total lack of comparability across companies. This total flexibility was not without its benefits, however, as it generated discussions and debates, as well as applications of a concept of funds as cash flows. This movement and support for a concept of cash flow resulted ultimately in official endorsement. In 1987, the FASB issued its Statement No. 95, *Statement of Cash Flows*, requiring that companies present a statement of cash flows for the accounting period, along with an income statement and balance sheet.[5]

14.2.2 Concepts of Funds Flow

From the historical perspective, it is apparent that the concept of funds flow has been changing over time. The alternatives used included a) short-term monetary asset flows, b) net monetary asset flows, c) working capital concept of funds, d) all financial resources concept of funds, and e) cash. Each is examined below:

1 A first concept of funds used is the short-term monetary assets, hence representing resources easily convertible into cash.

2 A second concept of funds used is the net monetary asset flows obtained by deducting short-term obligations from the current monetary assets. It is different from the first concept by considering both the net constructive inflows and outflows of cash.

3 A third concept of funds used is the working capital concept of funds. It differs from the net monetary asset flows concept by including nonmonetary assets such as inventories and prepaid expenses, and some nonmonetary liabilities such as advance receipts for services not yet performed.

4 The fourth concept of funds used is the all-financial resources concept of funds. It differs from the working capital concept of funds by disclosing the effects of all significant interfirm transactions.

5 The fifth concept of funds, adopted by FASB Statement No. 95, is cash. It is generally defined to include cash in hand or on-demand deposits, plus cash equivalents.

14.2.3   Cash Flows and the Conceptual Framework

The conceptual framework has taken a definite position in favor of the production and disclosure of cash flow information. The position starts with a definition of the needs of potential users. Investors, lenders, suppliers, and employees are assumed to perceive the business enterprise as a source of cash in the form of dividends or interests, appreciated market prices, repayment of borrowing, payments for goods and services, or salaries or wages.[6] It follows that general purpose external financial reporting which is to be directed towards the common interest of all these potential users will focus on the ability of firms to generate favorable cash flows. More specifically, in its Statement of Financial Accounting Concepts No. 1, the FASB stated that:

> Financial reporting should provide information about how an enterprise obtains and spends cash, about borrowing and repayment of borrowing, about its capital trans-actions, including cash dividends and other distributions of enterprise resources to owners, and about other factors that may affect an enterprise's liquidity or solvency ... information about cash flows or other funds flows may be useful in understanding the operations of an enterprise, evaluating its financing activities, assessing its liquidity or solvency, or interpreting earnings information provided.[7]

This statement is the best signal that the FASB was going ultimately to make the move to a cash flow statement and to its Statement No. 95. The FASB's move is also evident in their belief that

> [the] market's assessment of an enterprise's expected success in generating favorable cash flows affects the relative market prices of its securities although the level of market prices of its securities is affected by numerous factors — such as general economic conditions, interest rates, market psychology, and the like — that are not related to particular enterprises.[8]

It is also interesting that in SFAC 5, the FASB makes the following favorable assessments of a statement of cash flow:

> It provides useful information about an entity's activities in generating cash through operations to repay debt, distribute dividends, or reinvest to maintain or expand operating capacity; about its financing activities, both debt and equity; and about its investing or spending of cash. Important uses of information about an entity's current cash receipts and payments include helping to assess factors such as the entity's liquidity, financial flexibility, profitability, and risk.[9]

This is further reinforced in Statement No. 95 itself, as follows:

> The information provided in a statement of cash flows, if used with related disclosures and information in the other financial statements, should help investors, creditors, and others to (a) assess the enterprise's ability to generate positive future net cash flows; (b) assess the enterprise's ability to meet its obligations, its ability to pay dividends, and its needs for external financing; (c) assess the reasons for differences between net income and associated cash receipts and payments; and (d) assess the effects on an enterprise's financial position of both its cash and noncash investing and financing transactions during the period.[10]

14.2.4 Nature of the Cash Flow Statement

The statement of cash flows is intended to provide information on the change during an accounting period in cash and cash equivalents that can be useful in evaluating the firm's liquidity, financial flexibility, operating capability and risk. By cash equivalents is meant the short-term, highly liquid investments that are both a) readily convertible to known amount of cash and b) so near their maturity that they present insignificant risk of changes in value because of changes in the interest rate.[11] The statement of cash flows classifies the cash inflows and cash outflows as resulting from investing, financing or operating activities. This follows from the FASB's argument that analysis by external users to predict the amount, timing, and uncertainty of future cash flows requires financial information to be segregated into reasonably homogeneous groups.[12] As a result, the statement of cash flows must clearly show:

1 Net cash flow from operating activities.
2 Cash flows from investing activities.
3 Cash flows from financing activities.
4 The net increase or decrease in cash.
5 A reconciliation of the beginning cash balance to the ending cash balance.
6 A supplemental schedule of noncash investing and financing activities.

The statement of cash flows can be prepared using either the direct or indirect method. Under the direct method, the operating cash flows are deducted from the operating cash inflows resulting in the net cash flow from operating activities. Under the indirect method, net income is adjusted for differences between income flows and cash flows for operating activities to determine the net cash provided be operating activities. FASB Statement No. 95 requires, however, that the reconciliation of net income to net cash flow from operating activities be provided regardless of whether the direct or indirect method of reporting net cash flow from operating activities is used. An example of the suggested format is illustrated in Exhibit 14.1.

EXHIBIT 14.1

Illustration of the Cash Flow Statement

Presented below is a statement of cash flows for the year ended December 31, 19X1 for Company M, a US corporation engaged principally in manufacturing activities. This statement of cash flows illustrates the direct method of presenting cash flows from operating activities, as encouraged in paragraph 27 of this Statement.

COMPANY M
CONSOLIDATED STATEMENT OF CASH FLOWS
FOR THE YEAR ENDED DECEMBER 31, 19X1
Increase (Decrease) in Cash and Cash Equivalents

Cash flow from operating activities:	
Cash received from customers	$13,850
Cash paid to suppliers and employees	(12,000)
Dividend received from affiliate	20
Interest received	55

Interest paid (net of amount capitalized)	(220)	
Income taxes paid	(325)	
Insurance proceeds received	15	
Cash paid to settle lawsuit for patent infringement	(30)	
Net cash provided by operating activities		$1,365

Cash flows from investing activities:

Proceeds from sale of facility	600	
Payment received on note for sale of plant	150	
Capital expenditures	(1,000)	
Payment for purchase of Company S, net of cash acquired	(925)	
Net cash used in investing activities		(1,175)

Cash flows from financing activities:

Net borrowings under line-or-credit agreement	300	
Principal payments under capital lease obligation	(125)	
Proceeds from issuance of long-term debt	400	
Proceeds from issuance of common stock	(200)	
Net cash provided by financing activities		875
Net increase in cash and cash equivalents		1,065
Cash and cash equivalents at beginning of year		600
Cash and cash equivalents at end of year		$1,665

Reconciliation of net income to net cash provided by operating activities:

Net income		$ 760
Adjustments to reconcile net income net cash provided by operating activities:		
Depreciation and amortization	$ 445	
Provision for losses on accounts receivable	200	
Gain on sale of facility	(80)	
Undistributed earnings of affiliate	(25)	
Payment received on installment note receivable for sale of inventory	100	
Change in assets and liabilities net of effects from purchase of Company S:		
Increase in accounts receivable	(215)	
Decrease in inventory	205	
Increase in prepaid expenses	(25)	
Decrease in accounts payable and accrued expenses	(250)	
Increase in interest and income taxes payable	50	
Increase in deferred taxes	150	
Increase in other liabilities	50	
Total adjustments		605
Net cash provided by operating activities		$1,365

Supplemental schedule of noncash investing and financing activities:

The Company purchased all of the capital stock of Company S for $950. In conjunction with the acquisition, liabilities were assumed as follows:

Fair value of assets acquired	$1,580
Cash paid for the capital stock	(950)
Liabilities assumed	$ 630

A capital lease obligation of $850 was incurred when the Company entered into a lease for new equipment.

Additional common stock was issued upon the conversion of $500 of long-term debt.

Disclosure of accounting policy:

For purposes of the statement of cash flows, the Company considers all highly liquid debt instruments purchased with a maturity of three months or less to be cash equivalents.

Source: Financial Accounting Standards Board, Statement of Financial Accounting Standards No. 95, *Statement of Cash Flows* (Stamford, Ct.: FASB, 1987). Reprinted with permission.

14.3   NATURE OF CASH-FLOW ACCOUNTING

14.3.1   The Problems with Accrual Accounting

The call for cash-flow accounting does not originate solely from the academic world. A good example is the following statement, made in 1982 by a commissioner of the Securities and Exchange Commission:

> Over time, the accounting equation requires, of course, that accrual earnings equal cash earnings, but in the short term timing variations between accruals and cash flows may be quite significant; they may even make the crucial difference between continuing operations and bankruptcy. In other words, although accrual accounting, with its matching of revenues and expenses, may be important to the analysis of long-term profitability, cash flow is vital to survival.[13]

The most serious interest in cash-flow accounting was created by the limitations of accrual accounting. The advocates of cash-flow accounting questioned the importance and efficiency of accrual accounting, and identified a shift to the cash-flow approach in security analysis.[14] The efficacy of the accrual system was severely questioned in general as well. A.L. Thomas stated explicitly that all allocations, which are the basis of accrual accounting, are arbitrary and incorrigible.[15]

To be precise about allocation, Thomas defined it as follows:

1 The assignment of costs, revenues, income, cash flows, or funds flows to individual inputs or groups of inputs to the firm, including assignment to individual periods of time, divisions of the firm, etc.

2 The division of any total into parts.

3 The assignment of costs to revenues, called matching.[16]

Thomas claimed that many of the allocations used in conventional accounting are arbitrary and theoretically unjustified, in that they are unable to meet the following criteria:

1 *Additivity:* the whole should equal the parts; the allocation should exhaust the total, dividing up whatever there is: no more and no less.

2 *Unambiguity:* once the allocation method has been specified, it should be impossible to divide the total into more than one set of parts.

3 *Defensibility:* any choice among allocation methods should have a conclusive argument backing it, defending the methods against all possible alternatives.[17]

Thomas then concluded that no legitimate purpose for financial accounting that has been advanced to date is furthered by making allocations, urging that financial accounting allocations should cease.[18]

Amounts reported on income statements are allocations of input cost to the expenses of individual years, and most of what appears in the nonmonetary portions of the balance sheet are the cumulative result of allocation. Three kinds of conventional allocations are distinguished: (1) annual contribution, (2) input contribution, and (3) annual profit (annual rate of return). The matching allocation of individual input costs to individual years (allocation methods 1 and 2) can result in the amount assigned to any specified year varying anywhere between zero and the total cost itself. It is also easy to prove that the annual profit allocation (method 3) is ambiguous, because any such allocation requires making an assumption about the imput's book rate of return during each year.

All these problems arise because revenues are joint outputs of all inputs. Conventional matching attempts to associate joint revenue with cost. Actually, both joint revenue and all kinds of financial allocation have an identical form. In each case the fallacies of allocation are also identical.

Finally, Thomas concluded that we should forswear "matching fantasies," stop allocating, and prepare allocation-free financial statements. He recommended three possible kinds of such allocation-free statements:

1 Current exit value reporting.

2 Current entry value reporting.

3 Net quick asset reporting or cash-flow accounting.

The principles Thomas proposed for the preparation of allocation-free "cash-flow" financial (funds) statements are as follows:

1 The category of funds should be net quick assets, i.e., total cash, receivables, and any other current monetary assets less current monetary liabilities.

2 A statement of current activities (a combination of conventional income and fund statements) should be prepared. It would begin with a detailed calculation of funds from operations and would make whatever distinction between ordinary and extraordinary items was appropriate. This would be followed by a report of purchases of nonmonetary assets, less proceeds from nonoperating sales of such assets, leading to a figure for funds from operations less funds consequent to transactions in nonmonetary assets. The latter figure corresponds to conventional net income. Comparative funds statements would be disclosed.

3 The subtotal for funds from operations less funds consequent to transactions in nonmonetary assets would be followed by the dividend and other data which customarily appear on a funds statement.

4 The conventional balance sheet would be replaced by (a) a statement of monetary assets and liabilities, and (b) a statement of unamortized magnitudes of all nonmonetary assets presently in service.

5 There would be minor departures from conventional income statement and balance sheet reporting, consistent with the use of funds statements. For example, tax allocation would cease.

6 Insofar as possible, a rigorous orientation of inflow and outflow of net quick assets would be preserved throughout the reports; they would not be attempts to match or otherwise allocate.

7 Introduction of the new-style reports should require a lengthy transition period during which the old (accrual) reports continued to be prepared.

14.3.2   The Meaning of Cash-Flow Accounting

Thomas's call was heard, because the Study Group established by the American Institute of Certified Public Accountants stated in its report published in 1973: "An objective of financial statements is to provide information useful to investors and creditors for predicting, comparing, and evaluating potential cash flow to them in terms of amount, timing, and related uncertainty."[19] Thomas A. Lee also identified three common needs of the users of accounting information:

1 Each group is concerned with how well the company has survived in the past and how well it is likely to survive in the future.

2 Each group is concerned with making and monitoring decisions. Each of these decisions has financial consequences, and suitable information is needed to aid the decision makers.

3 There are common features to be found, the main one being that each group is concerned with the most basic resource in business — cash.[20]

These needs were to be met by cash-flow accounting. Although there are various definitions of cash-flow accounting, the best definition needs to differentiate it from other forms of accounting, namely, (a) the cash basis of accounting, (b) the accrual basis of accounting, and (c) the allocation basis of accounting. Barry E. Hicks provides a good definition of each as follows:

- The cash basis of accounting means reflecting only transactions involving actual cash receipts and disbursement occurring in *a given period* with no attempt to record unpaid bills (or amounts) owed to or by the entity.
- The accrual basis of accounting means keeping records, so that in addition to recording transactions resulting from the receipt and disbursements of cash, the firm also records the amount it owes others and others owe it.
- The cash-flow basis of accounting means recording not only the cash receipts and disbursements of the period (the cash basis of accounting), but also the future cash flows owed to or by the firm as a result of selling and transferring title to certain goods.

- The allocation basis of accounting not only does all that the cash-flow basis of accounting does, but it goes beyond, and subjects these cash flows to an allocation process. The allocation basis of accounting means: (a) taking the "real" cash flows and dividing them into parts until the parts no longer represent "real" cash flows, or (b) assigning the real cash flows or parts thereof to some period(s) other than the one in which they actually occur.[21]

14.3.3   Cash-Flow Accounting Systems

Various cash-flow accounting proposals have been made, as evidenced by a survey of articles by Lee.[22] Most of these systems share to a certain extent the same components and the same general philosophy. These major elements include the following:

N = Net cash inflow or outflow from operations
R = Replacement investment
G = Growth investment
RG = $R + G$ = Total cash investment
T = Cash payments for taxation
D = Cash payments for dividends
I = Loan interest payments
E = New equity receipts
B = Borrowing
C = Residual change in cash resources of the period (usually cash and bank balances and deposits, but could include some near-cash items such as accounts receivable if these credit transactions are included with cash transactions).[23]

Using the above components the cash-flow system proposed by G.H. Lawson[24] would appear along the lines of:

$$N - R - G - T - I + E + B - C = D$$

The Lawson system focuses on the determination of D, the disposable income or net surplus the firm can generate from its trading and productive (or service) activity. In addition, it makes a distinction between replacement and growth investment.

Using the same components, the cash-flow system proposed by Lee[25] would appear along the lines of:

$$N - [R + G] - T - I - D + E + B = C$$

which focuses on the cash residual, or

$$N - [R + G] - T - I - D = F$$

where $F = C - E - B$, which focuses on F, the residual financing charge during the period.[26] If the firm's transactions were financed internally, F would be positive; if it were financed out of cash balances and/or external sources, F would be negative.

Under both systems N could be expanded along these lines:

$$N = S - M - W = O$$

where
   S = Cash sales
   M = Cash payments for goods and services for resale
   W = Wage payments
   O = Overhead cash payments
Another refinement would be to dichotomize T, to distinguish foreign from nonforeign transactions.

Other variations on the above two proposals include approaches which would report both past and forecast cash flows.[27]

Yuji Ijiri makes the point for past and forecast cash-flow disclosure as follows:

> Of course, if forecasted future cash flows can be obtained, they will certainly provide a useful supplement to a statement of past cash flows. The two should be clearly separated so as not to mix hard figures and soft figures. The two statements on cash flows, one on past, the other on forecast, can provide a complete picture of what has happened and what is expected to happen in the future under the best estimate available now, all based on cash flows. Forecasts can then be checked with actual performance as time passes, as mentioned earlier. A reliability indicator may be prepared based on past discrepancy between forecast and actual. I think that this is a better approach than trying to capture the financial status of a company at one point in time in terms of a still picture of all of its assets and liabilities based on their current cost or current value. The latter covers all noncash assets, but is static. The cash flow approach concentrates on cash flows only, but is dynamic in the sense that its focus extends over time and is most realistic since the statements are based on what has happened and what is expected to happen.[28]

Another proposal made would link C (the residual change in cash resources) to a statement of changes in net realizable value of resources, thereby transforming a simple cash-flow system to one including a profit figure. The combination of cash-flow and net-realizable-value accounting is the subject of the proposal. It would be accomplished by the mere segregation of net-realizable-value accounting data into realized cash flows, as in cash-flow accounting, and unrealized cash flows, as in net-realizable-value accounting.

14.3.4   Evaluation of Cash-Flow Accounting

Like any accounting system, cash-flow accounting has its supporters and detractors. It has generated a debate in the profession and in research which has finally resulted in some of the standard setters paying attention to the concept.

The advantages attributed to cash-flow accounting are numerous. They include the following:

1 Cash-flow accounting would rely on the price/discounted flow ratio as a more reliable investment indicator than the present price/earnings ratio, because of the arbitrary allocations used to compute the present accrual earnings per share figure and the international differences in the computation of earnings per share.

2 As stated earlier, cash-flow accounting may be allocation-free.

3 Cash-flow accounting retains money as the unit of measurement, which is familiar and not confusing to people.

4 Cash-flow accounting, when expanded to include projected cash flows, may help the investor to assess the ability of the firm to pay its way in the future and also its planned financial policy.

5 If the investor's interest is in the survival of the firm, together with the ability to provide a stream of dividend, then cash-flow accounting will prove more useful by providing accounting information about the current and anticipated cash positions of the firm. Liquidity assessment is a critical aspect of performance evaluation in the sense that cash flow and net profit are the end result of a firm's activities.[29]

6 Cash flow does not require price level adjustments, because cash transactions reflect prices of the period in which they occur. It is, however, appropriate to note that some general price level adjustment is needed for cash plans occurring in different periods.

7 Cash-flow information fits as an important variable in the decision models of various users because of the concerns associated with the firm's ability to pay dividends to investors, interest and capital to lenders and bankers, amounts due to suppliers, wages and other benefits to employees, rectification and maintenance services for customers, and taxation to governments.[30]

8 Cash-flow information is argued to be more objective and relevant than accrual-based information. According to Lee,
First, in its historic form, it is perhaps the most objective information possible, avoiding most of the subjectiveness which enters into the technical adjustments involved in the traditional accrual accounting; it is the most relevant information for purposes of comparison with forecast information should this be measured on a cash basis. Second, forecast cash flows, although involving a great deal of uncertainty (however, no more so than budgeted profits on the accrual basis), clearly avoid the necessary subjectiveness of accrual judgments and opinions. Therefore, they appear to be far less subjective in a *total* sense than profit forecasts.[31]

9 There is the suspicion that the popularity of the all-embracing measures of performance such as profit may well have caused firms to underestimate the importance of performance measures such as market domination, productivity, and quality of products and services.[32]

10 Cash-flow accounting is the ideal system to correct the gaps in practice between the way in which an investment is made (generally based on cash flows) and the ways the results are evaluated (generally based on earnings).

Naturally, those opposed to cash-flow accounting question each of the above advantages, which leaves the debate at the hand of the researchers.

14.4   CONCLUSIONS

Cash-flow accounting is emerging internationally as a subject of research and interest to academics, practitioners, and/or standard setters. Although its alleged benefits, its impact on users' reactions, and its predictive ability are in need of more empirical evidence, its implementation seems to be gaining favor with the standard setters, who express fervent interest in its implementation. Cash-flow accounting has always been with us. It lost credibility for a while to the advantage of accrual accounting. Now it is making an international return. The return of cash-flow accounting to its well-deserved place of importance is best stated by Lee as follows:

> Cash-flow accounting and reporting has a long and honorable history in the develop-ment of business enterprises. It was superseded by the sophisticated statements of allocated data which are by now such a familiar part of financial reporting practice. Perhaps, with liquidity such a vital issue in business today, the wheel will turn full circle, and cash flow accounting will again be restored to its rightful place as a useful and relevant source of financial information about business enterprises for a variety of report users.[33]

NOTES

[1] Mason, Perry, Accounting Research Study No. 2, *"Cash Flow" Analysis and the Funds Statement* (New York: AICPA, 1961).

[2] Accounting Principles Board, APB Opinion No. 3, *The Statement of Source and Application of Funds* (New York: AICPA, 1963).

[3] Ibid., para. 9.

[4] Accounting Principles Board, APB Opinion No. 9, *Reporting Changes in Financial Position* (New York: AICPA, 1971).

[5] Financial Accounting Standards Board, Statement of Financial Accounting Standards No. 95, *Statement of Cash Flows* (Stamford, Ct.: FASB, 1987).

[6] Financial Accounting Standards Board, Statement of Financial Accounting Concepts No. 1, *Objectives of Financial Reporting by Business Enterprises* (Stamford, Ct.: FASB, 1978), para. 25.

[7] Ibid., para. 49.

[8] Ibid., para. 37.

[9] Financial Accounting Standards Board, Statement of Financial Accounting Concepts No. 5, *Recognition and Measurement in Financial Statements of Business Enterprises* (Stamford, Ct.: FASB, 1984), para. 52.

[10] Financial Accounting Standards Board, *Statement of Cash Flows*, op. cit., p. 5.

[11] Ibid., p. 7.

[12] FASB, *Recognition and Measurement in Financial Statements of Business Enterprises*, op. cit., p. 20.

[13] Thomas, Barbara S., "Reporting Cash Flow Information," *Journal of Accounting* (November, 1982), p. 99.

[14] Hawkins, D., and Campbell, W., *Equity Valuation: Models, Analysis and Implications* (New York: Financial Executives Institute, 1978).

[15] Thomas, A.L., Studies in Accounting Research No. 3, *The Allocation Problem in Financial Accounting Theory* (Sarasota, Fla.: American Accounting Association, 1969); Thomas, A.L., Studies in Accounting Research No. 9, *The Allocation Problem, Part Two* (Sarasota Fla.: American Accounting Association, 1974).

[16] Thomas, A.L., *The Allocation Problem in Financial Accounting Theory*, op. cit., p. 25.

[17] Ibid., p. 30.

[18] Ibid., p. 42.

[19] American Institute of Certified Public Accountants, Study Group on the Objectives of Financial Statements, *Objectives of Financial Statements* (New York: American Institute of Certified Public Accountants, 1973), p. 16.

[20] Lee, T.A., "The Simplicity and Complexity of Accounting," in *Accounting for a Simplified Firm Owning Depreciable Assets*, (eds) R.R. Sterling and A.L. Thomas (Lawrence, Kans.: Scholars Book Co., 1979), p. 4.

[21] Hicks, Barry E., "The Cash Flow Basis of Accounting," in *Cash Flow Accounting*, (eds) Barry E. Hicks and Pearson Hunt (Sudbury, Ontario: School of Commerce and Administration, 1981), p. 30.

[22] Lee, Thomas E., "Cash Flow Accounting and Reporting," in *Essays in British Accounting Research*, (eds) M. Bromwich and A. Hopwood (London: Pitman, 1981), pp. 63–78.

[23] The potential inclusion of near cash items is raised in Lee, Thomas A., "Cash Flow Accounting and Reporting," in *Developments in Financial Reporting*, (ed.) Thomas A. Lee (London: Philip Allan, 1981), p. 150.

[24] Lawson, G.H., "The Cash Flow Performance of UK Companies," in *Essays in British Accounting Research*, (eds) M. Bromwich and A. Hopwood (London: Pitman, 1981), pp. 79–100.

[25] Lee, T.A., "A Case for Cash Flow Reporting," *Journal of Business Finance* (Summer, 1972), pp. 27–36.

[26] Lee, T.A., "What Cash Flow Analysis Says about BL's Finances," *Financial Times* (October 23, 1981), p. 15.

[27] Briston, R.J., and Fawthrop, R.A., "Accounting Principles and Investor Protection," *Journal of Business Finance* (Summer, 1971), pp. 9–10; Jones, C.J., "Accounting Standards: A Blind Alley?," *Accounting and Business Research* (Autumn, 1975), pp. 273–9; Climo, T.A., "Cash Flow Statements for Investors," *Journal of Business Finance and Accounting* (Autumn, 1976), pp. 3–14.

[28] Ijiri, Yuji, *Historical Cost Accounting and Its Rationality*, Research Monograph No. 1 (Vancouver, BC: Canadian Certified General Accountants' Research Foundation, 1981), p. 75.

[29] Lee, T.A., "Cash Flow Accounting, Profit and Performance Measurement: A Response to a Challenge," *Accounting Business Research* (Spring, 1985), p. 93.

[30] Lee, T.A., "Cash Flow Accounting and Reporting," op. cit., p. 152.

[31] Lee, T.A., "A Case for Cash Flow Reporting," op. cit., p. 31.

[32] Kaplan, R.S., "Measuring Manufacturing Performance: A New Challenge for Managerial Accounting Research," *Accounting Review* (October, 1982).

[33] Lee, T.A., "Cash Flow Accounting and Reporting," op. cit., p. 169.

REFERENCES

Anton, Hector R., *Accounting for the Flow of Funds* (New York: Houghton Mifflin, 1968).

Accounting Standards Committee, Statement of Standard Accounting Practice No. 6, "Extraordinary Items and Prior Year Adjustments (1974), pp. 15–25.

Arnold, J., and Hope, A., "Reporting Business Performance," *Accounting and Business Research* (July, 1975), pp. 96–105.

Barlev, B., and Levy, H., "On the Variability of Accounting Income Numbers," *Journal of Business Finance and Accounting* (Summer, 1983), pp. 305–15.

Beaver, W.H., and Dukes, R.E., "Interperiod Tax Allocation, Earnings Expectations, and the Behavior of Security Prices," *Accounting Review* (April, 1972), pp. 320–32.

Beaver, W.H., and Morse, D., "What Determines Price–Earnings Ratios?," *Financial Analysts Journal* (July–August, 1978), pp. 65–76.

Belkaoui, Ahmed, *Accounting Theory*, First Edition (New York: Harcourt Brace Jovanovich, 1981).

Belkaoui, Ahmed, "Accrual Accounting and Cash Accounting: Relative Merits of Derived Accounting Indicator Numbers," *Journal of Business Finance and Accounting* (Summer, 1983), pp. 299–312.

Bird, Peter, "Objectives and Methods of Financial Reporting: A Generalized Search Procedure," *Accounting and Business Research* (Fall, 1975), pp. 162–7.

Bodenhorn, Diran, "Balance Sheet Items as the Present Value of Future Cash Flows," *Journal of Business Finance and Accounting* (Winter, 1984), pp. 493–510.

Bodenhorn, Diran, "An Economic Approach to Balance Sheets and Income Statements," *Abacus* (June, 1978), pp. 3–30.

Bromwich, Michael, "Standard Costing for Planning and Control," *Accountant* (April–May, 1969), pp. 16–21.

Canning, J., *The Economics of Accountancy* (New York: Ronald Press, 1929).

Chambers, R.J., *Accounting, Evaluation and Economic Behavior* (Englewood Cliffs, N.J.: Prentice-Hall, 1966).

Chambers, R.J., "Continuously Contemporary Accounting: Additivity and Action," *Accounting Review* (October, 1967), pp. 751–7.

Chambers, R.J., "Income and Capital: Fisher's Legacy," *Journal of Accounting Research* (Spring, 1971), pp. 137–49.

Chambers, R.J., "Second Thoughts on Continuously Contemporary Accounting," *Abacus* (September, 1970), pp. 39–55.

Chambers, R.J., "Third Thoughts," *Abacus* (December, 1974), pp. 129–37.

Climo, T.A., "Cash Flow Statements for Investors," *Journal of Business Finance and Accounting* (Autumn, 1976), pp. 3–14.

Daily, R.A., "The Feasibility of Reporting Forecast Information," *Accounting Review* (October, 1971), pp. 686–92.

Edey, H.C., "Accounting Principles and Business Reality," *Accountancy* (November, 1963), pp. 998–1002.

Edwards, E.O., "The Fundamental Character of Excess Current Income," *Accounting and Business Research* (Autumn, 1980), pp. 375–94.

Edwards, E.O. and Bell, P., *The Theory and Measurement of Business Income* (Berkeley: University of California Press, 1961).

Eggington, D.A., "Cash Flow, Profit and Performance Measures for External Reporting: A Rejoinder," *Accounting and Business Research* (Spring, 1985), pp. 109–112.

Eggington, D.A., "In Defense of Profit Measurement, Some Limitations of Cash Flow and Value Added as Performance Measures for External Reporting," *Accounting and Business Research* (Spring, 1984), pp. 99–111.

Fama, E.F., and Miller, M.H., *The Theory of Finance* (New York: Holt, Rinehart and Winston, 1972).

Ferrara, W.L., "A Cash Flow Model for the Future," *Management Accounting* (June, 1981), pp. 12–17.

Financial Accounting Standards Board, *Statement of Financial Accounting Concepts No. 1* (Stamford, Ct.: FASB, November, 1978).

Glautier, M.W.E., and Underdown, B., *Accounting Theory Practice* (London: Pitman, 1976).

Gombola, M.L. and Ketz, J.E., "A Note on Cash Flow and Classification of Patterns of Financial Ratios," *The Accounting Review* (January, 1983), pp. 105–14.

Gordon, M.J., "Postulates, Principles and Research in Accounting," *Accounting Review* (April, 1964), pp. 221–63.

Grimlund, Richard A., and Capettini, Robert, "Sign Tests for Actual Investments with Latter Period Net Cash Outflows," *Journal of Business Finance and Accounting* (Spring, 1983), pp. 83–193.

Gross, M.J., Jr., *Financial and Accounting Guide for Nonprofit Organizations* (New York: Ronald Press, 1972).

Hawkins, D., and Campbell, W., *Equity Valuation: Models, Analysis and Implications* (New York: Financial Executives Institute, 1978).

Heath, Loyd. C., "Let's Scrap the Funds Statement," *Journal of Accountancy* (October, 1978), pp. 94–103.

Hendriksen, E.S., *Accounting Theory*, Revised Edition (Homewood Ill.: Irwin, 1970).

Hicks, Barry E., *The Cash Flow Basis of Accounting* (Sudbury, Ontario: Laurentian University, 1980).

Ijiri, Y., "Cash-Flow Accounting and Its Structure," *Journal of Accounting, Auditing and Finance* (May, 1978), pp. 331–48.

Ijiri, Y., "A Simple System of Cash-Flow Accounting," in *Accounting for a Simplified Firm Owning Depreciable Assets*, (eds) Robert R. Sterling and A.L. Thomas (Houston: Scholars Book Company, 1979).

Ketz, J.E., and Largay III, J. A., "Reporting Income and Cash Flows From Operations," *Accounting Horizons* (June, 1987), pp. 5–17.

Lawson, G.H., "Accounting for Financial Management: Some Tentative Proposals for a New Blueprint," *Problems of Investment*, (ed.) R. Shone (London: Blackwell, 1971), pp. 36–64.

Lawson, G.H., "Cash-Flow Accounting I and II," *Accountant* (October 28 and November 4, 1971), pp. 15–20.

Lawson, G.H., "The Cash Flow Performance of UK Companies," in *Essays in British Accounting Research*, (eds) M. Bromwich and A. Hopwood (London: Pitman, 1981), pp. 79–100.

Lawson, G.H., "Initial Reactions to ED 18," *Certified Accountant* (December, 1976), pp. 13–20.

Lawson, G.H., "The Measurement of Corporate Performance on a Cash Flow Basis: A Reply to Mr. Eggington," *Accounting and Business Research* (Spring, 1985), pp. 99–108.

Lawson, G.H., "Measuring Divisional Performance," *Management Accountant* (May, 1971), pp. 147–52.

Lawson, G.H., "Memorandum Submitted to the Inflation Accounting Committee," *Working Paper No. 12* (Manchester: Manchester Business School, 1975).

Lawson, G.H., "Profit Maximization via Financial Management," *Management Decision* (Winter, 1969), pp. 6–12.

Lawson, G.H., "The Rationale of Cash Flow Accounting," *Analyst* (December, 1976), pp. 22–30.

Lee, T.A., "The Accounting Entity Concept, Accounting Standards and Inflation Accounting," *Accounting and Business Research* (Spring, 1980), pp. 176–86.

Lee, T.A., "A Case for Cash Flow Reporting," *Journal of Business Finance* (Summer, 1972), pp. 27–36.

Lee, T.A., *Cash Flow Accounting* (London: Van Nostrand Reinhold, 1984).

Lee, T.A., "Cash Flow Accounting and the Allocation Problems," *Journal of Business Finance and Accounting* (Autumn, 1982), pp. 341–52.

Lee, T.A., "The Cash Flow Accounting Alternative for Corporate Financial Reporting," *Trends in Managerial and Financial Accounting*, Vol. 1, (ed.) C. Van Dam (London: Martinus Nijhoff, 1978), pp. 63–84.

Lee, T.A., "Cash Flow Accounting and Corporate Financial Reporting," in *Essays in British Accounting Research*, (eds) M. Bromwich and A. Hopwood (London: Pitman, 1981), pp. 63–78.

Lee, T.A., "Cash Flow Accounting, Profit and Performance Measurement: A Response to a Challenge," *Accounting and Business Research* (Spring, 1985), pp. 93–7.

Lee, T.A., "Cash Flows and Net Realizable Values: Further Evidence of the Intuitive Concepts," *Abacus* (December, 1984), pp. 125–37.

Lee, T.A., "The Contribution of Fisher to Cash Flow Accounting," *Journal of Business Finance and Accounting* (Autumn, 1979), pp. 321–30.

Lee, T.A., "Goodwill: An Example of Will-o'-the-Wisp Accounting," *Accounting and Business Research* (Autumn, 1971), pp. 318–28.

Lee, T.A., "Laker Airways: The Cash Flow Truth," *Accountancy* (June, 1982), pp. 115–16.

Lee, T.A., "A Note on the Nature and Determination of Income," *Journal of Business Finance and Accounting* (Spring, 1974), pp. 145–7.

Lee, T.A., "Reporting Cash Flows and Net Realizable Values," *Accounting and Business Research* (Spring, 1981), pp. 163–70.

Lee, T.A., "A Survey of Accountants' Opinions on Cash Flow Reporting," *Abacus* (December, 1981), pp. 130–44.

Lee, T.A., "Towards a Practice of Cash Flow Analysis," Discussion Paper 13 (Edinburgh: University of Edinburgh, 1981).

Lee, T.A., "What Cash Flow Analysis Says About BL's Finances," *Financial Times* (October 23, 1981), p. 15.

Lee, T.A., and Stark, A.W., "A Cash Flow Disclosure of Government-Supported Enterprises' Results," *Journal of Business Accounting* (Spring, 1984), pp. 1–11.

Lee, T.A., and Tweedie, D.P., *Institutional Use and Understanding of Corporate Financial Information* (London: Institute of Chartered Accountants in England and Wales, 1981).

Lee, T.A., *The Private Shareholder and the Corporate Report* (London: Institute of Chartered Accountants in England and Wales, 1977).

Loscalzo, William, *Cash Flow Forecasting* (New York: McGraw-Hill, 1982).

Mason, Perry Empey, *Cash Flow Analysis and Funds Statement* (New York: American Institute of Certified Public Accountants, 1961).

Meyer, P.E., "The Accounting Entity," *Abacus* (December, 1973), pp. 116–26.

Milling, Bryan E., *Cash Flow Problem Solver: Procedures and Rationales for the Independent Businessman* (Radnor, Pa: Chilton, 1981).

Ortina, R.E., and Largay III, J.A., "Pitfalls in Calculating Cash Flow from Operations," *The Accounting Review* (April, 1985), pp. 314–26.

Paton, W., *Accounting Theory* (Chicago: Accounting Studies Press, 1962).

Revsine, L., *Replacement Cost Accounting* (Englewood Cliffs, N.J.: Prentice-Hall, 1973).

Rutherford, B.A., "Cash Flow Reporting and Distributional Allocations: A Note," *Journal of Business Finance and Accounting* (Summer, 1983), pp. 313–16.

Rutherford, B.A., "The Interpretation of Cash Flow Reports and the Other Allocation Problem," *Abacus* (June, 1982), pp. 40–49.

Stamp, E., "Financial Reports on Entity: Ex Uno Plures," *Accounting for a Simplified Firm Owning Depreciable Assets*, (eds) R.R. Sterling and A.L. Thomas (Houston: Scholar Books, 1979), pp. 163–180.

Stamp, E., "Useful Arbitrary Allocations," *Accounting Review* (July, 1971), pp. 472–9.

Staubus, G.J., *Making Accounting Decisions* (Houston: Scholars, 1977).

Staubus, G.J., "The Relevance of Cash Flows," *Asset Valuation*, (ed.) R.R. Sterling (Houston: Scholars, 1971).

Staubus, G.J., *A Theory of Accounting to Investors* (Berkeley: University of California Press, 1961).

Sterling, R.R., "In Defense of Accounting in the United States," *Abacus* (December, 1966), pp. 180–3.

Sterling, R.R., "Earnings Per Share Is a Poor Indicator of Performance," *Omega* (1974), pp. 11–32.

Sterling, R.R., *Theory of the Measurement of Enterprise Income* (Lawrence: University of Kansas Press, 1970).

Sterling, R.R., *Towards a Science of Accounting* (Houston: Scholars, 1979).

Thomas, A.L., *The Allocation Problem in Financial Accounting Theory*, Studies in Accounting Research No. 3 (Evanston, Ill.: American Accounting Association, 1969).

Thomas, A.L., *The Allocation Problem: Part Two*, Studies in Accounting Research No. 9 (Sarasota, Fla.: American Accounting Association, 1974).

Thomas, A.L., *A Behavioral Analysis of Joint-Cost Allocation and Transfer Pricing* (Houston: Stipes Publishing, 1970).

Thomas, A.L., "Matching: Up From Our Black Hole," in *Accounting for a Simplified Firm Owning Depreciable Assets*, (eds) R.R. Sterling and A.L. Thomas (Houston: Scholars, 1979).

Tweedie, D.P., "Cash Flows and Realizable Values: The Intuitive Accounting Concepts? An Empirical Test," *Accounting and Business Research* (Winter, 1977), pp. 2–13.

Vatter, W.J., *The Fund Theory of Accounting and Its Implications For Financial Reports* (Chicago: University of Chicago Press, 1947).

Whittington, G., "Accounting and Economics," *Current Issues in Accounting*, (eds) B. Carsberg and T. Hope (London: Philip Allan, 1977).

QUESTIONS

14.1 Describe the historical development of the statement of cash flows.

14.2 What is the conceptual framework?

14.3 Describe the problems of accrual accounting.

14.4 Present an evaluation of cash flow accounting.

14.5 Financing and Investing Activities Not Involving Cash

The statement of cash flows is normally a required basic financial statement for each period for which an earnings statement is presented. The statement should include a separate schedule listing the financing and investing activities not involving cash.

Required

1 What are financing and investing activities not involving cash?

2 What are two types of financing and investing activities not involving cash?

3 What effect, if any, would each of the following seven items have on the statement of cash flows?

   a. Accounts receivable.

   b. Inventory.

   c. Depreciation.

   d. Deferred income taxes.

   e. Issuance of long-term debt in payment for a building.

   f. Payoff of current portion of debt.

   g. Sale of a fixed asset resulting in a loss.   (*AICPA adapted*)

CHAPTER 15

FUTURE TRENDS IN ACCOUNTING

The objective of financial accounting is to communicate the information that results from the transactions of a firm. These transactions are primarily the exchanges of goods and services between two or more entities. Several limitations are inherent in this definition. First, the exchanges recognized by conventional accounting theory are limited to goods and services and do not include changes in *human capital*. Second, this definition limits the transactions to exchanges between two or more legal, economic entities; thus, exchanges between a firm and its *social environment* are ignored for all practical purposes. Third, most transactions are actual or past events, so that the *future* financial position and performance of a firm are not reflected in the financial statements. Fourth, the cost of debt capital is recognized by conventional accounting theory, but the cost of equity capital is not. Finally, a need exists for cash-flow reporting, employee reporting, and value-added reporting.

The future scope of accounting should embrace solutions to these and other problems and controversial issues. In this chapter, we will discuss some of the procedures presented in the literature and in practice that may be employed to deal with these new challenges. Seven principal new developments will be examined — socioeconomic accounting, human-resource accounting, accounting for the cost of capital, public reporting of financial forecasts, cash-flow reporting, employee reporting, and value-added reporting.

15.1   SOCIOECONOMIC ACCOUNTING

15.1.1   The Nature of Socioeconomic Accounting

Conventional financial accounting focuses on the results of transactions between two or more entities. Exchanges between a firm and its social environment are practically ignored. *Socioeconomic accounting*, which is aimed at correcting this omission, is based on the following thesis:

> The technology of an economic system imposes a structure on its society which not only determines its economic activities but also influences its social relationships and well-being. Therefore, a measure limited to economic consequences is inadequate as an appraisal of the cause-effect relationships of the total system; it neglects the social effects.[1]

Socioeconomic accounting is therefore the process of ordering, measuring, and disclosing the impact of exchanges between a firm and its social environment. Socioeconomic accounting is an expression of a corporation's social responsibilities and a new call for general corporate accountability. Exchanges between a firm and society consist primarily of the use of *social resources*. If the activities of a firm lead to a depletion of social resources, the result is a *social cost*; if they lead to an increase in social resources, the result is a *social benefit*. The objective of socioeconomic accounting is to measure and disclose the costs and benefits to society created by the production-related activities of a business enterprise. More precisely, the objective is to *internalize* these social costs and benefits to determine a more relevant and exhaustive result that represents the *socioeconomic profit* of a firm. Because this may require the use of techniques from other relevant disciplines, Linowes defines socioeconomic accounting as "the application of accounting in the field of social sciences. These include sociology, political science, and economics."[2]

Among the suggested dimensions of socioeconomic accounting are *national income accounting*, the *evaluation of social programs*, the *role of accounting in economic development*, the *development of social indicators*, and the *measurement and disclosure of the social performance of profit-oriented firms*. The last dimension is of primary interest in corporate accounting and is the basic objective of socioeconomic accounting. It involves the recognition, measurement, and disclosure of social costs and benefits, followed by a *social audit*.

15.1.2   Social Costs and Benefits: Externalities

Most economists agree that perfect competition in all markets leads to a position of maximum social welfare, given the underlying assumptions of this analysis. If markets are highly competitive and consumers and producers rationally attempt to reach a maximum level of satisfaction, then the available resources will be allocated in a way that maximizes social welfare. Thus, prices provide automatic, socially valid guidelines for investment and production. When an obstruction of private market prices exists, however, the *marginal social cost* does not equal the *marginal social benefit*, and maximum social welfare cannot be achieved. The indirect effects of this situation (variously labeled in economics as "third-party effects," "spillover effects," and, more clearly, "external economies or diseconomies") are the social costs and social benefits that the private marginal-cost pricing rule does not encompass. Thus, an *externality* arises whenever a firm's activities have a negative or positive impact on the environment for which the firm is not held accountable. If the impact is positive, it is an *external economy*, or social benefit; if the impact is negative, it is an *external diseconomy*, or social cost.

To date, attempts by economists to ascertain the monetary value of externalities and bring them within the scope of economic analysis has not been successful. We will discuss some of the reasons for this in the following paragraphs.

Some manifestly important categories of external diseconomies do not lend themselves easily to measurement. Also, the chain of causality may be quite complex. For example:

> Air pollution is not only the result of, and not only proportionate to, the volume of production and the emissions of residual waste products, it is also governed by the interactions of a whole series of variables that may react on one another.[3]

It is difficult to attribute to a specific sector of the economy the consequences of some external diseconomies that depend on complementary economic activities. As Knapp explains

> Environmental and social costs must be looked on as the outcome of an interaction of several complex systems (economic, physical, meteorological, biological, etc, ...) in which a plurality of factors interplay through a "feed-back" process.[4]

The measurement of external diseconomies and social costs depends on the magnitude of the perception and awareness of the issue in a particular society. In other words, it is a question of *social evaluation*. How much importance does organized society attribute to the tangible and intangible values involved?

Moreover, some of the consequences of externalities are intangibles (Ridker speaks of "psychic costs").[5] As such, even if the available monetary estimates of social costs were complete, the measures would have to be considered fragmentary because some of the social losses, which are intangible in character, must be evaluated in nonmonetary terms.

Otto A. Davis and A.B. Whinston distinguish between *separable* and *nonseparable* externalities.[6] In the case of *separable externalities*, only total costs are affected; marginal (incremental) costs are unaffected. For example, if Firm A builds installations that so reduce the natural ventilation that the management of a neighboring hotel must install a central air conditioner, the total cost function of the hotel would be increased by a fixed outlay but its marginal cost would remain constant. In the case of *nonseparable externalities*, marginal costs are affected. In other words

> ... the difference between the separable and nonseparable cases lies in the fact that externality enters the cost function in a multiplicative manner rather than in a strictly additive way.[7]

The distinction between separable and nonseparable externalities increases the difficulties of measuring and computing the appropriate charges to be levied.

Davis and Whinston also address the complex problem of assessing the value of *reciprocal externalities*.[8] A reciprocal externality raises the costs for Firm B when a production process conducted by Firm B creates another externality that raises the costs for Firm A. *Nonseparable reciprocal externalities* are likely to lead to a merger between two firms, because neither firm can reach maximum profit without the other firm.

Such measurement difficulties may explain some of the reluctance on the part of firms to adopt socioeconomic accounting and the urgency to develop a taxonomy for the measurement of social performance that embraces not only social costs but also social contributions, or social benefits. In fact, one economist considers the primary social costs of business enterprises to be:

1 The social costs resulting from the impairment of *human factors of production*.
2 The social costs of *air pollution*.
3 The social costs of *water pollution*.
4 The social costs of the *depletion and destruction of animal resources*.
5 The social costs of the *premature depletion of energy resources*.
6 The social costs of *technological change*.
7 The social costs of *soil erosion, soil depletion, and deforestation*.
8 The social costs of *unemployment and idle resources*.[9]

Similarly, the Committee on Accounting for Corporate Social Performance of the National Association of Accountants has classified the major domains of corporate concern for social performance as: (1) community involvement, (2) human resources, (3) physical resources and environmental contributions, and (4) product or service contributions.

Community involvement is comprised of activities that primarily benefit the general public, such as corporate philanthropy, housing construction and financing, health services, volunteer activities of employees, food programs, and community planning and improvement.

Classified under *human resources* are areas that benefit employees, such as training and job-enrichment programs, working conditions, promotion policies, and employee benefits.

Physical resources and environmental contributions encompass such concerns as air and water quality, the control of noise pollution, the conservation of resources, and the disposal of solid wastes.

Product or service contributions examine the impact of a company's product or service on society, taking into account such considerations as product quality, packaging, advertising, warranty provisions, and product safety.[10]

15.1.3   The Desirability of Socioeconomic Accounting

The desirability of socioeconomic accounting may be indicated by three factors: (1) corporate response, (2) individual user responses, and (3) the market response.

Although social reporting is still in an early state of development, the corporate response is encouraging. To varying degrees, more and more companies are making some form of *social disclosure* regarding the social impact of their activities.[11] The most comprehensive social report is the "Social Audit" of Abt Associates, Inc., presented in the appendix to this chapter. The social reports include a social income statement and a social balance sheet. The social income statement records the social costs and social benefits to the company and shareholders, to the staff, to clients and the general public, and to the community. The social balance sheet discloses staff assets, organizational assets, the use of public goods, financial assets, and physical assets.

Two field studies have been conducted to determine the impact of social disclosure on investment decisions. In a survey of institutional investors, Longstreth and Rosenbloom found that 57 percent of the respondents indicated that they consider social factors in addition to economic factors when making investment decisions.[12] In a field experiment, Belkaoui presented different forms of social reports, varying in the accounting treatment of pollution costs, to groups of bank officers, practicing accountants, and students. The results of the experiment suggest that pollution cost has an influence on investment decisions.[13]

Similarly, market-based studies have been conducted to empirically assess the relevance to investors of certain social-responsibility disclosures by firms in terms of the impact of such disclosures on security returns.[14] Belkaoui reports that the price behavior of firms making social disclosures differs from the price behavior of firms not making the social disclosures. Spicer finds pollution-control records useful in assessing a firm's total systematic risk. Finally, Ingram reveals that the informational content of a firm's social-responsibility disclosure depends on the market segment with which the firm is identified. Implicitly, such market studies investigate two views of the possible impact of social disclosure on the market. One view maintains that "ethical investors" form a clientele that responds to demonstrations of social concern.[15] A second view is summed up in the Beams-Fertig thesis, which holds that corporations that report the least activity in avoiding social cost will appear more successful to investors and will be favored by the market.[16]

15.2   HUMAN-RESOURCE ACCOUNTING

15.2.1   The Usefulness of Human Resources

The objective of financial accounting is to provide information that is relevant to the decisions users (investors) must make, including adequate information about one "neglected" asset of a firm — the human asset. More specifically, investors may greatly benefit from a knowledge of the extent to which the human assets of an organization have increased or decreased during a given period. The conventional accounting treatment of human-resource outlays consists of *expensing* all human-capital formation expenditures and *capitalizing* similar outlays on physical capital. A more valid treatment would be to capitalize human-resource expenditures to yield future benefits and to reveal when such benefits can be measured.[17] In fact, this treatment has created a new concern with the measurement of the cost or value of human resources to an organization and has led to the development of a new field of inquiry in accounting, known as *human-resource accounting*. A broad definition of human-resource accounting is

> The process of identifying and measuring data about human resources and communicating this information to interested parties.[18]

This definition implies that there are three major objectives of human-resource accounting: (1) identification of "human-resource value," (2) measurement of the cost and value of people to organizations, and (3) investigation of the cognitive and behavioral impact of such information.

Human-resource accounting has led to a few applications, including those of the R.G. Barry Corporation, Touche Ross & Company, and a midwest branch of a mutual insurance company.[19] Despite the lack of enthusiasm of many firms to disclose the value of their human assets, most empirical studies investigating the cognitive and behavioral impact show a favorable predisposition of users to human-resource accounting information.[20] We may wonder, in fact, why the R.G. Barry Corporation, a small shoe-manufacturing company listed on the American Stock Exchange, would develop a human-resource accounting system. As one of its officers rhetorically observed:

> Why in the world is a little company with good — but unspectacular — growth, good — but unromantic — products, good — but unsophisticated — technology, good — but undramatic — profitability interested in the development of a system of accounting for the human resources of the business? This is a fair question and deserves an answer.[21]

To answer this question — and any similar questions asked by other corporations — we may cite three facts:

1 Capitalizing human-resource costs is conceptually more valid than the expensing approach.
2 The information concerning "human assets" is likely to be relevant to a great variety of decisions made by external or internal users, or both.
3 Accounting for human assets constitutes an explicit recognition of the premise that people are valuable organizational resources and an integral part of a mix of resources.

15.2.2   Human-Resource Value Theory

The concept of *human value* may be derived from the general economic value theory. Values may be attributed to individuals or groups like physical assets, based on their ability to render future economic services. In line with the economic thinking that associates the value of an object with its ability to render benefits, the individual or group value is usually defined as the present worth of the services rendered to the organization throughout the individual's or the group's expected service life.

How do we determine the value of a human asset? To measure and disclose *human-resource value*, we must devise a theoretical framework, or *human-resource value theory*, to explicate the nature and determinants of the value of people to an organization. Basically, two models of the nature and determinants of human-resource value exist — one advanced by Flamholtz and one advanced by Likert and Bowers.[22] We will discuss each of these models here.

Determinants of Individual Value

In Flamholtz's model, the measure of a person's worth is his or her expected realizable value. Flamholtz's model suggests that such a measure of *individual value* results from the interaction of two variables: (1) the individual's expected conditional value, and (2) the probability that the individual will maintain membership in the organization.

The individual's *conditional value* is the amount the organization would potentially realize from that person's services. Conditional value is a multi-dimensional variable comprised of three factors: *productivity, transferability* and *promotability*. The elements of conditional value are perceived to be the products of certain attributes of the person and certain dimensions of the organization. Two important individual determinants are identified as the person's *skills* and *activation level*. Similarly, the organizational determinants that interact with the individual values are identified as the *organizational role* of the individual and the *rewards* that people expect from the different aspects of their membership in a firm.

The probability of maintaining the organizational membership is considered to be related to a person's degree of job satisfaction.

Determinants of Group Value

Flamholtz's model examines the determinants of an individual's value to an organization; the Likert–Bowers model examines the determinants of *group value*. Intended to represent the "productive capability of the human organization of any enterprise or unit within it,"[23] the model identifies three variables that influence the effectiveness of a firm's "human organization":

1 The *causal* variables are independent variables that can be directly or purposely altered or changed by the organization and its management and that in turn determine the course of developments within an organization. These causal variables include only those that are controllable by the organization and its management. General business conditions, for example, although an independent variable, are not viewed as causal because they are not controllable by the management of a particular enterprise. Causal variables include the structure of the organization and management's policies, decisions, business and leadership strategies, skills, and behavior.

2 The *intervening* variables reflect the internal state, health, and performance capabilities of the organization; that is, the loyalties, attitudes, motivations, performance goals, and perceptions of all members and their collective capability for effective action.

3 The *end-result* variables are the dependent variables that reflect the results achieved by that organization, such as its productivity, costs, scrap loss, growth, share of the market, and earnings.[24]

The Likert–Bowers model states that certain casual variables induce certain levels of intervening variables, which yield certain levels of end-result variables. The *casual variables* are managerial behavior, organizational structure, and subordinate peer behavior. The *intervening variables* are such organizational processes as perception, communication, motivation, decision making, control, and coordination. The *end-result variables* are health, satisfaction, productivity, and financial performance.

15.2.3 Measures of Human Assets

Monetary measures of human assets are historical cost (acquisition cost), replacement cost, opportunity cost, the compensation model, and adjusted discounted future wages. The principal nonmonetary measure is the "survey of organizations" model.

The Historical-Cost (Acquisition-Cost) Method

The historical-cost, or aquisition-cost, method consists of capitalizing all of the costs associated with recruiting, selecting, hiring, training, placing and developing an employee (a human asset), and then amortizing these costs over the expected useful life of the asset, recognizing losses in case of liquidation of the asset or increasing the value of the asset to offset any additional cost that is expected to increase the benefit potential of the asset. Similar to the conventional accounting treatments for other assets, this treatment is practical and objective in the sense that the data are verifiable.[25]

However, the use of these measurements is limited in several ways. First, the economic value of a human asset does not necessarily correspond to its historical cost. Second, any appreciation or amortization may be subjective and have no relationship to any increase or decrease in the productivity of the human assets. Third, because the costs associated with recruiting, selecting, hiring, training, placing, and developing an employee may differ from one individual to another within a firm, the historical-cost method does not result in comparable human-resource values.

The Replacement-Cost Method

The replacement-cost method consists of estimating the costs of replacing a firm's existing human resources. Such costs include all of the costs of recruiting, selecting, hiring, training, placing, and developing new employees until they reach the level of competence of existing employees. The principal advantage of the replacement-cost method is that it is a good surrogate for the economic value of the asset in the sense that market considerations are essential in reaching a final figure. Such a final figure is also generally intended to be conceptually equivalent to a concept of an individual's economic value.[26]

However, the use of the replacement cost method is also limited in several ways. First, the value of a particular employee may be perceived by the firm to be greater than the relevant replacement cost. Second, there may be no equivalent replacement for a given human asset.[27] Third, as noted by Likert and Bowers, managers may have difficulty estimating the cost of completely replacing their human organization, and different managers may arrive at quite different estimates.[28]

The Opportunity-Cost Method

Hekimian and Jones propose the opportunity-cost method to overcome the limitations of the replacement-cost method.[29] They suggest that human-resource values be established through a competitive bidding process within the firm, based on the concept of "opportunity" cost. More specifically, investment-center managers are to bid for the scarce employees they need to recruit. These "scarce" employees include only those employees within the firm who are the subject of a recruitment request by an investment-center manager. In other words, employees who are not considered "scarce" are not included in the human-asset base of the organization.

Obviously, the opportunity-cost method has several limitations. First, the inclusion of only "scarce" employees in the asset base may be interpreted as "discriminatory" by other employees. Second, less profitable divisions may be penalized by their inability to outbid more profitable divisions to acquire better employees. Third, the method may be perceived as artificial and even immoral.[30]

The Compensation Model

Given the uncertainty and the difficulty associated with determining the value of human capital, Lev and Schwartz suggest the use of an individual employee's future compensation as a surrogate of his or her value. Accordingly, the "value of human capital embodied in a person of age τ is the present value of his or her remaining future earnings from employment."[31] This valuation model is expressed

$$V_\tau = \sum_{t=\tau}^{T} \frac{I(t)}{(1 + r)^{t-r}}$$

where

$\quad V_\tau =$ the human-capital value of an individual τ years old.
$\quad I(t) =$ the individual's annual earnings up to retirement.
$\quad \tau =$ a discount rate specific to the individual.
$\quad T =$ retirement age.

Because V_τ is an ex-post value, given that $I(t)$ is obtained only after retirement and V_τ ignores the possibility of death before retirement age, Lev and Schwartz have refined the valuation model as follows:

$$E(V_T^* = \sum_{t=\tau}^{T} P_\tau(t + 1) \sum_{t=\tau}^{T} \frac{I_1^*}{(1 + r)^{t-\tau}}$$

where

$\quad I_1^* =$ future annual earnings.
$\quad E(V_T^*) =$ *the expected value of an individual's human capital.*
$\quad P_\tau(t) =$ the probability of an individual dying at age t.

The principal limitation of the compensation model is the subjectivity associated with the determination of the level of future salary, the length of expected employment within the firm, and the discount rate.

The Adjusted Discounted-Future-Wages Method

Hermanson proposes using an adjusted compensation value to approximate the value of an individual to a firm.[32] Discounted future wages are adjusted by an *efficiency factor* intended to measure the relative effectiveness of the human capital of a given firm. This efficiency factor, which is a ratio of the return on investment of the given firm to all other firms in the economy for a given period, is computed

$$\text{Efficiency Ratio} = \frac{5\,\dfrac{RF_0}{RE_0} + 4\,\dfrac{RF_1}{RE_1} + 3\,\dfrac{RF_2}{RE_2} + 2\,\dfrac{RF_3}{RE_3} + \dfrac{RF_4}{RE_4}}{15}$$

where

RF_i = the rate of accounting income on owned assets for the firm for the year i.
RE_i = the rate of accounting income on owned assets for all firms in the economy for the year i.
i = years (0 to 4).

The justification of this ratio rests on the thesis that differences in profitability are primarily due to differences in human-asset performance. Thus, it is necessary to adjust the compensation value by the efficiency factor.

Nonmonetary Measures

Many nonmonetary measures of human assets may be used, such as a simple inventory of the skills and capabilities of individuals, the assignment of ratings or rankings to individual performances, and the measurement of attitudes. The most frequently used nonmonetary measure of human value is derived from the Likert–Bowers model of the variables that determine "the effectiveness of a firm's human organization." A questionnaire based on the theoretical model called "survey of organizations" is designed to measure the "organizational climate."[33] The results of such a questionnaire may serve as a nonmonetary measure of human assets in terms of employee perceptions of the working atmosphere in the firm.

15.3   ACCOUNTING FOR THE COST OF CAPITAL

15.3.1   The Nature of Anthony's Proposal

In conventional financial accounting the cost of equity is not taken into account and allocated to operations like other costs. Consequently, *accounting for the cost of capital* is a process of allocating the costs of various types of capital to a firm's operations along with other normal production costs. Anthony suggests that such an absorption of the cost of equity would make financial accounting reports more meaningful guidelines for management.[34] In conventional financial accounting, interest, which refers only to the cost of using debt captial, is accounted for as a period cost and no charge is recognized for the use of equity capital. Under Anthony's proposal, interest refers to both the cost of debt and the cost of equity and is accounted for like other costs. In other words, the interest incurred for the use of capital in the production process should be included in inventory and cost of goods sold, in the same way that to a firm's labor, material, and factory overhead are included. Anthony argues that accounting principles concerning interest should be identical to accounting principles concerning economics and that accounting for the cost of capital would define "accounting profit" in the same way that "economic profit" is defined. Young visualizes four substantial and interrelated changes in current accounting procedures if Anthony's proposal is adopted by the Financial Accounting Standards Board:

- An interest charge would be applied to common shareholders' equity.
- Costs of goods sold would include an interest charge for capital tied up in the plant and equipment used for manufacturing.
- The cost of inventory held for sale or use in future periods would include an interest cost if the holding period were significantly long.
- The cost of new plant assets would include the interest cost for equity capital used during the construction period.[35]

15.3.2 A Method of Accounting for the Cost of Capital

Anthony's proposal may be subject to two problems: (1) the problem of measuring the cost of equity capital, and (2) the problem of accounting for the cost of capital *per se*.

The measurement of the cost of debt capital or, more precisely, of the cost of debt interest, is not an insurmountable problem in most cases. However, the measurement of the cost of equity capital does present certain difficulties that are well recognized in the field of corporate finance. Despite these difficulties, management may use judgment to compute the cost of equity capital explicitly or implicitly. One expedient method is to estimate the cost of equity by deducting the cost of debt from a total cost of capital, debt, and equity combined.

To solve the problem of accounting for the cost of capital, Anthony suggests creating an "interest pool" similar to any overhead cost pool, which is debited by the debt interest and equity interest incurred, with an offsetting credit to retained earnings and cash or debt interest payable. The interest pool is divided by the total capital employed to determine a weighted interest rate for the year. This weighted interest rate is then used to determine the amount of interest cost to be applied to cost objectives. More precisely, the interest pool is credited, and one or several accounts are debited: cost of goods sold, inventory, plant, and/or general. This account contains the following entries:

Interest Pool

from Debt	X	*to* Cost of Goods Sold	T
from Equity	Y	*to* Inventory	U
		to Plant	V
		to General	W
	Z		Z

This approach affects a firm's financial statements in four ways:

1 The cost of sales is increased by the amount of interest added as a cost of goods sold.

2 Inventory, plant, and other assets are increased by the amount of interest added as a product cost.
3 Income is decreased by the amount of interest added as a period cost.
4 Retained earnings are increased by the amount of equity interest.

15.3.3 Illustration of the Use of Anthony's Proposal

To illustrate Anthony's proposal in actual practice, assume that the Winger Manufacturing Company has $10,000 in 5-percent bonds and $10,000 in common stock and retained earnings and that the cost of equity capital to the firm is 10 percent. The firm manufactures a particular brand of cognac, which is not sold until the fifth year after production. The income statements and balance sheets for the firm (1) under present practice and (2) applying Anthony's proposal are shown in Exhibits 15.1 and 15.2 respectively.

EXHIBIT 15.1
Present Practice
Winger Manufacturing Company
Income Statements

	Each of Years 1–4	Year 5
Sales	$ 0	$10,000
Cost of Goods Sold	0	5,000
Gross Margin	0	5,000
Interest on Debt	$(500)	$ 500
Net Income (loss)	$(500)	$ 4,500

Winger Manufacturing Company
Balance Sheets

			Year			
	0	1	2	3	4	5
Cash	$15,000	$14,500	$14,000	$13,500	$13,000	$22,500
Inventory	5,000	5,000	5,000	5,000	5,000	0
Total	$20,000	$19,500	$19,000	$18,500	$18,000	$22,500
Debt	$10,000	$10,000	$10,000	$10,000	$10,000	$10,000
Capital	10,000	9,500	9,000	8,500	8,000	12,500
Total	$20,000	$19,500	$19,000	$18,500	$18,000	$22,500

EXHIBIT 15.2
Anthony's Proposal
Winger Manufacturing Company
Income Statements

	Each of Years 1–4	Year 5
Sales	$ 0	$10,000.00
Cost of Goods Sold	0	(13,605.10)
Gross Margin and Net Income	$ 0	$(13,105.10)

Winger Manufacturing Company
Balance Sheets

	Year					
	0	1	2	3	4	5
Cash	$15,000	$14,500	$14,000	$13,500	$13,000	$22,500
Inventory	5,000	6,500	8,100	9,810	11,641	0
Total	$20,000	$21,000	$22,100	$23,310	$24,641	$22,500
Debt	$10,000	$10,000	$10,000	$10,000	$10,000	$10,000
Capital	10,000	11,000	12,100	13,310	14,641	12,500
Total	$20,000	$21,000	$22,100	$12,310	$24,641	$22,500

15.3.4   Evaluation of Anthony's Proposal

The following arguments may be made in favor of accounting for the cost of capital. First, such an accounting will properly record the increasing investment necessary when holding an asset over time and will reflect an appropriate economic value for the asset. Second, it will reduce the over-estimation of the accounting profit that does include the cost of equity. Third, it will provide a comparable valuation of self-constructed assets and purchased assets. In conventional accounting, purchased assets include the cost of the supplier's equity and debt capital; self-constructed assets are assumed to have used no capital. Finally, Anthony suggests that reporting interest as an element of cost would facilitate the work of governmental agencies that rely on accounting information when formulating public policy.[36] Anthony cited as examples rate setting, price control, defense contracting, and public concepts about profit.

Some limitations also may be associated with Anthony's proposal to account for the cost of capital. First, a determination of the cost of equity is not sufficiently accurate and reliable, although Anthony suggests that the cost of equity figure from firm to firm be set by the Financial Accounting Standards Board. Second, the proposal to account for the cost of capital may be viewed as violation of the principle of conservatism in the sense that it recognizes revenue before it is realized. Third, problems are related to the cost of equity *per se*. Should the cost of equity be assumed to be constant over time, or does it vary with the interest rate? Should the cost of equity and the cost debt be obtained by applying the rate to the book value or the market value of debt?

15.3.5   Toward Capitalizing the Cost of Capital

The issue of accounting for interest cost has been continually debated in the accounting literature and has resulted in a number of attempts by the standard-setting bodies to resolve the questions. In 1971, a Special Committee on Interest in Relation to Cost established by the American Institute of Accountants (as it was then known) suggested that interest on investment should not be included in production cost. A committee appointed by the Accounting Principles Board in 1971 to study the question of capitalizing interest cost was terminated before a position could be issued. Because an increasing number of registrants were capitalizing interest, the Securities and Exchange Commission issued Accounting Research Study No. 163, *Capitalizing of Interest by Companies Other Than Public Utilities*, on June 21, 1974, declaring a moratorium on the trend to capitalize interest by other-than-public utilities. The SEC explained its action as follows:

> It does not seem desirable to have an alternative practice grow up through selective adoption by individual companies without careful consideration of such a change by the Financial Accounting Standards Board, including the development of systematic criteria as to when, if ever, capitalization of interest is desirable.[37]

In approaching the issue, the FASB considered three alternatives:

1 Accounting for interest on debt as an expense of the period in which it is incurred.
2 Capitalizing interest on debt as part of the cost of an asset, when prescribed conditions are met.
3 Capitalizing interest on debt and imputed interest on stockholders' equity as part of the cost of an asset, when prescribed conditions are met. (This corresponds to Anthony's proposal.)

In its Statement No. 34, the Financial Accounting Standards Board adopted the second method.[38] Assets that qualify for interest capitalization include facilities under construction for a company's own use and assets intended for sale or lease that are constructed as separate or discrete projects, such as ships and real-estate developments. Inventories that are routinely manufactured or otherwise produced in large quantities on a repetitive basis do not qualify. The capitalization period begins once three conditions are met: (1) the company has made expenditures for the asset, (2) work on the asset is in progress, and (3) interest cost is being incurred.

FASB Statement No. 34 fails to give comprehensive accounting recognition to an imputed interest cost for equity capital, as proposed by Anthony. The FASB position recognizes the capitalization of interest on debt only for a narrow range of qualifying assets. For example, inventories that require a long time to age, such as whiskey, wine, and tobacco, do not qualify for interest capitalization under the standards set forth in FASB Statement No. 34.

15.4 PUBLIC REPORTING OF CORPORATE FINANCIAL FORECASTS

Faced with the challenge from diverse users to develop more relevant financial reporting techniques, accountants and nonaccountants alike have recommended that forecasted information can be incorporated into financial statements. Proposals vary from the suggestion that budgetary data be disclosed to the suggestion that public companies provide earnings forecasts in their annual or interim reports and prospectuses. One objective of financial reporting set forth in the "Trueblood Report" supports this type of disclosure:

> An objective of financial statements is to provide information useful for the predictive process. Financial forecasts should be provided when they will enhance the reliability of users' predictions.[39]

Although the objective does not constitute a strong recommendation for corporate financial forecasts, steps have been taken to ensure that forecasts are included in accounting reports. In Great Britain, the revised version of the English *City Code on Takeovers and Mergers* requires profit forecasts to be included in takeover-bid circulars and prospectuses.[40] In the English case, the interest of the accounting profession was created by the requirement that not only must "the assumptions, including the commercial assumptions," be stated but the "accounting bases and calculations must be examined and reported on by the auditors or consultant accountants."[41] In the United States, in February 1973, the SEC first announced its intention to require companies disclosing the forecasts to conform with certain rules to be laid down by the Commission. In April 1976, in reaction to public criticism, the SEC called for voluntary filings of forecasts. The SEC's amended position presents some problems in terms (1) of the definition of earnings forecasts, (2) of whether disclosure should be mandatory or optional, and (3) of the possible advantages of such disclosures.

The first problem concerns determining which forecasted items are to be disclosed. The two possible solutions are disclosing budgets or disclosing probable results (forecasts). This distinction may be made because budgets are prepared for internal use and, for motivational reasons, may be stated in a way that differs from expected results. Ijiri makes the distinction as follows:

> Forecasts are estimates of what the corporation considers to be the most likely to occur, whereas budgets may be inflated from what the corporation considers to be most likely to occur in order to take advantage of the motivational function of the budget.[42]

From the point of view of the user, therefore, the disclosure of forecasts, rather than budgets, may be more relevant to his or her decision-making needs. In fact, the trend seems to be in favor of the disclosure of forecasts of specific accounts in general and earnings in particular.

The second problem is whether the disclosure of earnings forecasts should be mandatory or optional. Each position may be easily justified. The principal argument in favor of mandatory disclosure is that it creates a similar and uniform situation for all companies. However, mandatory disclosure could create an unnecessary burden in terms of competitive advantage, and certain firms would have to be viewed as exceptions (for example, private companies, companies in volatile industries, companies in the process of major changes, and companies in developmental stages).[43] Another argument against mandatory disclosure is that some firms lack adequate technology, experience, and competence to disclose forecasts adequately and that the outlays to correct this situation may create an unnecessary burden on these firms. Such a firm may doubt the benefits of a forecast-disclosure procedure that justifies the cost of installing a new reporting system.

The third problem concerns the desirability of forecast publication. Several arguments have been advanced against the reporting of corporate financial forecasts. One argument is that both companies and analysts have been unsuccessful in accurately forecasting earnings. Daily points out that budgeted "information must be reasonably accurate to be relevant; otherwise, investors will have no confidence in the information and consequently not utilize it."[44] Both his study and McDonald's study[45] support the contention that, on the average, management earnings forecasts are likely to be materially inaccurate. A number of factors may affect the accuracy of forecasts — for example, the length of time covered by the forecast, the nature of the industry in which the company operates, the external environment, and the degree of sophistication and experience of the company making the forecast. Ijiri classifies the primary issues involved in corporate financial forecasts as (1) reliability, (2) responsibility, and (3) reticency.[46] *Reliability* is related to the relative accuracy of the forecasts; *responsibility*, to the possible legal liabilities of firms making forecasts and accountants auditing these forecasts; and *reticency*, to the degree of silence and inaction of forms that are at a competitive disadvantage due to forecast disclosure. Similarly, Mautz suggests that three kinds of differences must be considered in evaluating the overall usefulness of published forecasts:

- Differences in the forecasting abilities of publicly owned firms.
- Differences in the attitudes with which managements in publicly owned companies might be expected to approach the forecasting task.
- Differences in the capacities of investors to use forecasts.[47]

Finally, given the difficulties associated with identifying and estimating forecasts, to what is an accountant expected to attest? Mautz suggests the following range of possibilities: (1) arithmetic accuracy, (2) internal integrity of the forecast data, (3) consistency in the application of accounting principles, (4) adequacy of disclosure, (5) reasonableness of assumptions, and (6) reasonableness of projections.[48]

15.5   CASH-FLOW ACCOUNTING AND REPORTING

A dominant characteristic in early views of the purpose of financial statements is the *stewardship function*. According to this view, management is entrusted with control of the financial resources provided by capital suppliers. Accordingly, the purpose of financial statements is to report to concerned parties to facilitate the evaluation of management's stewardship. To accomplish this objective, the reporting system favored and deemed essential and superior to others is the *accrual system*. Simply stated, the *accrual basis of accounting* refers to a form of record keeping that records not only transactions that result from the receipt and disbursement of cash but also the amounts that the entity owes others and that others owe the entity.[49] At the core of this system is the *matching* of revenues and expenses. Interest in the accrual method has generated a search for the "best" accrual method in general and the "ideal income" in particular. For a long time, this accounting paradigm governed the evaluation of accounting alternatives and the asset-valuation and income-determination proposals. However, this approach was constantly challenged by proponents of *cash-flow accounting*. The *cash-flow basis of accounting* has been correctly defined as the recording not only of the cash receipts and disbursements of the period (the *cash* basis of accounting) but also of the *future cash flows* owed to or by the firm as a result of selling and transferring the titles to certain goods (the *accrual* basis of accounting).[50] The advocacy of cash-flow accounting is more evident in a questioning of the importance and efficacy of accrual accounting and a shift toward the cash-flow approach in security analysis.[51]

The question of the superiority of accrual accounting over cash-flow accounting is central to the determination of the objectives and the nature of financial reporting. Accrual accounting facilitates the evaluation of mangement's stewardship and is essential to the matching of revenues and expenses, which is required to properly align efforts and accomplishments. The efficacy of the accrual system has been questioned, however. Thomas states that all allocations are arbitrary and incorrigible and recommends the minimization of such allocations.[52] Hawkins and Campbell report a shift in security analysis from earnings-oriented valuation approaches to cash-flow-oriented valuation approaches.[53] Many decision-usefulness theorists advocate a cash-flow accounting system based on the investor's desires to predict cash flows.[54,55] Most advocates of cash-flow accounting feel that the problems of asset valuation and income determination are so formidable that they warrant the derivation of a separate accounting system and propose the inclusion of a comprehensive cash-flow statement in company reports. For instance, Lee describes how cash-flow accounting and net-realizable-value accounting can be combined in a series of articulating statements that provide more relevant information about cash and cash management than either system can provide individually.[56]

Cash-flow accounting is viewed by supporters as superior to conventional accrual accounting because:

1 A system of cash-flow accounting might provide an analytic framework for linking past, present, and future financial performance.[57]
2 From the perspective of investors, the projected cash flow would reflect both the company's ability to pay its way in the future and its planned financial policy.[58]
3 A price-discounted flow ratio would be a more reliable investment indicator than the present price–earnings ratio, due to the numerous arbitrary allocations used to compute earnings per share.[59]
4 Cash-flow accounting may be used to correct the gap in practice between the way in which an investment is made (generally based on cash flows) and the way in which the results are evaluated (generally based on earnings).[60]

The important question remaining is whether or not cash-flow accounting will be restored to its predominant position as an important and relevant source of financial information. All trends seem to indicate that the answer is in the affirmative. Witness the following eloquent and optimistic statement:

... of all the available systems of financial reporting, cash-flow accounting is one of the most objective and understandable. It attempts to state facts in financial-accounting terms, without the accountant having to become involved in making subjective judgments as to which period the data relate. And it is expressed in terms that should be familiar to all nonaccountants — cash resources and flows are things that anyone in a developed economy has to administer from day to day. Thus, cash-flow reports are potentially comprehensible, a matter that is of increasing concern to accountants as the number of report users and groups increases year by year.[61]

How would users react to cash-flow information? Evidence to date seems to indicate that security analysts use earnings information more often than they use cash-flow information in their professional reports.

15.6   EMPLOYEE REPORTING

The provision of financial and other relevant information to company employees and labor unions is a subject of growing interest. *The Corporate Report* is one of the first accounting documents to show concern for employees as users of published financial statements.[62] In fact, one of its primary recommendations, the *employment report*, is intended to show "the size and composition of the work force relying on the enterprise for its livelihood, the work contribution of employees, and the benefits earned."[63] The following data are recommended for inclusion in an employment report:

Number employed.
Location of employment.
Age distribution of permanent work force.
Hours worked during year.
Employee costs.
Pension information.
Education and training (including costs).
Recognized trade unions.
Additional information (race relations, health and safety statistics, etc.).
Employment ratios.[64]

As a result of the requirements of *The Corporate Report*, employee reporting is becoming more the rule than the exception in the United Kingdom. Other countries are demonstrating a growing awareness of information provision to company employees. These countries include: (1) the German Federal Republic, where, since 1972, employees have been considered the most important constituents to whom reports on the activities and performance of companies are addressed;[65] (2) France, where, since 1979, companies have been required to conduct social audits and present social reports to the enterprise council, as well as to employees;[66] and (3) Sweden, where the unions have free access to company information and the right to examine any company documents.[67] In North America, the major disclosures in annual reports seem to occur in the areas of occupational safety and health in the United States[68] and work stoppages in Canada.[69]

At this point in time, two questions arise: (1) What is triggering this movement toward the provision of financial information to employees? and (2) What kind of information is needed by employees?

The pressure to provide information to employees may be attributed to a number of wider societal changes. Purdy classifies these changes in four categories: "(1) the general pressure for greater company disclosure; (2) the practice and problems associated with industrial relations; (3) the emergence of a debate about industrial democracy; and (4) an awareness of information provision in other countries."[70] Of particular importance is the concept of industrial democracy, which suggests that employees and management be brought together in such a way that decisions of management are likely to motivate the employees. To implement industrial democracy, both employees and management would have to have access to the same information.

The information needs of employees are determined by their desire to forecast the outcome of collective bargaining. To date, no really solid prediction model of such outcome based on accounting data has presented a reasonable description of the information needs of employees.[71] However, it may be argued that employees (like investors) basically have a two-parameter utility function that encompasses a measure of expected earnings and a measure of risk. Maunders uses such reasoning to argue that "like investors, rational employees will therefore need information that will assist them in forecasting future values of these two parameters."[72] With regard to the parameter of "forecasting expected earnings," Maunders deduces the following information needs on the part of employees:

- Information identical to that used by investors for forecasting expected security earnings and risk attached to these.
- Labor-force data for the company as a whole: levels and patterns of employment, structure and distribution of rewards, etc.
- Disaggregated labor-force data: by plant, division, etc.[73]

With regard to "forecasting earnings (job) security," Maunders deduces the following information needs on the part of employees:

- Information for forecasting *total* risk attached to company earnings.
- Labor-force data, disaggregated; manpower-planning data in particular.
- Health and safety at work information.[74]

Although these employee-information needs may not constitute an exhaustive list, they provide a step toward the improvement of disclosure adequacy by providing vital information to employees — one of the most important constituencies of firms and potential user groups. The net benefit will surely be the improvement of communications between employees and management.

15.7 VALUE-ADDED REPORTING

Following favorable recommendations in *The Corporate Report*, a new form of accounting statement — the *value-added statement* — is gaining popularity in the corporate reports of the largest companies in the United Kingdom. This new statement may be viewed as a modified version of the income statement. Like the income statement, the value-added statement reports the operating performance of a company at a given point in time, using both accrual and matching procedures. Unlike the income statement, however, the value-added statement is interpreted not as a return to shareholders but as a return to a larger group of capital and labor providers. As a result, the value-added statement can be easily derived from the income statement, according to the following steps:

Step 1: The income statement can be expressed

$$R = S - B - DP - W - I - DD - T \tag{1}$$

where

$$
\begin{aligned}
R &= \text{retained earnings.} \\
S &= \text{sales revenue.} \\
B &= \text{bought-in materials and services.} \\
DP &= \text{depreciation.} \\
W &= \text{wages.} \\
I &= \text{interest.} \\
DD &= \text{dividends.} \\
T &= \text{taxes.}
\end{aligned}
$$

Equation (1) expresses the profit as a return to shareholders.

Step 2: The value statement may be obtained by rearranging Equation (1) as

$$S - B - DP = W + I + DD + T + R \tag{2}$$

or

$$S - B = W + I + DD + T + DP + R \tag{3}$$

Equation (2) expresses the *net* value added; Equation (3) expresses the *gross* value added. In either case, the left part of the equation shares the value added (net or gross) and the right part of the equation divides the value added among the group involved. Exhibit 15.3 shows how the value-added statement can be derived from a regular income statement.

What are the advantages and disadvantages of such a report? Various advantages of including a value-added statement in the company's annual report have been cited:*

1 It is generally believed that value added may be more favorable and acceptable to employees than profit and may motivate employees to work harder, because the value-added statement perceives them as responsible participators in a team effort with management. Witness the following statement:

    This improvement should come about because value added reflects a broader view of the company's role and objectives than profit does. Profit is regarded by some as being narrow, sectional, selfish, and predatory, and few workers are really keen to maximize it. Value added, however, is the achievement of a team: workers, managers, and providers of capital. Workers would prefer to see themselves as responsible participators in the value-added earnings team, rather than as hired hands who maximize their employer's profits.[75]

---

* The advantages and disadvantages of the value-added report cited here are largely inspired by Michael F. Morley's works, which are cited in the references.

EXHIBIT 15.3
Deriving the Value-Added Statement

The conventional income statement of a company for 19X6 was:

Sales		$1,000,000
Less: Materials Used	$100,000	
Wages	200,000	
Services Purchased	300,000	
Interest Paid	60,000	
Depreciation	40,000	
Profit Before Tax		$300,000
Income Tax (assume 50% tax rate)		150,000
Profit After Tax		$150,000
Less: Dividends Payable		50,000
Retained Earnings for the Year		$100,000

A value-added statement for the same year would be:

Sales		$1,000,000
Less: Bought-in Materials and Services and Depreciation		440,000
Value Added Available for Distribution or Retention		$ 560,000
Applied as follows:		
To Employees		$200,000
To Providers of Capital		
Interest	$60,000	
Dividends	50,000	110,000
To Government		150,000
Retained Earnings		100,000
Value Added		$ 560,000

2 The value-added statement is expected to facilitate the introduction of productivity incentives for employees — primarily in the form of the payment of incentives for the maximization of value-added-based ratios.
3 Value-added-based ratios are interpreted as more indicative and predictive of the strength of the company than conventional ratios.
4 Value-added measures are believed to constitute a better measure of the size and importance of companies.

Similarly, some disadvantages of including a value-added statement in the company's annual report have been cited:

1 Value added may be the wrong variable to maximize when making internal decisions pertaining to resource allocation. Morley uses the example of a company that buys a component for £5 that it could manufacture for £14 (£4 for direct material; £10 for direct labor).[76] Based on a relevant cost analysis, the decision would be to continue to buy the component. However, based on a maximization of value-added criterion, the decision would be to manufacture the component, thereby

raising the value added to £1 per component, even though profits would be lowered by £9 — in short, a disastrous decision.

2 Value added may lead to information overload and confusion, given the amount of information already included in the annual report and the small degree of familiarity with the concept by users.

15.8   CONCLUSIONS

The new scope of financial accounting requires a more extensive disclosure of information by business entities, because a greater variety of information is deemed relevant for economic decision making. The new data result from attempts to account for the social impact of firms' activities, changes in human capital, costs of equity capital, financial forecasts, cash-flow reporting, employee reporting, and value-added reporting. Such extensive disclosure is a new and different challenge that will require not only the development of new measurement and reporting techniques, but also the possible expansion of the boundaries of the attest function. The accountants and users of tomorrow will need to have a better grasp of the relationship between accounting and other disciplines in the social sciences, of the extent of their responsibilities, and of the need for continuous education.

NOTES

[1] Mobley, S.C., "The Challenges of Socioeconomic Accounting," *The Accounting Review* (October, 1970), p. 767.

[2] Linowes, D.F., "Socioeconomic Accounting," *Journal of Accountancy* (November, 1970), p. 37.

[3] Knapp, W., "Environmental Disruption and Social Cost: A Challenge to Economics," *Kylos* (December, 1970), p. 836.

[4] Ibid., p. 834.

[5] Ridker, R.G., *Economic Costs of Air Pollution* (New York: Praeger, 1978).

[6] Davis, Otto A., and Whinston, A.B., "Externalities, Welfare, and the Theory of Games," *Journal of Political Economy* (June, 1962), p. 120.

[7] Ibid., p. 120.

[8] Ibid., p. 120.

[9] Knapp, W., *The Social Costs of Private Enterprises* (Cambridge, Ma.: Harvard University Press, 1950), p. 13.

[10] National Association of Accountants, Committee on Accounting for Social Performance, "Accounting for Social Performance," *Management Accounting* (February, 1974), pp. 39–41.

[11] Epstein, M., Flamholtz, E., and McDonough, J.J., "Corporate Social Accounting in the United States of America: State of the Art and Future Prospects," *Accounting, Organizations, and Society,* Vol. 1, No. 1 (1976), pp. 23–42.

[12] Longstreth, B., and Rosenbloom, D., *Corporate Social Responsibility and the Institutional Investor* (New York: Praeger, 1973).

[13] Belkaoui, A., "The Impact of Socioeconomic Accounting Statements on the Investment Decision: An Empirical Study," *Accounting, Organizations, and Society* (September, 1980), pp. 263–83.

[14] Belkaoui, A., "The Impact of the Disclosure of the Environmental Effects of Organizational Behavior on the Market," *Financial Management* (Winter, 1976), pp. 26–31; Spicer, B., "Investors, Corporate Social Performance, and Information Disclosure: An Empirical Study," *The Accounting Review* (January, 1978), pp. 94–111; Ingram, R.W., "An Investigation of the Information Content of (Certain) Social-Responsibility Disclosures," *Journal of Accounting Research* (Autumn, 1978), pp. 270–85.

[15] Simon, G., Pavers, C.W., and Gunnerman, J.P., *The Ethical Investor* (New Haven, Ct.: Yale University Press, 1972).

[16] Beams, Floyd A., and Fertig, Paul E., "Pollution Control Through Social-Cost Conversion," *Journal of Accountancy* (November, 1971), pp. 37–42.

[17] AAA Committee, *A Statement of Basic Accounting Theory* (Evanston, Ill.: American Accounting Association, 1966), p. 35.

[18] Report of the Committee on Human-Resource Accounting," *Committee Report*, supplement to Vol. 48, *The Accounting Review* (1973), p. 169.

[19] Woodruff, R.L., "Human-Resource Accounting," *The Canadian Chartered Accountant Magazine* (September, 1970), pp. 2–7; Alexander, M.O., "Investments in People," *The Canadian Chartered Accountant Magazine* (July, 1971), pp. 38–45; Flamholtz, E., "Human-Resource Accounting: Measuring Positional Replacement Costs," *Human-Resource Management* (Spring, 1973), pp. 8–16.

[20] Elias, N.S., "The Effects of Human-Asset Statements on the Investment Decision: An Experiment," *Empirical Research in Accounting: Selected Studies*, supplement to Vol. 10, *Journal of Accounting Research* (1972), pp. 215–40.

[21] Woodruff, R.L., "Human-Resource Accounting," p. 2.

[22] Flamholtz, E., "Toward a Theory of Human-Resource Value in Formal Organizations," *The Accounting Review* (October, 1972), pp. 666–78; Likert, R., and Bowers, D.G., "Improving the Accuracy of P/L Reports by Estimating the Change in Dollar Value of the Human Organization," *Michigan Business Review* (March, 1973), pp. 15–24.

[23] Likert, R., and Bowers, D.G., "Improving the Accuracy of P/L Reports by Estimating the Change in Dollar Value of the Human Organization," p. 15.

[24] Ibid., p. 17.

[25] Glautier, N.W.E., and Underdown, B., "Problems and Prospects of Accounting for Human Assets," *Management Accounting* (March, 1973), p. 99.

[26] Flamholtz, E., *Human-Resource Accounting* (Los Angeles: Dickenson Publishing, 1974), p. 190.

[27] Hekimian, J.S., and Jones, J.G., "Put People on Your Balance Sheet," *Harvard Business Review* (January/February, 1967), p. 108.

[28] Likert, R., and Bowers, D.G., "Organizational Theory and Human-Resource Accounting," *American Psychologist*, Vol. 24, No. 6 (September, 1969), p. 588.

[29] Hekimian, J.S., and Jones, J.G., "Put People on Your Balance Sheet," pp. 108–109.

[30] Elovitz, D., "From the Thoughtful Businessman," *Harvard Business Review* (May/June, 1967), p. 59.

[31] Lev, B., and Schwartz, A., "On the Use of the Economic Concept of Human Capital in Financial Statements," *The Accounting Review* (January, 1971), p. 105.

[32] Hermanson, R.H., "Accounting for Human Assets," Occasional Paper No. 14 (East Lansing, Mi.: Bureau of Business and Economic Research, Graduate School of Business Administration, Michigan State University, 1964).

[33] Taylor, J.C., and Bowers, D.G., *The Survey of Organizations* (Ann Arbor, Mi.: Institute for Social Research, 1972).

[34] Anthony, R.N., "Accounting for the Cost of Equity Capital," *Harvard Business Review* (November/December, 1973), pp. 88–102; and *Accounting for the Cost of Interest* (New York: Lexington Books, 1975).

[35] Young, D.W., "Accounting for the Cost of Interest: Implications for the Timber Industry," *The Accounting Review* (October, 1976), p. 788.

[36] Anthony, R.N., "Accounting for the Cost of Equity," p. 96.

[37] Accounting Research Study No. 163, *Capitalizing of Interest by Companies Other Than Public Utilities* (Washington, D.C.: Securities and Exchange Commission, 1974), p. 4.

[38] FASB Statement No. 34, *Capitalization of Interest Cost* (Stamford, Ct.: Financial Accounting Standards Board, October, 1979).

[39] *Objectives of Financial Statements*. Report of the Study Group on the Objectives of Financial Statements (New York: American Institute of Certified Public Accountants, 1973), p. 13.

[40] *The City Code on Takeovers and Mergers* (Great Britain), revised February, 1972.

[41] Ibid., Rule 16.

[42] Ijiri, Yuji, "Improving Reliability of Publicly Reported Corporate Financial Forecasts," in *Public Reporting of Corporate Financial Forecasts*, (eds) P. Prakash and A. Rappaport (Chicago, Ill.: Commerce Clearing House, 1974), p. 169.

[43] Sycamore, R.J., "Public Disclosure of Earnings Forecasts by Companies," *The Chartered Accountant Magazine* (May, 1974), pp. 72–75.

[44] Daily, R.A., "The Feasibility of Reporting Forecasted Information," *The Accounting Review* (October, 1971), pp. 686–92.

[45] McDonald, Daniel L., "An Empirical Examination of the Reliability of Published Predictions of Future Earnings," *The Accounting Review* (July, 1973), pp. 502–59.

[46] Ijiri, Yuji, "Improving Reliability of Publicly Reported Corporate Financial Forecasts," op. cit., p. 163.

[47] Mautz, Robert K., " A View from the Public Accounting Profession," in *Public Reporting of Corporate Financial Forecasts*, (eds) P. Prakash and A. Rappaport (Chicago, Ill.: Commerce Clearing House, 1974), p. 102.

[48] Ibid., p. 110.

[49] Gross, M.J., Jr., *Financial and Accounting Guide for Nonprofit Organizations* (The Ronald Press, 1972).

[50] Hicks, B.E., "The Cash-Flow Basis of Accounting," *Working Paper No. 13* (Sudbury, Ontario: Laurentian University, 1980).

[51] Hawkins, D., and Campbell, W., *Equity Valuation: Models, Analysis, and Implications* (New York: Financial Executives Institute, 1978).

[52] Thomas, A.L., Accounting Research Study No. 3, *The Allocation Problem in Financial Accounting Theory* (Sarasota, Fl.: American Accounting Association, 1969); Accounting Research Study No. 9, *The Allocation Problem: Part Two* (Sarasota, Fl.: American Accounting Association, 1974).

[53] Hawkins, D., and Campbell, W., *Equity Valuation: Models, Analysis, and Implications*, p. 5.

[54] Staubus, G.J., *A Theory of Accounting to Investors* (Berkeley, Ca.: University of California Press, 1961).

[55] Revsine, L., *Replacement-Cost Accounting* (Englewood Cliffs, N.J.: Prentice-Hall, 1973).

[56] Lee, T.A., "Reporting Cash Flows and Net Realizable Values," *Accounting and Business Research* (Spring, 1981), pp. 163–70.

[57] Lawson, G.H., "Cash-Flow Accounting I & II," *The Accountant* (October 28–November 4, 1971), pp. 586–9.

[58] Lee, T.A., "A Case for Cash-Flow Reporting," *Journal of Business Finance* (1972), pp. 27–36.

[59] Ashton, R.H., "Cash-Flow Accounting: A Review and a Critique," *Journal of Business Finance and Accounting* (Winter, 1976), pp. 63–81.

[60] Lee, T.A., "Cash-Flow Accounting and Reporting," in *Developments in Financial Reporting*, (ed.) T.A. Lee (Oxford: Philip Allan Publishers, Ltd., 1981), pp. 148–70.

[61] Govindarajan, V., "The Objectives of Financial Statements: An Empirical Study of The Use of Cash Flow and Earnings by Security Analysts," *Accounting, Organizations, and Society* (December, 1980), p. 392.

[62] The Accounting Standards Steering Committee, *The Corporate Report* (London: The Institute of Chartered Accountants in England and Wales, 1975).

[63] Ibid., p. 48.

[64] Ibid., pp. 88–91.

[65] Van Den Bergh, R., "The Corporate Social Report — The Deutsche Shell Experience," *Accountancy* (December, 1976), pp. 111–18.

[66] *Le Bilan Social*, supplement to *Revue Française de Gestion* (December, 1977).

[67] Grojer, J.E. and Stark, A., "Social Accounting: A Swedish Attempt," *Accounting, Organizations, and Society*, Vol. 2, No. 4 (1977), pp. 349–86.

[68] Chan, J.L., "Corporate Disclosure in Occupational Safety and Health: Some Empirical Evidence," *Accounting, Organizations, and Society*, Vol. 4, No. 4 (1979), pp. 273–81.

[69] Nelson, M., "Accounting Disclosures of Strikes and Lockouts," *Cost and Management* (November/December, 1982), pp. 30–32.

[70] Purdy, D., "The Provision of Financial Information to Employees: A Study of the Reporting Practice of Some Large Public Companies in the United Kingdom," *Accounting, Organizations, and Society* (December, 1981), p. 327.

[71] Foley, B.J., and Maunders, K.T., *Accounting Information Disclosure and Collective Bargaining* (London: Macmillan, 1977).

[72] Maunders, K.T., "Employee Reporting," in *Developments in Financial Reporting*, (ed.) T.A. Lee (Oxford: Philip Allan Publishers, Ltd., 1981), p. 179.

[73] Ibid., p. 179.

REFERENCES

Socioeconomic Accounting

Alhashim, Dhia D., "Social Accounting in Egypt," *The International Journal of Accounting, Education, and Research*, Vol. 12, No. 2 (Spring, 1977), p. 128.

American Accounting Association, "Report of the Committee on Accounting for Social Performance," supplement, *The Accounting Review*, Vol. 46 (1971), pp. 39–69.

American Accounting Association, "Report of the Committee on Environmental Effects of Organization Behavior," supplement, *The Accounting Review*, Vol. 48 (1973), pp. 75–119.

American Accounting Association, "Report of the Committee on External Reporting," supplement, *The Accounting Review*, Vol. 44 (1969), p. 118.

American Accounting Association, "Report of the Committee on the Measurement of Social Costs," Supplement, *The Accounting Review*, Vol. 49 (1974), pp. 98–113.

American Accounting Association, "Report of the Committee on Measures of Effectiveness for Social Programs," Supplement, *The Accounting Review*, Vol. 47 (1972), pp. 337–96.

American Accounting Association, "Report of the Committee on Social Costs," Supplement, *The Accounting Review*, Vol. 50 (1975), p. 53.

Anderson, John C., and Frankle, Alan W., "Voluntary Social Reporting: An Iso-Beta Portfolio Analysis." *The Accounting Review* (July, 1980), pp. 467–79.

Beams, Floyd A., "Accounting for Environmental Pollution," *The New York Certified Public Accountant* (now *The CPA Journal*), (August, 1970), pp. 657–61.

Beams, Floyd A., and Fertig, Paul E., "Pollution Control Through Social-Cost Conversion," *Journal of Accountancy* (November, 1971), pp. 37–42.

Belkaoui, A., "The Impact of the Disclosure of the Environmental Effects of Organizational Behavior on the Market," *Financial Management* (Winter, 1976), pp. 26–31.

Belkaoui, A., "The Impact of Socioeconomic Accounting Statements on the Investment Decision: An Empirical Study," *Accounting, Organizations, and Society* (September, 1980), pp. 263–83.

Belkaoui, A., *Socioeconomic Accounting* (Westport, Ct.: Greenwood Press, 1984).

Bragdon, Joseph H., and Marlin, John. "Is Pollution Profitable?," *Risk Management* (April, 1978), pp. 3–10.

Buzby, Stephen L., and Falk, Haim. "Demand for Social Responsibility Information by University Investors," *The Accounting Review* (January, 1979), pp. 23–37.

Buzby, Stephen L., and Falk, Haim, "A Survey of the Interest in Social Responsibility Information by Mutual Funds," *Accounting, Organizations, and Society* (May, 1979), pp. 99–201.

Chugh, Lal C., Haneman, Michael, and Mahapatra, S., "Impact of Pollution-Control Regulations on the Market Risk of Securities in the U.S." *Journal of Economic Studies* (May, 1978), pp. 64–70.

Churchill, Neil C., and Shank, John K., "Accounting for Affirmative Action Programs: A Stochastic-Flow Approach," *The Accounting Review* (October, 1975), pp. 643–56.

Colantoni, C.S., Cooper, W.W., and Deitzer, H. J., "Budgeting Disclosure and Social Accounting," *Corporate Social Accounting*, (eds) Meinolf Dierkes and Raymond Bauer (New York: Praeger, 1973), pp. 376–77.

Cooper, David, and Essex, Simon., "Accounting Information and Employee Decision Making." *Accounting, Organizations, and Society*, Vol. 2, No. 3 (1977), p. 201.

Corcoran, Wayne, and Leininger, Wayne, E., Jr., "Financial Statements — Who Needs Them?," *Financial Executive* (August, 1970), pp. 34–38, 45–47.

Dierkes, Meinolf, "Corporate Social Reporting in Germany: Conceptual Developments and Practical Experience." *Accounting, Organizations, and Society*, Vol. 4, No. 1/2 (1979), p. 92.

Dilley, Steven C., "External Reporting of Social Responsibility." *MSU Business Topics* (Autumn, 1975), p. 18.

Dilley, Steven C., and Weygandt, Jerry J., "Measuring Social Responsibility: An Empirical Test," *Journal of Accountancy* (September, 1973), p. 64.

Epstein, M., Flamholtz, E., and McDonough, J.J., *Corporate Social Performance: The Measurement of Product and Service Contributions* (New York: National Association of Accountants, 1976).

Estes, Ralph. *Corporate Social Accounting* (New York: John Wiley & Sons, 1976), p. 62.

Francis, Mildred, "Thoughts on Some Measures of Effectiveness of Social Programs." Unpublished paper prepared for Robert E. Jensen, College of Business Administration, University of Maine (Orono: March, 1971), p. 3.

Grojer, J.E., and Stark, A., "Social Accounting: A Swedish Attempt," *Accounting, Organizations, and Society*, Vol. 2, No. 4 (1977), pp. 349–86.

Ingram, Robert W. "An Investigation of the Information Content of (Certain) Social Responsibility Disclosures." *Journal of Accounting Research* (Autumn, 1978), pp. 270–85.

Ingram, Robert W., and Frazier, Katherine Beal, "Environmental Performance and Corporate Disclosure." *Journal of Accounting Research* (Spring, 1980), pp. 603–13.

Jaggi, Bikki, and Freedman, Martin. "An Analysis of the Information Content of Pollution Disclosures," *The Financial Review* (forthcoming).

Keller, Wayne, (Chairman, Committee on Accounting for Social Performance). "Accounting for Corporate Social Performance," *Management Accounting* (February, 1974), pp. 39–41.

Marlin, John Tepper, "Accounting for Pollution," *Journal of Accountancy* (February, 1973), pp. 41–46.

The Measurement of Corporate Social Performance, (New York: American Institute of Certified Public Accountants, 1977).

Morley, Michael F., "The Value-Added Statement in Britain," *The Accounting Review* (July, 1979), p. 629.

Nikolai, Loren A., Bazley, John D., and Brummet, R. Lee, *The Measurement of Corporate Environmental Activity*. New York: National Association of Accountants, 1976.

"Pollution Price Tag: 71 Billion Dollars," *U.S. News & World Report* (August 17, 1970), p. 41.

Robertson, John, "Corporate Social Reporting by New Zealand Companies," *Journal of Contemporary Business* (Winter, 1978), pp. 113–33.

Schoenfeld, Hanns-Martin, *The Status of Social Reporting in Selected Countries*, (Urbana, Ill.: Center for International Education and Research in Accounting, 1978), pp. 1–19.

Schreuder, Hein. "Corporate Social Reporting in the Federal Republic of Germany: An Overview," *Accounting, Organizations, and Society*, Vol. 4, No. 1/2 (1979), p. 111.

Schreuder, Hein, "Employees and the Corporate Social Report: The Dutch Case," *The Accounting Review* (April, 1981), pp. 294–308.

Seidler, Lee J., "Dollar Values in the Social Income Statement," *World* (Peat, Marwick, Mitchell, and Co.) (Spring, 1973), pp. 14, 16–23.

Social Measurement. (New York: American Institute of Certified Public Accountants, 1972).

Spicer, B., "Investors, Corporate Social Performance, and Information Disclosure: An Empirical Study," *The Accounting Review* (January, 1978), pp. 94–111.

Spicer, B., "Market Risk, Accounting Data, and Companies' Pollution-Control Records," *Journal of Business Finance and Accounting* (Spring, 1978), pp. 67–84.

Sudreau, P., *Rapport du Comité d'Etudes pour la Reforme de l'Entreprise*. (Paris: La Documentation Française, 1975).

Sudreau, P., "The Reform of the Enterprise," *Accounting, Organizations, and Society*, Vol. 1, No. 1 (1976), pp. 97–99.

Tokutani, Masao, and Kawano, Masao. "A Note on the Japanese Social Accounting Literature," *Accounting, Organizations, and Society*, Vol. 3, No. 2 (1978), p. 184.

Trotman, K.T., and Bradley, G.W., "Associations Between Social Responsibility Disclosure and Characteristics of Companies," *Accounting, Organizations, and Society*, Vol. 6, No. 4 (1981), pp. 355–62.

Wiseman, J., "An Evaluation of Environmental Disclosures Made in Corporate Annual Reports," *Accounting, Organizations, and Society* (February, 1982), pp. 53–64.

Social Auditing

Abt, Clark, "Managing to Save Money While Doing Good," *Innovation* (January, 1972).

Allard, J. Claude, "Comprehensive Auditing in Crown Corporations," *The Chartered Accountant Magazine* (February, 1981), pp. 38–43.

Bauer, Raymond A., Cauthorn, L. Terry, and Warner, Ranne P., "Auditing the Management Process for Social Performance," *Business and Society Review* (1979), pp. 39–45.

Bauer, Raymond A., and Fenn, Dan H., Jr., "What Is a Corporate Social Audit?," *Harvard Business Review* (January/February, 1973), pp. 37–48.

Blake, David H., Frederick, William C., and Myers, Mildred S., *Social Auditing: Evaluating the Impact of Corporate Programs.* (New York: Praeger, 1976).

Blum, Fred., "Social Audit of the Enterprise," *Harvard Business Review* (March/April, 1958).

Boyles, Jesse V., III, "Energy Accounting," *Management Accounting* (February, 1979), pp. 35–41.

Brooks, Leonard J., and Davis, William R., "Some Approaches to the Corporate Social Audit," *The Chartered Accountant Magazine* (March, 1977), pp. 34–45.

Butcher, Bernard L., "The Program-Management Approach to the Corporate Social Audit," *California Management Review* (Fall, 1973), pp. 11–24.

Charnes, A., and Cooper, W.W., "Auditing and Accounting for Program Efficiency and Management Efficiency in Not-For-Profit Entities," *Accounting, Organizations, and Society*, Vol. 5, No. 1, pp. 87–107.

Churchill, N.C., Cooper, W.W., San Miguel, J., Govindarajan, V., and Pond J., "Comprehensive Audits and Some Suggestions for Research," *Symposium on Auditing Research II.* Department of Accountancy, University of Illinois at Urbana-Champaign, 1977.

Churchill, N.C., and Cyert, R.M., "An Experiment in Management Auditing," *Journal of Accountancy* (February, 1966), pp. 39–43.

Corson, John J., Steiner, George A., and Meehan, Robert C., *Measuring Business's Social Performance: The Corporate Audit.* (New York: Committee for Economic Development, 1974).

Council on Economic Priorities. *Efficiency in Death*, (New York: Harper & Row, 1970).

Dewhirst, James, "Truest and Fairest: The Case for Social Audits," *The Accountant* (August 2, 1973), pp. 143–4.

Dilley, Steven C., "What Is Social Responsibility: Some Definitions for Doing the Corporate Social Audit," *The Chartered Accountant Magazine* (November, 1974), pp. 24–28.

Fetyko, D.F., "The Company Social Audit," *Management Accounting* (April, 1975), pp. 31–34.

Gartenberg, Morris, "How Dow Accounts for Its Energy Use." *Management Accounting* (March, 1980), pp. 10–12.

Gray, Daniel H., "Methodology: One Approach to the Corporate Social Audit," *California Management Review* (Summer, 1973), pp. 108–109.

Hay, Robert D., "Social Auditing: An Experimental Approach," *Academy of Management Journal* (December, 1975), pp. 871–7.

Higgins, James M., "A Proposed Social Performance Evaluation System," *Atlanta Economic Review* (May/June, 1977), pp. 4–9.

Humble, John, *Social Responsibility Audit: A Management Tool for Survival.* (London: Foundation for Business Responsibilities, 1973).

Industrial Energy Efficiency Program: July 1977 Through December, 1978 (Annual Report). (Washington, D.C.: U.S. Government Printing Office, 1979).

Katugampola, B., "The Energy Audit," *Internal Auditor* (October, 1978), pp. 93–5.

Linowes, D.F., "An Approach to Socioeconomic Accounting," *The Conference Board Record* (March, 1972), pp. 58–61.

Linowes, D.F., "Let's Get on with the Social Audit: A Specific Proposal," *Business and Society Review/Innovation* (November, 1978).

McDonnell, James, J., "Auditing the Government of Canada: A Centennial Conspectus," *The Chartered Accountant Magazine* (December, 1978), pp. 22–31.

Roth, Harold P., "A New Outlet for Energy Audit Data," *Journal of Accountancy* (September, 1981), pp. 68–82.

Ryder, Charles, "Energy Audits and Case Histories," *Energy World* (November, 1976).

Ryder, Charles, "The Need for an Energy Audit," *Management Accounting* (England), (May, 1976).

Sethi, S. Prakash, "Getting a Handle on the Social Audit," *Business and Society Review/Innovation*, (Winter, 1972/1973).

Tipgos, Manuel A., "A Case Against the Social Audit," *Management Accounting* (November, 1976), pp. 23–26.

Ullman, Arieh A., "The Corporate Environmental Accounting System: A Management Tool for Fighting Environmental Degradation," *Accounting, Organizations, and Society*, Vol. 1, No. 1, pp. 71–9.

Human-Resource Accounting

Alexander, Michael O., "Investment in People," *The Canadian Chartered Accountant Magazine* (July, 1971), pp. 38–45.

Allen, Albrecht, D., "Accounting for and Controlling Staff Work," *Management Accounting* (February, 1968).

Barret, James, E., "The Case for Evaluation of Training Expenses," *Business Horizons* (April, 1969).

Basset, Glenn A., "Employee Turnover Measurement and Human-Resource Accounting," *Human-Resource Management* (Fall, 1972).

Becker, Gary S., "Investment in Human Capital: A Theoretical Analysis," Supplement, *Journal of Political Economy* (October, 1962).

Blaine, E., and Stanbury, W.T., "Accounting for Human Capital," *The Canadian Chartered Accountant Magazine* (January, 1971).

Bowers, D.G., and Franklin, J.L., "Survey-Guided Development: Using Human-Resource Measurement in Organizational Change," *Journal of Contemporary Business* (Summer, 1972).

Bowman, Mary Jean, "The Human Investment Revolution in Economic Thought," *Sociology of Education* (Spring, 1966).

Braunstein, Daniel N., "Management Science: A Behavioral View," *Interfaces*, The Institute of Management Sciences (May, 1972).

Brummet, R.L., "Accounting for Human Resources," *Journal of Accountancy* (December, 1970).

Brummet, R.L., "Accounting for Human Resources," *The New York Certified Public Accountant* (July, 1970).

Brummet, R.L., "Total Performance Measurement," *Management Accounting* (November, 1973).

Brummet, R.L., Flamholtz, E.G., and Pyle, W.C., "Accounting for Human Resources," *Michigan Business Review* (March, 1968).

Brummet, R.L., Flamholtz, E.G., and Pyle, W.C., "Human-Resource Accounting: A Tool to Increase Managerial Effectiveness," *Management Accounting* (August, 1969), pp. 12–15.

Brummet, R.L., Flamholtz, E.G., and Pyle, W.C., "Human-Resource Accounting in Industry," *Personnel Administration* (July/August, 1969), pp. 34–46.

Brummet, R.L., Flamholtz, E.G., and Pyle, W.C., "Human-Resource Measurement — a Challenge for Accountants," *The Accounting Review* (April, 1968), pp. 217–24.

Deangelo, L.E., "Unrecorded Human Assets and the 'Hold Up' Problem," *Journal of Accounting Research* (Spring, 1982), pp. 272–4.

Dittman, D.A., Juris, H.A., and Revsine, L., "On the Existence of Unrecorded Human Assets: An Economic Perspective," *Journal of Accounting Research* (Spring, 1976), pp. 49–64.

Dittman, D.A., Juris, H.A., and Revsine, L., "Unrecorded Human Assets: A Survey of Accounting Firms' Training Programs," *The Accounting Review* (October, 1980), pp. 640–48.

Eggers, H.C., "The Evaluation of Human Assets," *Management Accounting* (November, 1971).

Elias, N.S., "The Effects of Human-Asset Statements on the Investment Decision: An Experiment," *Journal of Accounting Research*, Vol. 10, supplement, *Empirical Research in Accounting: Selected Studies* (1972), pp. 215–40.

Elias, N.S., "Some Aspects of Human-Resource Accounting," *Cost and Management* (November/December, 1971).

Flamholtz, E.G., "Assessing the Validity of a Theory of Human-Resource Value: A Field Study," *Journal of Accounting Research,* Vol. 10. *Empirical Research in Accounting: Selected Studies* (1972), pp. 241–66.

Flamholtz, E.G., "Human-Resource Accounting: Measuring Positional Replacement Costs," *Human-Resource Management* (Spring, 1973), pp. 1–12.

Flamholtz, E.G., "A Model for Human-Resource Valuation: A Stochastic Process with Service Rewards," *The Accounting Review* (April, 1971), pp. 252–67.

Flamholtz, E.G., "Should Your Organization Attempt to Value Its Human Resources?" *California Management Review* (Winter, 1971), pp. 40–45.

Flamholtz, E.G., "Toward a Theory of Human-Resource Value in Formal Organizations," *The Accounting Review* (October, 1972), pp. 666–78.

Flamholtz, E.G., "On the Use of the Economic Concept of Human Capital in Financial Statements: A Comment," *The Accounting Review* (January, 1972), pp. 148–52.

Gilbert, Michael H. "The Asset Value of Human Organization." *Management Accounting* (July, 1970), pp. 23–35.

Glauthier, M.W.E. "Human-Resource Accounting: A Critique of Research Objectives for the Development of Human-Resource Accounting Models." *Journal of Business Finance and Accounting* (Summer, 1976), pp. 3–21.

Hekimian, J.S., and Jones, J.G. "Put People on Your Balance Sheet." *Harvard Business Review* (January/February, 1967), pp. 105–13.

Herzberg, Frederick. "One More Time: How Do you Motivate Employees?" *Harvard Business Review* (January/February, 1968).

Kelley, Roger T. "Accounting in Personnel Administration." *Personnel Administration* (May/June, 1967).

Kollaritsch, Felix P. "Future Service Potential Value." *Journal of Accountancy* (February, 1965).

Krein, Ted J. "People — Assets That Talk Back." *The Internal Auditor* (July/August, 1969).

Lawrence, Susanne. "Putting People on the Balance Sheet." *Personnel Management* (January, 1971).

Lev, B., and Schwartz, Aba. "On the Use of the Economic Concept of Human Capital in Financial Statements." *The Accounting Review* (January, 1971), pp. 103–12.

Lev, B., and Schwartz, Aba. "On the Use of the Economic Concept of Human Capital in Financial Statements: A Reply." *The Accounting Review* (January, 1972), pp. 153–4.

Likert, R. "Human Organizational Measurements: Key to Financial Success." *Michigan Business Review* (May, 1971).

Likert, R. "Human-Resource Accounting: Building and Assessing Productive Organizations." *Personnel* (May/June, 1973).

Likert, R. "Human Resources — The Hidden Assets of Your Firm." *Credit and Financial Management* (June, 1971).

Likert, R. "Recognizing the Value of People." *International Management* (March, 1973).

Likert, R., and Bowers, D.G. "Improving the Accuracy of P/L Reports by Estimating the Change in Dollar Value of the Human Organization." *Michigan Business Review* (March, 1973), pp. 15–24.

Likert, R., and Bowers, D.G. "Organizational Theory and Human-Resource Accounting." *American Psychologist,* Vol. 24, No. 6 (September, 1969), pp. 585–92.

Likert, R., Bowers, D.G., and Norman, R.M. "How to Increase a Firm's Lead Time in Recognizing and Dealing with Problems of Managing Its Human Organization." *Michigan Business Review* (January, 1969).

Likert, R., and Pyle, W.C. "A Human Organizational Measurement Approach." *Financial Analysts Journal* (January/February, 1971), pp. 75–84.

Likert, R., and Seashore, S.E. "Making Cost Control Work." *Harvard Business Review* (November/December, 1963), pp. 96–108.

McRae, T.W. "Human-Resource Accounting as a Management Tool." *Journal of Accountancy* (August, 1971), pp. 32–38.

Marangell, Frank. "How to Establish a Human-Resource Data Base." *Personnel* (January/February, 1972).

Miles, Raymond E. "Human Relations or Human Resources?," *Harvard Business Review* (July/August, 1965).

Newell, Gale E. "Should Humans Be Reported as Assets?," *Management Accounting* (December, 1972).

Norton, H.S., and Kiker, B.F. "The Public Utility Concept and Human Capital." *Public Utilities Fortnightly* (April 11, 1968).

Ogolin, Earl J. "Human-Resource Accounting." *The U.S. Army Audit Agency* (Spring, 1970).

Paine, Frank T. "Human-Resource Accounting — The Current State of the Question." *The Federal Accountant* (June, 1970).

Peterson, Sandra E. "Accounting for Human Resources." *Management Accounting* (June, 1972).

Pyle, W.C. "Human-Resource Accounting." *Financial Analysts Journal* (September/October, 1970).

Pyle, W.C. "Monitoring Human Resources — 'On Line'." *Michigan Business Review* (July, 1970), pp. 19–32.

Ross, G.H.B. "Social Accounting: Measuring the Unmeasurables?," *The Canadian Chartered Accountant Magazine* (July, 1971).

Schultz, T.W. "Capital Formation by Education." *Journal of Political Economy* (December, 1960).

Shephard, Clarence D. "Missing from the Balance Sheet: People as Our Greatest Asset." *The Certified General Accountant* (December, 1969).

Simpson, Robert R., Jr. "The Management of Human Resource." *Journal of Accountancy* (September, 1971).

Singer, Henry A. "The Impact of Human Resources on Business." *Business Horizons* (April, 1969).

Stone, Florence. "Investment in Human Resources at AT&T." *Management Review* (October, 1972).

Tomassini, L.A. "Assessing the Impact of Human-Resource Accounting: An Experimental Study of Managerial Decision Preferences." *The Accounting Review* (October, 1977), pp. 904–14.

Weisbroad, Burton A. "Education and Investment in Human Capital." *Journal of Political Economy* (October, 1962).

Weiss, Marvin. "Accounting for Human Resources." *The Magazine of Bank Administration* (December, 1972).

Weiss, Marvin. "Where 'Human-Resource Accounting' Stands Today." *Administrative Management Society Report* (November, 1972).

Wingfield, Mervyn W. "Another Look at Human-Resource Accounting." *The Virginia Accountant* (September, 1971).

Winpisinger, William. "Human Resources." *Managerial Planning* (September/October, 1971).

Woodruff, Robert L., Jr. "Human-Resource Accounting." *The Canadian Chartered Accountant Magazine* (September, 1970), pp. 2–7.

Woodruff, Robert L., Jr. "Measuring Staff Turnover." *The Canadian Chartered Accountant Magazine* (February, 1973).

Woodruff, Robert L., Jr. "What Price People?," *The Personnel Administrator* (January/February, 1969), pp. 17–20.

Wright, Robert. "Managing Man as a Capital Asset." *Personnel Journal* (April, 1970).

Accounting for the Cost of Capital

Anthony, R.N. "Accounting for the Cost of Equity Capital." *Harvard Business Review* (November/December, 1973), pp. 88–102.

Anthony, R.N. *Accounting for the Cost of Interest.* New York: Lexington Books, 1975.

Anthony, R.N. "Equity Interest: A Cure for the Double Taxation of Dividends." *Financial Executive* (July, 1977), pp. 20–23.

Anthony, R.N. "Equity Interest — Its Time Has Come." *Journal of Accountancy* (December, 1982), pp. 76–90.

Bartley, J.W., and Davidson, L.F. "The Entity Concept and Accounting for Interest Costs." *Accounting and Business Research* (Summer, 1982), pp. 175–87.

Bierman, H., Jr., and Dyckman, T.R. "Accounting for Interest During Construction." *Accounting and Business Research* (Autumn, 1979), pp. 267–72.

Brennan, W.J., and Silvester, W.H. "Accounting for Interest Cost." *The Chartered Accountant Magazine* (October, 1981), pp. 74–76.

Defliese, P.L. "Defliese Calls for 'Cost of Capital Disclosures'." *Journal of Accountancy* (May, 1975), p. 25.

Paton, W.A. "Interest and Profit Theory — Amended from an Accounting Stance." *Journal of Accountancy* (June, 1976), pp. 76–82.

Russell, F. "Accounting for the Cost of Capital." *Cost and Management* (July/August, 1974), pp. 50–52.

Young, D.W. "Accounting for the Cost of Interest: Implications for the Timber Industry." *The Accounting Review* (October, 1976), pp. 788–99.

Public Reporting of Corporate Financial Forecasts

Abdel-Khalik, A.R., and Thompson, R. "Research on Earnings Forecasts: The State of the Art." *Accounting Journal* (Winter, 1977/1978), pp. 180–217.

Abdelsamad, M.H., and Gilbreath, G.H. "Publication of Earnings Forecasts: A Report of Financial Executives Opinions." *Managerial Planning* (January/February, 1978), pp. 26–30.

American Institute of Certified Public Accountants. *Presentation and Disclosure of Financial Forecasts.* New York: American Institute of Certified Public Accountants, 1975.

Asebrook, R., and Carmichael, D. "Reporting on Forecasts: A Survey of Attitudes." *Journal of Accounting* (August, 1973), pp. 38–48.

Backer, M. "Reporting Profit Expectations." *Management Accounting* (February, 1972), pp. 33–37.

Barefield, R.M., and Comiskey, E. "The Accuracy of Analysts Forecasts of Earnings Per Share." *Journal of Business Research* (July, 1975), pp. 241–52.

Barnes, A., Sadan, S., and Schiff, M. "Afraid of Publishing Forecasts." *Financial Executive* (November, 1977), pp. 52–58.

Basi, B. "The CPA's Liability for Forecasts." *The CPA Journal* (February, 1976), pp. 13–17.

Basi, B., Carey, K., and Twark, R. "A Comparison of the Accuracy of Corporate and Security Analysts Forecasts of Earnings." *Accounting Review* (April, 1976), pp. 244–54.

Bedingfield, J.P., and Lubell, M.S. "Extension of the Attest Function to Published Forecasts — An Opinion Survey." *The CPA Journal* (January, 1974), pp. 40–45.

Benjamin, J., and Strawser, R. "The Publication of Forecasts: An Experiment." *Abacus* (May, 1974), pp. 138–46.

Bissell, G. "A Professional Investor Looks at Earnings Forecasts." *Financial Analysts Journal* (May/June, 1972), pp. 73–7.

Blum, J., and Chadwick, L. "Accounting Educators' Views on Financial Forecasting." *The CPA Journal* (March, 1974), pp. 15–16.

Brown, L., and Rozeff, M. "The Superiority of Analysts Forecasts as Measures of Expectations: Evidence from Earnings." *Journal of Finance* (March, 1978), pp. 1–15.

Carpenter, C., and Daily, R. "Controllers and CPA's: Two Views of Published Forecasts." *Business Horizons* (August, 1974), pp. 73–8.

Clark, J., and Elgers, P. "Forecasted Income Statements: An Investor Perspective." *Accounting Review* (October, 1973), pp. 668–78.

Copeland, R., and Marioni, P. "Executives Forecasts of Earnings Per Share Versus Forecasts of Naive Models." *Journal of Business* (October, 1972), pp. 497–512.

Corless, J., and Norgard, C. "User Reactions to CPA Reports on Earnings Forecasts." *Journal of Accounting* (August, 1974), pp. 46–54.

Craig, J., and Malkiel, B. "The Consensus and Accuracy of Some Predictions of the Growth of Corporate Earnings." *Journal of Finance* (March, 1968), pp. 67–84.

Crichfield, T., Dyckman, T.R., and Lakonishok, J. "An Evaluation of Security Analysts' Forecasts." *Accounting Review* (July, 1978), pp. 651–66.

Daily, R. "The Feasibility of Reporting Forecasted Information." *Accounting Review* (October, 1971), pp. 686–92.

Dev, S. "Statements of Company Prospects." *Accounting and Business Research* (Autumn, 1974), pp. 270–74.

Dev, S., and Webb, M. "The Accuracy of Company Forecasts." *Journal of Business Finance* (Autumn, 1972), pp. 26–39.

Elton, E., and Gruber, M. "Earnings Estimates and the Accuracy of Expectational Data." *Management Science* (April, 1972), pp. B409–B424.

Epstein, M. "A Shareholder's View of Earnings Forecasts." *Managerial Planning* (November/December, 1975), pp. 33–6.

Fess, P., and Martin, S. "Company Forecasts and the Independent Auditor's Inexorable Involvement." *The CPA Journal* (October, 1973), pp. 868–76.

Foster, G. "Stock-Market Reaction to Estimates of Earnings Per Share by Company Officials." *Journal of Accounting Research* (Spring, 1973), pp. 25–37.

Fraser, D.R., and Richards, R. "Forecasting Bank Earnings." *Magazine of Bank Administration* (August, 1975), pp. 40–45.

Gillis, I. "Legal Aspects of Corporate Forecasts." *Financial Analysts Journal* (January/February, 1973), pp. 72–6.

Gonedes, N.J., Dopuch, N., and Penman, S. "Disclosure Rules, Information Production, and Capital Market Equilibrium: The Case of Forecast Disclosure Rules." *Journal of Accounting Research* (Spring, 1976), pp. 86–129.

Gray, W. "Proposal for Systematic Disclosure of Corporate Forecasts." *Financial Analysts Journal* (January/February, 1973), pp. 64–71.

Gray, W., Gilles, J., and Stewart, S. *Disclosure of Corporate Forecasts to the Investor.* (New York: Financial Analysts Research Foundation, 1973).

Green, D., and Segall, J. "The Predictive Power of First-Quarter Earnings Reports: A Replication." *Journal of Accounting Research.* Supplement, *Empirical Research in Accounting: Selected Studies* (1966).

Grenside, J.P. "Accountants Report on Profit Forecasts in the U.K." *Journal of Accountancy* (May, 1970).

Griffin, P. "Competitive Information in the Stock Market: An Empirical Study of Earnings, Dividends, and Analysts' Forecasts." *Journal of Finance* (June, 1972), pp. 631–50.

Guy, D.M. "Auditing Projected Financial Statements." *Management Accounting* (November, 1972), pp. 33–37.

Imhoff, E.A., Jr. "The Representativeness of Management Earnings Forecasts." *The Accounting Review* (October, 1978), pp. 836–50.

Jaggi, Bikki. "A Note on the Information Content of Corporate Annual Earnings Forecasts." *The Accounting Review* (October, 1978), pp. 961–7.

Kapnick, H. "Will Financial Forecasts Really Help Investors?" *Financial Executive* (August, 1972), pp. 50–54.

Kidd, R. *Earnings Forecasts.* Toronto: The Canadian Institute of Chartered Accountants, 1976.

Killough, L. "Arguments for Published Forecasted Financial Data." *The National Public Accountant* (December, 1973), pp. 15–17.

Lorek, K.S. "A Commentary on Research on Earnings Forecasts: The State of the Art." *The Accounting Journal* (Winter, 1970–1971), pp. 210–17.

Lorek, K.S., McDonald, C., and Patz, D. "A Comparative Examination of Management Forecasts of Earnings." *The Accounting Review* (April, 1976), pp. 321–9.

MacDonald, Daniel L., "An Empirical Examination of the Reliability of Published Predictions of Future Earnings." *The Accounting Review* (July, 1973), pp. 502–59.

Mandel, J.D., and Atschul, D. "Financial Forecasts and Projections: A Pitfall for the Uninitiated Accountant." *Journal of Accountancy* (May, 1977), pp. 46–9.

Nichols, D.R., and Tsay, J.J. "Security Price Reactions to Long-Range Executive Earnings Forecasts." *Journal of Accounting Research* (Spring, 1979), pp. 140–55.

Nickerson, C., Pointer, L., and Strawser, R. "Published Forecasts: Choice or Obligation?" *Financial Executive* (February, 1974), pp. 70–73.

Niederhoffer, V., and Regan, P. "Earnings Changes, Analysts' Forecasts, and Stock Prices." *Financial Analysts Journal* (May/June 1972), pp. 65–71.

Patell, J. "Corporate Forecasts of Earnings Per Share and Stock-Price Behavior: Empirical Tests." *Journal of Accounting Research* (Autumn, 1976), pp. 246–76.

Richards, R. "Analysts' Performance and the Accuracy of Corporate Earnings Forecasts." *Journal of Business* (July, 1976), pp. 350–57.

Richards, R., and Fraser, D. "Management's Role in Profit Forecasting." *Review of Business and Economic Research* (Spring, 1977), pp. 34–41.

Ruder, D. "Civil Liability for Corporate Financial Forecasts — A View From the Legal Profession." *Public Reporting of Corporate Financial Forecasts.* (New York: Commerce Clearing House, 1976).

Ruland, W. "The Accuracy of Forecasts by Management and by Financial Analysts." *The Accounting Review* (April, 1978), pp. 439–46.

Ruland, W. "Management Forecasts, Stock Prices, and Public Policy." *Review of Business and Economic Research* (Winter, 1978/1979), pp. 16–29.

Shank, I. "The Pros and Cons of Forecast Publication." *Business Horizons* (October, 1973), pp. 43–9.

Shank, I., and Calfee, I. "Case of the FUQUA Forecasts." *Harvard Business Review* (November, 1973), pp. 34–6.

Smith, L., and Murphy, G. "Earnings Forecasting — Investment Analysts Versus Exponential Models." *Journal of Business Administration* (Fall, 1976), pp. 11–21.

Stewart, S. "Research Report on Corporate Forecasts." *Financial Analysts Journal* (January/February, 1973), pp. 75–85.

Westwick, C. "Profit Forecasts in Bid Situations." *Accountancy* (July, 1972), pp. 10–16.

Cash-Flow Accounting

American Accounting Association, Committee on External Reporting. "An Evaluation of External Reporting Practices." A report of the 1966–1968 Committee on External Reporting. Supplement, *The Accounting Review* (1969), pp. 79–123.

Ashton, R.H. "Cash-Flow Accounting: A Review and Critique." *Journal of Business Finance and Accounting* (Winter, 1976), pp. 63–81.

Barlev, B., and Levy, H. "On the Variability of Accounting Income Numbers." *Journal of Accounting Research* (Autumn, 1979), pp. 305–15.

Belkaoui, A. "Accrual Accounting and Cash Accounting: Relative Merits of Derived Accounting Indicator Numbers." *Accounting and Business Research* (Summer, 1983), pp. 299–312.

Climo, Tom "Cash-Flow Statements for Investors." *Journal of Business Finance and Accounting* (Autumn, 1976), pp. 3–16.

Edey, H.C. "Accounting Principles and Business Reality." *Journal of Accountancy* (November, 1963), pp. 998–1002, and (December, 1963), pp. 1083–8.

Govindarajan, V. "The Objectives of Financial Statements: An Empirical Study of the Use of Cash Flow and Earnings by Security Analysts." *Accounting, Organizations, and Society* (December, 1980), pp. 383–92.

Hawkins, D., and Campbell, W. *Equity Valuation: Models, Analysis, and Implications.* (New York: Financial Executives Institute, 1978).

Hicks, B.E. "The Cash-Flow Basis of Accounting." *Working Paper No. 13*, (Sudbury, Ontario: Laurentian University, 1980).

Ijiri, Yuji, "Cash-Flow Accounting and Its Structure." *Journal of Accounting, Auditing, and Finance* (Summer, 1978), pp. 331–48.

Ijiri, Yuji. "A Simple System of Cash-Flow Accounting." In *Accounting for a Simplified Firm Owning Depreciable Assets*, (eds) Robert R. Sterling and A.L. Thomas. (Houston: Scholars Book Co., 1979), pp. 57–71.

Lawson, G.H. "Cash-Flow Accounting I & II." *The Certified Accountant* (October 28 and November 4, 1971), pp. 586–9, 620–22.

Lawson, G.H. "Some Arguments for Cash-Flow Accounting." *The Certified Accountant* (April/May, 1973).

Lee, T.A. "A Case for Cash-Flow Reporting." *Journal of Business Finance* (Summer, 1972), pp. 27–36.

Lee, T.A. "The Contribution of Fisher to Cash-Flow Accounting." *Journal of Business Finance and Accounting* (Autumn, 1979), pp. 321–30.

Lee, T.A. "Goodwill — An Example of Will-o'-the-Wisp Accounting." *Accounting and Business Research* (Autumn, 1971), pp. 318–28.

Lee, T.A. "The Relevance of Accounting Information, Including Cash Flows." *The Accountant's Magazine* (January, 1972).

Lee, T.A. "Reporting Cash Flows and Net Realizable Values." *Accounting and Business Research* (Spring, 1981), pp. 163–70.

Stanbus, G. "The Relevance of Cash Flows." *Asset Valuation*, (ed.) Robert R. Sterling. Houston: Scholars Book Co., 1971.

Staubus, G. *A. Theory of Accounting to Investors.* (Berkeley, Ca.: University of California Press, 1961).

Thomas, A.L. Accounting Research Study No. 3, *The Allocation Problem in Financial Accounting Theory*, (Sarasota, Fl.: American Accounting Association, 1969).

Thomas, A.L. Accounting Research Study No. 9, *The Allocation Problem: Part II.* (Sarasota, Fl.: American Accounting Association, 1974).

Whittington, G. "Accounting and Economics." *Current Issues in Accounting*, (eds) B. Carsberg and T. Hope. (Oxford: Philip Allan Publishers, Ltd., 1977).

Employee Reporting

Chan, J.L. "Corporate Disclosure in Occupational Safety and Health: Some Empirical Evidence." *Accounting, Organizations, and Society* (May, 1979), pp. 273–81.

Chan, J.L. "Occupational Safety and Health: Social Performance, Information Asymmetry, and Government Regulation." in *Research in Corporate Social Performance and Policy*, Vol. 5, (ed.) L.E. Preston. (New York: JAI Press, 1983).

Foley, B.J., and Maunders, K.T. *Accounting Information Disclosure and Collective Bargaining.* (New York: Macmillan, 1977).

Grojer, J. E., and Stark, A. "Social Accounting: A Swedish Attempt." *Accounting Organizations and Society* (May, 1977).

Hopwood, A.G., Burchell, S., and Colin, C. "The Development of Accounting in Its International Content: Past Concerns and Emerging Issues." Paper presented at the Third Charles Waldo Haskins Seminar on Accounting History. (Atlanta: Georgia State University, April 20, 1979).

Jones, D.M.C. *Disclosure of Financial Information to Employees.* (New York: Institute of Personnel Management, 1978).

Lau, C.T., and Nelson, M. *Accounting Implications of Collective Bargaining.* (Hamilton, Ontario: Society of Management Accountants of Canada, 1981).

Maunders, K.T. "Employee Reporting." in *Developments in Financial Reporting*, (ed.) T.A. Lee. (Oxford: Philip Allan Publishers, Ltd., 1981).

Nelson, M. "Accounting Disclosures of Strikes and Lockouts." *Cost and Management* (November/December, 1982), pp. 30–32.

Nelson, M. "Accounting for Strikes." *Cost and Management* (November/December, 1973), pp. 48–50.

Parker, L.D. "The Reporting of Company Financial Results to Employees' Research Committee." *Occasional Paper No. 12.* (London: The Institute of Chartered Accountants in England and Wales, 1977).

Pope, P.F., and Peel, D.A. "Information Disclosure to Employees and Rational Expectations." *Journal of Business Finance and Accounting* (Spring, 1981), pp. 139–46.

Purdy, D. "The Provision of Financial Information to Employees: A Study of the Reporting Practices of Some Large Public Companies in the United Kingdom. *Accounting, Organizations, and Society* (December, 1981), pp. 327–8.

Thompson, E.R., and Knell, A. *The Employment Statement in Company Reports.* (London: The Institute of Chartered Accountants in England and Wales, 1979).

Value-Added Reporting

Cox, B. *Value Added — An Appreciation for the Accountant Concerned with Industry.* (London: The Institute of Cost and Management Accountants, 1978).

Morley, Michael F. "Value-Added Reporting." In *Development in Financial Reporting*, (ed.) T.A. Lee. (Oxford: Philip Allan Publishers, Ltd., 1981), pp. 251–69.

Morley, Michael F. "The Value-Added Statement — A British Innovation." *The Chartered Accountant Magazine* (May, 1978), pp. 31–4.

Renshall, M., Allan, R., and Nicholson, K. *Added Value in External Financial Reporting.* (London: The Institute of Chartered Accountants in England and Wales, 1979).

International Accounting

Belkaoui, A. *International Accounting: Issues and Answers* (Westport, Ct.: Greenwood Press, 1985).

QUESTIONS

15.1 What is *socioeconomic accounting?*

15.2 Define *externality, social cost,* and *social benefit.*

15.3 Define *human-resource accounting.*

15.4 What are the determinants of *individual value* and *group value* to an organization?

15.5 Discuss each of the *monetary* measures of human assets.

15.6 Discuss each of the *nonmonetary* measures of human assets.

15.7 What do we mean by *accounting for the cost of capital?*

15.8 Explain the method of accounting for the cost of capital.

15.9 What are the principal advantages and disadvantages of the public reporting of corporate financial forecasts?

15.10 H.S. Kulshrestha makes the following statement in "Accounting as a Science," *The Chartered Accountant Magazine of India* (October, 1964), p. 208:

Accounting, when born, must not have been more dismal a subject than economics. At least, it has never been condemned as a "Gospel of Mammon." But later on, as all know, when economics aimed at the welfare of man as a member of society, it got popular and now occupies an important position among the social sciences. Accounting, however, continued serving individuals. As a result, the economist acted as a thinker, author, and orator on society; whereas the accountant worked at the desk, shabbily dressed and "sincere" to his master. The secret of this significant development in and popularity of economics lay in its social approach to the well-being of man, which unfortunately accounting failed to have.

Do you agree with this statement? Why or why not?

15.11 Are accountants required to care about the welfare of society?

15.12 What is a *social audit?*

15.13 Compare *Anthony's proposal* with FASB Statement No. 34.

15.14 It would seem that a firm's employees — its human resources — can be one of the most significant assets utilized by the firm. Despite this fact, conventional accounting procedures make no provision for entering the value of human resources on the balance sheet. Costs associated with the firm's employees are invariably charged to income as incurred.

  This fact has led many writers to conclude that more attention must be paid to the problems of accounting for human resources.

Required

a. Many different methods of accounting for the human resources of a company have been studied. List and briefly explain the six methods that Michael H. Gilbert examines in "The Asset Value of Human Organization," *Management Accounting* (July, 1970), p. 32.

b. In an attempt to develop an accounting system for human resources, Robert L. Woodruff, Jr., describes seven functional accounts in "Human-Resource Accounting," *The Canadian Chartered Accountant Magazine* (September 1970), pp. 2–7. List and briefly explain five of these functional accounts.

(SMA adapted)

15.15 The All-Mark Company operates several plants at which limestone is processed into quicklime and hydrated lime. The Breaker Plant, where most of the equipment was installed many years ago, continually deposits a dusty white substance over the surrounding countryside. Citing the unsanitary condition of the neighboring community of Pivelletown, the pollution of the Pivelle River, and the high incidence of lung disease among workers at Breaker, the state's Pollution Control Agency has assessed a substantial penalty on All-Mark, which will be used to clean up Pivelletown. After considering the costs involved (which could not have been reasonably estimated before the Agency's action), All-Mark decides to comply with the Agency's orders, the alternative being to cease operations at Breaker at the end of the current fiscal year. The officers at All-Mark agree that the air-pollution control equipment should be capitalized and depreciated over its useful life, but they disagree about the period(s) to which the penalty should be charged.

Required

Discuss the conceptual merits and reporting requirements of accounting for All-Mark's penalty as (1) a charge to the current period, (2) a correction of prior periods, and (3) a capitalizable item to be amortized over future periods.

(AICPA adapted)

15.16 All-Mark's Sensor Plant causes approximately as much pollution as its Breaker Plant. However, Sensor is located in another state, where there is little likelihood of government regulation, and All-Mark does not plan to install air-pollution control equipment at this plant. One of All-Mark's officers, Mr Haze, says that uncontrolled pollution at the Sensor Plant constitutes a real cost to society, which is not recorded anywhere according to current accounting practice. Haze suggests that this "social cost" of the Sensor Plant be included annually on All-Mark's income statement. Further, Haze suggests that this social cost can easily be measured by referring to the depreciation on Breaker's air-pollution control equipment.

Required

a. Is Mr Haze necessarily correct when he states that the costs associated with Sensor's pollution are entirely unrecorded? Explain your answer.
b. Evaluate Haze's proposed method of measuring the annual "social cost" of Sensor's pollution.
c. Discuss the merits of Haze's suggestion that a "social cost" be recognized by a business enterprise.   *(AICPA adapted)*

15.17 "Conventional accounting procedures make no provision for entering the value of human resources on the balance sheet." This fact has led many writers to conclude that more attention must be paid to the problems of accounting for human resources.

However, many accountants still believe that the problems of accounting for human resources have not been properly settled and that it is preferable to charge these costs to income as they are incurred.

Required

a. Give arguments or reasons that writers may use to support the accounting treatment of entering the value of human resources on the balance sheet.
b. Give arguments or reasons that *accountants* may use to support the accounting treatment of charging all human resource expenses to income.

(SMA adapted)

15.18 Gerhard G. Mueller and Lauren M. Walker make the following statement in "The Coming of Age of Transnational Financial Reporting," *The Journal of Accounting* (July, 1976), p. 67:

Multinational business is the prime generator of transnational financial reporting needs. Thus, with all the current political, legal, and moral attacks unleashed on the multinational corporation, we might simply assume that before long the multinational corporation will meet its fate on one guillotine or another and that the problem of transnational financial reporting will go away.

Do you agree with this statement? Discuss your answer.

CHAPTER 16

INTERNATIONAL ACCOUNTING

16.1 INTRODUCTION

International accounting is gaining an important posture in the field of accounting generally, in response to the demands of the global economy, the increasing number of multinational corporations, and the international user of information. While still lacking a unifying theme, the field of international accounting is the subject of increased theoretical and empirical scrutiny to investigate the numerous financial and managerial international accounting issues, as well as the standard-setting issues in both developed and developing countries. This chapter constitutes an introduction to the practical and theoretical facets of the field of international accounting.

16.2 DEFINITIONS OF INTERNATIONAL ACCOUNTING

There is definitely a confusion in the literature about the meaning of international accounting, evidenced by the various definitions encompassing different scopes. A useful clarification of these definitions was provided by Weirich et al., by their identifying three major concepts:

1 Parent–foreign subsidiary accounting or accounting for subsidiaries,

2 Comparative or international accounting,
3 Universal or world accounting.[1]

The concept of *universal* or *world accounting* is by far the largest in scope. It directs international accounting to the formulation and study of a universally accepted set of accounting principles. It aims for a complete standardization of accounting principles internationally. The definition adopted by Weirich *et al.* is as follows:

> *World Accounting.* In the framework of this concept, international accounting is considered to be a universal system that could be adopted in all countries. A world-wide set of generally accepted accounting principles (GAAP), such as the set maintained in the United States, would be established. Practices and principles would be developed which were applicable to all countries. This concept would be the ultimate goal of an international system.[2]

While very commendable, this goal is unlikely to be achieved in the near future, and may be safely characterized as highly idealistic by some, and even utopian by others. Pessimistic attitudes are based on the many obstacles to a complete standardization of accounting principles.

The concept of comparative or international accounting directs international accounting to a study and understanding of national differences in accounting. It involves:

(a) an awareness of the international diversity in corporate accounting and reporting practices,
(b) understanding of the accounting principles and practices of individual countries, and
(c) ability to assess the impact of diverse accounting practices on financial reporting.[3]

There is a general consensus in accounting literature that the term "international accounting" refers to comparative accounting principles. The definition is:

> *International Accounting.* A second major concept of the term "international account-ing" involves a descriptive and informative approach. Under this concept, international accounting includes all varieties of principles, methods and standards of accounting of *all* countries. This concept includes a set of generally accepted accounting principles established for each country, thereby requiring the accountant to be multiple principle conscious when studying international accounting. . . . No universal or perfect set of principles would be expected to be established. A collection of all principles, methods and standards of all countries would be considered as the international accounting system. These variations result because of differing geographic, social, economic, political and legal influences.[4]

The concept of *parent–foreign subsidiary* accounting, or *accounting for foreign subsidiaries*, is by far the oldest and narrowest in scope. It reduces international accounting to the process of consolidating the accounts of the parent company and its subsidiaries and translating foreign currency in local currency. The definition is:

> *Accounting for Foreign Subsidiaries.* The third major concept that may be applied to "international accounting" refers to the accounting practices of a parent company and a foreign subsidiary. A reference to a particular country or domicile is needed under the concept for effective internal financial reporting. The accountant is concerned mainly with the translation and adjustment of the subsidiary's financial statement. Different accounting problems arise and different accounting principles are to be followed

depending upon which country is used as a reference for translation and adjustment purposes.[5]

The advent of new international accounting paradigms expanded the framework to include new motions of international accounting. As a result, an exhaustive list of international accounting concepts and theories was provided by F.E. Amenkhienan to include the following:

1 universal or world theory;
2 multinational theory;
3 comparative theory;
4 international transactions theory;
5 translation theory.[6]

These theories imply respectively:

1 A universal concept being nurtured by the pragmatists who believe that the solutions to the problems raised in internal reporting lie in worldwide uniformity in accounting.
2 A multinational concept which suggests that international accounting includes all the varieties of principles, standards, and practices of all countries.
3 A comparative concept which suggests an analytical classification of national accounting systems, as has been done in the other social sciences such as economics, politics and law.
4 An international concept built around accounting information needed in international trade and international investment decisions.
5 A transnational concept which is used to characterize accounting for parent companies and foreign subsidiaries.[7]

Each of these theories provides some grounds for the development of a conceptual framework for international accounting. While arguments can be made for the desirability of one theory over the others, the first three — universal, multinational, and comparative — have generated better followings than the other two. The debate lies between those favoring uniformity leading to a universal theory, those favoring standardization leading to a multinational theory, and those favoring analysis of different national accounting systems leading to a comparative theory.

16.3   INTERNATIONAL ACCOUNTING PROBLEMS

Most accounting issues could qualify easily as international accounting issues, which may explain why international accounting is often referred to as a subarea of accounting. There are, however, some issues relevant to international business which create special accounting problems and which constitute the accepted domain of international accounting. These issues, in fact, make international accounting an essential functional area in international business. They have been effectively subdivided into several areas as follows:

Private Sector Accounting

1 Comparative analysis:
   a. national accounting, reporting, and auditing *practice* (principles, procedures, standards and disclosure);
   b. national accounting *theory* (including historical dimensions).
2 Policy at the international level (standardization).
3 Accounting for mutinational operations:
   a. Financial accounting (translation, consolidation, segmental reporting, inflation accounting, disclosure, auditing);
   b. managerial accounting (risk and exposure measurements, foreign investment analysis, information systems, transfer pricing, control and performance evaluation, operational auditing, behavioral dimensions).
4 Taxation (of international operation in different countries).

Public Sector Accounting

1 Comparative analysis of national systems (GNP measurement, balance of payments, balance of trade, employment statistics and so on).
2 Accounting for governmetal agencies and public not-for-profit organizations (overlaps with private sector accounting, because certain industries are nationalized in some countries).[8]

Most of these areas, especially those related to private-sector accounting, are the subject of theoretical and empirical research. The most important international accounting problems are in the area of comparative international accounting policies. Financial reporting practices vary from country to country. The most important differences are in the following areas:[9]

1 *Basis of presentation*: the financial statements may be prepared on any one of the asset valuation bases examined in Chapter 9–11. Differences exist among countries. The predominant method in the US is to use historical cost or lower of cost or market value, with the option of including five years of inflation-adjusted selected financial data as a supplemental footnote disclosure for large companies.
2 *Consolidation reporting practices*: the differences between reporting center on the need to include the financial conditions and results of operations of all worldwide wholly-owned subsidiaries in their consolidated financial statements. The predominant method in the US is to include majority-owned subsidiaries, and exclude minority-owned subsidiaries. In addition, discretion is allowed when control is anticipated to be temporary or separate disclosure is deemed more informative.
3 *Business consolidations*: the two most commonly-used accounting methods are:
   a. the purchase method where the net assets of the acquired company are revalued from their individual book value to "fair value"), and the difference between the fair value and the amount paid accounted for as goodwill, and
   b. the provoking of interests method where the two independent units are merged. The predominant method in the US is the purchase method, while the pooling of interests is prescribed in certain situations.
4 *Minority ownership*: two alternative methods are used for accounting for an investee's results of operations by less than fifty percent:

   a. the equity method, where the investor's share of the investee's earnings is included in the investor's earnings and the investor's investment account is also increased by its share of the investee's earnings and reduced by the investee's dividends given to the investor;

   b. the cost method where the investor's earnings are not affected by the investee's earnings and the investor reports any dividends received as income rather than as a reduction of the investment account.

   The predominant methods in the US are:

   a. the equity method in case of significant influence of minority ownership;

   b. the cost method in case of no significant influence.

5 *Valuation of fixed assets*: the methods used are either historical costs or a revaluation of historical cost to some form of fair value. The predominant method in the US is historical cost depreciated by a straight-line method. However, accelerated depreciation may be used for more purposes. Deferred taxes are recognized for the impact in income from the use of two depreciation techniques.

6 *Goodwill*: the goodwill resulting from the use of the purchase method for business combinations may be either capitalized and then amortized over its estimated useful life or written off in the year of acquisition. The first method is predominant in the US.

7 *Inventory costing*: The methods of inventory costing include FIFO, LIFO and weighted average. All these three methods are used in the US, including a valuation at lower of cost or market.

8 *Contingency reserve policy*: the reserve refers to the accruals established to account for the ultimate resolution of uncertain situations arising from abnormal business conditions. The US allows the establishment of reserves if an event has occurred from which it is probable that a liability has been incurred and the amount of that liability can be reasonably estimated.

9 *Deferred income taxes*: when the economic effect of a transaction is temporarily treated differently for tax purposes and book purposes, the resulting deferred income taxes are accounted for either under:

   a. the deferral method, where the temporary book/tax differences are accrued at the tax rate in effect when the transaction was recorded for book purposes and added to the entity's actual results of operations:

   b. the liability method, where the differences are accrued at the tax rate anticipated to be in effect when the tax is expected to be paid. In addition, the identification of transactions giving rise to deferred income taxes are solved by either:

      (1) the comprehensive allocation method, where all the differences are included in the calculation of the deferred taxes, or

      (2) partial allocation where certain differences whose alternate reversal is not reasonably assured are excluded. Liability method is required in the US.

10 *Pension disclosure*: practice varies widely. The US recognizes over- or under-funded pension liability on the balance sheet, as well as the actuarial present value of projected benefits in relation to plant assets available for benefit. The annual cost is based on the present value of benefits currently earned.

11 *Research and development costs*: practice varies among countries, including either:

   a. capitalization then amortization;

   b. expensing.

The US favors expensing immediately and capitalization only for certain software development costs.

12 *Foreign currency translation*: methods used include:
   a. the current–noncurrent method, where current assets and liabilities are translated at the current exchange rate, and noncurrent assets and liabilities are translated at historical exchange rates;
   b. the monetary–nonmonetary method, where monetary assets and liabilities are translated at current rates and nonmonetary assets and liabilities are translated at historical rates;
   c. the current rate method, where all assets and liabilities are translated at the current exchange rate;
   d. the temporal method where accounts carried at past exchange rates are translated at historical rates, while accounts carried at current purchase or sale exchange prices or future exchange prices are translated at current rates.

In the US, the translation process may be divided in two categories. Category one is where the US dollar is the functional currency. In that case the temporal method is required, and translation gains and losses are reported in the income statement as a nonoperating item. Category two is where the foreign currency is the functional currency. In that case the current method is used and the translation gains and losses are reported in the stockholder's equity section of the balance sheet as a translation adjustment.

13 *Long-term leases*: the methods used are either to
   a. capitalize then amortize;
   b. expense.

The US favors capitalization under the following criteria:
   a. ownership is transferred at the end of the lease term.
   b. the lease contains a bargain purchase option.
   c. the lease term is at least 75 percent of the property's estimated economic life.
   d. the present value of future lease payments is 90 percent or more of the property's fair value.

16.4 DETERMINANTS OF NATIONAL DIFFERENCES IN INTERNATIONAL ACCOUNTING

The differences in international accounting and in accounting for foreign subsidiaries, which result primarily from differences in the business environment from one country to another, are problems in need of correction. Mueller identifies four elements of differentiation:

- *State of economic development*: national economies vary in terms of their extent of development and in terms of nature, from the developed to the developing countries.
- *State of business complexity*: national economies vary in terms of their technological and industrial know-how, creating differences in their business needs as well as their business output.
- *Shade of political persuasion*: national economies vary in terms of their political systems, from the centrally-controlled economy to the market-oriented economy.

- *Reliance on some particular system of law*: national economies vary in terms of their supporting legal system. They may rely on either a common-law or code-law system; they may have protective legislation and unfair trade and antitrust laws, for example.[10]

These differences in the business environment cause differences in multinational accounting practices and a clustering of financial accounting principles. Mueller, for example, employs the four elements of differentiation to identify ten distinct sets of business environments:

- *United States/Canada/The Netherlands*: there is a minimum of commercial or company legislation in the environment. Industry is highly developed; currencies are relatively stable. A strong orientation to business innovation exists. Many companies with widespread international business interests are headquartered in these countries.
- *British Commonwealth (excluding Canada)*: comparable company legislation exists in all Commonwealth countries, and administration procedures and social order reflect strong ties to the Mother country. There exists an intertwining of currencies through the so-called "sterling block" arrangement. Business is highly developed but often quite traditional.
- *Germany/Japan*: rapid economic growth has occurred since the Second World War. Influences stemming from various United States military and administrative operations have caused considerable imitation of many facets of Unites States practices, often by grafting United States procedures to various local traditions. The appearance of a new class of professional business managers is observable. Relative policital, social and currency stability exists.
- *Continental Europe (excluding Germany, The Netherlands, and Scandinavia)*: private business lacks significant government support. Private property and the profit motive are not necessarily in the center of economic and business orientation. Some national economic planning exists. Political swings from far right to far left, and vice versa, have a long history in this environment. Limited reservoirs of economic resources are available.
- *Scandinavia*: here we have developed economies but characteristically slow rates of economic and business growth. Governments tend toward social legislation. Company acts regulate business. Relative stability of population numbers is the rule. Currencies are quite stable. Several business innovations (especially in consumer goods) originated in Scandinavia. Personal characteristics and outlooks are quite similar in all five Scandinavian countries.
- *Israel/Mexico*: these are the only two countries with substantial success in fairly rapid economic development. Trends of a shift to more reliance on private enterprise are beginning to appear; however, there is still a significant governmental presence in business. Some specialization in business and the professions is taking place. The general population apparently has a strong desire for higher standards of living.
- *South America*: many instances are present of significant economic underdevelopment, along with social and educational underdevelopment. The business base is narrow. Agricultural and military interests are strong and often dominate governments. There is considerable reliance on export/import trade. Currencies are generally soft. Populations are increasing heavily.

- *The Developing Nations of the Near and Far East*: modern concepts and ethics of business have predominantly western origins. These concepts and ethics often clash with the basic oriental cultures. Business in the developing nations of the Orient largely means trade only. There is severe underdevelopment on most measures, coupled with vast population numbers. Political scenes and currencies are mostly shaky. Major economic advances are probably impossible without substantial assistance from the industrialized countries. OPEC member countries have developed more rapidly since 1973.
- *Africa (excluding South Africa)*: most of the African continent is still in early stages of independent civilization, and thus little native business environment presently exists. There are significant natural and human resources. Business is likely to assume a major role and responsibility in the development of African nations.
- *Communist Nations*: the complete control by central governments places these countries in a grouping all their own.[11]

These groupings are likely to affect the development of accounting and the formulation of accounting principles, and to explain the diversity of practices used from one country to another. In fact, the comparative accounting literature includes various attempts to classify the accounting patterns in the world of accounting in different historical "zones of accounting influences." A good explanation for the various zones of accounting influence is that the accounting objectives, standards, policies and techniques result from environmental factors in each country; if these environmental factors differ significantly between countries, it would be expected that the major accounting concepts and practices in use in various countries would also differ. It is generally accepted in international accounting that accounting objectives, standards, policies and techniques reflect the particular environment of the standard-setting body. The environmental conditions likely to affect the determination of accounting standards include the following:

1 Cultural relativism, whereby accounting concepts in any given country are as unique as any other cultural traits.[12]
2 Linguistic relativism, whereby accounting as a language with its logical and grammatical characteristics will affect the linguistic and nonlinguistic behavior of users.[13]
3 Political and civil relativism, whereby accounting concepts in any given country rest on the political and civil context of that country.
4 Economic and demographic relativism, whereby accounting concepts in any given country rest on the economic and demographic context of that country.
5 Legal and tax relativism, whereby accounting concepts in any given country rest on the legal and base concept of that country.[14]

16.5 HARMONIZATION OF ACCOUNTING STANDARDS

16.5.1 The Nature of Harmonization of Accounting Standards

Harmonization has for a long time been erroneously associated with complete standardization. It is in effect different from standardization. Wilson presents this useful distinction:

The term harmonization as opposed to standardization implies a reconciliation of different points of view. This is a more practical and conciliatory approach than standardization, particularly when standardization means that the procedures of one country should be adopted by all others. Harmonization becomes a matter of better communication of information in a form that can be interpreted and understood internationally.[15]

This definition of harmonization is more realistic and has a greater likelihood of being accepted than standardization. Every host country has its own sets of rules, philosophies, and objectives at the national level, aimed at protecting or controlling the national resources. This aspect of nationalism gives rise to particular rules and measures which ultimately affect a country's accounting system. Harmonization consists of recognizing these national idiosyncracies and attempting to reconcile them with other countries' objectives as a first step. The second step is to correct or eliminate some of these barriers, in order to achieve an acceptable degree of harmonization.

16.5.2 Merits of Harmonization

There are various advantages to harmonization. First, for many countries, there are still no adequate codified standards of accounting and auditing. Internationally accepted standards not only would eliminate the set-up costs for those countries but would allow them to immediately become part of the mainstream of accepted international accounting standards. Some of this work is already being accomplished by the major accounting firms in their international practice. For example, Macrae states:

> Each of these forms of course has only been able to set and enforce the standards for its own organization, but combined, they determine the standards followed in a substantial portion of international audit engagements.[16]

Second, the growing internationalization of the world's economies and the increasing interdependency of nations in terms of international trade and investment flows is a major argument for some form of internationally-accepted standards of accounting and auditing. Such internationalization will also facilitate international transactions, pricing, and resource allocation decisions, and may render the international financial markets more efficient.

Third, the need for companies to raise outside capital, given the insufficiency of retained earnings to finance projects and the availability of foreign loans, has increased the need for accounting harmonization. In effect, suppliers of capital, here and abroad, tend to rely on financial reports to make the best investment and loan decisions, and tend to show preference for comparable reporting.

16.5.3 Limits to Harmonization

Current trends seem to indicate that there is little chance of ever achieving international harmonization. The following arguments are usually advanced to justify this pessimistic attitude. First, tax collections in all countries are one of the greatest sources of demand for accounting services. Because tax-collection systems vary internationally, it can be easily expected that it will lead to a diversity in the accounting principles and systems used internationally. Seidler states:

> Since tax collection systems vary widely between countries, and since governments show little sign of desiring to harmonize tax systems (except in the collection of maximum amounts from multinational corporations), there is little reason to expect that this barrier to international accounting harmonization will disappear.[17]

Second, accounting policies are known to be fashioned sometimes to achieve either political or economic goals compatible with the economic or policital system espoused by a given country. Since there is little hope of having a single political or economic system internationally, it can be expected that the differences in political and economic systems will continue to act as a barrier to international accounting harmonization.

Third, some of the obstacles to international harmonization are created by accountants themselves through strict national licensing requirements. An extreme example occurred in 1976, when the French profession required foreign accountants practicing in France to sit for an oral examination. As a result of the French experience, the EEC became involved with the qualifications of auditors. The first published version of the draft Eighth Directive created several restraints on the ability of foreign accountants to practice in the EEC member countries. Consider the following paragraphs from the first version of the draft of the Eighth Directive:

> The partners, members, persons responsible for management, administration direction or supervision of such professional companies or associations who do not personally fulfill the Directive (i.e., non-EEC qualified accountants) shall exercise no influence over the statutory audits carried out under the auspices of such approved professional companies or associations.
>
> The law shall, in particular, ensure:
> - that the above mentioned persons may not participate in the appointment or removal of auditors and that they may not issue to the latter any instructions regarding the carrying out of audits . . .
> - that the confidentiality of audit reports produced by the auditors and all documents relating thereto are protected and that these are withheld from the knowledge of the above-mentioned persons.

16.6   ACTORS INVOLVED IN HARMONIZATION

Whatever strategy for standard setting is chosen by the developing countries, they cannot escape the fact that there is an ongoing international harmonization drive. They could either learn from it, or become a legitimate partner, depending on the strategy they choose.

16.6.1   Accountants International Study Group (AISG)

The AISG was formed as a three-nation group to study accounting and auditing requirements and practices in the United States, The United Kingdom, and Canada. Its terms of reference were as follows:

To institute comparative studies as to accounting thought and practice in participating countries, to make reports from time to time, which, subject to the prior approval of the sponsoring Institutes, would be issued to members of those Institutes.

Before being disbanded, the AISG issued 20 studies, which are listed in Exhibit 16.1. Most of the studies were comparative and were not binding on the sponsoring institutes.

EXHIBIT 16.1
Studies Produced by the Accountants International Study Group (AISG)

1. *Accounting and Auditing Approaches to Inventories in Three Nations* (1968)
2. *The Independent Auditor's Reporting Standards in Three Nations* (1969)
3. *Using the Work and Report of Another Auditor* (1970)
4. *Accounting for Corporate Income Taxes* (1971)
5. *Reporting by Diversified Companies* (1972)
6. *Consolidated Financial Statements* (1972)
7. *The Funds Statement* (1973)
8. *Materiality in Accounting* (1974)
9. *Extraordinary Items, Prior Period, Adjustments, and Changes in Accounting Principles* (1974)
10. *Published Profit Forecasts* (1975)
11. *Comparative Glossary of Accounting Terms in Canada, the United Kingdom and the United States* (1975)
12. *Accounting for Goodwill* (1975)
13. *Interim Financial Reporting* (1975)
14. *International Financial Reporting* (1976)
15. *Going Concern Problems* (1976)
16. *Audit Committees* (1976)
17. *Independence of Auditors* (1977)
18. *Accounting for Pension Costs* (1977)
19. *Related Party Transactions* (1978)
20. *Revenue Recognition* (1978)

16.6.2 International Federation of Accounting Committee (IFAC)

Various international organizations preceded the creation of the IFAC. First, the International Congress of Accounts (ICA) was founded in 1904, with the general objective of increasing interaction and exchange of ideas between accountants of different countries. Second, in 1972 the ICA founded the International Coordination Committee for the Accounting Profession (ICCAP), with the objective of conducting specific studies of professional accounting ethics, eduation and training, and the structure of regional accounting organizations. Third, the ICCAP dissolved in 1976 to be reconstituted as the International Federation of Accounting Committee (IFAC). The goals of the IFAC are best expressed by the following twelve-point program to guide its efforts:

1 Develop statements that would serve as guidelines for international auditing practices.

2 Establish a suggested minimum code of ethics to which it hoped that member bodies would subscribe and which could be further refined as appropriate.

3 Determine the requirements and develop programs for the professional education and training of accountants.

4 Evaluate, develop, and report on financial management and other management accounting techniques and procedures.

5 Collect, analyze, research, and disseminate information on the managment of public accounting practices to assist practitioners in conducting their practices more effectively.

6 Undertake other studies of value to accountants such as, possibly, a study of the legal liability of auditors.

7 Foster closer relations with users of financial statements, including preparers, trade unions, financial institutions, industry, government, and others.

8 Maintain close relations with regional bodies and explore the potential for establishing other regional bodies, as well as for assisting in their organization and development, as appropriate. Assign appropriate projects to existing regional bodies.

9 Establish regular communication among the members of IFAC and with other interested organizations through the medium of a newsletter.

10 Organize and promote the exchange of technical information, educational materials, and professional publications and other literature emanating from other bodies.

11 Organize and conduct an International Congress of Accountants approximately every five years.

12 Seek to expand the membership of the IFAC.[18]

As of 1984, IFAC's membership reached 85 professional accountancy bodies from 63 countries. Its governing bodies consist of an assembly comprising one representative designated as such by each member of the IFAC and a council comprising fifteen representatives of member bodies from fifteen countries. The agenda of the IFAC is set by the following seven standing committees: education, ethics, international auditing practices, international congresses, management accounting, planning, and regional organizations. The International Auditing Practices Committee (OAPC) of the IFAC is the most active and most important.

16.6.3 International Accounting Standards Committee (IASC)

The IASC was founded in 1973 with the following objectives contained in its constitution:

1 To formulate and publish in the public interest accounting standards to be observed in the presentation of financial statements and to promote their worldwide acceptance and observance.

2 To work generally for the improvement and harmonization of regulation, accounting standards and procedures relating to the presentation of financial statements.[19]

This translates into a goal of developing a common international approach to standards setting in accounting, aimed at a worldwide harmonization and improvement of accounting principles used in the preparation of financial statements for the benefit of the public.

The IASC has an operating structure composed of the ISAC board, the consultative group, and various steering committees. Its procedure of exposure and comment is as follows:

1 After discussion, the IASC Board selects a topic that is felt to need an International Accounting Standard, and assigns it to a Steering Committee. All ISAC member bodies are invited to submit material for consideration.

2 The Steering Committee, assisted by the IASC Secretariat, considers the issues involved and presents a point outline on the subject to the Board.

3 The Steering Committee receives the comments of the Board and prepares a preliminary draft on the proposed standard.

4 Following review by the Board, the draft is circulated to all member bodies for their comments.

5 The Steering Committee prepares a revised draft, which, after approval by at least two-thirds of the Board, is published as an Exposure Draft. Comments are invited from all interested parties.

6 At each stage in the consideration of drafts, member bodies refer for guidance to the appropriate accounting research committees in their own organizations.

7 At the end of an exposure period (usually six months), comments are submitted to IASC and are considered by the Steering Committee responsible for the project.

8 The Steering Committee then submits a revised draft to the Board for approval as an International Accounting Standard.

9 The issue of a Standard requires approval by at least three-quarters of the Board, after which the approved text of the Standard is sent to all member bodies for translation and publication.[20]

As of 1990 the following fiscal standards had been produced:

IAS1   *Disclosure of Accounting Policies* (1975)
IAS2   *Valuation and Presentation of Inventories in the Context of the Historical Cost System* (1975)
IAS3   *Consolidated Financial Statements* (1976)
IAS4   *Depreciation Accounting* (1976)
IAS5   *Information to be Disclosed in Financial Statements* (1976)
IAS6   *Accounting Responses to Changing Prices*
IAS7   *Statement of Changes in Financial Position* (1977)
IAS8   *Unusual and Prior Period Items and Changes in Accounting Policies* (1978)
IAS9   *Accounting for Research and Development Activities* (1978)
IAS10 *Contingencies and Events Occurring After the Balance Sheet Data* (1978)
IAS11 *Accounting for Construction Contracts* (1979)
IAS12 *Accounting for Income Taxes* (1979)
IAS13 *Presentation of Current Assets and Current Liabilities* (1979)
IAS14 *Preparing Financial Information by Segment* (1981)
IAS15 *Information Reflecting the Effects of Changing Prices* (1981)
IAS16 *Accounting for Property, Plant and Equipment* (1982)
IAS17 *Accounting for Leases* (1982)

IAS18 *Revenue Recognition* (1983)

IAS19 *Accounting for Retirement Benefits in Financial Statements of Employers* (1983)

IAS20 *Accounting for Government Grants and Disclosure of Government Assistance* (1983)

IAS21 *Accounting for the Effects of Changes in Foreign Exchange Rates* (1983)

IAS22 *Accounting for Business Combinations* (1983)

IAS23 *Capitalization of Borrowing Costs* (1984)

IAS24 *Disclosure of Related Party Transactions* (1984)

IAS25 *Accounting for Investments*

IAS26 *Accounting and Reporting of Retirement Benefit Plans* (1987)

The success of the IASC's efforts naturally rests on acceptance of the standards by member countries and recognition and support internationally. Noncompliance with international standards has been attributed to the following reasons, by Sir Henry Benson, the founder of IASC:

> Some countries take the view that they cannot require compliance locally until they are satisfied that the Standards are internationally acceptable. Some see local legislation as an obstacle to the introduction of international standards. Some accounting bodies do not have the power of discipline over their members, and cannot therefore impose compliance with either national or international standards. Some countries have not yet overcome stubborn local resistance from the business community.[21]

Besides these obstacles, there is definite evidence that efforts toward harmonization are not shared equally by all members of IASC. T.R. Douglas summarized the situation as follows:

> Some accountancy bodies have declared to their members that international accounting standards are to be accorded the same status as domestic accounting standards. Each IAS is accompanied by an explanation of the relationship between the international standards and any domestic standard dealing with the same subject.
>
> Other accountancy bodies have issued statements declaring support for the concept of international standards and strongly encouraging their members to accept them. Some of these bodies indicate the extent to which an international standard differs from the related domestic standard. They often offer to review, or encourage the relevant body to review, the basis of the domestic standard, with the objective of eliminating any differences.
>
> There are some member countries, however, that have not yet presented any formal statement of the status of IAS's to the members of the accountancy profession.[22]

However, one piece of evidence of increasing compliance and national support of IASC pronouncements is a letter written in November 1980 by member bodies in Canada to the 300 largest companies quoted on the Toronto Stock Exchange, urging them to include a reference such as:

> The accompanying financial statements are prepared in accordance with accounting principles generally accepted in Canada and conform in all material respects to International Accounting Standards.[23]

In fact, the IASC's success rests on the best efforts of local professional organizations to ensure that published financial statements in their countries comply with the International Accounting Standards in all material respects.

A second piece of evidence has been provided by the International Finance Corporation (IFC), which is an investment institution established by its member governments to further economic development by encouraging the growth of productive private enterprise in developing member countries. A recent publication of IFS *Financial Reporting Requirements (Manufacturing and Commercial Enterprises)* contains the following statement:

> IFC recognizes that accounting policies vary from country to country. This could result in IFC receiving financial statements which are based on differing accounting policies. Hence, it is essential to include a summary of accounting policies applied as the first note to the financial statements as is adherence, in general, to generally accepted standards of reporting and disclosure. In deciding on accounting policies reference should be made, whenever applicable and practicable, to International Accounting Standards issued by the International Accounting Standards Committee (IASC). The IASC formulates and publishes basic standards to be observed in the presentation of audited accounts and financial statements.

16.6.4 United Nations

The United Nations (UN) became interested in accounting and the need for improved corporate reporting when the Group of Eminent Persons appointed to study the impact of multinational corporations advocated the formulation of an international, comparable system of standardized accounting and reporting. It also recommended the creation of a Group of Experts on International Standards of Accounting and Reporting. The group was created in 1976 with the following objectives:

1 To review the existing practice of reporting by transnational corporations and reporting requirements in different countries.
2 To identify gaps in information in existing corporate reporting and to examine the feasibility of various proposals for improved reporting.
3 To recommend a list of minimum items, together with their definition, that should be included in reports by transnational corporations and their affiliates, taking into account the recommendations of various groups concerned with the subject matter.[24]

As a result the group issued a report which included a 34-page list of recommended items to be disclosed by the "enterprise as a whole," that is, consolidated data, and by individual member companies, including the parent company. Following issuance of the report, an Intergovernmental Working Group of Experts on International Standards of Accounting and Reporting was formed with the objective of contributing to the harmonization of accounting standards. It does not function as a standards-setting body: its mandate is to review and discuss accounting and reporting standards. The group will consider, among other issues, whether the UN should promulgate accounting standards. Needless to say, this effort by the UN has created mixed international reaction. Most of the concerned institutions have expressed the feeling that accounting standards at the domestic or the international level are best set in the private sector. These same institutions are united in their support for the work of the IASC and national accountancy groups.

It is regrettable, however, that some nations do not agree with the UN effort. On May 20, 1986, the Permanent Representative of the United States to the UN informed the UN that the United States government had decided to resign from its position on the Intergovernmental Working Group. The reason for this withdrawal had been stated on February 26, 1986:

> The current work of the Working Group is of little usefulness to either the United States government or to the business community. Discussions of accounting and reporting practices and standards is covered adequately by international professional groups such as the International Accounting Standards Committee (IASC). Harmonization of standards, to the extent feasible, is best handled in more limited groupings such as the Organization of Economic Cooperation and Development (OECD).

While nobody is contesting the efforts of the IASC and OECD, it is still regrettable than the United States is withdrawing from an international effort to further accounting development. One would sincerely hope that this irrational act will be corrected with a more international and developing country-oriented administration in the White House.

16.6.5   Organization for Economic Cooperation and Development

The OECD is an organization whose members include twenty-four relatively industrialized noncommunist countries in Europe, Asia, North America, and Australasia. A Declaration on International Investment and Multinational Enterprises was issued in 1976, including an annex titled, "Guidelines for Multinational Enterprises," a section of which is subtitled "Disclosure of Information." The major elements suggested to be disclosed are listed below.

Enterprises should publish within reasonable time limits, on a regular basis, but at least annually, financial statements and other pertinent information relating to the enterprise as a whole comprising in particular:

- The structure of the enterprise, showing the name and location of the parent company, its main affiliates, its percentage ownership, direct and indirect, in these affilities, including shareholdings between them.
- The geographical areas where operations are carried out and the principal activities carried on therein by the parent company and the main affiliates.
- The operating results and sales by geographical area and the sales in the major lines of business for the enterprise as a whole.
- Significant new capital investment by geographical area and, as far as practicable, by major lines of business for the enterprise as a whole.
- A statement of the sources and uses of funds by the enterprise as a whole.
- The average number of employees in each geographic area.
- Research and development expenditure for the enterprise as a whole.
- The policies followed in respect of intra-group pricing.
- The accounting policies, including those on consolidations, observed in compiling the published information.[25]

16.6.6   European Economic Community (EEC)

The EEC has also been active in achieving regional harmonization of accounting principles through a series of directives which, within the Treaty of Rome, are not as binding as regulations. The directives anticipate given results, but the mode and means of implementation are left to the member countries. The EEC is in fact the first supranational body to have important authority in financial reporting and disclosure. Its influence is so pervasive that its directives are perceived to have important effects on non-EEC-based multinationals operating in the community. Particularly relevant to international accounting are the Fourth, Fifth, and Seventh Directives.

The Fourth Directive

The Fourth Directive, formally adopted in 1978, deals with the annual financial statements of public and private companies, other than banks and insurance companies.[26] Its purposes have been summarized as follows:

1 Coordinating national laws for the protection of members and third parties relating to the publication, presentation, and content of annual accounts and reports of limited-liability companies, and the accounting principles used in their preparation.
2 Establishing in the EEC minimum equivalent legal requirements for disclosure of financial information to the public by companies which are in competition with one another.
3 Establishing the principle that annual accounts should give a true and fair view of a company's assets and liabilities, and its financial position and profit or loss.
4 Providing the fullest possible information about limited companies to shareholders and third parties (with some relief to smaller companies).[27]

The major aspects relevant to international accounting were Articles 1 and 2 on types of companies covered by the directive and the general reporting requirements; Articles 3–27 on the format of annual reports; Articles 28–39 on the valuation rules; Articles 40–50 on publication requirements; and Articles 51–52 on the procedural, statutory changes in national laws required for compliance.

The Fifth Directive

The proposed Fifth Directive, revised in 1984, deals with the structure, management, and external audit of limited liability corporations. In the revised draft, the directive proposes to require a company that employs more than 1,000 workers in the EEC (or is part of a group of companies that employs more than 1,000 workers in the EEC) to allow the employees to participate in the company's decision-making structure. In addition, the proposal specifies certain rules concerning annual meetings of shareholders, the adoption of the company's annual financial statments, and the appointment, compensation, and duties of the company's auditors.

The Seventh Directive

The Seventh Directive, issued in June 1983, addresses the issue of consolidated financial statements and offers some guidelines for more standardization of accounting reporting. Companies in EEC member countries and non-EEC corporations with subsidiaries in a member country are required to file consolidated financial statements in the country. However, each of the ten EEC countries has five years to pass legislation to implement the directive, and annual reports do not have to conform until 1990.

16.6.7   Other Actors

The preceding sections identify the most important actors involved in the harmonization drive. Various other national, regional, and international groups are emerging as active in the same drive. They include basically the following:

1 ASEAN Federation of Accountants (AFA)
2 African Accounting Council (AAC)
3 Union Européene des Experts Compatables Economiques et Financiers (UEC)
4 Asociacion Interamericana de Contabilidad (AIC)
5 Confederation of Asian and Pacific Accountants (CAPA)
6 Nordic Federation of Accountants (NFA)
7 Association of Accountancy Bodies in West Africa (ABWA)
8 American Accounting Association (AAA)
9 Canadian Association of Academic Accountants (CAAA)
10 European Accounting Association (EAA)
11 Japan Accounting Association (JAA)
12 Association of University Instructors in Accounting (AUIA)
13 Financial Analysts Federations (FAF)
14 Financial Executives Institute (FEI)
15 Arab Society of Certified Accountants (ASCA)

Given the proliferation of actors involved or willing to be involved in the harmonization drive, one would expect a lot of interrelationships among these bodies and cross-representation in an attempt to exercise some influence in the international accounting arena.

16.7   STANDARD-SETTING STRATEGIES FOR THE DEVELOPING COUNTRIES

The developing countries are characterized by relatively inadequate and unreliable accounting systems and generally new and untested standard-setting institutions. Theory development and academic and professional accounting research add to the economic, social, political, and institutional problems that may be acting as deterrents to an effective standard setting. In spite of these limitations the development of basic accounting systems and procedures and the process of standard setting has accelerated, as evidenced by the increasing number of professional organizations, standard-setting books, and academic accounting associations, as well as by the increasing membership of these groups in international standard-setting bodies.

The standard-setting process in the developing countries has not followed a unique strategy proper to these countries and their context. In fact, four strategies may be identified:

1 the evolutionary approach;
2 the development through transfer of accounting technology;
3 the adoption of international accounting standards;

4 the development of accounting standards based on analysis of accounting principles and practices in the advanced nations against the backdrop of their underlying investment.[28]

16.7.1   The Evolutionary Approach

The evolutionary approach consists of an isolationist approach to standard-setting whereby the developing country develops its own standard without any outside interference or influences. The particular developing country defines its own specific accounting objectives and needs and proceeds to meet them by developing its own techniques, concepts, institutions, profession, and education in isolation. The particular country may feel its context to be unique enough to justify this drastic approach of standard setting. The learning process in this approach has to come from the local experiences rather than the international experiences. It assumes the foreign partners will adapt to its own idiosyncratic rules and may have to if they want to continue to trade with the country and/or maintain operations. Naturally, it may create an additional cost to the foreign partners, who may feel the conditions onerous enough to justify complete cooperation. In addition, the absence of an adequate local accounting technology may hamper not only the local firms, but also the foreign firms operating in the country.

16.7.2   The Transfer of Technology Approach

The development through transfer of accounting technology may result from either the operations and activities of international accounting firms, multinationals, and academicians practicing in the developing countries, or the various international treaties and cooperative arrangements called for exchanges of information and technology. Adolf Enthoven, for example, describes the benefits of US accounting assistance to the developing world as follows:

> US accounting and accountants have already had a positive effect on accounting systems, procedures and training in many developing economies. For example, the affiliates of US MNEs have developed sound financial management systems. Other US companies have entered into joint ventures with foreign companies or have set up their own organizations in these countries for the production and sale of goods and services. Good financial and managerial accounting methods have accompanied these investments. Many US CPA firms have either established corresponding relationships with foreign firms or set up branch offices abroad. Although much of value has been accomplished by US accountants in CPA firms and in industry-developing economies, such activities have generally been directed toward certain companies or to serve CPA firm clients. More might be done; however, I recognize that this task isn't the first priority of accountants in public practice and industry.[29]

Because most developing countries may not have given formal attention to the formulation and implementation of a strategy which facilitates the transfer of accounting technology, or the development of an indigenous accounting profession, Belverd Needles, Jr., proposed a conceptual framework by which a country may formulate a strategy for the international transfer of accounting technology as part of its overall economic plan.[30] Basically, national goals combine with the social, political, and economic environment and general resources and constraints to influence the overall economic plan. The economic plan itself contains as a subplan a strategy for the transfer of accounting technology, composed of:

1 objectives for the accounting technology transfer;
2 strategy;
3 channels of transfer;
4 levels of accounting technology.

The three types of technology, individual, organizational, and independent professional, are defined as follows:

T_1 — level of technical accounting knowledge possessed by individuals.
T_2 — level of sophistication of accounting techniques used by government and business organizations.
T_3 — level of advancement of an independent accounting profession.[31]

While the mere transfer of accounting technology may appear to be a direct benefit to the developing countries, there is the cost associated with (a) the transfer of the wrong or inapplicable technology, (b) the lack of appropriate infrastructure for the correct application of the technology, (c) the increased dependence on outside experts, (d) the lack of incentives for developing local standards, and (e) the horrible loss of pride by some culture groups. These costs ought to be compared with the benefits of technology transfer by each of the developing countries. It is a strategic decision which is an integral part of the overall economic plan, as suggested earlier. The whole process of development ought to include not only economic growth strategies but accounting growth strategies, and therein lies the question of the desirability of accounting technology transfer by the developing countries.

16.7.3   The Adoption of International Accounting Standards

The strategy available to the developing countries consists of joining the International Accounting Standards Committee (IASC) or some of the other international standards bodies identified earlier and adopting "wholesale" their pronouncements. The rationale behind such strategy may be to (a) reduce the setup and production costs of accounting standards, (b) join the international harmonization drive, (c) facilitate the growth of foreign investment which may be needed, (d) enable its profession to emulate well-established professional standards of behavior and conduct, and (e) legitimize its status as a fully-fledged member of the international community. In fact, some of the developing countries give more credence to the IASC and other standards than do some of the developed countries that have a dominant influence in the preparation of such standards.

The question is whether the benefits described as accruing to the developing countries from the mere adoption of the international accounting standards may be outweighed by the misspecifying of costs. Indeed, the international standards for accounting for various transactions occurring in the advanced countries may be totally irrelevant to some of the developing countries, as these transactions have little chance of occurring or may be occurring in a fashion more specific to the context of the developing countries. The particular situations occurring in the developing countries call for specific and local standard setting. In addition, the institutional and market factors of these countries are different enough in some contexts to justify a more "situationist" approach to standard setting. Amenkhienan makes the same point as follows:

> The case against the adoption of international standards by developing nations as an alternative to developing their own local standards is a conclusive one. Accounting in each country should develop in a manner relevant to the needs and objectives of that country. The situational variables should determine the patterns of development.[32]

This situationist strategy has also been labeled as the zero-based option, or what George Scott refers to as "fresh start," because its use established international standards as a basis toward a better fitting with the particular economic development context of the developing country. Scott elaborates as follows:

> The major alternative is to effect a relatively clean break with accounting tradition in developing nations and to attempt to develop accounting with a "fresh start" on the basis of the standards of accounting education, practices and professionalism that are embodied in economic evaluation accounting.[33]

16.7.4   The Situationist Strategy

The situationist strategy was also labeled as "the development of accounting standards based on an analysis of accounting principles and practices in the advanced nations against the backdrop of their underlying environments."[34] Basically, it calls for a consideration of the diagnostic factors which determine the development of accounting in the developing countries. A standard meeting the constraints imposed by these factors can be deemed relevant and useful to the developing countries. The total of these standards constitutes the system of reporting and disclosure of the developing country. The factors influencing it may be represented as being influenced by cultural linguistics, political and civil rights, economic and demographic characteristics, and legal and tax environment of the country in question. In other words, based on cultural relativism, linguistic relativism, and legal and tax relativism, the accounting concepts and the reporting and disclosure systems in any given country rest on the varying aspects of that country.

16.8   CONCLUSIONS

As this chapter has shown, the field of international accounting is full of practical and theoretical problems in need of investigation and inquiry. One may assume that every practical and theoretical issue in accounting has an international dimension that needs special treatment and investigation. The informational demands of the global economy makes it an important and crucial necessity to address the issues surrounding the setting, preparation, dissemination, and use of accounting information internationally. Special theoretical endeavors are necessary to capture the intricacies and complexities of situations faced by accountants internationally. This special situation of the field of international accounting places it as an important area of research and inquiry in accounting.

NOTES

[1] Weirich, T.R., Avery, C.G., and Anderson, H.R. "International Accounting: Varying Definitions," *International Journal of Accounting Education and Research* (Fall, 1971), pp. 79–87.

[2] Ibid.

[3] Qureshi, M., "Pragmatic and Academic Bases of International Accounting," *Management International Review* (2, 1979), p. 62.

[4] Ibid.

[5] Ibid.

[6] Amenkhienan, F.E., *Accounting in the Developing Countries: A Framework for Standard Setting* (Ann Arbor, Mich.: UMI Research Press, 1986), p. 20.

[7] Ibid., p. 20.

[8] Schoenfeld, Hanns-Martin, W., "International Accounting: Development, Issues, and Future Directions," *Journal of International Business Studies* (Fall, 1981), pp. 83–4.

[9] Merril Lynch, *Comparative International Accounting Policies* (New York, New York, Merril Lynch, 1989).

[10] Mueller, G.G., "Accounting Principles Generally Accepted in the United States Versus Those Generally Accepted Elsewhere," *International Journal of Accounting Education and Research* (3, 2, 1986), pp. 92–3.

[11] Ibid., pp. 93–5.

[12] Belkaoui, Ahmed, "Cultural Studies and Accounting Research," Report of the Cultural Studies and Accounting Research Committee, *Advances in International Accounting* (Vol. 4, 1991).

[13] Belkaoui, Ahmed, "Language and Accounting," *Journal of Accounting Literature* (Vol. 8, 1989).

[14] Belkaoui, Ahmed, "Economic Political and Civil Indicators and Reporting and Disclosure Adequacy," *Journal of Accounting and Public Policy* (2, 1983).

[15] Wilson, J.A., "The Need for Standardization of International Accounting," *Touche Ross Tempo* (Winter, 1969), p. 40.

[16] Macrae, E.W., "Impediments to a Free International Market in Accounting and the Effects on International Accounting Firms," in *The International World of Accounting Challenges and Opportunities*, (ed.) J.C. Burton (New York: Arthur Young, 1981), p. 150.

[17] Seidler, Lee J., "Technical Issues in International Accounting," in *Multinational Accounting: A Research Framework for the Eighties*, (ed.) F.D.S. Choi (Ann Arbor, Mich.: UMI Research Press, 1981), p. 41.

[18] Cummins, J.P. and Chetkovich, M.N., "World Accounting Enters a New Era," *Journal of Accountancy* (April, 1978), p. 52.

[19] International Accounting Standards Committee, *Objectives and Procedures* (London: IASC, January 1983), para. 8.

[20] Ibid., para. 27.

[21] Benson, Sir Henry, "The Story of International Accounting Standards," *Accounting* (July, 1976), p. 34.

[22] Douglas, T.R., "International Accounting Standards," *CA Magazine* (October, 1977), pp. 49–50.

[23] "The Time is Now," *CA Magazine* (November, 1980), p. 68.

[24] Group of Experts on International Standards of Accounting and Reporting, *International Standards of Accounting and Reporting for Transnational Corporations* (New York: United Nations, 1977), p. 7.

[25] Office of Economic Cooperation and Development, "Declaration on International Investment and Multinational Enterprises," *OECD Observer* (July — August, 1976), p. 14.

[26] Commission of European Communities, *Amended Proposal for a Fourth Council Directive for Coordination of National Legislation Regarding the Annual Accounts of Limited Liability Companies* (Brussels, 1974).

[27] *The Fourth Directive* (London: Deloitte, Haskins and Sells, 1978), p. 1.

[28] Amenkhienan, F.E., *Accounting in the Developing Countries: A Framework for Standard Setting*, op. cit., pp. 22–6.

[29] Enthoven, Adolf J., "US Accounting and the Third World," *Journal of Accountancy* (June, 1983), p. 112.

[30] Needles, Jr., B.E., "Implementing a Framework for the International Transfer of Accounting Technology," *International Journal of Accounting Education and Research* (Fall, 1976), p. 51.

[31] Ibid., p. 51.

[32] Amenkhienan, F.E., *Accounting in the Developing Countries*, op. cit., p. 74.

[33] Scott, G.M., *Accounting and the Developing Nations* (Seattle: University of Washington, 1970), p. 12.

[34] Ibid., p. 25.

REFERENCES

Amenkhienan, F.E., *Accounting in the Developing Countries: A Framework for Standard Setting* (Ann Arbor, Mich.: UMI Research Press, 1986).

Belkaoui, Ahmed, *Judgement in International Accounting* (Westport, Ct.: Quorum Books, 1990).

Belkaoui, Ahmed, *Multinational Management Accounting* (Westport, Ct.: Quorum Books, 1991).

Belkaoui, Ahmed, *Multinational Financial Accounting* (Westport, Ct.: Quorum Books, 1991).

Belkaoui, Ahmed, *Value Added Reporting: The Lessons for the US* (Westport, Ct.: Quorum Books, 1991).

Belkaoui, Ahmed, *The New Environment in International Accounting* (Westport, Ct.: Quorum Books, 1988).

Belkaoui, Ahmed, *International Accounting* (Westport, Ct.: Quorum Books, 1985).

Bursten, R.J., "The Evolution of Accounting in Developing Countries," *International Journal of Accounting Education and Research* (Fall, 1978).

Choi, F.D.S., and Bavishi, V.B., "Diversity in Multinational Accounting," *Financial Executive* (August, 1988), pp. 46–9.

Cooke, T.E., and Wallace, R.S.O., "Financial Disclosure Regulation and Its Environment: A Review and Further Analysis," *Journal of Accounting and Public Policy* (9, 1990), pp. 79–110.

Enthoven, A.J.H., *Accounting Education in Economic Development Management* (Amsterdam: North Holland, 1981).

Meek, G., "Competition Spurs Worldwide Harmonization," *Management Accounting* (August, 1984), pp. 47–9.

Perera, M.H.B., "Accounting in Developing Countries: A Case for Localized Uniformity," *The British Accounting Review* (21, 2, 1989), pp. 41–57.

Previts, G.J., "On the Subject of Methodology and Models of Accounting Education and Research (10, 2, 1975), pp. 1–12.

Weirich, T.R., Avery, C.G., and Anderson, H.R., "International Accounting: Various Definitions," *International Journal of Accounting Education and Research* (Fall, 1971), pp. 79–87.

QUESTIONS

16.1 Enumerate and discuss the various definitions of international accounting.

16.2 Identify the main accounting problems in international accounting.

16.3 Identify the main determinants of National Differences in International Accounting.

16.4 Discuss the harmonization problem.

16.5 Who are the main actors in the harmonization drive?

16.6 Discuss the main standard-setting avenues for the developing countries.

CHAPTER 17

ACCOUNTING: A MULTIPLE PARADIGM SCIENCE

The History of thought and culture is, as Hegel showed with great brilliance, a changing pattern of great liberating ideas which inevitably turn into suffocating straight-jackets, and so stimulate their own destruction by new emancipatory, and at the same time, enslaving conceptions. The first step to understand of men is the bringing to consciousness of the model or models that dominate and penetrate their thought and action. Like all attempts to make men aware of the categories in which they think, it is a difficult and sometimes painful activity, likely to produce deeply disquieting results. The second task is to analyze the model itself, and this commits the analyst to accepting or modifying or rejecting it and in the last case, to providing a more adequate one in its place[1]

Not long ago, a contempt for accounting existed within and without the university. Fortunately, the situation has changed. Various surveys of research findings attest to the academic status of accounting.[2] Accounting researchers have employed different methodologies and theories to examine all possible issues of interest in the field. Initially, in the early 1970s, such a priori research was criticized as theoretically deficient, or of doubtful value.[3] In 1970, Gonedes and Dopuch contended that an a priori model that justified the superiority of a set of accounting procedures is not possible. Fortunately, Wells, in a seminal article in 1976, defended a priori research as a necessary step in a revolution in accounting thought.[4]

Wells proceeded to show that events in accounting seem to follow the pattern of successful revolution Kuhn describes, and thus that the discipline of accounting is emerging from a state of crisis. Briefly stated, Kuhn's thesis is that a science is dominated by a specific *paradigm* at any given point. Anomalies and a crisis stage may follow, ending in a revolution in which the reigning paradigm is replaced by a new, dominant paradigm. Central to Kuhn's revolutionary pattern is the definition of a "paradigm." Assuming for the time being that such a definition is possible, the next step is to identify the paradigms in accounting. This step was taken in 1977 by the American Accounting Association with the publication of its *Statement on Accounting Theory and Theory Acceptance* (SOATATA).[5] This statement considers developments in accounting thought from a "philosophy of science" perspective — that is, in terms of Kuhn's ideas about how progress occurs in science. SOATATA identifies three dominant theoretical approaches:

1 The "classical" (true-income/inductive) approach, used by both the "normative deductionists" and the "chiefly positive, inductive writers."
2 The "decision-usefulness" approach, used by those who stress decision models and focus on decision makers (behavioral accounting and market-level research).
3 The "information/economics" approach, with a distinction made between the "single-individual case" and the "multi-individual case."

One of the arguments made in the AAA *Statement*, which is of great relevance to this study, is that the increasing varieties of accounting theories and approaches suggests the existence of several competing paradigms. The statement even suggests what these competing paradigms might be:

> For example, one paradigm, which could be labeled the "anthropological approach," specifies the professional practices of accountants as the empirical domain of account-ing. Following this paradigm, accounting theory is formulated as a rationalization of, and by drawing inferences from, extant accounting practices. Another paradigm rests largely on the behavior of stock markets to provide the empirical domain over which accounting theory is constructed and applied. Still another general view of accounting specifies the decision processes of individuals and/or extant decision theories as the empirical domain of accounting theory. This tripartite categorization can be further expanded to incorporate both the ideal income approach and the information/ economics approach, each of which suggests a somewhat unique empirical domain of accounting.[6]

First, if the application of Kuhn's concepts to Wells's interpretations is accepted, accounting qualifies as a *science*. Second, if SOATATA's suggestions are accepted, accounting is a *multiple-paradigm science*. Two issues emerge from the acceptance of both Wells's and SOATATA's suggestions. First, to offset the confusion between theories and paradigms, an adequate definition of a "paradigm" must:

1 categorize theories as mere components of paradigms and
2 differentiate between competing paradigms — two of the limitations of Wells's and SOATATA's suggestions.[7]

Second, accounting, like most sciences, lacks a single comprehensive paradigm; thus, competing accounting paradigms should be properly identified and delineated to achieve a proper conception of the state of accounting.

17.1   THE CONCEPT OF A PARADIGM

Central to Kuhn's ideas of how science progresses is the concept of a *paradigm*. Before the publication of Kuhn's "The Structure of Scientific Revolutions," "paradigm" was primarily a grammatical term, as Kuhn himself admits, that described

> an accepted model or pattern...for example, "amo, amas, amat" is a paradigm because it displays the pattern to be used in conjugating a large number of latin verbs, as in producing "laudo, laudas, laudat."[8]

Unfortunately, Kuhn's use of the term is different and inconsistent.[9] In the first edition of "The Structure of Scientific Revolutions," Kuhn says that "paradigm" encompasses "the entire constellation of beliefs, values, techniques, and so on, shared by members of a given community."[10] In the application to accounting, Wells uses "paradigm" as a disciplinary matrix. In SOATATA, "paradigms" are defined as conceptual and institutional frameworks that "provide models from which spring particular coherent traditions of scientific research." In fact, Masterman identifies 21 different senses in which Kuhn uses the term "paradigm."[11] Kuhn responded to these criticisms with a narrow definition of paradigm in an epilogue to his second edition:

> The concrete puzzle solutions that, when employed as models of examples, can replace explicit rules as a basis for the solution of the remaining puzzles of normal science.[12]

This definition is still vague and does not alleviate the major criticisms directed toward Kuhn's change from the view that paradigms rise and fall as a result of political factors, to the view that one paradigm wins over another for good reasons, including "accuracy, scope, simplicity, fruitfulness, and the like."[13] The first view is eloquently explained by Ritzer:

> One paradigm wins out over another because its supporters have more *power* than those who support competing paradigms and *not* necessarily because their paradigm is "better" than its competitors. For example, the paradigm whose supporters control the most important journals in a field and thereby determine what will be published is more likely to gain preeminence than paradigms whose adherents lack access to prestigious outlets for their work. Similarly, positions of leadership in a field are likely to be given to supporters of the dominant paradigm, and this gives them a platform to enunciate their position with a significant amount of legitimacy. Supporters of paradigms that are seeking to gain hegemony with a field are obviously at a disadvantage, since they lack the kinds of power outlined above. Nevertheless, they can, by waging a political battle of their own, overthrow a dominant paradigm and gain that position for themselves.[14]

Philips argues that the reason advanced in the second view are in fact paradigm-dependent.[15] Ritzer agrees with Philips that the emergence of a paradigm is essentially a political phenomenon, and offers the following definition of a paradigm:

A paradigm is a fundamental image of the subject matter within a science. It serves to define what should be studied, what questions should be asked, how they should be asked, and what rules should be followed in interpreting the answer obtained. The paradigm is the broadest unit of consensus within a science and serves to differentiate one scientific community (or subcommunity) from another. It subsumes, defines, and interrelates the exemplars, theories, methods, and instruments that exist within it.[16]

Central to Ritzer's definition is that a paradigm has the following four basic components:

1 An *exemplar*, defined as "a piece of work that stands as a model of those who work within the paradigm."
2 An *image of the subject matter*.
3 *Theories*.
4 *Methods* and instruments.

The paradigm concept, as defined by Ritzer, may be used to analyze scientific communities or subcommunities in accounting. As stated earlier, accounting lacks a single comprehensive paradigm and is a multiple-paradigm science. Each accounting paradigm is striving for acceptance, even dominance within the discipline. We will use Ritzer's paradigm concept to identify and delineate the competing paradigms in accounting. In agreement with SOATATA's suggestions, we will consider the basic accounting paradigms to be:

1 The anthropological/inductive paradigm.
2 The true-income/deductive paradigm.
3 The decision-usefulness/decision-model paradigm.
4 The decision-usefulness/aggregate-market-behavior paradigm.
5 The decision-usefulness/decision-maker/individual-user paradigm.
6 The information/economics paradigm.

17.2 THE ANTHROPOLOGICAL/INDUCTIVE PARADIGM

17.2.1 Exemplars

Several studies qualify as exemplars of the *anthropological/inductive paradigm* — namely, the works of Gilman, Hatfield, Ijiri, Littleton, and Paton.[17] The authors of these studies share a concern for a *descriptive-inductive approach* to the construction of an accounting theory and a belief in the value of *extant accounting practices*. For ecample, Ijiri considers the primary concern of accounting to be the functioning of accountability relationships among interested parties. The objective measurement is the economic performance of the firm. On the basis of discussions concerning research methodology and the role of logic in theory construction and policy formulation in accounting. Ijiri presents *accountability* as a descriptive theory of accounting:

What we are emphasizing here is that current accounting practice can be better interpreted if we view accountability as the underlying goal. We are also suggesting that unless accounting is viewed in this manner, much of the current practice would appear to be inconsistent and irrational.[18]

In defense of his paradigm refuting the criticisms of advocates of current-cost and current-value accounting, Ijiri also presents an axiomatic model of existing accounting practice that evaluates the significance of historical cost in terms of accountability and decision making.

Littleton arrives at his accounting principles from observations of accounting practices. Such inductively derived principles, supported by the test of experience, incorporate the goals implicit in accounting practice. For example, Littleton states:

> Teachers of bookkeeping and later of accounting and auditing found it necessary to supplement the accumulated rules and descriptions of procedure with explanations and justifications. This was done in order that study should be something more than the memorizing of rules. Hence, it is appropriate to say that both the methods of practice and the explanations of theory were inductively derived out of experience.[19]

> Good theory is practice-created and, moreover, is practice conditioning. Finally, whenever evidence of integration among accounting ideas is found, it wil strengthen the conviction that accounting doctrine contains the possibility of being built into a system of coordinated explanations and justifications of what accounting is and what it can become.[20]

Two other studies by Gordon and by Watts and Zimmerman[21] qualify as exemplars of the anthropological/inductive paradigm. Both studies argue that management will select the accounting rule that will tend to smooth income and the rate of growth in income. Gordon theorizes on *income smoothing* as follows:

> *Proposition 1*: The criterion a corporate management uses in selecting among accounting principles is the maximization of its utility or welfare . . . .
> *Proposition 2*: The utility of a management increases with
>   1 its job security
>   2 the level and rate of growth in the management's income, and
>   3 the level and rate of growth in the corporation's size . . . .
> *Proposition 3*: The achievement of the management goals stated in Proposition 2 is dependent in part on the satisfaction of stockholders with the corporation's perform-ance; that is, other things the same, the happier the stockholders, the greater the job security, income, etc., of the management . . . .
> *Proposition 4*: Stockholders' satisfaction with a corporation increases with the average rate of growth in the corporation's income (or the average rate of return on its capital) and the stability of its income. This proposition is as readily verified as Proposition 2.
> *Theorem*: Given that the above four propositions are accepted or found to be true, it follows that a management would within the limits of its power, that is, the latitude allowed by accounting rules,
>   1 smooth reported income, and
>   2 smooth the rate of growth in income.
> By "smooth the rate of growth in income," we mean the following: If the rate of growth is high, accounting practices that reduce it should be adopted, and vice versa.[22]

Several empirical tests in the income-smoothing literature leave Gordon's model unconfirmed. Also, Gordon's assumptions that shareholder satisfaction is solely a positive function of income and that increases in stock prices always follow increases in accounting income have been seriously contested. To avoid the pitfalls that may exist in Gordon's model, Watts and Zimmerman attempt to provide a positive theory of accounting by exploring the factors influencing management's attitudes regarding accounting standards.[23] At the outset, Watts and Zimmerman assume that management's utility is a *positive* function of the expected compensation of future periods and a *negative* function of the dispersion of future compensation. Their analysis shows that the choice of accounting standards can affect a firm's cash flow through taxes, regulation, political costs, information-production costs, and management-compensation plans:

> The first four factors increase managerial wealth by increasing the cash flows and, hence, the share price. The last factor can increase managerial wealth by altering the terms of the incentive compensation.[24]

17.2.2 Image of the Subject Matter

To those who adopt the anthropological/inductive paradigm, the basic subject matter is:

1 existing accounting practices, and
2 management's attitudes toward those practices.

Proponents of this view argue in general either that the techniques may be derived and justified on the basis of their tested use or that management plays a central role in determining the techniques to be implemented. Consequently, the accounting-research objective associated with the anthropological/inductive paradigm is to understand, explain, and predict existing accounting practices. For example, Ijiri views the mission of this paradigmatic approach as follows:

> This type of inductive reasoning to derive goals implicit in the behavior of an existing system is not intended to be pro-establishment to promote the maintenance of the status quo. The purpose of such exercise is to highlight where changes are most needed and where they are feasible. Changes suggested as a result of such a study have a much better chance of actually being implemented.[25]

17.2.3 Theories

Two kinds of theories may be considered to be part of the anthropological/inductive paradigm. The first type of theory deals with all attempts to explain and justify existing accounting practices — the historical-cost approach to asset valuation, conventional cost-allocation techniques, bookkeeping techniques, and so on. The second kind of theory deals with attempts to explain management's role in the determining of techniques and includes the income-smoothing hypothesis and the beginnings of a positive theory of accounting.

17.2.4 Methods

Those who accept the anthropological/inductive paradigm tend to employ one of two kinds of techniques. Those interested in explaining and justifying existing accounting practices rely on analytic reasoning or on survey-research and observational methods. Those primarily interested in explaining management's role in the determination of techniques rely basically on empirical techniques.

17.3 THE TRUE-INCOME/DEDUCTIVE PARADIGM

17.3.1 Exemplars

Studies that qualify as exemplars of the *true-income/deductive paradigm* are the works of Alexander, Canning, Edwards, and Bell, MacNeal, Moonitz, Paton, Sprouse and Moonitz, and Sweeney.[26] These authors share a concern for a normative-deductive approach to the construction of an accounting theory and, with the exception of Alexander, a belief that, ideally, income measured using a single valuation base would meet the needs of all users. These researchers are also in complete agreement that current price information is more useful that conventional historical-cost information is to users in making economic decisions. Paton, for example, refutes the propriety theory of accounts view by restating the theory of accounting in a way that is consistent with the conditions and needs of the business enterprise as a distinct entity or personality. According to Paton, accounting plays a significant and relevant role in the firm and in society:

> If the tendencies of the economic process as evidenced in market prices are to be reflected rationally in the decisions of business managers, efficient machinery for the recording and interpreting of such statistics must be avilable; and a sound accounting scheme represents an essential part of such a mechanism . . . .
>
> To put the matter in very general terms, accounting, insofar as it contributes to render effective the control of the price system in its direction of economic activity, contributes to general productive efficiency and has a clear-cut social significance, a value to the industrial community as a whole.[27]

Paton's theory of the accounting system consists of a logical discussion and justification of the accounting structure in terms of the fundamental classes of accounts; the proprietorship and liabilities; the property and equity accounts; the types of transactions; the expense, revenue, and supplementary accounts; the account classification; the periodic analysis; and the concepts of debit and credit. Paton states:

> The liberal view that, ideally, all bona fide value changes in either direction, from whatever cause, should be reflected in the accounts has been adopted without argument. To show that all possible types of situations and transactions can be handled in a rational manner in accordance with the principles enunciated is a chief reason for this attitude.[28]

17.3.2 Image of the Subject Matter

To those who adopt the true-income/deductive paradigm, the basic subject matter is:

1 the construction of an accounting theory on the basis of logical and normative reasoning and conceptual rigor, and
2 a concept of ideal income based on some other method than the historical-cost method.

MacNeal argues for an ideal-income concept as follows:

> There is one correct definition of profits in an accounting sense. A "profit" is an increase

in net wealth. A "loss" is decrease in net wealth. This is an economist's definition. It is terse, obvious, and mathematically demonstrable.[29]

Alexander, who also argues for an ideal-income concept, states:

> We must find out whether economic income is an ideal from which accounting income differs only to the degree that the ideal is practically unattainable, or whether economic income is appropriate even if it could conveniently be measured.[30]

17.3.3   Theories

The theories that emerge from the true-income/deductive paradigm present alternatives to the historical-cost accounting system. In general, five theories or schools of thought may be identified:[31]

1 Price-level adjusted (or current-purchasing-power) accounting.[32]
2 Replacement-cost accounting.[33]
3 Deprival-value accounting.[34]
4 Continuously contemporary (net-realizable-value) accounting.[35]
5 Present-value accounting.[36]

Each of these theories presents alternative methods of asset valuation and income determination that allegedly overcome the defects of the historical-cost accounting system.

17.3.4   Methods

Those who accept the true-income/deductive paradigm generally employ analytic reasoning to justify the construction of an accounting theory or to argue the advantages of a particular asset-valuation/income-determination model other than historical-cost accounting. Advocates of this paradigm generally proceed from objectives and postulates about the environment to specific methods.

17.4   THE DECISION-USEFULNESS/DECISION-MODEL PARADIGM

17.4.1   Exemplars

Chambers was one of the first to point to the *decision-usefulness/decison-model paradigm:*

> It is therefore a corollary of the assumption of rational management that there shall be an information-providing system; such a system is required both as a basis for decisions and as a basis for reviewing the consequences of decisions. . . . A formal information-providing system would conform with two general propositions.
>   The first is a condition of all logical discourse. The system should be logically consistent; no rule or process can be permitted that is contrary to any other rule or process. . . . The second proposition arises from the use of accounting statements as a basis for making decisions of practical consequence. The information yielded by any

such system should be relevant to the kinds of decision the making of which it is expected to facilitate.[37]

Chambers does not pursue this view of the decision-usefulness/decision-model paradigm. He prefers to base an accounting theory on the usefulness of "current cash equivalents," rather than on the decision models of specific user groups. Similarly, May[38] offers a list of uses of financial accounts without explicitly employing the decision-model approach to the formulation of an accounting theory. According to May, financial accounts are used as:

1 A report of stewardship.
2 A basis of fiscal policy.
3 A criterion of the legality of dividends.
4 A guide to wise dividend activity.
5 A basis for the granting of credit.
6 Information for prospective investors.
7 A guide to the value of investments already made.
8 An aid to governmental supervision.
9 A basis for price or rate regulation.
10 A basis for taxation.

In fact, the works of Beaver, Kennelly, and Voss and of Sterling[39] may be considered the true exemplars of the decision-usefulness/decision-model paradigm. Beaver, Kennelly, and Voss examine the origin of the *predictive-ability criterion*, its relationship to the facilitation of decision making, and the potential difficulties, associated with its implementation. According to the predictive-ability criterion, alternative methods of accounting measurement are evaluated in terms of their ability to predict economic events:

> The measure with the greatest predictive power with respect to a given event is considered to be the "best" method for that particular purpose.[40]

The predictive-ability criterion is presented as a purposive criterion in the sense that accounting data ought to be evaluated in terms of their purpose or use, which is generally accepted in accounting to be the facilitation of decision making. The predictive-ability criterion is assumed to be relevant, even when applied in conjunction with a low specification of the decision model:

> Because prediction is an inherent part of the decision process, knowledge of the predictive ability of alternative measures is a prerequisite to the use of the decision-making criterion. At the same time, it permits tentative conclusions regarding alternative measurements, subject to subsequent confirmation when the decision models eventually become specified. The use of predictive ability as a purposive criterion is more than merely consistent with accounting's decision-making orientation. It can provide a body of research that will bring accounting closer to its goal of evaluation in terms of a decision-making criterion.[41]

Sterling develops criteria to be used in evaluating the various measures of wealth and income. Given the conflicting viewpoints about the objectives of accounting reports, Sterling chooses *usefulness* as the overriding criterion of a measurement method, emphasizing its importance over such requirements as objectivity and verifiability.[42]

Due to the diversity of decision makers and the inherent economic and physical impossibility of providing all of the information that users want, Sterling opts for usefulness as the relevant criterion of decision models:

> The basis for selection that I prefer is to supply information for rational decision models. The modifier "rational" is defined to mean those decision models that are most likely to allow decision makers to achieve their goals . . .[43]
>
> In summary, an accounting system should be designed to provide relevant information to rational decision models. The accounting system cannot supply all the information desired by all decison makers and, therefore, we must decide to exclude some kinds of information and to include other kinds. Restricting the decision models to rational ones permits the exclusion of a raft of data based on the whims of decision makers. It permits us to concentrate on those kinds that have been demonstrated to be effective in achieving the decision makers' goals.[44]

17.4.2   Image of the Subject Matter

To those who adopt the decision-usefulness/decision-model paradigm, the basic subject matter is the usefulness of accounting information to decision models. Information relevant to a decision model or criterion is determined and then implemented by choosing the best accounting alternative. *Usefulness* to a decision model is equated with relevance to a decision model. For example, Sterling states:

> If a property is specified by a decision model, then a measure of that property is relevant (to that decision model). If a property is not specified by a decision model, then a measure of that property is irrelevant (to that decision model).[45]

17.4.3   Theories

Two kinds of theories may be included within the decision-usefulness/decision-model paradigm. The first type of theory deals with the different kinds of decision models associated wth business decision making (EOQ, PERT, linear programming, capital budgeting, buy versus lease, make or buy, and so on). The information requirements for most of these decision models are fairly well specified. The second kind of theory deals with the different economic events that may affect a going concern (bankruptcy, takeover, merger, bond ratings, and so on). Theories to link accounting information to these events are still lacking. Developing such theories is the primary objective of those working within the decision-usefulness/decision-model paradigm.

17.4.4   Methods

Those who accept the decision-usefulness/decision-model paradigm tend to rely on empirical techniques to determine the predictive ability of selected items of information. The general approach has been to use discriminant analysis to classify into one of several a priori groupings, dependent on a firm's individual financial characteristics.

17.5   THE DECISION-USEFULNESS/DECISION-MAKER/AGGREGATE-MARKET-BEHAVIOR PARADIGM

17.5.1   Exemplars

The exemplars of the *decision-usefulness/decision-maker/aggregate-market-behavior paradigm* are the works of Gonedes and of Gonedes and Dopuch.[46] In this pioneering paper, Gonedes extends the interest in decision usefulness from the *individual-user* response to the *aggregate-market* response. Arguing that market reactions (for example, anticipatory price reactions) to accounting numbers should govern the evaluation of the informational content of these numbers and of the procedures used to produce these numbers, Gonedes develops the *aggregate-market paradigm*, which implies that accounting produces numbers that have informational content dictated by market reactions. To the counter-arguments

1 that the procedures used to produce the numbers may induce market inefficiencies, and
2 that recipients may be conditioned to react to accounting numbers in a particular manner,

Gonedes argues that if both cases were true, the opportunity for those who possess this knowledge to earn an abnormal profit would provide a basis for the demise of the market paradigm within the context of an efficient capital market. In the award-winning paper, Gonedes and Dopuch provide a theoretical framework for assessing the desirability and/or effects of alternative accounting procedures. Their approach relies on the use of prices of (rates of returns on) firms' ownership shares. Gonedes and Dopuch conclude that the price-domain analysis is sufficient for assessing the effects of alternative accounting procedures or regulations, but insufficient for assessing the desirability of alternative accounting procedures or regulations. This conclusion is based primarily on one case of market failure in which information of a public-good nature cannot be excluded from nonpurchasers (the *free-rider problem*). In such a case, the prices of firms' ownership shares cannot be used to assess the desirability of alternative accounting procedures or regulations.

Other market-failure possibilities are the issue of *adverse selection*[47] and the effect of information on the completeness of markets and efficient risk-sharing arrangements.[48] Gonedes and Dopuch also note that some criticisms of work based on capital-market efficiency, including the works of Abdel-Khalik and of May and Sundem,[49] treat remarks on assessing *effects* as if they were remarks on assessing *desirability*.

A contemporary piece of work by Beaver[50] may also be viewed as an exemplar of the decision-usefulness/decision-maker/aggregate-market-behavior paradigm. Beaver raises the issue of the importance of this relationship between accounting data and security behavior. He argues that it is inconceivable that optimal informational systems for investors can be selected without a knowledge of how accounting data are impounded in prices, because the prices determine wealth and wealth affects the multiperiod investment decisions of individuals.

17.5.2   Image of the Subject Matter

To those who adopt the decision-usefulness/decision-model/aggregate-market-behavior paradigm, the basic subject matter is the aggregate-market response to accounting variables. These authors agree that in general the decision usefulness of accounting variables can be derived from aggregate-market behavior, or as presented by Gonedes and Dopuch, only the effects of alternative accounting procedures or speculations can be assessed from aggregate-market behavior. According to Gonedes and Dopuch, the selection of the accounting-information system is determined by aggregate-market behavior.

17.5.3 Theories

The relationship between aggregate-market behavior and accounting variables is based on the theory of *capital-market efficiency*. According to this theory, the market for securities is deemed efficient in the sense that (1) market prices "fully reflect" all publicly available information and, by implication, that (2) market prices are unbiased and react instantaneously to new information. The theory implies that, on the average, the abnormal return (the return in excess of the equilibrium-expected return) to be earned from employing a set of extant information in conjunction with any trading scheme is zero.[51] Thus, any change in the information set will automatically result in a new equilibrium.

17.5.4 Methods

Those who accept the decision-usefulness/decision-model/aggregate-market-behavior paradigm tend to use a variant of either the two-parameter, asset-pricing model or the dividend (earnings)-capitalization model when they conduct empirical research.

The *capital-asset pricing* model asserts that there is a linear relationship between the systematic risk of an individual security and its expected return, such that the greater the risk, the higher the expected return.[52] This model also states that the only variable that determines differential expected returns among securities is the *systematic risk* (either the security's covariance with the market portfolio or β, which is a measure of the security's responsiveness to the market factor). The capital-asset pricing model is then an equilibrium-pricing model. In general, accounting research has relied instead on the "market model," which specifies the *stochastic process* generating individual security returns. Simply, the market model assumes that the return on each security is linearly related to the market return:

$$R_{it} = a_i + \beta_i R'_{mt} + u_{it}$$

where

$$E(u_{it}) = 0$$
$$\sigma(R'_{mt}, u_{it}) = 0$$
$$\sigma(u_{it}, u_{jt}) = 0$$

R_{it} = return on security i in period t.

R'_{mt} = aggregate rate of return on all securities in the market.

u_{it} = stochastic portion, or the individualistic factor expressing that portion of the return on security i that varies independently of R'_{mt}.

a_i, β_i = the intercept and slope associated with the linear relationship.

The parameters (u_{it}, a_i, and β_i) are estimated from an ordinary time-series, least-squares regression of the individual security returns against the market returns. The differences between actual returns and the estimated returns are the *abnormal returns*. These abnormal returns are then aggregated and used to assess the effect(s) of information on the behavior of capital-market agents. One variant of this approach is to construct an *Abnormal Performance Index* (API). Used initially in the seminal Ball and Brown study,[53] API is computed

$$\text{API}_T = \frac{1}{N} \sum_{i=1}^{N} \prod_{t=1}^{T} (1 + u_{it})$$

where

> T = number of time periods.
> N = number of securities.

The API reflects the abnormal return that would be caused by holding a portfolio and knowing the earnings figure in advance of the market. The API is a measure of information in a foreknown sense. More specifically, a positive (negative) API associated with a positive (negative) earnings-forecast error is assumed to indicate a positive association between unexpected earnings and prices. Evidently, the effectiveness of this method depends on the earnings-expectation model used.

Under the *dividend (earnings)-capitalization model*, the equilibrium price of ownership shares equals the value of all future dividends to be received, discounted at the cost of equity capital. To account for uncertainty, various *ad hoc* adjustments are introduced, rather than implied by some explicit theory of valuation under uncertainty.

17.6 THE DECISION-USEFULNESS/DECISION-MAKER/INDIVIDUAL-USER PARADIGM

17.6.1 Exemplars

The works of Birnberg and Nath, of Bruns, and of Hofstedt and Kinard[54] may be considered exemplars of the *decision-usefulness/decision-maker/individual-user paradigm*. Bruns proposes hypotheses that relate the user of accounting information, the relevance of accounting information to decision making, the decision maker's conception of accounting, and other available information to the effect of accounting information on decisions. These hypotheses are also developed in a model that identifies and relates some factors that may determine when decisions are affected by accounting systems and information. Hofstedt and Kinard argue in favor of *behavioral accounting research* that stems from the realization that an accounting system can be designed to influence behavior. They define behavioral accounting research as the study of how accounting functions and reports influence the behavior of accountants and nonaccountants. These authors show that such endeavor is a proper area of inquiry worthy of research, and they propose a research strategy.

Birnberg and Nath investigate the implications of behavioral science for managerial accounting and present examples of how behavioral science may be used to perceive the accounting process and to develop testable hypotheses about it. The principal rationale for this endeavor is that the implementation of accounting techniques depends on human-element responses and on interactions of the individual or group with the accounting system.

17.6.2 Image of the Subject Matter

To those who adopt the decision-usefulness/decision-maker/individual-user paradigm, the basic subject matter is the individual-user response to accounting variables. Advocates of this paradigm argue that in general the decision usefulness of accounting is viewed as *behavioral process*. The American Accounting Association's Committee on the Behavioral-Science Content of the Accounting Curriculum hypothesizes that "the very process of accumulating information, as well as the behavior of those who do the accumulating, will affect the behavior of others."[55] Consequently, the objective of behavioral-accounting research is to understand, explain, and predict human behavior within an accounting context. This paradigm is of interest to internal and external users of accounting, producers and attesters of information, and the general public or its surrogates. Behavioral-accounting research related to the external reporting environment addresses four overall issues:

1 the adequacy of financial statement disclosure;
2 the usefulness of financial statement data;
3 attitudes about corporate reporting issues;
4 materiality judgments.[56]

Behavioral-accounting research related to the internal reporting environment addresses two overall issues:

1 behavioral budgeting, and
2 behavioral control.

17.6.3 Theories

Much of the research associated with the decision-usefulness/decision-maker/individual-user paradigm has been conducted without benefit of the explicit formulation of a theory. In general, the alternative to developing appropriate behavioral-accounting theories has been to borrow theories from other fields and disciplines. Most of these borrowed theories adequately explain and predict human behavior within an accounting context. Some examples are the use of linguistic relativism to explain the impact of accounting information on the user's behavior,[57] the use of socio-linguistics to explain the differences in the linguistic behavior of users and producers,[58] the use of the entropy concept to study aggregation in accounting,[59] the use of Weber's Law from psychophysics to study judgments of numerical data,[60] the use of models from the psychology of information processing to study the decision-making process,[61] the use of dissonance theory to explain compliance with APB opinions,[62] the use of functional fixity to study the impact of data on users,[63] and the use of information inductance, whereby the behavior of an individual is affected by the information he or she is required to communicate.[64]

17.6.4   Methods

Those who accept the decision-usefulness/decision-maker/individual-user paradigm tend to employ all of the methods favored by behaviorists — observation techniques, interviews, questionnaires, and experimentation. Because a laboratory provides a controlled setting, *experimentation* is the preferred method. Laboratory experiments also may be popular because the decision-usefulness/decision-maker/individual-user paradigm is a quite recent development. Such experiments may be only starting points for further validation. For example, Hofstedt and Kinard contend that the success of laboratory experiments "leads to more general hypotheses and to theories whose validity and applicability can be tested by subsequent field studies, both quasi-experimental and purely observational."[65]

17.7   THE INFORMATION/ECONOMICS PARADIGM

17.7.1   Exemplars

Exemplars of the information/economics paradigm are the works of Crandall, Feltham, and Feltham and Demski.[66] In his pioneering paper, Feltham provides a framework for determining the value of a change in the information system from the viewpoint of the individual making an informational decision (the decision maker). The framework relies on the individual components that are required to compute the *expected payoff* (or *utility*) for a particular information system. The components are:

1 a set of possible actions at each period within a time horizon;
2 a payoff function over the events that occur during the periods;
3 probabilistic relationships between past and future events;
4 events and signals from the information system, including past and future signals;
5 a set of decision rules as functions of the signals.

The framework states that the value of changing from one information system to another is equal to the difference between the expected payoffs of the two alternatives.

Crandall examines the usefulness of the information/economics paradigm to the future development of accounting theory and offers the "applied information economics" approach as a new mainstream accounting theory. Simply, this approach consists of recognizing explicitly each component of the information/economics model and broadening the scope of accounting design to include all of these components. Crandall defines the components as the "filter," the "model," the "channel," "decoding," and the "decision rule." The implications for the future development of accounting theory are stated as follows:

The ideal for the development of accounting theory would be the development of a constructive theory of information economics where, in some significant areas of the model, one could develop algorithms that pointed out the theoretically "best" design of the system, given a set of assumptions. . . .[67]

[The purpose is] to permit the construction and evaluation of information systems for the purpose of maximizing the utility to each user, subject to constraints as to the cost of the system, the decision rules available, the state of the technology, and the feasibility of obtaining information from the real world.[68]

The third exemplar, Feltham and Demski's "The Use of Models in Information Evaluation," presents and discusses a model of information choice that views information evaluation in *cost-benefit terms* and as a *sequential process*. The entire process is summarized as follows:

. . . specification of a particular information system results in a set of signals being supplied to the decision maker; the decision maker may then use the resulting information in selecting his or her action; and this action may determine, in part, the events x of the subsequent period. The information evaluation must predict the relationship between each of the above elements: the signal-generation process, $\varphi(y|\eta)$; $a(y|\eta)$; the decision maker's prediction- and action-choice process, and the relationship between the actions selected and the events that will occur, $\varphi(x|y, \eta, a)$ w(x). In addition, the decision maker must predict the gross payoff he or she will derive from the events of the subsequent period, as well as the cost of operating the particular information system $w'(y, \eta)$.[69]

17.7.2   Image of the Subject Matter

To those who adopt the information/economics paradigm, the basic subject matter is:

1 information is an economic commodity, and
2 the acquisition of information amounts to a problem of economic choice.

The value of information is viewed in terms of a cost-benefit criterion within the formal structure of decision theory and economic theory. This is best stated as follows:

. . .the case of the argument on behalf of accrual accounting rests on the premise that (1) reported income under accrual accounting conveys more information than a less ambitious cash flow-oriented accounting system would, (2) accrual accounting is the most efficient way to convey this additional information, and, as a corollary, (3) the "value" of such additional information system exceeds its "cost."[70]

Accounting information is evaluated in terms of its ability to improve the quality of the optimal choice in a basic choice problem that must be resolved by an individual or a number of heterogeneous individuals. A single individual must select among different actions that have different possible outcomes. Assuming a consistent, rational choice behavior governed by the *expected utility hypothesis*, the action with the highest expected payoff (or utility) is preferred by the individual. Information in this context is required to revise the probabilities of the original outcomes. Thus, the individual may face a two-stage process:

1 a first stage, during which the information system produces different signals, and
2 a second stage, during which the observance of a signal results in a revision of probabilities and a choice of the conditional best action.

The information system with the highest expected utility is preferred. The information required for a systematic probability-revision (*Bayesian-version*) analysis in turn facilitates information analysis on the basis of the subjective, expected-utility-maximization rule.

17.7.3   Theories

The information/economics paradigm draws on insights from the "theory of teams," developed by Marschak and Radner,[71] on statistical decision theory, and on the economic theory of choice. What results is a normative theory of information evaluation for the systematic analysis of information alternatives. Central to the information/economics paradigm is the traditional economic assumption of consistent, rational choice behavior.

17.7.4   Methods

Those who accept the information/economics paradigm generally employ analytic reasoning based on statistical decision theory and the economic theory of choice. The approach consists of isolating the general relationships and effects of alternative scenarios and applying Bayesian-revision analysis and a cost-benefit criterion to analyze questions of accounting policy. The primary assumption of this approach is *rationality*.

17.8   EVALUATION OF ACCOUNTING RESEARCH

The situation in accounting research has drastically improved over the years. Witness the following description of the situation made on the 20th of December, 1923, in an address to the American Association of University Instructors in Accounting made by Henry Rand Hatfield:

> I am sure that all of our colleagues look upon accounting as an intruder, a Saul among the prophets, a pariah whose very presence detracts somewhat from the sanctity of the academic walls. It is true that we ourselves speak of the science of accounts, or the art of accounting, even of the philosophy of accounts. But accounting is, alas, only a pseudo-science unrecognized by J. McKeen Cattel; its products are displayed neither in the salon, nor in the national academy; we find it discussed by neither realist, idealist, or phenomenalist. The humanists look down on us as beings who dabble in the sordid figures of dollars and cents instead of toying with infinities and searching for the illusive soul of things; the scientists and technologists despise us as able only to record rather than perform deeds.[72]

Needless to say the situation has changed in favor of a dynamic research agenda, as evidenced by the transformation of accounting into a full-fledged "normal science" with competing paradigms striving for dominance. Accounting research is grounded in a common set of assumptions about social science and society, and has generated a healthy debate about how to enrich and extend our understanding of accounting in practice. These issues are examined next.

17.8.1   A Framework of the Nature of Accounting Research

Nature of the Framework

Burrell and Morgan[73] made two main sets of assumptions: about social science and about society.

The assumptions about social science relate to the ontology of the social world, epistemology, human nature and methodology. These assumptions can also be thought of in terms of the subjective-objective dimension.

First, the ontological assumption, concerning the very essence of the accounting phenomenon, involves nominalism-realism differences. The debate is whether the social world external to the individual cognition is a compound of pure names, concepts, and labels that give a structure to reality as in normalism or whether it is a compound of real, factual, and tangible structures, as in realism.

Second, the epistemological debate, concerning the grounds of knowledge and the nature of knowledge, involves the antipositivism-positivism debate. This debate focuses on the utility of a search for laws or underlying regularities in the field of social affairs. Positivism supports the utility. Antipositivism refutes it and argues for individual participation as a condition of understanding the social world.

Third, the human-nature debate, concerning the relationship between human beings and their environment, involves the voluntarism-determinism debate. This debate focuses on whether humans and their activities are determined by the situation or environment, as in determinism, or are the result of their free will, as in voluntarism.

Fourth, the methodology debate, concerning the methods used to investigate and learn about the social world, involves the ideographic-nomothetic debate. This debate focuses on whether the methodology involves the analysis of the subjective accounts obtained by participating or getting inside the situation, as in the ideographic method, or whether the methodology involves a rigorous and scientific testing of hypotheses, as in the nomothetic method.

The assumption about the nature of society relates to the order-conflict debate or, more precisely, the regulation-radical change debate.

The *sociology of regulation* attempts to explain the society by focusing on its unity and cohesiveness and the need for regulation. The sociology of radical change, in contrast, seeks to explain society by focusing on the radical change, deep-seated structural conflict, modes of domination, and the structural contradictions of modern society. As highlighted by Burrell and Morgan, the sociology of regulation is concerned with status quo, social order, consensus, social integration and cohesion, solidarity, need satisfaction, and actuality, whereas the sociology of radical change is concerned with structural conflict, models of domination, contradiction, emancipation, deprivation and potentiality.

Any social science discipline, including accounting, can be analyzed along metatheoretical assumptions about the nature of science, the subjective-objective dimension, and about the nature of society, the dimension of regulation-radical change. Using these two dimensions, Burrell and Morgan were able to develop a coherent scheme for the analysis of social theory in general, and organizational analysis in particular.[74] The scheme consists of four distinct paradigms, labeled as:

1 the radical humanist paradigm, characterized by the radical change and subjective dimensions;

2 the radical structuralist paradigm; characterized by the radical change and objective dimensions;

3 the interpretive paradigm, characterized by the subjective and regular dimensions;

4 the functionalist paradigm, characterized by the objective and regulation dimensions.

The framework is illustrated in Exhibit 17.1. It comprises of four views of reality to be used in analyzing a wide range of social theories, including accounting. As Burrell and Morgan stated:

> Given the cross linkages between rival intellectual traditions, it becomes clear to us that our two sets of assumptions could be counter-posed to produce an analytical scheme for studying social theories in general: the two sets of assumptions defined four basic paradigms reflecting quite separate views of social theory. On attempting to relate this scheme to the social science literature we found that we possessed an extremely powerful tool for negotiating our way through different subject areas, and one which made sense of a great deal of the confusion which characterizes much contemporary debate within the social science.[75]

This framework is very much applicable to accounting, to explain four accounting paradigms — the functionalist, interpretive, radical humanist, and radical structuralist. Various attempts were made to classify accounting literature using the Burrell and Morgan framework.[76]

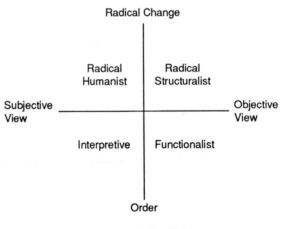

EXHIBIT 17.1

The Functionalist View in Accounting

Functionalists are interested in explaining the social order from a realist, positivist, deterministic and nomothetic standpoint. It is very characteristic of mainstream accounting. It views accounting phenomena as concrete real-world relations possessing regularities and causal relationships that are amenable to scientific explanation and prediction. The assumptions characterizing the functionalist view and mainstream research in accounting are shown in Exhibit 17.2.

EXHIBIT 17.2
Dominant Assumptions of Mainstream Accounting

A. Beliefs About Knowledge
Theory is separate from observations that may be used to verify or falsify a theory. Hypothetic-deductive account of scientific explanation accepted.

B. Beliefs About Physical and Social Reality
Empirical reality is objective and external to the subject. Human beings are also characterized as passive objects; not seen as makers of social reality.
Single goal of utility-maximization assumed for individuals and firms. Means-end rationality assumed.

C. Relationship Between Theory and Practice
Accounting specifies means, not ends. Acceptance of extant institutional structures.

Source: Chua, Wai Fang, "Radical Developments in Accounting Thought," *The Accounting Review* (October, 1986), p. 611.

The Interpretive View in Accounting

The interpretive alternative in accounting focuses on explaining the social order from a nominalist, antipositivist, voluntarist, and ideographic standpoint. The objective is to understand the subjective experience of individuals involved in the preparation, communication, verification or use of accounting information. The assumptions characterizing the interpretive view in accounting are shown in Exhibit 17.3.

EXHIBIT 17.3
Dominant Assumptions of Interpretative Perspective

A. Beliefs About Knowledge
Scientific explanations of human actions sought. Their adequacy is assessed via the criteria of logical consistency, subjective interpretation, and agreement with actors' common-sense interpretation.

B. Beliefs About Physical and Social Reality
Social reality is emergent, subjectively created, and objectified through human inter-action.
All actions have meaning and intention that are retrospectively endowed and that are grounded in social and historical practices.
Social order is assumed. Conflict mediated through common schemes of social meanings.

C. Relationship Between Theory and Practice
Theory seeks only to explain action and to understand how social order is produced and reproduced.

Source: Chua, Wai Fang, "Radical Developments in Accounting Thought," *The Accounting Review* (October, 1986), p. 615. Reprinted with permission.

The Radical Humanist View in Accounting

The radical humanist view or critical view in accounting focuses on explaining the social order from a nominalist, antipositivist, voluntarist, and ideographic perspective and places emphasis on forms of radical change. The focus is on the notion that the individual creates the world in which he/she lives and tries to change it to escape alienation or face consciousness. Accordingly the scope of the radical humanist view is stated as follows.

> The work of theorists located within the radical humanist paradigm is underwritten by a common concern for the freedom of human spirit. Radical humanists focus upon human consciousness within the context of the totality which characterizes a particular social formation. There tends to be a concern with what may be described as the "pathology of consciousness," by which men come to see themselves as trapped within a mode of social organization which they both create and maintain in everday lives. Radical humanists are concerned with understanding the manner in which this occurs, with a view to setting human consciousness or spirit free and thus facilitating the growth and development of human potentialities.[77]

Critical theory in accounting will assume that theories, bodies of knowledge, and facts are mere reflections of realistic world views. It views accountants, accounters and accountees as prisoners of a mode of consciousness that is shaped and controlled through ideological processes. All aspects of accounting are to be scrutinized for their alienating properties.

The Radical Structuralist View in Accounting

Radical structuralists are interested in challenging the social order from a realist, positivist, deterministic, and nomothetic standpoint. The focus is on radical change, emancipation and potentiality using an analysis emphasizing structural conflict, modes of domination, contradiction, and deprivation. As stated by David Cooper:

> From the point of view of these radical structuralists, organizations are instruments of social forces concerned to maintain the division of labor and distribution of wealth and power in society. To these researchers, whose perspective seems almost completely missing in current accounting research, there is an actuality of organizations that includes sexual and racial discrimination, patterns of social stratification and unequal distributions of wealth, power, and rewards . . . . The failure to acknowledge these characteristics and consider the relationship of accounting practices to them seems a curious omission for studies that explicitly seek to account for accounting.[78]

17.8.2   Mainstream Accounting Research

Mainstream accounting research sees a parallel between physical and social sciences and accounting, justifying in the process a hypothetic-deductive account of scientific explanation and the need for confirmation of hypotheses.

The first question of whether accounting is a science has never been adequately answered. A good definition of a science, provided by R. Buzzell, is as follows:

a classified and systematized body of knowledge... organized around one or more central theories and a number of general principles... usually expressed in quantitative terms... knowledge which permits the prediction and, under some circumstances, the control of future events.[79]

Accounting meets the above criteria. It has a distinct subject matter and includes underlying uniformities and regularities conducive to empirical relationships, authoritative generalizations, concepts, principles, laws, and theories. It definitively can be considered a science. If one subscribes to the unity-of-science argument, a single scientific method is equally applicable to accounting and other sciences. As Carl Hempel observed:

> The thesis of the methodological unity of science states, first of all, that, notwithstanding many differences in their techniques of investigation, all branches of empirical science test and support their statements in basically the same manner, namely by deriving from them implications that can be checked intersubjectively and by performing for those implications the appropriate experimental or observational tests. This, the unity of method thesis holds, is true also of psychology and the social and historical disciplines. In response to the claim that the scholar in these fields, in contrast to the social sciences, often must rely on empathy to establish his assertions, logical-empiricist writers stressed that imaginative identification with a given person often may prove a useful heuristic aid to the investigator who seeks to guess at a hypothesis about that person's beliefs, hopes, fears, and goals. But whether or not a hypothesis they arrived at is factually sound must be determined by reference to objective evidence: the investigator's emphatic experience is logically irrelevant to it.[80]

There is, therefore, a common acceptance by all sciences of a methodology for the justification of knowledge. That methodology rests in determining whether a true value can, in principle, be assigned to a hypothesis—that is, whether it can be refuted, confirmed, falsified, or verified, respectively. *Confirmation* is the extent to which a hypothesis is capable of being shown to be empirically untrue, that is, of failing to describe the real world accurately. *Falsification* is the extent to which a hypothesis is capable of being shown to be empirically untrue, that is, of failing to describe the real world accurately. Confirmation of hypotheses does not necessarily imply that they are falsifiable, and vice versa. In fact, hypotheses that are naturally grounded in theory can be either purely confirmable, purely refutable, or both confirmable and refutable. *Purely confirmable hypotheses* come from existential statements, that is, statements that propose the existence of some phenomenon. For example, the hypothesis "There are CPAs within public accounting firms who view inflation accounting as useless" is a purely confirmable hypothesis.

Purely refutable hypotheses come from universal laws, that is, statements that take the form of universal generalized conditionals. An example of such a hypothesis is "All accountants are CPAs." If the hypothesis is stated as "There are accountants who are CPAs," it becomes an existential statement, which is purely confirmable. Therefore, it appears that universal laws are basically negative existential statements that are purely refutable or falsifiable.

Both confirmable and refutable hypotheses come from singular statements, that is, statements that refer only to specific phenomena that are bound in time and space. For example, the hypothesis "All individuals tolerant of ambiguity process more information cues than those who are intolerant of ambiguity" can be both confirmed and refuted. However, there are hypotheses that are neither strictly confirmable or strictly refutable.

They are the hypotheses arising from statistical or tendency laws, that is, statements specifying a "loosely specified" statistical relationship between a phenomenon and a large number of variables. Most accounting hypotheses fall within this category, which makes them neither strictly confirmable nor strictly falsifiable. The market model, the accounting predictive models of economic events, the positive theory of accounting, the human information-processing models, and most empirical accounting research fit the description. If the data contradict the hypothesis derived from these theories or models, defenders can always claim different excuses, including contamination of the data, or small or biased sample size. The rhetoric of research plays a crucial role in challenging whatever results are provided by the data. Is this a cause for alarm, given that statistical laws abound in accounting research? Bunge suggested that this would be a mistake:

> Some die-hard classical determinists claim that stochastic statements do not deserve the name of law and are to be regarded, at their best, as contemporary devices. This anachronistic view has no longer currency in physics, chemistry, and certain branches of biology (notably genetics), especially ever since these sciences found that all major laws within domains are stochastic laws deducible (at least in principle) from laws concerning single systems in conjunction with definite statistical hypotheses regarding, e.g., the compensation of random deviations. Yet the prejudice against stochastic laws still causes some harm in psychology and sociology, where it serves to attack the stochastic approach without compensating for its loss by a scientific study of individuals.[81]

The refutation or confirmation is done by repeated testimony and new evidences.

17.8.3   Deconstruction

Various accounting texts about specific accounting paradigms and/or theories claim that they should be privileged over other forms of accounting knowledge and discourses. The text is used to ensure the hegemony of the paradigm and of special interests, as well as the closure around knowledge production. A philosophical phrase, termed deconstruction, introduced by Derrida[82] is intended to subvert these attempts. Because knowledge production is grounded and experienced in language, deconstruction uses the author's own system of grounding to reveal how the text violates that system. As stated by Norris:

> Derrida refuses to grant philosophy the kind of privileged status it has always claimed as the sovereign dispenser of reason. Derrida confronts this claim to power on its own chosen ground. He argues that philosophers have been able to impose their various systems of thought only by ignoring, or suppressing, the disruptive effects of language. His aim is always to draw out these effects by a critical reading which fastens on, and skilfully enriches, the elements of metaphor and other figurative devices at work in the texts of philosophy.[83]

What deconstruction implies is an exegesis of the texts to illustrate the construction of meanings within texts and subvert the hegemonic authority of a text to indicate the "truth" emanating outside the text. As stated by Arrington and Francis:

> Deconstructive readings of texts reveal how unruly and unstable meaning is and efface the veil of linguistic law and order we place over texts.[84]

In fact, Arrington and Francis are the first to use deconstruction to show that positive theory and the empirical tradition are not entitled to the kind of epistemic privilege and authority they have for a good number of accounting researchers. Their choice of a good exemplar of positive theory to deconstruct was Michael Jensen's "Organization Theory and Methodology."[85] Deconstruction in accounting research calls for more attempts to reveal the hidden assumptions of accounting texts. It assumes that all accounting discourse, even all historical narrative, is essentially rhetoric. The accounting deconstructionist will criticize the accounting text through various techniques including demythologizing, decanonizing, dephallicizing, dehegemonizing, or de-faming.

17.9 CONCLUSIONS

Accounting may be approached from the point of view of the "philosophy" of science. Research output in accounting is not considered to be of doubtful value or theoretically deficient. Rather, accounting research findings provide indications that accounting events follow the pattern of successful revolutions theorized by Kuhn. In this chapter we have adopted a definition of a "paradigm" that is relevant to accounting. The essential components of such a paradigm are exemplars, the image of the subject matter, theories, and methods. Our definition helped us to identify and delineate the competing paradigms in the accounting field:

1 the anthropological/inductive paradigm;
2 the true-income/deductive paradigm;
3 the decision-usefulness/decision-model paradigm;
4 the decision-usefulness/decision-maker/aggregate-market-behavior paradigm;
5 the decision-usefulness/decision-maker/individual-user paradigm;
6 the information/economics paradigm.

Each of these paradigms is the object of investigation and research by established scientific communities. In each of these communities, a paradigm creates a coherent, unified viewpoint—a kind of *Weltanschauung*—that determines the way in which members view accounting research, practice, and even education. In the interests of continuity and progress within the accounting discipline, these paradigms should never be considered absolute and final truthful knowledge. Instead, they should be subjected to constant verification and testing in a search for possible anomalies.

Most scientists and philosophers hold the view that scientific knowledge can never be "proved." Popper argues that although a theory cannot be proved "true" with finality, it can be proved "false" with finality.[86] Generally known as the notion of *falsification*, or the *theory of refutability*, Popper's theory holds that to be accredited as scientific, a theory must be refutable in the sense that if its results turn out to be wrong, the theory is falsified. The type of falsification that comes closest to Kuhn's view is termed *sophisticated falsification*, which Lakatos summarizes as "no experiment, experimental report, observational statement, or well-corroborated, low-level falsifying hypothesis alone can lead to falsification. There is no falsification before the emergence of a better theory.[87] A "better theory" is one that "offers any novel, excess information, compared with its predecessor," in which "some of the excess information is corroborated."[88] The difference between

Popper's *naive falsification* and the *sophisticated falsification* is that the latter requires the existence of a better theory. Lakatos tells us that the sophisticated falsificationist:

> ... makes unfalsifiable by fiat some (spatio-temporally) singular statements which are distinguishable by the fact that there exists at the same time a "relevant technique" such that "anyone who has learned it" will be able to decide that the statement is "acceptable."
>
> ... This decision is then followed by a second kind of decision concerning the separation of the set of accepted basic statements from the rest . . . . The methodological falsificationist realizes that in the "experimental techniques" of the scientist, fallible theories are involved, "in the light of which" he or she interprets the facts. In spite of this, the methodological falsificationist "applies" these theories — he or she regards them in the given context not as theories under test but as *unproblematic background knowledge* "which we accept (tentatively) as unproblematic while we are testing the theory."
>
> ... Furthermore, probabilistic theories may qualify now as "scientific:" although they are not falsifiable, they can be made "falsifiable" by an *additional (third type)* decision that the scientist can make by specifying certain rejection rules that may make statistically interpreted evidence "inconsistent" with the probabilistic theory.[89]

This may be the attitude to adopt in dealing with the competing paradigms in accounting.

NOTES

[1] Berlin, I., "Does Political Theory Still Exist?," in *Philosophy, Politics and Society*, 2nd Series, (eds) P. Laslett and W.G. Runaiman (Basil Blackwell, 1962), p. 19.

[2] Accounting Research 1960–1970: A Critical Evaluation," Monograph No. 7, (eds) N. Dopuch and L. Revsine (Urbana, Ill.: Center for International Education and Research in Accounting, University of Illinois, 1973); Gonedes, N.J., and Dopuch, N., "Capital-Market Equilibrium, Information Production, and Selecting Accounting Techniques: Theoretical Framework and Review of Empirical Work," in *Studies on Financial Accounting Objectives: 1974*, supplement to Vol. 12, *Journal of Accounting Research* (1974), pp. 48–129; *The Impact of Accounting Research in Financial Accounting and Disclosure of Accounting Practice*, (eds) A.R. Abdel-Khalik and T.F. Keller (Durham, N.C.: Duke University Press, 1978).

[3] Kuhn, Thomas S., "The Structure of Scientific Revolutions," *International Encyclopedia of Unified Science*, Second Enlarged Edition (Chicago: University of Chicago Press, 1970), pp. 10–15; Nelson, Carl L., "A Priori Research in Accounting," in *Accounting Research 1960–1970: A Critical Evaluation*, Monograph No. 7, (eds) N. Dopuch and L. Revsine (Urbana, Ill.: Center for International Education and Research in Accounting, University of Illinois, 1973), pp. 3–18; Gonedes, N.J., and Dopuch, N., "Capital-Market Equilibrium, Information Production, and Selecting Accounting Techniques: Theoretical Framework and Review of Empirical Work," op cit., p. 32.

[4] Wells, M.C., "A Revolution in Accounting Thought," *The Accounting Review* (July, 1976), pp. 471–82.

[5] American Accounting Association, Committee on Concepts and Standards for External Financial Reports, *Statement on Accounting Theory and Theory Acceptance* (Sarasota, Fl.: American Accounting Association, 1977).

[6] Ibid., p. 47.

[7] Danos, Paul, "A Revolution in Accounting Thought? A Comment," *The Accounting Review* (July, 1977), pp. 746–7; Peasnell, K.V., "Statement on Accounting Theory and Theory Acceptance: A Review Article," *Accounting and Business Research* (Summer, 1978), pp. 217–25: Hakansson, Nils H., "Where We Are in Accounting: A Review of 'Statement on Accounting Theory and Theory Acceptance'," *The Accounting Review* (July, 1978), pp. 717–25.

[8] Kuhn, Thomas S., "The Structure of Scientific Revolutions," op. cit., p. 23.

[9] Shapere, Dudley, "The Structure of Scientific Revolutions, *Philosophical Review*, Vol. 73 (1964), pp. 383–94.

[10] Kuhn, Thomas S., "The Structure of Scientific Revolutions," op cit., p. 175.

[11] Masterman, Margaret, "The Nature of a Paradigm," in *Criticism and the Growth of Knowledge*, (eds) Imre Lakatos and Alan Musgrave (Cambridge: Cambridge University Press, 1970).

[12] Kuhn, Thomas S., "The Structure of Scientific Revolutions," op. cit., p. 105.

[13] Kuhn, Thomas S., "Reflections on My Critics," in *Criticism and the Growth of Knowledge*, op. cit., pp. 231–78.

[14] Ritzer, George, "Sociology: A Multiple-Paradigm Science," *The American Sociologist* (August, 1975), pp. 15–17.

[15] Philips, D., "Paradigms, Falsification, and Sociology," *Acta Sociologica*, Vol. 16 (1973), pp. 13–31.

[16] Ritzer, George, "Sociology: A Multiple-Paradigm Science," op. cit., p. 157.

[17] Hatfield, Henry Rand, *Accounting* (New York: D. Appleton & Company, 1927); Gilman, S., *Accounting Concepts of Profit* (New York: The Ronald Press, 1939); Paton, W.A., and Littleton, A.C., "An Introduction to Corporate Accounting Standards," Monograph No. 3 (Sarasota, Fl.: American Accounting Association, 1953); Ijiri, Yuji, "Theory of Accounting Measurement," *Studies in Accounting Research*, No. 10 (Sarasota, Fl.: American Accounting Association, 1975).

[18] Ijiri, Yuji, "Theory of Accounting Measurement," op. cit., p. 37.

[19] Littleton, A.C., "Structure of Accounting Theory," Monograph No. 5, p. 185. (Fl.: American Accounting Association, 1953).

[20] Ibid., p. 31.

[21] Gordon, M.J., "Postulates, Principles, and Research in Accounting," *The Accounting Review* (April, 1964), pp. 251–63; Watts, R.L., and Zimmerman, J.L., "Towards a Positive Theory of the Determination of Accounting Standards," *The Accounting Review* (January, 1968), pp. 112–34.

[22] Gordon, M.J., "Postulates, Principles, and Research in Accounting," op. cit., pp. 261–2.

[23] Watts, R.L., and Zimmerman, J.L., "Toward a Positive Theory of the Determination of Accounting Standards," op. cit., p. 14.

[24] Ibid., p. 14.

[25] Ijiri, Yuji, "Theory of Accounting Measurement," op. cit., p. 28.

[26] Paton, W.A., *Accounting Theory* (New York: The Ronald Press, 1922); Canning, J.B., *The Economics of Accountancy* (New York: The Ronald Press, 1929); Sweeney, Henry W., *Stabilized Accounting* (New York: Harper & Row, 1936); MacNeal, Kenneth, *Truth in Accounting* (Philadelphia: University of Pennsylvania Press, 1939); Alexander, Sidney S., "Income Measurement in a Dynamic Economy," *Five Monographs on Business Income* (New York: The Study Group on Business Income, The American Institute of Certified

Public Accountants, 1950). *See also:* Edwards, E.O., and Bell, P.W., *The Theory and Measurement of Business Income* (Berkeley: University of California Press, 1961); Moonitz, Maurice, Accounting Research Study No. 1, *The Basic Postulates of Accounting* (New York: American Institute of Certified Public Accountants, 1961); Alexander, Sidney S., "Income Measurement in a Dynamic Economy," (rev.) David Solomons, in *Studies in Accounting Theory*, (eds) W.T. Baxter and Sidney Davidson (Homewood, Ill.: Richard D. Irwin, 1962); Sprouse, R.T., and Moonitz, Maurice, Accounting Research Study No. 3, *A Tentative Set of Broad Accounting Principles for Business Enterprises* (New York: American Institute of Certified Public Accountants, 1962).

[27] Paton, W.A., *Accounting Theory*, op. cit., p. 8.

[28] Ibid., pp. 8–9.

[29] MacNeal, Kenneth, *Truth in Accounting*, op. cit., p. 295.

[30] Alexander, Sidney S., "Income Measurement in a Dynamic Economy," op. cit., p. 159.

[31] Wells, M.C., "A Revolution in Accounting Thought," op. cit.

[32] Jones, Ralph Coughenour, *The Effects of Price-Level Changes* (Sarasota, Fl.: American Accounting Association, 1956); Mason, Perry, *Price-Level Changes and Financial Statements* (Sarasota, Fl.: American Accounting Association, 1971).

[33] Edwards, E.O., and Bell, P.W., *The Theory and Measurement of Business Income;* Mathews, Russel L., "Price-Level Accounting and Useless Information," *Journal of Accounting Research* (Spring, 1965), pp. 133–55; Gynther, R.S., *Accounting for Price-Level Changes: Theory and Procedures* (New York: Pergamon, 1966); Revsine, L., *Replacement-Cost Accounting* (Englewood Cliffs, N.J.: Prentice-Hall, 1973).

[34] Baxter, W.T., "Accounting Values: Sale Price Versus Replacement Cost," *Journal of Accounting Research* (Autumn, 1967), pp. 208–14; Wright, F.K., "A Theory of Financial Accounting," *Journal of Business Finance* (Autumn, 1970), pp. 51–69; Stamp, Edward, "Income and Value Determination and Changing Price Levels: An Essay Toward a Theory," *The Accountant's Magazine* (June, 1971), pp. 277–92; Whittington, Geoffrey, "Asset Valuation, Income Measurement, and Accounting Income," *Accounting Business and Research* (Spring, 1974), pp. 96–101.

[35] Chambers, R.J., *Accounting, Evaluation, and Economic Behavior* (Englewood Cliffs, N.J.: Prentice-Hall, 1966); Sterling, Robert R., "On Theory Construction and Verification," *The Accounting Review* (January, 1971), pp. 12–29.

[36] Solomons, David, "Economic and Accounting Concepts of Income," *The Accounting Review* (July, 1961), pp. 374–83; Lemke, Kenneth W., "Asset Valuation and Income Theory," *The Accounting Review* (January, 1966), pp. 33–41.

[37] Chambers, R.J., "Blueprint for a Theory of Accounting," *Accounting Research* (January, 1955), pp. 21–2.

[38] May, G.O., *Financial Accounting* (New York: Macmillan, 1943), p. 19.

[39] Beaver, W.H., Kennelly, J.W., and Voss, W.M., "Predictive Ability as a Criterion for the Evaluation of Accounting Data," *The Accounting Review* (October, 1968), pp. 675–83; Sterling, Robert R., "Decision-Oriented Financial Accounting," *Accounting and Business Research* (Summer, 1972), pp. 198–208.

[40] Beaver, W.H., Kennelly, J.W., and Voss, W.M., "Predictive Ability as a Criterion for the Evaluation of Accounting Data," op. cit., p. 675.

[41] Ibid., p. 680.

[42] Sterling, Robert R., "Decision-Oriented Financial Accounting," op. cit., p. 198.

[43] Ibid., p. 199.

[44] Ibid., p. 201.

[45] Ibid., p. 199.

[46] Gonedes, N.J., "Efficient Capital Markets and External Accounting," *The Accounting Review* (January, 1972), pp. 11–21; Gonedes, N.J., and Dopuch, N., "Capital-Market Equilibrium, Information Production, and Selecting Accounting Techniques: Theoretical Framework and Review of Empirical Work," op. cit., 48–125.

[47] Spence, M., "Job-Market Signaling," *Quarterly Journal of Economics* (August, 1973), pp. 356–74.

[48] Radner, Roy, "Competitive Equilibrium Under Uncertainty," *Econometrica* (January, 1968), pp. 60–85; Akerloff, George A., "The Market for 'Lemons': Quality Uncertainty and the Market Mechanism," *Quarterly Journal of Economics* (August, 1970), pp. 488–500; Kihlstrom, Richard, and Pauly, M., "The Role of Insurance in the Allocation of Risk," *American Economic Review* (May, 1971), pp. 100–130; Radner, Roy, "Existence of equilibrium of Plans, Prices, and Price Expectations in a Sequence of Markets," *Econometrica* (March, 1972), pp. 71–82.

[49] Abdel-Khalik, A.R., "The Efficient Market Hypothesis and Accounting Data: A Point of View," *The Accounting Review* (October, 1972), pp. 791–3; May, Robert G., and Sundem, Gary L., "Cost of Information and Security Prices: Market Association Tests of Accounting Policy Decisions," *The Accounting Review* (January, 1973), pp. 80–90.

[50] Beaver, W.H., "The Behavior of Security Prices and Its Implications for Accounting Research (Methods)," in American Accounting Association, *Report of the Committee on Research Methodology in Accounting*, supplement to Vol. 47, *The Accounting Review* (1972), pp. 407–37.

[51] Fama, E.F., "The Behavior of Stock-Market Prices," *Journal of Business* (January, 1965), pp. 34–105.

[52] Sharpe, William F., "A Simplified Model for Portfolio Analysis," *Management Science* (January, 1963), pp. 377–92; Lintner, John, "The Valuation of Risk Assets and the Selection of Risky Investments in Stock Portfolios and Capital Budgets," *Review of Economics and Statistics* (February, 1965), pp. 13–37; and "Security Prices, Risk, and Maximal Gains from Diversification," *Journal of Finance* (December, 1965), pp. 587–616; Mossin, Jan, "Equilibrium in a Capital-Asset Market," *Econometrica* (October, 1966), pp. 768–82.

[53] Ball, R., and Brown, Philip, "An Empirical Evaluation of Accounting Income Numbers," *Journal of Accounting Research* (Autumn, 1968), pp. 159–78.

[54] Birnberg, J.G., and Nath, Raghu, "Implications of Behavioral Science for Managerial Accounting," *The Acounting Review* (July, 1967), pp. 468–79; Bruns, William J., Jr., "Accounting Information and Decision Making: Some Behavioral Hypotheses," *The Accounting Review* (July, 1968), pp. 469–80; Hofstedt, T.R., and Kinard, J.C., "A Strategy for Behavioral Accounting Research," *The Accounting Review* (January, 1970), pp. 38–54.

[55] American Accounting Association, "Report of the Committe on Behavioral-Science Content of the Accounting Curriculum," *The Accounting Review*, supplement to Vol. 46 (1971), p. 247.

[56] Dyckman, T.R., Gibbons, M., and Swieringa, R.J., "Experimental and Survey Research in Financial Accounting: A Review and Evaluation," in *The Impact of Accounting Research in Financial Accounting and Disclosure on Accounting Practice*, (eds) A.R. Abdel-Khalik and T.F. Keller (Durham, N.C.: Duke University Press, 1978), pp. 48–105.

[57] Belkaoui, A., "Linguistic Relativity in Accounting," *Accounting, Organizations, and Society* (October, 1978), pp. 97–104.

[58] Belkaoui, A., "The Interprofessional Linguistic Communication of Accounting Concepts: An Experiment in Sociolinguistics," *Journal of Accounting Research* (Autumn, 1980), pp. 362–74.

[59] Abdel-Khalik, A.R., "The Entropy Law, Accounting Data, and Relevance to Decision Making," *The Accounting Review* (April, 1974), pp. 271–83.

[60] Rose, J., Beaver, W.H., Becker, S., and Sorter, G.H., "Toward an Empirical Measure of Materiality," supplement to Vol. 8, *Journal of Accounting Research* (1970), pp. 138–56.

[61] Libby, R., and Lewis, B.L., "Human Information Processing Research in Accounting: The State of the Art," *Accounting, Organizations, and Society* (September, 1977), pp. 245–68.

[62] Ritts, Blaine A., "A Study of the Impact of APB Opinions on Practicing CPAs" *Journal of Accounting Research* (Spring, 1974), pp. 93–111.

[63] Ijiri, Yuji, Jaedicke, R.K., and Knight, K.E., "The Effects of Accounting Alternatives on Management Decisions," (eds) R.K. Jaedicke, Yuji Ijiri, and O. Nielsen, *Research in Accounting Measurement* (Sarasota, Fl.: American Accounting Association, 1966), pp. 186–99.

[64] Prakash, P., and Rappaport, A., "Information Inductance and Its Significance for Accounting," *Accounting, Organizations, and Society*, Vol. 2, No. 1 (1977), pp. 29–38.

[65] Hofstedt, T.R., and Kinard, J.C., "A Strategy for Behavioral Accounting Research," op. cit., p. 54.

[66] Feltham, Gerald A., "The Value of Information," *The Accounting Review* (October, 1968), pp. 684–96; Crandall, Robert H., "Information Economics and Its Implications for the Further Development of Accounting Theory," *The Accounting Review* (July, 1969), pp. 457–66; Feltham, Gerald A., and Demski, Joel S., "The Use of Models in Information Evaluation," *The Accounting Review* (July, 1969), pp. 475–66.

[67] Crandall, Robert H., "Information Economics and Its Implications for the Further Development of Accounting Theory," op. cit., p. 464.

[68] Ibid., p. 458.

[69] Feltham, Gerald A., and Demski, Joel S., "The Use of Models in Information Evaluation," op. cit., p. 626.

[70] Beaver, William, and Demski, Joel, "The Nature of Income Measurement," *The Accounting Review* (January, 1979), p. 43.

[71] Marschak, Jacob, and Radner, Roy, *Economic Theory of Teams* (New Haven: Yale University Press, 1972).

[72] Hatfield, H.R., "A Historical Defense of Bookkeeping," *Journal of Accounting* (April, 1924), pp. 241–53.

[73] Burrell, G., and Morgan, G., *Sociological Paradigms and Organizational Analysis, Elements of the Sociology of Corporate Life* (Heinemann Educational Books Ltd., 1979).

[74] Ibid., p. 2.

[75] Ibid., p. 75.

[76] Belkaoui, Ahmed, *Inquiry and Accounting: Alternate Methods and Research Perspective* (Westport, Ct.: Quorum Books, 1987), Ch. 2; Chua, Wai Fong, "Radical Developments in Accounting Thought," *The Accounting Review* (October, 1986), pp. 601–32; Cooper, D.J., "Tidiness, Muddle, and Things: Commonalities and Divergencies in Two Approaches to Management Accounting Research," *Accounting, Organizations, and*

Society (2, 3, 1983), pp. 269–86; Hopper, T., and Powell, A., "Making Sense of Research into the Organizational and Social Aspects of Management Accounting: A Review of its Underlying Assumptions," *Journal of Management Studies* (September, 1985), pp. 429–65; Dirsmith, Mark W., Covaleski, Mark A., and MCallister, J.P., "Of Paradigms and Metaphors in Auditing Thought," *Contemporary Accounting Research* (Fall, 1985), pp. 46–68.

[77] Ibid., p. 305.

[78] Cooper, David, "Tidiness, Muddle, and Things: Commonalities and Divergencies in Two Approaches to Management Accounting Research," op. cit., p. 277.

[79] Buzzell, Robert D., "Is Marketing a Science?," *Harvard Business Review* (January–February, 1963), p. 37.

[80] Hempel, C.G., "Logical Positivism and the Social Sciences," in *Legacy of Logical Positivism*, (eds) P. Achinstein and S.F. Barker (Baltimore: Johns Hopkins University Press, 1969), p. 151.

[81] Bunge, Marie, *Scientific Research I: The Search for System* (New York: Spring, 1967), p. 336.

[82] Derrida, J., *Writing and Difference* (transl. by Boss, A.) (Chicago: The University of Chicago Press, 1978).

[83] Norris, C., *Deconstruction: Theory and Practice* (New York: Methuen, 1982), pp. 18–19.

[84] Arrington, C. Edward and Francis, Jere R., "Letting the Cat Out of The Bag: Deconstruction, Privilege, and Accounting Research," *Accounting Organization and Society* (January, 1989), p. 7.

[85] Jensen, Michael, "Organization Theory and Methodology," *The Accounting Review* (April, 1983), pp. 319–39.

[86] Popper, Karl, *Conjecture and Refutations* (London: Basic Books, 1963).

[87] Lakatos, Imre, "Falsification and the Methodology of Scientific Research," in *Criticism and the Growth of Knowledge*, (eds) Imre Lakatos and Alan Musgrave (Cambridge: Cambridge University Press, 1970), p. 119.

[88] Ibid., p. 120.

[89] Ibid., pp. 106–109.

REFERENCES

American Accounting Association, Committee on Concepts and Standards for External Financial Reports, *Statement on Accounting Theory and Theory Acceptance* (Sarasota, Fl.: American Accounting Association, 1977).

Danos, Paul, "A Revolution in Accounting Thought? A Comment," *The Accounting Review* (July, 1977), pp. 746–7.

Hakansson, Nils H., "Where We Are in Accounting: A Review of Statement on Accounting Theory and Theory Acceptance'," *The Accounting Review* (July, 1978), pp. 717–25.

Kuhn, Thomas S., "The Structure of Scientific Revolutions," in *International Encyclopedia of Unified Science*, Second Enlarged Edition (Chicago: University of Chicago Press, 1970).

Peasnell, K.V., "Statement on Accounting Theory and Theory Acceptance: A Review Article," *Accounting and Business Research* (Summer, 1978), pp. 217–25.

Ritzer, George, "Sociology: A Multiple-Paradigm Science," *The American Sociologist* (August, 1975), pp. 156–7; and *Sociology: A Multiple-Paradigm Science* (Boston: Allyn & Bacon, 1975).

Wells, M.C., "A Revolution in Accounting Thought," *The Accounting Review* (July, 1976), pp. 471–82.

OTHER NOTES

Arrington, C.E., and Francis, J.R., "Letting the Cat Out of The Bag: Deconstruction, Privilege, and Accounting Research," *Accounting, Organizations and Society* (January, 1985), pp. 1–88.

Belkaoui, Ahmed, *Socio-Economic Accounting* (Westport, Ct.: Quorum Books, 1984).

Belkaoui, Ahmed, *Public Policy and The Problems and Practices of Accounting* (Westport, Ct.: Quorum Books, 1985).

Belkaoui, Ahmed, *Inquiry and Accounting: Alternative Methods and Research Perspectives* (Westport, Ct.: Quorum Books, 1987).

Belkaoui, Ahmed, *The Coming Crisis in Accounting* (Westport, Ct.: Quorum Books, 1989).

Burrell, G., and Morgan, G., *Sociological Paradigms and Organizational Analysis* (London: Heinemann, 1979).

Chua, Wai Fong, "Radical Developments in Accounting Thought," *The Accounting Review* (October, 1986), pp. 601–32.

Chua, Wai Fong, "Interpretive Sociology and Management Accounting Research — A Critical Review," *Accounting, Auditing and Accountability* (1, 2, 1988), pp. 59–79.

Cooper, D.J., and Sherer, M.J., "The Value of Corporate Accounting Reports: Arguments for a Political Economy of Accounting," *Accounting, Organizations and Society* (1984), pp. 207–32.

Derrida, J., *Writing and Difference* (transl. by Bass, A.) (Chicago: The University of Chicago Press, 1978).

Hopwood, A.G., "On Trying to Study Accounting in The Contexts in Which it Operates," *Accounting, Organizations and Society* (1983), pp. 361–74.

Hunt, Herbert G. III and Hogler, Raymond L., "Agency Theory as Ideology: A Comparative Analysis Based on Critical Legal Theory and Radical Accounting," *Accounting, Organizations and Society* (August, 1990), pp. 437–54.

Laughlin, Richard C., "Accounting Systems in Organizational Contexts: A Case for Critical Theory," *Accounting Organization and Society* (October, 1987), pp. 479–507.

Neimark, M., "The King is Dead. Long Live the King," *Critical Perspectives on Accounting* (March, 1990), pp. 103–14.

Tinker, Tony, *Paper Prophets: A Social Critique of Accounting* (Praeger, 1985).

Tomkins, C.R., and Groves, R., "The Everyday Accountant and Researching His Realities," *Accounting, Organizations and Society* (1983), pp. 361–74.

QUESTIONS

17.1 Show how the pattern of events in accounting follows the pattern of *scientific revolution* described by Kuhn.

17.2 Define and discuss *paradigm* as it applies to accounting.

17.3 Is accounting a *multiple-paradigm science*? Discuss your answer.

17.4 Explain the following accounting paradigms:

    a. The *anthropological/inductive* paradigm.

    b. The *true-income/deductive* paradigm.

    c. The *decision-usefulness/decision-model* paradigm.

    d. The *decision-usefulness/decision-maker/aggregate-market-behavior* paradigm.

    e. The *decision-usefulness/decision-maker/individual-user* paradigm.

    f. The *information/economics* paradigm.

17.5 What are the primary contributions of Kuhn, Popper, and Lakatos to the "philosophy" of science?

17.6 What role does *falsification* play in accounting? What is the difference between *naive falsification* and *sophisticated falsification*?

INDEX